L. A. Carlyon was born in northern Victoria, Australia, in 1942. He has been editor of the Melbourne *Age*, editor-in-chief of the *Herald* and *Weekly Times* group and a visiting lecturer in journalism in a career that has established him as one of his country's most respected journalists, receiving the Graham Perkin Australian Journalist of the Year Award in 1993. *Gallipoli* was researched in Australia, Britain, New Zealand, and, most importantly, on the Gallipoli peninusla itself.

GALLIPOLI

L. A. Carlyon

BANTAM BOOKS

LONDON • NEW YORK • TORONTO • SYDNEY • AUCKLAND

GALLIPOLI
A BANTAM BOOK: 0 553 81506 7

Originally published in Great Britain by Doubleday,
a division of Transworld Publishers
First published in Australia by Pan Macmillan Australia Pty Limited 2001

PRINTING HISTORY
Doubleday edition published 2002
Bantam edition published 2003

3 5 7 9 10 8 6 4

Copyright © Les Carlyon 2001

Maps copyright © Pan Macmillan Australia Pty Limited 2001

The right of Les Carlyon to be identified as the author of
this work has been asserted in accordance with sections 77
and 78 of the Copyright Designs and Patents Act 1988.

Set in 11/13pt Sabon by
Falcon Oast Graphic Art Ltd.

Bantam Books are published by Transworld Publishers,
61–63 Uxbridge Road, London W5 5SA,
a division of The Random House Group Ltd,
in Australia by Random House Australia (Pty) Ltd,
20 Alfred Street, Milsons Point, Sydney, NSW 2061, Australia,
in New Zealand by Random House New Zealand Ltd,
18 Poland Road, Glenfield, Auckland 10, New Zealand
and in South Africa by Random House (Pty) Ltd,
Endulini, 5a Jubilee Road, Parktown 2193, South Africa

Printed and bound in Great Britain by
Cox & Wyman Ltd, Reading, Berkshire.

Papers used by Transworld Publishers are natural, recyclable products
made from wood grown in sustainable forests. The manufacturing
processes conform to the environmental regulations of the country of origin.

Contents

List of maps

Imperial measurements have been used in this book as they were in documents from the First World War. Exceptions to this are some gun calibres, which were measured in centimetres; and contour heights, which were recorded in metres on contemporary maps of the Gallipoli area.

1 inch	25.4 millimetres	1 centimetre	0.394 inches
1 foot	30.5 centimetres	1 metre	3.28 feet
1 yard	0.914 metres	1 metre	1.09 yards
1 mile	1.61 kilometres	1 kilometre	0.621 miles

Was it hard, Achilles,
So very hard to die?
Thou knowest and I know not –
So much the happier I.

I will go back this morning,
From Imbros, over the sea;
Stand in the trench, Achilles,
Flame-capped, and shout for me.

Patrick Shaw-Stewart,
who survived Gallipoli
to die in France in 1917

PART ONE

Of mice and men

1

The earth abideth forever

Spring is coming to the Gallipoli Peninsula, so surely there is a pulse to it. The shepherd bends down, cups his hand under a new lamb, all clanging heart and spongy ribs, and tucks it under his arm. The lamb wears yellow smears of foetal fluid down its hind legs and a speckle of gore on its forehead. The mother stares up at the shepherd, half-trusting: he gave it back last time. The other ewes mill around the car, hoofs clicking like castanets on the bitumen. They are old and daggy and heavily in lamb, and they are trying to be skittish. The warm wind has set off something in their heads. They smell the sappy grass in the culvert and blunder into a trot, trampling the bluebells in the roadside gravel.

The shepherd owns a stick, too rough to be called a crook, and three yellow dogs with pitiless eyes. He wears a woollen fez and a brocaded vest and grins through stubble. He appears to be straight from antiquity, doing what shepherds have been doing here for thousands of years. So long as the Athenians weren't fighting the Peloponnesians, that is, or the Ottomans the Venetians. And so long as the city-state at one end of the Dardanelles wasn't scrapping with the Persian stronghold at the other end. Then you notice that the shepherd wears an earpiece that leads to a transistor radio in his shirt pocket and that his lunch of bread and olives is flopping about in a super-market bag tucked through his belt.

Doesn't matter. Antiquity – or timelessness, its near-relation – is easy to find here. You stand at the foot of the Kilitbahir massif, layer upon layer of wavy sandstone known to the locals as the 'place of gigantic ghosts', and stare across the water to the Asian shore of the Dardanelles. This is where the British–French battle fleet ran into a minefield in 1915 and limped off determined not to fight another day if it could possibly get out of it. This is also close to where, 3000 years earlier, the ships of the Achaean Greeks arrived for the Trojan War. There are no skyscrapers, no petrochemical plants or corporate signs. History's stadium is much as it was. You are seeing pretty much what Alexander the Great saw. Close your eyes and you can see St Paul trudging behind a caravan and wondering whether the villagers up ahead will want to pelt him with stones or fete him. Everyone came to the Dardanelles, but only to get somewhere else. In 1915 the British and French were going to Constantinople. This was to be a stopover.

The tortoises are out grazing today, poking their heads from under black-and-khaki helmets, as though they have been outfitted by an army surplus store and are shy about their new clothes. A dolphin performs languid arcs beneath the castle on Kilitbahir harbour and sardines boil in the creek at Kum Tepe. A fisherman pulls on a wetsuit and begins to herd fish into the net he has set off the Anzac battlefield. Purple irises are poking through in the cemeteries and the wild pear trees wear white blossom. The Judas trees among the headstones at Shrapnel Gully are a blaze of pink and purple, so gorgeous that no betrayer of a messiah would consider hanging himself from a lesser tree. A hawk glides in the fairy blue sky over Anzac, surveying the great boneyard for signs of life.

Anzac was never farmed like the rest of the peninsula. General Otto Liman von Sanders, the German who commanded the Turkish land forces during the Gallipoli campaign, called this coast a 'waste landscape'. Here is a tangle of gullies and ridges that is eroding away, bleeding its yellow sludge into the Aegean every time the rains come.

All that blood and bone from 1915, and still this place refuses to bloom. As an Australian soldier wrote home in 1915, it wouldn't feed a bandicoot. At the other battle-fields on the peninsula, on the plains of Helles to the south and Suvla to the north, poppies appear like blood clots in fields of bright green wheat. Farmers work the stubble with chisel ploughs, their tractors rocking and throbbing like tramp steamers in a swell. Behind the plough you still pick up the flotsam of war. A brown-and-beige shard from an English rum jar. A curling piece of shrapnel, splintery and rusty and leaden in your hand. A tobacco tin that disintegrates as you force the hinges and falls through your hand like dust.

The tomatoes are going in on the red-brown dirt of the Suvla plain. Everyone is out in the fields, as if to celebrate the land coming alive again. Old men lean on whatever is handy and occasionally lift something heavy; mostly they give advice. Women in great bloomers of trousers tamp in the seedlings. Young men unravel the black irrigation pipes that lead to the pump on the well. At dusk the family clambers on to the trailer behind the tractor and goes home exhausted, except the old men. They light cigarettes and explain how things might have been done better.

No-one, neither locals nor tourists, much visits the cemeteries of Suvla. Anzac and Helles, though defeats for the British and French empires, are thought to have honour and the hint of romance. Suvla is untrodden; the cemeteries seem to say 'Lest we remember'. Suvla is for tomatoes and wheat and peppers. And goats, large herds of them, a black-and-tan breed from the Greek islands. They browse the ridges, a bite here, a bite there, all the time going forward, their neck-bells tinkling.

This land has been farmed and fought over for 5000 years that we know of. Along the coasts are the ruins – sometimes nothing more than a litter of broken tiles or a burial mound – of fabled cities: Troy and Dardanos on the Asian side of the Dardanelles, Elaeus down at Cape Helles, Sestos and Abydos up near Nagara Point. Australian sappers in 1915 came on pottery and other artefacts while tunnelling towards the Turkish trenches at Lone Pine. French soldiers at Morto Bay dug into a grave-yard thought to be 3400 years old; the corpses were in jars. Some of the Frenchmen tried to protect the relics and were killed – by artillery fire from near Troy. The warriors come and go but the rhythms of the land are eternal.

The caravans from the east once came to Çanakkale, the largest town in these parts, on the Asian side of the Narrows. The shores of the Dardanelles are only 1400 yards apart here. Pilgrims came on their way to Jerusalem or Mecca. Çanakkale was the cockpit of the world; here, Westerners liked to think, European virtue met Asian vice. In old Çanakkale, home to 16,000 people in 1915, the houses were of wood or sun-dried bricks and minarets towered over all. Muslims lived near the docks, gypsies behind the castle guarding the Narrows, Jews along what is now the main street and Greeks behind the waterfront north of the docks. Over on the peninsula, Maidos (now

Eceabat) and Krithia (now Alçitepe) were Greek villages, as was Kum Kale, at the entrance to the Dardanelles on the Asian side. Gallipoli, the English word for this place, is derived from a Greek word meaning 'fair city'.

Çanakkale is now a university town of 62,000 people. Apartment blocks of white concrete rise behind the sweep of the esplanade. The old part of Istanbul (which the British called Constantinople in 1915) is still Byzantine and dark and teeming with street vendors, all of whom have relations in Sydney and Melbourne and, should you be foolish enough to confess that you come from there, Dubbo as well. Çanakkale is Mediterranean and sunny, too relaxed to be on the make.

Fish are for sale in panniers on the docks; they flop and send up frantic bubbles and skinny cats with the hearts of thieves crouch near a bollard, waiting for someone to get careless. Across the esplanade, youths are playing basketball and ponies hitched to gypsy carts nuzzle into feedbags tied with twine behind their ears. The corn vendor leans over his griddle with a cigarette hanging from his mouth and a boy hurries past with sesame rings on a tray on his head. The locals stroll along the esplanade, day and night, hot or cold. The view is too lovely to hurry.

The water is never the same: blood-red, then pastel blue, then slate, then silver, then pink. It is sometimes all these colours at once, like the tail of a gigantic peacock, as someone once said. Most days you can see, across the water from Çanakkale, the New Zealand memorial high on Chunuk Bair; sometimes Chunuk Bair hides in the mists like a mysterious and faraway country, which it is. University students in jeans and Nike tops go hand in hand along the esplanade, giggling into mobile phones; alongside them are women in veils and ankle-length gaberdine coats and whiskered men in woollen fezzes.

That's how it goes in Turkey: some think the spiritual capital is Mecca and others, mostly the young, lean towards Hollywood. As in 1915, the country doesn't know whether it belongs in the East or the West.

Çanakkale now receives pilgrims of a different sort. Near the clocktower the Troy-Anzac Travel Agency looks across at the Hotel Anzac. Down the street is the Aussie and Kiwi Restaurant; around the corner is Anzac House, which advertises that its tours are 'hassle free'. In spring the peninsula tizzies itself up for the annual invasion.

A few days before Anzac Day the crosses in the French cemetery at Morto Bay are sticky with black paint. There is something honest about them. They have the starkness of iron fencing stakes, which is what they look to have been made from; you expect to see barbed wire twitched to them. With their rose beds and open spaces, the British cemeteries seem to be saying that war is sad but ennobling; the French crosses say it is black and grubby. Graders and tip-trucks lumber over the Anzac and Helles battlefields. Walls are being patched, lawns watered, towers installed so that mobile phones will work. Bitumen is sprayed straight on to the gravel roads like paint.

Matthew Taylor, a landscape architect from Sydney, is preparing the new site for the dawn service at North Beach. Several dozen Turkish labourers have not turned up for work today. No explanations; they simply aren't here. In the afternoon Taylor discovers why. They had to plant tomatoes. New ceremonial sites are interesting; tomatoes are the stuff of life.

The dawn service draws about 15,000 pilgrims: old men with their uncles' medals jangling on sportscoats, Vietnam vets with medals pinned on yellow rugby guernseys, backpackers lumping bedrolls, 20-year-olds with Australian flags draped over their shoulders, school kids on trips, matrons from Sydney's North Shore. Around 3 am the mood is like a sports stadium before the teams run out: whistles, catcalls, skylarking, half-hearted Mexican waves, a turmoil of emotions looking for an outlet. The Australians murder a few slabs of beer and the New Zealanders murder a few vowels. In the coldest hour of all, just before dawn, the mood becomes serene, just the odd murmur behind the flames from hundreds of candles.

What this beach symbolises to the crowd is beyond reason and probably beyond knowing. Jean Cocteau, the French writer who drove an ambulance in World War I – what did he say? 'What is history after all? History is facts that become lies in the end; legends are lies which become history in the end.'

This is far from being Australia's costliest battlefield. In 1916 two battles at Fromelles and Pozières produced roughly the same number of Australian casualties – around 28,000 – as the eight months of the Gallipoli conflict. Three times as many British and French troops died here as did Australians and New Zealanders. Gallipoli was a defeat, not at all like the triumph of the Light Horse in Palestine, yet no-one lights candles as dusk falls at Beersheba on the night of October 31. Good and evil did not meet on the field here. Gallipoli was about strategy, not ideology. Gallipoli did not threaten Australia as did the fall of Singapore in 1942. As a battle, Gallipoli did not change the world as Stalingrad did. Gallipoli was all about the British empire, which is as dead as Rudyard Kipling and just as quaint, and a world where the test of manhood and of a nation's right to exist was thought to be on the battlefield. This is Australia's largest memorial, and it isn't even in Australia. And another curious thing:

the Australians and New Zealanders who died here were, in truth, fighting for Nicholas II, last Tsar of Russia. He had been promised Constantinople.

None of this matters. The siren-call of this beach has little to do with facts or common sense or the desiccated footnotes of academics. It is rooted in myth and nostalgia – and imagining. Everyone who comes here tries to paint pictures on the empty landscape, to bring it back the way it was. Dugouts and tents and piles of stores. Woolly clouds of shrapnel. Battleships rocking and half-hidden behind mustard clouds as they bombard the hills. Lighters hovering around frail-looking piers and, behind one of these piers, a post office and a telephone exchange. A biplane droning overhead. A mule squealing and trying to buck off its load. Troops swimming to drown their lice. The crackle of rifle fire up on the escarpment. The music of a smithy's hammer. The smell of upturned earth and open latrines and pipe tobacco and creosol and cordite. The smell of corpses, the ripeness of death in your nostrils all day and all night. The hollow pop of rifle shells being ejected, like no other sound there is. The wind blowing pages from the *Bulletin* and the *Ballarat Courier* into the Turkish trenches. Bayonets bobbing above the Turkish parapets, the occasional glimpse of an Ottoman soldier in a cloth helmet. Bundles that were once men, arms and legs at grotesque angles, lying out in no-man's land. Men hefting water up the ridges. Men stumbling down the ridges, bloodied and befuddled, heading for the beach, following the same instinct that tells a wounded animal to go home. Flies. Flies everywhere. Blue flies, green flies, black flies. And the scent of thyme.

And how did the Anzac soldier look? Lean and laconic, as he is supposed to be, wearing torn shorts and a cheeky grin as he brews tea, everything about him saying that war

20

is just another hindrance and will you take a squiz at the Pommie joker over there with the monocle. Or was he scared and bewildered and wasted by dysentery, as he isn't supposed to be, because these things don't sit too well with mythology? Anyway, we shouldn't be too scornful of mythology. Where would religion be without it? And this part of the peninsula is rather like Golgotha, a place of skulls, quiet now but loaded up with old agonies.

What were these Australians doing *here*? They had joined up to fight Germans in France and Belgium, and here they were lost in antiquity, in this place some of them had never heard of until a few weeks before they landed. We know what they wrote in their letters and diaries. But what did they really think?

Imaginings. Young Australians come here for one, maybe two, days in the European spring and wander these hills trying to discover their past, to unearth truths about an Australian nation, white and rustic and British, that no longer exists and is not coming back. Gallipoli, as a wise man once said, is a country of the mind. Everyone who comes here sees the story the way they want to see it.

Tiny waves caress the shore an hour before dawn. A flash of phosphorescence, the rattle of shingle, then silence. A shooting star cascades through the night and the moon begins to slide down behind the Sphinx, the jagged spur, fluted and sharp like a rotten tooth, that dominates this part of the beach. The master of ceremonies tells the crowd the service is being broadcast live on television to Australia. 'Hi, mum,' a girl shouts.

Australians and New Zealanders swarm over the Anzac battlefield as soon as the service ends. Black figures are silhouetted on the skyline of Walker's Ridge, clambering upward, as though there is still some need to get inland before the sun is properly up. Near Shell Green cemetery a retired Australian army officer points in the direction of Bolton's Ridge and says, half to himself: 'Now if we'd landed over there, where we were bloody well supposed to . . . ' A 25-year-old Turkish schoolteacher smiles at him and says in English: 'You Australians never learn.'

Here is one of the peculiar things about the Anzac tradition, or myth or legend or whatever it is. The Australians and the Turks, the enemies of 1915 who didn't much bother about taking prisoners in the first weeks of the campaign, have ended up friends. They laugh with each other easily and share a dry sense of humour. Their war, they feel, had honour; there is no incident that festers, no Burma–Thailand railway, no Babi-Yar, hardly a dead civilian. It was a soldiers' war.

The service at Lone Pine cemetery, on the ground where Australians won seven Victoria Crosses, begins in bright sunshine at 9 am. The dawn service was subdued and respectful; this one has an air of triumph, as though this is really Australian ground and everyone can behave as they would back home. Australians stand shoulder to shoulder on three of the four walls. The cemetery lawn is like an island rookery in spring: teeming with life, territorial plots marked out by rucksacks and tracksuit tops. Backpackers who have been up all night fall asleep among the graves. One sleeps through the Turkish national anthem but lurches to her feet, as if by instinct, when the first few bars of *Advance Australia Fair* ring out. A couple from the Hunter Valley stands with an air of proprietorship at the grave of Private Oliver Cumberland, from Scone, New South Wales. They know his family and have brought a red rose.

Next day the pilgrims have gone. It rained overnight, just as on the first night at Anzac Cove 85 years ago. The ground is greasy, dull brown rather than orange-yellow, and the leaves of the dwarf oak are glossy and beaded with tears. The Aegean is a sheet of pale-blue glass and the rain has dissolved the haze. You can see the yellow streaks of beaches on the island of Imbros, from where General Sir Ian Hamilton directed the campaign and began his long journey down the Via Dolorosa. For the first time in three weeks you can see Samothrace, home of Poseidon, god of the sea and of horses. Samothrace looks like a mountain peak exploding out of the Aegean, which it is. It also looks like a proper home for a god: a corona of mist swirls just below the summit.

After its one wild day of the year Anzac has reverted to type. Hawks ride the currents. A shepherd near a village behind the battlefield holds up his flock while an old ewe stares at her flanks, then finally lies down and starts to lamb. The tomato seedlings are standing up erect and bright today. Politicians and pilgrims come and go but the earth abideth forever. The wind keens and burns your face.

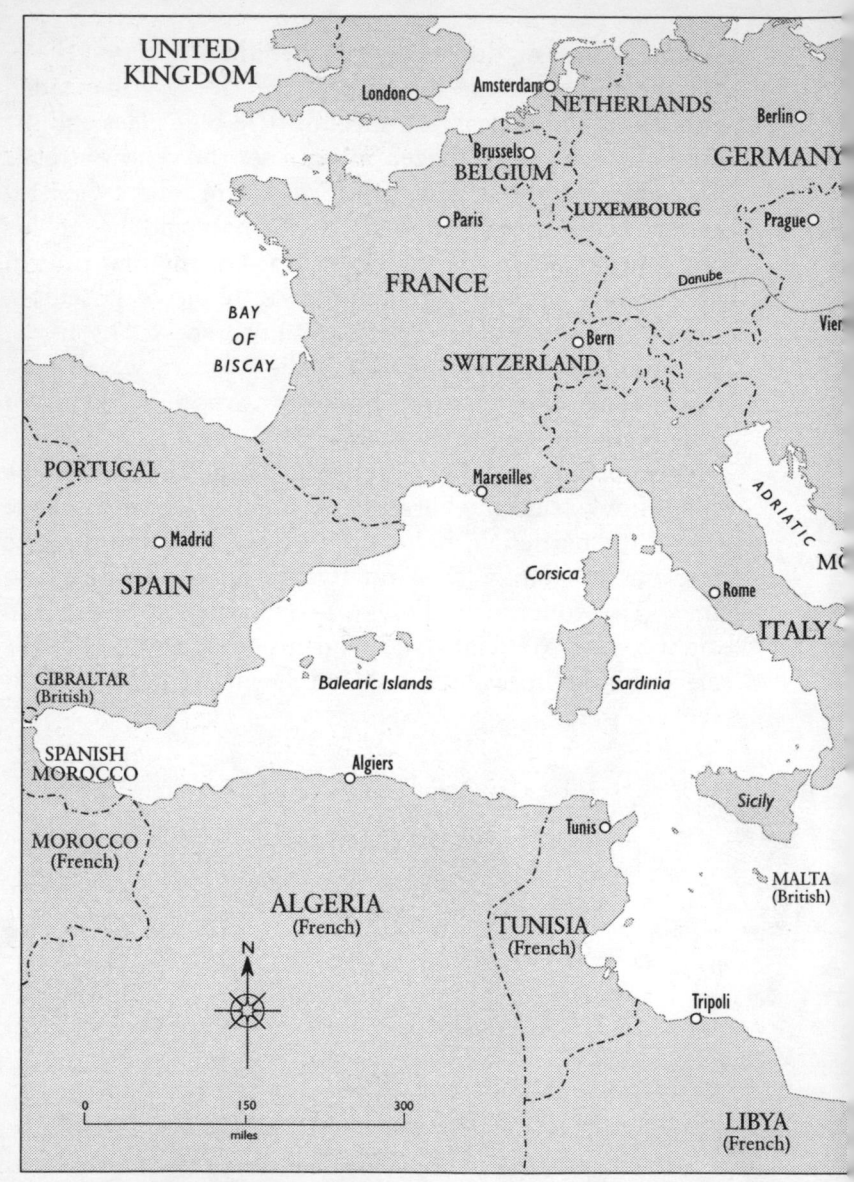

The theatre of operations

2

Four men and the road from Omdurman

The melting point of warfare [is] the temperament of the individual commander.

Barbara Tuchman

The war that came to these parts in 1915 began with assumptions that now seem so careless that they carry the whiff of innocence, but this is nothing much. If they are to get started, wars need innocence the way religion needs sin. This is the tale of how little wars, much like tumours, sometimes turn into big wars, not because those in charge intend this to happen, but because the thing they have created develops a life of its own. It grows on them, muddling their senses and slipping into places it shouldn't, until finally it gets away from them, so big and so painful that all they wish is for it to go away.

And this is the tale of how such wars are sometimes seen to get better with time, so that three or four generations on they become like the sunsets behind Imbros, back-lit with romantic glows that blot out all the mean gullies underneath. Such wars become epics or tragedies and myths follow them like cats padding behind the fish cart in Çanakkale.

Because it was fought so close to his old home ground, Homer might have seen this war on the Gallipoli Peninsula as an epic. Brief by his standards, but essentially heroic. Shakespeare might have seen it as a tragedy with splendid bit-parts for buffoons and brigands and lots of graveyard scenes. Those thigh bones you occasionally see rearing out of the yellow earth of Gully Ravine, snapped open so that they look like pumice, belong to a generation of young men who on this peninsula first lost their innocence and then their lives, and maybe something else as well.

Maybe these sons of the British, Ottoman and French empires are also condemned to eternal torment. We keep tramping over their potter's field, casting about for clues and telling ourselves that if we climb one more ridge, endure the barbs of the dwarf oaks one more time, the revelation of what went wrong will finally be upon us. We kid ourselves that the battle was lost by five minutes here and five minutes there. We blunder about these wounded hills and kid ourselves that we are starting to work things out. But maybe we aren't. Too many of the answers lie in another place.

This is how it starts, this war of ours, in the imperial capital of London on March 12, 1915. It is just after 10 am and General Sir Ian Hamilton, responsible for the land defence of England, spare and wiry on the outside and a poet on the inside, leaves his office in Horse Guards. The oaks in St James's Park show the fine tracery of winter and there is mud on the pavement, but Hamilton feels good. He is an old cavalry horse and he has heard a bugle. He is sure it is for him. His left hand is all but crippled, wrecked 35 years earlier by a Boer bullet; his left leg has been smashed in a fall from a horse, so that it is shorter than his right and makes him look bandy-legged. These things tell of his physical hardness.

The vaulting forehead, the nervous movements, the slender fingers, the warm and bright eyes: these hint at a sensitivity unusual in a military man. He is 62 and he has seen more of war than just about any senior British officer. He knows he has one big gallop left in him. It can't be in France, though. The generals running the war there don't want him. They think him too much of a free-thinker, too friendly with politicians, too intellectual, too *different*.

He likes to write. He has the gift of clarity and a good ear and occasionally produces a metaphor so right that you read it three times. He has the ability to seduce you with his words, to get you on side. He is close to those in power. Winston Churchill, now First Lord of the Admiralty, is a friend. The two first met in 1897. Hamilton failed to have Churchill decorated for gallantry during the Boer War. The trouble was that no-one, least of all the brazen Winston, seemed to know whether he was in South Africa as a soldier, a journalist or a show-off.

'Johnny' Hamilton is famous for his charm, yet few people truly know him and fewer still understand him. He is too ambiguous: too many layers, too many characters. He looks frail yet hums with nervous energy. He is brave. He has been recommended for the Victoria Cross twice; the first time he was judged too young and the second time too old. He is best of all in adversity. Yet he is not ruthless and thus is unlikely to become a 'great general'.

There is too much of what Lord Kitchener, the Secretary of State for War, calls the 'bloody poet'. Hamilton has no hatred of his enemies, be they Indian tribesmen, Boers or Germans. He does, however, detest capitalists and money-grubbers, even though he is wealthy himself. He has been a soldier for 42 years, toughened in Afghanistan, Burma, India, the Sudan and South Africa, but he is against conscription and always will be. He has inspected troops all over the world, including Australia and New Zealand. He loves a parade and is forever writing of some 'splendid body of men' he has just come upon, and sometimes it is even true. Yet another part of him yearns to be Keats or, better still, Rupert Brooke. He has written a volume of verse and a novel that the critics called risqué. His politics are liberal rather than Tory. He speaks German, French and Hindustani. He is an Edwardian gentleman, yet not much given to class-consciousness. He is in the killing business and admits he loves a fight, yet he is courtly and kindly.

He has seen the new age of war as an observer during the Russo-Japanese conflict of 1904–05 and been reckless enough to write that cavalry is obsolete, a heresy that still rankles with his brother generals in France, who have squadrons cantering behind the trenches as if the howitzer is a fad. He is a modernist, a 'scientific soldier', and at the same time trapped in the age of chivalry. Nearly four decades ago he saw the folly of infantry advancing shoulder to shoulder. He even believes in night attacks and aircraft. But, as his biographer John Lee will write, he is fascinated and repelled by the modern in equal measure. He tells people he was born two or three centuries too late.

People call him sanguine. He sees a rose where others see a cabbage. Like Don Quixote, he is seldom aware of his defeats. If forced, he will play at politics, and sometimes his wife, Jean, helps him, but he often underestimates his enemies. He is well read and independent of mind – many say too independent for a soldier – yet so often in the coming seven months he will show himself to be too deferential and a poor judge of men. Some people say he is deep and others say he is shallow. Herbert Asquith, the Prime Minister, thinks he has 'too much feather in his brain'. Charles Bean, the official Australian war historian, will write that he has 'a breadth of mind which the army does not in general possess'.

Hamilton appears in the war documentary *Forgotten Men*, made in 1934, when he was 81. He introduces the film wearing a glengarry, jodhpurs, top boots, spurs and gloves. He moves his right hand across to clasp his crippled left, which rests on his sword. His moustache has turned white and wispy. There is the trace of a Scots burr in his voice but mostly it is English twee and a touch high-pitched. His words are crafted and there is a hint of self-parody. He looks kind and avuncular, like a character from another British film that would appear nine years later, *The Life and Death of Colonel Blimp*. The war on the western front, he says, was war with the individual humanity abstracted. One of the last photographs of Hamilton shows him taking the salute at a march past of Boer War veterans in Whitehall in 1946. He is 93, stooped and wintry looking, leaning on a walking stick and so frail that a gust of wind might carry him away. There is something touching about this photograph, and it is not the fact that he has only a short time to live. To the end, no-one and no event managed to abstract the humanity from Ian Hamilton.

On leaving Horse Guards that day in 1915 Hamilton crosses Whitehall near where the statue of Lord Haig now stands. Field Marshal Sir Douglas Haig, commander-in-chief on the western front from 1915, is depicted trying to strangle a horse with a neck on it like an Angus bull. Haig did not have the imagination or humanity of Hamilton and, as in most of his photographs, his countenance here reminds one of a large terrier suffering from constipation. When the Great War was done, however, Haig would be a hero and Hamilton close to a pariah, and all because of this walk Hamilton is now taking.

He is heading towards the river, to the War Office. Lord Kitchener has summoned him. No-one in government understands Herbert Horatio Kitchener either, but the British people worship him. Hundreds of thousands of boys from the mill towns and pits are rushing to enlist because he has told them to. In the public mind he is Wellington and Marlborough, part man and part god.

The one thing the British people know about Kitchener is that he understands war better than anyone on earth. Beyond this myth – and its force is not to be mocked – all that those in government know is that the man is massive and square-headed and cross-eyed, that he seldom smiles, and that when he loses his temper, which he does easily and often, mainly because all his life he has been surrounded by nincompoops, his spectacles are said to blaze. David Lloyd George, Prime Minister from 1916 until 1922, likened Kitchener to 'one of those revolving lighthouses which radiate momentary gleams of revealing light far out into the surrounding gloom and then suddenly relapse into complete darkness'.

Kitchener's eyes are blue and cold, very cold. In the newsreel footage of him that survives the right eye stares vaguely to the front. The rogue eye, the left, seems to be trying to inspect his posterior for traces of lint. Compared with others on the newsreel, he seems tall and big-bellied. He looks better on a horse, back ramrod straight.

Kitchener is a bachelor who collects porcelain and likes flowers, the son of a cranky army officer who thought blankets were unhealthy and made his family sleep under newspapers. According to one biographer, Kitchener formed 'warm masculine friendships' with which he 'solaced a congenital loneliness'.

> Apart from one romantic attachment during his middle thirties, he remained throughout his life a natural celibate. He never married and a great loneliness descended upon him . . . Kitchener's sexual instincts were wholly sublimated like those of a Catholic priest . . . The key to his character . . . was a belief that he was defrauding the Almighty if he did not carry out his task. Kitchener placed the fulfilment of any task he had set himself, or which others had set him, ruthlessly before all else.

Or, as one of Kitchener's aides-de-camp put it, he preferred to be misunderstood than be suspected of human feeling. Or, as Hamilton would write many years later, Kitchener lived in an 'Arctic loneliness'. During the Boer War he kept a starling as a pet. He fed it worms and talked to it. One day the bird disappeared from its cage. Staff officers were sent to find it; the war could wait.

Hamilton did not pass the statue of General Charles Gordon on his way to meet Kitchener; it would have been right if he had. Gordon the martyr created Kitchener the martinet. Gordon, again indirectly, had much to do with the rise of the young Churchill. The empire loved Gordon so well that hysteria followed the news that he had been killed by followers of the Mahdi at Khartoum in January, 1885. Gordon could have slipped away and saved himself but didn't; Calvary beckoned and beguiled him, and he was half mad anyway.

Britain decided in 1897 that the Sudan needed to be conquered to protect the Nile from the French. Sixty thousand followers of the Mahdi met a British army of

20,000 outside the mud city of Omdurman, just short of Khartoum, on September 2, 1898. Lieutenant Winston Churchill rode a polo pony in the charge of the 21st Lancers. The battle, he wrote in 1930, 'was the last link in the long chain of those spectacular conflicts whose vivid and majestic splendour has done so much to invest war with glamour'.

> It was not like the Great War. Nobody expected to be killed. Here and there in every regiment or battalion, half a dozen, a score, at the worst thirty or forty, would pay the forfeit; but to the great mass of those who took part in the little wars of Britain in those vanished light-hearted days, this was only a sporting element in a light-hearted game . . . We may perhaps be pardoned if we thought we were at grips with real war.

Ancient met modern at Omdurman. The Dervishes threw themselves at the British with spears; some rode horses clanking with chain mail. The British had artillery, machine guns and gunboats. The 'war' was over by lunchtime. The British took Omdurman and the Mahdists fled. This enterprise was about politics; the British commander, General Kitchener, continued up the Nile and told the French to stay out of the Sudan. To the empire at large, however, this had been about something else. The cross-eyed crusader had avenged Gordon and slain the non-believers. The historian Barbara Tuchman wrote that after Omdurman the public had an almost religious faith in Kitchener. There was a 'mystic union' between him and the people.

Kitchener received a peerage, the thanks of Parliament and a grant of £30,000 for his victory at Omdurman. Reference points had been mislaid. Omdurman was not

Waterloo or Trafalgar. Compared with Robert E. Lee or Count von Moltke, Kitchener was a few battles short of genius. He was merely good at handling a colonial spat. The people thought otherwise. They didn't so much put him on a pedestal as hoist him, still breathing and cranky, high in the pantheon.

Kitchener in 1900 became commander-in-chief of the British forces in South Africa, succeeding Lord Roberts, Hamilton's friend and patron. Kitchener ended the Boer War by setting up concentration camps in which thousands of civilians died. In Britain his prestige grew anew. He received a viscountcy and a grant of £50,000.

So here he is in 1915, the obvious choice for War Minister, trying to run the Great War as though it is another of those colonial skirmishes he understands so well. Kitchener makes up the rules as he goes. He does not believe in delegation or explanation, or wheedling or coaxing. He cannot finesse and manipulate like Churchill. He is not clever with words. His way of winning an argument is to keep restating the same case, as though those who have already demolished it have never spoken. We do not know what drives him, but we suspect his mind is full of demons.

We do know he is by instinct a dictator and a loner, a doer rather than a talker, all of which sits curiously with his new position as a Cabinet minister in perhaps the world's most sophisticated democracy. With the blessing of Asquith and Cabinet, Kitchener is behaving like a feudal baron. The war he is trying to run single-handedly is 70 miles away in France and Belgium. Next year, even though it will still be in much the same place, it will seem closer. People in Kent will hear the artillery barrage before the first battle of the Somme and their windows will tremble the way animals do in the presence of danger.

This is the first big conflict of the industrial age, short on ideology and long on opportunism. The war between Russia and Japan had provided hints of how this one would go, but no-one in Britain took much notice, probably because they didn't want to. Barbed wire and machine guns and trenches sat badly with the imperial opera that had played so well for generations: cavalry wheeling in open country, bits clanking, the Union Jack humming in the breeze, delinquent natives trembling at the sight of so much pageantry. It wasn't like this in Picardy and Flanders. Kitchener had been right about one thing: almost alone, he had predicted that this war would be long.

By Christmas, 1914, in only its fifth month, the war against Austria and Germany had become a stalemate. It was about trenches: thousands upon thousands of them, thousands of miles of them. Frontline trenches, reserve trenches, support trenches, communications trenches, saps and traverses and funk holes and galleries, an underground world from Dante's *Inferno* that smelt of rum and earth and blood. As a German prisoner told his captors: 'It is the suicide of nations.' So much had changed. One man with a machine gun firing 500 rounds a minute had the power of 40 infantrymen. Howitzers were more important than bayonets, and just about anything else for that matter. For every man impaled on a bayonet, 70 would die from shrapnel or high explosives or gas. This was not about one-day battles like Borodino or Waterloo, or even three-day battles like Gettysburg. This was about attrition. Machine guns and howitzers had tipped the balance in favour of defenders. The stalemate was complete. Those two lines of trenches stretched from the North Sea to Switzerland, which left no opportunities for flanking movements. Any flanking movement had to be outside western Europe.

Hamilton knows that Kitchener is attracted to a flanking manoeuvre at the Dardanelles. It is conceived as a naval operation, and if it works, it will take Turkey out of the war, encourage the Balkan nations to join the Allied camp and return to the Russians their warm-water supply route through the Black Sea. The plan finally rests on one proposition: that the Turkish people, misused by their rulers for so long, will not fight when British battleships appear off Constantinople. The troops to be attached to the naval force will help the navy smash the forts along the Dardanelles and garrison Constantinople, which will eventually be handed to the Russians.

The author of this scheme is Churchill, a direct descendant of the first Duke of Marlborough, an adventurer more interested in ends than means and inclined to see war as an epic rather than a tragedy. Young Winston is now 40. Smouldering eyes burn in a face that is handsome but not kind. He has a fine mind and is full of derring-do. He is also impetuous: detail is for clerks. He charms and blusters; he is conciliatory and confronting; he has a gift for rhetoric that so baffles his opponents that they think of what they should have said hours after he has won them around. He understands theatrics. He is on his way to becoming (as an opponent once said of him) the greatest artist who ever entered British politics. The lobbying doesn't bother him too much; the important thing is to keep the momentum of the Dardanelles scheme rolling forward.

Kitchener loathed the young Churchill. He thought him bumptious, a part-time journalist and part-time soldier who drew his own lines of demarcation and was dedicated to getting his name in the papers and making friends who would be useful in a later political career. Kitchener tried and failed to keep Churchill out of the Omdurman campaign and was annoyed when he turned up to cover the Boer War. Ambitious men, however, make accommodations. Churchill and Kitchener now tolerate each other and maybe the relationship is mellowing into something warmer.

Kitchener and Hamilton, though not the least alike, have always understood each other well. A mere two years separate them – Kitchener is 64 – and this makes the relationship even stranger. It is that of father and son, headmaster and prefect. Hamilton's loyalty is so complete it amounts to hero-worship. When Hamilton was his chief-of-staff in South Africa, Kitchener would tell him to go to the front and find out what was happening. Kitchener would simply say 'Git' and Hamilton would pack his gear and leave. Hamilton would not ask for the instructions he was entitled to. It usually worked out and Hamilton saw the rough truth. He later confessed he was the 'so-called' chief-of-staff: 'The one-man show carried on royally in South Africa and all the narrow squeaks we had have been completely swallowed up in the final success . . . '

On this London morning in 1915, Hamilton tells us, it is as though he is back in Pretoria. He walks into Kitchener's office, wishes him good morning, and approaches the desk. Kitchener goes on writing like a 'graven image'. Eventually he looks up and announces: 'We are sending a military force to support the fleet now at the Dardanelles, and you are to have command.'

Hamilton is not as surprised as he implies in his *Gallipoli Diary*, a memoir he published in diary form in 1920, constructed in part from notes he dictated in 1915. He knows Churchill has been lobbying to have him appointed. Hamilton writes in *Gallipoli Diary* that Kitchener, having made his 'tremendous remark', wishes him to bow and go straight to the Dardanelles. Nothing has changed. Kitchener is telling him to go to the front and do something. Hamilton knew the pink escarpments of the Transvaal.

> But my knowledge of the Dardanelles was nil; of the Turk nil; of the strength of our own forces next to nil. Although I have met K. almost every day during the past six months, and although he has twice hinted that I might be sent to Salonika, never once, to the best of my recollection had he mentioned the word Dardanelles.

This is how wars start: with a 20-word sentence and a dismissal, the briefest of meetings in the headmaster's office. This time, however, Hamilton acts out of character. He needs to know more. He stands mute in front of the desk. Kitchener has gone back to writing. He looks up and makes another tremendous remark: 'Well?'

'We have done this sort of thing before, Lord Kitchener,' Hamilton begins. 'We have run this sort of show before and you know without saying I am most deeply grateful and you know without saying I will do my best and that you can trust my loyalty – but I must say something – I must ask you some questions.'

Kitchener frowns and offers grudging answers. Hamilton is one of the better lads; he will indulge him. Kitchener tells Hamilton he will be given the 29th Division from the British regular army, two divisions of Australian and New Zealand troops now in Egypt, the Royal Naval Division and a French contingent – all up, about 70,000 men.

Kitchener is starting to walk about now, happier to

talk. Hamilton must understand that the 29th Division is a loan to be repaid immediately the job is done. The job, one might conclude from this, isn't much, merely the conquest of European Turkey and the pacification of Constantinople, capital of the Ottoman empire. We do not know whether Kitchener bothers to tell Hamilton that Constantinople will be handed to the Russians so that Tsar Nicholas, a stranger to victories of any sort, can reclaim it for the Christian Church. There is talk of a Greek plan to take the Dardanelles with 150,000 troops. 'But,' says Kitchener, 'half that number of men will do you handsomely. The Turks are busy elsewhere. I hope you will not have to land at all. If you *do* have to land, why then the powerful fleet at your back will be the prime factor in your choice of time and place.'

There is also talk of getting a British submarine through the Dardanelles and into the Sea of Marmara. 'Supposing,' Kitchener says, 'one submarine pops up opposite the town of Gallipoli and waves a Union Jack three times – the whole Turkish garrison on the peninsula will take to their heels and make a bee line for Bulair.'

Kitchener calls in Lieutenant-General Sir James Wolfe Murray, chief of the Imperial General Staff and General Sir Archibald Murray, Inspector of Home Forces. Hamilton feels that this is the first either general has heard of the scheme. Hamilton should report to the general staff. And Sir James should know all about the scheme, which should also be written down on lots of pieces of paper and accompanied by maps and lists and estimates and intelligence reports. But Kitchener doesn't worry about such trifles and no-one is going to make him. He is his own chief-of-staff. He never consults Wolfe Murray and treats the general staff with scorn. As Hamilton will later write, Kitchener is like a powerful engine from which all controls, regulators and safety valves have been removed.

Kitchener tells Hamilton his chief-of-staff for the Dardanelles expedition will be Major-General Walter Braithwaite. He doesn't give Hamilton any choice; happily, Hamilton knows and likes Braithwaite, which is a pity because Braithwaite's speciality will turn out to be etiquette. Braithwaite is called in. The expedition, he says quite reasonably, needs aircraft for spotting. Hamilton tells us that 'K. turned on him with flashing spectacles and rent him with the words: "*Not one!*"' Braithwaite did not speak to Kitchener again during the interview.

Kitchener reminds Hamilton that the army is the second string; the navy thinks it can force the Dardanelles alone. The army will only have to land if the fleet fails. Kitchener asks Hamilton how he proposes to hold Constantinople. This is, after all, what the flanking movement is about: the ancient city on the Bosphorus with its soaring mosques and the beautiful church of Sancta Sophia, its murderous politics and fantastic intrigues, peopled by Turks, Greeks, Armenians, Jews, Muslims, Christians, Albanians, Egyptians, Serbs, Syrians, Bulgarians and dozens of other nationalities. Even if the Ottoman empire is falling apart, largely because for nearly 300 years it has been run by reactionaries, this is still one of the fabulous cities of the world. Constantinople is the prize; the Dardanelles are merely the approach route. This enterprise is conceived in optimism. No-one envisions that the yellow soils of the Gallipoli Peninsula will be thrown up to make a network of trenches and tunnels like those in France. This little war is going to be fast and light. France is mud-wrestling; this is chess, Churchill's Gambit Rampant.

Churchill wants to rush Hamilton to the Dardanelles. He has ordered a special train for that afternoon.

Hamilton is happy to leave, which suggests he doesn't see the need for too much preparation, but Kitchener says, no, wait a day. So on the 13th – Friday the 13th – Hamilton and Braithwaite return to see Kitchener, who is 'splashing about with his pen at three different drafts of instructions'. Hamilton thinks they are too vague and asks questions. The enemy's strength? Maybe 40,000. The enemy's heavy guns? No-one knows. Who commands the Turks on the peninsula? Jevad Pasha, it is believed. Kitchener's instructions are headed 'Constantinople Expeditionary Force', which rather gives the plot away. Hamilton begs him to alter them and the title becomes the 'Mediterranean Expeditionary Force'.

The document, with Kitchener's alteration, is in the Imperial War Museum in London. Kitchener uses less than 1000 words to tell Hamilton that landings are contemplated only if the fleet fails to break through the Dardanelles 'after every effort has been exhausted'. Plans can be worked out on how to defeat the Turkish army or persuade it to surrender when the Russians arrive at Constantinople from the other side. The final point – number 12 – tells Hamilton that all his messages should be sent directly to Kitchener. In short, he should forget about the general staff. Under the Field Service Regulations, Hamilton is entitled to receive detailed information not only on his own forces but also on those opposed to him, a survey of the theatre of war and a plan of campaign. He doesn't even receive the intelligence reports on the Dardanelles that have been sent back by Britain's military attaché in Constantinople.

Lots of armies had been to the Dardanelles. Most, like Hamilton's, were trying to get somewhere else. Xerxes, the Persian king, crossed above the Narrows, near Nagara Point, on his way to Athens in 480 BC. Alexander the

Great crossed from the other side on his way to India in 334 BC. We don't know too much about these campaigns. There remains the probability, however, that Xerxes and Alexander had a clearer picture of what they were supposed to be doing, and how they were going to do it, than Johnny Hamilton.

Hamilton says goodbye to Kitchener on March 13 as casually as if they are to meet for dinner. 'Actually my heart went out to my old chief. He was giving me the best thing in his gift and I hated to leave him amongst people who were frightened of him.' Kitchener does not wish him good luck, but as Hamilton picks up his cap from the table, the War Minister offers another tremendous remark: 'If the fleet gets through, Constantinople will fall of itself and you will have won, not a battle, but the war.'

Hamilton buys only two items for his journey: a Colt automatic and a notebook. He leaves London on a special train at 5 pm. Churchill comes to see him off. Hamilton tells his old friend that he cannot write to him: Kitchener would think it disloyal. Hamilton's new staff officers are at Charing Cross and look 'bewildered'. 'I haven't a notion of who they are,' Hamilton writes. A few of them have put on a uniform for the first time that day, spurs upside down and belts over shoulder straps. Orlo Williams had been a clerk in the House of Commons a few days earlier. Jack Churchill, younger brother of Winston, carries a large revolver in his belt and what Williams calls 'a vicious bludgeon' in his hand. Compton Mackenzie, the novelist, will join them in the Aegean.

Hamilton turns to Captain Cecil Aspinall, who will later write the official British history of the campaign after changing his name to Aspinall-Oglander. 'This is going to be an unlucky show,' Hamilton says. 'I kissed my wife through her veil.'

Hamilton and his staff cross the Channel in a destroyer before another special train takes them to Marseilles, where the cruiser *Phaeton* awaits. At sea, literally and figuratively, Hamilton takes inventory of the information he has to help him conquer Turkey: a few rough notes he and Braithwaite have got up, a textbook on the Turkish army written in 1912 and two small guide books.

In the night the *Phaeton* passes Corfu. Hamilton was born there in 1853 when it was garrisoned by the British army. His father was a captain, his mother the daughter of a viscount. Hamilton begins thinking about his mother, who died when he was three. As she lay dying, gasping in pain, she refused an opiate. A clergyman had told her the drug might dim the clearness of her thoughts ascending heavenwards. 'What pluck,' he writes. 'What grit – what faith – what an example to a soldier.'

It is easy to like Ian Hamilton. It is also easy to feel sorry for him. For most of his military life he has been close to strong commanders like Roberts and Kitchener. If he had doubts, all he had to do was to walk into their offices and ask advice. Now he is alone, the commander-in-chief. In two days his little war will start to become a big war, nothing like the scheme that Kitchener and Churchill sold him. In two days the tumour will start to grow. And slowly, ever so slowly, Ian Hamilton, at the tender age of 62, will start to lose his innocence.

In 1913, after the second Balkan War in which the Turks recovered much of the territory they lost in the first, the British general Sir Henry Wilson visited Turkey and met Enver and Djemal, two of the three revolutionaries running the country. Enver and Djemal were army officers; Talat, the third member of the triumvirate and the shrewdest, had been a telegraph operator. Wilson wasn't much impressed with Enver, who fancied himself as Napoleon, or Djemal, or the other officers he met, bar one. 'There is a man called Mustafa Kemal,' Wilson said. 'Watch him. He may go far.'

Mustafa Kemal was a young man who was hard to forget. He combined an inner sureness with the waft of danger that a predatory animal in a cage gives off. If he ever got loose, he might be hard to stop. Kemal was born in Salonika, Macedonia, in 1881 into a family that might be described as lower middle-class. His father was a customs clerk and later a timber merchant. Kemal was fair-haired and good-looking, slight of build but with a proud air that sometimes amounted to disdain. What everyone noticed was his stare. The eyes were hard and blue. They intimidated; they saw too much and knew too much. In group photographs, Kemal is always the one staring down the camera.

He was a loner from boyhood. It was as if he knew he had to be because he understood things other people didn't. His head nearly always ruled his heart; sentiment, he thought, led to weakness, although in later life he felt sentimental about trees and animals. He loved the Turkish people, but in the abstract. He liked women but would later say the quality he admired most in a woman was 'availability'. He could not be corrupted by money; he had no interest in it. At school he had enjoyed maths and was good with maps: it was said that he could look at a map once and visualise all the country it encompassed.

Patrick Kinross, his biographer, saw Kemal as an amalgam of East and West. The 'Western' part was logical and practical and enchanted by ideas. It knew that Constantinople and its empire had been run by boring old men who wouldn't acknowledge the rise of science and enlightened thought elsewhere. It thought the Muslim religion had become an impediment to progress because it supplied too many simple answers. Kemal was so radical he wanted a secular state. While still in his early twenties he told people he was a 'man of tomorrow'. The 'Eastern' part of Kemal mostly showed in the way he did things. His political style was about Byzantine intrigues and a revolver on the bedside table. He was often overbearing; consensus was for timid men. He didn't worry too much about the means if the end was good. As Kinross wrote, Kemal was a democrat by conviction and a dictator by temperament. In short, he was nothing like Ian Hamilton.

By 1915, however, the lieutenant-colonel, now 34, had not fulfilled General Wilson's prediction. He had fallen out with Enver and his cronies. Kemal's support was too qualified, too subtle, and they knew he was uneasy about their embrace of Germany. As a form of exile Kemal was sent to Sofia as military attaché. When Turkey entered the war Kemal wanted to command a division; patriotism was stronger than his distrust of Germany. Enver eventually gave him the 19th, which was being formed on the Gallipoli Peninsula, where Kemal had served during the first Balkan War. He arrived there late in February and made his headquarters around the village of Bigali, a few miles behind what would become known as Anzac Cove. The 19th was a typical Turkish division: three regiments each of three battalions, in all around 10,000 men. Arab soldiers made up two of the regiments, the 72nd and the 77th. Those in the 57th came from Thrace and Anatolia.

Bigali was – and is – a seedy old village, lived-in and worked hard: narrow streets, an avenue of mulberry trees, crowing roosters, stone walls that lean like petrified drunks, tumbledown sheepfolds. Its back streets carry the wool-and-ammonia smell of sheep. Turkeys, their wattles quivering like matrons in high dudgeon, pick grass along the verges of the road.

The double-storey house where Kemal stayed before the landings is now a museum. His clothes are laid out for posterity: socks, dressing gown, waistcoat, bow tie, blue shirt, scarf. In the dining room everything is set out on the floor the way it used to be in rural Turkey: a tray and serving spoon in the centre with cushions around them, a mortar and pestle for pounding garlic and onion. A lynx skin lies next to a brazier.

This was the headman's house, the best in the village, and Kemal, as the divisional commander, was taken in as a guest. The headman's wife stayed and, in the Muslim tradition, was forever trying to get out of Kemal's way and acting coy. Kemal tired of these games and eventually moved into a tent. The locals still tell you that one morning in April, 1915, Bigali awakened to the clatter of horses' hoofs and shouts. The 'British' were landing below the yellow ridge.

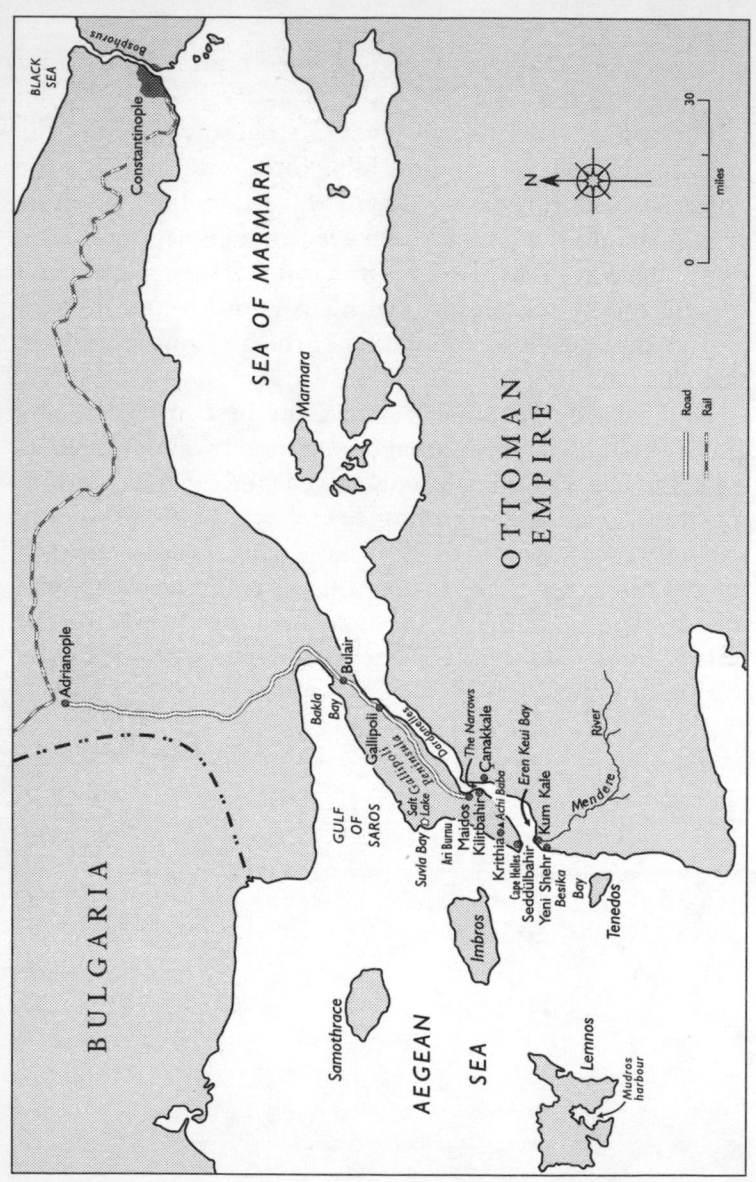

The cockpit of the world

3

The devil at two-and-a-half fathoms

No-one was writing in the style of Joseph Heller in 1915. War was not thought absurd and prose was about good manners. Henry James fitted in well: as another writer said, his characters had neither bowels nor sexual organs. Other authors fitted in better. Readers in England and Australia admired Thomas Hardy, Rider Haggard and Kipling. If Rupert Brooke hadn't written much, he was still the 'gifted and golden youth' and thoroughly wholesome. Things would change after the world war with the arrival of realists such as Graves, Remarque and Hemingway. In 1915, however, prose of all sorts, including letters between soldiers and their families, tended to gentility and euphemisms.

Soldiers weren't killed. They were *the fallen*; they had *paid the supreme sacrifice* or *perished*. Our chaps were invariably *plucky*; those who weren't were *cowards*; there were few colours in between. Superlatives were mandatory: there were few gallant officers but *most gallant* officers were everywhere. When our side suffered a defeat, it was said to have made *good progress*. Words such as *honour*, *duty* and *manliness* had clear meanings they do not have today. *Empire* meant the British empire, and a fine and paternal thing it was, not like the conglomerations of other powers, which were ill-gotten. The public school system produced *first-class chaps* and the odd *rotter*, and God was an Anglican. If you needed to write a strong swearword, you wrote d--n.

Joseph Heller, his riddles and his lunatics, would not have fitted in; yet the battle for the Dardanelles – and remember it was conceived as a naval operation – is about a riddle worthy of *Catch-22*. There were these forts with big Krupp guns along both sides of the Dardanelles. Above them were howitzer batteries that were moved around the escarpments by teams of buffalo. Below them were ten lines of mines moored across the straits between Çanakkale and Kephez Bay. And the riddle goes like this: the navy couldn't get in close enough to destroy the forts and batteries until the mines had been cleared; the mines couldn't be cleared because the forts and batteries kept firing on the minesweepers.

Mines are the main item of display at the maritime museum in Çanakkale: big ones and little ones, mines that float and mines with mooring rings, mines with short horns and others with long horns, grey ones and black ones. One is not told that this display is symbolic and it may not be intended so; but it is right enough. The hero of the Gallipoli campaign, the thing that best explains the course of events, is a metal sphere with horns on it, the devil at two-and-a-half fathoms.

The Turks began to mine the straits in November, 1914. Before that, there had been a struggle for the soul of the Ottoman empire.

In the 11th century the Turk men who would later be known as the Ottomans rode west from the steppes around the Caspian Sea. So well did they conquer in

Anatolia and eastern Europe that eventually they bred themselves out of existence. They were nomads and Muslims, as hard as the grasses that sustained their flocks. They worshipped their horses, rough-headed ponies that could live on water and a long rope, and sallied into battle with horsetails raised as standards. Their life was about lightness and movement. Saddles, tents, sheep, horses, bowstrings, gourds of yoghurt, the Koran, the paraphernalia of the caravan: these were the things that mattered. If you needed buildings or ploughed fields, you took them from some softer tribe to the west. The Ottomans conquered Anatolia and moved on, village by village, towards the fabled Christian city on the Bosphorus that has been called Byzantium, Constantinople and Istanbul. They crossed the Dardanelles, defeated the Serbs and others in Kosovo, and captured Constantinople in 1453. Mehmet the Conqueror dismounted outside Sancta Sophia, then, as now, the most affecting Christian building in the world, and sprinkled dirt on his turban as a gesture of humility. Lest this create a false image, it should be said that rape, butchery and looting were going on all around him.

By the 16th century the empire took in Greece, the rest of the Balkans, the Crimea, Rumania, Hungary, Syria, Iraq, Palestine, Arabia, Egypt and Libya. It stretched from the Danube to the Sahara. But the thing was too diverse, too loose. It owed its customs to too many nationalities. It was the ultimate in multiculturalism: one part Slavic, another Hellenic, another Arabic. There were Greeks, Bulgarians, Macedonians, Arabs, Serbs, Tartars, Armenians, Jews, Christians, Bedouins, Hungarians and Albanians, all united by – what? The empire spoke too many languages and worshipped too many gods. By the 17th century its rulers had grown fat and reactionary.

Western Europe, alive with ideas, saw the Ottoman empire as sensual, Oriental and brutal, even though the Ottomans often treated their minorities, particularly Jews, rather better than the 'civilised' nations to the north.

As Jason Goodwin wrote in *Lords of the Horizon*, the empire's early genius for lightness and speed had given way to a reputation for lumbering sloth. The descendants of the horsemen of the plains had become the fops of Constantinople. European statesmen were forever predicting the collapse of the empire. Tsar Nicholas II called it 'the sick man of Europe' and, since this diagnosis came from a member of the Romanov dynasty, it qualifies as expert opinion. As someone else said, the Ottoman empire that had been born in blood was strangling in its own cobwebs.

The empire was bankrupt by 1875. It had lost the Crimea and parts of the Balkans; Greece had become independent and Russia eyed Constantinople; in 1912 the Greeks took Salonika and the Italians grabbed Libya. The Ottoman empire at the outbreak of the Great War was like some giant beast that was down but still breathing. Vultures sailed around it in ever-decreasing circles. Russia, Bulgaria, Greece, Italy and France had long ago worked out which parts of the carcase they wanted.

There were two other body-snatchers looking on, but they were different. Britain was disdainful. Parts of the Middle East were attractive to her, but this was the Unspeakable Turk, cast out from the 'civilised world' for atrocities against minorities, notably Armenians, and for a history of impalement, strangling, rapine and bastinado. Germany was cynical. She thought she could coax one rousing gallop out of the beast before it died.

The Young Turks had grabbed power in 1908. Young Turkish officers in Salonika set up a secret society, the

Committee of Union and Progress, in which Major Enver was prominent. Mustafa Kemal was a member but he had reservations. Members had to swear to kill any person the Committee might condemn to death. The Committee demanded the restoration of the constitution of 1876. Threatened with dethronement, the Sultan agreed. Enver was a hero and the mood was euphoric. Enver told a crowd in Salonika: 'Today arbitrary government has disappeared. We are all brothers. There are no longer in Turkey Bulgarians, Greeks, Serbians, Rumanians, Mussulmans, Jews. Under the same blue sky, we are all proud to be Ottomans.'

On that day he might have meant it. Banners talked of liberty, equality, fraternity and justice, as though an empire built on despotism and corruption could, bloodlessly and overnight, reinvent itself as a benevolent democracy, and as though countries and cultures with little in common could hang together as an empire. Kemal was no romantic: he made himself unpopular by hinting that Enver didn't have the intellect or the ideas to lead the empire into the light.

The revolutionaries were really reformers with a single-issue platform: the restoration of the 1876 constitution, which was along Belgian lines and had lasted less than 13 months. The Young Turks flushed out the true revolutionaries. Turkey quickly lost Bosnia and Herzegovina to Austria. Bulgaria declared its independence. Crete went over to Greece. And Kemal, who was still criticising the Committee, was sent to Tripoli. In 1909 he was part of the army division organised by the Young Turks that marched on Constantinople to put down a counter revolution. The Sultan, Abdul Hamid, was exiled to Salonika. His brother, Mehmed Reshad, had been imprisoned in the palace for 30 years. He was led, bewildered, into the sunlight and told that he wanted to be the Sultan.

Kemal kept saying that soldiers couldn't also be politicians. A party member came to kill him. He entered Kemal's office on a pretext. Kemal thought there was something shifty about him and casually took a revolver from his drawer and laid it on the desk as they talked. The young man became more nervous and confessed he had come to kill him, but said he now didn't think it was a good idea.

During the next few years the Committee dropped any pretence that it would deliver democracy. It became another clique obsessed with personal power and making money – for itself. Its 40 or so members ran the country. The empire was still bankrupt, still falling apart. The Young Turks had fought two wars against the Balkan states and had lost their European lands bar Constantinople and Thrace. The Young Turks needed a friend.

Russia was the obvious enemy. The 'friend' had to be either Britain (even though she was lined up with Russia) or Germany. Britain wasn't much interested; she appeared to think the young upstarts would soon be tossed out. Britain had a naval mission in Constantinople and Germany a military mission. Germany was interested in a deal. But it was hard to negotiate with the Young Turks. Half-patriots, half-gangsters, more Oriental than Western, they weren't at all like the players in Europe, although they had one characteristic in common. With their posturing and bluffing, they too were doing their bit to make a European war inevitable.

Sir Harold Nicolson, a secretary in the British embassy, had the Young Turks to dinner.

There was Enver in his neat little uniform, his hands resting patiently upon his sword-hilt, his little hairdresser face perked patiently above his Prussian collar. There was Djemal, his white teeth flashing tigerish against his black beard: there was Talat with his large gypsy eyes and his russet gypsy cheeks: there was little Djavid who spoke French fluently, and who hopped about, being polite.

Henry Morgenthau, the American ambassador, said they were not a government so much as a secret society that by intrigue and assassination had grabbed all the high offices. He found Talat, the telegraph operator who had become the party boss and Minister of the Interior, the most interesting. Talat was thought to be of Bulgarian blood, a hulking man with fleshy jowls, bulging eyes and outsized wrists. He liked to drink and scorned religion. He lived, surrounded by cheap furniture, in a tumbledown wooden house. His favourite plaything was a morse key.

Whenever I think of Talat now, I do not primarily recall his rollicking laugh, his uproarious enjoyment of a good story, the mighty stride with which he crossed the room, his fierceness, his determination, his remorselessness – the whole life and nature of the man take form in those gigantic wrists . . . Of all the Turkish politicians I met, I regarded Talat as the only one who really had extraordinary innate ability. He had great force and dominance, the ability to think quickly and accurately, and an almost superhuman insight into men's motives.

Talat, Morgenthau wrote, knew that he was living dangerously. 'I do not expect to die in bed,' he said, and he got that right. Of the triumvirate that controlled the Committee, Talat seems to have been the best liked by foreigners, probably because he was too earthy to be earnest. Aubrey Herbert, the British parliamentarian and writer who later served at Gallipoli, wrote that Talat had 'a light in his eyes rarely seen in men, but sometimes in animals at dusk'.

It was Enver, however, who fascinated the wider world. He was the public face of the revolution: small and rather too pretty with his smooth face and delicate hands, well mannered, charming in public and vain in private, hopelessly vain. Like Kemal, he came from a relatively poor family – his mother, an Albanian, used to lay out the dead – but by now he had married a princess and lived in a large villa that he should not have been able to afford. Like Kemal, he had entered the army as a youth and fought in Tripoli and the Balkans. But whereas Kemal was a chess-player who thought four moves ahead, Enver was a gambler. Now in his early thirties, he was Minister for War and talked of himself as a 'man of destiny'. He didn't know enough and hadn't done enough to have earned either the high office or his nickname of 'the little Napoleon'. The wonderfulness of his being was mostly in his own mind.

According to Morgenthau, Enver had 'a remorselessness, a lack of pity, a cold-blooded determination, of which his clean-cut handsome face, his small but sturdy figure, and his pleasing manner, gave no indication'. He always gave the appearance of calmness and made decisions quickly. Enver spoke German and was pro-German. Talat was more interested in using the Germans rather than imitating them.

Djemal might have been pro-French; he was certainly anti-German and embarrassed Talat and Enver by swearing in Turkish at German diplomats and soldiers. Unlike Talat and Enver, Djemal lacked any veneer of charm that might lend ambiguity to his character. He had black eyes that darted everywhere and a bushy beard that made him look like a terrorist, which probably wasn't too far from the reality. He was the Minister of Marine, which didn't fit with his ambitions. He wanted to grab one of Turkey's southern provinces and run it as a personal fiefdom with lots of rough justice and much tribute for the ruler.

This was Turkey as Europe lurched towards war. Yes, there was a sultan and a Chamber of Deputies, but everyone knew that the Committee of Union and Progress ran the country, and that Talat and Enver ran the CUP and that these two were also putting their country up for tender. While the estate was rundown and seedy, there was one jewel: the Dardanelles.

Unlike World War II, the Great War did not grow out of a clash of ideologies. There was no champion of the master race throwing tantrums to sell-out crowds in Bavaria, and thereby reminding outsiders that liberal democracy had its virtues and might be worth fighting for. There was so little ideology around in the first months of the war that to encourage enlistment Britain had to embellish German atrocities in Belgium to create the Unspeakable Hun who raped nuns, tortured children and was generally an affront to civilised values. It is true that the Hohenzollern, Romanov and Hapsburg dynasties were clinging to an idea that was close to the divine right of kings; but this was more a yearning for the old certainties than ideology. The origins of the Great War mostly had to do with balance-of-power politics, with a tangle of alliances and mobilisation plans stored in drawers all over Europe.

Britain, France and Russia were lining up against Germany and the Austro-Hungarian empire. Lesser powers – Greece, Italy, Bulgaria and others – were trying to divine the likely winner before committing themselves. Even though she needed financial help, Turkey didn't need to auction herself; she could have contrived to stay neutral. Her army was certainly unready for war. Enver had purged more than 1000 officers in January, 1914. Ordinary soldiers had not been paid for years; some went bare-footed. When he arrived in 1913 to head the German military mission, General Otto Liman von Sanders decided to inspect troops around the country. He soon discovered he was inspecting the same clothing over and over again. New uniforms would be issued to whatever detachment he was known to be inspecting, then taken back and rushed to wherever von Sanders was headed next. Cavalry horses were covered with abscesses. In military hospitals one thermometer sometimes served 300 patients.

Turkey needed a friend, not a war. The German ambassador to Constantinople, while posing as a friend, was determined to give Turkey a war. Baron von Wangenheim, a friend of Kaiser Wilhelm, was in his mid-fifties, tall and erect, hard-eyed and arrogant, yet also given to outbursts of boisterous humour. He was not a Junker from Prussia; he simply played the part so well everyone assumed he was. He had ideas on racial purity and world domination that would surely have appealed to a painter of Vienna street scenes, shortly to enlist, called Adolf Hitler. Morgenthau, always a severe moralist, called von Wangenheim 'fundamentally ruthless, shameless and cruel'. He was also, Morgenthau admitted, a canny negotiator. He had 'the jovial enthusiasm of a college student, the rapacity of a Prussian official, and the happy-go-lucky qualities of a man of the world'.

Von Wangenheim needed to be good at his job. Germany

needed Turkey more than Turkey needed Germany. Sooner or later, the Germans were going to take on Britain, France and Russia. They needed Turkey to cut Russia off from her allies by closing the Dardanelles; which meant they first had to convince the Young Turks that Germany was going to win the coming war and, more important, that there would be spoils for Turkey in the Balkans and the Middle East.

Enver was Germany's trump. He was already more than half-won; if he could bring Talat around, the two of them could probably bring the whole Committee in behind Germany. The behaviour of the other ambassadors to Constantinople was curious. Russia had the most to lose – half her exports went through the Dardanelles – yet her ambassador appears to have been off-handed in his deal-ings with the Young Turks, as though they wouldn't be around for long. The British ambassador, Sir Louis Mallet, and his French counterpart appeared to think much the same. If so, this was a misreading of the game. The Young Turks needed to strike a deal with one of the great powers to establish their legitimacy and stay in power. Von Wangenheim knew this; no matter how often he failed to live up to Morgenthau's ideals, he understood how power worked.

Mallet went on leave in July, 1914, just as Europe was sliding towards war. On August 2, two days before Britain went to war with Germany, Turkey and Germany signed an alliance that pitted them against Russia. Then the British did Enver and von Wangenheim a favour.

There was still a British naval mission in Constantinople under Rear-Admiral Arthur Limpus. Britain was building two battleships for Turkey. One ship had been built; the other was weeks away from com-pletion. Turkish crews had arrived in Britain to sail them home. The ships had cost Turkey seven-and-a-half million pounds, huge money in those days, particularly for a bankrupt. The cash had been raised by public subscription. Villagers in Anatolia had put aside their poverty to drop a few coins in collection boxes so that Turkey might have a modern navy, because back then a modern battleship was the equivalent of a network of missile-launching sites. Turkish women had even sold their hair to raise money.

And here, on August 3, was Churchill announcing that the British navy would be confiscating the two ships that had already been given Turkish names. There was no mention of compensation, not even an offer of older ships, of which Britain had dozens. As an essay in provocation, it was breathtaking, although this is not the way Churchill tells it in his *The World Crisis*. The Turks were furious; if they were not much enamoured of Enver and his gang, the British were even worse. Morgenthau argued that the seizure was right, but conceded that it gave von Wangenheim 'the greatest opportunity of his life'. He was about to prove that Germany was Turkey's best friend.

On August 4 Britain sent Germany an ultimatum, demanding by midnight that Berlin respect Belgium's neutrality. At 11.05 pm – 12.05 am in Berlin – Britain declared war on Germany. The declaration also committed Australia and New Zealand to war as British dominions. Before the declaration British warships in the western Mediterranean were shadowing the German battle-cruiser *Goeben* and the light-cruiser *Breslau*. The *Goeben* was fast – she could make 26 knots – and carried 11-inch guns. She had already been to Constantinople, the largest warship to have passed through the Dardanelles. The Germans anchored her off the Golden Horn, festooned her with lights, and said, in effect: 'Look at what we can build.'

When darkness came on August 4, and with Germany and Britain certain to be at war in a few hours, the two German cruisers speeded up and lost their British pursuers. The British thought the *Goeben* would try to attack French ships coming from North Africa. Instead she and the *Breslau* headed for Messina, Sicily, to take on coal. They left there late in the afternoon on August 6. The British now assumed they would turn west or north. Instead they sailed south-east into the Greek islands. Admiral Wilhelm Souchon had received orders in Messina to take the *Goeben* and *Breslau* to Constantinople. On August 10 the cruisers were off the castle at Seddülbahir asking for permission to enter the Dardanelles.

The auction appeared to have reached its climax. Turkey was being asked to commit. If she wished to remain neutral, Turkey was bound by treaties to prohibit foreign warships from entering the Dardanelles. She was bound to intern any warship that remained in the straits for more than 24 hours. These treaties existed to preserve the balance of power, to prevent any of the great powers, particularly Russia, gaining control of the straits.

Morgenthau called at the German embassy on August 11. He found von Wangenheim with face flushed and eyes shining and unable to sit still. 'Something is distracting you,' Morgenthau said. 'I will go and come back again some other time.'

'No, no!' said von Wangenheim. 'I want you to stay right where you are. This will be a great day for Germany!'

Soon after he received a radio message.

'We've got them!' he shouted to Morgenthau.

'Got what?'

'The *Goeben* and the *Breslau* have passed through the Dardanelles.'

A few days before this, Enver had proposed to the Russian embassy a Turkish–Russian alliance directed against Germany. He didn't tell the Germans about this and presumably didn't then know the whereabouts of the *Goeben* and the *Breslau*.

On August 10 a German lieutenant-colonel named von Kress had arrived at Enver's office. Enver was talking with Colonel Hans Kannengiesser of the German military mission. Von Kress announced that the two German cruisers were at the mouth of the Dardanelles. Did they have permission to enter? Enver said he needed to consult others. The German demanded an immediate answer. The Minister for War said, yes, they could enter. Von Kress now demanded that the forts be ordered to fire on any British ships that attempted to follow the cruisers. Enver again began to dissemble. Von Kress again demanded an immediate answer – and got the one he wanted. Kannengiesser, who would serve prominently in the Gallipoli land war, later wrote: 'We heard the clanking of the portcullis descending before the Dardanelles.'

The auction was over: Turkey had been knocked down to Germany. There was a sub-plot nearly as good as the main story. That's why von Wangenheim was so excited when he saw Morgenthau on August 11.

Morgenthau recalled that, having made his first grand announcement, von Wangenheim was waving his radio message with 'all the enthusiasm of a college boy whose football team has won a victory'.

Then, momentarily checking his enthusiasm, he came up to me solemnly, humorously shook his forefinger, lifted his eyebrows, and said: 'Of course, you understand that we

have sold these ships to Turkey! And Admiral Souchon,'
he added with another wink, 'will enter the Sultan's
service!'

The ships would replace the two the British had con-
fiscated. Turkey would get around her treaty obligations:
she wasn't admitting foreign warships, merely taking
delivery of two she had bought. Now she could dominate
the Black Sea; Russia had nothing as smart as the *Goeben*.
Any thoughts of an alliance with Russia, the old enemy,
were forgotten. And now Turkey didn't need the British
mission under Vice-Admiral Limpus. It was 'banished'
from Turkish ships and forbidden to go on board the two
former German ships. On September 9 the mission was
withdrawn.

The crews of the *Goeben* and the *Breslau* were wearing
fezzes and insisting in perfect German that they were
Turkish. And, by the way, their ships were now called
the *Sultan Selim* and the *Medilli*. One day the Goeben
sailed up to the Russian embassy and anchored. The
sailors removed their fezzes and donned German caps.
The band played *Deutschland über Alles*. The sailors
then changed headgear again and left. Germans were
running the Turkish army and navy. As some wit in
the Constantinople diplomatic corps said, it was
'*Deutschland über Allah*'.

For all that, in mid-August there remained hope that
Turkey would at least stay neutral. German armies were
tramping through Belgium and into France. Von
Wangenheim believed the war would be over in a few
months. Germany would of course win. If she had Turkey
as an ally, she would have to hand over spoils. Anyway
speculation over how long Turkey's neutrality would last
was working well for Germany. It was tying up a

squadron of British ships off the Dardanelles, Russian troops in the Caucasus and British empire troops in Egypt. Constantinople, beautiful and corrupt, the whore and the grand lady, was in a fever and doing what it had always done best: intrigue. British, French and Russian diplomats worked on Enver and Talat to keep Turkey neutral, even offering to guarantee the borders of the Ottoman empire.

Von Wangenheim realised by September that he had been wrong: the war would not be short. Worse, Germany and Austria, fighting on two fronts, might lose. Now Germany needed Turkey on side to cut off Russia from her eastern allies. Von Wangenheim needed an incident.

On September 27 the British squadron off the Dardanelles intercepted a Turkish torpedo-boat. This was as tactless as the confiscation of the two Turkish battle-ships. Turkey closed the straits. Who made the decision? The Cabinet seems to have been taken by surprise. Aspinall, the official British war historian, says Jevad Bey, the Turkish commandant of the Dardanelles, was persuaded by Vice-Admiral Merten, his German artillery adviser, to close the waterway. Morgenthau says Weber Pasha, the German general in charge of fortifications along the Dardanelles, made the decision without consulting anyone. Morgenthau went to see the Grand Vizier.

> He presented a pitiable sight. This was, in title at least, the most important official of the Turkish Government, the mouthpiece of the Sultan himself, yet now he presented a picture of abject helplessness and fear. His face was blanched and he was trembling from head to foot. He was so overcome with his emotions that he could hardly speak.

Morgenthau cheered him up by delivering a line that would have been perfect for a B-grade movie 25 years later. 'You know this means war,' he said.

It didn't. Not yet, anyway. Turkey was merely living on the edge. Hundreds of ships from Russia, Bulgaria and Rumania dropped anchor in the Bosphorus and the Golden Horn waiting for the Dardanelles to re-open. They waited a month, then turned back. The Turks began mining the straits. More and more German soldiers and technicians appeared in Constantinople. German eagles were everywhere. It was now simply a question of where Turkey would put itself into the war, and that wasn't hard to guess. Russia was the country the Germans needed to hurt.

On October 28 the Turkish fleet sailed into the Black Sea under Germany's Admiral Souchon and fired on Odessa and nearby towns. The *Goeben* sank a Russian minelayer and fired on Sevastopol; a Russian gunboat was sunk. The facts about this raid, and who knew about it, will probably never be clear; one can only make assumptions.

One is that Souchon's voyage was no typical German attack with timetables and objectives. It was provocation, like louts setting fire to a police station on the basis that this must compel those inside to come out and chase them, a political exercise with the single aim of putting Turkey into the war.

A second assumption is that Enver and Talat knew this incident, or something like it, was going to happen. Djemal, the Minister of Marine, was playing cards when told of the attack. 'I know nothing about it,' he said. 'It has not been done by my orders.' Talat at first told Morgenthau that he had no advance knowledge of the attack. Later he said: 'Well, Wangenheim, Enver and I prefer that the war shall come now.'

A third assumption is that Enver and Talat saw the attack as a way of tightening their grip. Four prominent Cabinet members resigned afterwards and the Grand Vizier at least once burst into tears, although he stopped short of resigning because he liked the fancy dress of office too well.

Russia declared war on Turkey on November 2 and nothing would ever be the same again. The closure of the Dardanelles so hurt Russia it probably hastened the revolution and the rise of Lenin. The closure so hurt the Ottoman empire that when the Great War was over there was no Ottoman empire.

On November 3, after the British ambassador had left Constantinople but before London had declared war on Turkey, the British squadron off the Dardanelles bombarded the outer forts at Kum Kale and Seddülbahir for 20 minutes and got lucky. A shell hit the magazine at Seddülbahir castle, built in 1659, knocking all ten guns off their mountings and killing 86 Turks. Then, on December 13, the tiny British submarine *B11*, with a crew of 13, glided in under five lines of mines and from 600 yards torpedoed the old Turkish battleship *Messudieh* at anchor about four miles below Çanakkale.

Both incidents gave the British false hope. Never in their subsequent bombardments did they do as much damage as with one or two fluke shots on Seddülbahir in November. The Turks abruptly realised what they had to do. Jevad Bey said after the war: 'The bombardment of November 3 warned me, and I realised that I must spend the rest of my time in developing and strengthening the defence by every means.'

The Turks knew the British could stand out of range and shell the outer forts, which stood up on the horizon. The main defence of the Dardanelles had to be the inner forts along both sides of the straits, which were hard to see and even harder to hit with low trajectory naval guns, and the mobile howitzer batteries that were being brought up – and the mines. The Turks began laying more mines.

In November the Turks announced a *Jihad* against the infidels, although German Protestants were obviously exempted. Enver and Djemal, meanwhile, were dreaming big dreams. Djemal, though Minister of Marine, went south with an army to toss the British out of Egypt and to grab a personal kingdom for himself. Enver in December took an army of 100,000 into the Caucasus to toss out the Russians and reclaim Turkish provinces. Von Sanders had told Enver the plan was unsound; Enver said it was fine. Von Sanders wrote: 'At the conclusion of our conversation he gave utterance to fantastic, yet noteworthy ideas. He told me that he contemplated marching through Afghanistan to India.'

Enver's army and the Russians closed on each other high in the mountains in a blizzard. Enver made a wrong move and 30,000 Turks froze to death and more again surrendered. Enver returned, followed by about 12,000 frostbitten soldiers. He finally had something in common with Napoleon.

Enver's presence in the east bothered the Russian commander-in-chief, the Grand Duke Nicholas, who was losing men as carelessly as Enver. In early January, 1915, he asked the British if they could arrange a 'demonstration' to draw the Turks away from Russia. The obvious place was the Dardanelles.

The Dardanelles are about two-and-a-half miles wide at their mouth. On the left, under a pale blue haze, is Seddülbahir castle, tawny and crenellated like something from Arthurian legend. On the right, on a low marshland, is the fort at Kum Kale, close to the mouth of the Mendere River, the Scamander in Homer's *Iliad*. Behind Kum Kale lies the Trojan Plain and Troy.

After you pass through the mouth the waterway widens out for about four miles. This is Eren Keui Bay, a good place for battleships to turn around. Above it on the Asian side are pine-covered hills, a good place to conceal artillery. On the European side the hill the English called Achi Baba rises 700 feet high. It appears to dominate everything, and doesn't. It stares at the sulky massif of the Kilitbahir plateau to the north but offers no view of the Narrows or the Turkish intermediate forts under the plateau.

Beyond Achi Baba, about 10 miles up the Dardanelles, the yellow hills of the Sari Bair range rise to close to 1000 feet. This is the roughest country on the peninsula. On the Dardanelles side the range falls away to the narrow Maidos plain, which in 1915 was marshy, dotted with windmills and farmed by Greeks. The plain runs across the peninsula, from behind the promontory of Gaba Tepe on the Aegean to Maidos (now Eceabat), just above the Narrows. On the Aegean side the Sari Bair range tumbles down to the water's edge in a shambles of razorbacks and erosion gullies. The water's edge here now carries the name Anzac Cove.

The Narrows are 13 miles from the mouth of the Dardanelles. The heart-shaped castle at Kilitbahir stares across at the two larger and square-shaped forts at Çanakkale. There were five lines of mines at and below the Narrows, and another five at and below Kephez Point. If you walk both sides of the Dardanelles, you are sure of one thing: in 1915, before air power, this would be a better place to defend than to attack.

About 25 miles above Eceabat the peninsula narrows to

just three miles at Bulair, a flat and marshy plain. You are now on the edge of the Sea of Marmara, which runs for 170 miles before it narrows again into the Bosphorus at Constantinople.

The Bosphorus, in turn, leads into the Black Sea, 750 miles from east to west, 40 times larger than the Marmara, the drainage lake for the Danube and the Dnieper, the Dniester and the Don. It takes you deep into the lands of the Tartars and the Cossacks. But in 1915 you could get there only if you could shoot your way up the first 13 miles of the Dardanelles without being blown up by a mine.

Britain began thinking about forcing the Dardanelles more than a month before the Turks closed them. In August the Russians had asked the Greeks if they would help in an attack on the Dardanelles. The Greeks were neutral, but they hated the Turks, coveted the peninsula and understood its terrain better than any other nation. Yes, they were interested. Churchill on September 1 asked the army and the navy to work out a plan under which a Greek army would take the peninsula while the British navy steamed up the Dardanelles to Constantinople. General Charles Callwell, the Director of Military Operations, promptly submitted a rough plan that, in his own words, 'was intended to be dissuasive'.

Churchill was not a man to be dissuaded. The Greeks were asked for more details of their plan. They planned to land at Gaba Tepe, Kum Kale and Bulair. Then they lost interest: there were problems about what Bulgaria should do and King Constantine's wife was a sister to the Kaiser.

Churchill didn't lose interest. On November 3 he ordered the British squadron off the Dardanelles to fire on the outer defences of the Dardanelles. As mentioned earlier, this encouraged the Turks to improve their intermediate and inner defences, double their infantry strength and to put their best hopes in mines.

And then, in January, came the appeal from the Grand Duke Nicholas for a 'demonstration'. This is probably the point at which Britain's 'drift towards the Dardanelles' began. Britain now had a War Council. Its members comprised as fine a group of intellects as Britain has ever put together. There was Asquith, the Prime Minister; Arthur Balfour, a former prime minister; Sir Edward Grey, the Foreign Secretary; David Lloyd George, the Chancellor of the Exchequer, as well as Churchill, Kitchener, Lord 'Jackie' Fisher, the First Sea Lord, and Sir James Wolfe Murray, the Chief of the Imperial General Staff. The Council met at 10 Downing Street and followed the protocol of a Cabinet. The secretary was Lieutenant-Colonel Maurice Hankey.

4

The old man and the sea

John Arbuthnot Fisher, 73 years old, mercurial, neurotic and quick-witted, had been First Sea Lord from 1904 until 1910. He was recalled when Prince Louis of Battenberg, the First Sea Lord at the outbreak of war, was forced to step down because of his German pedigree (the family changed its name to Mountbatten in 1917). Fisher's specialities were gunnery, innovations and vendettas. His vendettas were Sicilian. He was tough and fragile, clear-headed and erratic. He loved to write letters. They were a form of catharsis. The prose was frantic and larded with underlines, capitals and exclamation marks. There was a nervous energy about it that suggests a man struggling against hysteria and just keeping it out. An excerpt from a typical letter:

> I was up till 2 am with Winston. *He is a genius without doubt.* He was very affectionate and so was Lloyd George. But ON THE WHOLE I'm sorry I went!

Churchill and Fisher: it was a weird combination, even though they started out liking each other. Both were in-telligent, eccentric and intolerant of humbug. Both liked

to get on with things. Both did a nice line in invective.
Fisher was sentimental about ships and Churchill wasn't.
Churchill was relatively young; he wanted to do something that would put him in the history books. Fisher was
so old he had served on the navy's first ironclad ship; he
wanted to protect the place he already had in the history
books. A naval colleague wrote in January, 1915, that
Fisher was

> old and worn-out and nervous. It is ill to have the destinies
> of the empire in the hands of a failing old man, anxious
> for popularity [and] afraid of any local mishap which may
> be put down to his dispositions.

When the War Council held its first meeting on
November 25, 1914, Churchill talked of an attack on
the Dardanelles. So far in the war the British navy, the
strongest in the world and the pride of the empire, had
found little glory. Kitchener had given Churchill an
opportunity to raise the Dardanelles by mentioning the
Turkish threat to Egypt. Kitchener said no troops were
available for a second front at the Dardanelles and the
Council did not share Churchill's eagerness for a naval
attack without troops. Churchill wasn't put off. After the
meeting – and this was to change forever the little worlds
of Australia and New Zealand – Churchill ordered that
the transport ships that had brought the two Anzac
divisions to Egypt remain there. Afterwards, too, Lloyd
George wrote a note for the Council that put into words
what everyone was thinking: the Allies needed a victory
'somewhere'.

Jackie Fisher put the Dardanelles on the agenda on
January 3. He suggested a joint naval and military attack
and argued his case in typical style:

But ONLY if it's IMMEDIATE! However, it won't be! Our Aulic Council will adjourn to the following Thursday fortnight! (N.B. When did we meet last? and what came of it???)

Fisher wanted to land 75,000 troops from the western front at Besika Bay, just south of Kum Kale. Greek troops would land on the Gallipoli Peninsula and the Bulgarians would attack Constantinople through Adrianople. The Russians would do something to tie down the Austrians. Old British battleships would be used to flatten the Dardanelles forts. But it had to be done quickly. Without 'CELERITY' there would be 'FAILURE'.

Even Churchill thought the scheme fantastic: for one thing, Greece and Bulgaria were neutral. But old battleships, the pre-dreadnoughts that were going to the scrap heap anyway: there was a thought. Churchill cabled Vice-Admiral Sackville Carden, commanding the British squadron off the Dardanelles. The cable was short and, as Churchill later admitted, loaded. 'Do you consider the forcing of the Dardanelles by ships alone a practicable operation?' Churchill asked. And one sentence later: 'Importance of result would justify severe loss.'

Carden two days later replied: 'I do not consider Dardanelles can be rushed. They might be forced by extended operations with large numbers of ships.' The admiral was playing games: his words could mean whatever he chose them to mean. It could be done; it could not be done. Churchill naturally decided that Carden was saying the first thing. Fisher wasn't so sure; he was starting to fret. The War Council was told of the idea and asked Carden to provide a detailed plan. On January 11 he outlined a scheme to force the Dardanelles by careful stages. He couldn't estimate how long this would take. He asked for 12 battleships (he had four at the time), extra sub-marines as well as 4 seaplanes and 12 minesweepers. The Admiralty was so impressed it decided to send him the *Queen Elizabeth*, the most modern battleship in the world, sporting eight 15-inch guns.

The War Council sitting of January 13 lasted almost all day. Field Marshal Sir John French, the old cavalryman who was now commander-in-chief on the western front, wanted to stage a new offensive there. Most councillors sided with him. Lloyd George and Balfour didn't. French's credit was running out; he had not only a genius for failure but also for being rewarded each time he failed. Everyone was tired and the table was strewn with papers. Then, as Hankey put it, events took a dramatic turn.

> Churchill suddenly revealed his well-kept secret of a naval attack on the Dardanelles! The idea caught on at once. The whole atmosphere changed. Fatigue was forgotten. The War Council turned eagerly from the dreary vista of a 'slogging match' on the western front to brighter prospects, as they seemed, in the Mediterranean. The navy ... was to come into the front line. Even French ... caught something of the general enthusiasm.

The decision on French's new offensive was deferred; all bar Jackie Fisher seemed entranced by the Dardanelles. Maybe they were sick of the stalemate in France, or tired, or won over by Churchill's gifts of oratory, which (as Aneurin Bevan wrote many years later) included an ability to persuade people not to look at facts. How, precisely, were those minefields to be cleared if the forts and batteries were still firing? If the fleet got through, how would it subdue Constantinople? How would the capture of Constantinople win the war against Germany? These questions didn't seem to matter – not then, anyway. The attack was to go ahead in February. But what was it? A probe, or something to be won at all costs? Was it a gambit or a second front? No-one knew.

Fisher began to worry. What about the Baltic and the North Sea? These were the theatres that interested him. He wrote to Admiral Sir John Jellicoe on January 19.

> There is only one way out, and that is to resign! But you say 'no!', which simply means I am a consenting party to what I absolutely disapprove. *I don't agree with one single step taken . . . the way the war is conducted both ashore and afloat is chaotic! We have a new plan every week!*

Two days later, in another letter to Jellicoe, he dropped an interesting number: 'I just abominate the Dardanelles operation, unless a great change is made and it is settled to be a military operation, with 200,000 men in conjunction with the fleet.' Two hundred thousand? Fisher might have been flighty, but he understood about the numbers needed to win a war.

Carden received all the ships he requested, plus the *Queen Elizabeth*. The French sent a squadron to serve under Carden; the Russians sent a light cruiser. The Russians were also asked to make a simultaneous attack on the Bosphorus. It was all happening so quickly that Carden began to fret.

Fisher was past fretting. He told Asquith the Dardanelles scheme was 'unjustifiable' as a purely naval operation. He wanted a military operation as well. He didn't want to lose ships, not even old ones. When the Dardanelles scheme came up at the War Council meeting of January 28, Fisher said he thought the matter was not going to be mentioned and that the Prime Minister knew what he, Fisher, thought anyway. Fisher headed for the door. He was staging a tantrum. Kitchener intercepted him and took him to a window.

Here was a very English tableau: at the Cabinet table, discussion continued as though nothing had happened; at the window, Fisher told Kitchener he was going to resign. Kitchener talked him into returning to the table. Fisher said nothing. Churchill and Fisher talked afterwards. Fisher agreed to support the Dardanelles scheme.

Churchill, Fisher admitted, could always get round him. They would talk. Fisher would be charmed and disarmed. Then he would go away, think about the conversation, and realise he hadn't changed his mind at all. Churchill had hypnotised him again. He must tell him so at once. Pen and ink and paper. Frantic strokes. Underlines, capitals, exclamation marks. The whole thing signed 'F'. Another discussion, and Churchill would finesse him again.

Churchill thought the doubts had been settled during his talk with Fisher after the War Council meeting; now he could get on with bombarding the hell out of the Turks. Fisher, later events make clear, had not been won over. One suspects he owned other fears that had not been spoken. The navy had been just about all of his life. He didn't like to lose ships or sailors. He thought that the First Sea Lord ran the Admiralty. And here was this young politician, cleverer and more manipulative than politicians are supposed to be, virtually saying: 'I don't care if the navy loses a dozen battleships. If the thing works it will shorten the war and, yes, people probably will say what an acute mind I have and that will be good for my career.' Fisher had built his reputation on husbanding ships; this Churchill wanted to build a career on sinking ships for the greater good. This young politician thought he ran the day-to-day affairs of the Admiralty. Why have a First Sea Lord?

The trouble with the Gallipoli campaign, as early as January 1915, was that everyone saw it differently. Asquith and others saw it as a good idea that could be abandoned if events went poorly. Churchill saw it as the idea. Kitchener sometimes thought it should have a military element and sometimes didn't. Wolfe Murray thought whatever Kitchener thought. Fisher's instincts told him it was all wrong, especially if the army was not part of it. One has the feeling – and this is important in light of what was about to unfold – that most at the Admiralty agreed with Fisher.

In September, 1914, Churchill had written: 'A good army of 50,000 men and sea power – that is the end of the Turkish menace.' Now he was planning to do it without the good army of 50,000. By February, 1915, most involved in the Gallipoli enterprise, whatever their differences, were starting to think the idea would be sounder with a military element. Admiral Sir Henry Jackson wrote in mid-February that the scheme for a naval bombardment was unsound 'unless a strong military force is ready to assist in the operation, or at least to follow it up immediately the forts are silenced'.

There was one crack division left in England, the 29th, regulars with a sprinkling of territorials. One of its regiments, the Lancashire Fusiliers, from the cotton town of Bury, near Manchester, had been around in various guises since William of Orange's march on Exeter in 1688. A meeting attended by Asquith, Churchill, Kitchener, Fisher and others in mid-February decided to send the 29th to Lemnos, the Greek island south-west of the Dardanelles. Some Australian troops in Egypt would also be sent there. The Admiralty was told to think about ways of landing maybe 50,000 men on the peninsula. With Greek permission, Rear-Admiral Rosslyn Wemyss was to become governor of Lemnos, which really meant he was allowed to set up a war base around Mudros harbour. As would happen to Hamilton the following month, Wemyss went off without clear instructions. How many troops was he supposed to accommodate? What were they going to do? No-one knew. The nature of the Gallipoli adventure changed every day.

It was like the hayshed that grew: a lean-to tacked on this side, a tool shed tacked on the other; now a fowl house at this end and a stable at the other. Soon it was a very big hayshed. Maybe it wasn't a hayshed any more. Kitchener suddenly decided he might need the 29th in France. He countermanded the order to send it to Lemnos. He was wavering. He consulted Captain Wyndham Deedes, an intelligence officer who would shortly join Hamilton's staff. Deedes had served with the Turkish army. When Deedes told Kitchener the operation was flawed, Kitchener turned on him angrily.

Carden began his 'extended operations' on February 19 with a bombardment of the outer defences. The fleet had 274 medium and heavy guns; the outer forts had 19 and only 4 of these had a range beyond 8000 yards. The attack began at 7.30 am with two destroyers heading into the mouth of the Dardanelles. At 7.58, the Turkish battery at Orkanie, near Kum Kale, opened up. Carden sent in the pre-dreadnoughts *Cornwallis* and *Vengeance* to pound Orkanie with their 12-inch guns. The *Vengeance* took a few shots in her foretops and splinters littered her decks. A gunnery officer on the *Cornwallis* wrote home: 'We blew No. 1 fort [near Cape Helles] to a perfect inferno, rocks & smoke, flame, dust & splinters all in the air together. We then got under fire from another fort, so we switched onto her then & never in my life have I had such a ripping time.' For all that, the day's action was, as they say, inconclusive.

Carden found none of the luck of November 3: no flukey shot hit a magazine. Few shells seem to have hit anything that mattered; in the capital cities of the Balkans, however, they exploded in men's minds and caused their limbs to quiver in anticipation. If this was the start of 'dismemberment', each vulture wanted the limb he had picked out long ago. The Greeks again offered soldiers to take the Gallipoli Peninsula. How did three divisions sound? The Russians talked of attacking Constantinople from the other side. There was, of course, a problem here: the Greeks and the Russians both felt they had a divine right to Constantinople. The Bulgarians, meanwhile, thought this might be a poor time to throw in with Germany and Austria.

Gloom enveloped Constantinople. Pallavicini, the Austrian ambassador, told Morgenthau he thought the British attack would succeed. Von Wangenheim was outraged at the prospect of British ships shelling his embassy, which meant he thought the same as Pallavicini. Talat told Morgenthau he was sorry Turkey had come into the war. Rumours flew and dissent festered. Morgenthau claims there were plans to burn the city – in 1915 most of the houses were wooden – and blow up Sancta Sophia with dynamite. Morgenthau asked Talat that the great church (it had been turned into a mosque) be spared, and the Minister for the Interior revealed a side of himself and his colleagues. 'There are not six men in the Committee of Union and Progress who care for anything that is old. We like new things!' Enver alone seemed unworried.

By now the Royal Naval Division (RND) had been ordered to Lemnos. Lieutenant-General Sir John Maxwell, the commander-in-chief in Egypt, had been told by Kitchener that the two Anzac divisions would almost certainly be going there too. Kitchener, however, had not told the navy about this. He ordered Lieutenant-General Sir William Birdwood, commander of the Anzac Corps, to go to the Dardanelles and look things over. Maxwell hated to lose troops. He wasn't sure whether the Anzac divisions were to be used for a landing on the peninsula or to garrison Constantinople; he wasn't sure whether he was losing the Anzacs or lending them. 'Who is co-ordinating and directing this great combine?' he wrote. It was a good question. By early March the enterprise had too many interpreters.

Carden had been held up by rough weather. He resumed his attack on the outer defences on February 25. The ships kept out of range of the forts and the four modern guns at the entrance stopped firing. The warships crept closer and the Turks evacuated the outer forts. The next day three warships steamed into the straits and shelled the intermediate defences. They came within the range of the Turkish mobile howitzer batteries. These didn't much bother the warships but there was a warning here of how the howitzers might worry the minesweepers, which were really just trawlers with no armour. Another problem became apparent: the howitzer batteries weren't like the fixed guns at Seddülbahir castle, sitting on the skyline and easy to hit with low-trajectory fire. These batteries were up on the escarpments, out of sight.

Marines landed at the Camber, a jetty on the bank below Seddülbahir, and at Kum Kale to blow up the fixed guns. They met little opposition. There were no casualties at Seddülbahir; one man was killed and two wounded at

Kum Kale. It all seemed easy. The next day another demolition party raided Seddülbahir without a casualty. On March 1 four battleships resumed the attack on the intermediate defences; again they were bothered by fire from the hidden batteries. That night trawlers crewed by fishermen tried to sweep the Kephez minefield. The heavy fire from the batteries bothered them and the current, running against them at five knots, slowed them down.

Carden's 'piecemeal' destruction of the Dardanelles defences was ten days old and a pattern was emerging. The fixed guns of the outer forts were easy to deal with; that battle had been won. The hidden guns of the intermediate defences were a problem; that battle had so far been lost. The unprotected minesweepers couldn't work in the current and the gunfire; that battle had been lost too. And, all around the peninsula, the Turks could be seen throwing up earthworks and stringing barbed wire in readiness for a landing.

Churchill asked Carden about progress. Carden said on March 2 that he required only 14 fine days to reach the Marmara. How could he be so precise? That night another attempt to sweep the Kephez minefield failed. And now the landing parties began to meet opposition. Twenty marines died at Kum Kale on March 4. The Turkish fire at Seddülbahir on the same day was so heavy that the marines had to withdraw with three killed. Everything was getting harder.

Birdwood thought Carden lacked energy. He cabled Kitchener that if a landing were necessary, Cape Helles looked the best spot. Kitchener cabled Birdwood on March 4 to remind him that the troops were there for operations around Constantinople, not for major landings on the peninsula. Birdwood replied tartly: 'I have already informed you that I consider the admiral's forecast too sanguine, and I doubt his ability to force the passage unaided . . . ' Kitchener was reading the situation from cables and maps; Birdwood had seen the reality from the deck of a ship.

The bombardment continued. Carden moved the *Queen Elizabeth* to the waters off Gaba Tepe to fire across the peninsula on the Narrows forts. Then he sent the *Queen Elizabeth* into the straits. Neither foray changed anything. The intermediate defences were still hard to hit, the mines were still there, the minesweepers could manage only three knots against the rippling current, and ammunition was starting to run low.

Kitchener told the War Council he would release the 29th Division for the Dardanelles. He said there were about 130,000 troops available for the attack on Constantinople; his figure was 15,000 too high and included a Russian force of 40,000. Kitchener then appointed Hamilton in the circumstances recounted earlier and sent him hurtling towards the Dardanelles without an administrative staff. Alexandre Millerand, the French Minister for War, raised a nice question. The French had contributed battleships and a division of troops to this adventure. What, Millerand wanted to know, was the plan?

Carden had broken off his bombardment but was still trying to clear the Kephez minefield. Commodore Roger Keyes, his chief-of-staff, wrote to his wife:

> The position is – we can silence – temporarily – I think the guns at The Narrows and at Chanak whenever we wish – but in order to take advantage of this we must have a clear channel through the minefield for the ships to close to decisive range to hammer the forts and then land men to destroy the guns.

Keyes' nicknames were 'the thruster' and 'the chief instigator'. Unlike Carden and his second-in-command Vice-Admiral John de Robeck, Keyes was a hothead who loved a 'stunt'. He shaved with a copy of Kipling's *If* beside the mirror. An attempt to sweep the minefield on the night of March 10 offended his sense of gallantry.

To put it briefly, the sweepers turned tail and fled directly they were fired upon. I was furious and told the officers in charge that . . . it did not matter if we lost all seven sweepers; there were 28 more and the mines had got to be swept up. How could they talk of being stopped by heavy fire if they were not hit?

Keyes was being unfair: the fishermen in the trawlers were not career officers like him and did not share his sense of heroics. Keyes shortly afterwards took charge of the sweeping. He added naval volunteers to the trawlers' crews and used the cruiser *Amethyst* as support. After dark on March 13 six trawlers and the *Amethyst* tried to bring up the Kephez mines. Searchlights blazed, hidden guns barked and shrapnel fizzed. Four trawlers were hit hard. The *Amethyst* was hit and her steering gear damaged. A shell burst among stokers washing in a bathroom. So badly were their bodies mangled that only after a muster could it be decided that 19 men had died. A few mines had been prised loose but the field was as formidable as ever. The problem was not the forts: they could be bombarded into silence, temporarily anyway. The problem was the mobile batteries that could not be silenced because they could not be found. And the mines. Always the mines.

Churchill was becoming as frustrated as Keyes. On March 11 the Admiralty told Carden to get on with it.

After thinking for two days, Carden said, yes, he would get on with it. He would do what he had said he would not do: attack in daylight with his whole force, sending the minesweepers in to work under cover of the attack. De Robeck held a meeting of senior officers to discuss the rush at the Dardanelles. A gunnery officer who attended wrote in his diary:

> Everyone, or nearly so I believe, knew really that it would be madness to try & rush them. The Narrows are sure to be mined. It has been proved the bombardments silences forts but does little material damage to guns & only silences because gunners take cover. Personally I feel sure that it is pressure from our cursed politicians on the VA [Vice-Admiral] which is making him even consider such a thing.

On March 15 the Admiralty agreed to Carden's plan for all-out attack. Carden replied that he would attack on the first fine day. The next day he was too ill to go on. Explanations of his illness include indigestion, a nervous breakdown, strain and worry and the inability to eat or sleep; one account has Carden locked in his lavatory signing orders that had to be slid under the door. It may also have been that, as with Jackie Fisher, Churchill was pushing Carden too rudely to do something he didn't believe in.

De Robeck took over Carden's command. He was 52 and had been recalled from half-pay at the outbreak of war. Ellis Ashmead-Bartlett, who covered the land war on Gallipoli for Fleet Street, described de Robeck as 'a most delightful man, a perfect replica of the courteous type of old English sportsman and country gentleman of bygone days'. De Robeck was cautious the way Keyes was rash.

Churchill wrote in *The World Crisis* that he had regarded de Robeck as a good sea officer and a 'fine disciplinarian', whatever that meant. 'One could not feel that his training and experience up to this period had led him to think deeply on the larger aspects of strategy and tactics.' Like Carden, like most old sailors, de Robeck hated to lose ships. Like Carden, he was not made for Churchill.

Hamilton had arrived and taken his first look at the peninsula. He saw the new trenches the Turks had dug at likely landing spots and barbed wire sparkling and bluish in the sun. 'Here,' he wrote to Kitchener, 'Gallipoli looks a much tougher nut to crack than it did over the map in your office.'

Maps can be fraudulent things. No map can ever explain the terrain of the peninsula, particularly the maze behind and to the north of Anzac Cove and the fissures that break up the Helles plain. And there was now another trouble. The Turks had had a month's warning of Britain's intentions.

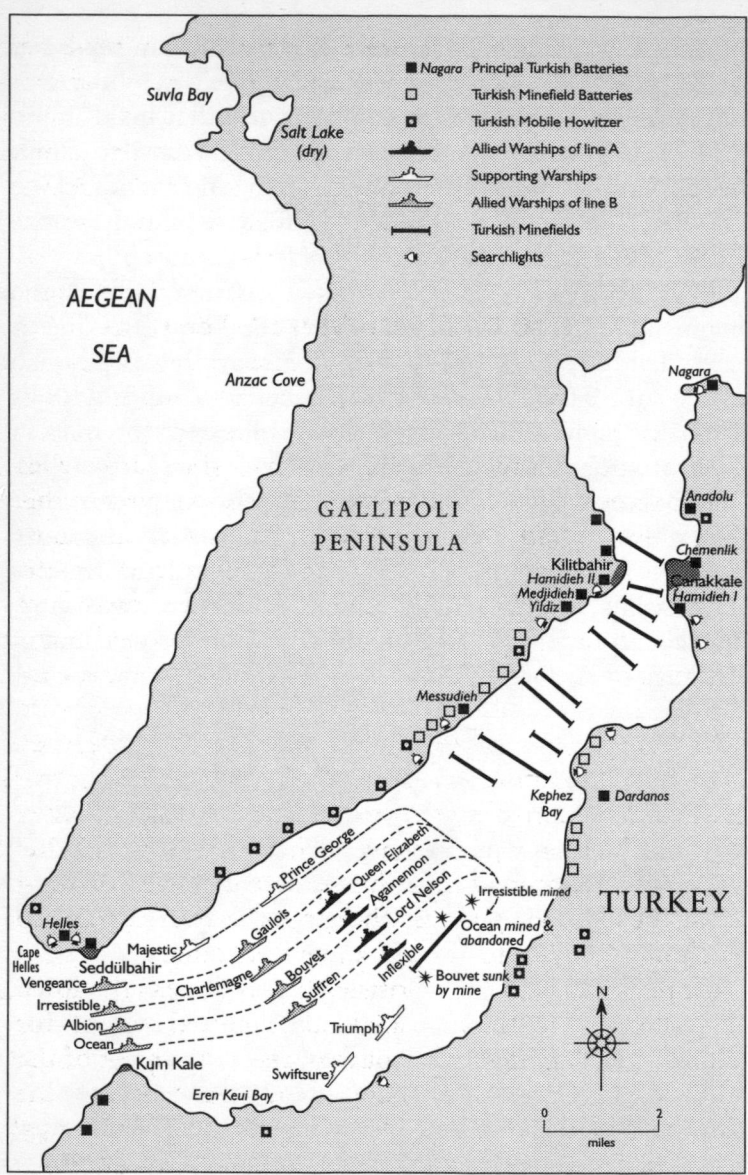

The battle of March 18

5

The battle of March 18

Enver took Morgenthau on a tour of the Dardanelles defences a few days before de Robeck began his attack. Enver had merely lost an army in the Caucasus; his self-belief was intact. He told Morgenthau the Dardanelles defences were impregnable and talked of the 'silly panic' in Constantinople. He also handed out a few lines of *realpolitik*. 'The Turks and the Germans care nothing for each other,' he told the ambassador. 'We are with them because it is our interest to be with them; they are with us because that is their interest. Germany will back Turkey just so long as that helps Germany; Turkey will back Germany just so long as that helps Turkey.' One worry with Morgenthau is his apparent power of total recall. His observations at the straits, however, explain much of what was to happen a few days later.

Morgenthau heard the British guns from near the town of Gallipoli. He found Çanakkale deserted except for soldiers. At Hamidiye fort, south of the town, most of the officers were German and many of the men were from the *Goeben* and the *Breslau*. The ten guns were the Krupp model of 1885 and showing rust. Turks ran the Dardanos emplacement, near the site of the ancient city. The ground for nearly half a mile around had been churned up by thousands of British shells, but not one gun had been hit. The bombardment had exposed water jugs and other relics from the old city. 'After the war,' Morgenthau was told, 'we are going to establish a big tourist resort here, build a hotel, and sell relics to you Americans.'

Morgenthau saw a team of 16 water buffalo hauling a howitzer from one concrete emplacement to another on the hills above Eren Keui Bay. As soon as the British had the range of the gun, the buffaloes were brought in to move it. The Turks had also rigged up lengths of sewer pipe as dummy guns on the ridge overlooking the bay. When a real gun was about to be fired, the crew would telephone the men at the sewer pipe, who lit a pile of black powder that sent forth a plume of smoke. The fleet fired at the smoke. One dummy gun had attracted 500 shots. Across the Dardanelles, at the forts under the Kilitbahir plateau, shell holes were everywhere but the guns were intact.

Before Morgenthau's visit, on the night of March 8, the Turkish minelayer *Nusrat*, straight of prow, no bigger than a trawler, crept into Eren Keui Bay. The *Nusrat* was entirely functional, built around three railway lines that conveyed the mines to her shallow stern. She was commanded by Captain Hakki Bey, who had suffered a heart attack several days earlier.

There were no mines in Eren Keui Bay. The Turks had laid 370 across the straits in ten lines. At the widest part of Eren Keui the straits open out on the Asian side to a width of about five miles. The Turks had noticed that the British were using the bay to turn around, swinging to starboard under the Asian shore.

Hakki Bey now laid an 11th line of mines not across the

channel but *parallel* to the shore, a mile or so off the Asian coast. British accounts say there were 20 mines in the line; the Turks say there were 26. The mines were moored about two-and-half fathoms below the surface at intervals of roughly 100 yards. Here was a new minefield, perhaps 2600 yards long, that any battleship turning to starboard was likely to cross. Most important of all, the fleet didn't know this line existed. The water is very clear here and the naval seaplanes could spot mines even if they were a few fathoms down. These mines had not been spotted.

Old rituals were playing for the battle of March 18. The lead-up had been leisurely. Each side pretty much knew what the other was doing. They had been staring at each other for more than a month. The Turks could name the Allied ships without reaching for binoculars. The British and the French knew where the Turks' heavy guns lay and in many cases the year of their manufacture; they thought they knew where the mines were. The stadium had been selected and its boundaries marked. There was little that was sly or clever.

And here, in another way, was a clash unlike any other. This wasn't a naval battle, as it is sometimes called, and it wasn't a land battle. It was ships against artillery. Legend says that the most famous war here was about the abduction of Helen by Paris, the son of the Trojan king. In truth, that war was probably about the same thing as this war of 1915: the right to trade with the Black Sea ports.

The British and French ships left their anchorages around Tenedos and steamed towards the Dardanelles at 10.45 am, a gentleman's hour for combat. The sun was bright and the water glistened under a blue sky blotched with the odd high cloud. The grey-blue haze over the mouth of the Dardanelles began to lift. The few sailors above deck could see snow-topped mountains in Asia Minor and, to the left, along the edge of the channel, the Kilitbahir plateau, sulky and ghost-like.

De Robeck's main force comprised 17 battleships, all pre-dreadnought bar the *Queen Elizabeth*, and the battle cruiser *Inflexible*. Cruisers, destroyers and minesweepers attended them, equerries buzzing back and forth. The idea was to silence first the forts at the Narrows and the batteries protecting the five lines of mines at Kephez Bay. The minesweepers would then clear the Kephez mines, working through the night. The next day, the 19th, the battleships would steam on to Sari Sighlar Bay, about two-and-half miles below the Narrows. From there they would demolish the Narrows forts at close range. Then, after the five lines of mines at the Narrows had been swept, on into the Marmara and into another battle, somewhere between the Narrows and Constantinople, with the *Goeben* and the *Breslau*.

De Robeck went forth with his ships in three lines. Line A comprised the *Queen Elizabeth*, the *Agamemnon*, the *Lord Nelson* and the *Inflexible*. The *Prince George* flanked this line on the European side and the *Triumph* on the Asian coast. About a mile astern came the French squadron: *Gaulois*, *Charlemagne*, *Bouvet* and *Suffren*. Flanking those were the *Majestic* and the *Swiftsure*. The third line comprised *Vengeance*, *Irresistible*, *Albion* and *Ocean*. De Robeck held the battleships *Canopus* and *Cornwallis* in reserve.

The first line steamed forward slowly under fire from the Turkish mobile batteries, which did little harm. Just after 11 am, Line A, by now deep into Eren Keui Bay, opened up on the Narrows forts. The *Queen Elizabeth* pounded the two forts at Çanakkale, the other three the forts around Kilitbahir. The *Prince George* and the *Triumph* from the flanks fired at the batteries under the Kilitbahir plateau and on the Asian heights. The Narrows forts fell silent and a pall of smoke rose over Çanakkale.

Just after noon, de Robeck, on *Queen Elizabeth*, decided to engage the Narrows forts at closer range. He ordered the French squadron to slip through the British line and steam a half-mile ahead of it. The forts on either side opened a heavy fire on the French. The ten battleships inside the straits eventually silenced the fire but all took hits. *Gaulois* was holed below the waterline, *Agamemnon* had taken perhaps a dozen hits, and the *Inflexible*'s foretop was smashed. Casualties, however, were few – maybe a dozen across the whole fleet – and the ships kept firing.

The Turks couldn't keep firing. Their guns were buried under debris; others had jammed or been dismounted. Communications had broken down. The air was full of smoke and dust. As the official account of the Turkish General Staff put it, 'the situation had become very critical'. The British and French had not come close to destroying the batteries and forts: the batteries were too well hidden and the battleships were not yet close enough to the forts. But by 1.25 pm the fleet had temporarily silenced most of the guns.

De Robeck decided to withdraw the French squadron and bring up *Vengeance*, *Irresistible*, *Albion*, *Ocean*, *Swiftsure* and *Majestic*. The French squadron turned to starboard, into the widest part of Eren Keui on the Asian side. *Suffren* turned first followed by Bouvet. At 1.54 pm, in the words of de Robeck's report to the Admiralty, the *Bouvet*

was seen to be in distress; large volume black smoke suddenly appeared on starboard quarter, and before any assistance could be rendered she heeled over and sank in 36 fathoms north of Eren Keui village in under three minutes. Explosion of *Bouvet* appeared to be an internal one.

It happened so quickly that the *Bouvet*, capsized and with jets of smoke and steam blasting out of her, plunged downwards with her engines still running. More than 600 men, including the captain, went down with her; ships' boats picked up several dozen survivors. One was carried so deep by the suction from the ship that blood burst through his ears and nose.

The probability is that the *Bouvet* sank in less than the three minutes mentioned by de Robeck. The near certainty is that she hit one of Hakki Bey's mines. The British at first thought that either a shell had struck her magazine or that she had been hit by a torpedo fired from a mobile tube that the Turks were known to have. There was also speculation that the Turks were using the current to float mines down the channel. A Turkish observer in the Asian hills wrote that he thought the *Bouvet* had hit a mine. But he mentioned a second, more violent, explosion. 'We believed that a shell from Mejidiye [fort] had blown up the magazine.' As the *Bouvet* died, Turkish morale soared.

The heavy guns at the Narrows opened up again. The six battleships in the channel crept closer as they fired back. The forts fell silent again. De Robeck sent in the minesweepers and three mines were brought up. But when the trawlers came under fire, they turned and left the channel; two didn't even bother to put their sweeps out.

Just after 4 pm the *Inflexible*, which had taken several heavy hits to her tops from the Turkish guns, left the line, struck a mine with her bow and lurched to starboard.

Thirty men were killed. The *Inflexible* was near where the *Bouvet* sank. The cruiser *Phaeton*, with Ian Hamilton on board, and an escort of destroyers attended her as she left the straits and headed for Tenedos. Around the same time *Irresistible* began to list to starboard. She flew a green flag, suggesting that she thought she had been torpedoed, but she too had probably hit a mine. She was on the same line as *Bouvet* and *Inflexible*. A destroyer took the *Irresistible*'s crew off. The battleship was drifting towards the shore and an easy target for Turkish gunners.

De Robeck sent Keyes in a destroyer to see what could be done to salvage the *Irresistible*. The *Ocean* and *Swiftsure* were still close by. Keyes came alongside around 5.20 pm as the *Irresistible* was being rocked by Turkish shellfire. He signalled the *Ocean*: 'The admiral directs you to take *Irresistible* in tow.' The *Ocean* signalled back that the water was too shallow for her to do so, which was not true. *Ocean* steamed up and down, sending thunderous salvoes at the Turkish guns. Keyes told the *Ocean* and *Swiftsure* to withdraw. Then, at 6.05 pm, the *Ocean* struck a mine. She was on the same line as *Bouvet*, *Inflexible* and *Irresistible*. Her steering gear jammed. She began to turn a crazy circle. Destroyers took her crew off. The Turkish gunners now had two easy targets.

Keyes returned to de Robeck and obtained permission to torpedo the *Irresistible* and, after a brief meal, the intrepid commodore steamed back into the straits in a destroyer. He cruised up and down for four hours, and found nothing. All was quiet on the darkened battlefield. Keyes' imagination became fevered.

Except for the searchlights there seemed to be no sign of life, and I had the almost indelible impression that we were in the presence of a beaten foe. I thought he was beaten at 2 pm. I knew he was beaten at 4 pm – and at midnight I knew with still greater clarity that he was absolutely beaten; and it only remained for us to organise a proper sweeping force and devise some means of dealing with drifting mines to reap the fruits of our efforts. I felt that the guns of the forts and batteries and the concealed howitzers and mobile field guns were no longer a menace. Mines moored and drifting must, and could, be overcome.

Every navy needs a Roger Keyes, just as every army needs a George Patton. They provide the Homeric stuff; they make war seem grander than a trip to the abattoir. All that really matters is that such people never become supreme commanders. Keyes had a buccaneering spirit that was at odds with the caution of de Robeck. Throughout the Gallipoli campaign that was to come, Keyes wanted to try things when others wanted to do nothing.

On the night of March 18, however, Keyes was wrong about the Turks. Compared with the fleet, they had taken few casualties and most of their guns were intact. By the medieval rules, they had won the day: they were still in possession of the field. But Keyes was also right about the Turks for reasons he could not have been aware of: they were running out of ammunition.

The British and French losses for the day amounted to about 700 sailors killed. Three battleships – *Bouvet*, *Irresistible* and *Ocean* – were on the bottom. Three other ships were crippled. The *Inflexible* had been run aground at Tenedos. *Gaulois* had been beached in the Rabbit Island group nearby. *Suffren*, another French ship, had been badly damaged by shell fire. By any sensible assessment, the day had ended, as Aspinall was to write, in 'complete failure' for the Allied fleet.

The Turkish account said that 8 of their 176 guns had been hit. Forty men had been killed and 70 wounded. In short, fewer Turks had died than when a British shell hit the magazine at Seddülbahir on November 3. The Turkish account concedes that ammunition was running low. The official German account says the medium howitzers and minefield batteries had fired half their shells. The Narrows forts had fired most of their high-explosive shells. There were only ten left at Kilitbahir. And there was no reserve of mines.

The mines: they were still everything. If de Robeck was to return, as the Turks and Germans were sure he would, he had still to find a way of clearing the mines. He told Churchill on March 20 that he was reorganising his armada of minesweepers. The tone of the cable suggested the attack would resume as quickly as possible. The day before he wrote to Hamilton that he was preparing for another 'go'. Churchill told him he was sending four ships immediately to replace those lost.

Constantinople expected another 'go'. According to Morgenthau, no-one there believed the Allies would accept defeat after the sinking of just three ships. All the Allies had to do was steel themselves to the loss of a few more. No grit, no glory. And there was the Turks' problem with ammunition. The neutrality of Bulgaria and Rumania cut Turkey off from her allies. Any ammunition had to come from Constantinople. An Associated Press journalist who witnessed the March 18 battle told Morgenthau that the Turks felt they could only hold out for a few hours if the fleet returned on March 19. Talat, according to Morgenthau, had two cars, one of which was loaded with spare tyres and cans of petrol, parked on the Asian side of the city, ready for a 'protracted journey'.

De Robeck on March 23 telegraphed the Admiralty that, in effect, the Carden plan had been tossed out and that the navy would need the army before it could get to Çanakkale, let alone Constantinople. De Robeck had been commanding Churchill's 'dispensable' navy for a week and he was confused. In his sailor's mind, just about the worst thing a commander could do was to keep losing ships. On the night of March 18 he wrote: 'After losing so many ships I shall obviously find myself superseded tomorrow morning.'

Now, with this cable of March 23, Gallipoli had become a joint operation – and of the worst sort. There was a navy commander and an army commander, but no supreme commander. Instead of being planned for months in London, down to the last artillery shell and the last bandage, this venture was being cobbled up on the spot, and only after another enterprise, the naval attack, had failed. The original numbers now made no sense. Hamilton had been given 75,000 troops to keep order in Constantinople and maybe make brief sorties ashore at the Dardanelles. Were 75,000 enough to *invade* the Dardanelles and knock out the batteries and howitzers along two coastlines? And, worst of all, surprise had been lost. When there were no signs of a resumption of the naval attack, the Turks began to sense there would be a landing. When the harbours at Lemnos and Alexandria became clogged with troop transports, they knew there was going to be a landing.

Cabinet hadn't ordered this combined operation; neither had the War Council, the Admiralty or the Imperial General Staff. It had just happened. Another annexe, a huge one this time, was being tacked on to the hayshed. All through, the adventure had lacked methodical planning; at this moment it also seemed to lack resolution, to be as soft and windblown as the haze over the Dardanelles.

In Constantinople, late in the afternoon of March 24, Enver called in von Sanders and asked him to take command of the Dardanelles defences. Von Sanders was very methodical.

It is spring in 2000 and we are at the third fort under Kilitbahir plateau. Corporal Seyyid, though long dead, owns this place. A statue of him carrying a shell stands near the fort. Alongside are the graves of 15 gunners killed during the battle of March 18. Seyyid was exceptionally strong. He was a timber collector in his village; he would often be seen walking around with a log under each arm. During the battle of March 18 the machinery that conveyed shells to the guns failed. Seyyid single-handedly hefted shells to the Krupp cannon. Each weighed about 600 pounds. Next day Seyyid, now and forever a Turkish hero, was asked to pose for a photograph with a shell under his arm. The battle was over, his blood had cooled. He couldn't lift the shell. The photographer settled for an imitation projectile made of wood.

Nature is reclaiming the forts now. The grey stones that once walled them in are strewn about and coated with moss. Wildflowers sprout out of cracks in the gun emplacements. The underground magazines and tunnels are intact. These walls, six feet thick, are forever. The magazine smells of mould and wild thyme.

No-one comes here much. One is hypnotised by an unusual beauty and led – perhaps by the solitude, perhaps by the fact that so little has changed – to imaginings. You can see the current below, phalanxes of vee-shaped ripples marching to the Aegean, as though this is a river rather than the strait that connects two great seas. Stare for a few moments and you can see the North Sea trawlers, which could barely make six knots when everything was right, struggling against the current, trying to get upstream, not to spawn but to feel for mines. You think you can see the fear on the faces of the upward-staring fishermen, see an elbow come up to protect a face as shrapnel bursts overhead and the sea spits and fizzes and splinters are stripped off the mast to bounce and clatter on the deck.

Across the water, and it seems so near, touchable almost, is Kephez Point, under a grey-blue haze. The sea is like shimmering glass. This is not some watery battlefield where ships fired at smoke smudges from nine miles; this is a stadium, small and intimate, with bleachers up both sides of the Dardanelles. You see the *Bouvet*, huge and stolid, veer to starboard just before Kephez Point. You hear the explosion, muffled and flat, that kills her, see the smoke and steam, yellow and black and red-tinged, hissing out of her, saying that the artery has burst and that it's all over. You see her capsize with her screws still turning, as though, like a harpooned whale, she is fighting death and, by struggling, hastening it. You see men running drunkenly across her slippery keel.

There, up the slopes, is the site of the ancient city of Dardanos, named for the son of Zeus. And there, further down the coast, is Kum Kale on its marshy spit, and Tenedos lying under a dreamy haze. You can see the line of British ships advancing, heavy with intent, battle ensigns flying, shells splashing in the water around them, the panoply of a new empire come to punish an old empire. And every now and then the ships rock to starboard and yellow-brown smoke boils from their turrets and the *crump* rolls across the water, and behind you, up the pale yellow cliff where the ghosts live, you hear the fall of rubble and then the dust cloud rolls down over you. When the guns aren't firing, you can hear the bands playing on the French ships. You spot the red flame of a howitzer near Dardanos and, nearby, dirty black puffs from sewer-pipe guns.

Black smoke rolls down the channel from Çanakkale. You cannot see the town and neither can the British gunners; they just keep firing those 12-inch shells and hoping one will land on a Krupp gun rather than a vegetable garden. You think of what would have been lost if the mines had not been there and if, as the fleet bore down on Constantinople, the Young Turks had blown up Sancta Sophia and the mosaic of Jesus. With his wispy beard, this Jesus looks human and Oriental, hook-nosed and thin with long fingers and a stare that challenges you not to believe.

Then the reverie is broken. A roar grows until it becomes the whole world. A Turkish pilot is barrelling a silver F-16 fighter up the Dardanelles. He's so low he is actually below you. It's as though he's reminding you who won.

In the maritime museum at Çanakkale remnants from the land war lie under glass. English water bottles, originally painted a lurid purple, now chipped and dented; a clip of rifle ammunition with the shells fused together as if they had come from a coral reef; a rusted fob watch, the hands like fuse wire; English marmalade jars; a doctor's syringe, a great metal barrel of a thing, better suited to a horse that has, ideally, first been blindfolded. These, however, are the lesser things. Outside are the rows of mines, Exhibit A for the Turks.

The Dardanos battery, its turrets removed, is on a ridge above the narrow coastal plain, near a tomb from the ancient city and overlooking a sweep of water the Turks call Dark Bay. This is now 'lovers' hill', a place for petting and what follows. A wheat crop comes right up to the five 1905 Krupp guns. Old guns are interesting; wheat is useful. These guns hit the *Irresistible* 19 times on March 18 and also the *Ocean*. A month later they pulverised the British submarine *E15*.

There are memorials and cemeteries here and at other batteries along this Asian coast. The Turks have remembered their hundreds of dead here rather better than their tens of thousands of dead on the peninsula. 'Beloved martyrs,' the inscriptions on the monuments say, 'the motherland is grateful to you.'

The real Scamander, a stream winding through marshes and broken by sandbars, isn't so handsome as the Scamander in *The Iliad*, but this land has changed. Troy used to be between two headlands; now it is three miles from the sea. The land between the headlands has filled with silt and when the plough goes in the soil comes up chocolate and red. Sheepfolds are thatched with rushes and enclosed by intertwined branches. The Turks call the land on the seaward side of the Scamander bridge 'Bloody Marsh' in memory of the fighting against the French here on April 25 and pines have been planted for the 'martyrs'. The wildflowers are out: bright reds, pinks, yellows, whites, mauves, all with a black centre.

From here you have a better view of the stadium than from the fort at Kilitbahir on the other side. Over your right shoulder is the mound of Troy, over your left Besika Bay, which the Allies considered as a landing spot. Down below the old castle at Kum Kale stares across at the old castle at Seddülbahir. You can see Achi Baba, a fraud disguised as a hill. It deceives you from here, just as it deceived the British on the water in 1915.

On the way back to Çanakkale we stop at the four-gun

battery of Turgut Reis with its dormitories and store-rooms still intact underneath. The guns were fired in the 1915 battles, but not from here. They were then on two old Turkish cruisers. The caretaker comes out. Alone every day in the pine forest, he is in his late thirties and, like many Turkish men, wears an old double-breasted suitcoat, stained and creased, over an open-necked shirt. He was born near Kephez Point and has never been across the straits.

He is so lonely he wants us to sit with him, patting the wooden seat and beckoning. He speaks not a word of English and we know a dozen words of Turkish, three of which we can pronounce. He uses sign language to ask for a cigarette. He smokes it slowly, sometimes holding it out in front of him and studying it, as though a Mexican firing squad awaits him in the pine trees. The war of 1915, whatever it was about, was long ago. What a man needs now is companionship, and it doesn't matter too much that these foreigners smile a lot and talk babble.

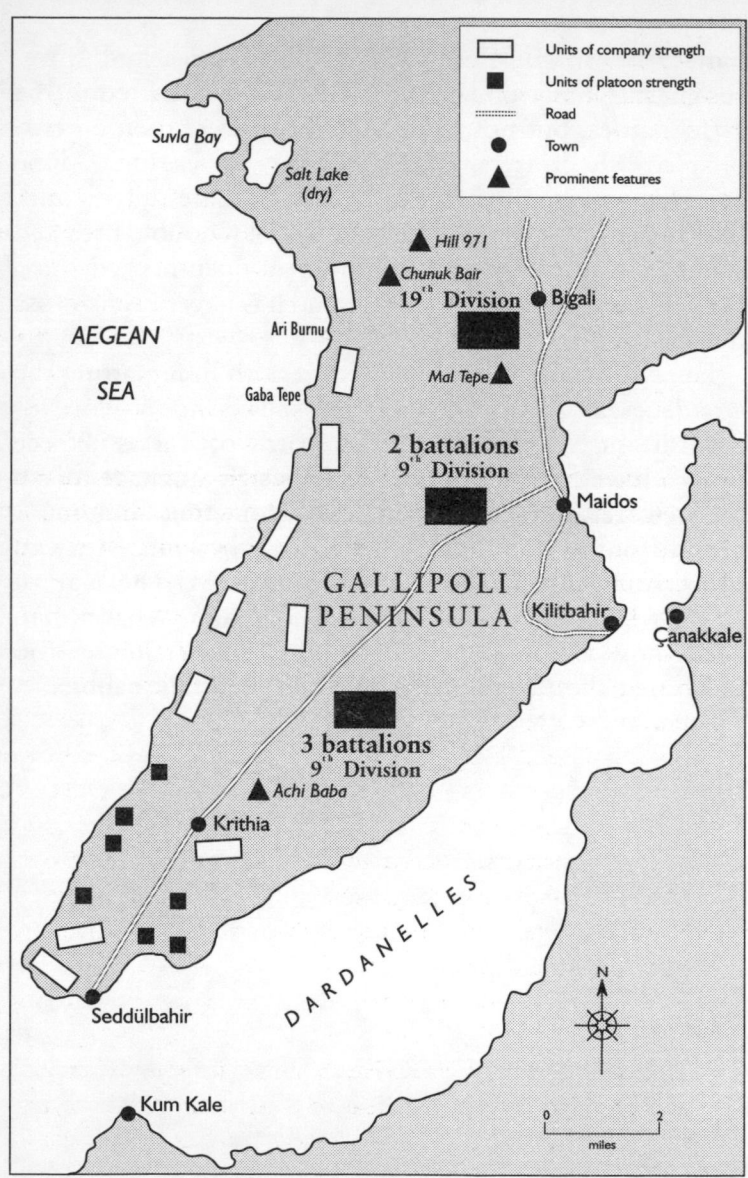

Turkish defences before the landings

6

By Chaos out of Pandemonium

We don't need to try to imagine what Ian Hamilton was thinking during the four days after March 18. He has told us in his diary entries. In edited form, they go like this:

March 19
The sailors are using highly coloured expletives about the mines the Turks floated down yesterday. Sheer bad luck, they say. I've cabled Lord K. and told him that the straits are unlikely to be forced by battleships alone and that this must also become a military operation carried out at full strength. I need to take my troops back to Alexandria and get things sorted out for a landing. Wemyss has a telegram from de Robeck describing yesterday as 'disastrous'.

March 20
The reply came in from K. He says that if large military operations are necessary to clear the way for the fleet, then I must carry them through. Very well. It all hinges on the admiral.

March 21
Received a letter from de Robeck. 'I was sad to lose ships,' he writes. 'My heart aches when one thinks of it. We are all getting ready for another "go" and not in the least beaten or downhearted.' Little Birdie, now grown up into a grand general, turned up. He thinks the navy have shot their bolt.

March 22
Went to a conference aboard *Queen Elizabeth*. Also present were Wemyss, de Robeck, Birdwood and Braithwaite. As soon as we sat down de Robeck told us *he was now quite clear he could not get through without the help of all my troops*. Birdwood, Braithwaite and I had agreed beforehand that we would say nothing for or against land operations until the sailors told us they had abandoned the idea of forcing the passage by ships alone. They have done so. The fat – that is us – is fairly in the fire.

So there was no discussion. We turned to the land scheme. Very sketchy. How could it be otherwise? Had I been a German general, plans for a landing in Gallipoli would have been in my pocket – up-to-date and worked out to a ball cartridge and a pail of water. In matters of supply, transport and administration, our ways are amateurish. Here I am without my Adjutant-General, my Quartermaster-General and my medical chief. Yet I have to decide whether the army pushes off from Lemnos or Alexandria. Nothing in the world to guide me beyond my own experience. Lemnos is practically impossible – no facilities. I'll have to do it from Alexandria. Fancy having to decide these things off the reel, without any administrative staff. Anyway, I've told K. it has to be Alexandria.

I have had to cable for engineers, trench mortars,

bombs, hand grenades and periscopes. I know K. hates being asked for more men but I have asked for a brigade of Gurkhas from Egypt. I've had to risk the fury of the army bureaucrats in London by telling the War Office their transports are so loaded – water carts in one ship, water-cart horses in another; guns in one ship, limbers in another – that they must be emptied and reloaded before we can land.

How many Turkish soldiers are on the peninsula? I told the conference there may be 40,000 – that's what my intelligence folk tell me. There may be another 30,000 above Bulair. There's at least a division over on the Asian side. There could be several. My 75,000 men could be taking on 100,000.

The sailors say special craft are being built back home for possible landings on the Baltic coast. Each lighter can carry 500 men and has bullet-proof bulwarks. They call them 'beetles'. Landing from these would be child's play. Winston would lend us some. But how do I get a cable to Winston? If it falls into the hands of Fisher it fails. The sailors tell me he is obsessed by the North Sea and the Baltic and grudges us every rope's end or halfpenny-worth of tar. Rotten luck to have cut myself off from wiring to Winston. Still, I see no way out of it. With K. as jealous as a tiger, what can I do? The sailors won't cable themselves. Frightened of Fisher. So I've asked K. for the beetles myself.

When to land? To a man of my temperament, there is a temptation to go in forthwith and revenge the loss of the battleships. We might sup tomorrow night on Achi Baba. But landing in face of an enemy is the most complicated and difficult operation in war. The attempt would be happy-go-lucky. There are no small craft. How do we carry water? There is no information about springs or wells ashore. How do I get the wounded off? My Principal Medical Officer and his staff won't be here for a fortnight. The 29th Division is our *pièce de résistance* and it won't be here, we reckon – not complete – for another three weeks.

Still, I might chance it. We would surprise the Turks. The certainties of common sense – that's what puts me off. I could be on Achi Baba tomorrow night. But I still could not counter the inevitable reaction of numbers, time and space. The Turks would have a fortnight to concentrate their whole force against my half force. Must wait for the 29th. By the time they arrive, I can get things organised for a smashing blow. Everything can be worked out and carefully rehearsed.

De Robeck, Wemyss and Keyes agree the army shouldn't try to do anything now. Like us, they think the military force should have been ready before the navy began to attack. What we have to do now is repair a first false step. De Robeck will keep pegging away at the straits while we in Alexandria are putting on our war paint. He will see to it, he says, that the Turks think more of battleships than of landings. He is glad that I have practically made up my mind to go for the south of the peninsula and to keep in closest touch with the fleet. Keyes says he hopes to reorganise his minesweeping fleet. There shouldn't be any danger from mines by April 3rd or 4th. Then, he says, with us to do the spotting for the naval guns, the battleships can smother the forts. So I may say that all are in full agreement – a blessing.

The mission was not blessed. And all were not in agreement. There had been, to put it in its kindest light, a misunderstanding. Hamilton believed his landings would be accompanied by a fresh naval attack. De Robeck appears to have decided against risking his ships again until the army took the southern end of the peninsula. De Robeck's version of the conference differs from Hamilton's. De Robeck cabled Churchill on March 27 and seemed to be saying that he had changed his mind about attacking after Hamilton put 'proposals' to him. Birdwood's diary confirms Hamilton's account and one is inclined to accept it. Hamilton, a poor politician, probably made it easy for de Robeck by offering his troops so readily.

Churchill wasn't going to make it easy for de Robeck, who was like a man who had been bitten by a dog and didn't want to go near it again. Churchill didn't like the idea of landing an army after giving the Turks at least another three weeks' notice of intent. He wanted to send de Robeck a cable telling him to renew his attack. Fisher and others at the Admiralty wouldn't agree to the cable and it was never sent. The way Churchill tells it, Fisher said: 'What more could we want? The army were going to do it. They ought to have done it all along.'

The political game had changed. Fisher and others at the Admiralty had never wanted to buy the Dardanelles with old ships. Ships weren't chips in a poker game. Churchill, this outsider who thought he knew so much, had bullied them and, until the conference at the Dardanelles on March 22, there wasn't much they could do. Now, three sunken battleships, plus de Robeck and Hamilton in polite conversation, had given them the means to stall and slide away. As Churchill put it, they had learnt to say no, and from now on all they would say was no. Churchill eventually sent de Robeck a cable that fell well short of an order and included this sentence: 'What has happened since the 21st to make you alter your intention of renewing the attack as soon as the weather is favourable?' What had happened, of course, was that Hamilton had made it easy for de Robeck. He had offered to take over the main offensive.

Hamilton is a decent man without much guile. He has a sense of chivalry: his army is scattered and incomplete and improperly equipped, yet he is tempted to dive straight into the fight. He also has a little in common with Hamlet. Will I or won't I? Should I or shouldn't I? What will Kitchener think? Would it be good form to demand the equipment I need?

There is a nice counterpoint in von Sanders, who is cold and clear-eyed. He arrives at the peninsula and is immediately like a prosecutor preparing a brief. Work out what the other side will do. Prepare for every trick. Play to your strengths. Exploit their weaknesses. Work out a plan and stick to it. Don't consult too much. Sack any Hamlets stricken with indecision. Don't be stood over by bureaucrats. Don't worry if you offend a few people.

Hamilton is a gentleman, von Sanders a technician. During his first month on the peninsula, von Sanders lived in a house in Gallipoli township that had belonged to the French consul. The house had been looted before he arrived. When von Sanders left, Greeks accused him of carrying out the plunder. 'I had something better to do than to carry away the round table and the wall mirror,' he sniffs in *Five Years in Turkey*.

His 5th Army comprised five divisions, about 50,000 troops, spread out along the European and Asian coasts. A sixth division, the 3rd, was on its way. Von Sanders wrote that the British gave him four full weeks before they landed. They had, in fact, given the Turks eight weeks: the local commanders had begun preparing for a landing after Carden's attack on the outer defences in February. But where were the British going to land?

The most important batteries were on the Asian side of the Dardanelles. Von Sanders thought Besika Bay, on the Aegean just south of Kum Kale, was 'the place of greatest danger'. Roads were reasonable there and the enemy could come up behind the batteries. The guns were sited to protect the waterway, not to repel an invasion from the rear.

Von Sanders saw three obvious spots on the peninsula. One was Cape Helles, where the terrain could be covered by the fleet's guns. Von Sanders thought that if the British took Achi Baba, they would be able to fire directly on the Turkish batteries under Kilitbahir. Like the British, von Sanders believed that Achi Baba commanded the Kilitbahir forts.

The second spot for a landing, von Sanders believed, was the coast on both sides of the headland called Gaba Tepe. From here a flat plain led straight to Eceabat. North of Gaba Tepe, there was a protected landing place below the steep heights of Ari Burnu. Von Sanders knew that those heights – they led on, tawny ridge after tawny ridge, to Hill 971 – were important if the British landed at Gaba Tepe. They commanded the plain to Eceabat as surely as Achi Baba did not command the Kilitbahir plateau.

The third spot von Sanders worried about was Bulair, where the peninsula was only a few miles wide. If the British landed here, they would be too far away to fire at the Dardanelles forts. But if they held Bulair and their fleet entered the Marmara, the peninsula would be cut off entirely, from Constantinople and Çanakkale, by land and by sea; the 5th Army would starve and die.

Having decided where the dangers lay, von Sanders split his six divisions into three groups. The 5th and 7th divisions went to Bulair. The 9th and the 19th (commanded by Mustafa Kemal) went to the southern part of the peninsula to guard against landings at Cape Helles or Gaba Tepe. The 11th and 3rd went to the Asian side to protect Besika Bay and Kum Kale.

Von Sanders also changed the plan of defence. The Turkish infantry had been spread lightly around the coasts like frontier detachments in the old days. 'The enemy on landing would have found resistance everywhere, but there were no reserves to check a strong and energetic advance.' Von Sanders ordered the divisional commanders to hold their troops together and to send only security detachments to the coast.

The plan was simple. Wherever the British landed, the Turkish defences would be light. Close to each likely landing spot, however, two divisions would be encamped, ready to move. Von Sanders was working to the maxim that says he who tries to defend all defends nothing.

Thus around the peninsula there were a dozen men here, maybe 100 there, at Gaba Tepe, Ari Burnu, Suvla, Seddülbahir and the beaches north of Cape Helles. Thus Colonel Sami Bey's 9th Division had its headquarters on Kilitbahir plateau and Mustafa Kemal's 19th at Bigali. Both could be sent relatively quickly to either Gaba Tepe or Cape Helles.

Von Sanders thought his troops had grown stiff in their coastguard positions. He sent them on manoeuvres, often at night to conceal them from the fleet and the British aircraft based on Tenedos (von Sanders had no aircraft). Labour battalions hacked into the scrub to widen pack trails into roads; boats were assembled so that troops might be ferried promptly, and beaches fortified with wood and wire taken from gardens and farms. The peninsula was toilworn and timeworn: a few Greek villages joined up by spidery donkey trails and old habits. Von Sanders imposed Teutonic order on the land; he had been all over it: by boat and by car, on horse and on foot. He imposed the same order on the army. It was short of equipment, particularly artillery, and many soldiers bandaged cloth over their feet in place of boots and used twine for rifle slings. Yet morale was good. They had beaten the English and French on March 18, hadn't they? The sick man of Europe had rolled out of bed and let fly with his crutch.

Hamilton arrived in Alexandria on March 24 and worked at first from a former brothel. His staff lit candles: there was no electric light. He had agreed to a landing before he knew where he was going to land or how he was going to do it. He had agreed to stage an amphibious attack against entrenched positions, an operation involving 75,000 men and hundreds of vessels of all sorts, at a few weeks' notice and before his administrative staff had arrived. (As a reference point, planning for the Normandy landings of June, 1944, began early in 1943.) Hamilton was in a worse position than von Sanders. Sometimes he seemed to know this and sometimes he didn't.

Take these two diary entries from his fortnight in Alexandria. In the first he is inspecting Général Albert d'Amade's French contingent, drawn from Africa for the Gallipoli landings. He likes what he sees.

High, high soared our hopes. Jerusalem – Constantinople? No limit to what these soldiers may achieve. The thought passed through the massed spectators and set enthusiasm coursing through their veins. Loudly they cheered; hats off; and hurrah for the infantry! Hurrah, hurrah for the Cavalry!!

Now consider the second diary entry:

Time presses; K. prods us from the rear: the Admiral from the front. To their eyes we seem to be dallying amidst the fleshpots of Egypt whereas, really, we are struggling like drowning mariners in a sea of chaos; chaos in the offices; chaos on the ships, chaos in the camps; chaos along the wharves . . . We cannot go rushing off into space leaving Pandemonium behind us as our Base!

The interesting thing about these entries is that they are from the same day, April 5, 1915.

Von Sanders could not have written either of them. He would never have tolerated chaos. Chaos was *verboten*, to be trussed up, tied to a stake and shot for the traitor to good order that it was. And to make it clear he was neither a romantic nor an easy touch, von Sanders might also have told the French cavalrymen they were riding with their stirrup leathers one hole too long, even if they weren't.

Hamilton's troubles started with his numbers. He might have had enough men for garrison duty around Constantinople and for raiding parties on the way there; he didn't have the numbers to make opposed landings against six Turkish divisions. His Mediterranean Expeditionary Force comprised five divisions: the 29th (17,649 troops), the Anzac Corps (30,638), the French contingent (16,762) and the RND (10,007). That was it: 75,056 troops.

Hamilton had no reserves for his British divisions. He had the 29th on loan. He had been refused the 'beetles' as landing craft; the men would go ashore in ships' cutters. He had been cheated on his artillery. According to *British War Establishments*, 1914, Hamilton's four 'British' divisions should have come with 304 guns; they had 118.

He had been cheated on ammunition too. He was short

of shells for his 18-pounders and there was no high-explosive ammunition, just shrapnel. London seems to have assumed that Hamilton's men would be racing forward like cavalry in pursuit of tax-dodging tribesmen. There were no mortars, no hand grenades.

The Turkish troop numbers were a worry. The terrain favoured the defenders. The British estimated that there were between 40,000 and 80,000 Turkish soldiers on the peninsula (von Sanders' army, as we have seen, amounted to about 60,000); they believed a further 30,000 could be brought across from Anatolia and that there were maybe 60,000 more within 'close call', providing Constantinople wasn't under attack from the Russians. In other words, Hamilton was looking at taking on a force of 40,000 to 150,000.

Why didn't Hamilton demand more men? He was an optimist and he didn't want to upset Kitchener. He asked him for more ammunition on March 30, but gently, deferentially, the schoolboy anxious not to provoke the headmaster. His diary entry for March 30 reads:

> Have just dictated a long letter to Lord K. in the course of which I have forced myself to say something that may cause the great man annoyance. I feel it is up to me to risk that. One thing – he knows I am not one of those rotters who ask for more than they can possibly be given so that, if things go wrong, they may complain of their tools. I have promised K. to help him by keeping my demands down to bedrock necessities. I make no demand for ammunition on the France and Flanders scale but – we must have *some*!

Kitchener suddenly became generous. He sent the 2nd Mounted Division, commanded by Major-General C. E.

Peyton, to Egypt in case Hamilton needed it. On April 6 he cabled Lieutenant Sir John Maxwell, the British commander-in-chief for Egypt:

> You should supply any troops in Egypt that can be spared, or even selected officers and men that Sir Ian Hamilton may want, for Gallipoli. You know that Peyton's Mounted Division is leaving for Egypt. This telegram should be communicated by you to Sir Ian Hamilton.

It wasn't. Maxwell didn't like Hamilton or his Gallipoli campaign. Both were taking troops he needed to defend the Suez Canal against Djemal's Turkish columns, or at least that was how Maxwell dressed up his bloody-mindedness. The Canal was in no serious danger; Maxwell was trying to protect his kingdom against the interloper Hamilton.

Maxwell's response to Kitchener's message of April 6 was to cable an account of a Turkish build-up east of Suez, most of which was baloney. Hamilton had in March asked Kitchener for the 29th Indian Brigade, under Major-General Vaughan Cox. Hamilton described this as like going up to a tiger and asking for a small slice of venison. Kitchener eventually said yes and Maxwell grudgingly handed over the 'Gurkha brigade'. Had Hamilton seen Kitchener's cable of April 6, had he been less of a gentleman, he might have obtained several extra brigades, even a whole division.

There was another reason Hamilton didn't demand more troops and artillery. In December, 1914, British sailors landed north of Alexandretta, near the Syrian border, to cut the Turkish railway line and a farce ensued. The Turks agreed to blow up two of their own loco-motives provided the British would lend them explosives.

They also demanded that the British lieutenant in charge of the demolition be made a Turkish officer for the day. According to the official British naval history, when the requests were agreed to, 'the comedy was ended by a party of Turkish cavalry rounding up the locomotives and bringing them to the place of execution, when they were duly blown up'. In early February, 1915, Djemal's troops attacked the Suez Canal, failed badly, and pulled back. Both incidents gave false pictures of the Turks' willingness to fight. Churchill later admitted that the buffoonery at Alexandretta persuaded him that 'we were not dealing with a thoroughly efficient military power'.

And, of course, there was the British assumption of superiority. In 1915 it was acceptable to talk about the virtues of one's 'race'. To do so was to identify oneself as a patriot rather than a racist. It was commonplace for clergymen, politicians, editorial writers and patrons of the public bars all over the British empire to talk about the pre-eminence of the 'British race', just as it was commonplace for Australian troops in Egypt to refer to Arabs as 'niggers', and for Australians generally to present themselves to the world as simultaneously 'Australian' and 'British'. The stalwarts of the British empire tended to dismiss soldiers who did not look, act and dress like them, as though a man who lacked the sense to fasten a kilt around his waist and a bearskin on his head must be from a lower caste and quite likely a heathen as well. They had made this mistake at Bunker Hill, Boston, in 1775, and at Isandhlwana, Zululand, in 1879. They would do the same at Singapore in 1942. It is not a British disease so much as one of all imperial powers. The French and then the Americans succumbed to the same thing in Vietnam.

Hamilton and his staff planned their attack on the basis that the Turks would contest the beaches, then shrink at the sight of so many Union Jacks and Sam Browne belts. Some Australians were offended upon being told they were going to Gallipoli. The Turk, they thought then, was a second-string opponent, barely worthy, and where the hell was Gallipoli anyway? Of the coming landings, Lieutenant-Colonel Andrew Skeen, one of Birdwood's staff officers, wrote: 'It will be grim work to begin with, but we have good fighters ready to tackle it, and an enemy who has never shown himself as good a fighter as the white man.'

The British forgot two things. The Turks had a long and brutal military history; and, second, while they had little of the ingenuity of their forebears in attack, what they were good at now was defence, dogged stonewalling defence. The soldiers from the Anatolian villages were fatalists raised on hardship. Most were illiterate. They didn't expect much from life; they were used to being mis-used by corrupt leaders. But, in defence, they knew how to hang on, to endure, to swallow bad food and go bare-foot, to baffle and frustrate the enemy with their perversity and their serenity in the face of pain and death.

And maybe there was another thing: in this coming battle, the Turks would be not be trying to hold on to some old conquest; they would be fighting for their heart-land and its capital and their identity. They knew a simple truth: a loss at the Dardanelles would turn *them* into a subject people.

If the British failed to take the Turks seriously, they also failed to take security in Egypt seriously; the likelihood is that the two things were connected, if only sub-consciously. To have any hope, a landing against an enemy well dug in needs surprise. As Aspinall wrote, 'no expedition was ever more loudly heralded'.

News of the arrival and departure of transports was common property in Alexandria and Port Said; the names of units were freely mentioned in the Egyptian press; and there were public reviews of the troops both at Alexandria and at Cairo. At this time, too, one of Sir Ian Hamilton's staff received an official letter from London, sent through the ordinary post and addressed to the 'Constantinople Field Force'.

Everyone knew what was coming. Because the expedition had to be outfitted in haste, tugs, lighters, horses, mules and water tanks were being bought for cash all around the Mediterranean. Général d'Amade even gave an interview to an Alexandria newspaper in which he pondered the chances of a successful assault on the Gallipoli Peninsula. Gallipoli, the word, was in the Egyptian newspapers just about every day. Hamilton protested to Maxwell, but softly.

Hamilton's problems with administration and logistics were spectacular. This was supposedly a joint operation, yet he was more than 500 miles from the naval commander. His administrative staff did not arrive in Egypt until April 1. Hamilton's general staff had to put strategy aside and become procurers of mules, kerosene tins and pack saddles. The general, however, kept his sense of humour. What, he wondered, would his former friends on the German staff say if they knew he had not one administrative staff officer to help him?

The Germans have tabulated the experiences and deficiencies of our leaders, active and potential, in peace and war – we have not! Every British general of any note is analysed, characterised and turned inside out in the bureau records of the great German General Staff in

Berlin. We only attempt anything of that sort with burglars.

Intelligence reports were not particularly useful. The War Office cabled Hamilton: 'Have you any good and recent information as to the water supply on the Gallipoli Peninsula? We have received a very bad account on this point.' Hamilton became concerned and asked the War Office to send him everything it had. The War Office replied that their main source of information was an official document dated 1905 and a report from an admiral that water in the villages was scanty.

When, on April 8, Hamilton left for Mudros on the liner *Arcadian* he took two delusions with him. One was that military expeditions in the Great War could be cobbled together by amateurs, as they might have been when Sudanese rebels needed a spanking. The other was that de Robeck would renew his attack on the Narrows as soon as the landings were completed, forcing the Turks to fight on two fronts.

As the *Arcadian* passed one lovely Aegean island after another, Hamilton refined his plans. The horse by Chaos from Pandemonium was about to be given a gallop.

In London, two days before the naval attack of March 18, Lieutenant-Colonel Hankey, secretary to the War Council, had sent a memorandum to the Prime Minister. No-one took much notice of it. It turned out to be one of the most prophetic documents of the campaign. Hankey had sensed that the army would be needed. 'Is it not desirable,' he asked, 'that the War Council should ascertain definitely the scope of the operations contemplated, and the extent of the preparations made to carry out these operations?' He wrote that combined operations required more careful preparation than any other military ventures. 'All through our history such attacks have failed when the preparations have been inadequate, and the successes are in nearly every case due to the most careful preparation beforehand.' Surprise had been lost at Gallipoli, Hankey wrote.

He raised a string of questions. How many troops would be used? Where would the hospitals be? Was the army thinking of a *coup de main*, one swift stroke, or was there the possibility of a siege? If the latter, would siege guns be available? What arrangements had been made for the supply of ammunition? In his final sentence Hankey said the hard thing: 'Unless details such as these, and there are probably others, are fully thought out before the landing takes place, it is conceivable that a serious disaster may occur.'

When Asquith received this, the naval attack was still expected to succeed. Besides, Britain and the War Council had Kitchener. He knew about these things. He wouldn't let us make a mistake.

Five days before he left Alexandria, Hamilton wrote to Kitchener:

> All goes well, and my chiefest worry is that three of our senior officers (excepting Braithwaite) now seem, for the first time, to see all the difficulties with extraordinary perspicacity. In fact, they would each apparently a thousand times sooner do anything else except what we are going to do.

The appreciation by the general staff, on which the battle plans were based, had been drawn up by March 23. The southern part of the peninsula was to be taken in a *coup de main.* Cape Helles was the favoured spot, mainly because the fleet could give support on three sides. Bulair looked to be too heavily defended, and Besika Bay and Kum Kale were out because Kitchener had ruled against landings on the Asian side. Birdwood, Major-General Aylmer Hunter-Weston, commander of the 29th Division, and Major-General Archibald Paris, commander of the RND, were all against Hamilton's scheme.

Hunter-Weston, a fox-hunting man, was 50 and had served as a staff officer and cavalry commander in the Boer War. Hamilton called the Scots general an 'acute theorist', which seemed generous. Like the French generals on the western front, Hunter-Weston could reduce all theory to one word: attack. At Helles he seemed without imagination or pity. He threw away troops the way lesser men tossed away socks, all the time bubbling with boisterous good humour. His friends called him 'Hunter Bunter' and his bushy moustache quivered when he laughed.

Compton Mackenzie in *Gallipoli Memories* recalls having tea with him at Helles a few months into the campaign.

'Shall we have tea in here, sir?' Hunter-Weston's aide-de-camp asked.

'Tea in here? Good God, no!' said Hunter-Weston. 'Why, it's a perfectly superb afternoon. We don't want to sit stuffing in here. The flowers that bloom in the spring, tra-la! The flowers that bloom tra-la, tra-la, tra-la!'

That night, Paris called on Hunter-Weston and they discussed the day's fighting.

'Many casualties?' Paris asked. He was bitter that his division was counting its dead in the thousands.

'Casualties?' snapped Hunter-Weston, eyes flashing, nose quivering. 'What do I care for casualties?'

Paris rose from his chair. 'I must be getting back,' he growled.

'You'll stay to tea?'

'No, thanks.'

Mackenzie writes that Hunter-Weston often spoke brutally and had a reputation as a butcher. 'Actually no man I have met brimmed over more richly with human sympathy. He was a logician of war, and as a logician he believed and was always ready to contend in open debate that, provided the objective was gained, casualties were of no importance.'

This is far too generous, but Hunter-Weston's appreciation of the Dardanelles campaign, written on his way to Egypt, suggests he was a realist. Surprise, Hunter-Weston said, had been lost. The peninsula had become an entrenched camp. He thought Helles the best landing spot but felt the army might still be 'tied up' in front of Kilitbahir plateau. There was not a reasonable chance of success. Better to have the moral courage to abandon the expedition.

Birdwood, who had come up through the Indian cavalry, wanted to land on the Asian side and force the Turks to withdraw most of their mobile artillery to meet the attack. This would give the navy a chance to sweep the mines. Birdwood had thought he would be commander-in-chief but deferred gracefully to Hamilton's appointment. He thought Hamilton shallow, unable to concentrate on detail and too interested in arty things. But he liked him and was happy to return to the command of his Anzac Corps, which he liked even more. He didn't like Braithwaite. Hardly anyone did. The chief-of-staff could offend people without knowing he was doing it.

Birdwood's chief-of-staff, Brigadier-General Harold Walker, was so appalled by the scheme that Birdwood offered to leave him behind. 'Hooky', as Walker was called, talked bluntly to his superiors. He turned out to be right about just about everything that mattered.

Paris touched on the biggest trouble: numbers. 'The enemy is of a strength unknown, but within striking distance there must be 250,000.' Surprise, he said, was impossible. The whole thing was cavalier.

Hamilton wrote: 'The truth is, every one of these fellows agrees in his heart with old von der Goltz [the German general who for years had been Turkey's military instructor], the Berlin experts, and the Sultan of Egypt that the landing is impossible. Well, we shall see . . . '

Most of the time one cannot take Maxwell seriously: he was trying to protect his own command in Egypt and offered help only when prodded by pieces of paper signed 'Kitchener'. Yet what he said to Birdwood on April 3 now seems prophetic. 'Gallipoli,' he said, 'gives us no liberty of manoeuvre; you are cramped and very liable to be held up and have a sort of miniature Flanders to fight.'

Polite dissent was everywhere. And there was the matter of the navy. What was it doing while the generals were arguing? It was now stronger than on March 18. Ships lost or sunk had been replaced, a naval aerodrome had been set up on Tenedos, the minesweeping fleet had been enlarged. This was still first of all a naval operation, yet the sailors were passive. Hamilton, of course, would not think of telling the admirals they were failing to honour their promises made after March 18.

Only in 1932, when he was almost 80, did Hamilton open up. In a speech at Birkenhead, he spoke of senior naval officers at home and at the front who began to tremble for their ships as soon as they saw a fort.

When Nelson saw a fort he began to tremble not for his

ship but for the fort, and I wish to tell you right now that we did possess at the Dardanelles the very spit and spirit of Nelson . . . and who, had he been given the chance, would have taken the fleet slap through the Narrows within one week of our landing.

He was referring to Roger Keyes. Keyes was no use to him in 1915. De Robeck was in charge and he had turned caution into an art form. One also suspects de Robeck was doing exactly what Fisher wanted him to do.

The navy did try something on April 17. The submarine *E15* attempted to get through to the Marmara, became caught in the current off Kephez Point and ran aground under the Dardanos battery. Her captain, Theodore Brodie, was killed in the conning tower. His twin brother, Charles, on a reconnaissance flight, was the first to sight the stricken submarine. The Turks regarded *E15* as a prize, better than the *Bouvet* because this one was lying there, on show to the world like a beached whale. Two British picket boats eventually torpedoed the submarine. This was probably the most dramatic incident between March 18 and the landings.

Hamilton arrived at Mudros without his administrative staff. This was another mistake. By now his doubting generals were starting to come around. Hamilton met de Robeck, Wemyss and Keyes on April 10, told them his generals had reservations, then outlined his scheme.

The more, I said, I had pondered over the map and reflected upon the character, probable numbers and supposed positions of the enemy, the more convinced I had become that the first and foremost step towards a victorious landing was to upset the equilibrium of Liman von Sanders . . . I must try to move so that he should be unable to concentrate either his mind or his men against us.

This was clever. Von Sanders' defence, as we have seen, was based on mobility, the ability to concentrate his forces. Prudence, Hamilton continued, was entirely out of place.

There will be and can be no reconnaissance, no half measures, no tentatives . . . this is neither the time nor the place for paddling about the shore putting one foot on to the beaches with the idea of drawing it back again if it happens to alight upon a land mine. No; we've got to take a good run at the peninsula and jump plump on – both feet together. At a given moment we must plunge and stake everything on the one hazard.

This, though more soldierly than the dilly-dallying of de Robeck, was perhaps not so clever. It is the mindset of a punter about to make one big bet. Hamilton did not have the bankroll to bet so bravely. And he could not be sure of Turkish troop numbers. As he put it, the Unspeakable Turk had become the Unknowable Turk.

Hamilton said he wanted to land as close as possible to Kilitbahir plateau, but the beach space beneath the cliffs was too cramped. So he would first attack Achi Baba with the 29th Division from the beaches at Cape Helles. He would attempt to flank the Turks defending those beaches by landing smaller detachments at Morto Bay, on the Dardanelles coast, and on the Aegean coast. Birdwood's Anzac Corps would land between Gaba Tepe and Fisherman's Hut, seize the high backbone of the peninsula and cut off any retreat from Kilitbahir plateau. There would be two important feints. Transports would be loaded with RND troops and sent to Bulair, as if there was going to be a landing there. And French troops would land briefly at Kum Kale to silence the guns and to prevent Turkish troops from being shipped across the Narrows.

> With luck, then, within the space of an hour, the enemy chief will be beset by a series of S.O.S signals. Over an area of 100 miles, from five or six places; from Krithia and Morto Bay; from Gaba Tepe; from Bulair and from Kum Kale in Asia, as well as, if the French can manage it, from Besika Bay, the cables will pour in. I reckon Liman von Sanders will not dare concentrate and that he will fight with his local troops only for the first forty-eight hours.

Hamilton's enthusiasm caught on. Hunter-Weston now thought Achi Baba could be taken on the first day. Birdwood became less critical and, in the words of a staff officer, a 'romantic sense of adventure' spread through the whole force.

Yet there were still riddles. How, precisely, would the capture of Achi Baba and Mal Tepe, the hill behind the Anzac landing place, lead to the conquest of the Narrows? How was the administrative staff going to get everything right, particularly the plans to evacuate the wounded, in just two weeks? Hamilton had thought out his strategy well but, as was his way, he didn't want to think too much about the detail and seemed to resent the work of the administrative staff. Surgeon-General Birrell and his staff arrived at Mudros less than a week before the date set for the landing to discover that there were only two hospital ships available. What would happen if the troops were unable to go forward on landing and hospitals could not be set up on the beaches? No-one had much thought about this. It was assumed that the hard part was getting the troops ashore. As Hamilton wrote: 'Once ashore, I could hardly think Great Britain and France would not in the long run defeat Turkey . . . '

And what were the Russians going to contribute? If they were going to get Constantinople, it was surely right to ask them to help from the Black Sea side. And when was the navy going to tackle the straits again? What was the navy's plan beyond putting troops ashore? One day Hamilton inspected the aerodrome on Tenedos. The navy fliers told him they felt the sea lords in London were half-hearted about Gallipoli. Hamilton could be slow to pick up on hints.

The landing plan was polished some more. At both Helles and Anzac a covering force would go in ahead of the main body. The covering forces would be landed from warships, the main bodies from transports. The troops would go ashore in ships' cutters towed by steam pinnaces. The cutters would be cast off near the shores and rowed to the beaches.

Commander Edward Unwin, a hardy 51-year-old who had first gone to sea in clippers, came up with an idea that was as old as Troy. One of the landing beaches at Cape Helles was tiny. It would be hard to get troops ashore quickly there. Unwin suggested running an old ship aground and landing 2000 troops from eight sallyports cut in her sides. The men would run along a wooden gangplank into grounded lighters and thence to the shore. For his Trojan horse, Unwin chose the *River Clyde*, a 4000-ton collier built in Glasgow. She had been used to ship mules from Africa.

Hamilton now came up with a sideshow of his own: the landing of some 2000 troops below undefended cliffs on the Aegean coast opposite Krithia at what was to be called

Y Beach. He thought these men could threaten the line of retreat of the Turks at Helles. Hunter-Weston appears to have grudgingly agreed to this. There was one more late change: the French would now stage a feint, in the fashion of Bulair, at Besika Bay.

Here then is how the final plan was to go. The 29th Division would land at Helles on five beaches. The main landings would be at W and V beaches. V Beach, a strip of sand about 10 yards wide and maybe 300 long, is an amphitheatre, made for defence, flanked by the ruined Seddülbahir castle and the village of the same name on the right and a newer fort on the left. There is a bank, four to five feet high, where the sand ends and from here the land rises to a height of 100 to 150 feet. The *River Clyde*, painted a yellowy brown for her mission, would be beached here.

W Beach lies between Tekke Burnu and Cape Helles. The beach is deeper and wider than V, but it also favours defenders; the way out is along a gully that narrows as it rises. V and W beaches were death traps unless navy guns could silence the defenders.

X Beach, less than a mile past Tekke Burnu, is a patch of sand at the base of cliffs. So is Y Beach. For obvious reasons, X and Y were unlikely to be defended. The fifth beach – S – was on the inside of the peninsula on Morto Bay. This would be the smallest landing, just three companies. The covering forces at Helles would protect the landing of the main body. The first-day objective was the peak of Achi Baba.

The Anzac landing would be on a front of about 2000 yards along a wide beach north of Gaba Tepe. The southern boats would land about a mile north of Gaba Tepe. The centre of the landing would be roughly opposite a hill that became known as Bolton's Ridge. The country here is hilly without being steep, with a few kind valleys. There is no point discussing it further because, as a result of miscalculations and bad luck, the Australians and New Zealanders landed in a tangle of gullies and ravines to the north. The covering force – the 3rd Brigade of the 1st Australian Division – was supposed to capture the southern spurs of the Sari Bair Range. The first-day objective of the main body at Anzac was Mal Tepe, the conical hill between the villages of Kojadere and Bigali.

At Helles 4900 troops would go ashore in the first wave at the five beaches. They would be followed by 2100 men in the *River Clyde*, then another 1200 in the second wave of tows. At Anzac the first wave of 1500 would land in tows from battleships, followed by another 2500 in tows from destroyers. The navy would bombard the straits on the third day after the landings.

Someone eventually thought of casualties. The estimate for wounded from the beaches was put at 3000. The two hospital ships could handle only 700 serious cases and would need to take them to either Egypt or Malta, voyages of three and four days respectively. When, finally, the administrative staff again caught up with the expedition, on April 18, the Adjutant-General and Surgeon-General Birrell said that the estimate for wounded should be 10,000. Eight transports should be added to the two hospital ships to take the wounded to hospital. This was agreed to; the trouble was the extra ships would not be available until two days after the landing. And there was the problem of how to get the wounded to the hospital ships. All the small craft would be needed for the landings. Hamilton finally ruled that small craft bringing troops ashore were not to be diverted to take off wounded. He had no choice: he was trying to do too much with too little. The landings might or might not succeed; either way, the wounded were in for a terrible time.

The landing was fixed for April 23. The armada at Mudros grew and grew: battleships, converted liners, chartered tramps, destroyers, lighters that had been hurriedly bought in Mediterranean ports, tugs, cruisers, colliers, trawlers from the North Sea and tugs from the Thames. The harbour was so crowded that ship-to-ship communication was impossible.

Then the gales came and the landings were postponed until the 25th. On the night of the 24th, 200 vessels were on the Aegean, heading for the peninsula, the RND transports bound for Bulair to the extreme north, the French ships bound for the Asian shore to the extreme south. The troops were full of hope. On the hull of one transport they had scrawled in white letters 'To Constantinople and the Harems'.

By April, 1915, bodies had been piling up for eight months from Belgium to the Caucasus. Massed artillery supplied the requiem music. There had never been killing like this, never a stalemate like this. Yet in Britain and her dominions innocence lingered, as it would until after the first battle of the Somme in 1916. Consider the obsequies for the poet Rupert Brooke of the RND.

The RND numbered among its officers a rare contingent of poets, scholars and what were called 'promising young men'. Because of the overcrowding at Mudros, the division was on the Greek island of Skyros, south-west of Lemnos. The sky on April 23 came up big and bright and melded into the sea so perfectly it was impossible to spot the seam. Spring, the gorgeous spring of the Aegean, had come; but not for Sub-Lieutenant Brooke. He was dying, probably from blood poisoning caused by an insect bite to his lip. It was all so improbable, as though Sir Lancelot had been diagnosed with terminal dandruff. Brooke lay on a French hospital ship, slipping away serenely, past fever and pain, past last words and hope. A pall fell over the expedition.

Brooke was the golden youth, friend of the famous (everyone from Churchill to Henry James), the spirit of an age, a hopeless romantic and just 27 years old. Men talked about his looks the way in later eras they would talk about women's looks. His poetry and prose gushed and bubbled like a burst water pipe; its appeal was to the heart rather than the head and it was aerated with the artless hope of youth. Here is Brooke in full flood on being told the RND was bound for Constantinople:

It's too wonderful for belief. I had not imagined Fate could be so kind . . . Will Hero's Tower crumble under the fifteen-inch guns? Will the sea be polyphloisbic and wine-dark and unvintageable? Shall I loot mosaics from St Sophia, and Turkish Delight and carpets? Should we be a Turning Point in History? Oh God! I've never been quite so happy in my life I think. Never quite so pervasively happy; like a stream flowing entirely to one end. I suddenly realise that the ambition of my life has been – since I was two – to go on a military expedition against Constantinople.

And there are the lines for which Brooke is remembered even today:

> If I should die think only this of me;
> That there's some corner of a foreign field
> That is for ever England.

By the end of the war, Brooke's innocence belonged to a lost world. Siegfried Sassoon ended his *Suicide in Trenches* thus:

> You smug-faced crowds with kindling eye
> Who cheer when soldier lads march by,
> Sneak home and pray you'll never know
> The hell where youth and laughter go.

Like Byron, Shelley and Keats, Brooke died young and in the Mediterranean. He left the world gently on the afternoon of April 23, the sun dappling the walls of his cabin as the light went out in his eyes. They buried him that night. The corner of a foreign field turned out to be an olive grove. Petty officers carried his body up the hill. Ratings held spluttering torches.

Hamilton had come upon Brooke in Egypt and offered him a staff job. Brooke refused, saying he wanted to land with his comrades in the Howe battalion. Now, on April 23, Hamilton wrote:

> Rupert Brooke is dead. Straightaway he will be buried. The rest is silence . . . Death grins at my elbow. I cannot get him out of my thoughts. He is fed up with the old and sick – only the flower of the flock will serve him now, for God has started a celestial spring cleaning, and our star is to be scrubbed bright with the blood of our bravest and our best.

Churchill, who had arranged for Brooke to be commissioned in the RND, wrote an obituary for *The Times*. Brooke, he said, expected to die.

> Joyous, fearless, versatile, deeply instructed, with classic symmetry of mind and body, he was all that one would

wish England's noblest sons to be in days when no sacrifice but the most precious is acceptable, and the most precious is that which is most freely proffered.

For better or worse, we don't talk about promising young men now. In the world of free-market economics, there are not large numbers of 27-year-olds who want to read Homer and Herodotus, write poetry and go skinny-dipping with Virginia Woolf (as Brooke apparently did). Promising young men were all around at Brooke's grave-side. They included Patrick Shaw-Stewart, the poet who would die in France, Bernard Freyberg, who would be much decorated before eventually becoming Governor-General of New Zealand, and Arthur Asquith, the Prime Minister's son, who would be badly wounded at Gallipoli.

We don't know whether Sub-Lieutenant Arthur Tisdall of the RND was there. He probably was. Like Brooke, he was a Cambridge man, a poet, good-looking and well liked.

Two days after Brooke's burial, Tisdall would win the Victoria Cross for rescuing wounded men during the landings at Helles. The award was not announced until March, 1916. By then Tisdall was dead, shot in the chest on May 6. A member of his platoon later wrote: 'All his men cried when he went because all the boys thought the world of him.'

At Gallipoli on April 25 romance and realism met on the battlefield. As it always does, romance lost.

7

'Him and me are mates'

Australia was a constitutional entity with a spiritual void at its core. It longed for a test of national character. That came at Gallipoli which, in turn, became a legend that was asked to do too much – to sustain a national identity.

Paul Kelly in *The End of Certainty*

The Turks tell a story about two New Zealanders they took prisoner in August. The Turks asked them where they were from.

New Zealand, they said.

Never heard of it, the Turks replied.

Several Germans nearby overheard the exchange. They told the Turks that New Zealand was in the South Pacific, literally at the other end of the world. The Turks were incredulous.

Why are you *here*? they demanded.

Well, the New Zealanders explained, they thought the war would be like playing rugby.

Australia tripped off to war much the same way: carefree, as full of dreams as a debutante going to a ball. She didn't know what was going to happen, but it was better than sitting at home, and when the ball was over she would be a bigger person than she had been before.

It is fashionable these days to ask why this was so and why Australia sacrificed so much in the Great War. The casualty lists are chilling: close to 60,000 dead, casualties of 215,000-odd out of the 332,000 men who left Australia, a rate of nearly 65 per cent, 15 points higher than the casualty rate of the 'mother country'. Why did Australia do it?

The past is easier understood when judged by the canons of its time. No-one in the Australian winter of 1914 envisioned casualties of 215,000. No-one in Britain, Australia or New Zealand envisioned the suicide of nations. For another thing, Australians saw themselves as transplanted Britons. A war against England was a war against them. There was an ambiguity in the Australian character, as much as a character could be said to exist. The best example of this was Alfred Deakin, perhaps Australia's best prime minister, referring to himself as an 'independent Australian Briton'. He could say that early in the century without being thought muddle-headed. As Gavin Souter wrote in Lion and Kangaroo: 'Like many of his fellow Australians, Deakin scarcely knew whether he was one thing or the other, or both.'

In one sense the Australians were nationalists. Like the Americans, they thought they had carried the best aspects of British civilisation to another place, held them up to the light, then modified some and discarded others to come up with a better society. Democracy in England co-existed with a class system. There were rules. If they were not written down, they were still rules. A coal miner, no matter how resourceful or intelligent, could only in unusual circumstances become an officer; a lad from Eton, though a twit, wore officer's pips as a right.

Australia, though a less sophisticated society than Britain, was kinder to train drivers and urchins. There was something honourable about the self-made man and it didn't matter too much that his great grandfather had clumped ashore in chains for nicking cutlery in Surrey.

Australia was far from classless; it was simply less hidebound than Britain. And there were things that were peculiarly Australian. One was the look of Australian men. They were generally bigger and stronger than working-class Englishmen of the same age. There was an obvious explanation: the Australians had grown up in sunlight, free of the smog and grime of English industrial towns. English officers would write rapturously of Australians stripped to the waist at Gallipoli. Here's Compton Mackenzie having a rush of blood:

> There was not one of those glorious young men I saw that day who might not himself have been Ajax or Diomed, Hector or Achilles. Their almost complete nudity, their tallness and majestic simplicity of line, their rose-brown flesh burnt by the sun and purged of all grossness by the ordeal through which they were passing, all these united to create something as near to absolute beauty as I shall hope ever to see in this world.

This is close to drollery – 'Diomed' was quite likely Merv from Wagga Wagga – and we would be wrong to read sexual innuendo into it. The worship of golden youths like Rupert Brooke was in vogue.

Another peculiarity was the Australian sense of mateship. Bean tells a story of the man who arrived at the front trench before the Australian assault on Lone Pine in August, 1915.

'Jim here?' he asked.

A voice on the fire-step answered: 'Right, Bill, here.'

'Do you chaps mind shiftin' up a piece,' said the first voice. 'Him and me are mates, an' we're goin' over together.'

Mateship was a child of the bush. Farming in Australia wasn't like farming in Europe. Australia's soils were old and worn out and the blazing summers burnt off the native grasses, which weren't worth much anyway. It took a lot of land to run a few sheep and life was lonely and brutish. Country life was, as it still is, built around the exchange of favours. A man broke his leg and his neighbours crutched his sheep; a mother came down with a fever and the neighbours nursed her and fed her children. It wasn't because bush folk had invented the sharing society; this was the only way life could exist out there. Neighbours helped each other and no-one kept score because over time it all evened out.

Nationalism had a few strident voices, notably Henry Lawson and the *Bulletin*. In 1887 Lawson's *A Song of the Republic* appeared.

> Sons of the South, awake! arise!
>   Sons of the South, and do.
> Banish from under your bonny skies
> Those old-world errors and wrongs and lies.
> Making a hell in a Paradise
>   That belongs to your sons and you.

There was an Australian sensibility in those words, even if most of the time it was unspoken. This was a place to make a fresh start, to experiment. A consensus had been reached on how Australia should be different. Manufacturing industry was protected by tariffs. Wages were set by arbitration, so that a share of the profits made behind the tariff wall flowed back to workers. This idea enshrined the Australian notion of a 'fair go' in a way that now seems radical. Order was imposed on the market-place; family welfare was linked to corporate profits. Introducing these laws in 1903, Deakin said: 'This bill marks, in my opinion, the beginning of a new phase of civilisation.' Deakin, as an admirer once observed, embodied Christ's view that man cannot live by bread alone.

A third element of the new society was state paternalism. And a fourth was White Australia. The new nation was terrified of Asia's hordes, and more so after Japan humiliated Russia in the war of 1904–05. Australia wasn't merely a haven for the white man. Specifically, it was a haven for white men whose descendants were English, Scots, Welsh or Irish. The 1911 census put the population at 4.8 million, including 590,722 born in the United Kingdom and just 36,442 born in Asia. Australia was about 96 per cent 'British'. Here was the final element in the consensus, a loyalty to the British empire and a belief in the protective power of the British navy.

This leads us back to the 'imperial' side of the national character, the bit that wasn't 'Australian'. The belief in the British empire was deep and just about universal. The assumption was that Britons, if not the master race, were definitely the superior race. And Australians saw them-selves as Britons. As Sir Henry Parkes said at the first Federation Conference in 1890: 'The crimson thread of kinship runs through us all. Even the native-born Australians are Britons, as much as the men born within the cities of London and Glasgow.' The Reverend Dr William Henry Fitchett, for 46 years principal of Methodist Ladies' College, Melbourne, in 1895 collected a series of pieces he had written for the *Argus* as *Deeds*

That Won the Empire. The book ran to 35 printings. The tales, Fitchett explained, were about the 'great traditions of the imperial race to which we belong'. A colonel from Toorak, John Monash, took Fitchett's book to Gallipoli. He thought it might be handy if his men wanted to know about British military tradition. One rather thinks that he soon decided it wasn't.

When war looked inevitable the two sides of the Australian character both seemed spontaneously to say that Australia must fight. As the historian Geoffrey Blainey wrote:

> Australians did not need to pause . . . Australia was emotionally and culturally tied to Britain. Her trade was largely with Britain. Her naval defences depended on Britain. She even entrusted, in most matters, her foreign policy to Britain.

The emotional tie was so strong that mostly there was no need to argue it. A federal election was being fought as Australia went to war. On July 31 Joseph Cook, the Liberal Prime Minister, born in the English Midlands and sent down the coal mines at the age of nine, spoke at the Victorian wheat town of Horsham, where many of the farmers in his audience were of German descent. 'Whatever happens,' he said, 'Australia is a part of the empire to the full. Remember that when the empire is at war, so is Australia at war.' Andrew Fisher, his Labor opponent, spoke at Colac in Victoria's western district on the same day. He declared that Australia would defend Britain 'to our last man and our last shilling', and you have to wonder about the possessive pronouns. Fisher, like Cook, was not truly an Australian son. A kindly and courteous man who disliked swearing and never touched alcohol, he had been born in Scotland. Like Cook, he had been a pit boy at nine. Three days later at Benalla, Fisher put the coming war in an election context with just two sentences.

> We are strongly opposed to the present [Cook] government . . . but, as I have stated frequently in parliament, in a time of emergency there are no parties at all. We stand united against the common foe, and I repeat what I said at Colac, that our last man and our last shilling will be offered and supplied to the mother country . . .

There it was: as an election issue, the war didn't rank; as an intellectual issue, it hardly seemed worth talking about. The people and the politicians were at one. They accepted the responsibilities of empire and, because they were innocent, saw the prospect of adventure. When Fisher won the election on September 5, Australia had officially been at war for a month. Australia didn't even have to think about an official declaration. That was an imperial matter. Once Britain had declared war, Australia as a dominion was committed. All Australia had to decide was the extent of its commitment.

If Australia's attitude to the war had been decided by pragmatism rather than filial ties, the result would have been the same. Australia could not defend itself and its sea lanes. Britain provided the insurance policy; Australia paid the premium by sending troops to Britain's wars. There was also the matter of Japan. The Japanese were eager to go to war against Germany in 1914 because there were spoils to be grabbed in the Pacific and Asia. Churchill was happy to have the Japanese as an ally: it meant he didn't have to divert ships from the North Sea to deal with Germany's Pacific squadron. Churchill was unworried if Japan picked up islands in the Pacific. He cared as little for Australia's security then as he did in 1942 when Britain lost Singapore to the Japanese. As things ended up in 1914, Japan acquired Germany's island possessions north of the equator, the Marshalls, the Marianas, and the Carolines.

In September, 1914, Australia captured Rabaul and German New Guinea, next door to Papua, which was already under Australian administration. Had Australia stayed out of the war, Japan would probably have ended up with a large chunk of New Guinea. Australians would not have wanted the Japanese so close.

Bean wrote that the war was like a crusade to Australians. This was certainly the way the story played in the newspapers. Germany was imposing its brutal culture on the world; the Kaiser was the anti-Christ; Belgium and Serbia were victims; democracy needed to be 'saved'. In *War and Peace*, Tolstoy occasionally spoils the tale by explaining, rather like a hack editorialist, that Russia won in 1812 because Napoleon was wholly evil and the Russians were wholly good. Bean sounded a little like Tolstoy when he wrote in the official war history, published in 1921, that the German philosophy was not based 'upon that sense of right which, whether evolved or implanted, exists in all modern civilisation'. It was based on the 'warped psychology or diseased ambition of powerful classes'. And it was 'utterly abhorrent to those nations which had been left free to develop according to the natural laws of human progress'.

Yes, the Prussian mindset was ugly. Yes, the Kaiser was a reactionary and not very bright, clinging to the divine right of kings while Britain and France worked at what Bean called 'human progress'. Yes, Germans committed atrocities across Belgium and behaved like Philistines, wrecking libraries and cathedrals. They, more than any nation, were responsible for the world war starting.

Yet it was not so simple as Bean and others saw it in 1914. The Romanovs of Russia, allies of Britain and France, were more reactionary than Kaiser Bill. Belgium indeed knew all about atrocities: it had been committing them in the Congo for decades. Even British democracy was a selective thing. It did not play in Bombay or Dublin (or among Australia's Aborigines) the same way as it did in London or Sydney. But no-one was thinking this way in 1914. As Ian Hamilton wrote after watching the naval battle of March 18: 'Once in a generation, a mysterious wish for war passes through the people. Their instinct tells them that *there is no other way* of progress and of escape from habits that no longer fit them.'

Australia's new Governor-General – he had arrived in May, 1914 – was Sir Ronald Craufurd Munro-Ferguson, a tall and handsome Scotsman, heir to a 27,000-acre estate, a lover of books and paintings, who had served in the Grenadier Guards before a 30-year career in the House of Commons. He was, as the *Sydney Morning Herald* put it, 'the representative of the King and of the race, and the racial ideals and traditions, the great institutions and the splendid history which the King symbolises . . . ' The Governor-General's office was different then. Though he was obliged to dress like a peacock, Munro-Ferguson was no figurehead who would only be drawn into the political process as an umpire of last resort. He was the conduit between the Colonial Office and the Australian Government. London, after all, behaved as if Australia was a colony that happened to be self-governing; Australia did not behave like an independent nation and didn't seem to want to. Munro-Ferguson was a true viceroy. On July 31, 1914, he telegraphed to the Prime Minister: 'Would it not be well, in view of latest news from Europe, that ministers should meet in order that imperial Government may know what support to expect from Australia?' In December he received a letter from the Colonial Secretary asking him to prepare the Australian Government for the possibility that, when the war ended, Japan would keep the German islands it had grabbed in the Pacific. His Excellency was a player; the governments in London and Melbourne expected him to be one. His main job was not to open agricultural shows but to recruit troops for the European war. He was furious when Australia voted against conscription in 1916.

Australia in 1915 was still a frontier society built on wool and gold and trying to forget that it had also been raised up on the transportation of convicts. It was not, as is often suggested, a rural society, peopled by characters from the pages of 'Banjo' Paterson or Steele Rudd. It was, however, a rural economy: most of its exports came from the farms and mines. The dream of land was still alive. And sometimes, just often enough to allow the dream to endure, a family could do well, even become wealthy, by working 12-hour days, knocking over the scrub, ripping the rabbit burrows, splitting lengths of yellow box into fence posts and tramping behind teams of Clydesdales and listening to the music of the chains. More often, the dream turned sour: all that work, only to be beaten by drought and the north wind and the wilfulness of a land that wasn't anything like England. Among those who survived it, the bush bred fatalism and dry humour.

The farmhouse was shaded by a few peppercorns and the garden consisted of three geraniums and a tangle of pumpkins. On the veranda stood a Coolgardie safe and a copper tub for doing the washing and heating the water for the weekly bath. Nearby was a harness box that smelt of mutton fat. Off to the side stood the kitchen, where the fire always burned and the toasting fork hung from a nail. In the killing shed, not far from the house but far enough, an old wether hung on a gambrel, his pink and blue flesh blotched with white globs of fat. Cold mutton was the staple diet; if it was particularly dark and gamey, one added more pickles. In the bedrooms stood brass bed-steads and kerosene lamps, and the lavatory, set aside from the house, was full of spiders.

The centrepiece of the farm was the woodheap. Here was an axe, the universal tool, and a grindstone. Lying among the chips were rabbits' heads and chooks' feet and heads and scraps of fencing wire and broken ploughshares and nearby a Kelpie cross with rheumy eyes and caved-in flanks lived on a chain, and past him was the clothes line, a piece of wire propped up with a forked stick. The farmers and their wives drove into town once a week in gigs, past the one-roomed schoolhouse with its corrugated-iron roof, past the river that smelled of mud and fecundity, past the blacksmith's shop with its junk-yard of broken hayrakes and mouldboards. They pulled up outside pubs with names like The Railway and The Commercial, where old men with rust-stained moustaches sat on benches, staring at nothing as they rummaged for tobacco in their waistcoat pockets. Most of the pubs were blood houses; on Saturdays they also became betting shops when the railway gangers and shearers came into town. Bank managers, teachers, clergymen and doctors didn't hang about the pubs; society said their vocations were 'respectable'. Women didn't go into them either. They went to the general store where there were bins of nutmeg and cloth was cut from bolts. The harness shop smelled of neatsfoot oil and the town kids, when they had nothing to do, which was most of the time, threw stones in the river.

Yet hope lived in these places. One good crop, a rise in wool prices, and the family would get by for another year. One day the patriarch might even be thought of as successful, although the odds were that when that day came he would be too worn out to do anything other than sit on a bench and rummage in his waistcoat for tobacco. But 1914 wasn't going to be a good year, and not because of the war. Australia was going through another drought and stock were dying around dams that had turned to puddles.

By 1914 most of the people and jobs were in the capital cities and large country towns. Factories, many of them employing 1000 workers, had sprung up behind Deakin's tariff wall: heavy engineering works, breweries, wool stores, woollen mills, tanneries, boot factories. A boot-maker earned £3 a week, a coal miner something between 48 and 54 shillings. The suburbs of Melbourne and Sydney crept outward. Private schools and universities were run in the English tradition and scholars were imported from Britain, as were newspaper editors and Anglican bishops.

The country took religion seriously. In 1915 some 4.2 million people said they were Christians and only 10,016 admitted they were godless. Sermons, no matter how banal, were reported in Monday's newspapers. Henry Montgomery, whose son would become an English field marshal, had been Bishop of Tasmania. When he returned to England in 1902, he wrote an instruction manual for clergymen heading to the colonies. He told them to clean their own boots when in Australia and to learn to shoe a horse. Don't use 'the affected voice manner', he advised.

And never speak about 'the lower classes'. Australians didn't like it.

A character, ambiguous and quirky, was forming in the old convict settlement. The people were proud to be 'British', part of the 'superior' race and of an empire that seemed to be short of its peak. Yet they didn't much like the mother country's class distinctions, particularly the notion that, when it came to classifying human beings, the past and the pedigree determined the future. Australians were cheekier and rougher and more inclined to look to the future rather than the past because there were too many things in the Australian past that were best forgotten. Bean was probably near to the truth when he wrote that 'Men passed among Australians for what in themselves they were worth.'

Bean was probably on one of his romantic flights in portraying the men of the first Australian Imperial Force as all of a kind. Bean tended to look at people the way farmers look at livestock: he had his idea of a 'good type'. He favoured a country lad, lean and sinewy, tough but big-hearted, equally good with a horse or a cricket bat but always modest. The lad looked better again if he had been a schoolteacher and was the son of a clergyman. Here is Bean explaining in the official history why the first recruits were easy to train:

The bush still sets the standard of personal efficiency even in the Australian cities. The bushman is the hero of the Australian boy; the arts of the bush life are his ambition; his most cherished holidays are those spent with country relatives or in camping out. He learns something of half the arts of a soldier by the time he is ten years old – to sleep comfortably in any shelter, to cook meat or bake flour, to catch a horse, to find his way across country by

day or night, to ride, or, at the worst, to 'stick on' . . .
Fires, floods, and even the concentration of sheep for
shearing, or the long journeys in droving bullocks down
the great stock routes across the 'back country', offer
many conditions similar to those of a military expedition.
The Australian was half a soldier before the war; indeed
throughout the war, in the hottest fights on Gallipoli and
in the bitterest trials of France or Palestine, the Australian
soldier differed very little from the Australian who at
home rides the station boundaries every week-day and sits
of a Sunday round the stockyard fence.

This might have been true of the light horsemen. By
1914, however, only about a quarter of the country's
workforce was on the land, although much of the temper
of the bush, its humour and the idea of mateship, had
been transplanted in the cities. New South Wales and
Victoria were the two most populous states with 3.2
million people between them. Half those people lived in
Sydney and Melbourne. Of the 416,809 men who enlisted
during the four years of war, only 57,430 fitted the
category 'country callings'. More than half were labourers
(99,252) and tradesmen (112,452), although some of
these would have come from the country. Suzanne
Welborn wrote in *Lords of Death* that a random
statistical survey of half of the original 11th Battalion
(raised in Western Australia) showed that the average age
was 25.8 years. Eighty-nine per cent of the men were
single. Fifty-eight per cent were Anglicans and 14 per cent
Roman Catholic. Thirty-four per cent were born in
Britain and another 31 per cent in Victoria; only 17 per
cent were born in the west. Across Australia in 1914,
about 30 per cent of those who enlisted had been born in
Britain.

* * *

Before Britain declared war on Germany, the Australian Cabinet offered its fleet, plus an expeditionary force of 20,000 volunteers, 'the force to be at the complete disposal of the Home Government'. Canada offered 2 cruisers and 20,000 men and New Zealand its navy and 8000 men. Munro-Ferguson cabled the Colonial Secretary: 'There is indescribable enthusiasm and entire unanimity throughout Australia in support of all that tends to provide for the security of the empire in war.' It was true enough. Australia was not a multicultural society in 1914. There were no significant groups of German and Austrian descent. Instead of the declaration of war being divisive, as such an event might have been in the United States, it was a force for unity. Trade unionists rushed to join up; Irish nationalists announced that they would put aside their grievances while the empire was in danger. People sang *Rule Britannia* and *God Save the King*. People who owned German Shepherds would shortly be saying that, while they still owned the same dog, it had always been an Alsatian. The Melbourne suburb of Heidelberg thought of changing its name. Anti-German feeling broke out and within a few months most German nationals had been interned and many Australians of German descent had been abused and spat upon.

From a distance of 86 years, it was as though Australians were *celebrating* war, sniffing the glory of it, as though, like the New Zealanders captured at Chunuk Bair, they thought it was going to be a game of rugby and that our side would win and walk away with the cup, and that afterwards other nations would take us more seriously. 'It is our baptism of fire,' the *Sydney Morning Herald* trumpeted on August 6. Innocence explains some of the headiness. Unlike France or Bulgaria, Australia had never been to a big war. It didn't know what it was like to lose the best spirits of a generation, to read casualty lists that took up whole columns in the newspapers, to see young men return home old and broken and wanting nothing much to do with anyone for the rest of their lives. And Australia probably had too much faith in the British empire; it looked stronger and smarter from Brisbane and Hobart than it really was.

Alan Moorehead, the Australian war correspondent who made writing look effortless, was four when his Uncle Harry left for Gallipoli. Uncle Harry loved to play with young Alan and toss him in the air. Moorehead wrote in a *New Yorker* piece that Harry thought going off to the other side of the world was 'the maddest, grandest thing on earth'.

> I don't think the prospect of fighting scared these young soldiers very much, or, if it did, their fear was coated over with the military trappings, the excitement, and a complete ignorance of war.

Uncle Harry was soon on his way home from Gallipoli and Moorehead worried that he would not want to play with him. Harry's right arm and right leg had been carried away by a shell.

Staff at Victoria Barracks in Melbourne on August 5 began registering the names of those eager to enlist. William Throsby Bridges, Inspector-General of Australia's permanent army, was organising the expeditionary force. Bridges, now a major-general, appointed Major Cyril Brudenell Bingham White as his chief-of-staff. Bridges and White decided to set up the expeditionary force as a division (plus a light horse brigade) with a national identity, rather than a series of smaller units that could be farmed out, a piece here and a piece there, within the British army, as Australian troops had been during the Boer War. If Bridges had not kept the Australians together, there would have been no Anzac Corps, no Gallipoli legend, no Gallipoli myths. Bridges had to raise a new force that was apart from the citizen army (Australia had brought in compulsory military training for home service in 1911) but there was no trouble finding volunteers.

John Simpson Kirkpatrick, an English merchant seaman, had jumped ship in Australia, so he enlisted in Fremantle as 'John Simpson' and became a stretcher-bearer. He wanted to fight Germans; he also wanted to get home to South Shields on the Tyne and see his widowed mother and sister. On October 14 he wrote home: 'We are expecting to leave at any moment for the Old Country . . . I am in the Australian Army Medical Core.'

Hedley 'Snowy' Howe, fair-headed and blue-eyed, was drinking in a hotel in Broome, Western Australia, where he worked in the pearling trade, when a telegram announcing the outbreak of war was pinned up. Howe at once walked to the shipping office, bought passage south to Fremantle and was off to war. Two German pearlers were also drinking at the bar. They at once set sail in the opposite direction.

Arthur Seaforth Blackburn, a law graduate in Adelaide, joined up on August 19 as a private. The son of a Woodville clergyman, he was 21. When he returned he would be wearing the pips of a captain and the red ribbon of the Victoria Cross. Walter McNicoll, principal of Geelong High School and a prominent citizen-soldier, telegraphed his willingness to serve the day war was announced. The Education Department grudgingly gave him leave of absence.

Bill Harney, who after the war would become well known as a 'bush writer' and raconteur, rode out of the Gulf country, caught a ship to Darwin, then another south to join up. Years later he told another writer: 'I was dead scared when I went to join up – scared it would be all over before I got there!'

Joe Cumberland from the Hunter Valley was said to be the youngest train driver in New South Wales. The 20-year-old enlisted at Sydney's Kensington racecourse within a month of the outbreak of war. His older brother, Oliver, who worked on a cattle property near Winton, Queensland, hurried south to enlist on October 17, just in time to leave for Egypt with the first contingent. Oliver joined up to look after his younger brother. Both were in the 2nd Battalion. 'I got in by the skin of my teeth,' Oliver wrote to his sister Una. 'I could not see Joe go alone and remain behind myself . . . I promise you I will never leave Joe wounded on the field whilst I have the strength to carry him off, and I know he will do the same for me.' Una wore a brooch of purple and green, the colours of the 2nd Battalion. The brothers both had big blue eyes and were more than six feet tall. From Cairo, Joe wrote to Una: 'If the boys are prepared to die fighting for their country, I reckon their sisters ought to be prepared to give them up if need be, when they know they are dying for a noble cause. So Una, I want to ask you one thing, that is to always look after little Doris [his younger sister] . . . ' Then a touch of bravado: 'There was never a Turk or German born, or a bullet made, that could kill a Cumberland. When Oliver and I get amongst them with the bayonet they will think all their birthdays have come together.'

Recruiting had begun in Sydney on August 11. That day the new army picked up 3600 men. Recruits needed to be between 19 and 38 years old, at least five foot six inches tall and to measure 34 inches around the chest. The doctors could pick and choose in a way they would not be able to do later in the war. They were particularly hard on men with bad teeth and flat feet. Fifty-two thousand men had enlisted by Christmas. Question Three on the enlistment form asked whether the applicant was a natural-born British subject or a naturalised British subject. This, and other rules, exempted Aborigines (or certainly those who looked like Aborigines) from the force that ended up at Gallipoli. Doctors were asked to certify that the recruits did not show 'traces of corporal punishment, or evidence of having been marked with the letters D. or B.C.'.

According to Bean, the rush to the recruiting offices brought out 'a class of men not quite the same as that which answered to any later call . . . all the romantic, quixotic, adventurous flotsam that eddied on the surface of the Australian people . . . ' War, Bean wrote, was a game to be played and these men were players by nature. Clergymen not accepted as chaplains enrolled as privates. A man four times rejected in Melbourne was accepted in Sydney. A bush worker rode 460 miles, then took a train, to join the Light Horse in Adelaide. There were no vacancies, so he sailed to Hobart. He finally enlisted in Sydney. Many of those who joined the 10th Light Horse Regiment in Western Australia brought their own horses and saddles. So heavy were the enlistments that on September 3 Australia was able to offer Britain a fourth brigade of infantry (the 1st Division comprised three infantry brigades) and a second brigade of light horse.

The Sydney recruits were sent to Randwick and Kensington racecourses. Everything was happening too fast. The contingent was supposed to sail in September.

There were no tents at Randwick, so recruits still in their civilian clothes slept on the wooden steps of the grandstand. Victorian recruits huddled on the windswept plain at Broadmeadows and caroused in Melbourne at night whenever possible. The South Australians were at Morphettville, the Queenslanders at Enoggera, the West Australians at Blackboy Hill and the Tasmanians at Pontville. They tried on their new uniforms: khaki woollen Norfolk jackets with four big pockets and the brass buttons oxidised black, slouch hats with the badge of the rising sun, webbing belts and packs, brown boots. All these men, hastily thrown together and barely trained, were supposed to converge on King George Sound in Western Australia where a fleet would take them to Europe. Privates serving overseas would be paid six shillings a day, six times the rate of English privates.

Bridges' 1st Division filled quickly. Its 631 officers included 68 from the permanent forces, 402 from the old militia forces and another 58 from the compulsory service scheme that had been introduced in 1911. About one-sixth of the officers had been to the South African or other wars. Or, to put it less optimistically, most of the officers had never commanded in battle before. Among the rank and file there were 1308 former British regulars and some thousands of trainees from the compulsory service scheme and the old militia; but 6098 men had come straight from civilian life, never having worn a uniform before. Twenty per cent of the force was under 21 years old, 40 per cent between 21 and 25, and 40 per cent over 25. A few officers were in their fifties. Close to 90 per cent of the men were single but one-quarter of the officers were married.

On October 24 the troopships began to assemble in King George Sound, off the port of Albany. One of the escort vessels turned up shortly afterwards: the Japanese cruiser *Ibuki*. The convoy had been delayed because of fears about the German raiders *Scharnhorst* and *Gneisenau*. These were now thought to be steaming for South America, although the German light-cruiser *Emden* was somewhere in the Indian Ocean. The convoy sailed on November 1 – 30,000 men, 7800 horses, 33 transports spread out over seven-and-a-half miles, three escorting cruisers, including the *Ibuki* and the *Sydney*. The convoy had sailed on the day Turkey came into the war. Had the men known this, they would not have made much of it.

On November 9, near the Cocos Islands, the *Sydney* headed west at speed to investigate reports of a 'strange warship' – and found the *Emden*. The Sydney signalled: 'Am briskly engaging enemy.' Twenty-five minutes later, the *Sydney* signalled: '*Emden* beached and done for.' The empire had triumphed again. Bridges gave the troops a half-holiday. When the convoy reached the Red Sea, Bridges and Godley, the commander of the New Zealanders, were told that the troops would disembark in Egypt. They were supposed to go to the Salisbury Plain, but a doctor said it would be 'criminal' to put men who had just passed through the tropics in tents during an English winter. The Australians would still go to the western front after further training in Egypt. They moved into their camp at Mena, outside Cairo, beneath the Pyramids and the Great Sphinx of Giza. They and the New Zealanders were formed into a corps – the 'Australian and New Zealand Army Corps' – under Birdwood. Bridges commanded the 1st Australian Division, Godley the New Zealand and Australian Division, consisting of the New Zealand Infantry Brigade, the Australian 4th Brigade, and two mounted brigades:

the 1st Australian Light Horse, under Colonel Harry Chauvel, and the New Zealand Mounted Rifles.

The first idea was to call the corps the 'Australasian Army Corps'. The New Zealanders rightly felt this was offensive. 'Australian and New Zealand Army Corps' was nevertheless a mouthful. Clerks began using a rubber stamp with one word – ANZAC – stamped on it. Anzac didn't come into general use until after the Gallipoli landing. Even then, no-one realised there was a Turkish word – *anjac* – which was sometimes used to mean 'almost' or 'but'.

The Anzacs were fortunate to be under Birdwood. Monash arrived with his 4th Brigade in January. In Birdwood he found

> a small, thin man, nothing striking or soldierly about him. [He] speaks with a stammer and has a rather nervy, unquiet manner, but there is no mistaking his perfectly wonderful grasp of the whole business of soldiering . . . I have been around with him for hours and heard him talking to privates, buglers, drivers, gunners, colonels, signallers and generals and every time he has left the man with a better knowledge of his business than he had before. He appeals to me most thoroughly.

This was Birdwood's gift: he got around, he talked and felt pulses. As Bean wrote, he looked upon men as men. When he waded ashore at Gallipoli, it was also apparent that he was very brave. He wrote to men who were decorated and to the families of men who died. He was not particularly gifted as a strategist or an organiser, but he had the power to inspire and lots of horse sense. He knew the Anzacs, and particularly the Australians, were not like English troops. The New Zealanders were mostly steady and sensible. The Australians were rough of manner and speech and not at all deferential. It was as though they were out to prove something, to themselves as well as to outsiders. They soon had a reputation for loutish behaviour in Egypt.

A joke went around Cairo. A sentry at one of the camps hears someone coming in the night.

Sentry: Halt! Who goes there?

Voice: Ceylon Planters' Rifles.

Sentry: Pass, friend.

[A little later:]

Sentry: Halt! Who goes there?

Voice: Auckland Mounted Rifles.

Sentry: Pass, friend.

[A little later again:]

Sentry: Halt, Who goes there?

Voice: What the ---- has it got to do with you?

Sentry: Pass, Australian.

Birdwood had the sense to accept the Australians for what they were and to make best use of their aggression and cheek. Birdwood was ambitious and, if necessary, he would use these dominion troops ruthlessly; but he would not try to change them too much. Birdwood was a tee-totaller, spartan in his personal habits and a neat horseman.

When he met Monash in Egypt, Birdwood wrote of 'an exceptionally able man on paper, observant – and with knowledge but I am doubtful about him being able to apply this knowledge in the field, partly because he does not seem to possess enough physical activity on horseback'.

Monash was not built to look good on a horse: he weighed better than 200 pounds and a large part of this was around his waist. Birdwood's observation tells us much about how the British saw war in the new century. Horses and bayonets: they were still what it was about. Though they were the same age – 49 – Monash was a modern man and Birdwood, at this stage anyway, was still living his past life as a cavalryman. Monash had three university degrees – law, arts and engineering – and a hopelessly curious mind. As Bean said, every piece of knowledge he picked up was docketed for future use. Monash had made his money from a relatively new idea in construction, reinforced concrete. He liked the theatre and opera, played the piano well, had a string of company directorships, and lived on a one-acre property in Toorak, where the library housed the works of Dickens, de Maupassant, Emerson and Shaw and paintings by Scheltema, Heysen and Norman Lindsay adorned the walls. He had been a citizen-soldier for 30 years. A biography of Thomas 'Stonewall' Jackson, the Confederate general, was his favourite text. He knew Napoleon's battles so well he would pull out a pencil and draw the disposition of forces at Austerlitz. Monash was methodical – he played chess for relaxation at Gallipoli – and cared about mastering detail and expressing ideas clearly and simply. His approach to soldiering was rational rather than emotional, and he wasn't shy about promoting his talents. He privately thought many of the English officers were dilettantes, their minds 'confined' by army training and gossip in the mess. Senior officers could talk well of their own speciality – gunnery or drill – and of polo, foxhunting and military lore, but were little interested in 'science, art or philosophy'.

Monash was still suffering for his ancestors. Louis Monasch, his father, grew up in Krotoschin in Prussia (the town is now in Poland) before immigrating to Victoria in 1854. John Monash was Jewish. Anti-Semitism was not only tolerated but published in the press in 1914, and people of German ancestry became victims of hysterical abuse. Munro-Ferguson had privately referred to Monash as a 'competent Jew'. A piece in Melbourne *Punch* in 1911 said Monash had 'the typical Hebrew mouth and the typical Hebrew eye'. On meeting Monash in Egypt and deciding that he couldn't ride, Birdwood also wrote: 'Lord Kitchener recently sent me a certain amount of nasty correspondence about him [Monash] from Australia with reference to his alleged German proclivities, but I told him [Kitchener] I am not prepared to take any action in the matter which I understand was fully enquired into in Australia.' In 1918, Monash, by then a corps commander in France, demonstrated his 'German proclivities' with a series of victories over the Kaiser at Amiens, Mont St Quentin and against the Hindenburg Line.

Bridges is the mystery among the Australian commanders. He didn't ride well either. Bean says he had a 'loose, awkward seat'. At Mena one day, he was cantering through the camp when his horse fell. The horse scrambled up with one of the general's feet caught in a stirrup. Had the horse galloped off, Bridges might have been killed. A young Australian from the Darling Downs leapt from his own horse while it was still cantering and grabbed Bridges' reins. Bridges never thanked him. White later said to Bridges: 'Foster deserved a VC today.' Bridges grunted. 'I suppose anyone else would have done it,' he said.

If Bridges lacked charm, he won over Bean, who didn't approve of Monash. The first chapter of Bean's biographical sketch of Bridges in *Two Men I Knew* is entitled 'The Rise of a Great Soldier'. One has to wonder about the adjective. Bean describes Bridges as 'a slow but deep thinker'. Again, one has to wonder whether a slow thinker should be a frontline general. Bridges was tall and thin, 53 when he came to command the 1st Division, with receding hair and the cold stare of an ascetic. He had been born in Scotland, the son of a captain in the Royal Navy and an Australian mother. The family moved to Canada, where Bridges graduated from the Canadian Military Academy, and then to Australia. After working as a roads inspector, Bridges served as a major in the Boer War. He spent time in England as Australia's representative on the Imperial General Staff before returning as commandant of Duntroon, the new military college at Canberra, where the national capital was to be built.

Bridges appeared to have the personality of a hermit with a headache. His favourite answer was a grunt. 'He was ruthless as to the feelings of others,' Bean wrote. 'He seemed to make no concessions to humanity; he expected none from it.' If he did not inspire men to do great things, he certainly made them afraid of him. 'He could not, by a kindly word or a tactful hint, help another out of difficulty,' Bean said. He also wrote that Bridges was 'really fond of some children'. In trying to make Bridges seem human, Bean only makes him seem more out of this world.

White, the chief-of-staff, was a nice foil to Bridges. The son of a grazier who had gone broke in the Queensland outback, White left school at 15 and became a bank clerk by day. By night he studied to be a barrister. He served with the First Commonwealth Horse in South Africa, then trained in England before returning to Australia as Director of Military Operations. White was 39, modest, intelligent, a quick thinker who was good at staff work, and easy to like. Also on Bridges' staff was Major Thomas Blamey, a 31-year-old schoolteacher who, in 1950, would become Australia's first and only field marshal, and Major Richard Casey, a 24-year-old Cambridge graduate who would become an Australian Governor-General.

Lieutenant-Colonel Ewen Sinclair-MacLagan was the most experienced soldier in the 1st Division, so it was right that he should lead the 3rd Brigade, the covering force that would go ashore first at Gallipoli. Born in Scotland in 1868, he had served in India and been decorated for bravery in the Boer War, where he was badly wounded. He had a sense of humour and got on well with Australians. MacLagan was worried about the plan for the Gallipoli landing. He thought it would be hard to carry out if the Turks were in strength on the ridges. He could even lose his whole brigade, he told Bridges. 'Oh, go along with you,' said Bridges, and laughed.

Major-General Alexander John Godley, Bridges' equivalent in the New Zealand and Australian Division, stood six feet two inches and had the cold stare and thin lips of a high-bred executioner. He was, however, charming to those above him. To those below he was unsmiling, seldom passing on praise and often finding fault. Monash later described him as bad-tempered, pernickety and selfish. Godley's mother was left 'very badly off' when his father, a lieutenant-colonel who had served in the Crimea, died suddenly. The family was socially prominent and Godley's relatives sent him through Sandhurst, but there was always the problem of money. Army officers needed a private income, particularly if they had Godley's tastes in travel and horseflesh, so in 1910, after service in the Boer War, he accepted an offer that wealthier British officers had refused. He would run the New Zealand army and introduce a system of compulsory military training. He was worried that he might be 'out of sight and out of mind', but he had to do it.

Godley published his memoirs as *Life of an Irish Soldier* in 1939 when he was 72. He writes with an easy charm and says very little. The book is one long garden party: Godley speaks ill of no-one and has no wisdom to impart. He is first of all a sportsman. Shooting, fishing, riding to hounds, watching the Melbourne Cup from the Victorian Governor's box, polo, socialising with the powerful: these are the things that move him. One day in Scotland he killed an otter in the morning, stalked and killed a stag, then finished the day with an 'excellent' afternoon's grouse-shooting. He shared a school dormitory with Rudyard Kipling – 'he was too clever for us, and rather different to most boys'. In 1898 he married Louisa Fowler – 'our honeymoon objective was the Devon and Somerset Staghounds . . . we enjoyed ourselves thoroughly'.

Louisa Godley was a strong personality. She and another woman drove a Cape cart from Mafeking to Pretoria as the Boer War swirled about them. At a parade of New Zealand troops in Egypt she was supposed to have said to her husband: 'Make 'em run, Alex.' The injunction became Godley's nickname among New Zealanders on Gallipoli. The chances are Louisa never spoke the words; they stuck because, said or unsaid, they were in character. There is another story, also un-confirmed, that she complained when wounded men from Gallipoli failed to lie at attention in their beds when she visited them in Egypt.

Godley proved a good administrator in New Zealand. He had the social graces Bridges lacked: he could finesse politicians and didn't look uncomfortable doing it. When war broke out New Zealand, though it had a population of only one million and was even more cut off from

Europe than Australia, owned a first-rate army, well equipped and ready to go. There was never a question of whether New Zealand should go. As with Australia, the war was about moral absolutes. More so than the Australians, New Zealanders saw themselves as Britons.

Under the system of compulsory training, boys from 14 to 18 served in the senior cadets. Men from 18 to 25 served as 'territorials' – in effect, citizen-soldiers – with the regional battalions and stayed in the reserve until they were 30. The territorials could be mobilised by proclamation for service in New Zealand. There were four military areas: Otago and Canterbury on the South Island, Auckland and Wellington on the North. The idea was to create two infantry divisions and four mounted brigades.

New Zealand went to war smoothly. Most of the volunteers came from the territorials. They had to sign on for the duration of the war, be between 20 and 34 years old, stand at least five foot four inches high and not be over twelve stone. Single men were preferred. Volunteers for the mounted brigades had to supply their own horses and tack, for which they were paid. Top price for a horse was £20 and no greys were accepted. New Zealand had slightly more people in the cities than on the land, but the method of recruiting gave the expeditionary force a rural bias.

Godley appointed Colonel Francis Johnston, a 42-year-old regular who had served with the British army in India, to command the centrepiece of his army, the New Zealand Infantry Brigade. The battalion commanders within the brigade included William Malone, a farmer and solicitor who had been born in London in 1859. Tall and domineering, Malone took over the Wellington Infantry Battalion. He had decided that war with Germany was inevitable and had prepared himself by sleeping on a military stretcher at home. Arthur Plugge (pronounced 'Pluggie'), a schoolteacher, commanded the Auckland battalion, and Colonel Andrew Russell, a farmer who had also served with the British army, took over the Mounted Rifles Brigade.

About a quarter of Godley's force had been born in Britain or other parts of the empire. Most were under 25 and 94 per cent gave their religion as Protestant. Where the New Zealand force differed from the Australian was in the depth of its experience. Out of 8417 men, only 1492 were without some form of military service. Malone, in a typical observation, wrote of his men in August:

> They are of all classes. Sons of wealthy run holders, farmers, school masters, scholars, M.A.s, B.A.s, musicians, tradesmen, mechanics, lawyers and all sorts. They will make good soldiers and the regiment, I trust, will lead the other regiments in the brigade. I will do my best to make it.

Just after dawn on October 16, the New Zealand contingent, plus 3818 horses, sailed for Hobart, then Albany. Not even Godley knew where they were going after that. England, then France, most probably. Perhaps India or Egypt as garrison troops. Maybe even South Africa, where the Boers were causing trouble. No-one would have thought that, a year hence and forever more after that, parts of the Dardanelles would be called Malone's Gully, Plugge's Plateau and Russell's Top.

Part Two

Attrition

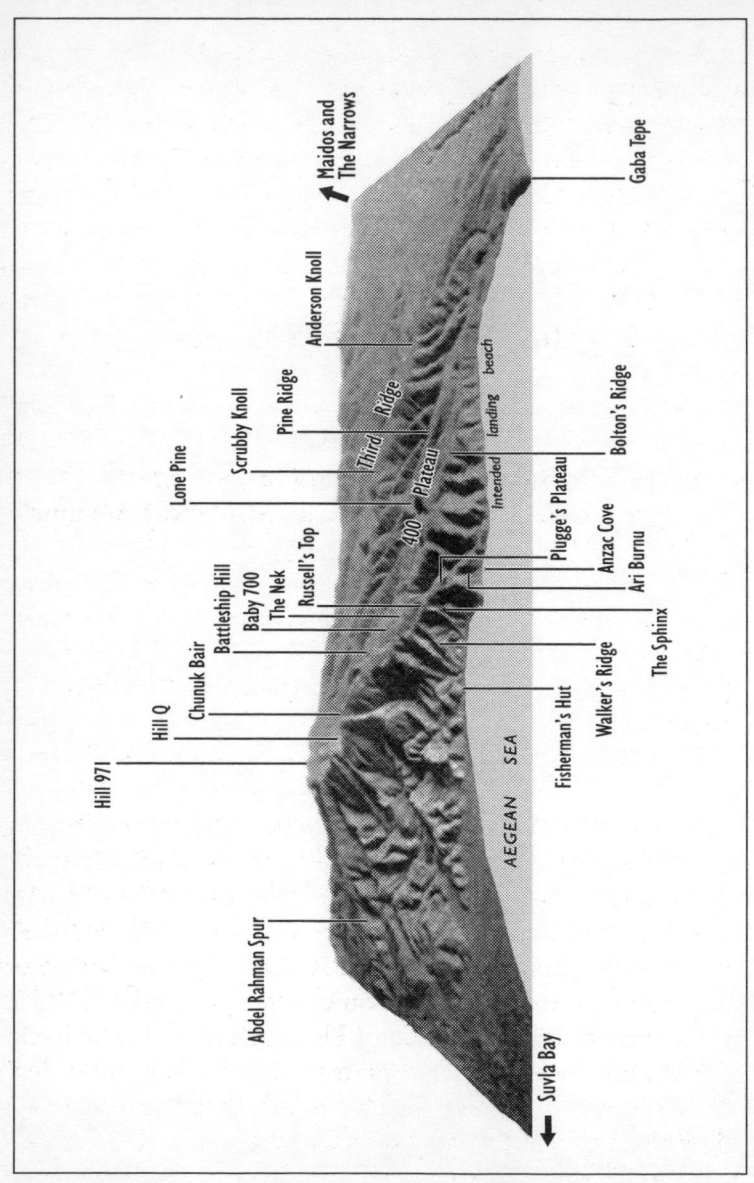

Anzac terrain

8

Almost a sight for the gods

Every fighter's got a plan – until he gets hit.
American boxing maxim

You are out to sea on the northern side of Anzac Cove. The dawn comes up like a thief: stealthily, out of grey shadows and smudges of inky blue. The first glimpse of the coast is of a mass, black and shapeless. It appears to erupt out of the sea. One cannot be sure whether it is a cliff face or a hill. It just looks dark and sullen. Don't come here, it says. Go somewhere less *foreign*.

You pick up a line of phosphorescence: waves lapping on the shingle, pebbles grinding and sighing. Now the mass begins to turn grey and to take on the shape of a sleeping elephant. The trunk, serrated and wrinkled, is the Razor Edge, pointing inland to Russell's Top and the Sari Bair range, none of which you can see. The great head is the knob on the inland side of Plugge's Plateau. The backbone and loins are the plateau itself. The hind legs stretched out behind are Ari Burnu, the headland that falls down to the sea, the hill you saw first.

It is so quiet, just the slop of the waves. The wind has gone down and the chill sends tingles down your arms.

Your watch says it is 4.30 am. The sea is a pane of glass and stars wink above Plugge's. It is, as Aspinall wrote of April 25, 1915, as if the elements are holding their breath.

Now you can see more of the elephant. It is covered with prickles and slashed by yellow scars. And to the left of it you can now pick up another ridge, much sharper, jagged and pitted, yellow from top to bottom because it is too steep for anything to take root on it. This is the Sphinx, an erosion in progress. It glowers down on you. There is still time to go away, to go somewhere you belong.

Around this time on the morning of the Anzac landing, boats from the first wave of the 11th Battalion were nosing towards the base of the Sphinx. They shouldn't have been anywhere near here, but it was too late to change course. Bullets were starting to fizz overhead and occasionally to thud into the men huddled in the boats. The sound of a wet sponge hitting the floor, a sigh, and a life was gone. A sergeant had told his men during training that bullets made a noise like small birds flying overhead. Now, as death first visited the 11th, a private looked up at the sky and said to Lance-Corporal 'Snowy' Howe: 'Just like little birds, ain't they, Snow?' Laughter broke out along the boat. A few men had been shot. Innocence, as yet, hadn't taken a hit.

Like most plans, this one did not survive first contact with the enemy. Birdwood wanted surprise. He had decided to land in the dark and without a naval barrage. The moon would set at 2.57. The first streaks of dawn would appear about 4.05 and the sun would come up at 5.15. The ships could not approach the coast while the moon was still up, lest the Turks spot their silhouettes. All this meant that the first wave needed to hit the beach about 4.30.

Not this beach in front of the Sphinx either, but the sandy one north of Gaba Tepe that looked so pleasant the English named it Brighton Beach. The bank there was a mere five feet or so and the coastal plain behind ran from 50 to 200 yards before the ground rose. The landing would be on a front of about a mile. Its right would be about a mile north of Gaba Tepe, its left near Ari Burnu, its centre in front of Bolton's Ridge. The ground here was rougher than at Gaba Tepe, but the headland had been fortified with wire and earthworks. Better to take Gaba Tepe from the flank rather than the front.

The coast north of Gaba Tepe falls into three sectors. The terrain at Bolton's Ridge is hilly but the slopes are tolerable and there are gentle valleys. Horses could be used here and a short march to the right brings you to the Maidos plain. Behind Anzac Cove is a confusion of ravines, gullies, razorbacks and cliffs. There is no pattern to this country, except that it rises to the heights of Chunuk Bair and Hill 971. Everything here favours the defender on the heights. Past Ari Burnu, inland from North Beach, the country is wilder still. Anzac is bedlam and North Beach is anarchy. No army would land at either place on purpose. From Bolton's Ridge one can reach the heights by following Legge Valley; at Anzac the invader must go cross-grain against the ridges.

Military historians and others talk of the three ridges that run out of the Sari Bair range and tumble to the sea between Ari Burnu and Gaba Tepe. We should be wary of this neatness: it brings too much order to shambles. On the ground it is harder to say where the first ridge ends and the second starts, mainly because, just as you are about to pronounce on the line of demarcation, you fall down a ravine. It is nevertheless true that the third ridge – from Chunuk Bair through Scrubby Knoll and on to

Anderson Knoll – is everything. To command the Maidos plain, you needed to have guns on the third ridge. Kemal knew this. The first thing he did on hearing of the landing was to head for Chunuk Bair. Birdwood knew it nearly as well, as his plans showed.

The landing was to be in two parts. The covering force, MacLagan's 3rd Brigade, roughly 4000 troops in four battalions, would strike quickly to the left and right. The 9th Battalion would land on the right. Two of its companies would clear Gaba Tepe; the other two would head for Anderson Knoll at the seaward end of third ridge. The 10th would land in the centre, capture the Turkish guns on 400 Plateau (part of second ridge), then cross Legge Valley and occupy Scrubby Knoll on third ridge. The 11th would land on the left and seize Chunuk Bair at the top end of third ridge. The 12th would be in reserve and the artillerymen would take their mountain guns to 400 Plateau.

The covering force would land in three waves. The first 1500 troops would be taken to within two miles of the shore by three battleships, then landed in 12 tows. The battalions were to be split up: 500 men from each of the 9th, 10th and 11th battalions would land in this first wave. The rest of these battalions, plus all the 12th, would land in the second and third waves. Seven destroyers towing ships' lifeboats would bring a second wave of 1250 men through the battleships to within 100 yards of the shore. Once the second wave had landed, the lifeboats would be used to bring ashore the third wave, also 1250 men.

The main body – the 1st and 2nd brigades, some 8000 men – would arrive from Mudros on eight transports. These would approach the shore around 5 am. Four of the transports would anchor and transfer their troops to the battleships' 12 tows. The other four would transfer their troops to the seven destroyers as soon as these had landed the covering force. If all went well, the three brigades and the mountain guns would be ashore by 9 am.

The 2nd Brigade would press on past Chunuk Bair and take Hill 971. It would also protect the left flank by holding the line along North Beach to Fisherman's Hut. The 1st Brigade would be in reserve.

One keeps writing *would*. One has to: this was merely the plan; it had nothing to do with what happened. In myth and legend the landing is about poetry and derring-do, Hector duelling with Ajax. In truth there was much derring-do but not much poetry. In truth the landing was mostly about confusion.

The 3rd Brigade has been called the 'all Australian' brigade. The 1st had been raised in New South Wales, the 2nd in Victoria. The 9th Battalion of the 3rd Brigade had been formed in Queensland, the 10th in South Australia and the 11th in Western Australia. The 12th was a composite: half from Tasmania, half from Western Australia and South Australia. The first wave of the 3rd Brigade landed at the foot of Ari Burnu at 4.30 am. 'Look at that!' an officer said as the boats came within 50 yards of the shore. The silhouette of a man showed up on the skyline of Ari Burnu. A voice called on shore. Then the flash from a rifle. Then lots of flashes. It had begun.

Ivor Margetts, a 24-year-old teacher from Hobart, was a lieutenant in the 12th. The battalion commander was Colonel L. F. Clarke, a 57-year-old shipping manager. Very soon Clarke would be dead, killed in mid-sentence as he wrote a message, crumpling into the damp clay of this foreign field with his book in one hand and a pencil in the other. And just before this happened he had probably never been so heart-thumpingly alive.

Despite his age – they called him 'the old colonel' – Clarke had climbed a cliff face on the south side of the Sphinx, a face so steep and slippery it would today bother a fit 20-year-old. Halfway up, a corporal came upon Clarke, panting and almost exhausted and still carrying his heavy pack.

Throw the pack away, said the corporal.

No, said Clarke.

All right, said Corporal Laing, let me carry the pack.

Clarke and Laing climbed the rest of the way together. And then Clarke was dead. Laing and Margetts lived through this mad day. Around nightfall, Margetts scribbled a few lines in his diary.

> Landed 0420. [He then mentions that three men were hit in his boat] Captain Lalor killed. Pat killed on left flank near me. Slept with Col. Smith on beach till 4 am. Rained.

Here is a masterpiece of understatement. Margetts later wrote a fuller account. He left Lemnos on the *Devahna*. At midnight, off Imbros, he clambered on to the destroyer *Ribble*. 'It was a wonderful sight to see the men smoking, quietly joking one with another, and perfectly cool and ready for whatever lay before them.' The captain gave the order for silence and for the men to stop smoking. 'In darkness and in silence, we were carried towards the land which was to either make or mar the name of Australia.' The *Ribble* came under fire and the captain gave the order: 'Man the boats, men.' The first tow left for the beach 'amid a perfect hail of bullets, shrapnel and the rattle of machine gun . . . I turned around to get the second tow ready, when a man just in front of me dropped, hit in the head.'

Margetts left in the second tow. He didn't know that the

boats were way off course, heading for the base of the Sphinx. Three men were hit in Margetts' boat. When it grounded the troops had to swim several strokes, then found it almost impossible to walk with their clothes and packs so sodden. Margetts fell twice before he reached the beach and the cover of a sand bank. He told his men to dump their packs, load their rifles and get their breath.

The men were heavily loaded. Each had 200 rounds of .303 ammunition, rifle and bayonet, an entrenching tool with two empty sandbags wrapped around it, a heavy backpack and two white bags containing two days' extra rations, which included a can of bully beef, biscuits, tea and sugar. The rifles were unloaded. There was to be no shooting before daybreak. Warfare had been turned back a couple of centuries. Before the sun was up the enemy could die only from stab wounds.

'It was just breaking dawn,' Margetts writes, 'and, as we looked towards the sound of the firing, we were faced by almost perpendicular cliffs about 200 feet above sea level, and as we were of the opinion that most of the fire was coming from this quarter, it was evident that this was the direction of our attack.'

Here we see the degree of confusion at dawn. The 12th had been spread around the seven destroyers. It was supposed to form up as a reserve at the foot of 400 Plateau. Yet here was Clarke, its commander, more than a 1000 yards north of the plateau, if indeed he had any idea of where he was, which he probably didn't. Instead of being in the centre, he was on the extreme left. Instead of looking at low hills, he was staring at the flutes of this mad ridge the men would call the Sphinx. Instead of looking out over a heart-shaped plateau, he was looking at a spur that led, over one hill and then another and another, to the heights of Sari Bair. Firing was coming from the ridge behind the Sphinx. It was more important to stop that firing than to turn right and try to find 400 Plateau and the rest of the 12th. For the rest of the day the 12th would not operate as a battalion; its men would fight in whatever battle they stumbled into.

Clarke didn't know it, but while he was catching his breath at the mouth of the tiny creek that took the run-off from the Sphinx, chaos was starting to unfold to his right on Plugge's Plateau. Though they knew they were on the wrong beach, the troops remembered their instruction to go forward strongly. The result was that companies of the 9th, 10th and 11th battalions all found themselves inter-mingled on Plugge's Plateau chasing a handful of Turkish coastal sentries. The 9th, which seemed particularly dis-organised, should have been on the right, the 10th in the centre and the 11th on the left. There was much enthusiasm, hardly any method.

Margetts waited a few minutes to regain his breath, then started to climb.

> Soon I came upon Col. Clarke and Lieut. Patterson and together on our hands and knees we climbed to the top of the first ridge [it was Russell's Top]. Up to this time I had not seen the sign of a Turk, but as we moved a little to our left we discovered a trench overlooking the beach and, fixing bayonets, we received the order to go for it but, unfortunately, the Turks had no desire to wait for us when they saw the bayonet.

Margetts and Clarke had about 50 men with them. Margetts ran forward with his revolver drawn. Clarke shouted from behind: 'Steady, you fellows! Get into some sort of formation and clear the bush as you go.' The Turks fled along a track bleached greyish-white that ran upwards and to the north-east, past the Nek, where the ridge narrowed to just 30 yards wide, and on towards the bare hill called Baby 700. There had been about 30 Turks in the trench. Two or three were shot as they ran; the rest lay down in the scrub on the seaward side of Baby 700. Margetts and his party advanced to the Nek.

Col. Clarke, who was about 20 yards to my right, called for a signaller, and commenced to write a report to Brigade Headquarters but was shot through the heart and died at once. Private Davis [Clarke's batman, waiting to take the message] was also killed here and Major Elliott [who would have taken over as battalion commander] going to the rescue of the C.O. was shot through the shoulder and elbow, fracturing his arm.

Elliott shouted to Margetts: 'Don't come here! It's too hot!'

Captain Eric Tulloch of the 11th, a brewer from Ballarat and an oarsman of some note, had landed even further north than Margetts at the foot of the spur that became known as Walker's Ridge. The 3rd Field Ambulance, which included Private John Simpson, also landed well up North Beach. Like the Sphinx, Walker's was a spur running from Russell's Top to the sea. Compared with the Sphinx, it was not too badly eroded and by following its narrow ridgeline one came out just below the Nek. After being shot at from the left as they ran and stumbled in single file along Walker's, Tulloch and his men reached Russell's Top in time to see an Australian bending over Clarke's body.

Captain Joseph Peter Lalor of the 12th arrived. He had a moustache with waxed ends and a sharp intelligent face. Like Clarke, Lalor had climbed a cliff alongside the

Sphinx. Lalor was the grandson of Peter Lalor, who led the gold diggers in the revolt at the Eureka Stockade, Ballarat, in 1854. Joseph had crowded much into his 30 years. After leaving Xavier College, Melbourne, he had enlisted in the British navy as a boy and deserted. He spent time in the French Foreign Legion, then fought in a South American revolution before joining the Australian Permanent Forces in Western Australia. He was said to be an accomplished linguist. He waded ashore at Gallipoli carrying a family sword that during the day would be lost, found and lost again.

Conscious that the 12th was supposed to be in reserve, Lalor decided to entrench at the Nek, much as this went against his impulsive nature. Tulloch's 11th Battalion, on the other hand, was supposed to seize Chunuk Bair, which was up the white track, past Baby 700 and its sister peak Battleship Hill. Tulloch moved off with about 60 men, including Lieutenant Mordaunt Reid, who had been born on the red plains of Elmore in northern Victoria and probably thought this was the most miserable piece of country he had ever seen. Tulloch didn't know where the other 900-odd men of the 11th were, let alone whether they could be expected to follow him.

A rare group was coming together on this northern flank under a clear blue sky. The main body had landed. Lieutenant Alfred Shout from the 1st Battalion arrived about 10 am, and didn't worry that the 1st was supposed to be in reserve. By this time reserves belonged to the plan and the plan was shot. Shout, a Sydney carpenter who had been born in New Zealand, would become the most decorated Australian soldier to serve at Gallipoli. With him came Major Blair Swannell, a 39-year-old English rugby international who had settled in Australia. He expected to be killed, and he was, on the seaward slope of

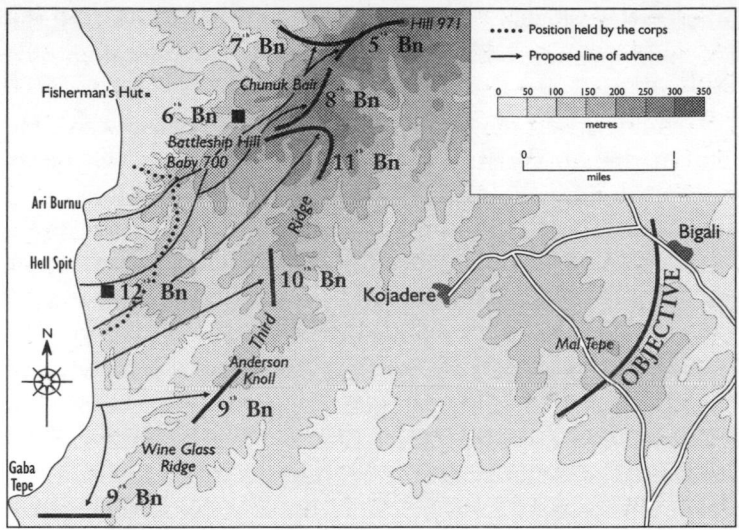

Anzac objectives

Baby 700. Later Captain Leslie Morshead of the 2nd Battalion arrived. He was then a young schoolteacher; in 1941 he commanded the Australian 9th Division at Tobruk and at the first and second battles of El Alamein.

Baby 700 would change hands five times this day. But there was another battle going on. It was out on the right, on 400 Plateau and beyond. Here, too, the Australians for a few hours occupied positions they would never hold again.

Even 85 years on, after all the reports have been held up to the light and rows of dots joined up, no-one is quite sure how the Australians landed on the wrong beach. Commander Charles Dix, who was in charge of landing the covering force, knew for sure that all had gone wrong when the boats were within 50 yards of the shore. 'Tell the colonel,' he shouted, 'that the damn fools have taken us a mile too far north!'

He had sensed the boats were off course before that. He was in the northernmost tow and he thought the boats were crowding each other towards the north. He steered across the stern of the boats inside him, shouting at them to keep to the south. This may be the reason the tows ended up in a bunch rather than spread out over a wide front as they should have been.

The first explanation for the error was a 'northerly current'. Later came the suggestion that the navy crews on the tows had mistaken Ari Burnu for Gaba Tepe. Others wondered whether the three battleships had anchored too far north, so that tows heading due east from them were bound to strike Anzac Cove rather than Brighton Beach. There has also been speculation about a late change of plans to move the Anzac landing up the coast.

We can probably forget about the current. The currents inside the Dardanelles are fierce; in the Aegean off Anzac Cove they hardly matter. There was, moreover, no wind on the morning of the landing. A northerly current would at worst have pushed the tows a few hundred yards north.

Ari Burnu looks nothing like Gaba Tepe. On a moonless night, however, one dark blob on the shore looks pretty much like another, so this allows the possibility of sailors mistaking one headland for another. Against that, the eye-catching feature around Ari Burnu, even in the treacherous light before sunrise, is not the headland itself but the Sphinx. There is nothing like the Sphinx at Gaba Tepe. It could be that by the time the navy crews picked up the outline of the Sphinx they were so close to the shore that it was too late to veer to starboard.

There exists the likelihood that the three battleships –

Queen, London and *Prince of Wales* – had anchored too far north, so that tows heading east from them were bound to land where they did. But why did the tows all end up so close to Ari Burnu? Assuming that the battleships were out of position, and that any northerly current would affect all tows equally, the boats should have landed on a wide front from the centre of Anzac Cove to Fisherman's Hut.

Where *were* the boats supposed to land? Braithwaite's written instruction to Birdwood dated April 13 refers to a landing 'on the beach between Gaba Tepe and Fisherman's Hut'. This is as precise as he gets. The distance between these two points is better than two-and-a-half miles, a 'broad front' indeed. Birdwood's order for the landing, dated April 17, simply says the corps is 'to land north of Gaba Tepe, and occupy the heights covering the beach'. This order also mentions the landing of artillery horses, which were to be harnessed before disembarkation, and there is perhaps a tiny clue here. Only a lunatic, and Birdwood was not that, would think of landing horses, harnessed or otherwise, on Anzac Cove or North Beach. Horses would, however, have been useful on the gentler country between Gaba Tepe and Bolton's Ridge.

General Bridges' order to the 1st Division for the landing, dated April 18, says: 'The division will land between Gaba Tepe and Fisherman's Hut.' This order also talks about the beach being divided into eight landing places. The arc of Anzac Cove is only about 600 paces, hardly long enough for eight separate landing places.

In a report to Braithwaite, dated May 8, Birdwood leaves no doubt about where he intended to land.

> I had originally intended landing with my right about one mile north of Kaba [Gaba] Tepe, as the advances from there up to the ridges of the Sari Bari [Bair] Hill, which I

hoped to take, were fairly easy, while the country further to the north was so difficult and precipitous that I feared troops would quite lose themselves in the dark, though the position there would probably be least guarded owing to the natural difficulties . . . As a matter of fact, the tows did not proceed quite due east on leaving the battleships but inclined to the north, *and landed me about a mile and a half north of where I intended our first disembarkation should take place.* [My italics]

Birdwood then made a virtue of the error.

As subsequent events turned out, I cannot help thinking that the hand of Providence directly guided us, for it so happened that the beach, on which we landed, and which we have since held, is one of the few places where the steepness of the cliffs has made us to a great extent immune from shell fire. Almost everywhere else we should probably have had to vacate owing to the heavy shell fire, which would most certainly have been poured on us.

Private Arthur Blackburn, the Adelaide solicitor with the 10th Battalion, probably got farther inland than any other Australian on the first day. The 10th was supposed to occupy Scrubby Knoll, across Legge Valley on the third ridge. Blackburn and Lance-Corporal Phil Robin, a bank accountant from South Australia, may even have passed beyond the crest of Scrubby Knoll. This says much about their mettle; it also says much about the madness of this first day. There was little point in scouting Scrubby Knoll unless a force was coming up behind to occupy it. It was the same on the left: Tulloch could hardly be expected to hold the heights below Chunuk Bair with 60 men.

Blackburn landed in the first tows from the battleships and everything he writes in a letter to his brother suggests an eagerness to rush forward. When he was 50 yards from the shore 'bullets started whizzing in all directions'. The men crouched low in the boats. Bullets splashed into the water. One clattered into a mess tin on a soldier's back but no-one in Blackburn's boat was wounded. He started half-swimming and half-wading for the shore. Three times he went right under. He had landed near the centre of Anzac Cove.

> The beach was very rocky and it was not the easiest thing on earth to clamber over big slippery rocks. All this time bullets were whizzing all around us and men were falling here and there. I rushed across the shore to the shelter of a small bank and there shed my pack and fixed my bayonet then straight on to drive the beggars away. The way our chaps went at it was a sight for the gods; no one attempted to fire but we just went straight on up the side of the cliff, pushing our way through thick scrub and often clambering up the steep sides of the cliff on all fours.

Blackburn reaches the top of first ridge and comes under fire from fleeing Turks on a ridge ahead 'looking right down on where we were'. Two men are hit on his right and one on his left. Dawn is breaking and 'the enemy can see us quite well'.

This is the story of the first few hours. The Anzac battlefield is a wilderness. The Turks did not know it that well – they never thought anyone would land there – but they knew it better than the Australians. The wilderness is easier to understand, as it still is, if you are on the higher ground, as the Turks were all day. And out on the right, where Blackburn was, the Turks had the sun behind them.

However we pushed on, forcing our way through the scrub and clambered and crawled up the second ridge, only to again practically find no enemy in sight. The country suited them beautifully for they could crawl forward in front of us through the scrub, firing all the time and we could hardly ever see them.

Blackburn and Robin had crossed Shrapnel Gully and were on 400 Plateau, near what would become known as Johnston's Jolly. No-one could know it then, but the plateau on the right would be like Russell's Top on the left. After the early rushes by the Australians had been repulsed, after groups had been cut off and killed, these places would become the frontline for the rest of the campaign. But it was early; the last thing Blackburn was thinking of was a siege.

Up till now I had seen no one that I knew, as all the battalions of our Brigade were completely mixed up. Just as I started down into the valley, however, I met Phil Robin and Micky Smith and together we pushed on after the enemy. Travelling across this valley was a decidedly lively time as the scrub was full of snipers and every little while a bullet would come closer than was pleasant. However we got to the top of the ridge in safety and there found several other chaps but no-one in charge. Just at that moment however, Captain Herbert came up and so Phil Robin reported to him. He had decided to entrench there and so sent Phil and me out to watch a valley on his front and flank while he did so, and this, by the way, was about the only bit of scouting I got to do on the first day. We stayed out there until driven in by the enemy who were coming to the attack in force . . .

Robin was killed three days later. From Robin's diary, which he wrote until the 26th, and a letter from Blackburn, Bean concluded that Blackburn and Robin had crossed Legge Valley and climbed the third ridge north of Scrubby Knoll. They scouted southwards and saw Turks approaching. This was Sami Bey's 27th Regiment coming to meet the landing from its camp near Eceabat. Blackburn also saw Australians to the southwest. This was a party under Lieutenant N. M. Loutit, also of the 10th, which had reached the third ridge south of Scrubby Knoll. Further south a handful of the 9th Battalion under Captain E. C. P. Plant reached the third ridge south of Anderson Knoll. The Turks arrived at Scrubby Knoll about 8 am. For the rest of the campaign this hill, just three miles from the Narrows, became Turkish headquarters.

Tulloch's men got farthest in on the left. They crossed the Nek and pushed through the prickly scrub on the inland crest of Baby 700. Walking with about seven paces between them the men toiled up the inland slope of Battleship Hill. Across Legge Valley to the right lay Scrubby Knoll. A Turkish machine gun opened up from there and ten Australians fell. The Turkish fire eased and Tulloch's party went forward again. Ahead was a bigger hill, Chunuk Bair, the objective for the 11th. The Australians now came under heavy fire from there. They rushed forward for perhaps 200 yards, then began to crawl. Survivors told Bean the Turkish fire chopped the dwarf oak and arbutus into chaff that flew under their collars and down their backs. They were still on Battleship Hill, maybe a few hundred yards inland from the crest. It was after 9 am and if they had looked to their right they would have seen a big sweep of the Dardanelles glinting like tinsel. More likely, however, they were looking to the front, at Chunuk Bair and the blue-grey puffs from Turkish rifles. They could see a lone tree up there. A man stood near it. Messengers would approach him and leave. Tulloch took him to be the Turkish commander and fired at him. The man did not move.

Tulloch's position became hotter. As well as the Turks in front he could see others to his right. Then the Turks opened up on his left. They were starting to roll down from the heights, not in a frontal rush but around his flanks. Mordaunt Reid was shot in the thigh. He began crawling back towards Baby 700 and was never seen again. Tulloch withdrew his skirmishers to Baby 700. He left half of them there and took the other half back to near where Lalor had dug a horseshoe trench at the Nek.

Shrapnel was bursting all over the battlefield now. The guns at Gaba Tepe had opened up soon after dawn and now others were joining in. The Australians quickly learnt the sequence. You heard the *crump* away to the south. Then you heard a whizzing sound, like a kettle going off the boil. Then there was the flash, just a pinpoint. Then the bang followed by a puffy white cloud and the whirr of pellets. The ground boiled and dust flew and men would cry in pain and others wouldn't because they were now just lumps of quivering flesh.

The first New Zealanders landed after the Australian main body. General Walker was leading them because the commander of the New Zealand Infantry Brigade, Colonel Francis Johnston, was ill. The New Zealanders found their way to Baby 700. Thus from Russell's Top up to Baby 700 were fighting men of the 11th and 12th battalions of the covering force, men from the 1st Brigade of the main body (who were supposed to be the reserve) and New Zealanders from Godley's division. Who was in charge up here? We know what these troops were *supposed* to be doing, but what were they trying to do now that the plan wasn't working? Out on the right, on 400 Plateau and along the rim of Monash Valley, things were going much the same.

The first hours of the landing and the misfortunes of the covering force are like a dream: full of loose ends and cameos that don't connect up with the sequences either side of them. The early clashes were without pity. Bean reports, without comment, that as Lieutenant Loutit's party was heading for 400 Plateau it chased a group of Turkish coastal sentries. 'As the Australians got in among them, the Turks threw down their rifles; but they were too many to capture, and were consequently shot.' When, later in the day, the Turks began to reclaim ground lost in the first few hours, they did the same. Groups of Australians on Baby 700 to the north and Pine Ridge to the south were cut off and never seen again. When the Australians returned in 1919, they found the skeletons of their countrymen, scraps of uniform and webbing still attached, lying in little semi-circles, the ground around them littered with .303 shells.

The landing of the covering force had in one sense gone well. Hamilton's biggest worry with all his landings had been *getting the men ashore*. Well, they were ashore at Anzac. They had not met heavy opposition on the beaches. There were barely two Turkish companies in the area and these had had the sense to retreat, shooting all the way. The Australians had incurred casualties – Birdwood estimated them at between 300 and 400 – but they had not been massacred by machine guns, as the English would be at Helles.

They were, however, on the wrong beach and the units were so badly mixed up there was no way they could be untangled. The maps had turned out to be useless. These suggested that Plugge's Plateau led on to Russell's Top, as it appeared to from the sea. And it did, but the 'link' was the Razor Edge, the thinnest of ridges that could only be crossed by straddling it. It was not a practical route for troops under fire; even today it is only attractive to those flirting with suicide. Plugge's led to nowhere in a straight line and this caused fearful confusion. Men needed on the heights above Russell's Top had to go around the Razor Edge. They spilled down the right-hand side of Plugge's into Shrapnel Gully and its extension, MonashValley, then climbed the steep sides of Russell's Top. If they went this way, however, there was a chance they would be caught up in skirmishes at the head of Monash Valley or diverted to the battle on the right on 400 Plateau. Or they might simply get lost. The other way to Russell's Top from Plugge's was to retrace one's steps to the beach, head north under the base of the Sphinx, then climb Walker's Ridge in single file.

The troops had rushed into the hills full of the verve that belongs to young men who have not seen much of death. They had remembered the instruction to go forward and not to get hung up on the beach. But there was no system to it. Nothing was connected up to a plan, either the written one or a new one that might have been devised on the beach. There was no *concentration* of the force. Hardly anyone was where they should have been. Instead there were dozens of running battles all the way from Battleship Hill in the north to Anderson Knoll in the south. Tulloch and Blackburn and dozens of others went forward as they were supposed to, but who was following to secure the ground? Who even knew where the forward parties were? Communications had broken down, partly because the country was so baffling and also because of the intermingling of units. And it probably didn't help that most of these men were volunteers who had never been under fire before.

By mid-morning the thing was far from lost, merely heading out of control. In these first hours chaos and the terrain caused more damage than the Turks. The rushes at the third ridge had produced nothing but bravery and bodies; now, as the Turks began to counter-attack, the operation took on the first characteristics of what it was never supposed to be. It began to look like a siege.

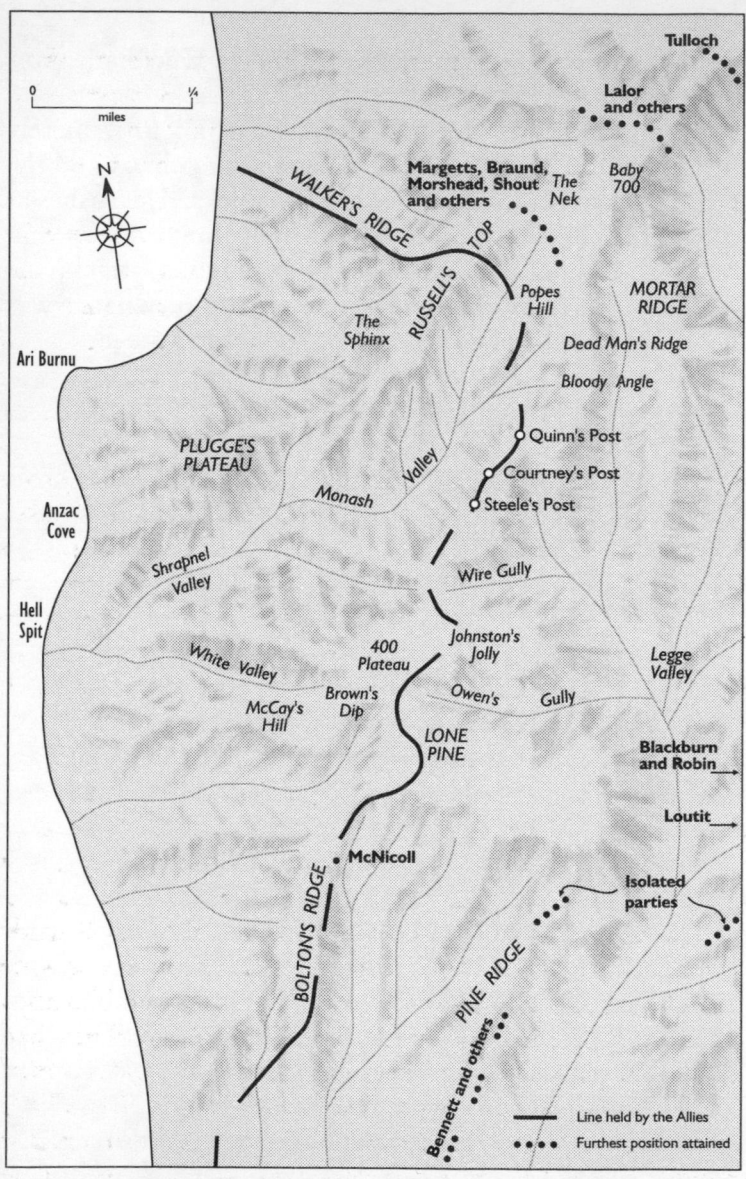

Anzac: the first day

9

The loss of the heights

Hamilton sailed past Anzac Cove in the *Queen Elizabeth* just after 5 am, unsure whether he was a general or a poet.

The day was just breaking over the jagged hills; the sea was glassy smooth; the landing of the lads from the South was in full swing; the shrapnel was bursting over the water; the patter of musketry came creeping out to sea; we are in for it now; the machine guns muttered as through chattering teeth – up to our necks in it now. But would we be out of it? No; not one of us; not for five hundred years stuffed full of dullness and routine.

Hamilton knew that the 4000 men of the 3rd Brigade were ashore; he didn't know they were on the wrong beach and all mixed up. The Australians looked like ants. Hamilton decided they were fighting for love. They had come 'all the way from the Southern Cross for love of the old country and of liberty. Wave after wave of the little ants press up and disappear. We lose sight of them the moment they lie down. Bravo!'
Whereupon Don Quixote and the *Queen Elizabeth*

turned south for Cape Helles, for the main battle and the main slaughter.

At about the same time in Gallipoli township Liman von Sanders heard of the landings. He was not moved to lyrical flights. Nor, the way he tells it, was he flustered, despite the 'pale faces' around him, when reports came in of so many landings and probable landings. Besika Bay, Kum Kale, four beaches near Cape Helles (the Turks were so far unaware of the landing at Y Beach), Ari Burnu, Gaba Tepe, Bulair: all were under some form of threat. The British and French, with their hundreds of ships, seemed to be everywhere.

'My first feeling,' von Sanders wrote with true aplomb, 'was that our arrangements needed no change. That was a great satisfaction! The hostile landing expedition had selected those points which we ourselves considered the most likely landing places and had specially prepared for defence.' Faced with so many threats, and not knowing which of them was the real thing, von Sanders kept his nerve. He would respond only when he knew the true nature of the threat.

As has been mentioned, von Sanders had two of his six divisions, the 5th and the 7th, at Bulair and another two, the 11th and the 3rd (which was meeting the French landing) around Besika Bay and Kum Kale. The 9th Division, under Lieutenant-Colonel Khalil Sami Bey, was responsible for the peninsula, which meant that at this moment it had to deal with six landings. The 19th, under Kemal, was in reserve and just happened to be camped within sound of the gunfire at Anzac.

Sami Bey's 9th Division was made up of three regiments, each of three infantry battalions, plus artillery. The 25th Regiment was in reserve at Serafim Farm on

Kilitbahir plateau so that it could quickly be diverted north to Gaba Tepe or south to Helles. The 26th Regiment was in the Helles area with a battery of field artillery. Two companies were guarding four of the beaches where the British landed; there were no coastal sentries at Y Beach.

The 27th Regiment, commanded by Lieutenant-Colonel Ali Sefik Bey, was at Anzac, although obviously to oppose a landing at Gaba Tepe rather than at Ari Burnu. Two battalions were in reserve near Eceabat. The other battalion, which included a mountain battery, watched the coast. One company was spread out between Ari Burnu and Gaba Tepe, another between Ari Burnu and the Aghyl Dere (valley). In short, the Australian covering force was opposed by several hundred Turks spread out in small detachments. The Gaba Tepe battery, which began firing from a clump of oak trees around dawn and didn't stop for eight months, comprised two 15-centimetre guns and two 12-centimetre guns.

Aspinall estimates that 17 Turkish battalions (nine in the 9th and Kemal's eight) were available to oppose the 24 British and Anzac battalions that had landed by noon on April 25. But how quickly could the Turkish troops be brought into the fight? Von Sanders had first to decide which landings were real and which were feints. Bulair, where no troops had come ashore, worried him more than Helles or Anzac.

The 7th Division was in Gallipoli town. Von Sanders sent it to Bulair. He galloped on ahead and looked upon an 'unforgettable picture'. He counted 20 warships and transports off Bulair. The warships gave off fire and smoke as they let fly with broadsides, yet no troops came ashore. Essad Pasha, in charge of the 9th and 19th divisions, arrived. The British landings around Cape

Helles had so far been repulsed by the 9th, he said, but the enemy was bringing up more troops. At Ari Burnu the 'British' held the heights along the coast. The 19th Division was marching from Bigali to recapture them. There were no detailed reports from the Kum Kale fighting. 'The preparations of the enemy were excellent,' von Sanders wrote in 1928, 'their only defect being that they were based on reconnaissances that were too old and that they underestimated the powers of resistance of the Turkish soldier.'

Von Sanders kept watching the sea at Bulair. This, he thought, could be a feint. He noticed that the transports were not as deep in the water as they should have been if they were fully loaded. And the decks were lined with rows of branches; it was impossible to see if there were troops behind them. Then came news that Besika Bay also looked to be a feint.

Von Sanders still wasn't prepared to denude Bulair, even though he now knew that Sami Bey had put his last available troops into the battle down south. He sent Essad five battalions from Bulair. Von Sanders stayed there for the night. Next morning he was sure Bulair was a feint. He sent more troops to Essad and decided to send all the Bulair force to Helles and Anzac if no landing was made in the next 24 hours. He then put Colonel von Sodenstern in charge at Helles; Essad would command at Anzac. Von Sanders went south to Essad's tents at Mal Tepe, about three miles from Anzac Cove. When the French left Kum Kale he ordered the 11th Division to cross the Dardanelles and join von Sodenstern. He was systematically carrying out the plan he had settled on weeks earlier.

Accounts of the Turkish response at Anzac on April 25 invariably stress the part played by Kemal, and this is proper. Kemal accepted more responsibility than he needed to. He literally rode to the sound of the guns, map and compass in hand. He brought all his troops into the fight without first asking permission. Kemal was certain he knew what the 'British' were doing. Ari Burnu was no feint. If it was, why were these khaki-clad figures from Tulloch's party advancing on him from the inland side of Battleship Hill? If Ari Burnu was a feint, the enemy would have been near the beach, making lots of noise but ready to re-embark. Yet here they were running forward so strongly and dying so carelessly that they had just about cut themselves off from help. Kemal also realised at once that the Anzac battle was about the high ground. He had to stop the enemy taking Chunuk Bair. If that meant sacrificing his division, he would do it. As his famous order of April 25 read: 'I do not order you to attack; I order you to die. In the time which passes until we die other troops and commanders can take our places.'

Kemal was inspirational, about as quick-witted as a military leader can be when taken by surprise. Afterwards he became the national hero for routing the vultures who in 1918 finally came down from the trees to start ripping apart the Ottoman corpse. Every village has a statue of him; his face is on lapel pins and above the podiums of university lecture halls and on every denomination of the local currency. The deification of Kemal has, however, tended to eclipse the part played by the 27th Regiment of Sami Bey's 9th Division on the first day of the Anzac landing.

The men of the 27th, mostly from Çanakkale province and European Turkey, were first into the fight. They were camped outside Eceabat. The regiment's coastal sentries telephoned Sefik Bey, the 27th's commander, around 5.30 and told him of the landings. Adil Şahin, from Big

Anafarta village, was in charge of a party of ten men guarding the coast near Hell Spit. Kenan Çelik, the best-known of the present-day battlefield guides, used to drink tea with the white-whiskered old man at Şahin's house just below the mosque in Big Anafarta. Adil Şahin was in his eighties but he remembered the day well. He had seen British warships, presumably before the moon went down, on the night of April 25. He went off sentry duty about 4 am. A soldier rushed into his tent and said the 'English' were landing in small boats. Adil Şahin ran back to his post and at once realised that his ten men would be overrun. He retreated to Scrubby Knoll and lived to grow tomatoes.

Sefik Bey had an observation post on Kakma Daği, a low hill outside Eceabat that looks over the Maidos plain, which is about two miles wide here. Across the plain is Scrubby Knoll, from where Loutit and Blackburn fleetingly glimpsed the Narrows, and beyond that, easily observed, Lone Pine and Pine Ridge.

The 27th was on the move by 6 am, skirting around Kakma Daği, keeping to the low ground to avoid being seen by the armada off Anzac. The regiment came into the fight from Scrubby Knoll, more than two hours before Kemal's 57th Regiment counter-attacked from the heights, and stopped the Australian rush across 400 Plateau. It is hard to estimate the part played by the 27th in those first few hours; but it perhaps counted for more, and maybe a great deal more, than has been conceded.

When Kemal heard the sounds of ships' guns he sent his divisional cavalry to Hill 971 to find out what was happening. He had expected a landing at Gaba Tepe, not Ari Burnu. He didn't even know the country at Ari Burnu. The 57th Regiment was already out on parade; an exercise towards Hill 971 had been scheduled for that morning. Kemal telephoned Essad, who was in Gallipoli township. Essad said he had no clear facts. Then at 6.30 am a report from Sami Bey arrived. The enemy had climbed the heights at Ari Burnu. Sami Bey asked Kemal to send a battalion, roughly 1000 men, to check the advance. Sami Bey appears at this stage to have thought that the landing at Ari Burnu involved only one battalion; he was more bothered by the landings at Helles. Kemal had read the situation rather better. If it was a feint, why was this 'one battalion' heading for Chunuk Bair?

Both from this report and as a result of the personal observation I had carried out at Mal Tepe, my firm opinion was, just as I had previously judged, that an enemy attempt to land in strength in the neighbourhood of Gaba Tepe was now taking place. Therefore I appreciated that it was impossible to carry my task with a battalion, but that as I had reckoned before, my whole division would be required to deal with the enemy.

He dictated a report to Essad outlining what he was doing. He told the 57th Regiment to head for Hill 971 and take a battery of mountain guns. (As he later told an interviewer: 'A famous regiment, this, because it was completely wiped out.') Kemal mounted his horse and led them out. So unfamiliar were they with the wild country behind Anzac that they were soon lost. Kemal himself worked out a route. Zeki Bey, commander of the 1st Battalion of the 57th, told Bean in 1919 that Kemal probably didn't know where Ari Burnu was. 'On the little maps which we then had it was not marked by name.' Anyway, Zeki Bey said, Kemal's main concern was not the beach but Hill 971; he had to reach it before the 'English'.

From the peak of 971, Kemal saw dozens of British ships and boatloads of troops coming ashore, but he could not see the beach at Ari Burnu, which is hidden from here. He passed word back that the 57th should rest out of sight of the sea while he rode downhill to Chunuk Bair. The ground turned out to be too rough, so he dismounted and walked.

A Turkish detachment had been on the southern shoulder of Chunuk Bair to watch the coast. Now the men were fleeing back towards him.

Let me tell you the conversation as it took place. Confronting these men myself I said: 'Why are you running away?'

'Sir, the enemy,' they said.

'Where?'

'Over there,' they said, pointing out Hill 261 [the southern shoulder of Chunuk Bair].

In fact a line of skirmishers of the enemy approached Hill 261 and was advancing completely unopposed. Now just consider the situation. I had left my troops, so as to give the men ten minutes rest. The enemy had come to this hill. It meant that the enemy were nearer to me than my troops were, and if the enemy came to where I was my troops would find themselves in a very difficult position. Then, I still do not know what it was, whether a logical appreciation or an instinctive action, I do not know, I said to the men who were running away: 'You cannot run away from the enemy.'

'We have no ammunition,' they said.

'If you haven't got any ammunition, you have your bayonets,' I said, and shouting to them, I made them fix their bayonets, and lie down on the ground . . . When these men fixed their bayonets and laid down on the ground the enemy also lay down. The moment of time that we gained was this one.

Kemal had seen Tulloch's party and Kemal was probably the officer Tulloch saw near the lone tree and fired at. Much has been made of the 'lying down' incident, as though it was a turning point. Patrick Kinross, Kemal's biographer, says it 'may well have decided the fate of the peninsula'. This is going too far. Tulloch, with less than 60 men and no reinforcements coming up behind him, could never have held the heights.

Kemal brought the 57th forward and had them open fire. The mountain battery opened up from Chunuk Bair. It was around 10 am. The Australians were now being attacked by Sami Bey on the right and Kemal on the left.

At 11.30 am, Kemal says he summed up the situation thus:

> The force which the enemy had landed was more than eight battalions. Now these eight battalions had been able to advance on an unfavourable and very wide front as far north as Point 261 and as far east as the western slopes of the ridge where Kemalyeri [Scrubby Knoll] was. But this long front was cut up by a number of valleys which were obstacles. For this reason the enemy was weak on nearly every part of his front ... But to my mind there was a more important factor than this tactical situation, that was that everybody hurled himself on the enemy to kill and to die.

Turkish oral tradition has Kemal describing the Australians coming towards him as 'unconnected'. If he did say this, it was a perceptive judgement.

Kemal later in the day put his two remaining regiments,

the 72nd and the 77th, both mostly Arab troops, into the fight. Neither was in the class of the 57th. The 77th spent the night of April 25 in a panic, shooting at whatever moved, which mostly meant that it was firing into the Turkish regiments on either side of it.

Kemal set up his headquarters on Scrubby Knoll, which frowns down on the Anzac perimeter and came to be called Kemalyeri – Kemal's Place. From here, a few days later, he issued an order of the day:

> Every soldier who fights here with me must realise that he is in honour bound not to retreat one step. Let me remind you all that if you want to rest there may be no rest for our whole nation throughout eternity. I am sure that all our comrades agree on this, and that they will show no signs of fatigue until the enemy is finally hurled into the sea.

The Unspeakable Turk had a voice. If it wasn't as lyrical as Hamilton's, it had a harder edge.

Most of the Australian main body, the 1st and 2nd brigades, some 8000 infantrymen, had waded ashore by soon after 9 am. They squelched and scrambled into rising chaos. The 2nd Brigade had begun landing from about 6.20. It was supposed to be on the left, so as to take Hill 971 and hold the line from there to Fisherman's Hut. This plan took no account of the terrain all along this line: the tawny knolls with sheer faces, valleys that broke three or four ways, little streams with muddy bottoms and bulrushes that rose six feet. It would have been close to impossible for 4000 men to hold such a line.

We need, however, think no more of this. The new plan, as much as there was one, was to fill the gaps, to deal with the emergency of the moment. The biggest problem was not yet the Turks; that would come later. The biggest trouble was the terrain, these ravines and washaways that had been thrown together by a lunatic. The reconnaissance had been from the sea and the view from a ship's bridge didn't reveal the Razor Edge for what it was, or show Walker's Ridge in its true narrowness and dizziness, or tell anything about Monash Valley at all. MacLagan didn't know whether to look left or right. The first threat appeared to be on the right where the 27th Regiment was starting its counter-attack from Scrubby Knoll. So the 2nd Brigade, instead of heading left for Hill 971, was sent to the right, out on to 400 Plateau.

MacLagan had his headquarters out there on MacLaurin's Hill. This was too close to the front for a HQ but, at this time, MacLagan couldn't know the advance would stop at the second ridge. No sooner did MacLagan see the threat on the right, near his HQ, than he saw a bigger one on the left. One thing he had learnt about the terrain from a few hours ashore was the importance of Baby 700. Whoever held it could direct fire down Russell's Top, into Monash Valley and along the rim at the head of it, and across towards 400 Plateau and Lone Pine. Baby 700 sat over Anzac, dominated it physically and mentally like a tyrannical parent. The maps didn't really make this clear, nor did the reconnaissance from warships. And now the 57th Regiment was rolling down the Sari Bair range, intent on pushing the Australians off Baby 700. So half of the 1st Brigade, instead of being held in reserve, was sent up to help Lalor and Margetts, to suffer and to die on that gentle and lonely hill. The first New Zealanders ashore were also sent there.

What happened to them tells much about the problem

with the ground. Birdwood signalled that he was landing one-and-a-half battalions of New Zealand infantry under the command of General Walker. Bridges decided to send them up Walker's Ridge to Baby 700. Walker, quite reasonably, thought the ridge too steep and exposed. Better to go via Plugge's Plateau. Walker assumed, as everyone had before the landing, that Plugge's led on to Russell's Top and thence Baby 700. He didn't know that the Razor Edge turned Plugge's into a dead end. The New Zealanders who climbed Plugge's had to tumble back down into Shrapnel Gully before they could start climbing Russell's Top. The units became mixed up. Some became lost. Some ended up on 400 Plateau, others at the head of Monash Valley. Less than one company reached the Nek before 1.30.

By 3 pm the Australians and New Zealanders around the Nek and Baby 700 came from seven battalions, all mixed up and worn out and with no-one in charge. They were being cut up by Turkish shrapnel and receiving no support from their own artillery or from the ships' guns. They didn't know what they were supposed to do or whether anyone cared about them.

When the New Zealanders started landing the 2nd Brigade had been out on 400 Plateau for hours. How it got there is another example of the confusion of the first day. When the 2nd started landing MacLagan, then the senior officer ashore, decided his biggest threat was on 400 Plateau. The Turks, he thought, would hit him hard there with men from the Gaba Tepe defences. He had given up on trying to take the third ridge there. There were too many gaps in his line. The main thing was to dig in and hold 400 Plateau. When Colonel James M'Cay, the commander of the 2nd, came ashore, MacLagan told him he had already diverted one battalion of the 2nd to the right. According to Bean, MacLagan said: 'I want you to take your whole brigade in on my right.'

M'Cay was not only senior to MacLagan; Irish-born and 50 years old, he was often cranky and sarcastic and a man of some standing. A teacher and a solicitor, he had also been Minister of Defence between 1904 and 1905. Now MacLagan was telling him that he should disobey his written orders, go right instead of left. Bridges, the divisional commander, wasn't ashore. M'Cay said he wanted to go forward and see things for himself.

Bean says MacLagan answered: 'There isn't time. I assure you my right will be turned if you do not do this.'

M'Cay then asked MacLagan to assure him that the left, where the 2nd should have been, was secure. MacLagan said it was. It wasn't: MacLagan merely thought it was at that moment. M'Cay then agreed to put his whole brigade on the right. What was unclear was whether the 2nd should try for the third ridge or simply dig in to hold the second.

We should mention one other example of the problem of command. Bridges came ashore at 7.20 under bursting shrapnel. There was no-one in authority on the beach to tell him what was happening. MacLagan and M'Cay were well forward. Bridges went forward himself. As he passed groups of troops he discovered that the plan had been changed and that the 2nd Brigade was out somewhere on the right. In Shrapnel Gully he came on men sheltering from fire behind a creek bank. He abused them and told them to remember they were Australians. He stood among the bullets lisping down from Baby 700 as though they were insects. Bridges found neither MacLagan nor M'Cay as he strode out to the right. He returned to the beach, set up headquarters, and eventually made telephone contact with his two brigade commanders.

* * *

In 1903 Walter McNicoll was a schoolteacher at Heathcote in central Victoria. Hildur Wedel, a Scandinavian beauty with golden hair and sea-blue eyes, taught at the nearby Kilmore school. Two years later they married. By 1914 Walter, now 37, was headmaster of Geelong High School, though more interested in soldiering than teaching. He also liked sailing and opera. McNicoll volunteered the day war was declared. After he sailed Hildur gave birth to a fifth son, David, who would in 1944 report the liberation of Paris as a war correspondent and later become a sparkling columnist for the *Bulletin*. Walter McNicoll left Australia as second-in-command of Harold 'Pompey' Elliott's 7th Battalion. McNicoll took over the 6th Battalion when its commander was declared medically unfit. This annoyed a prickly 27-year-old, Major Henry Gordon Bennett, who thought he should have got the job.

In the early morning of April 25 the men of the 6th and 7th were eating a hot meal on the transport Galeka. They could see the black mass of the peninsula beneath the stars. A year later McNicoll wrote:

Then began the strain of waiting. How would we face it? The question was never spoken aloud, but each man asked it of himself, and wondered if his neighbours were doing so too. They were trained to the minute – their bodies fit as a result of many weary days of tramping across the desert sand – their minds prepared to guide those bodies rightly to meet any and every emergency. But in all this training the big element of 'the man who hits back' had been absent. We had at last come to the end of those charges that stopped judiciously a hundred yards from a friendly opposing force. The bayonet would no longer be thrust viciously into an inoffensive and spineless sack. Our future targets would not wait patiently for the marker to flag the result. How would we face it?

After landing the 3rd Brigade the pinnaces and their tows were supposed to meet the *Galeka* and begin landing the 2nd. The tows didn't arrive on time. Shrapnel was bursting close to the ship. The captain decided to start landing the 7th Battalion from the *Galeka*'s boats. Four boatloads, some 140 men, were told to land about a mile north of the 3rd Brigade. They headed for the extreme left of the Australian position, straight for Fisherman's Hut and into a storm of rifle and machine-gun fire. When the boats grounded more than 100 men were dead, dying or badly wounded. So began the 7th Battalion's war.

McNicoll was luckier. The tows arrived in time to take the 6th ashore.

It was galling to be compelled to sit quietly in slow-moving boats and be fired at. Now we could do something, and as soon as the boat's keel touched the stony shore men jumped out up to their waist-belts in sea-water to the serious detriment of the rations of biscuit in their haversacks. So intent were our minds on the business ahead of us that no-one seemed to notice his wet condition for an instant nor can he remember when and how he dried.

Picks and shovels were thrown as far ashore as possible and recovered later. It did not take long for Australians to learn that in modern warfare the pick is almost as mighty as the rifle . . . Packs, containing the great coat, a few toilet necessaries, an emergency ration, etc., were taken off and stacked, and most of them were not again seen by their owners. It was two days before we could send for them, and the whole face of the country had changed in the meantime. There were many more packs than men by that time, and everyone was able to get a great coat at least. One noticed the novel shrubs growing thickly on the hillsides and smelt the fragrance of the flowers and grasses, still wet with morning dew, but no-one stayed to botanise this morning . . . The fragrant shrubs were hindrances in our paths, and were impatiently brushed aside, crashed through, or cut down later to be used in boiling the billy. As one crossed a ridge the 'Tzip Tzip' of Turkish bullets warned of the attention of some sniper who had the range to a yard . . .

McNicoll was sent out to the right. As with just about every commander, he was not told what he was to do. Like Elliott, who was sent out to the right before him, McNicoll was expected to plug a gap, create a presence – nothing more precise than that. He eventually set up his headquarters in the lee of Bolton's Ridge. He sent Bennett forward to control his forward companies, only to discover that his rear companies had been diverted on their way to Bolton's, swallowed up in some little emergency of the moment. Elliott had been wounded. McNicoll found himself commanding a line from the southern end of 400 Plateau to Bolton's. He found himself commanding men not just from the 6th and 7th but from a string of battalions. A disproportionate number of officers had been killed or wounded, partly because they kept standing up trying to see where their men were. McNicoll didn't know where his forward troops were or where his missing companies had gone. The Turkish artillerymen were bursting shrapnel all over 400 Plateau and a piece ripped into McNicoll's webbing. The Australian artillery was non-existent.

Bennett, meanwhile, advanced to Pine Ridge. Bennett couldn't be expected at this stage to understand a simple truth. If the Australians couldn't control 400 Plateau, there was no way Pine Ridge, which was much further forward, could be held. McNicoll sent whatever men he could to Bennett.

One met small parties composed of men of half a dozen units. 'Give us someone to lead us and tell us where to go.' The request was, in itself, an indication of the reliance placed upon leaders, and of the heavy losses of officers and NCOs. It was a case of a quick search for a man with 'that narsty fightin' face that all nice people 'ate.' A sharp order, 'You take charge!' and they were off to join Major Bennett . . .

Around 3.30 M'Cay told his battalion commanders to entrench on a line from Owen's Gully to Bolton's Ridge. In short, forget the third ridge, forget about attacking and think about defending. Half an hour later Bennett stood on Pine Ridge to direct fire and was shot in the wrist and shoulder, which probably saved his life. He was sent to a hospital ship and next day deserted and took himself back to the frontline. The men on Pine Ridge had been cut off and killed; the Turks took no prisoners. Among the dead was Bennett's brother, a 20-year-old sergeant. In 1919 Bean found skeletons in groups of three and four along Pine Ridge, the red and violet colours of the 6th Battalion still showing on the rags that lay around them. 'They needed no epitaph,' Bean wrote. 'It was enough that they lay on Pine Ridge.'

What happened to McNicoll's men told the story of the first day on 400 Plateau. Dozens of isolated struggles. Dozens of rash advances. Dozens of muddled retreats.

Groups of men rushed in to plug this or that gap. Parties cut off and not sure whether to advance or retreat. A frontline that did not connect up. A frontline that should have been a mile or two further inland. A failure of command with everyone from Bridges down giving orders but no-one in control. Clouds of dust on Scrubby Knoll as the Turks rushed up reinforcements. Scrub turned into chaff by machine-gun bullets. Nowhere to hide: the trenches weren't deep enough. Little hand-to-hand fighting. Because they were on the heights, because they had a better view, because they had artillery, the Turks could do most of their killing from the third ridge.

Colonel William Malone landed with the first of his Wellington Battalion around 4.30 pm. Malone was prickly and bossy and inclined to severe judgements that he often reversed a few days later. He read the mood of Anzac on the first day rather well.

> The beach was crowded with all sorts of beings, men, mules, donkeys, horses, ammunition supplies, naval beach parties ... There didn't seem much organisation on the shore, in fact it was disorganisation. We evidently haven't got a Kitchener about. On paper it was all right but in practice no good.

When you wander over 400 Plateau you have to keep reminding yourself it is a plateau: it dips and rises and is scored by shallow gullies. You do not sense how relatively flat it is, how big it is or that it is heart-shaped. From the heights, from Scrubby Knoll, Battleship Hill or Baby 700, it stands out, as Bean wrote, 'like the stage in a Greek amphitheatre'. Stand on Battleship Hill and the stage does look flat and heart-shaped, with Johnston's Jolly on its near lobe and Lone Pine (named for the Aleppo pine that stood there) on the far one and Owen's Gully where the two meet. The view is nearly as good from Scrubby Knoll. You try to imagine how this stage would have looked in 1915. Take out the bitumen road. Take out the pine trees that have been planted in recent years. Take out the great limestone memorial on Lone Pine. Now you are starting to see what the Turks saw. And what their artillery spotters saw was just about everything, every arrival, every advance and retreat, khaki figures digging in here, creeping forward there, the glint of bayonets, flying clods from a trench line. As Bean suggested, the Turkish artillerymen were like firemen playing with a hose.

Sometime after 11 am the mountain battery on Scrubby Knoll, less than a mile from the plateau, began bursting shrapnel over the Australians. Another battery on Anderson Knoll fired on the southern lobe and Bolton's Ridge. The plateau became a hailstorm of pellets and stayed that way all day, four or eight shells every minute. If men stood up to dig, or to look for a safer position, they were also exposed to machine-gun fire. The Turkish batteries near Chunuk Bair were meanwhile shelling the front on the left: Baby 700, the Nek and Monash Valley. And the Gaba Tepe guns, as they had been since first light, were peppering the beach.

Until noon there had been no reply from Allied guns. The Turks had been handed a psychological advantage that is hard to exaggerate. Where was the fabled British navy and its 12-inch guns? Well, the navy was there – it even had a balloon ship for spotting – but it couldn't fire for fear of hitting Australians. The navy didn't know where the frontline was, which was reasonable enough because most of the time the Australian commanders didn't know either. What messages the navy received came from hand signalling from the beach. The navy gunners knew the Turkish guns had to be on the third ridge. But where?

The first of the Indian mountain batteries landed about 10.30. The dismantled guns were packed on mules and taken to the head of White's Valley, on the edge of 400 Plateau. They opened up just before noon, the battery commander directing fire from the head of Owen's Valley. But the Turks above Battleship Hill could see exactly where the battery was. They rained shrapnel upon it from Chunuk Bair. Casualties were heavy. Around 2.25 the battery commander, bleeding copiously from a head wound, decided to withdraw his guns. Mules could not be brought up because of the hellish fire; many of them were already dead anyway. The little guns were manhandled away. The Australians had no support from their own field artillery. Only one 18-pounder had been landed by 6 pm. An officer on Pine Ridge had from about noon been trying to send back reports on the position of the Turkish guns on Anderson Knoll. All his messages 'miscarried' until 5 pm when a report finally reached the fleet. The navy opened up on Anderson Knoll and the Turkish guns there stopped firing for the first time in hours. Such was the way things happened on the first Anzac Day.

Things were going no better on the left front. Battleship Hill was lost when Tulloch withdrew. Baby 700 kept changing hands. Margetts was one of the few officers who survived. Early in the afternoon Margetts, though exhausted, ran to the crest of Baby 700 for the third time. He had gathered all the men he could find near him on Russell's Top – about ten. He found an officer from the 2nd Battalion in charge on Baby 700. The men were almost out of ammunition. Margetts went back to find some, then returned to Baby 700 for the fourth time, tripping over as he dodged shrapnel. The men he had taken up had left. Back down the hill again to find them. Apart from the shrapnel from Chunuk Bair, which was becoming worse, sometimes bursting only ten feet above the ground, Margetts noticed rifle fire coming from the left. The Turks were sneaking around the seaward side of Baby 700, near Malone's Gully. 'We could see people moving on our left flank,' Margetts wrote, 'but did not shoot at them as we were informed that the Indian troops were on our left. This we later found out must have been a ruse of the enemy.' The rumour was all over the lines that day and night – 'Indian troops'. There was no Indian infantry at Anzac this day.

Margetts reached the Nek and told Lieutenant P. J. Patterson of the 12th that he was just about 'done up'. Patterson said that he would take about 30 of his own men to reinforce the 2nd Battalion on Baby 700. No-one ever saw the 20-year-old Duntroon graduate again. Lalor came up and gave Margetts a drink from his whisky flask and told him to rest. Next to Margetts was an officer from Tulloch's party, asleep from exhaustion. Word now came that the 2nd Battalion on Baby 700 needed help. Lalor told Margetts to go up, then changed his mind. 'No, I'll go. You take your bugler and go down and see if you can bring up some support and stretcher-bearers.'

'I'll go forward, sir,' Margetts said.

'You'll do as you're told.'

It was about 3.15. Margetts never saw Lalor again. Lalor moved up the left-hand side of Baby 700 and met Morshead of the 2nd. Lalor had dropped his sword and, from the report of his conversation with Morshead, was becoming unstrung. He decided to charge and stood up.

'Now then, 12th Battalion . . . ' he shouted. And a Turkish bullet killed him. The '12th Battalion' he was summoning was just a handful of men. The left front was a shambles.

Captain Tulloch was wounded shortly afterwards. There were not many officers left and no-one was in charge of the front. The men remaining were a mixture of the 3rd and 1st brigades and New Zealanders. Corporal Laing was leading the remnants of the 12th Battalion. Then Laing, who had helped Colonel Clarke climb the cliff alongside the Sphinx, was shot in the thigh and crawled away. More New Zealanders arrived around 4 pm. The shrapnel fire increased. And now Kemal's troops were starting to roll down Baby 700.

To have a hope, the Australians and New Zealanders here needed strong reinforcements and artillery support. We know why there was no artillery. And there were no reinforcements. The only battalion Bridges had kept in reserve was the 4th. Bridges was agonising about what to do with it. Left or right? He was in trouble on both fronts. M'Cay was calling for reinforcements (throughout the day, the right appeared to have better communications with Bridges than the left) and at 5 pm Bridges gave him the 4th. There were no reserves. Most of Godley's division was still at sea.

Baby 700 was lost. Morshead and Shout, remnants from a string of Australian battalions, Aucklanders and Canterburys – all retreated to Russell's Top and the row of positions at the head of Monash Valley that would for eight months be the Anzac frontline. 'Snowy' Howe delayed leaving until Turks appeared on the skyline. A Turkish officer peered down through binoculars. Howe waited and shot him.

Lieutenant-Colonel G. F. Braund, the commander of the 2nd Battalion, had the remnants of two companies on the left of the Nek. A New Zealand sergeant now commanded the troops on his right. The carnage among New Zealand officers here had been fearful. Braund sent Shout to the beach with a message that ended: 'If reinforced can advance.' Braund didn't mean it to sound plaintive; it just sounds plaintive now.

At dusk Howe was with the New Zealand sergeant's party at the Nek. The sergeant was now wounded. The Turks shouted 'Allah' as they ran towards the Nek. All the Australians and New Zealanders signed a note asking for reinforcements and sent it back down the hill. Back came the message 'Reinforcements are on their way.' None came. There was no point staying on now. The Australians and New Zealanders fought a running battle back down Russell's Top.

Other Australians and New Zealanders around the head of Monash Valley fell back to the spots on the rim that would become famous as Pope's Hill and Quinn's Post. Dreams were as dead as the khaki bundles that would lie on Baby 700 for years. Conquest was no longer in the field of possibilities; the siege had started. In Australian memory this first day and the symbolism of the beach are just about everything. Some Australian visitors arrive at the peninsula, ask to see the beach, walk wistfully along the sand, pocketing the odd pebble, then announce that they have 'seen Gallipoli' and leave. It is probably folly to argue against the force of such a memory. Yet if there was an epic at Anzac, it was not on the beach or on the first day. An epic doesn't demand more heroics; it does demand rather less muddling. The epic at Anzac was up on the escarpment. The epic was in the hanging on.

Margetts left Lalor for the beach around 3.15 pm, looking for reinforcements and stretcher-bearers.

I rolled down into the gully, sniped at all the way, and made my way towards the beach. It was just as much as I could do to get back, as in places the mud was up to our knees, and I was thoroughly exhausted before I left the firing line. I met some stretcher-bearers and sent them up and reported to some Colonel that Captain Lalor wanted reinforcements and then went along to Div. Headquarters and reported myself. I then went back to the place where a few slightly wounded and exhausted men of the 12th had collected and here met Mr. Green who had received orders to collect stragglers. Here I lay down, utterly finished; for a while I was too stiff and sore to move. Later on the Provost Marshall told me to form my men up and report to Major Glasford, he ordered me to get ready to move out to the right . . . We were afterwards sent off to the right but met Captain Ross who ordered us back for the night.

Was Margetts a straggler because he went to the beach and lay down? The thought is offensive. Margetts had raced forward on landing, as he had been told to. He had been shot at for ten hours. Most of his fellow-officers had been killed or wounded or had disappeared never to be seen again. He had been to Baby 700 four times. He had been landed on the wrong beach. He had been let down by his superiors, although there is no evidence that he felt this. And now, after his first day in a real war, he was worn out and wanted to sleep.

Others, however, were straggling. Bean wrote in his diary that there might have been 600 to 1000 around the beach by nightfall. There had to be: confusion breeds stragglers, as does poor leadership. The beach was the logical destination for any soldier trying to find out what was going on or where his mates were.

This straggling takes on an importance. It affected a judgement Birdwood was about to make about the Anzac beachhead. And for 85 years it has influenced judgements about how the Anzacs performed on the first day. The mythology had taken on such rigid form by the nineteen-twenties that any mention of straggling offended Australian sensibilities. The centrepiece of the mythology was, as it perhaps still is, the glory of the first day, as reported by Ashmead-Bartlett of the London *Daily Telegraph*.

In 1926 the draft of Aspinall's early chapters of the British official history arrived in Australia. Aspinall had written that the landing was relatively easy. No argument here. In the afternoon, Aspinall wrote, a well co-ordinated attack could have carried the line to its objectives up the range. The afternoon? The only opportunity for a co-ordinated attack was in the early morning, before Kemal and Sami Bey threw in their troops. There was confusion among the Australians, Aspinall said. True. No one was in proper command at the front. True again. In the late afternoon the strain on untried troops was starting to tell. The gullies behind the beach were 'choked' with stragglers and lost soldiers. Probably true, although 'choked' may be an exaggeration. Aspinall then said the extent of the straggling caused Birdwood and others to wonder whether the beachhead could be held.

The historian Alistair Thomson is the authority on the strange interlude that began with the arrival of Aspinall's draft. Thomson wrote in *Australian Historical Studies* in 1993 that Aspinall's words were seen as heresy. Bean told the Australian Department of Defence that they would 'cause an outcry in Australia'. Here we run into another problem. Bean was a 35-year-old journalist from the *Sydney Morning Herald* when he landed at Gallipoli as a war correspondent; now, in the nineteen-twenties, he had become the keeper of the flame. He was Australia's official war historian, hard-working, meticulous, incorruptible, a kindly and modest man – and also obsessed with a vision of 'Australian manhood' that was built around the Anzac story and his idea of the rustic virtues.

The Defence Department agreed that Aspinall's chapter eight was unfair. Bean wrote to Aspinall and made the obvious point that being landed on the wrong beach and in broken country didn't help the Anzacs. He also told Aspinall that he had made too much of the straggling. Aspinall replied that his evidence of straggling had mostly come from Bean's history (published in 1921) and Australian unit diaries.

Then the newspapers discovered the story. The Sydney *Daily Guardian* spoke of the 'Vilest libel of the war' and of Australians being portrayed as a rabble. Honour was now the issue; heretics were trying to tear down the Anzac church. Billy Hughes, the Australian Prime Minister, talked of 'slander'. A genteel spat between two historians had become a storm that loured over Anglo-Australian relations. The easy way to make it go away was to censor Aspinall. Isolated and hurt, Aspinall toned down his manuscript.

The losers from this – apart from Aspinall, who was sacked in 1932 – were future generations. The truth about April 25 is still blurry, except for a few obvious things. The Anzacs might have been raw on their first day at war; many assumed, for instance, that if a mate was wounded it was all right to leave the frontline and take him to the field ambulance. Their mettle, however, should not have been in question. Think only of the spirit of Margetts, Tulloch, Shout, Morshead, Loutit, Blackburn, Howe, Baird and Lalor. In his efforts to explain the failures of the first day, Aspinall probably bothered too much with befuddled privates and too little with the failings of brigadiers and generals who were not new to war and who helped create the conditions that made straggling inevitable.

There *was* confusion on April 25 – everywhere and all day – and Bean probably should have written more of it. As much as the examples of 'Australian manhood' he offered in such plenitude, this confusion explained why the first day went the way it did. The forays of Tulloch and others who got 'farthest in' were important; but so was Bridges' muddling, the failure to get the field artillery ashore and firing, and the fact that no-one in authority seemed to understand the battle on the left.

How bad was the confusion? As night came and light rain fell on the wounded lying in their own blood on the beach, there came a flight of despair. Between 10 and 11 pm, by the light of two candles and a torch in a dugout behind the beach, Birdwood dictated a note to Hamilton suggesting that maybe the beachhead should be abandoned. Hamilton eventually received the note, even though Birdwood and his generals had forgotten to address it to anyone. It was that sort of day.

10

The legend begins

Bean went ashore around 9.30 am on April 25. He had not yet received his accreditation as a correspondent, so he couldn't send copy, although one suspects he had already decided he was writing for the ages rather than newspaper deadlines in Sydney or Perth. Ellis Ashmead-Bartlett of the London *Daily Telegraph* was covering the Anzac landing for all the Fleet Street papers. He had his accreditation; even if he hadn't, he would have found a way to get copy out. Ashmead-Bartlett was a journalist–adventurer, the sort of man who once made Fleet Street interesting, and he knew about war. He had served in the Boer War as a lieutenant and reported at least seven others, several of them involving Turkey. He was the sort of man who could write 'Hire of yak – £500' on an expense claim and not blush. He always needed money, mostly because he lived like the last surviving member of a class to which he had never belonged. He was on the edge of bankruptcy now, but he had been there so many times he could live with it, and his creditors, petty little shopkeepers all, would have trouble drawing out any of his blood while he was at the Dardanelles.

What he lacked in money, Ashmead-Bartlett made up

for in political connections and self-belief. If Cabinet ministers back home didn't know him personally, and most did, they knew him by reputation. He could say a lot with one sharp sentence and had a good eye. He described a destroyer dodging Turkish shells in the Dardanelles as writhing about as if she had a pain inside her. Of the light-heartedness of soldiers before a battle, he wrote: 'Wars are only carried on, and desperate enterprises carried out, owing to the lack of imagination amongst the rank and file.' Ashmead-Bartlett had already decided that jumped-up staff officers with smaller minds than his were bungling the Dardanelles campaign. He made himself unpopular by saying the landings should have been at Bulair and walked about with a sullen look that said the rest of the world had failed to live up to his expectations.

Commander Dix, who was in charge of the tows for the Anzac covering force, wrote in 1932 that everyone on the *London* was in high spirits before the landing – except Ashmead-Bartlett.

In conversation with me that evening [the 24th] he fore-told the run of events with almost uncanny exactitude. He insisted that only in the event of having another division both at Anzac and Helles could speedy success be obtained, and that long-delayed success might, and probably would, mean eventual failure.

Ashmead-Bartlett put his forebodings aside next day to report the Anzac landing. Tradesman that he was, he planned things carefully. He decided to watch from the battleship *London* so as to take in the whole panorama and stay close to the people orchestrating it. Later he would go ashore to pick up first-hand stuff and colour. So here he was on the *London*'s bridge, a slim man in his mid-thirties, wearing a khaki uniform and a soft green hat, a camera slung over his shoulder, listening to the rifle fire ashore, staring into the sun rising behind the Anzac hills, thinking of what he might write for Fleet Street and not knowing that his words would become the wellspring of the Anzac mythology on the other side of the world. At 9.30 pm he landed from a pinnace.

> I climbed ashore over some barges and found myself in the semi-darkness amidst a scene of indescribable confusion. The beach was piled with ammunition and stores, hastily dumped from the lighters, among which lay the dead and wounded, and men so absolutely exhausted that they had fallen asleep in spite of the deafening noise of the battle. In fact, it was impossible to distinguish between the living and the dead in the darkness. Through the gloom I saw the ghost-like silhouettes of groups of men wandering around in a continuous stream apparently going to, or returning from, the firing-line. On the hills above there raged an unceasing struggle lit up by the bursting shells, and the night air was humming with bullets like the droning of countless bees on a hot summer's day.

Ashmead-Bartlett didn't know where to go to find out things. Then he saw a small group of officers. He saw a short man at the centre and, though he had never met him, recognised Birdwood. Ashmead-Bartlett was still wearing his green hat. An Australian colonel shouted: 'Who are you and what are you doing here?'

The colonel didn't give Ashmead-Bartlett time to answer. 'Seize that man,' he shouted, 'he is a spy.' Ashmead-Bartlett thought it rather droll that a spy would draw attention to himself by wearing a green hat. Soldiers rushed up and the journalist, for the third time in the

Great War, was arrested as a spy. The colonel shouted: 'Does anyone here know this man?'

Out of the darkness, a gruff voice replied: 'Yes, I do.' It was a boatswain from a pinnace. He was worried, he explained later, that Ashmead-Bartlett would be 'hexecuted'.

Ashmead-Bartlett met Birdwood, who seemed calm and asked him how he had come ashore.

In a pinnace, Ashmead-Bartlett told him.

Could he keep the vessel here? There was an important message to be sent off.

The naval beach officer excitedly told Ashmead-Bartlett: 'We have to go round all the transports and get them to send in their boats. It is impossible for the Australians to hold out during the night . . . '

Ashmead-Bartlett headed off in the pinnace carrying the message.

The message, dictated by Birdwood to Godley and intended for Hamilton, was undated and said:

> Both my divisional generals and brigadiers have repre-sented to me that they fear their men are thoroughly demoralised by shrapnel fire to which they have been subjected all day after exhaustion and gallant work in morning. Numbers have dribbled back from firing line and cannot be collected in this difficult country. Even New Zealand Brigade which has been only recently engaged lost heavily and is to some extent demoralised. If troops are subjected to shell fire again tomorrow morning there is likely to be a fiasco as I have no fresh troops with which to replace those in firing line. I know my representation is most serious but if we are to re-embark it must be done at once.
>
> Birdwood

The wording is curious. *My divisional generals and brigadiers have represented to me* . . . Birdwood isn't saying it; his underlings are; he is merely passing it on. *Their men are thoroughly demoralised by shrapnel* . . . Of course they were. Is there a record somewhere of men being uplifted by shrapnel? And might not the men have felt less demoralised if some general had managed to get the Australian field artillery ashore to send a little shrapnel the other way? *If we are to re-embark* . . . Birdwood isn't saying he recommends such a course; he is inviting Hamilton to order him to re-embark.

The note suggests unanimity. Harold Walker, good general that he was, had argued against evacuation. We don't know what he said, but he is supposed to have spoken to Bridges 'in terms which could have jeopardised his career'. Birdwood didn't really want to evacuate either. There was something unsoldierly about it, and after just 17 hours on the beach.

Bridges and Godley had asked Birdwood to come ashore around 9.15 pm. They suggested evacuation and the thought appalled him. But they knew what was going on and he couldn't ignore them. His compromise was to dictate the note to Hamilton.

The note went off addressed to no-one. The pinnace went to Admiral Thursby's flagship, the *Queen*. Hamilton was on the *Queen Elizabeth*. Thursby opened the message thinking it was for him. He was about to have it signalled to the *Queen Elizabeth* when she suddenly turned up at Anzac. Thursby headed straight to her.

Hamilton had gone to sleep more worried, as he was entitled to be, about Helles than Anzac. At midnight Braithwaite was shaking his shoulder, saying, 'Sir Ian, Sir Ian', which is an unusual way to speak when you are waking someone to tell them the house is on fire, but these were gentlemen and this was 1915. 'Sir Ian, you've got to come right along. A question of life and death. You must settle it!'

Hamilton found de Robeck, Thursby, Keyes, Braithwaite and others in the dining saloon. Braithwaite was chewing his moustache. 'A cold hand clutched at my heart as I scanned their faces,' Hamilton wrote.

Hamilton read the curious note, then began behaving curiously himself.

'Admiral, what do you think?' he asked Thursby.

'It will take the best part of three days to get that crowd off the beaches.'

'And where are the Turks?'

'On top of 'em!'

'Well, then, tell me, Admiral, what do *you* think?'

'What do I think? Well, I think myself they will stick it out if only it is put to them that they must.'

Keyes supported Thursby. Then Keyes was called outside to be told that the Australian submarine *AE2* had passed through the Narrows and sunk a Turkish ship.

Hamilton had not discovered what was happening ashore. He had not offered his view of what should happen. He had merely asked Thursby if an evacuation was possible and Thursby had said no. Hamilton now dictated a note.

Your news is indeed serious. But there is nothing for it but to dig yourselves right in and stick it out. It would take at least two days to re-embark you as Admiral Thursby will explain to you. Meanwhile, the Australian submarine has got through the Narrows and has torpedoed a gunboat at Chunuk [Çanakkale]. Hunter-Weston despite his heavy losses will be advancing tomorrow which should divert pressure from you. Make a personal appeal to your men and Godley's to make a supreme effort to hold their ground.

Ian Hamilton

P.S. You have got through the difficult business, now you only have to dig, dig, dig, until you are safe. Ian H.

Rain was falling and white breakers were slapping the shore when Thursby took the note to Birdwood around 2 am.

In his memoir *Life of an Irish Soldier* – essential reading for anyone interested in pig sticking and grouse shooting – Godley writes the final act to this comic opera. He says Hamilton sent back a 'gallant reply'. And then: 'We were, of course, delighted to get it . . . ' Why would they be delighted when, a few hours earlier, they had predicted a fiasco if they stayed? Godley ends his book by saying he has had a 'wonderfully good innings'. Indeed. His performance at Gallipoli, however, often leaves the impression that he never understood why he had been sent in to bat.

Fifteen thousand men and 42 mules were ashore by 6 pm on the 25th. The Anzacs' casualties – dead, wounded and missing – on the first day are usually put at 2000. This is probably too low. Records show that by 3 am on April 26 more than 1700 wounded had been taken off. At one stage hundreds of wounded lay on the beach. The beach-master ignored Hamilton's order and sent the wounded off on tows, pinnaces, lighters – whatever was empty.

The Turkish casualties are also put at 2000. This is probably more of a guess than the Anzac figure. Let's assume, for a moment, that it is accurate. If so, the Turks suffered worse than the Anzacs, because until dusk no more than six Turkish battalions (about 6000 men) were in the fight. Kemal told the truth when he said the 57th Regiment had been wiped out. The commander of the regiment's 3rd Battalion could only find 90 of his men; the 2nd Battalion had disappeared. The 27th Regiment had also taken big losses, but they were probably lower than in Kemal's regiment because more of the fighting on 400 Plateau had been at long range.

Tulloch survived the first day and recovered from his wound. He later received the Military Cross and briefly commanded a battalion on the western front in 1918. He had flirted so well with death for four years and got away with it. He returned to the peace of his St Kilda home where he was shot dead by a burglar in 1926.

Lalor's body was not found. His widow was in England with their two-year-old son at the time of his death. She had followed the troops to Egypt, then left for London when the Australians were diverted to the Dardanelles. Shout lived to find death and glory at Lone Pine in August. Morshead found fame in North Africa 26 years later. Private John Simpson of the 3rd Field Ambulance was on his way to eternal fame but didn't know it. He had 'annexed' a donkey and was using it to carry men with leg wounds down Shrapnel Gully. He would become Australia's folk-hero from Anzac, even though he was as Australian as North Sea cod and peas. 'Snowy' Howe returned to Gallipoli in 1919 as a lieutenant with Bean's historical mission, climbed to the Nek, stared at a few pits shaped like graves, said, yes, that was Lalor's trench.

For Blackburn, the private who had gone past the crest of Scrubby Knoll, Gallipoli was the start of an extraordinary life. Next year at Pozières he won the Victoria Cross. He returned to Australia in 1917 as an invalid and spent three years as a member of the South Australian Parliament. During World War II he commanded a battalion in Syria. He wore black-rimmed glasses, a small moustache and the air of a coroner and believed in discipline and good order. In Java the following year he and his men were taken prisoner by the Japanese. Blackburn was freed in Manchuria in 1945. An Australian who served with him in Syria and Java said it was no wonder Blackburn got so far in at Gallipoli. 'When he was nearly 50 he took us on a 23-mile march through the Mount Lofty Ranges [in South Australia]. He marched in front the whole way.' Blackburn died in 1960, aged 67.

In 1916 Bennett, McNicoll's second-in-command, became one of the youngest brigadier-generals in the British armies and was eight times mentioned in despatches. But he couldn't get on with people; his divisional commander called him a 'pest'. He commanded Australia's 8th Division at Singapore in World War II. His men were taken prisoner; Bennett, so brave and rash at Pine Ridge, slipped out of Singapore in a sampan and into ignominy. Should he have stayed with his men? The argument still goes on. Bennett didn't help himself by always managing to say something that offended someone. He died in 1962.

In Melbourne, seat of the national government until Canberra was built, Sunday, April 25, was cool and cloudy. Families sat down to roasts, went to church and read Saturday night's *Herald*. The Australian rules football season had opened the day before and the inner-suburban families, as they usually did, had walked to the grounds. Others had gone to Caulfield racecourse where the mythology of Gordon Pasha was still playing: they ran the Khartoum Hurdle, worth 200 sovereigns.

Down the road at North Brighton there was a 15-event programme of starling shooting; the starlings lost.

Monday's *Argus* carried a report from Athens that troops had been landed at three points in the Dardanelles: Suvla, Bulair and Enos, near the Bulgarian border. There was no suggestion these troops were Australians. The big story was from the western front; the Germans were using poison gas. On Tuesday the main war story was from the famous journalist Philip Gibbs, who had been touring Belgium and France. The heroism of 'the race', he reported, was towering again above slime and slush. The Lord Mayor's relief fund for Serbia had reached £113.

On Friday, five days after the landing, the press for the first time linked Australian troops to the Dardanelles. The *Argus* didn't know what to do with the story. The war was supposed to be in France and Belgium, so the main story was about the fighting at Neuve Chapelle. A double-column story quoted the British War Office as saying the Allies were advancing steadily up the Gallipoli Peninsula. The Turks had prepared deep pits with spiked bottoms. The Allies had landed at Suvla, Helles, Kum Kale and Bulair. There was no mention of Gaba Tepe or the cove to the north of it. Temperance groups in England were objecting to British troops in France being given a rum ration.

On Saturday, May 1, the *Argus* ran the first casualty list from Gallipoli: 22 wounded officers. 'No information is available as to whether any Australians have been killed.' New Zealand declared a public holiday to celebrate the landing. Reports from Athens said 8000 Turks had been captured at Kum Kale. (For months the Australian papers would run 'reports from Athens', even though these invariably turned out to be wrong, mainly because they amounted to nothing more than journalists swapping rumours in bars, then leaving to write them as fact.)

On Sunday the *Argus* produced a 'special war edition'. The headlines were becoming larger. A four-column story said 18 Australians were dead and 15 wounded. Captain Tulloch was severely wounded in the thigh.

On Monday came the first mention of the Australians and New Zealanders landing near Gaba Tepe. And the first New Zealand casualties: four dead. Pen portraits of the Australian dead – the figure was now 41 – began to appear. 'He will also be sadly missed in lacrosse circles . . . His mother was writing a letter to him when the telegram arrived informing her of her son's death.'

The *Age* on May 5 said the Allies had occupied Maidos. Yes, the report was from Athens. Next day, from Athens again, the paper had the Allies 'steadily advancing' while their battleships bombarded the Dardanelles forts. The *Argus* said the Turks were burning every village from which they were driven.

The next day both papers carried reports from the Reuters correspondent in Cairo, who had interviewed returning wounded. 'Our big lads lifted some of the Turks on the end of their bayonets, and other Turks ran scream-ing and howling in fear . . . our casualties were heavy, but very many of the wounds are slight . . . ' The Reuters man reported that the Turks were using dum-dum bullets.

Then, on May 8, the Australian dailies carried Ashmead-Bartlett's story and everything changed.

The papers loved it, as did their readers, because it was the first on-the-ground account, well written – Ashmead-Bartlett had a sense of occasion Bean could never manage – and warm with praise for the Australians. It was also shot through with small inaccuracies and exaggerations that Bean would never have allowed into his copy. The papers and their readers liked the story best of all because it was written by an Englishman. England was the mother country and Australia, like all children, craved approval. The *Sydney Morning Herald* introduced his piece with what amounted to an editorial.

> Mr Ashmead-Bartlett has been through many campaigns; he has seen men of many nations win glory on the battlefield. Thus he has been able to watch the behaviour of our soldiers with a steady eye and to weigh it against the behaviour of some of the finest troops in the world. And he has not written this despatch for the special edification of Australians – he has written it solely for the London papers which he represents. So when he says that the Australasian troops . . . have proved their right to stand beside the heroes of Mons, the Aisne, Ypres, and Neuve Chapelle, we can read into that declaration a glorious meaning indeed.

In the *Age* Ashmead-Bartlett's story carried eight decks of heading:

GALLANT AUSTRALIANS
FULL STORY OF THEIR FIGHT
A Thrilling Narrative.
TROOPS LANDED IN DARKNESS
ATTACKED ON SEASHORE
British Correspondent's Tribute
'NO FINER FEAT IN THIS WAR.'
Heroes of Mons Equalled.

The report, some 2000 words, was generally cool and sensible. Several lines, however, exploded in people's minds.

The Australians who were about to go into action for the first time in trying circumstances were cheerful, quiet, and confident. There was no sign of 'nerves', nor of excitement . . . They did not wait for orders, or for the boats to reach the beach, but sprung into the sea and, forming a sort of rough line, rushed the enemy's trenches. Their magazines were not charged, so they just went in with cold steel . . . I have never seen anything like these wounded Australians in war before. Though many were shot to bits, without hope of recovery, their cheers resounded throughout the night . . . They were happy because they knew they had been tried for the first time and not found wanting . . . There has been no finer feat in this war than this sudden landing in the dark and storming the heights, and, above all, holding on while the reinforcements were landing. These raw colonial troops, in these desperate hours, proved worthy to fight side by side with the heroes of Mons, the Aisne, Ypres and Neuve Chapelle. Early on the morning of 26 April the Turks repeatedly tried to drive the colonials from their position. The latter made local counter attacks, and drove off the enemy with the bayonet, which the enemy would never face . . . The scene at the height of the engagement was sombre, magnificent and unique.

The dying Australians had not cheered too much; it is very hard to do so when half your face has been shot away or your stomach torn open by shrapnel. Nevertheless, without meaning to, Ashmead-Bartlett had produced an image that made Australians feel good about themselves. The nation was only 14 years old; it had never done anything much in the wider world before. Ashmead-Bartlett had started the Anzac legend and would now move on; Bean, whose first report ran seven days after

Ashmead-Bartlett's, would become the custodian of the legend. Bean would never move on. The yellow track up Shrapnel Gully was his Damascus road.

Bean's first piece was modestly displayed. His copy was flat, but left one with the impression that he had actually seen all he had written about. Ashmead-Bartlett's piece was cut out and pasted in scrapbooks; clergymen quoted from it in Sunday sermons; volunteers queued up at recruiting centres with the crumpled words in their pockets. Recruiting picked up again. Enlistments had fallen from 10,225 in January to 6250 in April; in May they rose to 10,526 and in June to 12,505.

On the day of Ashmead-Bartlett's story the Argus ran its first map of where the Anzacs had landed. An arrow pointed into Maidos. 'Taken by Allies' said the caption.

This was the trouble: Australians had become captivated by a story that, while mostly true in itself, left out larger truths that Ashmead-Bartlett, had he so wanted, would not have been allowed to write. Gallipoli sounded romantic and it wasn't. The casualties ran to thousands, not the hundreds the papers were reporting. Rather than running away, the Turks were fighting well. In military terms the landing had been nearer to a failure than a success. The Anzacs were not going forward; they were clinging to 400 acres of useless beachfront, as though staying there was a point of honour, which it was. This was not an advance but the start of a siege. Not in Australia, though. In Australia this was an adventure written by Kipling. There was still time to be part of it.

The papers were full of half-truths and propaganda. The day before Bean's first story ran, the Argus carried a report from London of Lord Bryce's findings on German atrocities in Belgium. 'Murder, lust, and pillage,' Bryce said, 'prevailed over many parts of Belgium on a scale unparalleled in any war between civilised nations during the last three centuries.' The report spoke of a 'holocaust'.

The Germans *had* committed atrocities in Belgium and around 5000 civilians were dead because of them. But, seven years later, a Belgian inquiry failed to substantiate most of Bryce's allegations. There was a holocaust going on in 1915. It wasn't in Belgium and it was perhaps as cruel and terrible as anything that had happened in the previous three centuries. The Turks had begun to massacre their Armenian minority. This was not yet being reported.

Nor was the fate of the Gallipoli wounded, especially those who had to endure days at sea before even a dressing was changed. The same day as Ashmead-Bartlett's report appeared, the Australian Defence Minister, Senator George Pearce, said that several 'lady doctors' had offered to serve at hospitals at the front. The War Office in London had told him it could not use female doctors.

Baby 700. Strange name. Mesmerising place. The name is easy to explain. British naval gunners could see two hills about the same height. They reckoned them both about 700 feet high. They named the larger one Big 700 – changed later to Battleship Hill – and the lesser one Baby 700. Baby 700 is in fact 590 feet and Battleship 100 feet higher. It is harder to explain why Baby 700 gets inside your head. Maybe because the wind is always in your ear, strumming at the brain, telling it to wake up. This is perhaps the loneliest cemetery at Anzac, squatting on the swell of the hill and marked by two pine trees so tortured by the wind that they are bent like bananas.

The first time you came here, in 1998, your hands ached with cold. It was snowing and the Aegean was blacky-blue and flecked with whitecaps. You walked among headstones on which are chiselled the Anglo-Saxon names of men from Anglo-Australian towns. And the place teased you to remember something. What?

Three days later it came. It was the bit in italics at the start of Ernest Hemingway's *The Snows of Kilimanjaro*, the bit about the body of a leopard being found high above the snowline and no-one knowing what the leopard was doing at that altitude. These Australians and New Zealanders under the snow here? What were they doing here? If they were in German New Guinea or on the outskirts of Paris, it would make better sense. But here? What was the prize? This erosion project, these yellow hills bleeding gravel and quartz into the Aegean? Where was the cause to die for?

It made sense in books. You could follow the political trails of Churchill and Kitchener, Tsar Nicholas and Kaiser Wilhelm, Enver and Talat. They all intersected here. But when you were on the ground it was different. What were these men from Sydney and the Waikato doing in a place considered so remote that their wives and children never thought to visit their graves? Their great-grandchildren came near the turn of the new century. They wandered among the graves until one of them stopped, rubbed dirt on the headstone to bring up the letters, and said: 'Here he is.' Then they squatted around the grave and wondered what he looked like and why he had died here, above the snowline.

Baby 700 cemetery is up a walking track off the bitumen road that leads to Chunuk Bair. From the cemetery you can see a glint from the water near the Narrows, nothing more. The Turks here, on the other hand, could see clearly into Monash Valley and across to Lone Pine. Lalor fought on the seaward side of this cemetery and below it. He may not have seen the water he died for. His memorial headstone carries the inscription 'Lord thou knowest best'.

When Bean came here in 1919, he found some 30 graves of Anzacs buried by the Turks. Bits of clothing lay about, including arm patches of the 1st and 2nd battalions. Bean found badges of the Waikato company and the insignia of a New Zealand major. Beyond the crest of Baby 700 he found the remains of another 20 or 30 men in precisely the position that Margetts told Bean he had reached. One of the farthest inland was a New Zealander.

As we walk around the cemetery again on a spring day in 2000, a Turk who has accompanied us is prospecting nearby, eyes down, right foot gently kicking at the dirt. He spots a flash of colour, a .303 shell case, slightly squashed, the brass tarnished, the imprint of the firing pin showing dead centre. Someone could have brought it here from down the range; if not, it is a relic from the first day.

You walk up Battleship Hill, where green lizards scurry in caved-in trenches. An erosion patch on the inland side marks the spot where Tulloch's advance ended. No plaques, no limestone columns, just a yellow scar. From here you can see a great triangle of the Dardanelles shining to the right. Tulloch probably gave it no more than a glance. The bullets were coming from the front and the left.

The bumpy track to the hill of Kakma Daği is the same road that was built in 1915. Kakma Daği is now Eceabat's rubbish tip. Plastic bags and cartons, sheep bones and old socks, straw and bottles are scattered willy-nilly, unburnt and putrid. Two pups with the poddy bellies of orphans slink from one pile to another. From here you look out over the neat fields of the Maidos plain, bordered by poplars coming into leaf and dotted with white farmhouses. The Turkish observation post here looked straight at Lone Pine. The Turks directing the 27th Regiment into battle from here would have seen the Australians swarming on to the plateau and down Pine Ridge.

Mal Tepe, the conical hill that was the first-day objective, should have something to mark its place in history. Xerxes reputedly watched his army cross the Dardanelles from here. Where he is thought to have stood a concrete water tower squats among pine trees that rustle in the spring wind. You can see the white apartments of Çanakkale and the grey castle at Kilitbahir. Artillery brought to this hill could fire on Çanakkale but not on Eceabat (unless the Anzacs had observers well forward) or the forts south of Kilitbahir. Gypsies have today conquered the base of the hill; headquarters is a plastic igloo.

From Scrubby Knoll you can see most of the Anzac perimeter, just about everything that matters except the beach. There's the yellow scar where Tulloch stopped. It is so silent here, like watching a film with the sound turned off. You see the tourist bus from Istanbul going to Chunuk Bair, but it makes no sound. Every so often the wind brings the scent of thyme and lavender. The Turks had the kinder country. You can work things out from here. The Anzac country baffles you day after day. You think you are coming to understand it, then find you have blundered the wrong way. The prickly oak stings your face and you know the terrain has won again.

The Sphinx is crumbling away. It was bigger when the Anzacs came. Everything probably seemed bigger then.

Down in Shrapnel Gully stands a headstone that sets the imagination racing. 'I've no darling now. I'm weeping. Baby & I you left alone.'

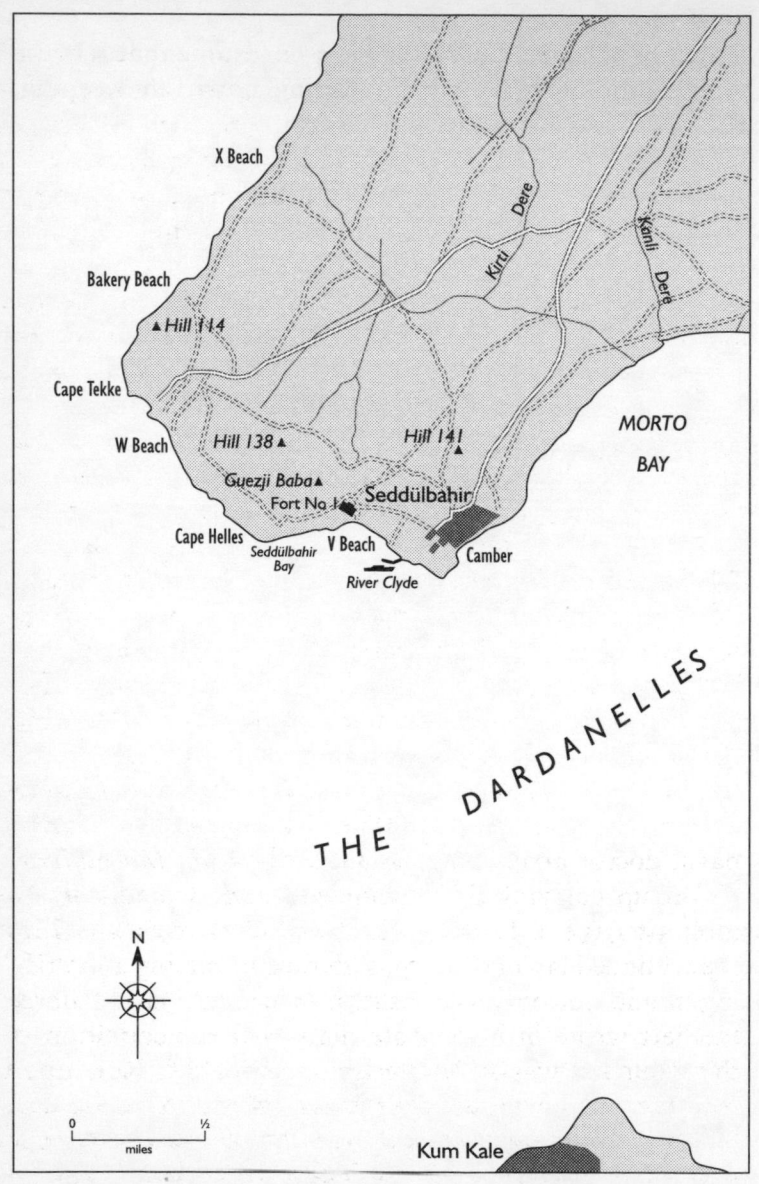

The Helles beaches

11

And the sea ran red

I never knew blood smelt so strong before.
Midshipman George Drewry

The Australians and New Zealanders had been mauled. Those who survived knew that war was not like the Reverend Fitchett's books or stuff in newspapers. Barges taking off wounded became slippery with blood as they hawked their cargoes around the transports. Meanwhile the wounded became seasick. The transport *Lutzow* still had horses on board, which is how a veterinary surgeon became the sole medical officer for 300 patients until a naval doctor arrived on the 26th. The *Clan Macgillivray* ended up carrying 850 wounded – and two doctors to look after them. In the dark at Anzac Cove on the 25th the wounded lay in the rain, sighing and cursing and drifting in and out of consciousness. A fortnight later Aubrey Herbert wrote in his private diary that the condition of the wounded was still 'utterly indescribable'. Row upon row lay on the sand, 'their faces caked with sand and blood'. Yet, compared with the British who had gone ashore at V and W beaches at Helles, the Anzacs had been relatively fortunate on their first day.

Hamilton slept for about three hours after saying no to the Anzac evacuation. About nine o'clock the next morning the *Queen Elizabeth* picked up a message from the commanding officer at Y Beach, the northernmost of the Helles landing spots, a cliff top almost on a line with Krithia and behind the Turkish troops defending the Helles beaches.

'We are holding the ridge till the wounded are embarked,' the message said. Why 'till'? Hamilton wondered. Were they thinking of leaving? He decided to look at Y Beach on his way south from Anzac. He saw wounded coming off and loose groups 'hanging about' the beach. 'I disliked and mistrusted the looks of these aimless dawdlers by the sea,' he wrote. The force was obviously coming off or, as Hamilton put it, 'making off'. Why? Had Hunter-Weston ordered this? If so, why hadn't he consulted his commander-in-chief? The landing at Y had been Hamilton's idea. It was a flanking manoeuvre, and a canny one. Hamilton had pressed it on Hunter-Weston, who mostly thought in straight lines. Hamilton was angry. He wanted to intervene. He said his staff talked him out of it. He probably meant Braithwaite talked him out of it. Braithwaite fussed over etiquette like a viceroy's butler. From the *Queen Elizabeth*, Hamilton thought Y Beach a fiasco. It was, and bigger than he realised.

He had caught the final act. By observing this and failing to intervene, by behaving like a gentleman rather than a general, Hamilton became an accessory to the fiasco. The main offender was Hunter-Weston. For ten hours, Lieutenant-Colonel Godfrey Matthews, the commander at Y Beach, had been sending frantic messages. The situation was 'serious', then 'critical'. He needed reinforcements and ammunition 'urgently'. Hunter-Weston ignored these messages. Matthews received no word from divisional headquarters for the 29 hours he was ashore at Y. Nothing to tell him what was happening at Helles, or what he should do. Not even a message to say that Hunter-Weston didn't have time to worry about Y Beach because massacres were going on at V and W. Matthews had not even ordered the 'evacuation'; it had just happened, born of panic and failures of command.

There are no signposts to Y Beach. You get there by walking south along the cliffs above the Aegean, past a ploughed field of rich brown earth where lumps of shrapnel and shards of bones lie among the clods. Whose bones are these? Maybe the company of Turks, about 100 of them, who were seen here by the *Queen Elizabeth* on April 28? At what amounted to rifle range, the *Queen Elizabeth* fired one of its 15-inch shells loaded with 24,000 pellets of shrapnel. Hamilton watched the shell burst right over the Turks. When the smoke cleared all the Turks were dead. 'We looked for a long time,' Hamilton wrote. 'Nothing stirred.'

The beach where the British landed on April 25 is narrow and rocky, so lonely that you think of smugglers. The cliffs to the left and right of the cove are too steep to climb. The slope in front of the beach, rent by a gully and about 200 feet high, can be climbed if you stick to the gully and grab an arbutus bush in your right hand while lunging for a pine trunk with your left.

This scrub wasn't here in 1915: goats had grazed the place close to bare. Ten men with a machine gun on the cliff top could have wiped out the British force. But there were no Turks here. The English made the cliff top without a shot being fired, brewed tea and lugged water up from the beach in kerosene tins. From the cliff top you can see the hump of Achi Baba. Gully Ravine, the gorge that runs down the west coast, is about 300 yards inland. Beyond this, a short walk across the wheat fields, you see the mosque of Krithia. The town was deserted on April 25: no Turkish soldiers, no Greek farmers.

Matthews and his adjutant crossed Gully Ravine and strolled to within 500 yards of Krithia. Matthews was way behind the Turkish lines; he had landed without a casualty and no-one was shooting at him. He had 2000 men: his own Plymouth Battalion of the RND, Scottish Borderers under Lieutenant-Colonel Archibald Koe, and a company of South Wales Borderers. They were all ashore by 5.45 am. His force was equal in number to all the Turks south of Achi Baba.

Matthews had verbal orders only from Hunter-Weston and they were vague. He was to advance inland, capture a Turkish gun thought to be nearby, and attract the Turkish reserves to his position, thereby denying reinforcements for the defence of V and W beaches. He was also to join up with the troops from X Beach and, late in the day, take part in the general advance on Achi Baba.

On the first day Hamilton had passed Y Beach in *Queen Elizabeth* on his way south from Anzac. He saw that the landing had gone well. Later, when Hamilton realised the landing at V was going badly, he signalled Hunter-Weston: 'Would you like to get some more men ashore on Y Beach? If so, trawlers are available.' Note the deferential tone: the last thing the commander-in-chief was going to do was crack out an order. Hamilton sent the signal even though Braithwaite warned him it could be a breach of etiquette, since Hunter-Weston had executive control of the southern invasion. Hamilton might have told his chief-of-staff that if the landings failed, he – Hamilton – would have to take the blame in Whitehall, but of course he didn't. Hunter-Weston failed to reply, so the message was repeated. Hunter-Weston now replied that Admiral Wemyss had told him that any changes to the plan would delay the landings at V and W beaches.

The idea lapsed for want of a seconder and because its proposer spoke too softly. Aspinall later wrote in the official history: 'Had the suggestion been acted upon, or had Sir Ian Hamilton seen fit to issue a definite order on this subject, the whole story of the Gallipoli campaign might well have been different.' This assumes too much. Still, a chance had been missed. And with the battles just five hours old we had already seen evidence of Barbara Tuchman's dictum that the melting point of warfare is the temperament of the individual commander. Sami Bey, commander of the Turkish 9th Division, had issued an order that day. 'I am sending you a battalion,' he wrote to the commander of the 26th Regiment at Helles. 'It is quite clear that the enemy is weak; drive him into the sea, and do not let me find an Englishman in the south when I arrive.'

Matthews' troops couldn't find any trace of the Turkish gun that was supposed to be nearby. They sat around on the cliff top when they could have occupied Krithia. At 3 pm Matthews ordered them to dig in. The regulars took the centre; the marines, volunteers and still raw, took the flanks.

The Turks had known for at least three hours that Matthews was there. At Serafim Farm, Sami Bey had committed his 27th Regiment to Anzac and his 26th to the Helles beaches. He had the 25th Regiment – three battalions – with him as a reserve. Now he sent it south. Two battalions went to Helles; the third reached Krithia at 2.30 pm and turned right for Y Beach. Sami Bey understood the importance of Y Beach rather better than Hunter-Weston.

At 5.40 the Turks attacked Matthews' force then pulled back when the warships off Y fired on them. When darkness fell and the ships stopped firing the Turks advanced again in the rain. They fought furiously even though they were then outnumbered two-to-one. The British were in trouble because their trenches were only 18 inches deep. Two further companies of Turks arrived at 11 pm.

Just before midnight Matthews signalled to Hunter-Weston via the battleship *Goliath*, which was lying offshore. 'Situation serious. One battalion to reinforce should arrive before dawn.' No reply. Five minutes later he sent another message saying he needed ammunition urgently. No reply. Around dawn he signalled again. 'A reinforcing battalion urgently required, also ammunition.' No reply. An hour later, the *Goliath*'s commander, apparently of his own volition, signalled Hunter-Weston: 'Y force in desperate position. Can you send reinforcements immediately.' No reply.

At dawn Matthews counted his casualties. The marines had lost 331 killed and wounded, the Scottish Borderers 296, the South Wales Borderers 70. Koe was dying. Matthews had lost a third of his force. Panic set in. Men started heading for the beach. At 6.30 am a young officer from the Scottish Borderers signalled to the *Dublin*: 'Will you please send help as we are cut off, and have no ammunition and also a number of wounded.' Boats were sent in to take off the wounded. Stragglers climbed into the boats. The evacuation, ordered by no-one, had begun.

The Turks attacked again shortly after 7 am, breaking the centre before being driven out with bayonets. The last shot had been fired for the day. Matthews discovered that the trenches on his right flank were empty. Down on the beach, unknown to him, men had been signalling for more boats to come in. Matthews signalled Hunter-Weston:

'Situation critical. Urgent need reinforcements and ammunition, without which cannot maintain ridge at Y. Alternative is to retire on to beach under cover ships' guns.' No reply.

Matthews decided to authorise the unauthorised evacuation. At 11.30, all his men were off, their kits strewn about the trenches and the beach. Late in the afternoon Lieutenant-Commander Adrian Keyes, brother of Roger, climbed the cliff to see if any wounded had been left. He walked the battlefield for an hour without being fired upon. The Turks had left for Helles.

Y Beach was a little incident in what would become a big war. It had lasted only 29 hours, yet it said much about how the war would be conducted, and more again about the character of those running it.

Hunter-Weston had treated Matthews outrageously. All that can be said in the general's defence is that his two major landings, at V and W, had turned into bloodbaths and may have distracted him. Or did they? On the evening of the 25th, Hunter-Weston boarded the *Queen Elizabeth* as Hamilton, de Robeck, Keyes, Braithwaite and others were finishing dinner. Hamilton says Hunter-Weston was 'cheery, stout-hearted, quite a good tonic and – on the whole – his news is good'.

Good? How could it be good? Hunter-Weston's troops at V Beach – those still alive, that is – were pinned down behind a bank; another 1000 were trapped inside the *River Clyde*. Maybe Hunter-Weston wasn't too surprised by the slaughter there. A few days earlier, in a typically tactful message to the 29th Division, he had emphasised that 'heavy losses by bullets, by shells, by mines and by drowning' could be expected. He had got that right, although it had an unexpected result. A soldier at X Beach carried a dead tortoise to his brigadier. 'I've found one of these here land mines, sir,' he said.

How could the news be good? Didn't the plan say that Hunter-Weston's troops were supposed to be surging up Achi Baba at this hour? On the first day of his war, Hamilton's natural optimism was already blinding him to reality.

From the sea off the toe of the peninsula, Achi Baba, about five-and-a-half miles inland, seems to glower over all, a squatting lump crowned with a knob that looks like an afterthought. The British in 1915 usually described it as a head-and-shoulders formation. Sometimes it reminds you of a man peeping over a hedge. Below Achi Baba on the extreme right of the toe of the peninsula is Seddülbahir castle and behind it the village of the same name. Immediately west of the castle is V Beach, about 300 yards long, 10 to 15 yards of sand running to a bank less than six feet high. About 500 yards inland is a small rise, Hill 141. From out to sea the left boundaries of V Beach are the cliffs of Cape Helles and Ertuğrul Fort, where a 28-centimetre Krupp gun still lies in the sand, its black barrel pointing impotently at a Russian container ship about to enter the Dardanelles. On the right-hand side of V Beach a spit of rocks juts into the sea.

This is where the Trojan horse called the *River Clyde* was run aground, which is right enough because you can just make out the mound of Troy across the water. This is where the slaughter happened. On the 25th the village on the right, what was left of it, was on fire and dust from the battered castle drifted over the men crouching on the beach. They couldn't look forward, to the wire entanglements above the beach; the Turks were too close and shooting too well. And they probably didn't want to look back, to that spit, and the lighters and the *River Clyde*. They would have seen a red rim in the sand left by the lapping waves. They could have raised their eyes and seen yellow-brown puffs as the battleships fired salvo after salvo. But what did these matter? The Turks still had the Munsters and Dubliners pinned down on the beach.

George Drewry, a handsome young midshipman from Essex, was here, out in the water, where bullets were splashing and whistling, a few yards from where you are standing. He was trying to position the lighters in front of the *River Clyde*; later, he helped to take the wounded off. 'I never knew blood smelt so strong before,' he wrote to his father. Drewry won the Victoria Cross here. Three days later, while walking through Seddülbahir village, now in British hands, he fainted at the sight of so many Turkish and British bodies. And Father Finn, Catholic padre to the Dubliners – he was here, too, on the other side of the spit, running back from the bank to the water's edge to administer the last sacraments to his flock. He was seriously wounded before he reached the bank the first time, then hit again. He died somewhere here, maybe a few yards away, maybe near that pile of kelp, from loss of blood.

So many died here. Looking down from the hill, a Turkish officer said the shore was strewn with corpses 'like a shoal of fish'. A British airman looked down on a sea 'absolutely red with blood'. The stain, he said, spread for 50 yards from the shore.

It is such a small theatre, this. Today it smells of seaweed and salt. Seddülbahir castle is so close that you could hit it with a well-thrown stone. The Turks had a machine gun there, enfilading the beach. The low plain in front of you offered a clear field of fire for the Turkish machine gunners and riflemen entrenched below Hill 141.

To borrow a metaphor of Hamilton's, the beach was the stage, open and well lit, and the Turks were in the balconies. The two-storeyed Mocamp motel now sits jauntily on the shoreline in front of where the *River Clyde* grounded. In the old village of Seddülbahir a dove coos from his perch on mildewed tiles and far away you hear the knock of tractor engines.

If we go back out to sea and look to the left of V Beach, we see the cliffs of Cape Helles tumbling into the sea for about 700 yards. Then comes W Beach, another amphitheatre, about 350 yards long with the sand running back 40 yards in places. There is no bank here. W Beach is pretty much as it was in 1915, wide open, a rising plain of tussocks and scrub, broken by a gully and closed off by the cliffs of Cape Helles to the right and Cape Tekke to the left. It is made for defence. The remains of two British piers poke out of the water and one still comes upon scraps of barbed wire, encrusted with rust and salt.

A walking track on the eastern side leads to a cave in rippling layers of sandstone. It is a black hole, nothing more, dank and musty, its mouth overgrown, its soft walls crumbling. You think of contraband and bandits. Outside are goat droppings and a Coke can. Nothing to say that this was once called Baronial Hall. Hunter-Weston gave it the name after it was built for him in June as a shelter from the Turkish guns firing from near Troy. When the Turkish gunners failed to do much damage in a 30-minute bombardment, Hunter-Weston, humming and singing, would exclaim: 'Wasteful rascals! Wasteful rascals!' From here orders were issued, again and again, for thousands of men to be sacrificed before the false god of Achi Baba. Now it is just a black hole. If you had walked out of here in 1915, you would have seen horse lincs, wagon parks, tents, dugouts, roads pock-marked with craters, makeshift hospitals, piles of stores, four piers, thousands of men in pith helmets trudging about in the dust and still half-believing in victory. Now all you hear is the keening of the wind and the tinkle of a goat's bell.

From out to sea you cannot see S Beach; it is around the corner on the right-hand side of the peninsula. Nor can you see X or Y; they are around the corner on the left. If you are the invader and believe you must land on the toe, there are only those two beaches, V and W. If you are the defender, and if you have come to terms with the warfare of the early 20th century, these beaches are just about perfect. Both allow the defender to pour enfilading fire on the enemy once he is ashore. Both offer clear fields of fire. Both are made for barbed-wire entanglements.

On these beaches on April 25 the battle of Omdurman was fought again. This time the British were the ancients, the Turks the moderns. At V Beach a company of Turks held up and inflicted frightful casualties upon battalions of Englishmen. At W Beach a company of Turks could not hold the advancing British but they shot them to pieces as they came ashore. From wooden boats, the British came ashore with bayonets. From earthworks, forts and the ruins of a village, the Turks fired on them from above with machine guns, pom-poms and rifles. (The Turks had four machine guns at V; the British say the Turks also had two at W, although the Turks say they had none.)

A man with a machine gun can create a firestorm. Trials at the British Musketry School in Kent during 1907 showed that at 600 yards two Maxim machine guns could wipe out a battalion (roughly 1000 men) advancing in the open in one minute if the troops did not go to ground. This trial offended Edwardian sensibilities. Infantry and cavalry: that's what warfare was about. Hundreds of years of tradition said this was so. Who were these modernists who would reduce warfare to a clash of technology rather than of men, so that the heroes would be called Vickers and Krupp rather than Hector and Achilles? What sort of world was that for a chap who liked to wear spurs and a plumed helmet? And how could war be 'manly' if the hero was a machine? We should not be too hard on the planners of the Helles landings on this point. In 1916 their comrades in France were still ordering infantry to advance across open ground towards machine guns.

Until 1919 the British believed a division of Turks had opposed their five landings at Helles, rather than bits and pieces of Sami Bey's 26th Regiment. The British had been opposed by two companies spread over V and W beaches, by a platoon at S Beach and by 12 men at X. The whole Turkish force below Achi Baba at daybreak on the 25th amounted to two battalions and a company of engineers.

Lieutenant-Colonel Weir de Lancy Williams, a staff officer from Hamilton's headquarters, stood on the bridge of the River Clyde as it approached V Beach on April 25 writing notes for his diary.

6.10 am.	Within half-mile of the shore. We are far ahead of the tows . . . It must cause a mix-up if we, 2nd line, arrive before the 1st line. With difficulty I get Unwin [captain of the *River Clyde*] to swerve off and await the tows.
6.22 am.	Ran smoothly ashore without a tremor. No opposition. We shall land unopposed.
6.25 am.	Tows within a few yards of shore. Hell burst loose on them. One boat drifting to north, all killed. Others almost equally helpless.

	Our hopper gone away.
6.35 am.	Connection with shore very bad. Only single-file possible and not one man in ten gets across. Lighters blocked with dead and wounded. Very little fire on this ship. Wedgwood's maxims in bows firing full blast, but nothing to be seen excepting a maxim firing through a hole in the fort [Seddülbahir castle] and a pom-pom near the skyline on our left front.
9.00 am.	Fear we'll not land today.
10.00 am.	. . . Very little directed fire against us on the ship, but fire immediately concentrates on any attempt to land. The Turks fire discipline is really wonderful.

V Beach was seen as the main landing and it wasn't supposed to go like this. Two battalions of the RND (the Plymouth and the Anson) had been added to the 29th Division for the five landings. This gave Hunter-Weston more than 12 battalions of fighting troops. Seven-and-a-half would go ashore as the covering force and the others as the main body. For V, W and X beaches, the covering force was the 86th Brigade, plus two companies of Hampshires. Brigadier-General S. H. Hare commanded. He would go ashore at W. The 86th comprised the Royal Dublin Fusiliers, the Royal Munster Fusiliers, the Lancashire Fusiliers and the Royal Fusiliers. The Royal Fusiliers were bound for X Beach, the Lancashire Fusiliers for W.

At V Beach most of the Dubliners would land in tows, like the Australians at Anzac Cove. The *River Clyde* was to be run aground as soon as the Dubliners' first tows arrived at the beach. Two thousand men would be on the

River Clyde: all the Munsters, the two companies of Hampshires, one company of Dubliners, a few RND troops, including Sub-Lieutenant Arthur Tisdall, the Cambridge poet, and two members of Hamilton's staff, Williams (whose diary entry appears above) and Lieutenant-Colonel Charles 'Dick' Doughty-Wylie.

Hamilton and others were keen to land at Helles, even though it was a long way from the forts, because the navy could support them on three sides. The naval gunners could see with the naked eye Seddülbahir castle, the village behind it, Fort Ertuğrul and the three hills overlooking the Helles beaches. They could drop a fantastic barrage on them, and they did. It began at 5 am. For an hour the warships flashed fire and belched yellow-brown smoke and great plumes of earth and masonry rose on the peninsula and it was thought that no-one could live in such a hell. There was no return fire, not a sign of life. What was not understood until afterwards was that the naval guns with their low trajectories and high-explosive shells were splendid when it came to demolishing buildings and making holes in the ground. They were not particularly effective against men well spread out. When the barrage lifted, the Turkish troops, deafened and unstrung but with barely a mark on them, came out of their shelters and ran to the firing steps. They didn't fire until the boats grounded; and they didn't waste bullets on the *River Clyde* itself. They fired at men and movement.

The tows carrying the Dubliners headed for the beach at 6 am. It was a lovely spring day, the sea glassy, the sun a blood-red orb over the Asian coast. The troops could see three lines of wire behind the beach but not a Turk. The Turks, it appeared, were dead or had fled. Not a sound. As the *River Clyde* touched bottom and the tows were a few yards off the beach, the Turks opened up. Machine guns from right, left and straight ahead, rifles, pom-poms. The Dubliners were slaughtered in the boats. Boats turned broadside on with every man in them dead. Dubliners jumped over the side to be mowed down. Others drowned under the weight of their packs. A few, many of them wounded, made the bank. Few of the boats made it back to the ships. A naval rating from the *Lord Nelson* ended up the only man unwounded on his cutter. He stood up and tried to pole the boat ashore. He died.

The men who had made the bank were trapped. If they tried to crawl forward to cut the first line of wire, or even put their heads up, they were shot. Seven hundred Dubliners had become 300, and many of those were wounded.

And the *River Clyde* scheme had gone wrong. The Argyll, a steam hopper, was supposed to beach itself in front of the *River Clyde*. The troops would burst out of the sally ports in the collier's sides, run along a wooden gangplank to a platform on the ship's bow, then drop into the *Argyll*, which would be their bridge to the shore. Three lighters had been brought along in case the collier grounded too far out, leaving a gap between it and the *Argyll*. When the *River Clyde* grounded, the *Argyll*, commanded by Drewry, touched bottom on the port side of the collier and turned broadside on to the beach – worthless.

Commander Unwin decided to use the lighters to make a bridge to the spit of rocks to his starboard. He climbed on to the lighters as bullets hissed into the sea and thudded into bodies around him. Unwin had escaped from an unwritten novel by Joseph Conrad. He was more than six feet tall, strongly made, with a small thin mouth and a jutting chin. He bawled out orders through a megaphone and didn't spare the stragglers or the slow-witted. He was impulsive, rough-mouthed and impatient. He knew about ships, didn't have time for fools and tended to see the world in absolutes of right and wrong. He had joined the merchant navy at 16 after receiving two dozen strokes of the birch at the end of his term on a training ship on the River Mersey. He spent 15 years on clippers and with P. & O. Then he joined the Royal Navy, where he fought in a skirmish in West Africa and the Boer War. He retired in 1909, only to be recalled just before war broke out in 1914 and given command of the destroyer *Hussar* in the Mediterranean. He had earned the right to roar out orders and he was well liked; colleagues described him as cheerful and good-humoured.

When Unwin went forward to the lighters, he took with him Able Seaman William Williams, a 34-year-old leading seaman on the *Hussar*. Unwin later told how Williams came to be on the *River Clyde*. 'I told him I was full up and that I did not want any more petty officers, to which he replied, "I'll chuck my hook [drop in rank] if you will let me come", and I did, to his cost but everlasting glory.' Another crewman from the *Hussar*, Seaman George Samson, was on the *Argyll* with Drewry.

Williams accompanied Unwin to the lighters because the commander had ordered him to stay at his side throughout the day. When Unwin gave orders you didn't ask questions. Unwin plunged into the water and Williams followed. They began hauling the lighters towards the spit with ropes, sometimes swimming, sometimes wading. Cutters full of dead and dying drifted nearby. The few sailors who had survived tried to bring the cutters under the ship's sides. In his *Gallipoli*, Michael Hickey quotes an eyewitness on the *River Clyde* who watches a wounded sailor trying to hold a cutter full of dead and dying in a safe place. The hand of a dying man in the boat continually strokes the sailor's hand.

Drewry, meanwhile, waded ashore, presumably to take the end of the rope. On his way, and with the help of a soldier, he tried to carry ashore a wounded Dubliner, 'but he was again shot in our arms, his neck in two pieces nearly, so we left him . . . ' Drewry tossed away his revolver, coat and hat and waded out to help Unwin and Williams. Waist deep in water, bullets splashing around them, they held the lighters in position. The landing from the *River Clyde* began.

Two companies of Munsters emerged from the sally ports. Captain Henderson's company ran out of the starboard side and fell in bloodied heaps along the gangway and on the lighters. A few made the shore and joined the Dubliners. Henderson was mortally wounded. Captain Geddes' company ran cheering out of the port side. The first 48 men behind him fell. A lieutenant lying on the gangway, hit in five places, shouted: 'Follow the captain!' Turkish batteries from the Asian coast were now bursting shells over V Beach. The machine guns on the *River Clyde*'s bows were still firing but not hitting much. The Turks, playing at classic defence, weren't offering targets. Commander Josiah Wedgwood, a Liberal parliamentarian who was in charge of the machine guns, wrote to Churchill: 'The wounded cried out all day – in every boat, lighter, hopper and all along the shore. It was horrible . . .'

A shell fragment hit Williams, straining on a rope alongside Unwin. Unwin dropped the rope to grab Williams, who died in his arms. The lighter nearest the shore drifted away. Geddes' men tried to swim ashore; some were shot and many drowned. In their first attempt to land the Munsters had suffered about 70 per cent casualties.

Unwin, suffering from cold and exhaustion, was taken

to the doctor on the *River Clyde*. Drewry later said: 'I stayed on the lighters and tried to keep the men going ashore but it was murder and soon the first lighter was covered with dead and wounded and the spit was awful; the sea around it for some yards was red.' Drewry was joined by Midshipman Wilfred Malleson, an 18-year-old from the battleship *Cornwallis*. Drewry, still trying to repair the bridge, was hit in the head by shrapnel. He worked on with rivulets of blood running down his face, left briefly to have his head bandaged, then returned. Malleson exposed himself to Turkish fire to get hold of a new rope. Eventually, around 9 am, a new bridge was completed.

A third company of Munsters tried to land. Another massacre. This time the attempt was called off after only two platoons had run along the gangway. The commander of the Munsters and Hampshires, still in the *River Clyde*, decided to wait for night before making another attempt to land the 1000 men left in the hold.

Hunter-Weston was off W Beach on the *Euryalus*. At 8.30 am, he ordered the main body to land at V and Brigadier-General Napier, its commander, set off. The reader may wonder how the main body was going to land if the covering force couldn't. The answer is that Hunter-Weston didn't know what was happening at V. Hamilton and Keyes did. They had arrived about 6.45 am aboard the *Queen Elizabeth* and saw the men trapped on the beach. Hamilton wrote:

Through our glasses we could quite clearly watch the sea being whipped up all along the beach and about the *River Clyde* by a pelting storm of rifle bullets. We could see also how a number of our daredevils were up to their necks in this tormented water trying to struggle on to land from the barges linking the *River Clyde* to the shore . . . Watching these gallant souls from the safety of a battleship gave me a hateful feeling: Roger Keyes said to me he simply could not bear it. Often a commander may have to watch tragedies from a post of safety. That is all right. I have had my share of the hair's breadth business and now it becomes the turn of the youngsters. But, from the battleship, you are outside the frame of the picture. The thing becomes monstrous; too cold-blooded; like looking on at gladiators from the dress circle.

Hamilton knew it was pointless to send in the main body at V. Keyes suggested putting it ashore at Y. Hence Hamilton's message, mentioned earlier, asking Hunter-Weston whether he would like to land more men at Y. Here we see how muddled things were among the army commanders on the ships. Hamilton *only* sent the message because of what he and Keyes had seen at V; Hunter-Weston could treat the message with disfavour because he *didn't* know what was happening at V. Hamilton was commander-in-chief but didn't want to issue a direct order; Hunter-Weston was in charge of the landing at V but didn't want to look at it.

Unwin went back to work on the lighters wearing a white shirt and was hit in the face and arms by pieces from a ricocheting bullet. A doctor on the *River Clyde* attended him again.

Still unaware of what was happening at V, Hunter-Weston signalled to the *River Clyde* that the covering force at V should move left to join up with the troops at W. This appears to be the reason why, at around 9.30, a company of Hampshires attempted the run from the sally ports to the beach. A few men reached the lighters alive. The third attempt to land troops was called off.

Napier arrived shortly after with a small detachment from the main force. His tow was headed straight for the beach. A colonel on the *River Clyde* hailed it to come alongside the collier. Napier saw the lighters full of men lying down. Not realising they were dead, Napier sprang on to a lighter intending to lead the men ashore. A voice from the *River Clyde* shouted: 'You can't possibly land!' Napier shouted back: 'I'll have a damned good try.' He was pinned down on the lighters for 15 minutes. Then he was killed.

Hamilton at 10.21 signalled Hunter-Weston: 'Not advisable to send more men to V Beach. We have 200 on shore unable to progress.' The rest of the force intended for V was diverted to W.

Wounded men still cried out on the beach. Unwin returned to the killing field for the third time. Now he crawled along the spit looking for wounded. According to one account he brought back seven. A petty officer helping him was shot in the stomach. Unwin tore a strip off his shirt to bind the wound. Both lay in the water, pretending to be dead. During a lull in the firing they made it back to the *River Clyde*. Unwin was just about played out.

Tisdall took over his work. He had heard the cries of the wounded and is supposed to have said: 'I can't stand it. I'm going over.' He may have made five trips to and from the beach, each time pushing a lifeboat loaded with three or four wounded men. A ricocheting bullet left Tisdall with splinters in his wrist. He worked under fire until at least midday. Seaman George Samson from the *Argyll* worked at recovering wounded until dark.

Unwin, Williams, Drewry, Samson, Malleson and Tisdall all received the Victoria Cross. Williams has no known grave. Samson was hit by shrapnel on the deck of the *River Clyde* on April 26. Some accounts have him receiving more than two dozen wounds, others 17. He returned to his home town in Scotland to be feted. He was wearing civilian clothes, which explains why someone handed him a white feather.

Tisdall could have been anything: at 24, he was a poet and had won the Chancellor's Gold Medal for Classics at Cambridge; he was interested in socialism, women's rights and economic theory. Tisdall might have become a professor or a writer or a Cabinet minister. He might have fathered children and owned an old Labrador and fussed over his roses and read Herodotus by a winter's fire. But when he was in the water at V, his future was just about all used up. He was killed on May 6.

The 1st Battalion of the Lancashire Fusiliers landed at W Beach as the *River Clyde* nudged into V. The battalion had left England for Egypt and Gallipoli 1029 strong; after the first day at W Beach, it was down to 410. Just after dawn on the 25th, about 2000 yards off the coast, the men climbed into cutters and headed for the shore once the naval barrage ended. They could see barbed wire strung on steel posts and the earth thrown up from the trenches; they could not see the trip wires in the water or the land mines. Several of the cutters heeled over as the picket boat towing them changed direction. 'I 'listed to get killed, not to get drowned,' a soldier informed the coxswain.

A and B companies, on the right, were to attack the trenches and redoubt on Hill 138, towards V Beach. C Company was to take the trenches in the centre and on the left and head towards Hill 114. D Company was to be in reserve under Cape Tekke.

The 32 cutters approached the beach. Dead silence. Not

a Turk. It was a re-run of V Beach. Captain Richard Willis, commanding C Company, recalled:

> It might have been a deserted land we were nearing in our little boats. Then, crack! The stroke oar of my boat fell forward to the angry astonishment of his mates, and pandemonium broke out as soldiers and sailors struggled to get out of the sudden hail of bullets that was sweeping the beach and the cutters from end to end. Men leapt out of the boats into deep water, encumbered with their rifles and their 70lb of kit, and some of them died right there, while others reached the land only to be cut down on the barbed wire.

Captain Shaw, commanding B Company, jumped into three feet of water, rushed up the beach, blundered through the wire, found cover and looked back.

> There was one soldier between me and the wire, and a whole line in a row on the edge of the sands. The sea behind was absolutely crimson, and you could hear the groans through the rattle of musketry. A few were firing. I signalled to them to advance. I shouted to the soldier behind me to signal, but he shouted back, 'I am shot through the chest.' I then perceived they were all hit.

Captain Clayton, commanding D Company, couldn't get his wire cutters to work. 'The front of the wire by now was a thick mass of men, the majority of whom never moved again . . . The noise was ghastly and the sights horrible.'

It was an ambush like V Beach. The difference at W was that the troops who lived were able to keep going forward. One soldier joked to his officer as he pulled out wire – while bleeding from seven wounds. Men who found their rifles jammed with sand forced the bolts open with their heels. More than 100 corpses lay between the water and the wire. More bodies were strung up in the wire.

Alfred Richards' right leg was almost severed by bullets. He was a 35-year-old sergeant with kind eyes and a shy smile. He kept shouting to his men to go forward as he crawled through the wire with them, dragging his twisted leg like an animal that has been shot far back in the spine. Brigadier-General Hare, commanding the covering force, landed safely under Cape Tekke but was soon badly wounded. His successor was killed.

The Lancastrians, however, rolled on. The three platoons of Turks defending the beach melted before them. By 7.15 the landing place was relatively safe; it merely looked like hell. Captain Willis took his objective, Hill 114. By then his company had been reduced to 87 men.

Willis, Sergeant Richards (whose leg was amputated) and four others won the Victoria Cross. Private William Keneally's VC was announced in the *London Gazette* of August 23. His family at Wigan, Lancashire, was very proud. Keneally had gone down the mines at 13; now, at 28, he had won his country's highest award for bravery. The local council was going to honour him. People would want to hear everything he had to say. He might receive a rose bowl or a plaque. His photograph would be in all the papers, even the Fleet Street dailies. What the family didn't know was that Keneally had been killed in the battle for Gully Ravine on June 28. They were told of his death in October.

The Turks hadn't been expecting a landing at X Beach, around the corner from Cape Tekke and about 1000 yards across country from W. In front of the beach stood an eroded cliff, not as severe as at Y, and 12 Turks. Two companies of Royal Fusiliers were on the cliff top by 6.30, without a casualty.

At S Beach, on the opposite side of the peninsula to X and less than two miles behind V, three companies of South Wales Borderers landed at 7.30. Fifteen Turks there surrendered. S was a good flanking position from which to attack the Turks at V. But this was not part of the orders and Hunter-Weston didn't want to change them. So the men stayed in the relative calm of Morto Bay for two days. Hunter-Weston sent them a message telling them to 'consolidate' their position. 'Well done, South Wales Borderers,' the general signalled the following afternoon. 'Can you maintain your position for another 48 hours?'

Which raises a nice point. How come Hunter-Weston had time to send messages to S, where nothing was happening, but not to Y, where a larger opportunity was being lost and hundreds were dying?

The diversion at Bulair went well. The warships bombarded the coast, the transports swung out their boats as if a landing was about to begin, and von Sanders didn't know what to think. A small force under Lieutenant-Commander Bernard Freyberg was supposed to land briefly in the night and make noise, as if a major assault was starting. Freyberg thought he could lose his whole force by doing this. He came up with another plan. Freyberg had been a good swimmer in New Zealand; he would fake a landing by himself.

He slipped into the cold waters of the Gulf of Saros carrying flares, a knife, a revolver and a signalling light in an oilskin bag. He swam for an hour to reach the shore. He set his flares at intervals, lit them one by one, looked for Turks, found only dummy trenches, then began swimming back to the pinnace, which picked him up as his cramps started to become intense.

The French next day worked a similar diversion at Besika Bay. Two destroyers bombarded the coast and six transports lowered boats and pretended they were about to land troops. At 10 am the feint was called off. The exercise may have fooled the Turks, if briefly.

Kum Kale is not made for defence like V or W. The old Greek village and its castle squatted on a low spit looking out across the Dardanelles to V Beach and Morto Bay. Behind Kum Kale the Trojan plain runs back to Troy. Where old Kum Kale stood looks like a good place to breed mosquitoes, low and marshy and open. Just east of it the Mendere River – the Scamander in Homer's tale – meanders around sandbanks. South of Kum Kale, following the line of the river, is an old Turkish cemetery and, further along, the Orkanie Mound, said to be the tomb of Achilles. Yeni Shehr, another Greek village, sat further south on a bluff. Yeni Shehr and its windmills are all gone now, just a rubble of broken tiles underfoot. In April, 1915, the castle at Kum Kale and the battery at Yeni Shehr had been wrecked by the fleet's gunfire and a raiding party of marines had blown up the battery at Orkanie Mound. There were still many Turks here, but they were not going to attempt a defence on the marshland around Kum Kale. They had not even laid wire.

The French came ashore on the 25th with little difficulty – and badly late. The 6th Regiment – one battalion of colonial infantry and two of Senegalese, less than 3000 men – finally landed below the castle around 10 am. The bombardment by the fleet had begun at 5.15. Three hours later Yeni Shehr was burning and the few Turks around

Kum Kale had crossed back over the river. The French troops began to clamber down into the boats at 6.20, but the steamboats towing them found the Dardanelles current too strong. Tugs and torpedo boats were brought in to get the troops ashore. By 11.15 the French had captured the deserted village. A French doctor wrote to his wife that a watchmaker's shop still had its signboard flapping in the wind and a display of cuckoo clocks.

The French began to advance on Yeni Shehr at 5.30 pm. They ran into heavy fire and stopped halfway between Kum Kale and Orkanie. During the night three battalions of Turks made four bayonet charges. In the morning Turkish dead lay all around Kum Kale. The French, having no posts, used the bodies to string wire.

The behaviour of the Turks here was at odds with their cleverness at V Beach, their doggedness at Anzac, and their heroics at both. And it becomes stranger because, unlike their brothers on all the peninsula beaches, they outnumbered the invader. The official Turkish account criticises the divisional commander for issuing 'many orders in great anxiety' and making 'arrangements without much meaning'. There was no pattern to the Turks' behaviour here. They died gamely in the night bayonet attacks; the next day many of them surrendered.

Colonel Ruef, the French commander, wrote of an 'incident' on the morning of the 26th. Turks were seen waving white flags. Eighty unarmed men were taken behind the French lines. Several hundred other Turks arrived but refused to lay down their rifles. A French captain pushed into the huddle, trying to persuade the Turks to drop their rifles. He was not seen again. While the negotiations were going on, Turks slipped back into the village, occupied several houses and opened fire. The French eventually drove the Turks out, taking 80 prisoners. They summarily executed the officer commanding and eight of his men. Colonel Ruef wrote that he sensed 'the whole thing was a misunderstanding', that the Turks really wanted to surrender and that the French interpreters did not explain things properly.

Général D'Amade appears to have decided that morning to pull out his troops. It was only a diversion and he couldn't take Yeni Shehr without reinforcements. Hamilton agreed to the withdrawal. About 3 pm, a battalion of Turks fled after a bombardment and another 450 surrendered. The French pulled out at night with their prisoners. The French had suffered 778 casualties. A monument outside Kum Kale lists the Turkish casualties at 1690.

As the French were leaving Hamilton decided that maybe they should stay another day and so delay the transfer of Turkish troops to the peninsula. He sent a signal telling the French to remain. The message arrived too late. This was the story of the first two days: so often Hamilton and Hunter-Weston issued orders without knowing what was happening on land. The war was on one planet and they were on another.

The Turks had fought poorly at Kum Kale, probably because they were badly led. Was this the way Churchill, Kitchener and Hamilton expected them to fight all over the peninsula? As any Allied soldier who had been at V Beach or on Baby 700 could have told them, Kum Kale was the exception.

The Turks had done well on their first day. The sick man of Europe fought for his hearth with a fury the British had not expected. The Turks made the terrain work for them, so that numerical superiority counted for little. The British landed more than 12 battalions on the Helles

beaches; the most the Turks could muster against them –
and this was not until late in the day – was two battalions.
At Anzac 8000 Australians were ashore by 8 am; the
Turks opposing them numbered about 500. Late in
the day, when 15,000 Australians and New Zealanders
had landed, the defenders could only muster 5000. At
Helles the Turks had set up the two main landing beaches
as shooting galleries; at Anzac, they held the heights. The
Turks were well led. Von Sanders did not panic when
the British appeared to be landing everywhere from Besika
Bay to Bulair. Kemal and Sami Bey instinctively did the
hard things they knew they had to do.

The Allies had suffered heavier casualties than they
expected; they had not achieved their first-day objectives,
hadn't even come close. The forts of Kilitbahir plateau
seemed far away. Still, the Allies were ashore; they had
won the battle of the beaches. It would not have been so
bad if Hamilton had shiploads of reserves standing offshore; or if those in London had understood what they
were asking him to do.

12

The morning after

The Allies were waylaid by reality on April 25. They fell into denial and confusion, then began to adapt to what was possible. Maidos and the Narrows faded from the vision after the first day at Anzac Cove. The war was about hanging on to the beachhead. It was about digging in, keeping the Turks behind a line that stretched from North Beach up Walker's Ridge to Russell's Top, across the escarpment, past Pope's and Quinn's and Courtney's, out on to 400 Plateau just below Lone Pine, and then back to the beach. Anzac was not a spearhead; Anzac was a fort in the shape of a triangle, 400 acres of very mean dirt.

After the first day at Helles the campaign came to be about how to get off V Beach. Once that was done and the British and the French, now on their right, moved inland, there was a new problem. The men were worn out: dead eyes stared out of faces that seemed all cheekbones. In four days these men had lost not only their youth but also the certainties of youth. Hamilton wrote early in May: 'The beautiful battalions of the 25th April are wasted skeletons now.' And, besides, there were no longer enough men. The casualties, particularly among the officers, had been severe. In truth there had never been enough men; now it was obvious. Just as no-one at Anzac was thinking about Maidos, no-one at Helles was thinking about the Dardanelles forts. Krithia and the slopes behind it became sensible goals. Reinforcements would be needed to take the forts. Constantinople? That was a dream, especially now that the navy appeared to be gun-shy.

The campaign at Anzac had gone from an invasion to a siege in one day. At Helles the same thing happened over a few weeks. Yet if this was going to be a siege, even temporarily, things were wrong. For trench warfare, one needed lots of artillery, particularly howitzers, as well as mortars, grenades and periscopes. Hamilton didn't have these things; he didn't even have reserves of infantry. Worse, London didn't understand the problems he was facing. He was only fighting Turks, wasn't he?

The Turks had taken heavy casualties too: whole regiments had been wiped out. The difference was the Turks' battle plan still made sense. Once it was clear that Kum Kale, Besika Bay and Bulair were diversions, the divisions guarding those places could fight at Helles and Anzac. But the Turks also had to lower their expectations. Early on their orders spoke of 'hurling the invaders into the sea'. They tried, but they couldn't do it.

On the grey morning of the 26th the clay at Anzac was slippery from the overnight drizzle and the scrub smelt of crushed thyme. The Australians and New Zealanders had grabbed a few hours' sleep in dugouts cut into the hills – Bean described them as something between a grave and a cave – in scrapes and behind biscuit boxes and kerosene tins and on the beach. Now they waited for a Turkish attack. The Turkish batteries opened up after daybreak but the hordes never came. The Turks were tired and disorganised too, and the warships off Anzac sent salvoes into the hills.

Bean met Birdwood on the beach before dawn. He seemed disappointed. 'First,' Birdwood said, 'there was the mistake of landing us a mile and a half north of where we should have landed, in this ghastly country. And then there's this enormous line.' The apex of the triangle – the head of Monash Valley below Baby 700 – was the weakest point. Braund was still up there, around Walker's Ridge and Russell's Top, with the shot-up remnants of his 2nd Battalion, and so were the New Zealanders. Oliver Cumberland of the 2nd had been wounded there on the first afternoon. He was in B company; Joe, his younger brother, was in C. Oliver later wrote to his sister, Una, from Cairo that he was in a bayonet charge when a bullet thudded into his hip and grazed the bone. 'I don't know how Joe is at present,' he said, 'but he was not hurt when I left the field.'

Australians had dug in on Pope's Hill, to the right of Braund. Between these two outposts the apex of the triangle was open. Turks could creep down between the two posts. Snipers were actually inside the Anzac line. The Turks higher up, at the Nek and on Baby 700, could shoot down Monash Valley and direct artillery fire on to 400 Plateau. The posts near the apex, particularly Pope's and Quinn's, were so vulnerable that it was fair to ask whether they could be held for more than a few days.

Simpson lit one of his precious Woodbines and began leading his donkey, a Red Cross brassard on its forehead, up Shrapnel Gully, which had become the highway to the war. Alongside him men carted water and ammunition to the firing lines, dodging shrapnel as they trudged beside the little gutter of a creek. That was the trouble with the Anzac triangle, that's why it would take so long to bring order to it. There was no safe area, nowhere to hold a quiet conference. The Turkish gunners could see so much from the hills above and from Gaba Tepe and Suvla. They could not see the beach, but they knew where it was. Stragglers – and there were still hundreds of them – were rounded up, but the corps remained a shambles. More than a week would pass before all the lost men of April 25 found their way back to their battalions. The generals sorted out spheres of influence. Godley and his New Zealand and Australian Division, which included Monash's Brigade, took responsibility for the left: Walker's Ridge, Russell's Top and the head of Monash Valley.

Monash came ashore around 10.30 am on the 26th. His tidy mind at once told him he had walked into chaos. Three of his battalions had landed the day before and were scattered from Russell's Top to 400 Plateau. A shrapnel pellet hit Monash as he tried to collect his men. It had burst too high and did no harm; he pocketed it as a souvenir. He took his men into the high-walled valley that would bear his name and set up his headquarters under Courtney's Post. He took over the left centre, which included the crazy position of Quinn's Post, exposed to flanking fire as well as to a frontal assault and where the troops in the front trench could not see over the crest and had a cliff immediately behind them. His dugout smelt of musty earth and cordite. It was not at all like Toorak, but it did have a telephone.

Casualties might have been light at Anzac on the 26th but for a blunder on 400 Plateau in mid-afternoon. Bridges said he wanted the line there straightened out, then left. Most of the 4th Battalion rushed from their trenches after receiving a muddled message about a 'general advance'. There was no order, which meant there could be no objective. Lieutenant-Colonel A. J. Onslow-Thompson, the battalion commander, ended up leading his troops up no-man's land, with the Australian trenches on the left and the Turkish on the right. The Turkish gunners burst shrapnel all over them. The battalion took Lone Pine, dislodged a few surprised Turks and reached Johnston's Jolly, where it also came under machine-gun fire. Then came the realisation that the 'orders' must be wrong. A panicky retreat began. Onslow-Thompson was killed. He had once managed Camden Park Estate, the famous merino stud founded outside Sydney by John and Elizabeth Macarthur. Two weeks later men of the 3rd Battalion came upon his body while digging a forward sap.

Bridges didn't know the 4th Battalion had 'advanced'. He had left 400 Plateau unhappy with the state of the trenches. 'What trenches are these?' he asked as he headed for McNicoll's headquarters. Upon being told, he snapped: 'They're no damned good anyway.' Bridges was seldom happy. Earlier he had been swearing at stragglers.

The trenches were too shallow. Trenches are dug by privates, not staff officers. Unlike the staff officers, the trench-diggers had not yet realised that they were stuck in this little triangle. The men thought their advance would resume at any moment. They thought the British and French were on their way north. There was a rumour on the 26th that the 29th Division was advancing up Legge Valley, just behind where Onslow-Thompson had died. The men still thought they would be marching through Turkey. Why else were they carrying ten-shilling notes overprinted in Ottoman script? Why else had they been told that on arrival in Constantinople they should be wary of 'grog-shop keepers and the hangers-on of disorderly houses'?

When Bridges eventually found McNicoll that day, he stood on the skyline to show McNicoll how he wanted the trenches realigned. As Bridges showed himself to the Turks, a voice from a trench cried out: 'For goodness sake come down here, sir – you'll be hit for certain.'

The general looked down at the man. 'Be damned,' he said.

On November 17, 1915, a woman stepped ashore at V Beach, which had become the main French base. She is thought to be the only woman to have landed during the Gallipoli campaign. She left the *River Clyde*, now being used as a pier, walked through the castle where the rubble smelled of mould and old wars, past the line of tottery walls and unearthed cellars that had once been Seddülbahir village, past the fig and pomegranate trees that had survived the bombardment, and began to climb Hill 141. On the summit she stopped at a lone grave fenced off with barbed wire, placed a wreath on the wooden cross, and left.

One report says she spoke to no-one ashore. We do not know what she was wearing. Probably black. Probably lace-up boots. Maybe a veil. Almost certainly a coat of some sort; the peninsula in November is cold and windswept. We do not even know for certain who she was. Most likely she was Lilian Doughty-Wylie, who at this time worked for the French Hospital Service. She may have been Gertrude Bell, the English writer and explorer.

We do know the grave she visited. It's still there, the only Allied cemetery on Gallipoli with just one grave. The cross, knocked up by a ship's carpenter, has gone now, the barbed wire too. A cypress tree guards each side of the headstone. Lavender bushes surround the grave. Here lies Lieutenant-Colonel Charles 'Dick' Doughty-Wylie,

Victoria Cross, shot through the head at this spot on April 26, 1915. Maybe one day they'll make a film about the mysterious woman who walked into a war to say goodbye to him. Only in the last reel will the veil be lifted to tell us whether Lilian or Gertrude trudged up the hill in 1915.

Doughty-Wylie was on the *River Clyde* as a member of Hamilton's staff, along with Colonel Weir Williams. Doughty-Wylie was 46, well on his way to going bald, with a neat moustache and a beak of a nose. Ashmead-Bartlett said he seldom spoke but 'seemed to think so much'. When he stepped aboard the Trojan horse his mind was tormented. Two women were in love with him; it is also possible he was in love with both of them. He certainly had affection for both. Both women had said they might commit suicide if he were killed. Now he was going where there was a good chance he would be killed. He had a premonition about it.

Charles Doughty married Lilian Wylie, a widow, in India in 1904. He shortly after changed his name by deed poll to Doughty-Wylie. Doughty had attended Winchester and Sandhurst, joined the Royal Welch Fusiliers and served in India, Crete, the Sudan, the Boer War (where he was wounded), China and Somalia. He was a transport officer in India, a mounted infantryman in South Africa, in charge of a camel detachment in Somalia. The Doughty-Wylies toured Baghdad, Babylon and Constantinople in 1906. The Middle East fascinated him and he liked the people. Later that year he became a military vice-consul in southern Turkey. In Adana in 1909 a massacre of Christian Armenians took 2000 lives. Doughty-Wylie put on his British army uniform and led 50 Turkish soldiers trying to stop the killings. Though shot in the arm by an Armenian who thought he was a Turkish officer, he confronted the mobs and ended up taking command of the town. For this, he was made a Companion of St Michael and St George.

Around this time he met Gertrude Bell, who was working at an archaeological dig. They wrote to one another but their affair did not begin for several years. Doughty-Wylie became consul-general in Addis Ababa. When the Balkan War broke out in 1912, he and Lilian moved to Constantinople. He became director of the Red Cross units, she a nursing superintendent. The Turkish Sultan awarded him the Imperial Ottoman Order of Medjidieh, second class. His own country made him a Companion of the Bath. Doughty-Wylie went back to Addis Ababa. 'Go I must,' he wrote to Gertrude Bell. 'There's anarchy out there, complete and beastly.' The affair with Bell had now begun. He saw her again in London on his way to join Hamilton's headquarters staff. Hamilton wanted him because of his knowledge of the Turks.

Doughty-Wylie was down to attend the Anzac landing but ended up on the *River Clyde* with Williams, who felt that Doughty-Wylie was suffering on the inside. 'I am firmly of the opinion,' he wrote a month after the landing, 'that poor Doughty-Wylie realised he would be killed in this war.' We know the talk of suicide by Lilian and Gertrude was bothering him. Before joining the *River Clyde*, he wrote to Gertrude:

When I asked for this ship, my joy in it was half strangled by that thing you said, I can't even name it or talk about it. As we go steaming in under the port guns in our rotten old collier, shall I think of it . . . Don't do it. Time is nothing, we join up again, but to hurry the pace is unworthy of us all.

At the same time he wrote to Lilian's mother. He said he

was taking on a dangerous job, 'namely the wreck ship of which you will see in the papers'. If anything happened to him, Lilian (who was in charge of a French hospital) would feel lonely and hopeless. 'She talks about overdoses of morphia and such things. I think that in reality she is too brave and strong minded for such things but the saying weighs on my spirits . . .'

Williams wrote that he and Doughty-Wylie 'sat and suffered until sunset' after the *River Clyde* had run aground. Captain Garth Walford arrived around midnight with orders from Hunter-Weston that the advance on the castle and village be resumed. Walford, an artillery officer, went ashore in the morning to fight with the Hampshires. A rough plan of attack had been worked out. One party would try to take the castle and the village; another would try to join up with the troops at W Beach on the left; and a third would drive up the centre, through the maze of barbed wire, towards Hill 141.

The troops took the castle easily enough. The village was different: the Turks fought for every wrecked house. Sometimes they sniped at the invaders as they emerged from the back door of the castle. Other times they let them pass, then fired into their backs from cellars and rubble.

Doughty-Wylie had been watching. It seems he decided this was Adana again: he would have to do it himself, set the example, maybe take charge. He headed for the village late in the morning carrying his walking stick. Walford was already dead, shot near the castle's back gate. Doughty-Wylie was almost killed at the same spot. A bullet knocked his cap off. A Munster officer wrote: 'I happened to be quite close at the moment, and remember being struck by the calm way in which he treated the incident. He was carrying no weapon of any description at the time, only a small cane.' As he advanced into the village, Doughty-Wylie briefly carried a rifle, then discarded it. The Munster officer said Doughty-Wylie walked into houses that might contain Turks as casually as if he were walking into a shop.

Seddülbahir village finally fell to the British. Doughty-Wylie now went for Hill 141. Dublins, Munsters and Hampshires surged through the wire cheering, Doughty-Wylie out in front. They reached the top and fired at the retreating Turks. And here, at the moment of victory, around 3 pm, Doughty-Wylie was shot dead.

Williams came upon Doughty-Wylie's body.

. . . the men round about were full of admiration and sorrow . . . I took his watch, money and a few things I could find and had him buried where he fell. I had this done at once, having seen such disgusting sights of unburied dead in the village that I could not bear to have him lying there. This was all done hurriedly . . . we just buried him as he lay and I said The Lord's Prayer over his grave and bid him goodbye. That night when things had quietened down I asked Unwin to have a temporary cross put up to mark his grave.

Next day the Munsters' chaplain read the burial service over the grave. Hamilton wrote that Doughty-Wylie's death had stripped victory of its wings.

Alas, for that faithful disciple of Charles Gordon; protector of the poor and of the helpless . . . He had no hatred of the enemy. His spirit did not need that ugly stimulant. Tenderness and pity filled his heart . . . He was a steadfast hero. Years ago, at Aleppo, the mingled chivalry and daring with which he placed his own body as a shield between the Turkish soldiery and their victims during a time of massacre made him admired even by the Moslems. Now; as he would have wished to die, so has he died.

Lilian was told of her husband's death at St Valery-sur-Somme. She wrote in her diary: 'The shock was terrible. I don't know quite what I did for the first 60 seconds. Something seemed to tear at the region of my heart. All my life was so much of his life, all his life mine . . . ' Lilian lived until 1960. Gertrude Bell died in 1926.

Doughty-Wylie and Walford received the Victoria Cross, as did Corporal William Cosgrove of the Munsters, which meant 15 Victoria Crosses were awarded for the first two days at V and W beaches. Cosgrove, a tall 26-year-old from County Cork, uprooted wooden posts supporting Turkish wire while under heavy fire. He rushed the Turkish trenches and didn't realise he had been shot several times until he collapsed.

Kemal had been given two more regiments. On Tuesday, April 27, he set out to throw the Anzacs into the sea. He decided to attack right along the line. He would have done better had he concentrated on the open apex of the triangle. The order he issued suggests that, this time, he was thinking more with his heart than his head.

Of the forces which the enemy brought in his ships only a remnant is left. I presume he intends to bring others. Therefore we must drive those now in front of us into the sea . . . There is no need to scheme much to make the enemy run. I do not expect that any of us would not rather die than repeat the shameful story of the Balkan War. But if there are such men among us, we should at once lay hands upon them, and set them up in line to be shot.

Before the Turks attacked, Braund, still up on Walker's Ridge, decided he would attack. He had just been re-inforced with troops from Malone's Wellington Battalion. He led them, and the troops of his own 2nd Battalion, who hadn't slept for three days, in a bayonet charge against the Turks creeping down Russell's Top. The Turks retreated. Braund's men started to dig in under fire from Baby 700. About 2.30 pm, Braund began to retreat. Men forward of his position came running back shouting: 'The Turks are coming in thousands.'

Six lines of Turks ran down Battleship Hill, the start of Kemal's general attack. The warships off Anzac opened up. Plumes of green smoke and yellow-brown dust rose all over Battleship Hill. Bean wrote that the Turks ran around like ants on a disturbed nest. The attack stalled. Braund and the Wellingtons now took a position across Russell's Top where they could finally see Monash's 16th Battalion on Pope's Hill. The apex had closed a little. Braund sent back a cryptic message: 'Will hold it until otherwise ordered. No officers but self and one other. Want picks and shovels, also water.'

The Turks came again in the dark, blowing bugles and shouting 'Allah'. For the first time they used bombs, grenades shaped like cricket balls. The Turks reached Braund's trenches but were driven back. Most of their bombs fell short. Kemal's attack failed all along the line, partly because of poor co-ordination. The Turks charged Monash's brigade at the head of the valley. A line of 300 in ragged uniforms, led by an officer with a flashing sword, rushed Pope's. Cavalrymen dismounted on Scrubby Knoll and attacked with swords. Others attacked at MacLaurin's Hill and Johnston's Jolly to be shot down in the open by machine guns.

Major F. D. Irvine, brigade-major to Colonel MacLaurin, commander of the 1st Brigade, stood up at Steele's Post to see where the Turks were coming from. Get down, the men told him. 'It's my business to be sniped at,' Irvine, a British regular, replied. A Turk on Russell's Top fired across the back of Pope's and Quinn's and killed him. Ten minutes later MacLaurin stood up on the ridge that carries his name. He was south of Irvine, but on almost the same line. He too was shot dead. Earlier in the day Brudenell White, Bridges' chief-of-staff, was hit by shrapnel while inside a dugout. The pellet didn't penetrate his clothing and he laughed. A truth, however, was apparent. No-one was safe at Anzac.

It was a tense night. Margetts, now at Wire Gully, wrote that the Turks 'did everything imaginable to raise their courage, blowing bugles, shouting "Allah" and shooting like hell'. Towards dawn Margetts fell asleep standing up. One hand, holding his revolver, rested on the parapet. His head rested on the arm.

Braund led his men down from Walker's Ridge to the beach after dawn on the 28th. His battalion, 970 strong at the landing, had been up there for three days and three nights. It had lost 16 officers and 434 men killed and wounded. The Australians and New Zealanders had fought up there as one. Bean says the jealousies that were obvious between them in Cairo quickly disappeared. They died as brothers, slumped against each other; and afterwards they were buried as brothers.

Malone and his Wellingtons relieved Braund. Malone didn't share Bean's ideas about brotherhood. He was furious with Braund. He thought the Australian had sacrificed the Wellingtons who had been sent up as reinforcements. Braund, Malone said, was a bungler. Malone pelted the Australians with stones and kicked them to get them moving. Malone thought of asking to have Braund court-martialled, even though he conceded he was a 'brave chap'. The idea was absurd. Braund had been to a hell Malone had not yet seen. This was Malone at his most high-handed. He was also, as ever, being protective of his own men; he didn't want some Australian ordering them to die. The first Wellingtons he had sent up to Braund had suffered nearly 200 casualties in an hour. The wounded were very brave, Malone wrote in his diary. 'No cries or even groans. One man kept saying "Oh, Daddy, Oh, Daddy" in a low voice . . . My men are wonderful.'

A week after leaving the ridge, Braund was returning to a rest camp. He was slightly deaf. He didn't hear the challenge of his own sentry. The sentry shot him dead.

On the afternoon that Kemal assailed the Anzacs, the British and French began to advance up the peninsula. The night before they had dug in, expecting a Turkish attack. They still thought they were fighting two divisions rather than two shot-up regiments. The Turks were outnumbered about three-to-one, but the British wouldn't know this for years. The British were nervy. Two days on the peninsula had told them the general staff had got it wrong: the Turks were ferocious fighters. One officer made his men count the headstones and cypresses in a cemetery in front of their position so that these would not be mistaken for advancing Turks during the night. The Turks never came.

They had withdrawn a few miles north. They too had dug in for the night; they expected a British assault. The local commanders wanted to retreat to the natural fortress of Achi Baba. Essad and von Sanders said, no, the line had to be held in front of the hill, around Krithia.

British patrols reported no sign of Turks on the morning of April 27. A balloon ship spotting for the *Queen Elizabeth* picked up a Turkish troop transport at the Narrows. The *Queen Elizabeth* fired across the peninsula at a range of about ten miles and sank the transport with her third shot.

Hunter-Weston put off his advance until 4 pm because the French were slow in coming ashore. He decided he couldn't take Achi Baba today; he would throw forward and take it tomorrow. In the soft sun of the late afternoon, the British and French advanced for about two miles through wheat fields and olive groves, bothered only by the odd sniper. The country looked easier than it was. Only when you walk this line do you realise that the interior of the peninsula below Achi Baba is like a saucer. You see low hills on three sides and the saucer itself is riven by tremendous gullies. It would turn out difficult to direct naval fire into this saucer, and Hunter-Weston had gone forward before he had landed sufficient field artillery to support his troops. There was another problem he could not have foreseen. He was entitled to think that the Turks were fading up the peninsula. In fact they were choosing their ground and waiting for reinforcements, their spirit unbroken.

Hunter-Weston decided against going for Achi Baba on the following day. He would advance in a right-wheeling movement. The pivot for this right wheel would be the French position above S Beach. Over on the left the British would capture Sari Tepe on the Aegean coast, Hill 472 north of Krithia and the village itself. At the end of the day, the top of the line would be facing east, straight at Achi Baba. As plans go, it was intricate and fussy, not the sort of operation one associates with Hunter-Weston. Mastery of detail was not his *métier*, as he demonstrated the night before the battle when, bluff and cheerful, he dined with Hamilton. No, he gave no order to evacuate Y Beach. Wasn't even consulted. Don't know *who* gave the order. Would you pass the butter?

Orders for what would be called the First Battle of Krithia on April 28 were issued so late that some commanders saw them only 20 minutes before they moved off. One officer wrote that 'it was practically impossible for everyone to understand in a hurry from the map the exact position we were to reach'.

The naval bombardment began at 8 am. At first Hunter-Weston's men went forward so easily that it looked as if they would walk into Krithia without firing a shot. But the wheeling manoeuvre became hard to carry out. The centre became disorderly. Some units ran into Turks, others didn't. Some advanced too quickly, others too slowly. The gullies baffled them. The British ran into Gully Ravine, the French Kereves Dere. The French were easy targets in their soft blue uniforms and white cork helmets. Aspinall, who had not envisioned the sexual revolution of the late-twentieth century, called them gay uniforms. A British unit fell into a panicky retreat near Y Beach, on the seaward side of Gully Ravine; this was where the *Queen Elizabeth* wiped out an entire Turkish company with one shot.

The Turks had at first withdrawn towards Achi Baba, then returned as reinforcements came up. They had managed to field nine battalions. They fought well, but the Allies perhaps made them look better than they were. Hunter-Weston's plan had become a shambles; it was too contemptuous of the Turks and the terrain. Communications were breaking down, just as they had during the landings. No-one was properly in charge of the battle, as had also happened during the landings; hares and hounds ran in all directions. Units became inter-mixed, as they had at Anzac. Ammunition ran out. And it was soon clear that the men were worn out and unstrung from the battles on the beaches. Hamilton had to send Aspinall ashore near Y Beach to stop stragglers slipping back towards Helles.

A few troops came close to Krithia, only to be told to fall back. Hamilton, on the *Queen Elizabeth*, began receiving messages that the 29th was being 'cut up'. At 3.30 he asked Hunter-Weston what was happening. Hunter-Weston was running the battle from Hill 138, except he wasn't in charge of it. No-one was. And it wasn't a battle so much as a series of skirmishes. Hunter-Weston, after waiting two hours, replied to Hamilton with splendid ambiguity.

Alarmist messages have been sent to me all day, but there is nothing yet to justify them. There have been local successes and local reverses, and since my first report we have made no progress. There is no doubt that in present exhausted state of the troops a Turkish counter-attack would have serious effects.

In short, there was nothing to be alarmed about, except that there was.

The battle was called off around 6 pm. The Allies had attacked with 13,500 men and 3000 of them were dead, wounded or missing. As darkness came the survivors wandered about like zombies, then lay down in the cold and the rain. Hamilton wrote that on the 28th he saw 'our men scatter right and left before an enemy they would have gone for with a cheer on the 25th or 26th'. Now he was worrying that he had no reserves. His diary takes on a dithery voice. It bothers him that the troops he had commanded before Kitchener sent him out here are 'loafing around London'. Von Sanders has reinforcements and he doesn't.

The First Battle of Krithia was a watershed, although such things always take on sharper form with hindsight. It said that the plans Hamilton and his staff had made in Egypt and Mudros were not going to work. The peninsula could not be taken in one bold stroke. And it could not be taken, either by *coup de main* or by attrition, with five divisions. As Aspinall wrote years later, on the 26th and the morning of the 27th the door to Achi Baba was still ajar. After the First Battle of Krithia it was bolted and barred.

Hamilton now behaves as we would expect. He is enough of a soldier to know things are going badly and, on the inside, becomes fluttery and anxious. He knows soldiers well enough to understand that the men of the 29th Division, good as they are, have been asked to do too much, to bleed too often, and that when they aren't bleeding they spend their time carrying water and supplies from the beach. He knows Hunter-Weston's handling of the Y Beach landing was unconscionable. Yet Hamilton, so brave in the field, shrinks from personal confrontation. He doesn't reprimand Hunter-Weston. 'Least said, soonest mended,' he writes in his diary. He knows he should tell Kitchener how badly things are going, but he doesn't want to sound like a malcontent, so he tells him 'all continues to go well'. He knows he needs reinforcements but doesn't want to anger Kitchener by behaving like the generals in the other theatres. Instead of asking for men, he asks for small-arms ammunition. He gets reinforcements only because two admirals make it easy for him.

Admiral Guépratte, the French naval commander,

signalled his superior in Malta on April 26 that Hamilton's force was 'insufficient for such extensive operations'. The message was repeated to London. On the 27th de Robeck told the Admiralty of Hamilton's difficulties. Kitchener at once cabled to Hamilton: 'If you want more troops from Egypt Maxwell will give you any support from Egyptian garrison you may require.'

That night Hamilton asked for more troops (his cable crossed Kitchener's) but timidly, like a man trying to obtain a bank overdraft by suggesting he won't use it.

Thanks to the weather and wonderfully fine spirit of our troops all continues to go well . . . May I have a call on 42nd East Lancs Territorial Division in case I should need them? You may be sure I shall not call up a man unless I really need him.

Note, in passing, another splendid example of military English from the period: all continues to go well – so well, in fact, that I need another division.

The 42nd Division, territorials from Lancashire, had been in Egypt for seven months. Kitchener now told Maxwell to send them to Gallipoli, where they arrived on May 6. Maxwell also offered the Australian Light Horse and the New Zealand Mounted Rifles as infantry; the first brigades of these sailed on May 9. The French also decided to send a second division.

The numbers looked better, but only because the Allies didn't know what von Sanders was doing. He quickly garnered three more divisions, two from Constantinople and one from Smyrna, as well as heavy guns from Adrianople. By April 30 von Sanders had 75 battalions to Hamilton's 53. And there was another matter: at both Helles and Anzac, the Turks held the high ground.

* * *

Helles was working its way towards a siege; Anzac had already got there. By the 28th many of Birdwood's troops had been fighting for four days without sleep. Hamilton sent four battalions of the RND to Anzac to take over part of the line while Australians and New Zealanders briefly rested near the beach south of Shrapnel Gully. By the standards of France, it was hardly a rest area: no bars, no girls and always the pitter-patter of shrapnel. Margetts said the men of the 12th Battalion, among the first to be relieved, scratched 'little holes' to protect them from Turkish artillery. But they were happy.

> No message was more gratifying as hardly any of us had had any sleep since the previous Friday night; we all had beards, no-one had washed, and very few of us had found time to respond to the calls of nature. I think another 24 hours and most of our nerves would have been absolutely ruined. For my own part I had no overcoat, my trousers were torn to ribbons, and my boots were laden with mud, but, nevertheless, dirty, weary, and cold though we were, we had the satisfaction of knowing we had done what was asked of us . . . It was almost pathetic to see how one man would greet a pal who had been separated from him in the fight and whom he thought was either wounded or killed.

Margetts thought the English marines in their sun helmets the 'most amusing' soldiers he had seen. 'The subaltern in charge of the party on my left was about 18 years old and a typical English Sub. Every time a big gun fired, either our guns or the enemy's, he bobbed his head and once he remarked: "They pop some!"' Malone wrote: 'Such *boys* they look.' Birdwood described the marines as 'children under untrained officers'. The children trudged up to the frontline in a thunderstorm and either died or grew up fast. The marines were certainly nervy.

McNicoll was worn out. On the night of the 28th he scraped a hollow, spread his greatcoat and fell asleep. He woke up after midnight. Rain was falling and the hollow was filling up. He decided he didn't care. He went back to sleep in the pool. Late next day the Deal Battalion of the RND relieved McNicoll's troops.

A few days later word came down that the Deal boys had the 'jumps'. McNicoll went to the firing line to see the Deal commander, Lieutenant-Colonel Bendyshe. One of the marines began to stare at McNicoll, who was dirty and unshaven. The marine began to stand up. 'Don't stand up, man,' Bendyshe said, 'your head will be over the parapet.'

'Yes, sir,' the man said, raising his rifle, aiming at McNicoll and firing. He missed McNicoll and shot Bendyshe dead. Marines ran along the trench firing. An English sergeant-major and several others fell shot. The marines tried to bayonet McNicoll. He caught one bayonet in his hand and it grazed his shoulder.

The marines knocked him down. A sergeant told a marine to rest his bayonet on McNicoll's chest and shoot him if he spoke. The 'spy' was relieved of his notebooks and revolver, trussed and blindfolded and marched to the rear. The first man the party met was the adjutant of the 6th Battalion, whose profanities were said to have upheld the highest standards of the AIF. McNicoll was taken to the field ambulance on the beach. Birdwood came to congratulate him on his escape from the British.

The night before this incident, a RND stretcher-bearer, wounded at least four times, became the first Victoria

Cross winner of Anzac. The award wasn't announced until June, 1917. By then Lance-Corporal Walter Parker had been invalided out of the marines with a war gratuity of £10.

If the Australians thought the marines strange, the Englishmen must have thought the same of the Australians. Bean told of the men who came out of the hills.

> Bearded, ragged at knees and elbows, their puttees often left in the scrub, dull-eyed, many with blood on cheeks and clothes, and with a dirty field dressing round arm or wrist, they were far fiercer than Turks to look upon. They had long since taken the wire hoops from their caps in order to break the obvious outline which too often had showed like a disc in the scrub. Many had learned to wear for camouflage a spray of holly over the peaks of their caps or in the bands of their battered and bullet-torn Australian hats. Officers were often indistinguishable from men . . . Many wandered in a half-sleep, like tired children . . . [Men] went to sleep with the food still in their hands.

Now, for the first time since the landing, the accounting could begin. Margetts' battalion assembled on the beach.

> . . . we were all surprised to see each other. Only six officers out of a total of 30 who landed, turned up . . . I was put in charge of B company and one strength was about 84 men out of a total of 213 who landed. Then we proceeded to eat, and we were well fed and had our first drink of tea; it was glorious.

The 12 battalions of the 1st Australian Division had

each landed with roughly 970 men. Eight battalions were down to half strength; the 7th had lost 524 men. Braund wept at the rollcall of his 2nd Battalion. Casualties over the 12 battalions to noon on April 30 amounted to 4931, or roughly one-in-three. Of this, 495 were known to be dead. Many of the 1963 listed as missing were also dead. And some of those walking about the rest area, officially alive and unhurt, were carrying wounds they had not bothered to report. (Late in the campaign, a private who had been in pain for months sought out a doctor and explained, half-apologising, that he was having 'a little trouble'. The doctor diagnosed him as having dysentery, a compound fracture of the arm, two bullets in the thigh and bullet wounds to the liver and diaphragm.) The figure for wounded from the 1st Division was put at 2468. Many of these too had died, either on the transports taking them off or in hospitals in Egypt.

On May 31 Oliver Cumberland was still in Cairo recovering from his wound on the first day. When he had left the firing line, his brother, Joe, was unhurt. Now he wrote to his sister, Una, at Scone.

I am quite well now and expect to go back to the front any time, but Una, prepare yourself to hear the worst if you have not already heard it – poor Joe is gone – he died of wounds in Alexandria hospital on the 5th of May. I did not know until yesterday, I went to headquarters offices in Cairo and saw the list of killed and wounded. I had been very anxious wondering where he was, and when I saw the list I did not know what to do. I wandered about the streets nearly mad, I felt so lonely . . . If I can get away for a couple of hours when I pass through Alexandria, on my way back to the front, I will visit the hospital where he died and see if he left any message.

We do not know when Joe was wounded, except that it was before May 1. Una eventually received a brown-paper parcel. Joe's effects comprised a pocket knife, a pencil, eraser, hairbrush, hymn books, a gift box, photos and cards.

For statistical purposes the 'landing' phase at Anzac is assumed to run to May 3. For these nine days casualties are put at about 8500 – Australians, New Zealanders and 600 British marines. Of these, 2300 were dead. Turkish casualties for the first ten days at Anzac are estimated at 14,000. Even at the start of June Australians at home had no notion of the extent of casualties or the truth about the Dardanelles war. The daily newspapers of June 1 listed casualties of 5034, including 688 killed. Readers were not told the Anzacs were clinging to the peninsula by their fingernails. A few days earlier the papers had carried a report from London 'confirming' that the fortress at Kilitbahir had been destroyed. The *Argus* of May 29 reported that 'everyone in the Allies' army in the Dardanelles is showing the most confident optimism'.

We should not be surprised that casualty figures were running months behind. The significance of the press reporting is simply this: young men were lining up at recruiting centres with a fraudulent picture of the war in their heads; and families who had sons at Gallipoli were living with false hopes.

British casualties at Helles to April 30 were 4453. The French had incurred 1779 at Kum Kale and in the First Battle of Krithia. On May 1 the strength of the 29th Division was down to 6746. The Dublin Fusiliers Battalion could field only one officer and 344 men.

Hamilton ran into a large batch of wounded from the First Battle of Krithia.

I spoke to as many of them as I could, and although some were terribly mutilated and disfigured, and although a few others were clearly dying, one and all kept a stiff upper lip – one and all were, or managed to appear – more than content – happy!

One can only wonder at the general's ability to see what he wanted to see.

Within a week Anzac had become a frantic city of caves and dugouts and sandbags and biscuit boxes. It had the bustle of a mining camp: piles of orange clay everywhere, smoke from cooking fires, the thud of picks and the scrape of shovels, as though the next stroke would expose some glittering reef. And of course it was nothing like a mining camp. Mining camps don't have corpses, bloated and sickly-sweet, lying within a few yards of the diggings. Maybe the better analogy is with a prison. That's the way a hawk soaring high above would have seen it. The hawk would have seen two lines of spewed-up earth. The Australians and New Zealanders were digging in so that the Turks would not get in. A few yards away the Turks were digging in, most noticeably in front of Pope's and Courtney's, so that the Anzacs would not get out.

Everyone who visited Anzac wondered at its theatricality. Hamilton went ashore on the 29th.

No-one has ever seen so strange a spectacle and I very much doubt if anyone will ever see it again. The Australians and New Zealanders had fixed themselves into the crests of a series of high sandy cliffs, covered, wherever they were not quite sheer, with box scrub. These cliffs were not in the least like what they had seemed to be through our glasses when we reconnoitred them at a distance of a mile or more from the shore. Still less were they like what I had originally imagined them to be from the map. Their features were tumbled, twisted, scarred – unclimbable, one would have said, were it not that their faces were now pock-marked with caves like large sand-martin holes, wherein the men were resting or taking refuge from the sniping. From the trenches that ran along the crest a hot fire was being kept up, and swarms of bullets sang through the air, far overhead for the most part, to drop into the sea that lay around us. Yet all the time there were full five hundred men fooling about stark naked on the water's edge or swimming, shouting and enjoying themselves as it might be at Margate. Not a sign to show that they possess the things called nerves.

On the same day Bean was sketching the scene in his diary, which is a better read than his official history. He sees four jetties made from pontoons, crowded with barges and trawlers, and warships out to sea. Mules line the beach; occasionally one goes mad, kicking and spinning, head down and snorting, until it dislodges its load. The kits the men left behind on the first day are scattered around piles of biscuit boxes. Every now and then one sees a flash from the warships followed by a *crump*. Bean says the noise seems to hit the hill 'as with a flat hand', shaking it, but one doesn't notice the noise or the earthquake. It's just part of life at Anzac. So is the tap-tap of rifle fire, although it seems to be right above rather than up on the second ridge. The 'overs' plop into the Aegean.

Imbros and Samothrace begin to show up grey against the evening rose – the scene is perfectly exquisite – rose pink on the horizon, the sun's track broad upon the sea, the transports and their smoke haze, the black shapes of

The odd couple: Winston Churchill, First Lord of the Admiralty, and Lord 'Jackie' Fisher, First Sea Lord. They started off liking each other, but the marriage was always going to fail. Fisher was sentimental about ships and Churchill wasn't; Churchill believed in the Dardanelles adventure and Fisher didn't; Fisher was too flighty and Churchill too ambitious.

The romantic: Rupert Brooke, the golden youth who saw the war as a grand adventure. His poetry gushed and bubbled like a burst water pipe. Brooke died, probably from blood poisoning, two days before he was to take part in the Gallipoli landings. Had he survived the war, Brooke would surely have thought his own poetry foolish. *[Imperial War Museum Q 71073]*

The reality: wounded being taken off Anzac Cove in early May. The wounded from Anzac and Helles went through ordeals as bad as anything in the Crimean War 60 years earlier. After the landings, one hospital ship ended up carrying 850 wounded – and two doctors to look after them.

[Australian War Memorial C02679]

Death of a battleship: under the Asian hills, the *Bouvet*, holed by a Turkish mine and hissing red-tinged steam, begins her death dive. *[IWM SP 682]*

Australian troops being towed towards the Anzac beachhead just after dawn, April 25, 1915. *[AWM P02194.003]*

One of the first things some of the Australians saw on April 25: the Sphinx to the north of Anzac Cove, sheer and fluted and yellow; an erosion in progress and just about unclimbable. The dawn service is now held below the Sphinx. *[AWM C01488]*

What the British saw as they tried to land from the *River Clyde* at V Beach. Note the dead and wounded in the bows and on the shore. Seddülbahir castle on the right looks much the same today, old and Arthurian and forever. *[AWM A03076]*

The Anzac beachhead: piles of stores and naked bathers, Australians and New Zealanders, mules and their Indian drivers, rickety piers and dugouts made from sandbags and tarpaulins, all the bustle of a mining camp. The cove is about 600 paces long. The headland of Ari Burnu and the lower slopes of Plugge's Plateau are on the horizon. Shrapnel Gully runs inland from the lower right of the photo. Corps headquarters lay on the slopes above the piers. A bitumen road now runs above the beach. North Beach, the Sphinx and Fisherman's Hut lie behind Ari Burnu. *[AWM H03500]*

Dugouts at Anzac with Plugge's Plateau in the background. Some dugouts were simply big rabbit burrows, heavy with the smell of clay; Charles Bean described them as a cross between a grave and a cave. Others were more elaborate, with galvanised-iron roofs on which earth had been piled as protection against shrapnel pellets, a waterproof sheet for a door and sandbags for walls. Candles provided the light. Thus did Australians and New Zealanders, privates and generals, live for eight months. *[AWM H03929]*

Mustafa Kemal (fourth from left) staring down the camera with those hard eyes that saw too much and knew too much. Kemal had the ruthlessness and sureness that Ian Hamilton lacked. As Atatürk, he became president of Turkey and one of the great reforming figures of the 20th century. *[AWM PO1141.001]*

Enver, who thought he was Napoleon. *[AWM H19408]*

General Otto Liman von Sanders, the methodical German cavalryman who commanded the Turkish forces at Gallipoli. *[IWM Q 95324]*

Talat of the gypsy eyes.

Sir Ian Hamilton, the Allied commander-in-chief, on the day he left Gallipoli after being sacked. He was always chivalrous and seldom ruthless. His strength of character as a man, that blithe spirit, was his weakness as a commander. *[AWM H10350]*

They called him the soul of Anzac and the Australians and New Zealanders were probably fortunate to have him as their corps commander. Sir William Birdwood got around the trenches at a brisk walk, feeling pulses, talking to gunners, grave-diggers, colonels, whoever he ran into. He liked Australians and didn't try to change them too much. In the 1930s he tried and failed to become Governor-General of Australia. *[AWM G01222]*

They called him the butcher of Helles, although others claimed he was a 'logician of war'. Lieutenant-General Sir Aylmer Hunter-Weston commanded the British forces at Helles until his 'breakdown'. Before that he had broken down several British divisions. His speciality was the frontal attack in daylight.
[AWM H10293]

Kitchener of Khartoum, massive, square-headed, russet-cheeked and cross-eyed. There was a 'mystic union' between him and the British people after he won the battle of Omdurman in 1898 and was seen to have avenged the killing of Charles Gordon. During the Great War, Kitchener was secretive, made up policy as he went along, tried to be a commander-in-chief and a Cabinet minister at the same time, and generally failed to live up to the promise he had never shown. *[AWM A03547]*

Looking like a mortician, which may have had a certain symbolism for the New Zealanders he once led, Sir Alexander Godley, commander of the New Zealand and Australian Division, attends an Anzac memorial service in London in 1948. *[AWM 134755]*

Brigadier-General Brudenell White (left), the outstanding Australian staff officer who had much to do with the planning of the Anzac evacuation, and Lieutenant-Colonel Howse, the country doctor from NSW who won the VC in the Boer War. Howse spoke of the 'criminal negligence' of the British medical authorities at Gallipoli. *[AWM G01329]*

William Throsby Bridges, commander of the 1st Australian Division, who died from a leg wound in May. Shy and gruff and unknowable, he found grace as death approached. *[Image Library, State Library of New South Wales P1/B]*

Lieutenant-Colonel Charles 'Dick' Doughty-Wylie, VC, one of the grand figures of the Gallipoli campaign. His grave, on a hill above Seddülbahir castle, is the only one-man Allied cemetery on Gallipoli.

Private John Simpson Kirkpatrick (right) with two friends at Blackboy Hill Camp, Western Australia, in 1914. The skeleton was used to instruct stretcher bearers. *[AWM A03116]*

Commodore Roger Keyes.
[IWM Q 22960]

Major-General Walter Braithwaite.
[AWM H10350]

Charles Bean. Phillip Schuler, the
Age correspondent at Gallipoli,
called him 'the most enthusiastic,
painstaking and conscientious
worker I have ever met'. [AWM G01561]

Vice-Admiral John de Robeck.
[AWM H10350]

A blindfolded Turkish envoy is carried by bathers into the Anzac position to negotiate terms for a truce to bury Turks killed in the mass attack of May 19. *[AWM G00989]*

This Turk died in a kneeling position during the attack of May 19. His body stayed in that position for several days, then toppled over. *[AWM P02321.011]*

The truce: Turkish and Anzac soldiers in no-man's land. A Turkish captain told an English officer: 'At this spectacle even the most gentle must feel savage, and the most savage must weep.' *[AWM H03954]*

the barges, the pinnaces dragging great creases across the yellow satin surface . . . today Samothrace is covered with a cap of snow . . .

Anzac had taken less than a week to assume a character and the character would stick. Anzac was grubby when you looked at the corpses and beautiful when you looked across the satin to Samothrace. You had to know you were alive here. Death was everywhere, in the air and in the sounds coming from second ridge. Death was there when you rolled a smoke or told a joke or carted water. Day and night it was there. And its nearness made you feel so thrillingly alive. Many who outlived this place could not settle down when they returned home. They had never been so aware they were alive as when they were here, close to death.

Helles at this time was far from safe; the Turks shelled it from Asia and Achi Baba. But there was space behind the beaches at V and W. Horses could be driven and bicycles ridden. The front was a few miles up the Krithia road. W and V beaches were like jumping-off places; the gold rush was inland. Hamilton likened W to an ants' nest in revolution.

Five hundred of our fighting men are running to and fro between cliffs and sea carrying stones wherewith to improve our pier. On this pier, picket boats, launches, dinghies, barges, all converge through the heavy swell with shouts and curses, bumps and hair's-breadth escapes. Other swarms of half-naked soldiers are sweating, hauling, unloading, loading, roadmaking; dragging mules up the cliff, pushing mules down the cliff: hundreds more are bathing, and through this pandemonium pass the quiet stretchers bearing pale, blood-stained, smiling burdens.

The blood-red poppies swayed in the wind along the Krithia road. Patches of them could be seen on Achi Baba. The hill was a long way off and they looked rust coloured – like a bloodstain, someone said.

The Turks counter-attacked at Helles on the night of May 1. Enver the politician had telegraphed from Constantinople that the British should be driven into the sea; von Sanders the soldier would know how to work out the details. Von Sanders had no trouble working out one thing: it had to be a night attack. That way his troops would be unseen by the fleet's guns. Colonel von Sodenstern, the German commander of the 5th Division, had taken charge at Helles. He tried to sound like Napoleon and even implied that he was a convert to Islam.

Soldiers! You must drive into the sea the enemy who are in Seddülbahir . . . You must believe that the greatest happiness awaits him who gives up his life in this Holy War. Attack the enemy with the bayonet and utterly destroy him! We shall not retire one step back; for if we do our religion, our country and our nation will perish! Soldiers! The world is looking at you! Your only hope of salvation is to bring this battle to a successful issue or gloriously to give up your life in the attempt.

The Turks attacked after 10 pm with bayonets. The orders said rifles were not to be loaded. Special squads were to burn the British boats on the beach so that no invaders could escape. The Turks shouted 'Allah' and broke the Allied line in two places, one in the British sector, one in the French. The British quickly reclaimed their lost trenches; the French were in trouble. It was a furious and confused battle, the night rent by bloodcurdling cries and lit up by star bombs and the green, red and white parabolas from Turkish signalling pistols. Hamilton, now on the *Arcadian*, watched it for several hours and wondered what was happening. Was his force being thrown back into the sea? Hunter-Weston eventually told him the attack had been repulsed and Hamilton gave the order for a counter-attack. The worn-out British took ground from the Turks at first, then had to return to their starting points. Two RND battalions were sent to reinforce the French line, where Senegalese troops, under artillery fire for the first time, had fled. The ground was strewn with Turkish dead. The French had suffered more than 2100 casualties and the British 678. Among the British casualties were five battalion commanders.

The Turks attacked the French again on the night of May 3. Again the Senegalese broke. Cooks and orderlies were rushed to the firing line. French artillery pieces grew so hot their paint melted. At dawn the Turks withdrew. Eight battalions of the Turkish 15th Division had landed near Eceabat on the morning of May 3. They had been marched 20 miles and thrown straight into the battle. It took a week to round up the survivors and get them back to their battalions.

Von Sanders couldn't go on losing men like this. Von Sodenstern had been wounded in the knee. Von Sanders told General Weber, the new commander at Helles, to revert to defence and to dig his trenches as close as possible to the enemy's. That way the fleet could not fire on them. Von Sanders refused requests that his forces be allowed to retreat and defend the peninsula from Achi Baba. His reasoning was simple. The further north one went, the wider the peninsula became. The wider it became, the more men were needed to defend it. Besides, Achi Baba was too easy a target for the fleet.

Hamilton also needed to change his style. He couldn't sit and let the enemy come to him, howling in the dark like a nightmare. He didn't have the numbers for an offensive, nor anything like the artillery ammunition needed; but he had to go forward.

Birdwood also needed to do something. The Turks had to be thrown off Baby 700, which meant they also had to be thrown off the Chessboard, their grid of trenches in front of Pope's, off Dead Man's Ridge and the Nek. The Turks at these places could fire into the back of Quinn's, the most forward of the Anzac positions, now held by Monash's 4th Brigade. Quinn's was an affront to military logic, a fortress built by desperates. The Australian and Turkish lines were only yards apart; the Turks knew Captain Quinn's name and imitated some of his common commands. Behind Quinn's and Pope's the east wall of Monash Valley is a cliff. Troops climbed it at night by hanging on to a rope. Someone said that one looked up at Quinn's as one might look at a haunted house.

Birdwood told Godley to take Baby 700. It was on Godley's side of the front. Godley agreed readily enough: he was always pleasant to his superiors. Birdwood wanted an attack involving Godley's troops – the New Zealand Infantry Brigade and Monash's 4th Brigade – and the 1st Australian Brigade, which would capture Mortar Ridge and advance along it. General Walker had taken over the 1st after MacLaurin's death. He thought the plan muddle-headed and said so. His concerns were the exhaustion of his troops and the gap between his forces and Godley's. Walker talked Bridges, his divisional commander, out of the attack. Monash also thought the plan flawed – his engineer's mind didn't like the half-baked – but Monash had not the sway of Walker, the professional soldier. He couldn't talk Godley out of it. Godley, Monash later said, belonged to the 'Army Clique'; he didn't take 'amateurs' seriously. His forces would attack alone.

The attack – it had to be at night – was set down for May 2. Monash received Godley's orders at 2.15 pm, five hours before the attack was to begin, which gave him little chance to discuss them with the Otago and Canterbury battalions which would be going forward on his left.

Monash's troops ran out into a storm of fire when the bombardment ended. Those waiting to support them could be heard singing *Tipperary* and *Australia Will Be There*. The Australians dug in about 100 yards ahead of their starting point. Baby 700 was too far away. And the Otagos had not turned up. They were still filing up Monash Valley when they should have been on the ridge. Johnston, now over his illness and commanding the New Zealand Infantry Brigade, had mistimed things; he would fumble many times more before this campaign was over. When they did arrive, the Otagos were promptly shot up badly. The earlier Australian attack had warned the Turks, who were now firing star shells over the Anzac front. Some of the New Zealanders took two or three steps over the crest and were killed. About half the Otago troops were killed or wounded; the Quinn's Post cemetery is thick with their headstones.

Chaos set in. Johnston and Godley didn't know what was happening. This didn't stop them assuming things they had no right to assume. Godley figured the Otagos must be near Baby 700 and ordered the Canterburys to attack over the Nek. He then sent British marines to support Monash.

Dawn revealed a panorama of confusion: dead and wounded Australians and New Zealanders all about, men dribbling back, others trying to hold the trenches they had dug in the night, men looking for their officers, men looking for orders, British marines unsure of what they were supposed to be doing. The last Australians returned to their starting trenches on the night of May 3. One thousand casualties for no ground gained. The Turks had been presented with new trenches that they worked into the Chessboard. Monash's brigade, which had a nominal strength of 4000, was down to 1770 men.

Bean went to see Monash after the battle and saw Australian dead 'lying like ants, shrivelled up or curled up, some still hugging their rifles'. Bean wrote in his diary that Monash 'seemed a little shaken' and talked of 'disaster'. He was entitled to. His brigade had been crippled for no gain. The plan had been flawed, scrambled together, and it was doomed when the Otagos turned up late. Godley and Johnston must have known the battalion had been delayed. Why hadn't Monash been told?

It was Monash's first offensive and he had learnt much. His superiors weren't that smart. They didn't understand about detail and preparation. The Godleys lived in the world of hunt clubs and the Indian Raj; they took pride in muddling through; they knew how to rationalise failure and to protect their own.

It was also Godley's first offensive at Gallipoli. As Christopher Pugsley points out in *Gallipoli: The New Zealand Story*, the general learnt nothing. He made no criticism of Johnston. The brigade commander, a regular from the British army, was a member of his 'club'. Godley's report was an essay in subterfuge.

The net result as regards gain of ground was nil but it is believed that heavy casualties were inflicted upon the Turks, and that the operation was very valuable in demonstrating to them that our force was capable of determined offensive effort. It also had the effect of completely stopping the enemy's sharpshooting for several days.

The affair rates one sentence in Godley's memoirs. If the attack on Baby 700 was just another of Gallipoli's lesser tragedies, it had an importance beyond that. Godley, Johnston and Monash would come together again in the August offensive and Godley and Johnston would do much the same things again.

Hamilton decided he had to go forward at Helles, and by May 6. By then he would have one brigade of the 42nd Division ashore. Birdwood met Hamilton on the *Arcadian* on the morning of May 3. Birdwood obviously didn't know how badly Godley's attack had failed. He told Hamilton he had straightened out his line on the left and felt safer. Hamilton asked him to send two infantry brigades to Helles for the coming advance. Which is how the 2nd Australian Brigade and the New Zealand Infantry Brigade came to be part of the Second Battle of Krithia.

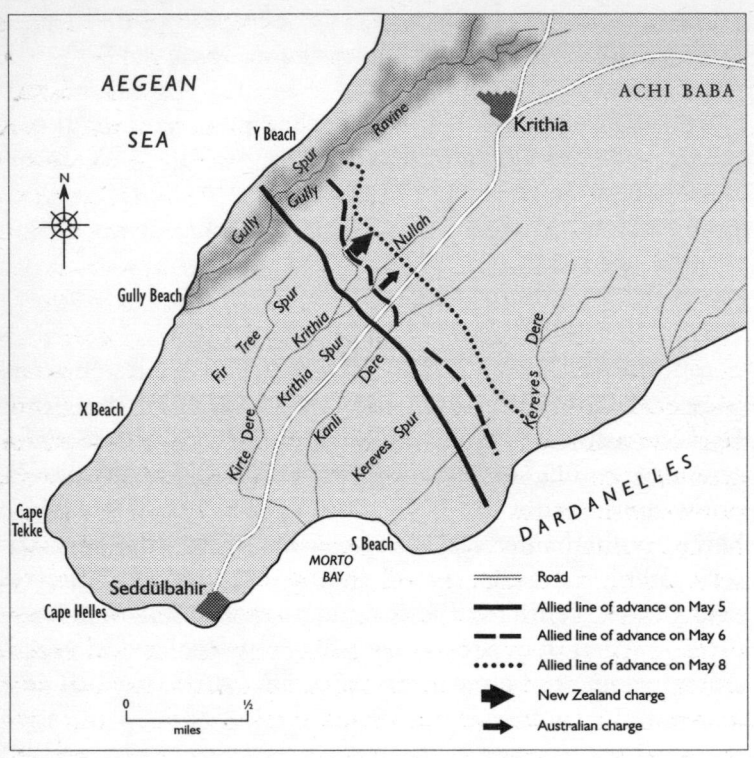

AEGEAN
SEA

ACHI BABA

Y Beach

Krithia

Gully
Ravine

Gully
Spur

Gully
Nullah

Gully Beach

Fir Tree
Spur

Krithia

Krithia Spur

Kirte Dere

Krithia
Dere

Kanli

Kereves Spur

Kereves Dere

X Beach

Cape
Tekke

DARDANELLES

S Beach

MORTO
BAY

Seddülbahir

Cape Helles

N

〜〜〜	Road
▬▬▬	Allied line of advance on May 5
▬ ▬ ▬	Allied line of advance on May 6
• • • • •	Allied line of advance on May 8
➤	New Zealand charge
→	Australian charge

0   ½
miles

The second battle of Krithia

13

Krithia, battle done badly

Once, after a conversation with the impish Lord Beaverbrook, Rudyard Kipling scribbled his ode to press barons. They were like harlots, he said. They wanted power without responsibility. Ian Hamilton was no press baron, which may explain why at the Dardanelles he settled to have things the other way around.

He was a gentleman and he had integrity, so of course he took the responsibility. He lacked arrogance and cared about good manners, so he allowed others to steal his powers, then felt sorry for himself after the thieves had gone off and created another shambles. After the second day of the Second Battle of Krithia, marooned on the *Arcadian* and receiving one bad report after the other, he wrote:

In France these reports would have been impersonal messages arriving from afar. In Asia or Africa I would have been letting off the steam by galloping to d'Amade or Hunter-Weston. Here I was neither one thing nor the other: neither a new-fangled commander sitting cool and semi-detached in an office; nor an old-fashioned commander taking personal direction of the show.

When the plans were being prepared, Hamilton wanted the attack of May 6 to begin an hour before dawn. There was sense to this. Much of the ground at Helles is open farmland, good for machine gunners waiting in the copses and the gullies, bad for infantrymen running with bayonets and hearts that threaten to pop out of their chests. And Hamilton was badly short of artillery ammunition: he couldn't put up much of a barrage for the men advancing in the sun. The navy was also short of ammunition because it was still living the dream: it was hoarding shells for use at Constantinople. There was another, and more serious, problem with the artillery. The British didn't know where the Turks were. Even the 15-inch guns of the *Queen Elizabeth* were just a loud noise if all they were hitting was standing wheat and mulberry trees.

Hunter-Weston was against an advance in the dark. He had lost too many company commanders, he said. The men might get lost. Throughout his time at Gallipoli, Hunter-Weston always wanted to do things within bankers' hours. Ten o'clock was a good time to start and eleven even better; six in the evening was a good time to finish. Hamilton deferred to him again. According to Hamilton, Hunter-Weston thought it was best to blaze away freely with the artillery 'and to trust to our bayonets when we get in'. Hamilton and Hunter-Weston ended up planning an old-fashioned battle. The Greeks outside Troy in 1184 BC might have thought it guileless.

The Allies would rely on luck: they would discover what they were up against as the battle went along. They would advance at 11 am, a sensible hour, capture Krithia sometime in the afternoon and take Achi Baba at another sensible hour, sometime before dark. With the arrival of the one brigade of the 42nd Division, the Indian Brigade and the two Anzac brigades, Hunter-Weston had about 25,000 troops, most of them worn out. How many Turks were in front of them? No-one knew. The guess was something between 15,000 and 20,000. (This turned out to be accurate.) Where were the Turks? No-one knew. Aircraft had spotted a few trenches in front of Krithia. But where was the main line? On the left facing the British or on the right facing the French and protecting the Dardanelles? Was it in front of Krithia or in front of Achi Baba? Did the Turks have a system of trenches or merely foxholes here and there? Hunter-Weston's troops would find out as they went along.

No-one had thought much about the terrain either. It wasn't as soft as it looked. It looks like one plain rising gently towards Achi Baba and it isn't. Four watercourses turn it into four fingers. On the left is Gully Ravine, the great gorge emptying into the Aegean. The land between this and the Aegean is Gully Spur. Around Krithia, two smaller watercourses start to flow south before turning abruptly to empty into Morto Bay. Krithia Nullah is the next gully on the left after Gully Ravine; the land between the two is Fir Tree Spur, about 1000 yards across and wooded. The next gully is Kanli Dere. The land between this and Krithia Nullah is Krithia Spur, about half-a-mile across and mostly bare in 1915. The big ravine on the right is Kereves Dere; the land between this and Kanli Dere is Kereves Spur.

The French had the front between Kanli Dere and the Dardanelles. They were to advance about a mile, get astride Kereves Dere and dig in. Their left flank would be the pivotal point for the British. When the 29th Division was in line with the French left flank, the British would swing right and take Krithia after moving up Gully and Fir Tree spurs. The British would do as little as possible on

Krithia Spur because it was too exposed. The capture of Krithia would complete stage two of Hunter-Weston's master plan. Orders for stage three were to be given later. In fact, they were never issued.

The orders for the first two phases arrived late. The brigades received them at 4 am on the morning of the battle. The French started 40 minutes late; for the day, they gained about 400 yards. On Gully Spur, around Y Beach, the British were halted by a storm of fire from machine guns. On Fir Tree Spur they made about 400 yards. Soon after noon the advance was in trouble everywhere, even though there had been no contact with the Turkish main body.

Around this time came an interlude of burlesque. A cable arrived at GHQ from the War Office. Hamilton had told London two days earlier that he urgently needed artillery shells. The cable now in front of him read: 'The ammunition supply for your force was never calculated on the basis of a prolonged occupation of the peninsula. It is important to push on.'

Hunter-Weston pushed on the next day. Plan A having failed the day before, he did the logical thing and used it again. Again the bombardment did little damage. As Aspinall wrote in the official history: 'Unaware of the enemy's positions, the gunners had to search the whole front and depth of the objective – an area of ten-and-a-half square miles – and the result was ineffective.' Hunter-Weston did start an hour earlier on the second day. Again the advance stalled just after noon. At 4.30 pm the 29th tried to go forward along Fir Tree Spur. The New Zealand Brigade moved up behind it. At dusk the British and French frontlines were in much the same positions as at the end of the first day. Casualties for the two days had been relatively light.

Plan A having failed twice, Hunter-Weston naturally gave it a third chance. There were small changes to the plan. This time the New Zealanders, rather than the 29th, were to attack along Fir Tree Spur and take Krithia. As Aspinall put it: 'Four weak [he meant numerically] battalions of New Zealanders were to attack, in full daylight, a position held by at least nine battalions of Turks.' This time Hamilton came ashore with Aspinall and set up a command post on a hill above Helles. Aspinall wrote of the scene and rather proved that a thing of beauty is not necessarily a joy forever, or even until noon.

> The grassy slopes that crown the cliffs are carpeted with flowers. The azure sky is cloudless; the air is fragrant with the scent of wild thyme. In front, beyond a smiling valley studded with cypress and olive and patches of young corn, the ground rises gently to the village of Krithia, standing amidst clumps of mulberry and oak; and thence more steeply to a frowning ridge beyond, its highest point like the hump of a camel's back. Away to the right, edged with a ribbon of silvery sand, lie the sapphire arc of Morto Bay, the glistening Dardanelles, and the golden fields of Troy.

Aspinall wasn't cavorting with fairies with names like Byron and Keats; on spring mornings, the peninsula can look as gorgeous as this and it steals your heart. It looks just as beautiful in the evening. By dusk on this day, however, no one would be much taken with the crimson lights behind Imbros. You do not admire sunsets when standing in a charnel house.

Ashmead-Bartlett watched the battle and thought it seemed like something out of antiquity. Hamilton could see the whole panorama. The world would not see many more battles like this: the general on the hill, staff fussing around him; horse lines on the beach; the music of bugles and drums; bayonets glittering on the plain; French troops protesting the drabness of modern war by lining up in blue jackets and red trousers and then wondering why the Turks seemed to like shooting at them. More so than Leipzig, Ashmead-Bartlett felt, this was the battle of the nations: Ottomans from Bulgaria to Syria and a hundred places in between; English, Scots and Irish; Australians and New Zealanders; French, Algerians and Senegalese; Sikhs, Punjabis and Gurkhas; émigré Jews from eastern Europe brought together as the Zion Mule Corps.

Everyone sees Achi Baba differently. Ashmead-Bartlett saw it as a Chinese idol with a 'stupid-looking head', short thick-set shoulders and two long arms stretching out either side to the sea. It looked to have been put there to devour all the soldiers, guns and material disgorged from the ships, he thought. Below Achi Baba lay a 'beautiful and fertile' garden: olives groves, Turkish oaks, Scottish firs, apricots and almonds, white orchids and rock roses, white marguerites and yellow clover. As he rode about, Ashmead-Bartlett also noted that the garden was tainted: over there a dead man crumpled up in a tattered uniform; over here a hastily dug grave; up ahead broken rifles and barbed wire.

The bombardment began at 10.15 am. If it was more impressive today, the ships and the batteries were still firing blind, aiming at clumps of scrub and shadows in ravines in the hope that they hid the Turkish army. Then the British lines began to go forward. The French couldn't go forward: the position in front of them, to the west of Kereves Dere, turned out to be the Turkish main body. By noon the attack had failed for the third successive day. And the New Zealanders had made their sacrifice on the altar of Achi Baba.

* * *

Colonel Malone, the farmer from Taranaki, liked the look of Helles, the spaciousness, these open plains, the olive groves and wheat fields, men on horses, roads even. This was the way war was supposed to be. A man could understand what was going on here. Anzac was an asylum, cramped and feverish. 'It is a relief to get in where war is being waged scientifically and where we are clear of the Australians,' he wrote in his diary.

At 8.55 am on May 8 Colonel Johnston received his orders to advance up Fir Tree Spur. He called in his battalion commanders and told them they were going to take Krithia. Malone's Wellingtons would be on the left, the Aucklanders in the centre and the Canterburys on the right. The Otagos, so badly mauled in the attack on Baby 700 a few days earlier, would stay in reserve. When Johnston finished talking the battalion commanders had only 20 minutes to brief their men.

The men went forward not knowing much more than that somewhere up ahead, somewhere past the Turkish lines, lay the windmills and granaries of Krithia. They ran into a storm of shrapnel and machine-gun fire, yet somehow made 400 yards. Machine guns from Gully Ravine tore into the side of the Wellingtons. Casualties piled up. The three battalions could not go forward and they could not go back. They began to crawl or to scrape rifle pits. They couldn't see the Turks but the Turks could see them. Any New Zealander reaching for a water bottle or trying to use an entrenching tool attracted a hail of fire.

Major C. B. Brereton of the Canterburys told how his men sprinted for 200 yards, 'thinking oddly how beautiful the daisies and poppies were'. Soon he was watching his men being slaughtered.

303

I was starting with the last platoon, but I had not gone ten yards before I felt the terrible pain of a bullet through the top of my head and as I fell I could see in imagination, but very vividly, great flames rushing out of my head. It crossed my mind instantly, 'Served you damned well right for ordering men into such a fire.'

Cecil Malthus, a teacher from Timaru who later wrote *Anzac: A Retrospect*, lay among dead and wounded.

A sledgehammer blow on the foot made me turn with a feeling of positive relief that I had met my fate, but it was a mere graze and hardly bled. Another bullet passed through my coat, and a third ripped along two feet of my rifle sling. Then the wounded man on my right got a bullet through the head that ended his troubles. And still without remission the air was full of hissing bullets and screaming shells. After an hour the fire slackened, but we continued working feverishly, in the cruel pain of sheer weariness, until each man, including the wounded had a shallow pit to lie in. By then it was nearly two o'clock in the afternoon and I devoured a tin of bully beef and fell asleep for awhile.

The three battalions were pinned down. Yet Hunter-Weston sent orders that they were to attack again at 5.30. This time the Otagos would be thrown in too. Johnston's battalion commanders told him the obvious: another advance like the last one and there would be no New Zealand Infantry Brigade. Johnston passed this on to 29th Division headquarters. He was told the order stood.

Hamilton watched the shambles on both fronts. He wrote that in mid-afternoon 'there was an opinion in some quarters that we had done all we could'. Hunter-Weston clearly wasn't part of this 'opinion' because he was already working on plans for the late-afternoon attack of the New Zealanders. Hamilton now made a wild throw. 'At 4 pm I issued orders that the whole line, reinforced by the Australians, should on the stroke of 5.30 fix bayonets and storm Krithia and Achi Baba.'

Malone by now knew that he had made a mistake: war here was not being waged 'scientifically'. Looking back on this day a month later, he wrote: 'I am quite satisfied that the New Zealand officer has absolutely nothing to learn from the imported man and that active service has taught the latter nothing.' That was the wonderful thing about Malone's opinions: he kept changing them.

The Australians had been in reserve for two-and-a-half days. Suddenly, at 5.05, came an order that they were to take Krithia and the ridge beyond. There was no time to discuss anything. The four battalions of the 2nd Brigade were 400 to 800 yards from their start line. Bean hurried forward with them through Turkish shrapnel. He could not write the thrilling music of Ashmead-Bartlett. Bean was a clerk of facts; he didn't understand what to leave out. His opening sentences often washed over the reader like an anaesthetic and in his fussiness to get the little things right he often overlooked the big things; eventually the *Age* and the *Argus* stopped taking his copy. Yet it is hard to think of a war correspondent, before or since, who was more conscientious, so obsessed with accuracy that he was careless with his own life. Here he is heading for the front trenches on Krithia Spur.

> . . . I was never in the midst of such an uproar – bang, bang, bang, from the front – bang, bang-a-bang, bang-whang, bang-a-whang – and so on from the rear. It was as

if the universe was a tin-lined packing case, and squads of giants with sledgehammers were banging both ends of it, and we tiny beings were somewhere in between . . . One boy to the left of me carried his spade, shovel end upwards like a fan in front of his head . . .

Bean finally reached the 'British trench', the starting point, a bank of red earth. He saw a wounded man 20 yards ahead. The youngster rolled over and tried to crawl. Bean ran out under fire and dragged the soldier back. He wasn't as brave as the lowest, simplest soldiers, Bean explained in his diary; his conscience made him do it. Bean was recommended for the Military Cross; he could not receive it because he was only an honorary captain.

M'Cay, the brigade commander, told him any more 'damn-fool' acts and he'd send him straight back. Next thing, Bean noted, M'Cay was on the parapet doing damn-fool things himself. 'Now then, Australians,' he shouted. 'Which of you men are Australians? Come on, Australians!' The men scrambled out of the trench on to the treeless plain where bullets kicked up puffs of dust.

McNicoll arrived with a batch of 6th Battalion troops and rested for three minutes. Then he rose to go forward and immediately slid back into the trench, gasping for air.

'Are you hit?' M'Cay asked.

'Only slightly, I think,' McNicoll said.

Two men ripped open his jacket and found a wound to the left shoulder. McNicoll rose again, blew his whistle, waved his good arm and disappeared out on to the plain. 'They'd have gone anywhere with him,' Bean wrote in his diary.

Bean crouched in the trench, watching men struggling back with throat and leg wounds while fresh batches arrived. The new men would rest for three minutes, then surge forward with a shout of 'Come on, Australians.' Bean heard the leader of one group shout: 'Come on, chaps, we've got to get it sometime.'

It was great to watch them as they went, absolutely un-affected by bullets. I never saw one man whose manner was changed by them, except in that moment when they got up and faced them; and rushed over the trench – then their faces were set, their eyebrows bent, and they looked into it for a moment as men would a dazzling flame. I never saw so many determined faces at once – Oh! what a photograph I missed.

M'Cay wanted a telephone reel taken forward. He was going to move his headquarters to where he could see more. He told Bean he would be better off to stay where he was. 'I knew I was, and stayed there,' Bean wrote. What M'Cay and Bean couldn't know was that the brigade was being butchered. The men had somehow advanced 500 yards, and when you stand on Achi Baba today you wonder that they got that far. But now those still unwounded were forced to the ground. The Turkish artillery could see them perfectly. A Turkish trench showed up ahead and fire spewed out of it and from skirmishers lying further forward. Fire came in from both flanks. The charge had stalled after 30 minutes and half those involved in it were dead or wounded. Ashmead-Bartlett watched from Helles. He knew before Bean that it was doomed.

The manner in which these Dominion troops went forward will never be forgotten by those who witnessed it. The lines of infantry were enveloped in dust from the patter of countless bullets in the sandy soil, and from the hail of shrapnel poured on them . . . The lines advanced steadily as if on parade, sometimes doubling, sometimes walking. I watched them melt away under this terrible fusilade [sic], only to be renewed again as the reserves and supports moved forward to replace those who had fallen. No man, except the wounded, attempted to return to the trenches.

Hamilton wrote approvingly that a wounded British officer had said it was worth ten years of tennis to see the Australians and New Zealanders go in. This must have been a comfort for the new widows of Ballarat and Nelson.

The short battle life of Sergeant George Fergus Greig of the 7th Battalion ended on the Krithia Spur not long after 5 pm. He was a printer's machinist from Melbourne, 23 years old. Every day he picked up a pencil and wrote in a spiderish hand in a black-jacketed notebook. It doesn't look much but it mattered to him. A note in the front says: 'The diary of my life with the 1st Australian Imperial Force . . . if this diary is found please deliver to [he gives his mother's address] . . . costs will be paid.'

His entry for April 26 reads: 'We lost a lot of men and the enemy lost a lot . . . I sent a Turkish sniper to h . . .' Greig could kill but he wasn't going to spell out a profanity. On May 1 he noted that he had not undressed for a week and felt dirty.

On May 7, at Krithia, he wrote: 'I did a lot of sewing and mending to my clothes . . . It was a lovely day . . . It is very cold and I had a poor sleep. The artillery are bombarding all night and they set a small village on fire. The enemy are having a very tough time for sure.'

Greig was killed the next day. His mother wanted to

know how and where he died. 'Pompey' Elliott, commander of the 7th, wrote and told her he didn't know how George died or where he was buried, only that he died early in the charge. 'Had he survived he would certainly have been granted a commission . . . '

Nearly two years later Greig's mother received a letter from Hector Bastin, who had been at Krithia. 'On the eve of the now famous Krithia charge,' Bastin wrote, 'George came along to me, held out his hand and said quite cheerfully to me: "Well, Hec, shake. I'm going to go out in this action." He evidently had a presentiment that he was going to be killed.'

Bastin did not see Greig fall. 'Another pal of mine Sergeant J. Rutherford buried your son. George did not suffer any pain when he was shot as the bullet that killed him struck him in the forehead directly between the eyes.'

The New Zealanders tried to go forward at the same time as the Australians. There had been a 15-minute bombardment first. Ashmead-Bartlett said it was the most stupendous he had ever seen. Yellow, green and white smoke covered the lower slopes of Achi Baba and 'great volcanoes seemed suddenly to burst into eruption'. This didn't help the New Zealanders or the Australians; the gunners still didn't know where the Turks were. Malone argued with Johnston about the silliness of the orders. Malone and Johnston had been grating against each other. Malone didn't think Johnston much of a leader. Johnston told Malone he was more trouble than the other three battalion commanders combined.

Malone was right to query this order. Fire was coming from both flanks; the Turkish artillery was bursting shrapnel overhead, range and height about perfect; and the Wellingtons couldn't even see the enemy up ahead.

Johnston told Malone he must 'push on', an expression much favoured by Johnston's good friend Godley.

The Aucklanders ran into open country at the Daisy Patch and, like the Australians on their right and slightly below them, were shot up badly. Finally they could see the Turks up ahead, or at least their trenches and rifle smoke. A New Zealand sergeant on the Daisy Patch watched a Turkish officer climb out of a trench several hundred metres ahead and wave a sword.

Well that was too much for me. I thought if he can stand up and do those things, I can. So I stood up and took a steady bead on the gentleman and squeezed the trigger and just as I did so I got a whale of a bang in the elbow, so my rifle dropped to the ground and I grabbed my arm and my hand felt hot and I looked down and there was blood squirting out.

I slithered down out of the fire and on the bank at the side was Captain Bartlett, wounded, lying in the scrub, bandaged up, and I remember saying to him, 'Sir, this is a sheer waste of good men . . . I'm going back, I'm going to take the risk and go back and see what I can do to stop this senseless waste of life.' So I took off my web equipment and I set off at the gallop and the ground was jumping and the bushes were swaying and it sounded as if I was running through a swarm of bees on the move, and I ran into a gap that had been cut by some Pommies who were down behind us. I was bone dry and I wanted a drink, and they didn't have any water. But they had the rum ration, so they gave me a good solid swig of rum – and I would have taken on anybody!

Hamilton watched from his command post. 'Bayonets sparkled all over the wide plain,' he wrote later. 'Under our glasses this vague movement took form and human shape: men rose, fell, ran, rushed on in waves, broke, recoiled, crumpled away and disappeared.' That was the story of the Australians and New Zealanders all right. And it was the story of the day, and of the three days. War was not being waged very scientifically here.

The French went forward on the right at about 6 pm. The spectacle belonged to the heyday of Napoleon, though not the outcome. This was all about pageantry and derring-do – and failure. Drums and bugles and lines of men in red and blue uniforms and white cork hats, lovely to look at, the way peacocks are when they spread their iridescent tails, and so easy, so very easy, to shoot. Turkey was not a modern country, but it had seen the future well enough to know that greenish-khaki was the new colour of war. The French briefly looked to have taken Kereves Spur, including that 'pivotal point' on the left. They had certainly done what had been impossible for the British and dominion troops on their left: they had got among the Turks and their earthworks. But the Turks plastered the ridge with high-explosive shell and the French were forced back, although they did capture the Bouchet redoubt.

Hamilton's binoculars shook as he watched. The poor man needed a win. Any sort of a win, anywhere. And this one looked promising. 'It seemed; it truly seemed as if the tide of blue, grey, scarlet specks was submerging the enemy's strongholds.' Then the Turks opened up with their six-inch howitzers.

The puppet figures we watched began to waver . . . All along the Zouaves and Senegalese gave way . . . The last thing – against the skyline – a little column of French

311

soldiers of the line charging back upwards towards the lost redoubt. After that – darkness!

While Hamilton was watching the French, Bean was in the 'British trench' on Krithia Spur. Bean had watched M'Cay's telephone reel going forward. He didn't yet know that along the line of that wire men he knew would be lying wounded, hit by machine gun and rifle fire, hit by shrapnel, hit from the front and the sides, bruised by flying clods of earth, burnt by the grass fires that had broken out: hundreds of men, thirsty and outraged and in the open. An unusual number of them had abdominal wounds; many had multiple wounds. In his history of the 6th Battalion, Ron Austin tells of Sergeant Sam Wilson, who had been watching his mates fall all about him.

. . . I thought I had a charmed life. This was not so, for when about 300 yards from the Turks' trenches, I got a bullet through the right ear. It just felt like the prick of a penknife. I called them a good Australian name and was going on further, when I got two more in the shoulder . . . I was smothered in blood, even my eyes were full and I could not see, and while I was trying to dig it out of my eyes, I got knocked on the right shoulder with shrapnel.

Wilson sat behind a bush, then headed back towards the dressing station. He met a British soldier wounded in the head and shoulder. Wilson gave him a drink and dressed his wounds. The Tommy gave him his watch in appreciation. Wilson carried him about 30 yards. 'I was putting him down behind a bit of cover, when a shell fell between us. It blew one of his legs off, and left his lifeless body in my arms. This was the end of the poor chap.'
A message was passed along the British trench for

'Captain Bean'. It was from M'Cay's orderly officer. 'Shot through both hands,' the message said. 'Please inform brigadier.'

Bean followed the telephone line forward for about 200 yards. Then he heard a voice in scrub to the left. 'Hullo, old man – you up here?'

McNicoll had been shot a second time. This one was in the abdomen, and serious. Soldiers had propped two packs in front of him as shelter. 'He was awfully plucky and cheerful. I told him I would get some stretcher-bearers and I got another pack from near a dead man and put it in front of him . . . ' Bean went on another 150 yards, found M'Cay and delivered the message. M'Cay called him a fool. They were about 70 yards from the frontline of the 6th Battalion. M'Cay told Bean the obvious: 'They set us an impossible task.'

Bean headed back along the telephone wire. Dusk was falling. He could just make out men on his left. Stretcher-bearers. He asked them to come with him. They said they were going to the right: there were hundreds of wounded out there. He told them about McNicoll. Bean and two stretcher-bearers brought McNicoll in.

McNicoll spent five days on a hospital ship before reaching Alexandria. It turned out that the bullet had entered his abdomen and deflected downwards, knocking splinters off his pelvis before lodging at the head of his right thigh bone, which was also splintered. Surgeons removed the bone fragments but couldn't reach the bullet. They were happy for it to stay there. McNicoll wasn't.

The foreign body inside him made him anxious. Neurasthenia, the doctors called it. In London a surgeon was prepared to operate. The day before the operation, McNicoll had the Distinguished Service Order pinned on his pyjamas. It was for gallantry during the Anzac landing, not for Krithia. He also received a 'parcel of lovely flowers' – tiger lilies, carnations and rare white heather – from Lady Hamilton. Next day, after a frustrating search, the surgeon found the bullet buried in the bone. A nurse tied a piece of red-white-and-blue ribbon around it and hung it on the bed post. It was the first thing McNicoll saw when he came out of the anaesthetic.

After rescuing McNicoll, Bean dragged a man with two leg wounds to a dimple in the ground and put packs around him. 'He had torn open his trousers, as they generally do, to see the wound, and was bleeding pretty freely. I don't fancy he can have lived – poor chap.'

He followed the wire up to M'Cay's headquarters again. Wounded were crying out all about him. Three or four in the headquarters trench were wounded too. A signaller was working with a broken leg. An 8th Battalion man, shot through the intestines, was weeping and crying out 'Doctor, doctor!' Bean gave him a lozenge of morphia. Wounded men were calling for stretcher-bearers in the darkness. A messenger coming up to headquarters heard the cry 'stretcher-bearer' and said: 'You won't see them tonight, my boy – they're rarer than gold.' The wounded man's voice came back feebly: 'You might let us think we will.'

Bean made trip after trip across the heath, as he called it. M'Cay asked him to see if he could get stretcher-bearers and water brought forward. The battlefield had to be cleared before daylight. If not, the men would die, either of wounds, new and old, or of thirst. Bean eventually discovered why the stretcher-bearers had not reached the frontline. There were no wagons to carry the wounded from the dressing station to the beach. The bearers were caught up doing this with stretchers.

It was after midnight. Bean went back to the trench from which the Australian attack had begun, half filled a petrol tin with water and was about to start his seventh trip over the battlefield when the news came that M'Cay had been hit in the leg. Bean looked for him but couldn't find him. Bean decided to take his tin of water right up to the firing line. First, though, he gave the wounded in the trench a drink, warning them they must not take much. 'They were as good as gold. Each fellow took about two sips and then handed it back – really you could have cried to see how unselfish they were . . . '

Bean left the battlefield around 4 am, furious about 'the dull, stupid, cruel, bungling that was mismanaging the medical arrangements'. Like Malone, he was starting to question the notions of 'British superiority' that he had grown up with. He wrote in his diary on May 20:

> . . . once the wounded leave our hands there seems to be the same general muddle which is the one thing that impresses you with almost everything this British staff has done as far as we have seen it. Everything is late – nothing up to time – no evidence of brains that I have seen, although I know brains do exist there. Braithwaite, Ward, Ian Hamilton, are undoubtedly good men, but I think there must be an impossible proportion of dugouts [old soldiers brought out of retirement]. As for the Medical Staff – the arrangements are a sheer scandal. They have foreseen nothing.

Hamilton was starting to sniff scandal too. He saw a fleet-sweeper tied up, full of wounded, mainly Australians.

> They had been sent off from the beach; had been hawked about from ship to ship and every ship they hailed had the

same reply – 'full up' – until, in the end, they received orders to return to the shore and disembark their wounded to wait there until next day . . . As soon as I heard what had happened I first signalled the hospital ship *Guildford Castle* to prepare to take the men in (she had just cast anchor); then I went on board the fleet-sweeper myself and told the wounded how sorry I was for the delay in getting them to bed. They declared one and all that they had been very well done but 'the boys' never complain; my A-G [Adjutant-General] is the responsible official; I have told him . . . that a Court of Enquiry must be called to adjudicate on the whole matter.

The Allied casualties for these three days in May came to about 6500, nearly one-third of the men engaged. Nowhere had the advance been more than 600 yards. Only the French on the final day had found the Turkish main body. Krithia had never looked like falling. Achi Baba still sat there, sulking and mocking. Hamilton's beautiful battalions had indeed become wasted skeletons. Between the landing and May 10 the 29th Division alone had suffered 10,000 casualties; French losses ran to about 12,000.

The New Zealand Infantry Brigade, a fighting force as good as any on the peninsula, had been almost ruined. It had run up 835 casualties in one mad day on Fir Tree Spur. The Auckland battalion – nominal strength 1000 men – was down to 268. Only two of its officers were unwounded. The brigade – nominal strength 4000 men – was down to 1700. A New Zealander wrote in his diary: 'One feels fearfully lonely with only one pal left.' Men from the newly arrived 42nd Division relieved the New Zealanders. Private Russell Weir of the Wellingtons recalled that they seemed like 'little kids'.

And they were blubbering, crying their eyes out. Terrified. We tried to help them by saying those trenches were safe. They weren't, of course. We were just trying to soothe those kids.

The New Zealanders felt sorry for the 'kids' from Lancashire; they were also weeping on the insides for themselves. And they were starting to come down with dysentery.

The Australian 2nd Brigade was about 2900 strong at 5 pm on May 8; when the battle was over its casualties ran to 1056. It was now below half its nominal strength. In the 6th Battalion Major Bennett was the only combat officer from the landing still walking.

Hamilton took responsibility. He told Kitchener the battle had been a 'failure'. Then he lapsed into fantasy. The Turkish 'fortifications' were 'too scientific'; his troops had done all that could be done against 'semi-permanent works'. The Turks did not yet have fortifications or even semi-permanent works. What trenches they had didn't connect up and they hadn't strung wire. Next day, wary of upsetting Kitchener, Hamilton gently suggested he could use two fresh divisions. Kitchener replied that he would send him one, the 52nd (Lowland) Division.

At least three big things had gone wrong. We should not be too hard on Hamilton about one of them. The techniques of war had changed more in the past eight months than they had in the whole of the 42 years he had been in the army. Like many of the generals in France, he had not yet glimpsed the new world. Bayonets were not enough; character was not enough. British claims to natural superiority were only worth something if the enemy believed them. In the new world one did not send men forward over bare ground without artillery support. And 'support' meant firing at where the enemy was known to be, rather than where they *might* be. Muddling through, that charming English way of doing things, didn't play in the industrial age. Brigade and battalion commanders needed to receive orders earlier than 20 minutes before a battle was to start.

There is less excuse for the second big error in the battle. What Hunter-Weston had done, what Hamilton had let him do, was repeat the same attack three times – four times if one counts the charges of the New Zealanders, Australians and French late on the third day. The attack failed on the first day. The ideas it was based upon were exposed as flawed on the first day.

The third error goes to Hamilton's character. Things would have gone better if he had forced his idea of a night advance on Hunter-Weston. He didn't. That was his way of doing things: responsibility without power. And he had this optimism that was now not only quixotic but dangerous. He told Kitchener on May 9 that everyone was in good spirits. This gave a false impression of the whole campaign. Helles was a stalemate and Kitchener should have been told so.

Kitchener was sufficiently worried by May 14 to ask Hamilton what force he needed to carry through the operation. Hamilton acted out of character and asked for three extra divisions in addition to the Lowland Division already promised.

It is a warm spring day, like those three days in May, 1915. Outside Krithia, three Friesian-cross heifers pick at a grassy strip between wheat fields, watched by a shepherd carrying a pine branch and a bored look. Goats frolic in a culvert nearby. Krithia, or Alçitepe as it is now called, is a cluster of white-washed brick and stone houses, shaded by birches and elms. The walls of the sheepfolds are of rough stone and the pens inside are slapped up from anything that is around: old planks, roofing iron, pine branches, rusty wire, angle iron. The backstreets smell of sheep; roosters and tractors provide the music. A private museum stands in the main street near a Coca-Cola sign. Here is debris from the battlefields: dentures, spectacles, cigarette lighters, tins of Eno's Fruit Salts and Tam O'Shanter tobacco, rusted silver razors, a piece of bone with a bullet embedded in it like a jewel set in a creamy stone.

In 1915 the village ended up looking like a back street of Hiroshima after the bomb: chimneys rising like headstones from a field of rubble. Krithia was an Ottoman Greek village. The Greeks had left before the shelling. They returned after the Great War, then left again in 1923 after Turkey's War of Independence. Bulgarian and Rumanian Turks took over the town. Krithia is now home to about 100 families; it is about nothing grander than wheat and olives and bringing up the kids and getting by. It moves to the rhythms of the land and of Islam.

One hundred families. The figure nags at you. It doesn't bear any sensible relationship to what happened here. In 1915 Krithia, the word, meant grieving in tens of thousands of families: Turkish, English, Scots, Irish, Australian, New Zealand. This was where a son or husband disappeared. It had to be something important. It had to be a great fort, a provincial capital, a city of gold. It couldn't be a village that mattered only because it was in front of Achi Baba.

In the Turkish cemetery at Morto Bay you are reminded of the size of the lost Ottoman empire. The headstones tell of men from Medina and Iraq, Baghdad and Rumania, Macedonia and Izmir, Ankara and Libya. And here, beneath the Turkish crescent, is the headstone of the youngest Turk to die in the campaign, Hasanoglu Ahmet, from Çanakkale province. He was 15. Not far away, in Skew Bridge Cemetery, lies the youngest Englishman to die. Drummer J. A. Townsend of the East Lancashire Regiment was also 15.

A magnificent fig tree sprouts out of a Turkish trench in Kereves Dere, its roots planted in blood and bone. Nearby is the concrete monument to Lieutenant-Colonel Hasan Bey, killed here by a wounded Frenchman. His last words, it is said, were: 'Don't kill the Frenchman – he did his duty.'

The ground where the 2nd Australian Brigade was cut down is no longer bare. Almond trees are coming into a delicate white flower. They stand in a fallow of grey soil shot through with rocks like currants in a pudding. The plough has turned up a tobacco tin, a buckle and the inevitable shrapnel. Seagulls wheel and scrap overhead. Looking back to where the Australians started, you see an olive grove intersown with wheat. The Turks tell you that in 1915 there was a vineyard back there owned by a Greek called Six Fingers. When – as you are expected to – you ask the obvious, they tell you he was called that because he was born with six fingers. Across the gully, on higher ground, you see the Daisy Patch where the New Zealanders fell. Up ahead the Krithia mosque peeps over a line of poplars. All is quiet, the fantastic silence of Gallipoli. The wind carries a chill.

The summit of Achi Baba is pocked with shell craters. Flakes of shell casing and shrapnel poke through the whitish soil. There is one tree, a scraggy pine, bent and misshapen by the north wind. A small bird is trying to build a nest in it. The bird arrives with twigs and the wind at once whisks them away. The tree is overshadowed by a new water tower being built for Krithia.

For the British, the hill was (as Roger Keyes later called it) a gigantic fraud, although they didn't know this until 1919. There is no view of the Dardanelles forts. For the Turks, it was the perfect observation post. Back towards Helles stretches a panorama of rustic peace: poplars and pines and olives, white farmhouses and fields of wheat. Look around to the right and you can see the Anzac battlefield.

A pile of rubbish lies near the new water tower, bottles and dregs of plastic. In 1915 tens of thousands died for this ground. This hill was everything back then; now someone is using it as a rubbish dump.

14

Heroes and myths

William Throsby Bridges, commander of Australia's 1st Division, didn't have many friends. Four or five maybe. Amiable people had friends; Bridges wasn't amiable. Friends were a risk: they could trick you into being human, make you laugh and make you care. Worse, they could make you vulnerable. In no time you would be smiling on human frailty.

By the time he strode ashore at Gallipoli, Bridges didn't have to turn away would-be friends. They had turned away from him. He grunted at people; he was shy. Tall and stoop-shouldered, he had the haunted look of the ascetic. He frightened people. He meant to. White, his chief-of-staff, and Lieutenant-Colonel Howse, supernumerary medical officer to the division and a Victoria Cross winner from the Boer War, were as near as he had to friends, along with Casey and Blamey and a few others. Howse and White weren't frightened of him.

Bridges was still stomping around the firing lines exposing himself to Turkish bullets. Maybe he was trying to rattle those who had to follow him around. He mocked staff officers when they took cover. Bean wrote that some staff officers felt what Bridges did was his own business.

What worried them was that Bridges would get White killed. Maybe Bridges was trying to set an example. If so, it was a silly one. Generals are supposed to direct battles, not behave like 20-year-olds who think they are immortal. And the Turkish snipers had been practising for weeks. They knew the thoroughfares and routines of Anzac, particularly along Shrapnel Gully and Monash Valley, which they overlooked from Baby 700 and Dead Man's Ridge. With the sun behind them they sometimes hit 20 men in a morning.

It was easy enough to get shot when you were being careful. Birdwood was peering through a periscope at Quinn's on May 14. A sniper hit the upper mirror and part of the bullet skidded along the top of Birdwood's head. He briefly collapsed, blood spurting freely. Pieces from the nickel jacket of the bullet were removed from the wound six months later.

Around this time Bridges had stood upright as a shell burst. Howse told him: 'General, you'll be caught if you go risking any more of those.' Because it was Howse, Bridges didn't say 'Be damned.' The next day Bridges again stood up during shellfire. White told him: 'General, I think it's no use giving them the chance they want.'

On Saturday, May 15, Bridges left his headquarters at around 9 am with White and Casey. He was going to visit Colonel Chauvel, commander of the 1st Light Horse Brigade. The brigade, along with the New Zealand Mounted Rifles, had arrived to fight as infantry. The Light Horse had gone to Monash's positions at the head of Monash Valley, the New Zealanders to Walker's Ridge and Russell's Top. Bridges headed up Monash Valley.

Engineers had built buttresses of sandbags, five-foot thick, some on the left of the track, some on the right. They had also hung screens of brushwood on wires. But sections were still exposed to the Turks on Dead Man's Ridge. The party reached the sandbags below Steele's Post, near the dressing station of Captain Clive Thompson, medical officer of the 1st Battalion. Bridges stopped to talk and light a cigarette. Thompson warned Bridges to be careful. Bridges darted out from behind the barrier.

'I don't quite know how it happened,' White said afterwards, 'but Casey and I were standing there waiting to follow, when, on a sudden, there was a commotion in the air – someone hit . . . Thompson dashed out, and we looked round from the shelter at the side of the path to see who it was, and I saw they were kneeling over the general.'

Bridges lay with a huge hole in his thigh. The shot had almost certainly come from Dead Man's Ridge. Bridges' femoral artery and femoral vein had been severed. Thompson managed to ligate them just in time; another five heartbeats would have finished Bridges. They dragged him behind the sandbags, his suntanned face now the colour of ivory. 'Don't have me carried down,' he said. 'I don't want to endanger any of your stretcher-bearers.'

Bridges went to the hospital ship *Gascon*. There were no blood transfusions then. The surgeons felt an amputation would kill him and ruled it out; they also knew that if the leg did not come off, gangrene would kill him anyway.

Hamilton visited Bridges the next day. He looked languid and pale, Hamilton recalled, but managed to laugh at a joke. 'Were he a young man, they [the doctors] could save him by cutting off his leg high up, but as it is he would not stand the shock.' The same day Bridges sent his cigarettes and tobacco to Casey.

Birdwood, White and Casey came to see him on the

17th before the *Gascon* sailed. The wound had turned gangrenous. Bridges knew he was dying, and he had at last found grace. 'Anyway,' he said to the doctor dressing his wound, 'I have commanded an Australian division for nine months.'

Bridges died at sea on May 18. George V made him a Knight Commander of the Bath the day before. His body was returned to Australia for a funeral in Melbourne on September 2. Sandy, Bridges' horse, was shipped back from Egypt to be led behind the general's coffin to the slow tap of a kettle drum. Of the 121,000 Australian horses sent overseas during the Great War, Sandy is thought to be the only one to have made it home. Bridges is buried at Duntroon, Canberra, the founder of the AIF and now largely forgotten. The *Argus* devoted thousands of words to his funeral service. In the same edition, under a report from Ian Hamilton, there appeared a paragraph saying: 'There is a general impression at home that Turkey's lack of ammunition will lead to the fall of Constantinople at an early date.' Then, as now, there were spin doctors.

A few days after Bridges' death, White, while praising his commander as a 'big soldier', touched on his failing. Bridges had been lucky that his first command had been a division, White said. 'A brigade is really the last command in which an officer comes into intimate contact with his men. He lacked just the little added touch which would have made him a big man.'

Bean, in the official history, wrote that had Bridges lived he probably would have become 'the greatest of Australia's soldiers'. Bean idolised White and danced around Bridges' character defects. Had Bridges lived, it is unlikely he could have ever have attained the heights of two colonels who lived in 'a somewhat dissolute-looking rabbit warren' at the head of the valley where Bridges fell. Their names were Monash and Chauvel.

A few days after Bridges' death Compton Mackenzie was walking up Monash Valley with other officers from Hamilton's staff. An Australian in shorts was holding up the pannikin that contained his daily allowance of water. 'Now, if I was a mucking canary,' he murmured, 'I might have a bath in this.'

One of the English staff officers tried to strike up a conversation with three Australians. He had a soft and somewhat ecclesiastical voice and meant well.

'Have you chaps heard that they've given General Bridges a posthumous KCMG [he meant KCB]?'

'Have they?' one of the Australians replied. 'Well, that won't do him much good where he is now, will it, mate?'

The day after the general died, another man was shot dead at much the same spot in Monash Valley. Bridges' name was well known in Australia. No-one in Australia knew a thing about this young private with blue eyes and wavy hair who died the next day. Few at Anzac knew him, except those who worked around the beach and Shrapnel Gully.

No-one had feted him when he was alive. He was gritty, but hundreds of men had surprised themselves at Anzac. This man was just another battler, cheery and a bit of a character, but still a nobody. He never expected much from life, least of all fame. Life had mostly just pushed him around. Before the war he was happy enough if he got paid, managed to scrounge a 'decent feed' at a rough boarding house and had enough left over to buy a packet of Woodbines and a lottery ticket.

John Simpson Kirkpatrick of the 3rd Field Ambulance led his mousy donkey into Shrapnel Gully on the morning of the 19th. He generally had breakfast on his way up to the valley, where he would pick up men with leg wounds. Breakfast wasn't ready this morning. 'Never mind,' Simpson said. 'Get me a good dinner when I come back.'

We don't know for sure what killed him, except that he was hit in the heart. And now it began, a process that defies easy explanation. Simpson was beatified, then canonised. In death he found a grace he never enjoyed in life. He lodged in Australia's collective mind and grew bigger and bigger. He was turned into things he never was, such as a 'six-foot Australian' (he was five foot nine). Out of the thousands who did heroic things at Gallipoli, he would be the chosen one. He would become one of the most tender of Australian folk heroes. Statues of him would stand outside the Australian War Memorial in Canberra and the Shrine of Remembrance in Melbourne. Australians would make a film about him, put him on postage stamps, celebrate him in poetry, hold him up as an example to school children and petition for him to be awarded a posthumous Victoria Cross. A sanctimonious clergyman would write his biography and leave out the unwholesome bits. Gallipoli veterans who had never seen Simpson would tell how they met him and what a saintly chap he was. The legend would be so carefully managed that for more than 40 years most would assume Simpson was an Australian.

Why did it happen? Australia likes quirky heroes and the Simpson poetry was right. He sounded like a bloke you could have met in a shearing shed or on a railway gang. He wasn't a toff; he was one of us. He was a soldier but he didn't kill. He was Christ-like, a one-man epic with a donkey. In one sense, his appeal was like that of Gordon of Khartoum; in another, it played to the way Australians like to see themselves. He didn't take himself too seriously.

He looked after his mates and whistled as the shrapnel kicked up dust around him. Simpson made war look nobler than it was.

Reports of Simpson's death appeared in the Australian press in mid-July. That's where the legend began and grew – at home rather than at the front. He was remembered and others, some perhaps more worthy, were forgotten. Bean gives Simpson around 300 words in the 1600 pages of his official history of Anzac. This is about right if one is trying to keep a sense of proportion. Myths and legends, however, are by definition out of proportion and bigger than the facts.

Simpson the man is more interesting than Simpson the legend, and sadder. He was brave; he wasn't a saint. He liked Australia but he was always a Geordie. His heart belonged not to the sunlit plains but to the familiar grime of northern England, to his widowed mother, Sarah, and his sister, Annie.

Simpson's letters, written in the blunt Geordie idiom, are creased and faded and a few have started to break up along the fold lines. They have a wafer-like feel, as though the ages have sucked the weight out of them. Here, on page after page, is Simpson's looping handwriting in black ink or pencil. He conveys meaning wonderfully because he is without affectation. And, before long, you are in thrall to his rhythms; before long, you have come to like him for reasons that have little to do with the legend. The legend is written in granite; these letters, with their misspellings and faulty punctuation, are flesh and blood.

Jack Simpson was Sarah Kirkpatrick's last surviving son; his three brothers died of scarlet fever. He left school at 12 to drive a milk cart. That was around the time his father was crippled in a shipping accident. Within days of his father's death in 1909 Jack became a merchant seaman. At 17 he jumped ship in Sydney. He carried a swag around the outback, worked in cane fields and coal mines and as a ship's stoker in the coastal trade. He sent much of his pay home to his mother, who took in lodgers and trembled on the fine line between poverty and penury. He liked to tease Annie. He regarded himself as the head of the family.

Not long after jumping ship, he carries his swag to Queensland.

Now Mother keep your heart up . . . There are no hardships about it at all. It is just about the best life that a fellow could wish for 'carrying his swag' or 'humping his bluey' as the colonials call it . . . Now Mother you would think we would be like the tramps in the Old Country but what a mistake. The best of respectable men with a house of his own when he gets out of work just packs his swag and off he goes to where he hears the work is on.

He works on a cattle station. He always thought it would be good to ride a horse all day – until he tried it. He tosses the job and goes down the mines. One job, south of Sydney, lasts only four shifts 'and then a gang of us were paid off for slackness. PS I am enclosing PO for a quid.'

Around the same time he writes: 'Only sent 15/- as only had 7 shifts this fortnight and after paying two quid board and paying for my fags I am about cleaned out.' But he promises to send a postal order to pay the licence fee on Lilly, the terrier he left behind at South Shields on the Tyne. Simpson likes animals. When the fair came to South Shields he would take children on donkey rides along the beach. He took a baby possum aboard the troopship to Egypt and let it run around inside his shirt.

He becomes a ship's stoker in the coastal trade. As with most itinerants, his spirits are up and down. He writes that England is 'lousebound', that Australia is kinder to the working man. He sometimes sounds homesick. He meets people easily and likes to joke, yet you suspect he is a loner.

He has a rough side that the myth-makers will later decide to ignore. He can sound like a bully, although this may be the bravado of a young man trying to impress his mother and sister. He threatens to return to South Shields to give someone a 'thick ear'. His mother writes that she has evicted a lodger called Antonio. Simpson writes back that he wishes he had been home. 'I would have made that Russian Jew bugger dance a hornpipe on his ars.'

One Christmas day at sea he dines on goose and plum pudding.

> . . . we drank each others health quite a number of times . . . my mate suggested going over and having a fight with the sailors . . . You couldn't see anything for blood and snots flying about until the mates and engineers came forward and threatened to log all hands forward . . . Someone bunged one of my eyes right up and by the look of my beak I think someone must have jumped on it by mistake when I was on the floor but as they say, all's well that ends well.

He also tells his mother of a boarding-house fight. A man hits Simpson over the head with a poker. Simpson retaliates by breaking a chair over the man's head. The man takes out a summons for assault. According to Simpson, the case is dismissed because the complainant was drunk and Simpson wasn't.

From Adelaide in 1912, he tells his mother:

I often wonder when the working men of England will wake up and see things as other people see them what they want in England is a good revolution and that will clear some of there Millionaires and lords and Dukes out of it and then with a labour Government they will almost be able to make their own conditions. I am enclosing PO for 3 quid.

On August 25, three weeks after Britain declared war on Germany, he jumps ship again – this time in Fremantle – and enlists. He is patriotic all right; he also sees the war as a ticket home. He tells his mother he has sent her a letter to hold for him. It contains Tasmanian lottery tickets, 'and I might have a prize in my Numbers'. He is annoyed when the Australians end up outside Cairo, 'this Godforsaken place'. He arranges for a large slice of his army pay to go into a London bank account, so his mother can draw on it. His writing of February 28 looks hurried. 'Just a line to let you know that we are leaving Egypt today I don't know where we are bound for but hope that it will England or France.' This is his last letter.

He sends a field postcard from Anzac, scrubbing out the alternatives to leave standing the words 'I am quite well'.

On June 15 Annie sits down in the tiny terrace house in South Shields and begins to write to her brother. She is either 19 or 20 and works as a clerk. She has a handsome face, dark hair and long elegant fingers. She is anxious but doesn't want to sound so.

How are you keeping? I expect you will be kept very busy tending the wounded as I see by the papers that there is a very heavy casualty list for the Dardanelles. Oh! if only this terrible war was finished, for it seems dreadful to think so many fine, healthy young men have to be used as fodder for guns. The brave Australians have lost very heavily too . . .

Mother and I have sent you a box of 50 Woodbines on chance with this mail, so I hope you get them alright . . . for I know you will enjoy them & think of Mother & I at home safe while you are just out there in the middle of danger. But you were always of a brave and sturdy nature . . . Mother is keeping a bit better just now but of course you are for ever in her thoughts & she can't be happy.

Your ever loving sister
Annie

P.S. We would like a few lines in your handwriting if you could spend the time dear Jack. Goodnight lad & God protect you for your poor old Mother's sake for Oh Jack! how we do love you.

Annie had also written on June 3 and May 24. She asks him to write to his mother – 'it would make your heart ache to see her waiting & watching for the post. XXXXXX.'

All three letters had of course been written to a corpse. The letters would shortly come back to her. Scrawled across one envelope in indelible pencil would be a single word: 'Killed'.

Hamilton hadn't been telling the truth in his cables to Kitchener. This was partly because he didn't want to make Kitchener cross; when this happened planets tended to collide and careers become puffs of dust. And it was partly because of Hamilton's optimism. His cables were long and writerly and meant to soothe, full of loose ends and omissions. The result was that Kitchener didn't truly know what was happening at the Dardanelles.

By mid-May the situation there was serious and Hamilton was too intelligent not to have realised this. What started as a naval adventure on March 18 had failed so badly on the first day that de Robeck and Fisher didn't want to try it again. What started as an army adventure on April 25 was now on the edge of failure. It certainly couldn't succeed in the form in which it had been conceived.

The Anzacs were clinging to a few hundred acres of beachfront, and tenaciously. They were not, however, threatening anything, not even the third ridge. By mid-May – as the aerial photographs showed – Anzac was taking on the formal shape of a siege. Both sides were sapping and mining to make their trenches continuous. The Turkish trenches in front of Pope's Hill looked like what they would be called: the Chessboard. The same thing was now starting to happen in front of Achi Baba. If Hamilton's force could not take Achi Baba, how could it take Kilitbahir plateau for the navy? Hamilton's casualties had been so severe that an extra division was not going to make much difference. And he still didn't have the tools for trench warfare: howitzers, grenades and mortars.

The assumptions had been wrong, although it took the landings to make this obvious. The terrain was harder than it looked on maps and from the sea. Helles was a poor place to land. There were too many obstacles – Achi Baba, Soğanli Dere and Kilitbahir massif – between the landing beaches and the Dardanelles forts. It was time for Hamilton to tell Kitchener these things. Much as the idea would have appalled him, he needed to do this to save his men – and himself.

Kitchener suddenly gave him an opportunity. The War Council met on May 14. Churchill described the mood as 'sulphurous'. As the impetuous author of the Dardanelles adventure, he was not a popular man. The council looked at three possibilities. It could abandon Gallipoli and risk nudging the Balkan nations into the German camp. It could send heavy reinforcements and hope that these would get Hamilton moving up the peninsula. This would involve taking men from the French theatre, where things were going badly for the Allies. Finally, the council could replace the troops lost in the first three weeks at Gallipoli, send out one fresh division, and hope that the Turks succumbed to pressure. The council reached no decision. It resolved to look at the idea of heavy reinforcements. It wanted Hamilton to say what forces he needed for victory.

Kitchener cabled Hamilton:

The War Council would like to know what force you consider would be necessary to carry through the operation upon which you are engaged. You should base this estimate on the supposition that I have adequate forces to be placed at your disposal.

Kitchener had not only given Hamilton a chance; he had made it easy for him. Hamilton's reaction was to fall into a series of soliloquies over three days. He calls this 'heart-searching' and 'head-scratching'.

On the face of it, we are invited to say what we want. Well, to steer a middle course between my duty to my force and my loyalty to K is not so simple as it might seem. The middle course is (if only I can hit it) my duty to my country. The chief puzzle of the problem is that nothing turns out as we were told it would turn out . . . At first, the fleet was to force its way through; we were to look on; next, the fleet and the army were to go for the straits side by side; today, the whole problem may fairly be restated on a clean sheet of paper, so different is it from the problem originally put to me by K. when it was understood I would put him in an impossible position if I pressed for reinforcements. We should be on velvet if we asked for so many troops that we must win if we got them; whereas, if we did not get them we could say victory was impossible. But we are not the only fighters for the empire. The admiral, Braithwaite, Roger Keyes agree with me that the fair and square thing under the circumstances is to ask for *what is right*; not a man more than we, in our consciences, believe we will really need – not a man less.

Why does Hamilton do this? He isn't the arbiter of where troops go: that's Kitchener's job; ultimately it is Cabinet's job. Yes, the campaign hasn't turned out as it was supposed to, but a commanding general's job is to keep a clear head; he can ruminate about outrageous fortune in his memoirs. His loyalty to K? Isn't this campaign bigger than the headmaster–prefect relationship?

Hamilton eventually replies in the strangest terms. Yes, he needs more troops but he doesn't know where to put them. There is no room on the beachheads. Kitchener's question is hard to answer. Will Turkey be left undisturbed in other parts of its empire? Will Bulgaria, Russia or Greece enter the struggle? If things stay as they are, he will need three more divisions in addition to the 52nd. He also badly needs artillery ammunition. Hamilton rambles and speculates. He still doesn't tell Kitchener what is happening on the peninsula.

Kitchener now confuses Hamilton. He cables on the 18th that it is a 'serious disappointment' to discover that his thoughts on how to conquer the Dardanelles were 'miscalculated'. Calls for large reinforcements and ammunition create a 'serious situation'. Hamilton's views are 'not encouraging'. And then this: 'I know that I can rely upon you to do your utmost to bring the present unfortunate state of affairs in the Dardanelles to as early a conclusion as possible, so that any consideration of a withdrawal, with all its dangers in the East, may be prevented from entering the field of possible solutions.'

This had obviously been prompted by the discussion of alternatives at the War Council meeting. Hamilton didn't know what had been said there. He interpreted the sentence to mean that he should not cable bad news that could be used by opponents of the campaign. The misinterpretation bordered on the tragic. Hamilton was an optimist and a dissembler by nature. He didn't need to be encouraged, even unintentionally.

He immediately cabled back to Kitchener: 'You need not be despondent at anything in the situation . . . we gain ground surely if slowly every day.' This was nonsense. Hamilton's forces had won the odd scrap; but nothing had changed. Hamilton was setting himself up for betrayal from within. There were some fine minds on his general staff, Aspinall, Guy Dawnay and Orlo Williams among them. They knew what was happening. They knew that Hunter-Weston had too much power and had been allowed to get away with too much. They knew that Braithwaite was making the general staff unpopular with the frontline commanders. Some thought Hamilton spent too much time writing press reports in which he dressed up setbacks as 'good progress' and managed (to borrow George Orwell's line about politicians) to give an appearance of solidity to pure wind. Now they had to watch him sending misleading messages to Kitchener.

Hamilton had to wait to find out what reinforcements he would receive. There was a political crisis at home.

Lord Fisher's departure from the Admiralty was a very English resignation. More accurately, it was a very upper-class English resignation. Churchill believed in the Dardanelles adventure; Fisher didn't and never had. Fisher hated the way Churchill cast spells over him, tricking him into agreeing to things he didn't agree with at all. How did he do it? He, Fisher, was so quick-witted and cunning, yet in the presence of this likeable upstart he sold pieces of his soul. The marriage could not last.

It ended on May 15 when Fisher sent Churchill a note of resignation that concluded: 'I am off to Scotland at once, so as to avoid all questionings.' Fisher was found holed up in the Charing Cross Hotel. He was the First Sea Lord and he could leave his post in wartime on a whim. Corporals from Durham who did similar things were court-martialled and occasionally shot as an example to the working classes. This was different. This was a gentleman's tantrum.

De Robeck had unwittingly caused Fisher to resign. Keyes had been pushing for a resumption of the attack of March 18. De Robeck agreed to put the idea to the Admiralty. He did so on May 10 in a curious way, as though he didn't believe in it, which he didn't. The cable included this sentence: 'The temper of the Turkish army in the peninsula indicates that the forcing of the Dardanelles and subsequent appearance of the fleet off Constantinople will not, of itself, prove decisive.'

Churchill knew things had changed since March 18. The navy now had to look after the army as well. And

German submarines had arrived in the Aegean; the *Queen Elizabeth* was in danger. Churchill decided on a limited operation: the fleet would engage the forts at the Narrows while destroyers swept the Kephez minefield. Fisher said no. On the night of May 12 a Turkish torpedo boat sank the old battleship *Goliath* in Morto Bay and 600 of her crew died. Churchill said Fisher had been showing 'great nervous exhaustion'; the *Goliath* incident made him worse. Churchill agreed to the withdrawal of the *Queen Elizabeth* and to de Robeck being told to stay out of the straits. Kitchener became angry on learning of the recall of the *Queen Elizabeth*; the navy was deserting the army at a critical moment, he said. Fisher threw a tantrum on hearing this. The *Queen Elizabeth* would come home that night or he would walk out of the Admiralty.

This explains much of the 'sulphurous' mood at the War Council meeting of May 14. Kitchener was still seething about the *Queen Elizabeth*; Churchill afterwards told Asquith he had never seen Kitchener in a 'queerer mood – or more unreasonable'. Fisher, for his part, announced that he had been against the Dardanelles scheme from the start. Churchill and Fisher that evening agreed on a list of new ships to be sent to the Dardanelles. When Fisher arrived at the Admiralty next morning he found that Churchill had added two submarines to the list. Fisher resigned. Churchill wrote him a conciliatory letter. Fisher replied with a classic of his genre: 'YOU ARE BENT ON FORCING THE DARDANELLES AND NOTHING WILL TURN YOU FROM IT – NOTHING. I know you so well! . . . *You will remain* and I SHALL GO . . .'

Asquith's Liberal Government was brittle and Fisher unintentionally cracked it open. The Prime Minister decided to form a coalition government with a Cabinet that included 13 Liberals, eight Conservatives and one Labour minister. Arthur Balfour, a cautious man, took over the Admiralty from Churchill, who, to his shock, became the Chancellor of the Duchy of Lancaster. He kept his position on the War Council, which would now be called the Dardanelles Committee; but he had been brought down, and his high-handedness had much to do with it. Sir Henry Jackson replaced Fisher. Jackson was lukewarm about the Dardanelles. The new government took three weeks to sort itself out. Fisher fled to Scotland and Hamilton lived in limbo.

15

Death by suicide

Von Sanders had made few mistakes. Now on May 19 he launched a night assault against Anzac, right along the line, charge after charge, lots of bugles, not much art. The idea was to drive the Australians and New Zealanders back to the beach, where they would be slaughtered. It was so artless Hunter-Weston could have thought it up. No artillery barrage, no concentration on the weak spot at the apex of the Anzac triangle. Just bayonets and religious fervour and a belief that superior numbers must prevail. Von Sanders ordered nothing more sophisticated than an avalanche.

Four divisions of Turks, about 30,000 to 40,000 men, would roll down the hill and crush about 12,500 Anzacs. Don't worry that in this sort of operation the terrain favoured the defenders. Afterwards, long after they had dragged the Turkish corpses away, von Sanders admitted he had made a mistake.

The defenders began to sense something was about to happen on the afternoon of the 18th. The Turkish rifle fire on the escarpment died down. The *crack-crack-crack* up there, all day, every day, was part of Anzac life, like the thump of a stamp mill in a mining town. Bean mentioned the silence to White. 'Yes,' said White, 'I wonder what it means.' Naval aircraft spotted troops forming behind Anzac and columns moving up from Krithia. Essad, the corps commander, wanted to concentrate the attack on the Nek and the head of Monash Valley. No, said von Sanders, it had to be all along the line. At the head of Monash Valley – at Pope's, Quinn's and Courtney's – the trenches were only a few yards apart and all the Anzacs had behind them was a cliff. On 400 Plateau, however, the Turkish trenches were several hundred yards from the Australian frontline. Apart from small hollows and craters, the ground between the lines here was relatively flat and bullets and shrapnel had trimmed the scrub. Birdwood wrote afterwards that if the Turks had concentrated their attack on one place, 'they must have got through'.

The moon went down before midnight. At 3 am the Anzacs, wrapped in greatcoats, stood to arms and peered into the night. The light was exceptionally good. It glinted on thousands of Turkish bayonets on 400 Plateau. Two shots rang out from the Australian line, then a shout. Fire broke out all along the Australian line. It was about 3.20. The bewildered Turks fell in heaps. The Australians climbed out on to the parapets and fired as fast as they could work the bolts, as fast as their thumbs could click another five rounds into the magazines. They could sit up like this because the Turkish commanders had provided no covering fire or artillery support for their shock troops. As an attack, this was about as crude as they came. The Australians sat on the parapets and traverses, waved their hats and taunted the Turks. 'Play ya again next Saturday,' a 3rd Battalion man shouted.

The Australians blazed off hundreds of thousands of rounds. The 14th Battalion history says that the woodwork of the rifles became hot to touch. Lieutenant Jack Merivale wrote to his mother that the men talked of the night as 'better than a wallaby drive – [they] shot them down in droves'. Private J. H. L. Turnbull wrote in his diary: 'Our men were sitting on top of the parapets in places shooting as fast as they could load. They could not miss at the distance . . . 18 Turks were captured in our communications trenches. They looked pretty ragged & miserable.' Lieutenant S. L. Milligan was opposite German Officers' Trench, where Turks were trying to file out of a trench under fire. 'One out – got him,' he counted. 'Two out – got him; three out – got him; four, five out – get that man, somebody.'

A Turkish band played martial airs as the Turks continued to run forward with shouts of 'Allah'. They made at least two charges on 400 Plateau and at least five at Quinn's. The New Zealanders had pushed out several new saps from Russell's Top towards the Nek. The Turks ran past these and were shot down from in front and behind. They broke into the line at Courtney's Post, held by the 14th Battalion, after throwing bombs into a trench-bay.

But they couldn't go on from here. If they went one way they had to pass the mouth of a communications trench down which Australians were firing. They couldn't go the other way because one man, Private Albert Jacka, was firing from a bay there. Lieutenant K. G. W. Crabbe shouted to Jacka, asking whether, if he were given support, he would charge the Turks. 'Yes,' Jacka shouted back, 'I want two or three.' Jacka, a cocky 22-year-old forestry worker from Wedderburn, Victoria, liked to fight.

Crabbe brought up four men. Jacka joined them in the communications trench. They ran into the firing trench, straight at the Turks, with bayonets. Two of the Australians were wounded. Jacka and Crabbe decided on a new plan. Crabbe and the two unwounded men would distract the Turks. Jacka would climb out into no-man's land and take the Turks from behind. Jacka leapt in among the Turks, shooting five and bayoneting two. Those still alive thought it best to leave. Crabbe found Jacka surrounded by dead Turks and Australians. His face was flushed and an unlit cigarette dangled from his lips. 'I managed to get the beggars, sir,' he said.

Jacka's diary entry also has him taking three prisoners and includes the line: 'Lieut Crabbe informed me that I would be recommended.' Jacka was on Imbros recovering from diarrhoea when the news came that he had won the Victoria Cross. At Pozières the following year Jacka burst into a group of Germans and killed about 20, despite being wounded seven times. He finished the war as a captain with a Victoria Cross, a Military Cross and Bar.

By 5 am, probably earlier, the Turkish attack was in disarray. It was over by mid-morning. Dead and wounded Turks lay all along the line. One Turk died in a kneeling position. He sat up in no-man's land for two or three days, then toppled over. Bean saw five Turks lying one on top of the other. One was a wounded officer. Australians were trying to get him into the trench by throwing a grappling hook to him as a Greek interpreter shouted instructions. Bean said some of the Turks had frightful head wounds. 'I saw one head wound like a star, or pane of broken glass; another more or less circular – you could have put your hand into either.' Many Australians had believed the Turks had been using dum-dum bullets and mutilating the dead. Now, in front of them, was the evidence of what ordinary rifle and machine-gun bullets did at close range.

About 3000 dead Turks lay in front of the Anzac trenches, from Russell's Top to Bolton's Ridge. Another

7000 had been wounded. One cannot be too sure of these figures. A week before the battle, the 2nd Division had arrived from Constantinople. Von Sanders afterwards wrote that it lost nearly 9000 men in the May 19 battle. If so, it would have ceased to exist: its strength when it arrived was only nine battalions. Von Sanders also wrote that 'on both sides the losses were so great'. The Anzac losses were about 600, of whom 160 were killed.

The Anzacs found on their prisoners several sheets of a new Turkish map of the peninsula. Other pieces of it had been captured at Helles. When all the pages were put together, the Allies had their first accurate map of the ground they were dying on. But maps aren't much use if you can't move. The Turkish offensive rather proved the nature of the stalemate at Anzac. Before May 19 it was obvious that the Anzacs could not break out of their triangle with a frontal attack. After May 19 it was obvious the Turks, even if they outnumbered the defenders three-to-one, could not roll the Anzacs into the sea with an assault right along the line. To have any hope of doing this, they needed more heavy guns. In winter, the gales and floods would work in the Turks' favour. For the summer, Anzac would endure; and it would be about sapping and tunnelling and bomb-throwing.

Birdwood had realised the nature of the stalemate before the Turkish attack. An idea was forming in his mind and he had written to Hamilton about it. The way out of Anzac had to be on the left. The New Zealanders had scouted this country. It was rougher than Anzac, much rougher, a maze of knolls and ravines and valleys that broke four and five ways. But there were fewer Turks there. And those valleys led to the heights of Chunuk Bair and Hill 971. If the Anzacs were reinforced and took those heights, they could still cut the peninsula. Hamilton liked the idea. He was also starting to understand the terrain at Helles. He told Birdwood on May 18 that once Achi Baba had been taken, 'we may not find it advisable to press on further from the south'.

Birdwood outlined a scheme to Hamilton on May 30. He would make a 'big sweeping movement' on his left flank and take the heights of Sari Bair. The attack would have to be a surprise, which meant it had to be at night. Some men would get lost; that was inevitable. Birdwood explained that once he had three brigades on Chunuk Bair, one would attack back towards Anzac, taking the Turkish trenches on Baby 700 and the Nek from behind. Meanwhile the Anzac troops on 400 Plateau would take Pine Ridge and Gaba Tepe. Birdwood reckoned he could do the job with his two divisions, about 19,000 men, plus the Indian Brigade. This was the start of the idea that became the August offensive.

At Anzac there was a more urgent problem. The thousands of Turkish corpses in front of the firing line were starting to bloat and stink. Swarms of flies buzzed over them. If the bodies were not buried the stench would become unbearable and the men who had survived Turkish bullets would die of disease, if they didn't go mad first.

Lieutenant Reg Garnock of the 6th Light Horse Regiment had just arrived at Anzac. He wrote in his diary on May 22: 'The smell of the dead Turks outside our trenches is getting appalling and must be doubly so for them . . . some of the bodies have been there for three weeks.'

16

The most savage must weep

Generals tend to be vain, especially if they are high-bred English or German chaps. If there was to be a truce at Anzac to bury the dead, neither commanding general could appear to ask for it. Thus von Sanders wrote in his memoirs that 'the local British commander requested a brief suspension of hostilities to bury his dead, which I granted for the 23rd of May'. In fact the date von Sanders agreed upon was the 24th. Birdwood had only 160 dead and most of them were behind his lines; he didn't need a truce to bury them. And thus Hamilton wrote that burying the dead would be all right, '*provided* it is clear we do not ask for the armistice but grant it to them – the suppliants'. Hamilton sent Braithwaite to Anzac to negotiate terms with a Turkish envoy. If there were protocols for armistices, Braithwaite would know them.

General Walker took command of the 1st Division after Bridges' death. Walker wasn't too concerned about protocol; he was concerned about the smell. The Australians liked 'Hooky', as Walker was called. Sergeant Cyril Lawrence, an Australian engineer and the author of one of Gallipoli's finest diaries, said Walker would appear attended by an entourage of 'flunkeys'. He was 'a small man dressed in light khaki and shorts, with not a sign of rank about him. Both he and the Australians have learned to know each other and, because he is not a funk or a dugout general, he is a favourite.' Lawrence said Walker seemed to enjoy the Australians' uncouth replies to his questions.

On May 20 Walker stood at MacLaurin's Hill when Turks came out under a white flag and began to attend to their dead and wounded. Walker was worried that this had happened spontaneously. He wanted to get the rules sorted out and, typically, sauntered out into no-man's land and began chatting in French with the Turks and handing out cigarettes. He told the Turks that if they wanted a formal truce they had to send an officer under a white flag along the beach from Gaba Tepe. That day Bean wrote in his diary:

> It is extraordinary how the men have changed in their attitude to the Turks. They were very savage the first day because they found some of their wounded (or dead) mutilated; but since the slaughter of May 19, and since they have seen the wounded lying about in front of the trenches, they have changed entirely. They are quite friendly with the Turks; anxious to get in the wounded if they can – give them cigarettes. The Indians with the mules down here also take the prisoners chocolates – they give our men some also.

The Turkish envoy came riding along the beach from Gaba Tepe. He dismounted and shared a cigarette with Australian officers. He agreed to be blindfolded before being led and carried along the beach to headquarters, where he survived an encounter with Braithwaite.

Compton Mackenzie tells of an incident during the negotiations. The Turk and the British were each anxious to uphold the dignity of their respective nations. Suddenly the flap of the tent was lifted and an Australian or New Zealand batman put his head through and called out: 'Heh! Have any of you muckers pinched my kettle?' One rather hopes the story was true.

Mackenzie came to Anzac on the 24th for the truce. It had rained. The sun worked its way through the haze and the air became rank and humid. Mackenzie arrived at the foot of Quinn's to be offered a cigar. Why the cigar? Then 'the smell of death floated over the ridge above and settled down upon us, tangible, it seemed, and clammy as the membrane of a bat's wing'. Mackenzie climbed up to Quinn's.

In the foreground was a narrow stretch of level scrub along which flags were stuck at intervals and a line of sentries, Australians and Turks, faced one another. Staff officers of both sides were standing around in little groups, and there was an atmosphere about the scene of local magnates at the annual sports making suggestions about the start of the obstacle race. Aubrey Herbert looked so like the indispensable bachelor that every country neighbourhood retains to take complete control of the proceedings on such occasions.

An Australian told Mackenzie he had his foot in an 'awkward place'.

Looking down I saw squelching up from the ground on either side of my boot like a rotten mango the deliquescent green and black flesh of a Turk's head. 'This parapet's pretty well made up of dead bodies,' said our friend below, putting out his hand to help me jump back into the trench, for he saw that I had had enough of it up there . . . I cannot recall a single incident on the way back down the valley.

Captain Aubrey Herbert had done more than anyone to bring the truce about. Now he was running it.

We mounted over a plateau and down through gullies filled with thyme, where there lay about 4000 Turkish dead. It was indescribable. One was grateful for the rain and the grey sky. A Turkish Red Crescent man came and gave me some antiseptic wool with scent on it . . . The Turkish captain with me said: 'At this spectacle even the most gentle must feel savage, and the most savage must weep' . . . One saw the results of machine gun fire very clearly; entire companies annihilated – not wounded, but killed, their heads doubled under them with the impetus of their rush and both hands clasping their bayonets . . . I talked to the Turks, one of whom pointed to the graves. 'That's politics,' he said. Then he pointed to the dead bodies and said: 'That's diplomacy. God pity all of us poor soldiers . . .'

At 4 o'clock the Turks came to me for orders. I do not believe this could have happened anywhere else. I retired their troops and ours, walking along the line. At 4.07 p.m. I retired the white-flag men, making them shake hands with our men . . . About a dozen Turks came out. I chaffed them, and said they would shoot me next day. They said, in horrified chorus: 'God forbid!' The Albanians laughed and cheered, and said: 'We will never shoot you.' Then the Australians began coming up, and said: 'Goodbye, old chap; good luck!' And the Turks said: 'Smiling may you go and smiling come again.'

Corporal J. M. Ranford, standing at Pope's Hill, tried to reconcile what he was seeing with his childhood memories from Adelaide.

> ... how as a young boy I remember going to Montiforte Hill to see the review of our old redcoats, etc., how that handful of men with their rifles and bayonets used to seem so wonderful and grand to me; today we have been witnessing some of the real dark side of the business ... The burying of the dead has been an awful business ... around our section of the trenches they were thick enough to satisfy the most martial, but further along on our right they were in thousands ... simply mowed down like hay before the mower ...

Private Victor Nicholson of Malone's battalion recalled years later that he grabbed a corpse by the arm to drag it to a hole and the arm came off in his hand. Most of the corpses, Nicholson said, were covered with only six to eight inches of soil during the armistice burials. This meant that with the first shower of rain, they were 'practically out and about again'.

Lieutenant-Colonel Percival Fenwick, a New Zealand medical officer, wrote:

> Everywhere one looked lay dead, swollen, black, hideous and over all a nauseating stench that nearly made one vomit. We exchanged cigarettes with the other officers frequently ... there was ... a swathe of men who had fallen face down as if on parade ... The Turkish officers were charming. The Germans were rude and dictatorial and accused us of digging trenches. I lost my temper (and my German) and told them the corpses were so

decomposed that they could not be lifted and our men were merely digging pits to put the awful things into.

Private Turnbull watched an Australian captain talking with a Turkish officer.

He did not understand Australians being a civilised white race. There were several German officers there. One of our men offered a German officer a packet of cigarettes. When he saw the brand 'Brittania' he went crook and threw them on the ground. Another German officer noticed a Turk pick up a bomb from our side of the line & make for his trench. The German followed and took the bomb from him & booted that Turk good and hard and apologised to one of our officers.

Malone had a gentle side. He arose on the morning of the truce and picked wildflowers from around his shelter to send to his wife. Then he went to the armistice. 'Poor shattered humanity,' he thought. Then he saw a German officer. 'I hated him at sight. His manner was most offensive.' The New Zealanders were digging a pit in which to bury Turks. The Turks were so badly decomposed that it was almost impossible to lift them. 'This pig [the German officer] accused us of digging a sap . . . I told some of our chaps if he said anything to squash a dead Turk on to him.'

The Turks and the Anzacs had agreed there would be no reconnaissance, sketching or photography during the truce. Well, there are plenty of photographs: men in shirt-sleeves bend over swollen bodies, others hold white flags; swords and bugles and rifles and shovels and scraps of webbing lie scattered through the dwarf oak. Stare at these photographs long enough and you can hear the buzz of flies and feel the clammy heat. Stare a little longer and you sense the elation of men who, even though they gag every now and then, are for the first time in a month moving, as they once moved in a previous life, upright and in the open. Absurd as it seems, you think, like Mackenzie, of children at a sports day.

Much reconnoitring also seems to have been done. Bean saw Birdwood, Godley, Monash and others doing just that. Bean, always the boy scout, was shocked. 'We wanted it [the truce] to clean the battlefield for our men,' Bean wrote in his diary. 'The Turks wanted it to get rifles. The Turks made no pretence of burying many of their fellows so far as I could see. We both frankly reconnoitred the other's position . . . '

Bean also made his first visit to Quinn's Post.

In one trench there is an archway such as you often find, left to avoid enfilading fire, I suppose. It is not four foot – scarcely three foot – thick; but in it is a dead Turk. His boot and his fingers of one hand stick out from the roof as you squeeze your way under.

Bean noted that the trenches here were within ten yards of each other, with bare ground in between. At one point they were joined by a communication trench that the Australians had dug when they had stormed the Turkish trench in front. When the Australians retreated they filled up one end and the Turks the other, but for a time the trench was open. Australians would throw biscuits or tins of bully beef to the Turkish end of the trench, then blaze away when a Turkish hand appeared. Turkish accounts tell of Australians and Turks shaking hands around the corners of trenches, although this was doubtless after May 24, when the Anzacs' view of their foe had mellowed.

If there is such a thing as an 'Anzac spirit', it belongs up here rather than on the beach. The beach was where the adventure started, but it was also about chaos. Quinn's and the other posts along the wall of Monash Valley were about hanging on and learning to live amid madness.

Captain Cuthbert Finlay tells of another truce at Quinn's in November. It lasted about 15 minutes.

> We could notice the Turks putting their head above the parapet and signalling to us – shortly afterwards there was a dull thud in the trench which we took to be one of the many bombs. However, as nothing transpired, in the course of a few minutes I picked the parcel up – it contained cigarettes and written underneath one of the boxes was the following inscription [written in French]: 'Take with pleasure our heroic enemies. Send some milk.' . . . After this, the Turks and ourselves intermingled in no-man's land for about [a] quarter hour and then 'finis' was announced – a few shots fired towards the sky and everything went on as usual.

There was also the story of 'Ernest', although he may not have been at Quinn's. Ernest was an old Turk who came out of his trench each morning to collect firewood. The Australians didn't shoot at him. Sometimes they threw him tins of bully beef and he'd salaam. Poor Ernest died suddenly one morning when a relieving body of troops took over the Australian line.

Cecil McAnulty, a 26-year-old private in the 2nd Battalion, told of a failed attempt to encourage Turks to surrender. A few Turks who surrendered in June were sent down to the beach, where they were well treated and given plenty of freedom. The idea was that they would escape and tell their comrades how handsomely they had been looked after and induce others to surrender. The Turkish prisoners showed no inclination to escape. McAnulty says they were given axes and sent to a hill near their lines to gather firewood. At sundown they staggered back to the beach 'with loads that a donkey couldn't carry'.

Major Quinn was killed on May 29 at the post that bears his name. Malone and his Wellingtons took over Quinn's on June 9. 'Such a dirty, dilapidated, unorganised post,' Malone wrote. 'Still I like work and will revel in straightening things up.' He at once imposed good house-keeping. Trenches were deepened, roofed over and swept; iron-roofed terraces arose behind the firing line; wire netting was strung along poles to keep bombs out; loop-holes were built into the front trenches. Rubbish was picked up and men were encouraged to keep themselves clean. Malone had an armchair made out of a box. He would bathe in a pint of water outside his dugout each day. 'Be like cats,' he told his men. 'Cats always cover up what they do and always go back to the one place.' He said he would have liked to grow roses. 'The art of warfare,' he explained to Bean, 'is the cultivation of the domestic virtues.'

Corporal Charlie Clark of the Wellingtons recalled in 1982:

> At Quinn's, looking out on the bodies of mates, and not being able to recover them, you got callous pretty quick. You couldn't be anything else. It was no use feeling any-thing else. We seen out the heat and the flies and the dysentery for months. We seen out the British generals too, and their mess-ups. We didn't hate them. We just treated them with contempt. We treated some of our own lot with contempt too, the officers that ran. Not our Colonel Malone, though.

Sergeant Dan Curham said Malone made Quinn's clean and tidy but it was still a 'restless place'. One could always hear Turks talking and coughing and the thud of shovels.

And of course there were the bodies between us and the Turks, and the smell. There was a particularly unpleasant corpse – one of ours or one of theirs – right in front of our firestep which someone tried to burn with inflammable liquid one night, and that made matters worse; we had to live, eat and sleep with the smell of roasted human flesh for days afterwards. I suppose you could say Quinn's wasn't boring.

Private Nicholson watched his mate Lofty die at Quinn's, shot through the eye as he peeped through a loophole.

I didn't cry, unless Gallipoli was one long cry. If you cried once you'd never stop. There were friends going every day and sometimes every hour of the day, wonderful friends. I grieved inwardly. That was all you could do. As a war went on you could forget the death of a very fine friend in five minutes.

In formal terms, Anzac was a British outpost; in spirit, it was laconically Australian. Before the landing this country might have run a goat to four or five acres. In a good year, that is, and if the goats were on the small side. Lieutenant Will Sheppard, an insurance surveyor from New South Wales, told his parents the country wouldn't carry a bandicoot to the square mile – 'and then it wouldn't get fat'. Anzac was now running 50 men to the acre. They could get away with this because it was summer. The price of overcrowding was merely flies and dysentery and other diseases. In winter this ground would have been impossible: the rivulets cascading down the range would have washed Malone's terraces into the Aegean and opened up the graves. Anzac would have been awash with skulls and thigh bones. But no-one was thinking of winter. There was still hope.

Chaplain E. N. Merrington arrived with the 1st Light Horse Brigade on May 12.

Before us passed the unique panorama of Anzac, Australians, New Zealanders, Tommies, mules, Turkish prisoners, mule-carts, donkeys, gun-carriages, came and went ceaselessly. Troops were arriving on the beach from transports; wounded were being sent away in barges; picket boats, in charge of cool, young, treble-voiced middies, were cruising in and out, while ever and anon the shells burst and churned the sea near the shore.

Merrington heads up Shrapnel Gully and Monash Valley.

It was bordered with scooped-out places and isolated graves, sometimes marked with rough wooden crosses . . . wounded limped with or without assistance down the track . . . traverses built of ammunition boxes and sandbags jutted out here and there, to afford a measure of shelter from the devastating rifle fire. A small mortuary contained some bodies . . . Chaplain Wray, a conspicuous figure with clerical collar and a brown neck-protector suspended from his cap, moved about busily. In his hand was a notebook, in which he was writing the names of dead and wounded, and making memoranda of the effects of the deceased . . . When the fusillade was at its height volumes of sound rolled from the cliffs with almost deafening effect. The sides of the track were frequently lined with wounded and even dead, while lint and blood were evidences of the unremitting nature of the terrible struggle . . .

Several days later Merrington sees Trooper Kane of the Light Horse being carried, wounded, down Shrapnel Gully. Kane's brother, from the same regiment, is with him. Merrington goes to the beach hospital and mentions to Lieutenant-Colonel J. L. Beeston that the Kane boys are sons of Captain Kane, a medical officer.

'Perhaps you know them?' Merrington ventured.

'Know them?' said Beeston. 'Why, sir, I brought them into the world.'

Trooper Kane, shot in the abdomen, died.

Ion Idriess, also of the Light Horse, hadn't been long at Anzac when he saw a man shot in front of him.

He was a little infantry lad, quite a boy, with snowy hair that looked comical above his clean white singlet. I was going for water. He stepped out of a dugout and walked down the path ahead, whistling. I was puffing the old pipe, while carrying a dozen water bottles. Just as we were crossing Shrapnel Gully he suddenly flung up his water bottles, wheeled around, and stared for one startled second, even as he crumpled to my feet. In seconds his hair was scarlet, his clean white singlet all crimson.

Idriess soon after watched an infantryman being carted off on a stretcher. 'Half his face was shot away and he was trying to sing *Tipperary*.'

Two months later he watched soldiers playing two-up. The Turks started shelling; the men took no notice.

Shrapnel bowled over three of them. 'So they picked up their wounded and retired casually into their dugouts, one of the wounded men arguing volubly that he had won the last toss.'

Some dugouts were simply big rabbit burrows, heavy with the dank smell of earth. Others were thought so ritzy they were given names. These had a galvanised iron roof on which earth had been piled as protection against shrapnel pellets. The door was a waterproof sheet hung from the roofing iron and the walls were sandbags. Candles provided the light. Once the troops received a shipment of rancid butter. A wag scooped up a tin full, stuck a wick in it and used it as a candle.

The food was frightful. Salty bully beef that brought on thirst, biscuits so hard that men broke teeth on them, a few ounces of jam, a little cheese, maybe a few desiccated vegetables, tea, condensed milk, sometimes a little treacle. Private Nicholson said the bully beef was 'cats' meat floating around in a tin of oil'. Letters from home were the most precious thing. Men read them over and over, maybe a dozen times. The other big pleasure was swimming in the Aegean, risky as it was. Private John Gammage of the 1st Battalion writes matter-of-factly in his diary on June 2: 'I went swimming with two men who were both killed, I got covered with blood.'

Like everything at Anzac, the latrines were exposed to shellfire. The men sat on a pole over a deep hole, 'like sparrows on a perch', as Sergeant Lawrence put it. He tells of a shell bursting over a latrine. 'In the scatter that followed, none waited to even pull their trousers up. The roar of laughter that went up could have been heard for miles. It's only these little humorous happenings that keep things going here.'

The shovel kept men going most of the time. The

ground at Anzac is unusual. There is no topsoil, just unconsolidated sediment, deep and yellow-orange and studded with rocks, small lumps of quartz and the occasional sea shell. It is relatively easy to dig, though heavy to lift because of the clay content. And that's what Anzac was about by the end of May: digging and tunnelling, making the earthworks bigger and better. The Anzacs were doing it and so were the Turks. Trenches were dog-legged to prevent men being wiped out by enfilading fire. Tunnels were used to start saps or to detonate mines under enemy positions. Tunnellers would often hear the picks of the other side going a few feet away. It then became a case of who could set off the mine first. The Anzac tunnels were going out into the ground in which Turks had been buried during the May 24 armistice.

'We are constantly digging them up,' Lawrence wrote. 'It's a treat I assure you to come across one of these gentry. Either we have to dig round him or take him out entirely. It's great either way. They have a peculiar smell of oily fat flesh. Ugh.' Tunnelling under 400 Plateau towards Lone Pine, Lawrence comes on what is obviously the ruins of an ancient city, 'great deposits of pottery buried as low as 20 feet'. No time for archaeology: vases and coffins and secrets of the peninsula are tossed out with the spoil.

Hamilton walked along Shrapnel Gully and Monash Valley to Quinn's Post late in May.

Along the path at the bottom of the valley warning notices were stuck up. The wayfarer has to be as punctilious about each footstep as Christian in the *Pilgrim's Progress*. Should he disregard the placards directing him to keep to the right or to the left of the track, he is almost certainly shot . . . The spirit of the men is invincible. Only lately have we been able to give them blankets: as to square meals and soft sleeps, these are dreams of the past, they belong to another state of being. Yet I never struck a more jovial crew. Men staggering under huge sides of frozen beef; men struggling up cliffs with kerosene tins full of water; men digging; men cooking; men card-playing in small dens scooped out from the banks of yellow clay . . . all the time from that fiery crestline which is Quinn's, there comes a slow constant trickle of wounded – some dragging themselves painfully along; others being carried along on stretchers. Bomb wounds all; a ceaseless, silent stream of bandages and blood. Yet three out of four of 'the boys' have grit left for a gay smile or a cheery little nod to their comrades waiting for their turn as they pass, pass, pass, down on their way to the sea . . . Men live through more in five minutes on that crest than they do in five years of Bendigo or Ballarat.

Many of those who made it back to Bendigo and Ballarat spent the rest of their lives reliving their time on the escarpment. They were with their families, back in their communities, honoured citizens, stalwarts of the empire; but they were as solitary as hermits and, had they wanted to, probably couldn't have explained why. The rest of the world moved on to the boom of the twenties and the bust of the thirties; these men kept shadow-boxing with a demon called Gallipoli.

17

If only . . .

As his submarine glided into the Dardanelles and headed for Constantinople, Commander Otto Hersing of the German navy felt the elation known only to assassins who do the job and get away as well. His *U21* had sunk two British battleships in three days. Just after noon on May 25 he torpedoed the *Triumph* off Anzac. According to one of its officers, the old ship went down growling like a wounded dog. The Australians and New Zealanders on the hills watched in disbelief. That night they penned diary entries that remind you of children writing of the sudden death of a parent: the subtext is abandonment. Higher on the hills the Turkish infantrymen cheered. Two days later Hersing sunk the *Majestic* off W Beach. The *Majestic* lay at anchor, surrounded by colliers and other sprats. Hersing torpedoed her, as Hamilton put it, like a hunter picking a royal stag out of a harem of does. Now the Turks on Achi Baba cheered.

Two battleships. One for each front. True, they were old, and their passing wouldn't change the war in the Dardanelles too much. But they were still battleships. Better than a trawler and a horse-boat. In truth Hersing had changed the course of the war far more than he could know. Ellis Ashmead-Bartlett was on the *Majestic*.

He didn't want to be there. Ashmead-Bartlett had decided that the *Majestic* would be torpedoed. He had watched the *Triumph* sink. The *Majestic* was the logical next target. He knew that. It was so obvious. Most of the fleet had fled into the Aegean after the sinking of the *Triumph*; the *Majestic* was the pick of what was left. But that was always the trouble: Ashmead-Bartlett could see things that smaller minds couldn't. There wasn't much fun in being bright. And these smaller minds kept calling you Jonah or Cassandra. The night before the *Majestic* went down Ashmead-Bartlett helped drink the last of her champagne and followed that with a few glasses of port. As he explained afterwards, it would have been a tragedy if either had gone down with the ship.

Then he went to his cabin. He didn't like the look of it now. It was on the seaward side. The torpedo would probably come from there. He had been given a lifebelt but couldn't be bothered inflating it himself. He meant to ask a marine to blow it up for him – well, that's what marines were for – but he forgot. He did ask a marine to carry his mattress up on to the deck. A chap like Ashmead-Bartlett couldn't be seen lumping a mattress like the help at a country hotel. If he slept on deck he would be able to get away more quickly once the torpedo struck. He wrapped his notes and documents in a water-proof coat and put them in a bag which he intended to take to the deck. Then he was overcome by *noblesse oblige*. What would the crew think if they saw him preparing to leave the ship before it was actually struck?

No-one likes a prophet who actually gets it right. Take the memorandum he had completed and handed to the censor a few days ago for transmission to London. This – it took the form of a letter to the press – said that

Hamilton's expedition was failing and that the British public was being misled. Hamilton wasn't making 'good progress', as he kept saying. There was not 'the smallest chance' of an advance from either Helles or Anzac. Very well-written, it was, cool and forensic. Not only had Hamilton failed to thank him for laying out the facts for him; the general appeared to be miffed. He was 'far from friendly' when Ashmead-Bartlett ran into him. Hamilton didn't actually mention the matter to Ashmead-Bartlett; but he told others that the memorandum, plague bacillus that it was, must not be allowed to infect the wider world. It would stay in the censor's office forever. Hamilton had even told people Ashmead-Bartlett was a Jeremiah. Braithwaite was rabid. Protocols had been breached. As he told Ashmead-Bartlett a month later, war correspondents had no right to any views other than those given to them officially. Ashmead-Bartlett had to stop thinking and seeing for himself. The notion seemed self-evident to Braithwaite. Why did he have to explain these things? Braithwaite would not have liked Martin Luther either.

Ashmead-Bartlett left for the *Majestic*'s deck wearing his pyjamas and carrying £30 in banknotes and his cigarette case. There he lapsed into the easy sleep of a man who knows he is going to be torpedoed. It was all absurd anyway. He wouldn't be lying out here, waiting to be blown up, if they had let him have the yacht.

Ashmead-Bartlett would have been well cast in Evelyn Waugh's *Scoop*. Had he been sent to Abyssinia in 1935, he would have immediately bought a mule train and hired a team of eunuchs to peel grapes for him. He belonged to an era when journalists didn't dress like tax lawyers or talk like merchant bankers. The *Majestic* was his fifth floating home during the Gallipoli campaign. He was tired of having to summon marines to move his kit from ship to ship. Before he had been dumped on the *Majestic*, he had asked Keyes if he might hire his own yacht. 'I think the London papers should have a yacht of their own,' he wrote. 'They can split up the cost between them and it will not hurt much.' Keyes told him he could not have a yacht but a motor boat would be all right.

Ashmead-Bartlett awoke on the *Majestic*'s deck and asked the sentry the time. Well, that's what sentries were for. 'Six-fifteen, sir,' the sentry replied. Ashmead-Bartlett went back to sleep. The torpedo would come in its own good time. At 6.40 am someone trod on his chest. Men were rushing by.

'What's the matter?' he called out.

'There's a torpedo coming,' a voice replied.

A dull explosion. The *Majestic* was hit low down. She listed to port. 'Then,' Ashmead-Bartlett wrote, 'there came a sound as if the contents of every pantry in the world had fallen at the same moment.' He decided to leave. Black smoke stung his eyes. The crowd swept him down to the quarter-deck where men were jumping into the sea. Ashmead-Bartlett had his legs over the side, coyly preparing to launch himself into the water, when he was pushed forward. He bounced off the shelf where the torpedo nets were stored and into the water. He swam to a cutter and clung to the side. A sailor dragged him aboard. The *Majestic* rolled to port and with a hiss turned upside down. A sailor ran the length of her green keel. She plunged to the bottom with a roar. It had taken less than 30 minutes and 50 men were dead.

Ashmead-Bartlett found himself on a French transport. The French, a civilised people, gave him what he needed – brandy. He also needed clothes. They gave him blue trousers, a singlet and rubber shoes. Taken ashore, he went to see Hunter-Weston, 'who was surprised to see me in such a strange get-up'. Ashmead-Bartlett left for Mudros. All his kit had gone down with the *Majestic*. How could a chap cover a war if he didn't look the part? He would have to go to Malta to buy new outfits. The indignity of walking around in a singlet was already obvious. He was greeted with jeers as he climbed aboard *Triad* to ask de Robeck's permission to leave for Malta. De Robeck had his valet fit Ashmead-Bartlett out in an old shooting suit; Keyes threw in a hat.

Ashmead-Bartlett sailed for Malta on a store ship. He came aboard carrying the largest lifebelt he could find. The captain told him he didn't need it. The ship was carrying 12-inch naval ammunition as ballast. If she were torpedoed, 'we shall go up so high that the only thing which could help you would be an aeroplane'. Ashmead-Bartlett tossed away the belt.

He could not buy the things he needed in Malta. He decided to go to London. Not only would he pick up a proper kit there; he would also tell everyone in authority – and he knew them all – the truth about the Dardanelles campaign.

At Anzac on May 25 Aubrey Herbert had asked Commander Dix if he believed there were enemy submarines about. 'Yes,' Dix said. Then he swore. 'There's the *Triumph* sinking,' he said. Destroyers and picket boats rushed to her, taking off most of the crew. The *Triumph* lingered for about 20 minutes, then turned upside down before making her death plunge. On the battleship *Swiftsure* Rear-Admiral Stewart Nicholson closed his telescope and announced: 'Gentlemen, the *Triumph* has gone.' As Ashmead-Bartlett said, they had all seen her go, 'but I suppose she had not officially sunk until the admiral announced the fact'. Ashmead-Bartlett returned to finish his lunch and to drink a few extra glasses of port. A tremor of panic ran through the navy.

The larger ships were sent to Imbros or out into the Aegean. It was all very undignified, like hounds bolting at the sight of a fox. De Robeck next day decided there should be a 'presence', which is how the *Majestic* happened to be lying off Helles waiting for a torpedo on the 27th. After her sinking more vessels were withdrawn. Now only destroyers with four-inch guns were 'protecting' the troops at Helles and Anzac. De Robeck, the most prudent of men, moved his command to the yacht *Triad*. The Turks grew bolder. No longer bothered by naval fire, the gunners near Troy began to lob more shells into the back areas of Helles.

Hamilton left the *Arcadian* – it was no longer considered safe either – and set up his headquarters on Imbros. He raised his tent on a sandbank 'whereon some sanguine Greek agriculturalist has been trying to plant wheat'. He was starting to feel sorry for himself.

> What a change since the War Office sent us packing with a bagful of hallucinations. Naval guns sweeping the Turks off the peninsula; the Ottoman army legging it from a British submarine waving the Union Jack; Russian help in hand; Greek help on the *tapis*. Now it is our fleet which has to leg it from the German submarine; there is no ammunition for the guns; no drafts to keep my divisions up to strength; my Russians have gone to Galicia and the Greeks are lying lower than ever.

As a summary of the campaign so far, this was neat. Hamilton was still an optimist, though. He and Hunter-Weston were going to try to take Krithia again.

*   *   *

Helles wasn't like Anzac. It was mostly flat and it had farms and fields of flowers: red poppies, yellow poppies, white orchids, bluebells, wild roses. And it had space. The Allies had penetrated a little more than three miles. The front stretched across the peninsula for about the same distance. The British, on the left, held about two-thirds of the line, the French the rest. The opposing trenches weren't as close as at Anzac. But, contrary to myths that have grown up, mostly in Australia, a soldier's life at Helles was no easier than at Anzac and often worse.

The finest diarist of the Helles campaign was Ordinary Seaman Joe Murray of the Hood Battalion of the RND, a young Scots miner from County Durham. He was digging a trench with others in May when he saw a soldier bringing them a dixie of tea. Something was wrong with the man. He seemed dazed and kept falling. When he reached the trench only one cupful of tea remained in the dixie.

> He was in a terrible mess . . . His right thigh muscle appeared to be completely shot away and he had two more bullets in his right arm. Goodness knows how many more he had in his body. Our thirst was made more acute by the sight of that cupful of cold tea but no man would dream of touching it whilst there was the least sign of life in the chap who had brought it. As he lay exhausted, almost unconscious, there was always someone in attendance, dipping a finger in the precious liquid and wetting the poor chap's lips. We sucked stones and moistened our own lips with urine, which made them smart but it was moisture and that was all that mattered at the moment.

Murray was worried that von Sanders, having failed at Anzac on May 19, would send his fresh troops against Helles.

His fresh troops won't have to be very fresh to be in a fitter condition than we. For over three weeks we have attacked and been counter-attacked. The shortage of food and water, the blazing sun, the stench from the rotting corpses everywhere and the millions of flies has sapped most of the life out of us. Why were the dead not buried? Easier said than done. Show your head for one second and you are on the list for burial. Day or night, anything that moves is fired on . . . Within a matter of hours corpses that are exposed to the sun swell to an incredible size.

All the time, Murray felt, Achi Baba mocked them. It looked uglier by the day. The food at Helles was no better than at Anzac.

Once a day, if you are lucky, there is bully beef and fly stew as the main meal. For breakfast you might get a rasher of salty bacon and a mug of fly tea. I am sure they boil the bacon in the tea. In the evening we have another mug of fly tea and either a piece of slimy, fly-covered cheese or share a small tin of apricot jam between the lot of us. As one opens the tin the flies are so thick that they are squashed in the process. One never sees the jam; one can only see a blue-black mixture of sticky, sickly flies. They drink the sweat on our bodies and our lips and eyes are always covered with them.

W Beach had changed. 'Once there was a little sand,' Murray wrote. 'Now it is a scrap-iron dump in the middle of a horse-and-mule fair.'

Compton Mackenzie went to Helles early in June. Shells dropped about him; the Turkish gunners were busier now that the fleet had fled. Mackenzie took it personally. Didn't the Turks realise that he was just a novelist doing a spot of staff work? He wasn't worth all that expensive ammunition. He watched two gravediggers laughing as shells fell around them. One of them dropped. The other looked at Mackenzie.

'Beg pardon, sir! Beg pardon!' he called out.

'You can't do anything,' Mackenzie snapped. 'You'd better get into cover yourself as quickly as you can.'

'No, sir, it's not that,' the man whimpered, forcing Mackenzie to stop while he saluted. 'But would you mind telling me if my friend's dead, sir, because I'm new at this job.'

His friend sat up, rubbing his head. 'Of course I'm not bloody well dead, you silly little cod,' he said.

Burials were quick and perfunctory. A New Zealand artillery battery stayed at Helles until August. In his account of the New Zealanders' war, Pugsley tells of a gunner who is shot and dies just as the doctor arrives. Another gunner writes in his diary:

> We have got used to this now and apart from being sorry that another of our mates has had to leave us, these scenes affect us but little. His wound is bound, his disc taken off, his uniform placed over him after all papers etc. have been taken out, he is then wrapped up in his blanket and pinned in . . . The minister arrives . . . we desert the guns for a few minutes and crawl along to the shallow grave . . . We have to lie or sit under cover so that the enemy may not 'spot' us and let fly. We gather around the grave, his own puttees are used to lower him into his last resting place. The chaplain speaks, all's over.

Leonard Thompson, a Suffolk farmhand, arrived at Helles early in June. One of the first things he saw on the beach was a large marquee, like the one they used to have

at the village fete. The new troops unlaced it and barged
inside. It was full of corpses.

Dead Englishmen, lines and lines of them, and with their
eyes wide open. We all stopped talking. I'd never seen a
dead man before and here I was looking at two or three
hundred of them. It was our first fear. Nobody had
mentioned this. I was very shocked. I thought of Suffolk
and it seemed a happy place for the first time.

By June 6, Thompson had been in action for three days.
Now he was burying corpses himself.

We pushed them into the sides of the trench but bits of
them kept getting uncovered and sticking out, like people
in a badly made bed. Hands were the worst; they would
escape from the sand, pointing, begging – even waving!
There was one which we all shook when we passed, saying, 'Good morning', in a posh voice. Everybody did it.
The bottom of the trench was springy like a mattress because of all the bodies underneath . . . We wept, not
because we were frightened but because we were so dirty.

Joe Murray lost his pal in June. Tubby put his thumb
over the muzzle of his rifle and pulled the trigger.

I caught hold of him with much difficulty and began to
bandage him up. The blood was squirting out like a
fountain . . . we decided it would be better to cut off
altogether what was left . . . with Tubby's approval, I
began the operation in cold blood, like a butcher cutting
up the Sunday joint. Tubby howled like the devil – he is
only a youngster, not yet nineteen. Come to think of it, he
is older than me! Well, I pushed and sawed for all I was

worth but, try as I might, could not sever the offending flesh. By now Tubby had lost a lot of blood. Something had to be done quickly and the alternative was to try chopping it off. I placed the thumb on the butt of his rifle, inserted the blade and, with a sharp tap with my fist, the operation was complete.

Tubby wasn't a bad soldier; he simply 'had the wind up'. It had become too much, gone on too long. If this had happened a few weeks earlier, Murray said, he would have slit Tubby's throat. Now it was different. Murray had been at Gallipoli for six weeks. He didn't approve; but he understood.

Hamilton misled Kitchener and Hunter-Weston misled Hamilton. After the Second Battle of Krithia, Hamilton preferred to wait until the new government told him what reinforcements and munitions he might expect. Besides, the Allies had crept forward at Helles after Second Krithia without getting caught up in a major battle. But Hunter-Weston kept telling Hamilton another attack could deliver Achi Baba; no need to wait for the 52nd Division, due to arrive around June 7.

Hunter-Weston lacked imagination. He reacted slowly to events, as he had proved during the landing and Second Krithia. He didn't like surprises. The sly flanking movement, the quick change of plan: these were for nimbler minds. Once his plans were laid, he didn't like to vary them. Compton Mackenzie claims otherwise, but everything Hunter-Weston did suggests that, unlike Birdwood and Walker, he had little affection for the men in his charge: they were sheep and he was the butcher of Helles. Aubrey Herbert wrote in his private diary that Hunter-Weston was 'more hated than most of the generals'.

Just about everything Hunter-Weston had done at Helles had failed. Which would explain why, on May 24, he was promoted to lieutenant-general and made a corps commander. Had he managed to take Achi Baba, he possibly would have been made Archbishop of Canterbury. His VIII Corps consisted of the long-suffering 29th Division, the RND, the 42nd Division and the 29th Indian Infantry Brigade. Brigadier H. E. Street became his chief-of-staff. Street, like Hunter-Weston, was an optimist.

What would come to be known as the Third Battle of Krithia was set down for June 4. The plans were more elaborate than for Hunter-Weston's earlier attacks. This was not going to be another leap into the dark: the deepest advance would be 800 yards, which ruled out taking Achi Baba. The first wave would take the Turk's forward trenches. The second would leapfrog over them and advance another 400 to 500 yards. Digging and mopping-up parties would follow. It was a plan for trench warfare, and was half-sensible because both sides now had continuous lines. Hunter-Weston, however, didn't have the means to fight trench warfare. He didn't have enough heavy guns or shells for them. His gunners couldn't be sure what they were shooting at. And he needed grenades. The Turks had plenty; the British had jam tins loaded with scraps of metal.

Hamilton came over from Imbros, along with Aspinall, Dawnay, Mackenzie and other members of his staff, to watch the battle from an iron-roofed dugout that had been built for him. Aspinall wrote in the official history that Hamilton could only be a 'spectator'. Other than being guaranteed the best seat in the house, he had the same rights as a cricket-lover at Lord's. Why? There were no immutable rules about these things. Kitchener would not have settled to be a spectator, nor von Sanders.

Summer had come. A north-easterly blew swirls of yellow dust over the Allied lines and gunners stripped to the waist. A tortoise crawled past Hamilton's dugout as the second bombardment ended and the advance began. That was another change: two bombardments this time. When the first finished at 11.20 am, the infantry cheered and waved their bayonets above the parapets. This was to draw the Turks to their firing steps. Then at 11.30 am, a second barrage, lasting 30 minutes, began. The troops went forward at noon, the Indian Brigade on the extreme left along Gully Spur, the 29th and 42nd divisions in the centre, the RND on the right centre, and the French on the right. The Allies had about 30,000 men, 10,000 of them in reserve. The Turks had about 25,000 to 28,000, half of them in the frontline.

The barrages looked spectacular and did little damage. The French attack failed quickly, partly because the artillerymen had dropped their shells too far back and also because the Senegalese troops again proved – in the twee language of military reports – 'unreliable'. Three battalions of the RND went forward strongly towards the centre. The Collingwood Battalion, which had been on the peninsula six days, made the second assault. The marines were caught by fire from their right flank where the French should have been. This is the trouble with straight-line assaults across a wide front: *all* the enemy trenches have to be taken; if not, those that are intact can direct enfilading fire to either side. The Collingwoods were wiped out in less than 30 minutes. An eyewitness wrote that their bodies looked like 'dead leaves in autumn'. There were so few left that no attempt was made to reconstitute the battalion. The other three RND battalions also took frightful casualties and lost all but ten of their officers.

In the centre the Manchester Brigade of the 42nd Division advanced about 1000 yards towards Krithia and took 217 prisoners. Again the problem of advances on a wide front: the Manchesters had done so well they were in danger of being marooned. Next to them on the left the 29th Division had gone forward strongly and taken 250 prisoners. Along Gully Ravine, a formidable battlefield, the Indian Brigade was held up.

By early afternoon Hunter-Weston had to decide how he would use his 18 battalions (12 British, 6 French) of reserves. Would he put them in the centre, where the 29th and the Manchesters had done so well? Would he put them in on the flanks where the attack had failed so badly? And how many extra battalions would he throw in? He decided on nine. To use them all would be to reduce the Gallipoli campaign to one wild bet. Hunter-Weston decided to use them on the flanks. The plan failed. Général Gouraud, who had taken over from d'Amade as the French corps commander, finally announced that his troops could not attack again that day. The Indian Brigade attacked again on the left and was hit hard around Gully Ravine. One battalion lost 23 officers out of 29 and 380 men out of 514. Another lost all its British officers.

The 29th Division and the Manchester Brigade in the centre were left isolated. The Manchesters eventually had to retreat. Their advance of 1000 yards became a gain of 250 to 500 yards. Brigadier-General Noel Lee, their commander, was shot in the throat. He was carried to the rear but got off the stretcher and walked towards the beach. A medical officer told him he should be on a stretcher. Lee had lost gouts of blood and could not speak. He wrote a note saying he wasn't going to leave on a stretcher. Surgeons operated on him on the beach but he insisted on getting up and going around his troops. He died on a hospital ship.

It was over before nightfall. Another failure, apart from the small gain in the centre. Hunter-Weston's corps had run up 4500 casualties, or about one-quarter of the troops he had sent forward. The French losses from the morning disaster were about 2000. The Turks had lost at least 9000. It was a typical Helles outcome: the British unable to exploit their advantage; the Turks unable to counter-attack in force; bodies everywhere attended by swarms of flies; survivors with faces bled white by shock.

Two days later the Turks forced the 29th Division back and a 'wild-looking' lieutenant in the Hampshires won the Victoria Cross for doing things that normally don't attract formal honours. The citation said Dallas Moor, an 18-year-old, 'stemmed' the retreat of British troops. He did this by shooting several of them. The Hampshires' history says he shot 'one or two panic-stricken fugitives'. Major-General Beauvoir de Lisle, who had the misfortune to take command of the 29th on the evening of June 4, said Moor 'had to shoot the leading four men and the remainder came to their senses'.

Depression settled over Hamilton's staff on June 4 as they left for Imbros. 'Nobody spoke a word,' Mackenzie wrote.

> Sir Ian Hamilton has been sneered at for claiming that we were within an ace of victory. Yet if a small entanglement of barbed wire on the left of our line had not escaped the ships' guns and if troops more reliable than the Senegalese had been on the right of it, Achi Baba would have fallen a few days later and the casualties of the fourth of June would not have been a quarter of what they were.

This campaign was coming to be all about 'if onlys' and bad luck. In his *The Uncensored Dardanelles*, Ashmead-Bartlett wrote a parody of Hamilton's battle reports.

> After a concentrated bombardment our infantry advanced against the demoralised enemy and speedily captured four lines of trenches. We were on the verge of taking Achi Baba when unfortunately something (generally the French) gave way on our right, leaving us with an exposed flank. Our centre then had to retire, suffering heavy casualties. On our left, something else gave way, and the enemy was unfortunately able to reoccupy his old positions. We are now back on the same line from which we started this morning. The enemy's counter-attacks were most gallantly repulsed with enormous losses. At least 10,000 of his dead are lying in front of our lines and it is reported that 30,000 wounded have been evacuated to Constantinople. Our troops are much elated by their success, and declare themselves ready to attack again at any time. We have made a distinct advance of at least five yards in some places.

Cruel? Yes. Unfair? Probably not. Something was always going wrong. No-one could be that unlucky all the time.

Mackenzie reached the pier with Guy Dawnay when a group of wounded officers from the RND arrived, wrapped in bloodstained bandages. Dawnay turned to Mackenzie, 'a look in his eyes not of pain exactly, nor of pity, nor of grief entirely, nor of wistfulness, nor yet quite of apology, but somehow compounded of all five'.

'Let's get out of their way,' he said, pulling Mackenzie aside. 'They won't want to see us just now.'

On the voyage back to Imbros, Dawnay and Aspinall looked at one another without speaking. Unlike

Mackenzie, they were professionals. They knew there was more to these disasters than lousy luck.

Mackenzie the next day met a young RND officer. His name was Oldfield and he looked about 18. They didn't talk about the battle. Oldfield eventually said with a nervous laugh: 'I'm the only officer left of the Collingwood.'

Hamilton had received a cable from Kitchener the day before the Third Battle of Krithia. 'Are you convinced,' Kitchener asked, 'that with immediate reinforcements to the extent you mention you could force the Kilitbahir position and thus finish the Dardanelles operations?' Hamilton told Kitchener he wanted to defer an answer until after the battle. When it was lost, Hamilton told Kitchener he still felt he could take the plateau, but he needed the four divisions he had asked for.

The Dardanelles Committee met three days after Third Krithia. Churchill had lost high office but he could still overwhelm slower minds. He argued that Hamilton should be reinforced. Kitchener agreed. Other forces were at work. The western front was more of a stalemate than when the Gallipoli campaign begun. There was a passion about the Dardanelles campaign in Australia and New Zealand. Both countries were eager to send more men. The Committee decided to send Hamilton three New Army divisions, volunteers who had responded to the famous Kitchener poster. The 10th, 11th and 13th divisions would reach the Dardanelles in mid-July. With the 52nd Division already on its way, Hamilton had got all the men he had asked for. As Aspinall wrote, Hamilton's force had been treated like an urchin; now, briefly, it was the favoured son.

Churchill lobbied for another two divisions again,

which is how Hamilton also came to get the 53rd and 54th as well as the other four. Churchill pointed out that since April the British and French had lost more than 300,000 men on the western front. For this, they had reclaimed 8 square miles of the 10,500 square miles of France and Belgium that lay in German hands. Would it have made any difference, Churchill asked, if all the troops at the Dardanelles had been in France? Constantinople was the 'only prize that lies within reach this year'.

Churchill was also aware, as others were not, of the relentless arithmetic working against Hamilton. Hamilton was the poker player who, when it comes time to bet, never has enough money in front of him. When he eventually rustles up the stake, he finds the ante has been raised. Five divisions might have captured the peninsula in February. Five were not enough to take it on April 25; seven or eight might have. Hamilton had seven by the time of Third Krithia but now this was not enough. The betting had gone up to ten. Would 13 be enough in August?

If Churchill and Kitchener wanted to help, they still didn't understand the nature of Hamilton's war. Hamilton needed howitzers and artillery ammunition, particularly high-explosive shells. He was still begging for these late in June. The three new divisions were being sent out without their normal artillery strengths. Neither Churchill nor Kitchener understood the terrain. Churchill wrote notes suggesting that, so long as Hamilton had sufficient troop numbers, all he had to do was stroll on to Kilitbahir plateau and watch the Turks bolt. Even if Hamilton took Achi Baba, he had to get across the Soğanli Dere, a terrible piece of country, then tackle the Turks on the Kilitbahir massif. The massif was a stronger defensive position than Achi Baba. And nowhere had the Turks shown a tendency to bolt.

Churchill and Kitchener were also talking about a new landing at Bulair. Both had been having confidential chats with a man who had an obsession about Bulair. His name was Ellis Ashmead-Bartlett.

At a harness-racing meeting at Ballarat in May, 1915, one of the races carried the name 'The Dardanelles Trot'. The organisers were caught up in the fever of patriotism; they didn't realise how right the name was. Summer had come to Gallipoli. Hot days and sunsets that dappled the sea with crimson and gold. And flies, millions of them, green and blue and black and all fat from the corpses they had been burrowing into. And maggots squirming in the trench walls. And lice that appeared to be immortal: they seemingly wouldn't drown, or burn up when chased with glowing cigarettes, or roll over when doused with insecticides. When the men ate bully beef or treacle or a slice of fat masquerading as bacon, they also swallowed flies. If they ate anything, they ate flies. And flies brought on a dysenteric diarrhoea that was called 'the Gallipoli trots'.

At Anzac things were relatively quiet compared with April and May. Hamilton had by now decided he would try to break the deadlock with an assault from here. Bulair was out: de Robeck feared for his ships and when he felt this way, which was most of the time, nothing happened. As for Helles, one suspects that Hamilton knew Achi Baba was unlikely to be taken by frontal assault and that, even if it was, there would be new battles, just as terrible as the old, to get on to the Kilitbahir plateau. No, the left of Anzac was the place for a break-out, and for that reason Hamilton didn't want to see any big offensives there. The fewer Turks at Anzac the better.

The big offensive at Anzac was against the flies and

disease. Lieutenant H. R. McLarty of the 3rd Field Ambulance wrote to his mother.

> By the way all the bunkum about Turkish atrocities is wrong. They are fair fighters and very brave. Of course in isolated instances there is often dirty work done . . . As a matter of fact, we don't mind the Turks so much, but it is the lice and flies that worry us. Flies are simply awful.

Private McAnulty wrote in his diary in mid-June:

> The flies are simply unbearable. They are here in millions, from the size of a pin's head to great bluebottles that bloated they can't fly. Other vermin irritate us very much at night & it is very troubled and restless sleep we get, when we get any at all.

On June 15, Bean and his batman fought the big fly offensive.

> We literally fought them for a quarter of an hour – waving towels, burning Keatings, scattering them. We must have killed 1000 or 2000 but only excited them. They swarmed in our faces, crawled all over us (I suppose the Keatings made them silly), dropped off the ceiling on to the floor. The place was filthy with them this morning – nothing but dead flies . . . The men find the flies at present far worse than the Turks.

While Ashmead-Bartlett was in London, buying new hairbrushes and working over everyone from the Prime Minister down, Bean kept going around the firing line with a diligence no war correspondent has shown before or since. He went to Quinn's after hearing a burst of firing there during the night. Men were dragging dead Turks away.

> Two men had just passed pulling a Turk by the leg when there was a general scatter . . . and down the path came rolling an innocent black ball, like a cricket ball. It reached the dead Turk, who was about 6 feet from me, and then exploded like a big Chinese cracker. There was a blue smoke and a bit of dust, something hit me on the hip – don't know what – and the dead Turk was lying there with his leg blown off. I expect it would have been mine if it hadn't been his. I was spattered over with bits of dead Turk – fortunately not very thickly . . .

Sergeant Lawrence was digging tunnels at Brown's Dip. He had dysentery and neuralgia.

> It's absolutely piteous to see great sturdy bushmen and miners almost unable to walk through sheer weakness, caused by chronic diarrhoea, or else one mass of Barcoo rot. We are all the same, all suffering from sheer physical weakness and yet we can't get relieved. I believe that our stay here constitutes a record for the Army for being constantly under fire. I wonder how those damn wasters whose photos we see in *Table Talk* would feel if only they could see the Boys: the way they work, their weakness, their undaunted spirit and, above all, hear their opinions regarding those stay-at-homes. Women's play things, that's all they are fit for.

Three days later he wrote:

Daily now the men are getting weaker ... If only those at home, fed on lies as they are, could see how the men really are: weak as kittens, one mass of sores, and yet as undaunted in spirit as ever; but that spirit can't last forever and soon these English idiots will have ruined one of the finest bodies of men that ever fought.

Eighty per cent of the men at Anzac and Helles had dysentery by August. It was particularly bad among Monash's 4th Brigade. Bean noted in his diary on July 5: 'We are now losing about 100 men a day – today in both divisions it was about 150 – almost entirely by sickness.' Aspinall said that in July the number of men evacuated from Anzac averaged 1400 a week; three-quarters of them were ill rather than wounded. The numbers stayed up at Anzac because the recruiting drives at home meant replacements were landing all the time. In July a Maori contingent, 500 strong, arrived.

The Turks were suffering from the same diseases, and others, and the likelihood is that they lost many more men to illness than the Allies. The clue is in the figures in the Turkish official history. More than 20,000 Turks died from disease during the campaign. Adil Şahin, the soldier from Big Anafarta village, said towards the end of his life: 'That smell! When the wind blew from the east the smell went across to the enemy ... but when the wind blew from the west it came all over us. There were even maggots, maggots feeding off and moving over all the dead bodies.' The Turkish soldiers' families were also suffering. Their men had been roughly conscripted. Often there was no money at home. Lieutenant McLarty wrote of two letters, 'very simple and sincere', found on a dead Turk:

To my dear Son-in-Law, Hussein Aga,

First I send my best salaams and I kiss your eyes. Your
mother Atif also kisses your eyes . . . Your mother kisses
your eyes and Abdullah kisses both your hands. Your
brother Bairham's wife has died – may your own life be
long – but before dying she brought into the world a child.
This child has also died. What can I say about the decree
of God? Your brother Bairham has also been taken as a
soldier. We pray God that his health may be preserved.
The money you send has arrived. Thank God for it, for
money is scarce these days. Everybody sends salaams,
everybody kisses your hands and your feet. God keep you
from danger.

Your father,
Faik

To my dear Husband,

Hussein Aga, I humbly beg to inquire after your blessed
health. Your daughter sends her special salaams, and
kisses your hands. Since you left I have seen no-one. Since
your departure I have had no peace. Your mother has not
ceased to weep since you left. We are all in a bad way.
Your wife says to herself, 'While my husband was here we
had some means'. Since your departure we have received
nothing at all. Please write quickly and send what money
you can.

All your friends kiss your hands and your feet. May
God keep you and save us from the disasters of this war.

Your wife,
Fatima

As with the Australians, the Turks in the trenches kept

their sense of humour. Private McAnulty wrote in his diary in June:

> The Turks are also busily engaged sapping or trenching. We can see the dirt flying over their parapets. Their trench opposite is about 100 yards away & we take pot shots as the shovels show up. If we hit it, it is dropped. If we missed it, it is waved back afterwards.

The Turks would attack shouting 'Allah'. The Australians would often shout back: 'Come on, you bastards.' The Turks asked, quite reasonably, whether 'bastard' was an Australian god.

Phillip Schuler, the *Age* correspondent, tells of a funeral being conducted near Hell Spit, probably in what is now Beach cemetery. 'Dust unto dust,' says the chaplain as a Turkish shell flings earth over the sad little party. 'Oh, hell!' says the chaplain, 'this is too ho-at for me! I'm aff!'

Schuler also tells of Birdwood going on his rounds one morning, alone and wearing no badges of rank. He comes upon two Australians brewing bully-beef stew. He begins talking to one of them about the stew and the war and this and that. When Birdwood leaves, the other Australian says: 'You ---- fool! Do you know who you were talking to?'

'No!'

'Well, that was General Birdwood, that was, yer coot!'

'How was I to know that? Anyway, he seemed to know me all right.'

After wounds, dysentery and skin infections, the big trouble among the Australians was broken and infected teeth. Hundreds left the peninsula with dental diseases. Unlike the New Zealanders, the Australians had no dental corps. Dentists from within the ranks sometimes improvised with blacksmith's pliers. Amateur dentists sometimes pulled the wrong tooth. Sergeant Lawrence had a tooth pulled in July. 'The chair is just a box and I think the dentist only has the one instrument; anyhow I thought that my jaw was broken.' Four days later he wrote: 'My toothache is still pretty bad. Evidently it was not the one I had pulled out.' Bean noted in his diary that after a shell landed in the dentists' dugout in July the hillside was covered with false teeth.

The Anzacs made several small-scale attacks in June, but they were mostly 'demonstrations' to distract the Turks from larger attacks at Helles. Turks from Kemal's 19th Division attacked Russell's Top, held by the 3rd Light Horse Brigade, on the night of June 29. The Light Horse had 26 casualties, the Turks about 800, including 13 taken prisoner. Mostly, though, Anzac was about sapping and tunnelling. Sometimes the tunnels were opened to make a sap, which would then be used to bring the firing line forward. Sometimes they were used as listening posts. And often they were used to explode mines under the enemy. Sergeant Lawrence was tunnelling towards the Turkish positions at Lone Pine. 'Just fancy,' he wrote, 'one can walk now (in the dark of course) for about one-and-a-half miles underground 90 feet out in front of our firing line.'

A few days earlier the Turks had blown up one of the Australian tunnels. The Australians, Lawrence said, had heard the Turks working on their tunnel for a week. On the morning that the Turks fired their mine they were so close that their pick blows knocked the candle off the wall in the Australian tunnel. The Australians heard the Turks laying their charge and tamping it home.

Few Australians owned up to fear. 'Jack' Gammage of the 1st Battalion did. On June 15 he wrote in his diary:

'For the first [time] my nerves are gone and felt as if each step is the last.' On July 21, he wrote: 'Dropped my bundle. I don't care if I get one or not. Just as well die of bullets as starvation and thirst and want of sleep and 30 hours stretches of work (pick and shovel) but the poor officers are all right so it doesn't matter.' Gammage didn't like officers or 'big capitalists'. Few were as honest as him. Fear was, of course, everywhere. In 1982 the New Zealander Russell Weir, a private in the Wellingtons, told an interviewer:

> On Gallipoli, from first to last, I lived with fear all the time, 24 hours a day, not just in spasms . . . Sometimes you felt obliged to put up a fight against fear – you might start digging madly, deeper and deeper, to get further down into the ground in the hope you might be free of fear. You didn't think of brave deeds at all. That was all gone. You just did your job. Even when I first shot a Turk I just took it as routine. I had no particular feelings. He was there to be shot and I shot him.

His countryman Vic Nicholson, interviewed the following year, said: 'Scared? Sometimes you were too scared to be scared. I would laugh at any individual who says he wasn't afraid.'

Late in July British troops began arriving at Anzac. 'Something big is going to happen,' Sergeant Lawrence wrote. He didn't like the look of the Tommies: 'Sheepish-looking country yobs, who gape about everywhere and appear to have not the slightest go in them.' He liked the English officers with their canes and monocles even less. 'They even take their canes to the latrine with them, and now all our boys are haw-hawing wearing their identification discs in their eyes.' Monocles fascinated the dominion troops, particularly the Maoris. One Maori wanted to know why the English became weak in one eye only.

Bean went to Imbros for a few days in July. He was struck by the novelty of hearing a dog bark at night, and only then realised how long he had been on Anzac. A press camp had been set up near Hamilton's headquarters. Hamilton had dysentery and it bothered him for years afterwards. He had become more remote since leaving the *Arcadian*. Some of his staff were starting to doubt whether he was the right man for what was becoming a big war. Maybe, some of his staff began to think, Hamilton was a muddler. He didn't have the trait that later made Monash such a good commander in France. He couldn't work through the detail.

On Imbros Bean caught up with Ashmead-Bartlett, whose new kit included a silk dressing gown and a movie camera. Ashmead-Bartlett said he had told people in London the campaign was 'going all wrong'. 'It seemed to be typically and exactly the thing that a war correspondent ought not to do,' Bean wrote, 'but I'm bound to say I think he's a competent man, though certainly inaccurate.' Had Ashmead-Bartlett been asked his opinion of Bean, he would doubtless have said he was a competent man, always accurate, who had difficulty making the English sentence move. Both would have been right.

18

Gehenna

On his first day in London – June 6 – Ashmead-Bartlett finished writing a résumé of the campaign. The same day he saw Sir Edward Carson, the Attorney-General in the new coalition government. Carson arranged for him to meet Bonar Law, the Colonial Secretary. Bonar Law took Ashmead-Bartlett's résumé and said he would give it to Arthur Balfour, who had taken over from Churchill at the Admiralty.

Ashmead-Bartlett a few days later dined with Churchill at Lady Randolph Churchill's home. Winston seemed years older, pale and unusually quiet. Suddenly he let fly with a diatribe about the Dardanelles, directed not at Ashmead-Bartlett or the other guests but at his mother. Lady Randolph listened 'most attentively'; it was apparently his habit to lecture her. Churchill complained that the battle of March 18 had never been fought to a finish. 'The loss of the ships leaves him undismayed,' Ashmead-Bartlett noted. 'His only regret . . . is that the sacrifices were stopped, before the full number of victims, waiting to be laid on the altar of chance, had reached their destination.'

When the women left Churchill rounded on Ashmead-Bartlett. He had been running down the expedition. Not true, said Ashmead-Bartlett. He merely wanted to see the operation 'handled in the right manner'. Churchill calmed down. He would arrange for Ashmead-Bartlett to see the Prime Minister.

Around midnight Ashmead-Bartlett walked to Admiralty House with Churchill, who had not yet moved out of his rooms there. Churchill became angry again once inside. 'They never fought it out to a finish,' he cried out. 'They never gave my schemes a fair trial.'

'But,' Ashmead-Bartlett replied, 'they did, and lost three battleships sunk, and three others badly damaged without ever reaching the minefields at the Narrows.'

'That is not the point! They ought to have gone on. What did it matter if more ships were lost? The ships were old and useless . . . '

It apparently didn't matter to Churchill that the crews of these old and useless ships were young and useful. He calmed down and talked to Ashmead-Bartlett until 3 am.

Ashmead-Bartlett and Churchill saw the Prime Minister the next day. Asquith was affable and benevolent. The three pored over maps Churchill had brought along. Asquith agreed a landing north of Bulair seemed a good idea. He asked Ashmead-Bartlett to prepare a memorandum for the following day's Cabinet meeting and to attend in case ministers wanted to question him.

Ashmead-Bartlett then lunched with Lady Jean Hamilton, wife of Sir Ian, who was troubled by the failures at Gallipoli. Ashmead-Bartlett says he tried to cheer her up, and one has trouble reading this without smiling. That night he dined with Balfour. He told Balfour the military authorities at the Dardanelles often failed to tell London the truth. Yes, Balfour said, he had discovered that already. Everyone was frightened of Kitchener. 'You will find him a harmless enough old gentleman, somewhat slow in grasping points when they are placed before him, but far from inspiring this vague terror.' Ashmead-Bartlett left to write his memorandum.

Anzac, he said, was a stalemate. The Helles troops might eventually reach Kilitbahir plateau, but Kilitbahir was no longer the key to the straits. The Allies had to get astride the peninsula at Bulair. Five divisions would be needed. It might be a good idea to include three Australian brigades. The Australians had 'dash and initiative'. The French should make a fresh landing at Kum Kale. Once the Allies were across the peninsula, the Turks could not hold out for ten days.

Ashmead-Bartlett went to Downing Street while Cabinet met and Kitchener came out to ask him questions. Kitchener looked older than his published photographs, his skin red and rough, his manner not at all fearsome. He thought a landing north of Bulair had advantages but said there would be troubles with the lines of communication. Besides, he didn't think he had enough troops to land there. Ashmead-Bartlett assured him that new attempts to storm Krithia or Achi Baba would fail. The Anzacs, he said, were trapped in their own fort.

And then Kitchener said something that revealed the extent of his understanding.

'But don't you think they [the Anzacs] might get on a bit and seize that hill?' (He presumably meant Hill 971.)

Ashmead-Bartlett explained about the terrain, the cliffs and the ravines.

Well, said Kitchener, why couldn't the Anzacs move south and take Kilitbahir and Achi Baba from behind?

Ashmead-Bartlett told him that the Australian right couldn't move forward until Gaba Tepe was taken.

'But why did they give up Gaba Tepe?' Kitchener asked.

Ashmead-Bartlett told him they had never held it.

The two men talked on amiably, then parted, never to meet again.

Assuming that Ashmead-Bartlett reported him accurately, why was Kitchener so muddled? Was he, as many suggested, attempting to do too much? And was part of the trouble that Hamilton, ever anxious to please, had failed to tell Kitchener about the difficulty of the terrain?

Ashmead-Bartlett headed back to the Dardanelles. In less than ten days in London he had lobbied Asquith, Kitchener, Churchill, Balfour, Carson and Bonar Law; his view of the war had been read out to Cabinet; he had seen his literary agent, learnt how to work a movie camera and bought a dressing gown of yellow silk shot with crimson.

He claimed not to have criticised Hamilton personally, yet everything he had said must have kindled doubts about the commander-in-chief. Ashmead-Bartlett found the mood at Hamilton's headquarters hostile. 'They fear any sort of criticism . . . they know that I have seen all the ministers and that is what they resent more than anything else.' He was told he now had to live on shore with the other correspondents. On a 'sandy wilderness', no less, 'burnt up by the sun, blown about by the siroccos, tormented by millions of flies'. The food was 'execrable'. And he had to live in a *tent*. A chap looked rather foolish walking through a tent flap wearing yellow silk shot with crimson.

Ashmead-Bartlett found Hamilton looking 'much older and worried'. He knew Hamilton wanted to get rid of him; Hamilton knew Ashmead-Bartlett had told Cabinet ministers that the campaign was being mismanaged. The two appear to have sniffed around each other like two battle-scarred dogs, each leery of the other's reputation, each careful not to provoke. Ashmead-Bartlett did, however, irritate Hamilton by explaining that the new offensive should be at Bulair. 'He seems to think he is mooting to me a spick-and-span new idea – that he has invented something.'

According to Hamilton, Ashmead-Bartlett also suggested that every Turk who deserted with his rifle and his kit be given a free pardon and ten shillings. This would get rid of the Turkish army very quickly. Hamilton thought the idea offensive – to the Turks.

According to Ashmead-Bartlett, Hamilton told him that he had originally thought the best plan was to attack the Turks right across the line. He now believed this was a mistake. Future attacks would be on narrow fronts. Two days later, Ashmead-Bartlett saw Hunter-Weston. 'He looked years older and very worried, but full of fight and confidence . . . Achi Baba still frowns defiantly down on Hunter-Weston, while Hunter-Weston frowns defiantly back . . . '

At Helles in June and July, Hunter-Weston and Gouraud continued to buy real estate with English and French bodies. Not much real estate, lots of bodies. They crept towards Achi Baba without looking likely to capture it. The French had already tried the new tactics mentioned by Hamilton with some success on June 21. Their objective was limited to capturing the crest of Kereves Spur on the right, including the two forts known as Haricot and Quadrilateral. The front was limited to 650 yards. The artillery barrage was heavy, much heavier than in the Third Battle of Krithia, when the French front was 1500 yards. Unlike the British, the French were not short of gun ammunition.

This bombardment also turned out to be extremely

accurate, throwing up plumes of earth and mangled bodies along the Turks' front trenches. Before the assault, timed for 6 am, the men were given soup, bread and coffee laced with spirits. Spirits were also added to the men's water bottles.

The French could not take the Quadrilateral (they finally took it on June 30) but they ended up on the crest of Kereves Dere, scrambling into trenches thick with Turkish dead. For the first time they could look down on the Turkish positions. The land was bought expensively: French casualties over four days ran to 2500. But it was a victory – the Turks lost more than 6000 – and it proved the value of heavy and accurate artillery fire.

The right flank had been pushed forward. Hunter-Weston now decided to take the left flank forward in similar fashion along both sides of Gully Ravine. The front would be across about 700 yards. The 29th Division and the Indian Brigade would advance along Gully Spur and the ravine itself. One brigade, the 156th, of the newly arrived 52nd Division would attack up Fir Tree Spur. The barrage would be heavy, even though ammunition was low, but most of the shells would be directed at Gully Spur rather than Fir Tree.

The first assault of the Battle of Gully Ravine began along Gully Spur under a blazing sun at 10.45 am on June 28. Hamilton watched the barrage from the destroyer *Colne*.

> The cliff line and half a mile inland is shrouded in a pall of yellow dust which, as it twirls, twists and eddies, blots out Achi Baba himself. Through this curtain appear, dozens at a time, little balls of white – the shrapnel searching out the communication trenches and cutting the wire entanglements. At other times spouts of green or black

vapour rise, mix and lose themselves in the yellow cloud. The noise is like the rumbling of an express train – continuous; no break at all.

The shelling was so effective that the British quickly captured the Boomerang redoubt and 100 prisoners. Fifteen minutes later the guns lengthened their range and the general assault began. To assist the artillery spotters, the men of the 29th went forward with triangular pieces of biscuit tin tied on their backs. Hamilton, now ashore and in his dugout, picked up the triangles as the smoke cleared. It was as if someone had flung a big handful of diamonds on the landscape, he thought.

Hamilton arrived at his dugout feeling 'indescribably slack', bothered by the heat and the flies, and probably also by dysentery. He came out of it 'radiant' and rushed off to congratulate Hunter-Weston. He had seen what could have been. If they only had enough shells to repeat this morning's bombardment, they could pick up another 1000 yards today. That would give them Achi Baba tomorrow or the day after. Hamilton's imagination was so fevered he neglected to mention the 156th Brigade.

The Battle of Gully Ravine had gone well on the left, where the advance along the cliffs above the Aegean stretched to about half a mile, and badly, very badly, on the right, where the 156th had received little artillery support. The forward troops were cut down by machine guns. The support and reserve troops were then ordered to go out and die the same way. This was the brigade's initiation to war and it was cruel. Lieutenant Leslie Grant of the 4th Royal Scots remembered thinking that the bullets kicking up puffs of sand were 'awfully funny'. He reached the Turkish trench.

... the place was in a fearful mess, blood everywhere, arms, legs, entrails lying around ... It sounds horrible in cold blood ... but at this time all that is savage in one seemed to be on top. I remember two things distinctly, one was wanting to cut off a man's ears and keep them as a trophy, the other was jumping on the dead, hacking their faces with my feet or crashing my rifle into them ... Men fought with their rifles, their feet, their bare fists, a pick, a shovel, anything.

The brigade commander, Brigadier-General W. Scott-Moncrieff, was 57; he had fought against the Zulus in 1879 and got about with a walking stick as a result of a wound in the Boer War. Now he was killed, probably only a few yards beyond the parapet, as he brought reserves forward, responding to a hurried order to take the trenches in front of him 'at all costs'. He almost certainly knew he was going to die. The reserve battalion he was leading, the 7th Scottish Rifles, ran out into a storm that had already wiped out half the 8th Scottish Rifles. In five minutes the 8th had lost 25 of its 26 officers and more than 400 men. The remnants of the 7th and the 8th were later rolled into a composite battalion. The 156th Brigade was itself a remnant, down to half strength after 1400 casualties of whom 800 were dead.

That's how, a few days later, Major-General Granville Egerton, commander of the 52nd Division, referred to his first brigade to go into action – remnants. As he was taking Hamilton around, Egerton would stop and say: 'These are the remnants of the ... ' Four times he did so; then Hamilton rebuked him.

Egerton smouldered for the rest of his life. He never forgave Hamilton, Hunter-Weston and Street. When Hamilton was told the 52nd was coming, he had warned

Kitchener that Egerton was 'highly strung'. There is a good chance Egerton was, but he now had much to be highly strung about. His first brigade to land had been sacrificed. They had given him no say in this: the brigade had been loaned to General de Lisle of the 29th for the day. When he arrived Egerton had been shown a document, put together by Compton Mackenzie, saying that the Turks 'are getting more and more depressed'. Mackenzie was not the first novelist to write hokum in the name of patriotism, but his timing was poor. As Egerton wrote in the margin: 'My 156th Brigade found the Turkish villagers anything but depressed.' Worst of all for Egerton, after the 156th had been torn to pieces, Hunter-Weston, who had been a master of fox hounds, announced that he had been glad to have had the opportunity of 'blooding the pups'.

The British casualties for the three days to June 30 came out at 3800. The Turkish losses were probably heavier. The Turks now began a series of wild counter-attacks back down Gully Spur. They bombed the Gurkhas out of their trench, then the Gurkhas took it back. Hamilton seemed pleased that the Gurkhas 'got into the enemy with their *kukris* and sliced off a number of their heads'.

Général Gouraud that day left the peninsula with his thigh, ankle and arm smashed. He was on his way to visiting his wounded at the hospital at V Beach when a shell from the Asian batteries landed near him. No metal touched him but the explosion threw him over a wall said to be seven feet high.

The Turks continued their desperate attacks down Gully Ravine and died by the thousands. Reinforcements were brought up. The Turks, it seems, could always find them. Von Sanders came to the front. The Turks made their heaviest attack at dawn on July 5. It failed everywhere and the Turkish losses were worse than at Anzac on May 19. According to their official account, the Turks lost 16,000 troops between June 28 and July 5, most of them around Gully Ravine, which explains why, 85 years later, one still sees so many bones there, and why, even on a smiling spring day, the place seems haunted and, in a way that is hard to explain, corrupted. If one believed in the devil, it would also be possible to believe that he lived in Gully Ravine.

Ashmead-Bartlett saw great fires burning there. They gave off 'a horrid, sickly stench'. Turkish dead were being burnt.

> The trenches are packed with debris, like the Gully. The same awful stench pervades everything, and the flies swarm in millions. In one corner seven Turks, with their rifles across their knees, are sitting together. One man has his arm round the neck of his friend and a smile on his face, as if they had been cracking a joke when death over-whelmed them. All now have the appearance of being merely asleep, for of the seven I only see one who shows any outward injury . . . On going up a deserted sap I suddenly came upon a wounded Turk, lying on his back all by himself, with his chest heaving and his hands clenched above his head. He was muttering to himself – I think praying – but was too far gone to live much longer.

The Turks asked Hamilton for a truce to bury their dead. Hamilton refused – 'though on grounds of humanity as well as health, I should like the poor chaps to be decently buried'. He believed the Turks had only made the request because they could not get their men to charge over the corpses of their comrades. Dead Turks, he thought, were better than barbed wire.

Wherever possible, the soldiers burned the Turkish bodies. A chaplain likened Gully Ravine to Gehenna, the rubbish dump at Jerusalem where fires were kept burning to purify the air.

Having advanced on the flanks, Hunter-Weston now tried to bring his centre into line. He wanted to use the RND as his main force in the attack. He was told the obvious: the marines were worn out. He should have known this. The 29th Division had taken tremendous casualties since the first day; besides, it was tied up holding on to the gains on Gully Spur. The 42nd Division had been mauled in the Third Battle of Krithia. The 52nd, Egerton's division, was in reasonable shape by Helles standards. Hunter-Weston could misuse only one of its brigades in the Battle of Gully Ravine, mainly because the other two hadn't landed. So now it was the turn of these two, the 155th and the 157th, neither of which had been in an assault before. They would attack east of the Krithia road. The French would attack to their right. The 155th would go over the top at 7.35 am and the 157th at 4.50 pm. This way the artillery could use all its guns to support one brigade at a time.

So now, on July 12, the men of the 155th, wearing the heavy serge uniforms they had brought from England, went forth in the fierce sun to make their sacrifice to Achi Baba. The battle went to the Helles rituals. The brigade found the Turkish frontline trenches easily enough. These were thick with Turks killed in the bombardment and splashed with blood. The British troops began to suffer heavy casualties when they ran on to the Turkish support trenches. Some battalions appear to have overrun their objectives. One of these, left in the open, quickly lost 60 per cent of its men. A lieutenant in this battalion asked his cousin to cut off the shreds and shards of his arm, lit a cigarette, cheered his men on, then fell dead.

It was chaos, also part of the Helles ritual. No-one behind the lines knew what trenches had been taken and where the various battalions were. Even at noon Hunter-Weston didn't know what was happening. He finally decided that the afternoon attack by the other brigade should go ahead.

The 157th captured the enemy's front and support trenches, but was cut down when it reached the third line, which was only 18 inches deep. By nightfall the battlefield was still confused. Those of the 52nd Division still alive were desperately thirsty and lying in gore-splashed trenches next to the bodies of Turks and Englishmen swollen by the sun. The frontline was a scene from some Dantesque hell. An eyewitness wrote that even the soil beneath the surface smelt poisonous.

Panic broke out in a section of the British line early next morning. A trickle of troops left, possibly because of an order to thin out the frontline, and this soon became a torrent. The retreating troops were quickly turned around, but word reached Hunter-Weston that two battalions had 'bolted'. He now decided to throw in the exhausted troops of the RND. He told Egerton and the RND commander that the attack must be renewed that afternoon. Another slaughter followed.

While this was going on, Hunter-Weston relieved Egerton of his command. The 13th Division, the first of Kitchener's five divisions of reinforcements, was landing. Its commander, Major-General Frederick Shaw, found himself in temporary command of the 52nd in the middle of a battle where no-one, either at the front or at corps headquarters, knew what was going on.

Why did Hunter-Weston do this? He and Egerton did

not get on and Egerton had been bitter since the sacrifice of his brigade in the Battle of Gully Ravine. The probability is that Hunter-Weston was himself becoming 'unstrung'. Egerton, having spent the night on a hospital ship, returned to his command the next day, more bitter still.

And the ritual was complete. One man in three in the 52nd was either dead or wounded; the RND had lost another 600; the Turks had lost another 9600, including 600-odd taken prisoner. The Allies had crept a little closer to Achi Baba, yet were further away than ever from capturing it. That was part of the rituals too.

Whether these attacks at Helles in June and July should have taken place is a fair question. Hamilton seemed to have decided, long before these battles began, that Achi Baba could not be taken from the front. The hope of the Mediterranean Expeditionary Force was the August offensive, which would come out of Anzac like a giant left hook. Hunter-Weston had butchered every division he had been given. The three big battles in June and July had produced 12,300 casualties, the equivalent of a division. The Turks had lost 30,000, but after each setback they always found more men. Hunter-Weston's force was forever 'fighting to a standstill'; when it made gains, it couldn't exploit them. And, because it didn't have enough artillery, all its gains came at an outrageous price. 'It was fortunate for us,' von Sanders wrote, 'that the British attacks never lasted more than one day, and were punctuated by pauses of several days. Otherwise it would have been impossible to replenish our artillery ammunition.'

Now Hunter-Weston fell ill and left the peninsula forever. What was wrong with him has never become clear. The explanations run from sunstroke and exhaustion to enteric fever and dysentery to a collapse and a breakdown. Hamilton noted on July 20 that his corps commander was staying aboard the *Triad*, and 'is quite worn out'. Hunter-Weston didn't want to see anyone. Hamilton saw him 'staggering' off to a hospital ship. 'He is suffering very much from his head.' Next day, Hamilton wrote, 'Hunter-Weston has to go home.' A few days later, he referred, in passing, to 'Hunter-Weston's breakdown'.

Did he mean a nervous breakdown? If so, it sounds so improbable. Here was a man who was without pity, whose idea of leadership was to push men hard, then harder and harder still, until eventually they broke. Here was a man who, like France's Général Foch, believed in attack, as if the machine gun had never been invented. Such a man should have gone down in the frontline, felled by a bullet, shouting with defiance to the swelling music of Elgar. He couldn't just fade away, and from something as eloquent of human frailty as a 'breakdown'. He couldn't crack up like a private from Lancashire. He couldn't come down with a condition that demands that its victim be possessed of an imagination.

Hunter-Weston left behind four shot-up divisions. Joe Murray wrote on July 13:

> It is pitiful to see men, not long ago strong and healthy, now with drawn faces and staring eyes, struggling towards the firing line. Most of them should be in hospital. They are cheating death but only just. They are walking corpses – the ghosts of Gallipoli.

In the coming month, however, Helles would no longer be the main theatre. An affable old gent named Freddie Stopford had arrived to command three fresh divisions.

PART THREE

The last throw

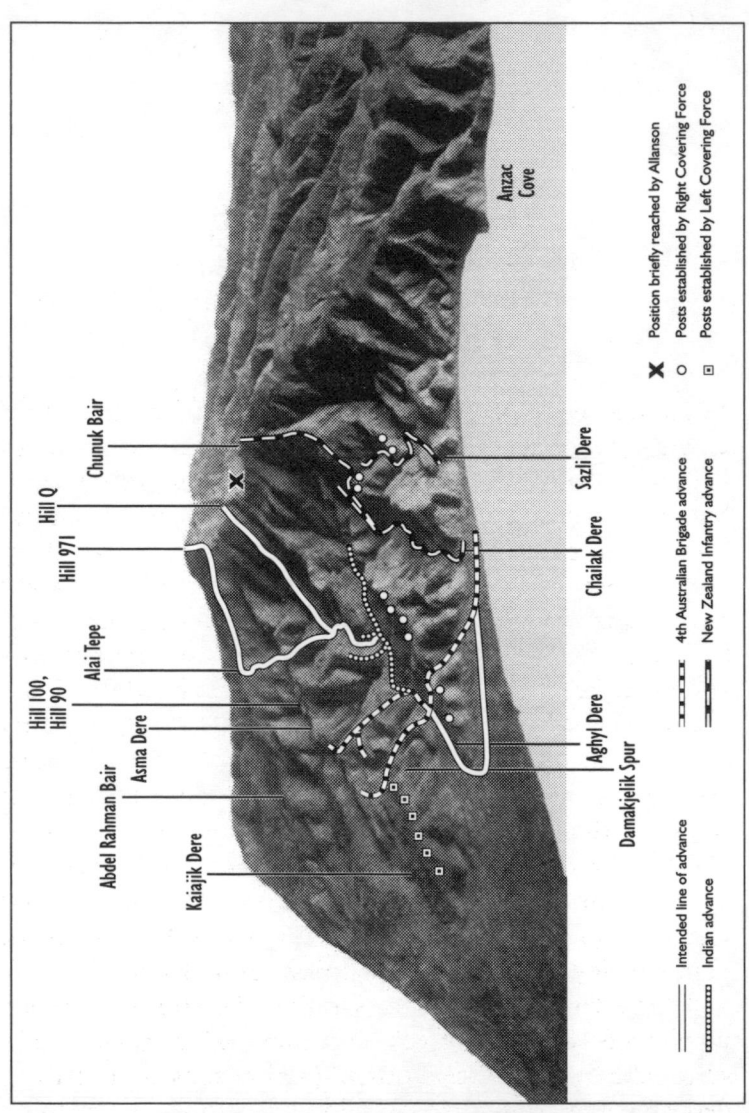

The August offensive

Chunuk Bair
Hill Q
Hill 971
Alai Tepe
Hill 100, Hill 90
Asma Dere
Abdel Rahman Bair
Kaiajik Dere

Sazli Dere
Chailak Dere
Aghyl Dere
Damakjelik Spur

Anzac Cove

X   Position briefly reached by Allanson

○   Posts established by Right Covering Force

▣   Posts established by Left Covering Force

——————   Intended line of advance

·········   Indian advance

▪▪▪▪▪▪   4th Australian Brigade advance

▬ ▬ ▬   New Zealand Infantry advance

19

A scapegoat, made to order

Some generals become corps commanders because they are irresistible, so good that no-one would think of appointing anyone else. Some get there through a combination of destiny and imagery: they are seen as natural leaders and photograph well in sunglasses. A few get there because they know the right people or belong to the right faction. Sir Frederick Stopford became the commander of IX Corps at Gallipoli through a process of elimination – and also because he was neither too fat nor too tall.

Kitchener decided to send three of the New Army divisions to the Dardanelles as a corps. These were the 10th (Irish) Division under Lieutenant-General Sir Bryan Mahon, the 11th (Northern) Division under Major-General Frederick Hammersley, and the 13th (Western) Division under Major-General Frederick Shaw. Shaw weighed close to 20 stone, or around 120 kilos. Hammersley came with a caution from Kitchener: 'He will have to be watched to see that the strain of trench warfare is not too much for him.' Hammersley had suffered a 'nervous breakdown' (a phrase used in 1915 to describe everything from mild exhaustion to frothing lunacy) before the outbreak of war. Mahon was one rank too high to be commanding a division; he was also very conscious of his seniority.

Corps are usually commanded by lieutenant-generals, divisions by major-generals. Kitchener suggested that, as Mahon was already a lieutenant-general, he was the obvious choice to command IX Corps. Hamilton said no. Mahon was 'good up to a point and brave, but not up to running a corps out here'. Hamilton asked for either Lieutenant-General Julian Byng or Lieutenant-General Henry Rawlinson, both serving on the western front. Kitchener said he couldn't spare either. Besides, there was the matter of Army List seniority: both were junior to Mahon. Kitchener said that since Mahon had raised and trained the 10th, he should be allowed to lead it in battle. Therefore, the corps commander, whoever he was to be, had to be senior to Mahon. This left two candidates only: Lieutenant-General John Ewart or Stopford.

Hamilton mumbled about the 'seniority fetish', as he was entitled to, but knew he couldn't talk Kitchener out of it. It had to be Ewart or Stopford. Hamilton ruled out Ewart because of his height and bulk. 'I greatly admire his character,' he told Kitchener, 'but he positively could not have made his way along the fire trenches I inspected yesterday.' And then he wrote the fateful words: 'Would not Stopford be preferable to Ewart?'

So Frederick Stopford sailed to Gallipoli as a corps commander, not because he was a brilliant soldier, or because he was pushy, or because he knew the right people, or even because he wanted to go; he went because he was the only candidate left. He was 61 and most of his future was behind him. He had once been seen as one of the 'coming men', but that was in 1895. Now he was tired and ill; had it not been for the fuss over seniority, the world would have quickly forgotten him, if indeed it had ever been aware that he existed. He could not lift his brief-case into the train as he left Victoria Station for the Dardanelles.

He had been retired since 1909 and had never com-manded men in battle. This was not his fault and need not have mattered; Eisenhower had never commanded in battle when in 1942 he took over the Allied forces in North Africa. The difference was that Stopford's fire, if it had ever burned, had gone out. Churchill described him as a 'placid, prudent, elderly English gentleman'. Others used words such as courteous, kindly and fatherly. He was a man grown soft with age and they were going to ask him to do hard things.

Compton Mackenzie sat next to Stopford at lunch a few days before the August offensive began. Mackenzie found him charming – and indulgent. A brigadier was criticising the general staff's plans for the August offensive; he was close to being truculent. Stopford tried to soothe him in a fatherly way. The brigadier persisted. Stopford continued to reassure. Mackenzie longed for Stopford to slap down his junior but he didn't. When the lunch ended Mackenzie was left without hope. How would this man frighten the Turks if he couldn't put down an underling? In the battle to come Stopford had already set himself up to be the perfect scapegoat.

He would choose to remember none of this. His entry in the 1920 edition of *Who's Who* mentions his decor-ations and postings, except that of corps commander at Gallipoli. In his mind it never happened.

While Stopford was pacifying his juniors, Kemal was roughing up his superiors. On April 25, as soon as he saw the line of Australian skirmishers on Battleship Hill, Kemal knew that the Sari Bair range was the prize. If the

Anzacs were going to try for the heights again, and by the most direct route, they needed to capture the Nek and Baby 700. That meant running uphill against trenches bristling with machine guns. The Anzacs and the Turks both knew this couldn't be done.

So, Kemal thought, what would the Anzacs do? Sit out the war on their 400 acres? Wait for the winter rains to wash them into the Aegean? No, they would go for the heights again, but indirectly. They would try to slip out along the left of Anzac, go north then turn sharply east.

The valley called Sazli Dere worried him. It began above North Beach and narrowed to a gully that finished just below the summit of Chunuk Bair. Kemal was vexed because Sazli Dere was the boundary between his command and that of Major Willmer, a Bavarian cavalry officer with a sabre slash across his left cheek. Willmer's main area was the Suvla plain and the Anafarta Hills, north of Anzac. Kemal wanted to know who was responsible for Sazli Dere: him or Willmer? He wrote note after note to Essad Pasha, his corps commander. It is obvious from Essad's replies that he was bemused. Sazli Dere was a 'little valley'. What did it matter?

Kemal was not going to be put off; Kitchener would have hated him. Kemal says in his memoir that he was frustrated at being unable to make his superiors see his point. He wrote Essad a memorandum on July 18 that he admitted was excessively long. The enemy could use Sazli Dere for a night attack on Chunuk Bair, he told Essad. 'I consider that it [Sazli Dere] should be made the responsibility of a commander who would clearly realise the importance of his task.' Essad arrived with his chief-of-staff. He wanted Kemal to show him this ground that was so important. Kemal took them out to Battleship Hill.

From here you see the panorama of Anzac and Suvla.

Down the hill is the Anzac frontline, stretching from the beach north of Walker's Ridge back to the Aegean south of Hell Spit. To the right, north of Anzac, lies the roughest country on the peninsula: deceitful little gullies that dart and swerve and seldom go the way you think they should, dried up watercourses thick with bulrushes, yellow-scarred knolls with flat tops, yellow-scarred razorbacks, plunging cliffs. And there, wending through this mayhem, is Sazli Dere and, above it, the razorback called Rhododendron Ridge.

No-one has described this country better, or with such perfect brevity, as Robert Rhodes James. 'It is a mad country,' he declared in *Gallipoli*. The land is not so much laid out as strewn about, possibly by some pagan god called Erosion. Only a bandit could feel good about it. You have to walk it to realise it is even rougher than it looks. Even with the soaring white pylon of the New Zealand memorial on Chunuk Bair offering itself as a reference point, it is easy to become lost, particularly when you are down in the creek beds being mocked by croaking frogs. The only logic to the country is that Hill 971 is the hub. From here, the spurs run out like spokes. Rhododendron Ridge runs vaguely parallel to the spur that passes through Baby 700 and ends at the Anzac beachhead. Abdel Rahman Spur runs north from 971 towards Suvla.

This is the panorama Kemal showed them that July day in 1915. The chief-of-staff looked to the north of Anzac and said: 'Only raiding parties could cross this ground.'

Essad turned to Kemal and said: 'Where will the enemy come from?'

Kemal pointed along the coast from Anzac to Suvla. 'From here,' he said.

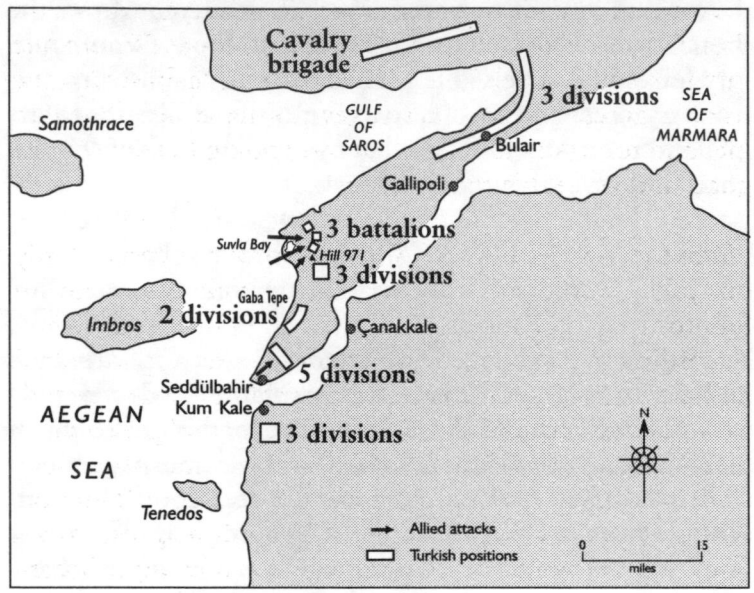

Turkish dispositions, August 6, 1915

'Very well,' said Essad, 'supposing he does come from there, how will he advance?'

Kemal pointed towards Anzac, then moved his hand in a semi-circle towards Hill 971. 'He will advance from here.'

Essad smiled and patted Kemal on the shoulder. 'Don't you worry,' he said. 'He can't do it.'

Kemal gave up. *'Insh'allah,'* he sighed. 'Let's hope you are right.'

Kemal recorded the conversation in his diary. After the August offensive, he underlined the passage in red ink and added a few stern words. Those who had disagreed with his theory had been 'mentally unprepared'; they had exposed the nation to danger.

Now, in the days before the offensive, he wrote in French to a woman friend in Constantinople. Would she buy him some novels? He needed them to 'help soften the hard character which present events have developed in me, and to make me capable of responding to some of the good and agreeable things in life'.

Hamilton wanted his new offensive to be a surprise. Only on July 22 did he and Aspinall outline the plan to Stopford. According to Hamilton, Stopford was 'keen'. According to Aspinall, Stopford said it was a 'good plan' and that whoever thought it up should be congratulated. Von Sanders began to hear rumours in mid-July that a new landing was imminent. He had been told that fresh troops – 50,000 to 60,000 – were arriving at Lemnos, where an armada was forming. Churchill had also given him, and everyone in Constantinople, a warning. Victory would come to the Allies, Churchill predicted in a careless speech at Dundee on June 5; Lord Kitchener knew what he was doing. This, von Sanders thought, had to mean a new landing. If the Allies were going to stay, and they obviously were, they had to try something new.

But where? The Anzacs had pushed out their north flank. Did this mean anything? Essad said it didn't. Kemal said it did. Kemal was a fine divisional commander but disputatious; no-one, not even a tyrant like the army, could ever own him. Bulair was a possible landing spot. Von Sanders had three divisions there. A landing on the Asian shore seemed less likely, but von Sanders kept three there too. The open space between Anzac and Helles? That was a worry. He had put Colonel Kannengiesser's 9th Division there. And Suvla? Perhaps. Von Sanders had 3 battalions there, along with 19 artillery pieces and some cavalry, less than 2000 men all told, under Major Willmer.

As von Sanders did the mental exercises, he was suddenly recalled. Plots were swirling in Constantinople. Field Marshal von der Goltz was to replace him. Von Sanders managed to have the decision postponed but was forced to accept the appointment of a new staff officer who, so one story goes, tried to poison him. Rumours of Hamilton's 'secret' landing were all over Constantinople. A member of the German military mission told von Sanders that the Allied offensive was considered so likely to succeed that windows were being rented in Pera Street for the entry of British troops. Von Sanders asked that a window also be rented for him.

Whenever one reflects on the Gallipoli campaign, there is a temptation to judge the men and events of 1915 by the values and the knowledge of today. To do so is not only unfair; it is also an obstacle to understanding. Events only seem reasonable when judged by the thinking of their time. Had Pilate known what he was starting, he would surely have given Jesus a suspended sentence. That acknowledged, one has to say that the plans for the August offensive – by the standards of any war in any era – were too complex. The possibility exists that only Hamilton, Aspinall and a few others at GHQ understood the scheme in its entirety. Too many events were contingent on each other. It was like an exotic bet on a series of horse races. If the first leg got up, the second leg was alive; if the third leg didn't get up, the whole bet was lost. There were to be three new fronts, two on the left of Anzac and one at Suvla, plus diversions at Anzac and Helles. One hundred thousand Allied troops would be in action on five fronts. Control of the battles would be dispersed over a string of commanders who quite likely wouldn't know what was happening on the other fronts.

This may not have mattered if the commander-in-chief could be counted on to take overall charge; but, as we know, this was not Hamilton's way.

The scheme was so fussy and over-cooked that mis-understandings persist about what it was supposed to do. The capture of the Sari Bair heights from Anzac, directed by General Godley, was the main event; the landing at Suvla under Stopford was the sideshow, if a big one. What Godley did was more important than what Stopford did.

Birdwood's original plan of May 30 was mainly the work of his staff officer Lieutenant-Colonel Andrew Skeen; it assumed that the offensive would be in July. Chunuk Bair would be captured in a night attack from the left of Anzac. The troops would next day attack back down the range, taking Battleship Hill and Baby 700. The Anzacs would take the rest of the third ridge over the next few days. Then, reinforced by four brigades, they would surge across the peninsula from Gaba Tepe to Maidos, as they had intended to do on April 26. There was no mention of a landing at Suvla.

Then Kitchener suddenly gave Hamilton the three New Army divisions that would become Stopford's IX Corps. Hamilton and Birdwood began to think more expansively. Anzac was already overcrowded. Three reinforcing divisions could not be hidden there for an offensive. Birdwood suggested that one of the new divisions should be landed at either Fisherman's Hut or Suvla, five miles north of Anzac.

Suvla appealed to Hamilton. Unlike Gaba Tepe, it was only lightly defended. From here the Turks could be attacked from outside Anzac as well as inside. There were several suitable landing beaches and the terrain was kinder than at Anzac, a big plain with hills on three sides. The Kiretch Tepe Ridge, rising to 650 feet, dominated the north, and the Tekke Tepe Ridge, rising to 900 feet, the east. The Anafarta Spur, about 350 feet high, formed the southern rampart. This spur ended in the W Hills (so called because the vegetation on them was, and still is, in the shape of a W) and Scimitar Hill. Further west lay Chocolate Hill and Green Hill. The Sari Bair Range and all its madness petered out before Suvla. The last feature that could be said to belong to Sari Bair was Hill 60, a little swell of a hillock that mattered only because it dominated the ground towards Suvla Bay.

Suvla would give Hamilton a new base, free from shelling. He could drive south-east from here, into the Sari Bair Range and the Turkish flank. This was the crucial point. Owning the Suvla beachfront was no prize. The troops at Suvla only mattered when they moved and threatened something.

Hamilton decided to land the 10th and 11th divisions there. These volunteers had never been to war but, compared to Helles or Anzac, Suvla would be an easy landing. The men wouldn't have to land in lifeboats either. The armour-plated 'beetles' (so called because they were black and the projecting arms of their ramps looked like antennae) were now available. Some had been built before the April landings and undoubtedly would have saved lives then, but Fisher had refused to let them go.

'Johnny' Hamilton was still an orphan, as he had been from the day Kitchener hurried him out of London. Reports of his haggard looks every now and then troubled the consciences of the men who ran the empire and they tossed him a few rounds of artillery ammunition, a couple of divisions of reinforcements, a fleet of beetles. But they weren't going to claim paternity – unless he gave them a whopping victory, in which case he would receive a measure of recognition, but only after Kitchener and

Churchill had walked off with the main prizes. Hamilton in mid-July asked, deferentially as ever, for two batteries of howitzers. Kitchener said no.

Birdwood's original plan now became more complex again. There would be *two* assaulting columns on the left of Anzac, one heading for Chunuk Bair and another taking a wider loop through the bandit country to Hill 971. The second column would advance in the dark through country that had not been scouted, but the plan was contemptuous of the terrain; these troops, it said, would be on the summit of 971 by dawn. Actually, there would be four columns out on the left because each main force would have a covering force in advance of it. The column going for 971 would also split as it approached the heights, with some of the troops going for Hill Q. The scheme was becoming very tangled.

Something had to be done at Helles and Anzac to keep the Turks tied down there. The feint at Helles needed to be modest. Thanks to the recently departed Hunter-Weston, the four British divisions there were down to 26,000 men, compared with their nominal strength of 46,000. Working like modern-day corporate planners, GHQ decided the most they could lose at Helles was 4000 men; therefore, a feint had to be thought up that involved a 'battle expenditure' of not more than that number. The planners decided to straighten the frontline in the centre. The feint at Anzac was to be nothing less than the capture of Lone Pine by the 1st Division on the afternoon before the night assault on the left. 'Hooky' Walker, then commanding the 1st, at once told Birdwood this was a bad idea.

Walker liked Birdwood. The two were alike and not alike. Birdwood was forever buzzing around the trenches at his brisk walk. He always refused a drink at the frontline, knowing that water was scarce. He once took a cup of tea from Malone at Quinn's. Malone insisted he drink it and Birdwood's courage had its limits. Malone described him as lovable and considerate. Birdwood was out with the troops but he didn't take infantile risks as Bridges had. Unlike Bridges, he didn't snarl at the men. 'Birdie' liked to talk with them, went out of his way to do so, and it doesn't matter that most of these exchanges involved platitudes being pushed one way and the other. He had the good sense to accept that, as Aubrey Herbert put it in his private diary, the Australians were 'uncivilised'. Phillip Schuler, the *Age* correspondent, told how Birdwood was returning to his headquarters one day when he accidentally trod on the roof of a dugout, causing stones and earth to fall on the occupant below. 'Quick, quick,' said the general, 'let me get away from this. I would rather face half a dozen Turks than that Australian when he comes out.' Birdwood never learned to yarn, to play at irony as Australians did. But he had affection for his men and it lasted all his life. They, in turn, thought he was a decent man who meant well. Walker, his hat at a jaunty angle, was also out among the men. He liked them too, but the Australians seem to have warmed to him more easily than to Birdwood. He was less formal and more like them and he understood Australian humour.

Walker's opposition to the Lone Pine attack, shared by White and other Australian officers, probably had a little to do with affection. Why ask good troops to run from 60 to 120 yards at machine guns for such a questionable gain? Walker's larger objection had to do with common sense. Lone Pine didn't lead out of Anzac as obviously as, say, Baby 700. And Baby 700 overlooked Lone Pine. The time to attack Lone Pine was after Baby 700 was taken, not before. Walker and White suggested that Lone Pine and Baby 700 be attacked simultaneously. Walker later suggested his 1st Division be used to seize the W Hills and form an outpost for the troops landing at Suvla. Birdwood wouldn't move. Walker eventually won one concession: he talked Birdwood into putting the Lone Pine attack back from 3 pm until 5 pm, thereby bringing the feint closer to the main attack.

Monash's 4th Brigade was chosen for the assault on Hill 971. It was in poor shape for such a leap into the dark. Monash, at 50, was too old and too rotund to be making the trek, although he couldn't know how rough it would be because no Allied soldier had been there. The 4th Brigade had been resting in Reserve Gully after its spell in purgatory at Quinn's. Dysentery was everywhere and the 4th was probably suffering worse than the other Australian brigades. The 4th had also taken severe battle casualties. Of the 132 original officers, only 37 remained. Reinforcements now made up half the brigade. Some had arrived from Egypt so poorly trained that they were loading rifles by pushing one round into the chamber for each shot instead of clicking ten into the magazine. In July Godley gave Monash the faintest hint of what was to come. He told Monash to think about night marches in rough country and compasses.

The offensive was to begin on August 6. Once it started Godley would become the most important commander. He would be in charge of the rush for the heights. Godley's New Zealand and Australian division consisted of Monash's brigade; the New Zealand Infantry Brigade under Johnston; the New Zealand Mounted Rifles Brigade under Russell; the 1st Australian Light Horse Brigade under Chauvel; and the 3rd Light Horse Brigade under Colonel Frederic Hughes. Godley would also control the 13th Division under Shaw; the 29th Indian Brigade under

General Vaughan Cox; and one brigade from the 10th Division. In short, Godley would become a *de facto* corps commander.

The other two New Army divisions – the 11th and the 10th – would land at Suvla. The 53rd Division would arrive in Mudros by August 6. It would be in reserve, then probably go to Suvla. Helles would not be reinforced. Hamilton would have six divisions at Helles, three (plus two extra brigades) at Anzac, two (less one brigade) at Suvla and one division in reserve at Mudros. The 54th Division, the last of the reinforcements promised by Kitchener, was also on the way.

It was becoming a big war. Hamilton would have 13 divisions (including the 54th), 8 more than he landed with. Von Sanders had 16, compared with 6 on April 25. Three of these were at Anzac, including Kemal's 19th. Essad, the corps commander at Anzac, could also draw on Kannengiesser's 9th, which was spread out south of Gaba Tepe. The numbers at Anzac on August 6 favoured the Allies, although such arithmetic took no account of terrain. Birdwood would have about 37,000 men and woeful artillery support. The Turks in front of him numbered about 20,000; two battalions of Turks, more or less, were out on the left where the night attack was planned.

The sequence was to go like this. Birdwood's reinforcements would come ashore at night from August 3 to be hidden in dugouts during the day. On the afternoon of August 6 the British would attack in the centre of the line at Helles. At 5.30 pm the Australians would storm Lone Pine (Birdwood had shifted this attack back another 30 minutes).

After dark New Zealanders would clear the foothills on the left of Anzac. The right assaulting column, all New

Zealanders, would then head for Chunuk Bair, some going up Sazli Dere, some up Chailak Dere. The left assaulting column, commanded by General Cox of the Indian Brigade, would head off along the coast, then turn right up Aghyl Dere, heading for Hill 971 and Hill Q. On the same night the 11th Division would land at Suvla and take Kiretch Tepe, Chocolate Hill and the W Hills.

At dawn the next day the 10th Division would also land at Suvla. The New Zealanders on Chunuk Bair would attack back down the range, towards Baby 700. At the same time Australians at the Nek, Pope's and Quinn's would attack up the range, towards Baby 700. The troops at Suvla would advance further along Kiretch Tepe and also take Tekke Tepe. At the end of the second day Suvla would be secure and joined up with Anzac, the Turks on Baby 700 and Battleship Hill would be under attack from front and rear, and the Turkish line would be broken at Lone Pine. The Allies would be poised to break out and head for Maidos. That was the theory anyway.

One of the troubles was that three New Army divisions were being used at Suvla and Anzac. The troops were keen; they had had more training than the Australians who landed on April 25, and their senior officers were regulars. Many of these regulars, however, were too old for field command; others would never have obtained such high ranks in peacetime or if seniority had been awarded on merit. And to ask untried troops to take part in an amphibious landing and night assaults and then to soldier on the next day in blazing heat – that was a gamble.

Hamilton wanted the 29th Division, which had been brought up to strength with reinforcements, to lead the attack at Suvla. His staff told him it would be unfair to ask the division to make two amphibious landings in three months. None of the other five divisions at Helles could be used; they had been wrecked. And, anyway, the Helles line had to be held. The 1st Australian Division was needed for Lone Pine and to hold the line elsewhere on 400 Plateau. The Australia and New Zealand Division was the centrepiece for the attack on the heights.

Another trouble arose from Hamilton's passion for secrecy, which he – or was it really Braithwaite? – carried to extremes. Birdwood early in July mentioned to Hamilton that he had shown his plan to Walker and Godley. Hamilton wrote to him sternly: 'Please find out at once how many staff officers each of them has told, and let me know.' Hamilton told Birdwood to tell Walker and Godley the scheme had been abandoned. Most commanders found out too late what they were supposed to do. Cox, quite reasonably, wanted to scout the country that would lead him to Hill 971 and Hill Q. He was told he couldn't. His Indians were to arrive at Anzac the night before the attack. They would be hidden in dugouts the next day. Then they would be sent out at night into country they had never seen. On the night of the Suvla landing many officers had never seen a map of the coast they were now blundering over. As has been mentioned, Stopford was not told what he was supposed to do until July 22.

Stopford – here was the biggest trouble, although Hamilton was such a poor judge of character that he didn't realise it. Stopford was trying to do something he wasn't equipped to do. He didn't know what was right and what was wrong. He was thus swayed by the last person he spoke to. And he didn't want to use up too much energy; he tired easily and it was so hot and everything was so confusing.

*   *   *

The memorandum of July 22 told Stopford that IX Corps' first task after landing and securing Suvla Bay was to capture the Chocolate and W Hills and to get a foothold on the Tekke Tepe ridge, the highest point above the plain. Specifically, it said: 'It is of first importance that the Chocolate and W hills should be captured by a *coup de main* before daylight.' Stopford was told that the 10th Division, landing at dawn on August 7, could quickly take the village of Big Anafarta, about four miles inland. This would bring the division in on the flank of Hill 971 and help Cox and Monash. Stopford was also told that few heavy guns would be landed until morning. The plan assumed there were five Turkish battalions defending Suvla (in fact there were three). If the landing went to plan the British would have 20 battalions ashore by the morning of August 7. Hamilton told Stopford there would be trouble with darkness, the rawness of the troops and unknown country, but inspired leadership could get around these things. Stopford said it was a good plan. Then he went off and talked to his chief-of-staff, Brigadier-General Hamilton Reed, and decided it was a bad plan.

Unlike Stopford, Reed, a Victoria Cross winner in South Africa, had frontline form and disliked sloppy planning. His recent experience on the western front told him that troops should not be asked to attack trenches without artillery support. He had been with the Turkish army as a liaison officer during the Balkan wars. He knew how dogged the Turks could be in defence. Reed was almost certainly the 'truculent brigadier' who so upset Mackenzie at lunch. We know now that there were only three battalions of Turks at Suvla and that they did not dominate the beaches the way their comrades had at Helles on April 25; we know now that Stopford's troops

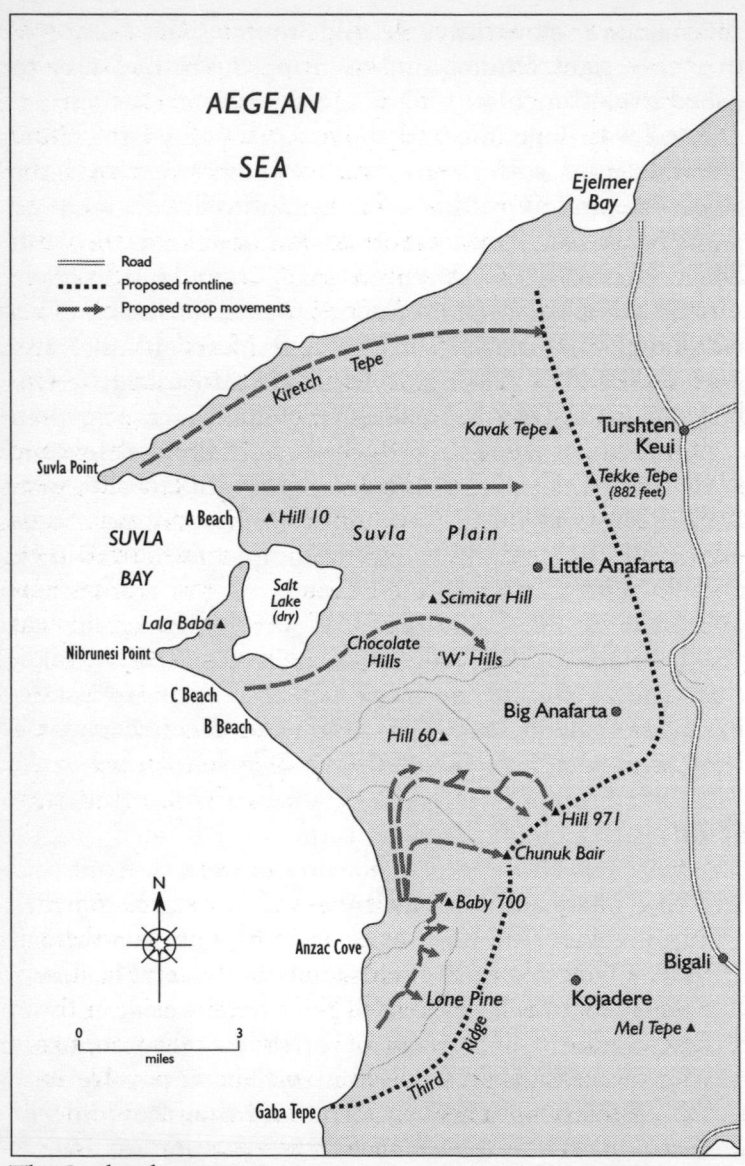

AEGEAN

SEA

Ejelmer
Bay

Road
Proposed frontline
Proposed troop movements

Kiretch Tepe

Suvla Point

Kavak Tepe ▲

Turshten
Keui

Tekke Tepe
(882 feet)

A Beach   ▲ Hill 10   Suvla   Plain

SUVLA

BAY

Little Anafarta

Salt
Lake
(dry)

▲ Scimitar Hill

Lala Baba ▲

Nibrunesi Point

Chocolate
Hills

'W' Hills

C Beach

B Beach

Big Anafarta ◉

Hill 60 ▲

N

Hill 971

▲ Chunuk Bair

Bigali

▲ Baby 700

Anzac Cove

0   3
miles

Lone Pine

Kojadere

Mel Tepe ▲

Third Ridge

Gaba Tepe

The Suvla plan

didn't need an artillery barrage. Reed, however, was probably right to object. Certainly Stopford was being asked to capture a huge amount of ground in the dark.

Reed was dogmatic and thought he knew a lot about war; Stopford was passive and conceded he knew little. Which meant Stopford now became a football, kicked one way by Reed and Mahon (who also disliked the plans) and another way by Hamilton and Aspinall, who were more concerned with the Anzac breakout than the Suvla sideshow. Stopford became more bewildered each time he was kicked. His first battle had not started and he was already a study in mental decline.

Stopford, urged on by Reed, now wanted the 'good plan' revised. The three brigades of the 11th Division were to land south of Nibrunesi Point rather than inside Suvla Bay itself. The navy was worried about uncharted reefs and sandbanks within the bay. Stopford now wanted one brigade landed within the bay; this was agreed to. He was worried about troops advancing without artillery. Since no howitzers would be available until the morning after the landing, Stopford said his troops could not capture the Chocolate and W hills by dawn. Nor could they make the Tekke Tepe ridge by that time. He received new orders.

> Your *primary objective* [my italics] will be to secure Suvla Bay as a base for all the forces operating in the northern zone. Owing to the difficult nature of the terrain, it is possible that the attainment of this objective will, in the first instance, require the use of the whole of the troops at your disposal. Should, however, you find it possible to achieve this object with only a portion of your force, your next step will be to give such direct assistance as is in your power to the General Officer Commanding Anzac in

his attack on Hill 305 [Hill 971], by an advance on Biyuk Anafarta, with the object of moving up the eastern spurs of that hill . . . Subject only to his final approval, the General Commanding gives you an entirely free hand in the selection of your plan of operations.

The instruction, dated July 29, was a nonsense. Hamilton had told Stopford a week earlier that he wanted the Chocolate and W Hills captured by dawn, presumably so that Turkish artillerymen there could not fire into the Anzac attack. The new order said: 'If, therefore, it is possible, without prejudice to the attainment of your *primary objective* [my italics], to gain possession of these hills at an early period of your attack, it will greatly facilitate the capture and retention of Hill 305.' There was no mention of Tekke Tepe.

Why would the beach be the primary objective? The beach was of no strategic value. Troops there threatened nothing. What, one might now ask, was the point of the Suvla landing? Was it simply to set up a northern base? Or was it to help Birdwood break out of Anzac and cut the peninsula? With the issue of the second set of orders, this was unclear. Whatever may be said against him, Stopford was now *entitled* to believe all he had to do was set up on the beach, then think about taking a few hills when he felt able. The imperative of speed had gone. What if Birdwood urgently needed help? Wouldn't Stopford be in a better position to help if he commanded the hills above Suvla? What if Stopford took so much time setting up on the beach that the Turks were able to rush up reinforcements? If that happened, the Suvla base could end up hemmed in like Anzac. And what was this about needing the 'whole of the troops' to secure the beach? This wasn't V Beach. Aerial photographs showed no defences overlooking the landing coast. The point of the Suvla landing had been smudged by the new orders. Humpty Dumpty was the author; the words meant whatever one wanted them to mean.

Stopford now issued an imprecise order for IX Corps. Hammersley, in turn, issued an imprecise order for the 11th Division; he would attack the W Hills 'if possible'. Hammersley's orders suggested that the point of the Anzac attack was to distract the Turks from the 11th Division's landing. Cox and Monash would be slogging up Aghyl Dere; the New Zealanders would be fighting their way up Rhododendron Ridge; the Australians would storm Lone Pine; light horsemen would run at machine guns at the Nek – all this so that the 11th Division could secure a beach at a place that, of itself, didn't matter? Maybe Hammersley really believed this, even though he had discussed the operation with Birdwood.

The confusion was fantastic. Hamilton had said a fortnight before that the Chocolate and W hills should be taken by dawn and that the Tekke Tepe ridge should be occupied. The orders now going out to the brigades said merely that Chocolate Hill and Green Hill, next to it, be captured – at no precise time. Hamilton and his staff didn't seem to realise that their scheme was being watered down and turned into something else.

Stopford wrote to Hamilton after the new orders came out, saying: 'I fear that it is likely that the attainment of the security of Suvla Bay will so absorb the force under my command as to render it improbable that I shall be able to give direct assistance to the G.O.C. Anzac in his attack on Hill 305.'

Here is the mindset of a general already defeated. Hamilton should have summoned him at once and disabused him. In his *The Decisive Battles of the Western*

World, Major-General J. F. C. Fuller describes Stopford as an incompetent with 'no conception of what generalship meant'. This is surely true. Yet Stopford was right to query the original orders; they were glib and perhaps asked him to do too much on the first night. The blame for the confusion, and for what flowed from it, lies mostly with Hamilton. He allowed the watered-down orders to go out; he allowed Stopford to wallow in defeatism. Aspinall is hard on Stopford in his official history, but Aspinall was in a curious position. Writing in 1932, he was the official historian; in 1915, he was head of the operations division at Hamilton's GHQ and largely responsible for the plans.

The Turks tell a story about Kemal. It is the nineteen-thirties and now he is known as Atatürk, President of Turkey. He does not read English. Someone is reading Aspinall's history to him, translating it into Turkish. The translator comes to the prelude to Suvla. Kemal suddenly interrupts him. *No*, Kemal says, Hamilton was to blame, not Stopford.

It is April, 2000, and a group of us stand near the fire-spotting tower on Hill 971, peering out over the country where Cox and Monash made their night advance. A taxi pulls up. An Englishman gets out with his son, who is perhaps ten years old. The Englishman obviously has plenty of money. He wears a shirt with a Dow Jones logo. He has hired the taxi in Istanbul, four-and-a-half hours away. He wants to show his son the battlefield. The taxi-driver looks lost, mainly because he is. In Istanbul he was the predator, the entrepreneur. Now this Englishman has waved millions of lire at him and he's been bribed into this wilderness with its dirt roads and cemeteries and these foreigners who just stand and stare at the ridges, as though if they stare long enough some revelation will eventually come to them. '*Insh'allah*,' he says in despair, '*Insh'allah*.'

The Englishman is breezy. 'Now where's Suvla?' he asks.

We point to the salt lake and the green farmland behind.

'Looks easier than here,' he says, pointing to the dark gullies below Chunuk Bair. 'Why didn't they move at Suvla?'

'Stopford,' someone says, as though that one name explains everything.

'Ah! *That's* Stopford. You know, I've always thought the Russians got that right.'

'The *Russians*?'

'Yes, the Russians. They shoot the generals who fail – makes the others better. Should I go to Helles? Anything worth seeing there?'

He decides to go to Helles. '*Insh'allah*,' the taxi-driver mutters. The second battle of Gallipoli has begun; this time the Turk is losing.

In early August Hamilton's headquarters on Imbros bristled with plots and not all of them were against the Turks. Many in London and Paris had resented the expedition all along. To them, Hamilton was a thief who took troops from France. Hamilton knew they thought this, even though he hadn't been home. He needed a success. He had dysentery and he was nervous about the coming offensive. Reed and Mahon didn't seem to believe in it. Stopford had no 'go' in him. Ashmead-Bartlett, that damned Jeremiah, was out there drinking champagne and telling everyone that the Allies should be landing at Bulair. God knows what Ashmead-Bartlett had said to Asquith and Kitchener. *Why did Kitchener see him?* Other gossips were about. And here he was, stranded on this rock called Imbros. Alone.

Hamilton didn't know that many on his own staff were losing faith in him. He had allowed Braithwaite to protect him too well and influence him too much. He wasn't good at detail. He gave in to Kitchener too much. He had let Hunter-Weston butcher the Helles divisions in July. He didn't tell London what was really happening. He didn't get around the trenches enough. He spent too much time writing press reports. Dawnay, particularly, was starting to wonder if Hamilton was the right man.

Into this hotbed walked Lieutenant-Colonel Maurice Hankey, Secretary to the Committee of Imperial Defence. He was to report on Gallipoli for Cabinet. He had come instead of Churchill. Cabinet had decided it didn't want Churchill at the Dardanelles. The Gallipoli campaign was his wayward son; he would be biased. The general staff resented Hankey's presence and declared him an 'amateur'.

Hankey wasn't put off. He was 38 and looked older, short and balding and with a benevolent air. His walk was as languid as his speech. He had a fine mind but didn't flaunt it; he crept up on people and picked the pockets of their minds. He asked Compton Mackenzie to have a talk with him. First he reassured Mackenzie. 'I want you, when you are talking to me quite frankly, to remember that you are not talking to the average soldier man. I have imagination.' Then he moved closer to where he wanted to be. 'First of all, do you think Sir Ian Hamilton is the right man to command out here?'

Mackenzie began a long defence of Hamilton that included this observation: 'In his heart Sir Ian must know that Lord Kitchener has no grasp at all of the situation out here; but he cannot bring himself to tell him as much in as many words. All our leaders suffer from an exaggerated sensitiveness over the feelings of other leaders.'

What was more interesting was that the representative of the Prime Minister was asking an Intelligence officer, a self-confessed amateur, whether the commander-in-chief was up to the job.

Ashmead-Bartlett early in August made what he called 'a most important discovery'. He boarded one of the monitor ships that had been sent out to provide artillery support after the German submarine scare. It was captained by a friend and carried in its holds everything Ashmead-Bartlett desired. Champagne, liqueurs, port, sherry, caviar, foie gras, hams, tongues, potted meats – they were all there. 'He [the captain] is going to see plenty of me this summer,' Ashmead-Bartlett declared.

Four days later, on the evening of August 6, he watched the New Army youngsters leave for Suvla and wondered how many would have enlisted if they had known the truth about Gallipoli. Mackenzie also watched. The empty tents on Imbros looked like ghosts in the twilight, he thought. By 7.30 all the ships had left. 'The metallic blues and greens and blood-reds in the water had turned to a cold dull grey. Eastward the ever increasing surge and thunder of the guns: here an almost horrible quiet.'

It wasn't like the night of April 24; the players knew not to hope too much. Hamilton thought the New Army boys seemed subdued. Nights like this, he wrote, held 'the same intoxicating mixture of danger and desire as fills the glass of the boy bridegroom when he raises it to the health of his enigma in a veil. But I don't know how it is; I used to feel like that; now I too am terribly anxious.'

Major Willmer had been going around his posts at

Suvla. After sunset he stood staring out to sea, looking for ships. Nothing. He rode home to the village of Little Anafarta. There, at 9.45 pm, they told him the English were landing at Nibrunesi Point.

20

Lone Pine

If Hunter-Weston had left the peninsula, his profligate spirit lived on in Brigadier-General Street, the chief-of-staff of VIII Corps. Lieutenant-General Francis Davies, Hunter-Weston's replacement, had arrived on August 5, but Hamilton thought it best that he wait until the Helles feint was over before taking command. Hamilton saw this attack, timed to begin at 3.50 pm on August 6, purely as a diversion, just enough noise to keep five Turkish divisions tied down in front of Krithia. Maybe Hamilton failed to make himself clear. Street and others at corps headquarters certainly saw the attack as something bigger. The corps order talked about the early capture of Krithia and Achi Baba.

Such an order might have been reasonable on April 24; now it was just bluster. Street didn't have enough artillery ammunition to advance his frontline 200 yards; Krithia and Achi Baba might as well have been suburbs of Constantinople. Aspinall wrote in the official history that Street was a 'very capable officer' with 'one blind spot': he couldn't admit to the increasing difficulties facing the troops at Helles. Cecil Aspinall was a polite man who wrote a polite, if wonderfully clear, history. What he was really saying was that Street was a dangerous optimist and not really a very capable officer at all.

Instead of a diversion, Street and his helpers delivered a typical Helles battle. Hunter-Weston could have sued him for plagiarism. The artillery support was inadequate. Trenches were taken and quickly lost again. Communications broke down. Corps headquarters had no notion of what was happening at the front, but they issued orders anyway; that was what they were good at. The communications trenches were choked with dead and wounded. Wounded lay in the blazing sun, going crazy with thirst. And the casualties bore no sensible relationship to the ground gained. How could they? As usual, hardly any ground was gained.

Because VIII Corps was still short of artillery, the attack was to come in two parts so that each would receive the support of every gun. The 88th Brigade of the 29th Division was to attack on the left on August 6. Two brigades of the 42nd Division would attack on the right the next day.

The bombardment began at 2.20 pm on August 6. The Turks immediately replied with their artillery. The casualties in the 88th Brigade piled up before a single man had left the trenches. Davies watched as a spectator. He had come from the western front and said he was 'horrified at the total inadequacy of the British bombardment'. He was getting a quick lesson on how things were done on the peninsula.

The troops finally surged forward on this hot and windless day. Few reached the Turkish trenches. They had gone out with metal discs on their backs. Those at corps headquarters were sure the attack had succeeded because they could see the discs all along the Turkish trenches. They didn't realise the wearers were all dead. The 88th Brigade had been destroyed – again.

The two brigades of the 42nd Division attacked next day. All they managed to capture and hold was a small vineyard west of the Krithia road. Again the losses were tremendous. In 24 hours VIII Corps had amassed 3469 casualties for the gain of a vineyard. Hamilton now ordered that there would be no more offensives at Helles while the new battles to the north were going on. In fact the frontline at Helles barely changed for the next five months. The dream was dead. Achi Baba would never be taken.

Not only had these two attacks failed; they had not even worked as diversions. By the morning of August 7 von Sanders knew that the main assault was at Anzac. He told Wehib Pasha, the commander at Helles and Essad's brother, to send his reserve division to help Essad. Wehib protested. Von Sanders ignored him. Wehib's chief-of-staff, a German, was so worried by the attacks around Anzac that he urged von Sanders to abandon Helles and move the troops to the Asian shore 'while there is still time'. Von Sanders sacked him.

Like the attack at Helles on August 6, the assault on Lone Pine was a diversion. As with the Helles attack, the casualties were high: more than 2000 Australians, about 7000 Turks. But Lone Pine was also that rare thing, an Allied victory. And something else again. On both sides it was an epic of savagery and sacrifice that leaves one wondering again at man's capacity to harbour, within the same brain and the same body, so much that is brutal and so much that is sublime.

A pilot flying above 400 Plateau from south to north would have seen two networks of trenches facing each other at distances varying from 60 to 150 yards. Each network looked like the anatomical diagrams that Leonardo da Vinci once sketched. That thick wavy line running vertically at the start of each maze – that was the fire trench, the artery. The other thick lines behind them, also running vertically – they were support and reserve trenches, the veins. And those lines running horizontally, hundreds of them, much thinner, short and faint – they were the communications saps, the capillaries.

Walker and White had argued against this attack and lost. They now planned it as carefully as any frontal assault across 100 yards of relatively flat ground could be. They had not attended the Hunter-Weston School for Cheery Bovines; they would try to bring sense to madness. Tunnels were pushed out towards the Turkish lines, from the Pimple, the Australian salient opposite Lone Pine, and either side of it. The ends of the tunnels were opened before the artillery barrage ended, which meant the men pouring out of them only had to run 40 yards or so. One tunnel almost reached the Turkish frontline. This was opened up along its entire length to provide a safe communications trench between the two frontlines. Three more tunnels were blown up to make craters to provide cover for the troops who had to make the long run from the trenches. The slow bombardment over three days smashed much of the wire in front of the Turkish trenches.

The Australians attacked on a front of about 220 yards. Two lines from the 1st Brigade dashed out of the tunnels when the barrage lifted. Another two lines from the same brigade charged across open ground. The Turks did not expect an attack. Lone Pine was one of their strongest posts. Behind it lay a gully called the Cup, running away to Legge Valley and out into open country towards the Turkish headquarters on Scrubby Knoll. The Cup was not entrenched; it was a bivouac and administrative area with dugouts and terraces. If the Australians broke through here and beyond, they were out of the Anzac prison. But surely they wouldn't be foolish enough to attack something as layered as Lone Pine? Some Turks apparently thought the barrage was a payback for placards they had raised to report the German capture of Warsaw. (A notice hoisted at Johnston's Jolly read 'Varsaw ash fallin'. As Bean noted, the Australians' attempts at Turkish were often worse.)

The trenches at Lone Pine, roofed with pine logs from Constantinople, were probably the most elaborate at Anzac. When the Australians reached the Turkish frontline, the anti-climax was surreal. The aerial photographs had not shown the pine logs. How to get in there? Some Australians fired through gaps in the logs. Others poked at them with bayonets. Some dropped down into the musty galleries below. Others ran on, past the frontline, towards the open communication trenches beyond and even as far as the Cup. Meanwhile reinforcements came running along the open tunnel that now joined their trenches to those of the Turks.

Considering this was a frontal assault, the casualties during the charge were light. The killing took place underground, in the galleries and saps, and on a scale out of all proportion to the tiny bit of ground involved. This was a reversion to war in its most primitive form. Men fought with bayonets and bombs; they kicked and punched; shrieks and shouts and sighs and curses came out of holes in the earth. Waves of Australians ran over the bodies of their own dead and wounded, sometimes piled three and four deep; there was nowhere else to step. One group of Australians reached Turkish battalion headquarters in the Cup. They were cut off and killed.

The Turks had been badly surprised. Zeki Bey, his

wound of April 25 healed, was ordered to take his battalion from German Officers' Trench and reinforce Lone Pine. When he arrived he met a battalion commander called Mustafa Kemal. 'What has happened?' Zeki asked. 'We're lost, we're lost!' the man replied, as if to prove he had nothing in common with his namesake. Turkish soldiers were lying down nearby, not knowing what to do. Australian bayonets and periscopes could be seen deep in the Turkish positions. The Turks were unnerved and confused. 'Things were clearly critical,' Zeki told Bean after the war. 'If any further attack came, we should lose the whole position.'

Zeki and others rallied the Turks. The fighting raged for several days. Australians from the 2nd and 3rd brigades came up as reinforcements. Troops in reserve begged to get into the fight; some offered bribes of £5 to be allowed through. Lone Pine came to be about bombs, or grenades, and the Turks had better bombs and more of them. Some Turkish bombs, set to an eight-second fuse, made three trips back and forth before they exploded. Men who lost a hand picking up the bombs took to throwing them back with their other hand. Others lay writhing from bomb wounds to the legs and buttocks. There were thousands upon thousands of bodies, some dead, some barely alive. A lieutenant from the 4th Battalion fought on even though one of his eyes had been shot away. Shreds from the socket were plastered down over his cheekbone. He went forward again rallying his men, and was shot dead.

By August 12 the worst of the fighting was over. The Australians had taken Lone Pine and the Turks, despite the fury of their counter-attacks, were not going to get it back. But the Australians could not take the Cup and beyond. The Australians blocked off the Turkish communications trenches with sandbags and earth and built a new frontline across them. Lone Pine was a diversion that worked, rather too well as we will see, and an epic in a way that the landing of April 25 was not; but it was not a breakout.

Private John Gammage of the 1st Battalion keeps thinking of his little niece as he waits to charge at Lone Pine. He decides not even a louse could live under the bombardment being dumped on the Turks. But the Turkish artillery replies and Australians begin to fall in the support trenches. Gammage receives a 'slight tap' on the face that bleeds freely and another on the knee. He rushes forward in the second wave, trips over a roll of barbed wire as bullets whistle around him, reaches the first trench and lands on a wounded Turk.

> The moans of our own poor fellows and also Turks as we tramped on their wounded bodies was awful. We rushed them out of their 2nd and third line of trenches in half an hour. The wounded bodies of both Turks and our own in the 2nd and 3rd line, especially the third, were piled up 3 and 4 deep . . . the bombs simply poured in but as fast as our men went down another would take his place. Besides our own wounded the Turks' wounded lying in our trench were cut to pieces with their own bombs. We had no time to think of our wounded . . . their pleas for mercy were not heeded . . . Some poor fellows lay for 30 hours waiting for help and many died still waiting.

Gammage thinks the place will be impossible to hold. 'But we would have sooner died than retreat.' Around 3am Gammage and others are sent over the parapet towards a Turkish trench. When daylight comes they are like 'mice in a trap', shot at and bombed. Gammage and a few others crawl back to their starting point about 11 am. Gammage's eyes are full of sand and his face is bleeding from gravel thrown up by bombs and shells. But he is happy. He doesn't much like officers, or the ruling classes generally, and now he hears that an officer he particularly dislikes – 'the drunken cad who sent many good men to their death' – has been shot (accidentally, one presumes) by his own men. 'I nearly had a foal when I heard it. A pity he never got one hours before.' On the evening of August 8 Gammage's group is relieved.

Seven hours later he is back in the firing line.

I got one most daring Turk from 12 yards off who was throwing bombs . . . We felt like wild beasts but were calm and never fired reckless but deliberate . . . Bombs all day. Our bomb throwers nearly all dead or wounded . . . 11 am nearly blinded but men are scarce so I must not throw the towel in. Only scratches from gravel and dirt thrown up by bombs. This was an awful place. 12 am hit again and put out of action [it was a leg wound]. It is not sore but bled freely. My rifle was blown to splinters . . . Since Friday [August 6, three days earlier] food was turned off. All I had was taken from dead comrades haversacks but its all for a good cause. Jews and big Capitalists. I could see a few weeks holiday sticking out. Didn't my comrades envy me being carried out with only a flesh wound. Today I left some of the best men ever god put breath in.

Gammage goes to a hospital at Lemnos and finds officers suffering from nervous breakdowns and other complaints from which, he says, privates are apparently immune, 'but officers are different, poor creatures'. He is back on the front line by September 30. He has a dark view of life and the various conspiracies it throws at him; but he has a big heart too.

Private Cecil McAnulty of the 2nd Battalion was reported killed at Lone Pine between August 7 and August 12. His diary was written on the backs of envelopes and other scraps of paper.

> On Friday when we got the word to charge Frank and I were on the extreme left . . . There was a clear space of 100 yards to cross without a patch of cover. I can't realise how I got across it. I seemed to be in a sort of trance, the rifle and machine gun fire was hellish. I remember dropping down when we reached their trenches, looked around and saw Frank and three more men alongside me . . . I yelled out to the other 4 chaps, 'This is only suicide, boys. I'm going to make a jump for it.' I thought they said alright we'll follow. I sprang to my feet in one jump

The diary stops in mid sentence.

Sergeant Lawrence, the engineer, had worked on the tunnels. Now, on August 7, he goes to Lone Pine to work on the communications trenches joining the old frontline to the new. He comes on a group of Australian wounded in a Turkish tunnel.

> These fellows have been crouched up in here all night; some of their wounds are awful yet they sit there not saying a word, certainly not complaining, and some have actually fallen off to sleep despite their pain. One has been shot clean through the chest and his singlet and tunic are just saturated with blood, another has his nose and upper lip shot clean away . . . Lying beside them was a man asleep. He had been wounded somewhere in the head, and

as he breathed the blood just bubbled and frothed at his nose and mouth . . . Yet all one gave him was simply a casual glance, more of curiosity than anything else. At ordinary times these sights would have turned one sick but now they have not the slightest effect.

Lawrence works on deepening the communications trench and looks back on the old Australian firing line.

The whole way across it is just one mass of dead bodies, bags of bombs, bales of sandbags, rifles, shovels and all the hundred and one things that had to be rushed across to the enemy trenches. The undergowth has been cut down, like mown hay, simply stalks left standing, by the rifle fire, whilst the earth itself appears just as though one had taken a huge rake and scratched it all over . . .

Right beside me, within a space of fifteen feet, I can count fourteen of our boys stone dead. Ah! it is a piteous sight. Men and boys who yesterday were full of joy and life, now lying there, cold – cold – dead – their eyes glassy, their faces sallow and covered with dust – soulless – gone – somebody's son, somebody's boy – now merely a thing. Thank God that their loved ones cannot see them now – dead, with the blood congealed or oozing out. God, what a sight. The major is standing next to me and he says, 'Well, we have won.' Great God – won – that means a victory and all those bodies within arms' reach – then may I never witness a defeat.

Lawrence sees a dead Australian with his head and shoulders hanging into a Turkish tunnel. 'The blood is drip, drip, drip into the trench. I sit watching it – fascinated.' Lawrence tries to find the soldier's identity disc. The soldier's head is heavy and full of dirt and now

Lawrence has blood all over his hands. He shudders and wipes his hands in the dirt. Lawrence sees another dead Australian with a congealed line of dark red running down his neck. He notices the man's hands. 'They are clasped before him just as though he was in prayer. I wonder what that prayer was.'

Lawrence writes home to his father.

Talking about Lone Pine . . . we could see our dead lying in all sorts of positions . . . amongst them was a wounded chap. After trying all we knew to get him in . . . one of our boys, who had had too much rum, insisted on going out alone . . . There were dozens of dead lying there and he went around shaking them all and asking, 'Are you dead? Come on, get up.'

Ivor Margetts, the Hobart schoolteacher, now promoted to captain, also wrote to his father shortly after Lone Pine.

I will try and describe what a captured trench looks like . . . The trench smelt just like a slaughter house in the cleanest parts . . . in others it is impossible to describe the smell . . . dead bodies were stacked in heaps in places where there was available room and in other parts where there was no room they were left in the floor of the trench and covered with a thin layer of earth and made a soft spongy floor to walk on. Of course as many as we could get rid of were thrown up to help make bullet proof parapets and also to make a barrier to block up communicating trenches leading from Turkish reserve trenches. As some of these bodies had been dead for some days when I went through, and were horribly swollen, remembering that the weather is so hot that one wears as little clothing as possible, it is necessary to try and describe the stench that the men were eating, fighting, and sleeping in. In the trench I counted 7965382165073982 flies who walked first on the perspiring live men and then, so as to cool their feet, they walked on the dead ones.

Margetts explained to his parents that he was telling them this so that next time they read in a newspaper that the British had captured and held a trench they would understand what this really meant. Margetts told his parents he had been 'wonderfully lucky' and his health was 'just splendid'. He had survived that first day up on Baby 700 and received a graze to the cheek from a shell burst at Lone Pine, even though he was not involved in the trench fighting. In December he played Australian football against the 10th Battalion. 'Beautiful match. Led at three-quarter time, lost by seven points.' He survived Gallipoli only to be killed in France in 1916, aged 24, dead when he should have been full of life. Perhaps he was the sort of man the historian Geoffrey Blainey was thinking of when he wrote that the worst effect of the war on Australia could never be enumerated. It was the loss of 'all those talented people who would have become prime ministers and premiers, judges, divines, engineers, teachers, doctors, poets, inventors and farmers, the mayors of towns and leaders of trade unions, and the fathers of another generation of Australians'. Between 1914 and 1918 Australia lost the most generous male spirits of a generation. There is no way of knowing whether the country ever recovered from this.

Lieutenant Jack Merivale of the 4th Battalion was killed on the first day at Lone Pine. Among his papers is a letter written by an unknown Australian. All we know is that he was an officer. He watched the first assault. 'My batman and I were fearfully excited, and I'm not ashamed to own we both wept with excitement at not being in it, but our turn was to come.' Of the next day, he wrote:

> The sights in the Lone Pine works were too terrible for words, so I won't describe that at all, but the way those chaps took the trenches, and the way they held on, was the equal of any feat of arms ever accomplished. One must remember that these men had been constantly fighting for four months, and are thin and worn. The Turks are magnificent fighters, and are very brave men . . . more honourable than those German swine.

Oliver Cumberland, the second of the two brothers from Scone, also died at Lone Pine, probably on the third day. No-one knows how or where he died. He was like so many, just another body to be tossed out on a parapet so that the living could breathe the air without gagging. In his last letter to his sister Una, dated July 26, he wrote: 'You can understand Una, that losing Joe has broken me up a bit, but Una it might be for the best – war is a terrible game especially this war, and those who are killed quick are sometimes better off.'

Una sewed children's clothes at night and fretted. She had been told early in September that Oliver had been wounded between August 7 and 14. Why wasn't he writing? What hospital was he in? In October she wrote to the Minister for Defence. Could he tell her what had happened to her brother? Back came a letter from a captain in Base Records. Oliver's wound was not serious. Although the captain didn't know what hospital Oliver was in or the nature of his wound, 'favourable progress may be assumed'. In March, 1916, Oliver was officially posted as 'wounded and missing'. Later the same month a court of inquiry decided that he had been killed in action.

When the Great War ended, there was no trace of his body. An exhumation party in 1922 found his remains in an old trench 35 yards from the present-day Lone Pine cemetery. The body was re-interred. 'This work,' the letter Una received from Base Records said, 'is carried out with the utmost care and reverence in the presence of a chaplain.' In October, 1922, Oliver's identification disc, caked with yellow dirt, arrived at Kelly Street, Scone. Una finally had something to hold on to.

In September, 1915, a month after the great attack, Ion Idriess of the Light Horse went up to Lone Pine. 'The route smelt like a cavern dug in a graveyard, where the people are not even in their coffins.'

> Of all the bastards of places this is the greatest bastard in the world. And a dead-man's boot in the firing-possy has been dripping grease on my overcoat and the coat will stink forever . . . The roof of this dashed possy is intermixed with dead men who were chucked up on the parapet to give the living a chance from the bullets while the trench was being dug. What ho, for the Glories of War!

The glories of war. Seven Australians won the Victoria Cross at Lone Pine, two of them posthumously. All the medals were won during the three days after the opening charge. All were about bomb-throwing and the subterranean anarchy of the second part of the battle. All were about furious little scraps around trench corners and over piles of sandbags. By 6 pm on the first day, the Australians held the Turkish frontline trenches; it was possible to talk of success almost straight away, yet it was a disorderly success. The Australians had established posts deep inside Lone Pine. These were not joined up, so there was no new frontline. And the Turks were counter-attacking.

The background of the seven VC winners tells much about Australian society in 1915. Lance-Corporal Leonard Keysor was a 29-year-old Jew who had emigrated to Sydney a few months before the outbreak of war. He returned to London after the war, lived quietly and said the war was the only adventure he ever had. Captain Alfred Shout was born in Wellington, New Zealand, and served with the New Zealand contingent in the Boer War, where he was twice wounded. He emigrated to Sydney in 1907. Three others – Lieutenant William Symons, Captain Frederick Tubb and Corporal William Dunstan, all born in country Victoria – were of Cornish stock. Before the war, Private John Hamilton worked as a butcher's boy, Dunstan as a messenger boy in a draper's shop, Symons as a clerk in a grocer's shop, Shout as a carpenter, Tubb as a farmer. Tubb and Corporal Alexander Burton, both from the Euroa area of Victoria, had joined up together.

Burton was killed by a bomb. Tubb was with him and later said: 'Just before he died he looked up at me, smiled quietly, and was then killed. His was a fine death, and I almost wish I had died too.' Tubb was killed in Belgium in 1917. Dunstan later became general manager of the Herald & Weekly Times newspaper group when it was run by Keith Murdoch. Dunstan never talked to his son, Keith, about that day at Lone Pine.

It was always presumed the events were so terrible, it was a forbidden subject in our house. Just occasionally my mother would take me to the little cupboard under the stairs and show me that dull little bronze cross made from cannon captured at Sebastopol during the Crimean War. There were also little oak clusters which told that he had been mentioned twice in despatches.

Dunstan was blind for almost a year after Lone Pine. Pieces of shrapnel came out of his body for years and the Dunstan children had to keep quiet around the house because of their father's headaches. Keith Murdoch, though he had only been on the peninsula for a few days as a journalist, was better remembered for his part in the Gallipoli campaign than Dunstan. Murdoch, as we shall see, had a myth built around him; Dunstan just had headaches.

Myths were constructed around Simpson and his donkey, but not around Shout, who died from his wounds at Lone Pine and became Australia's most decorated soldier at Gallipoli. Shout was the casual hero with the cheery manner; he made hard things look easy and made men around him feel better. He deserves to be seen as one of the larger figures of the Gallipoli campaign, and it doesn't much matter whether Australia or New Zealand claims him.

As a lieutenant at the landing he fought all day on Baby 700 and Walker's Ridge. Two days later he carried more than a dozen men out of the firing line, though repeatedly wounded himself. He received the Military Cross for this and was mentioned in despatches. Back at the front by May 11 he was wounded again and promoted to captain. At Lone Pine on August 9 Shout charged the Turks with bombs, cracking jokes and cheering his men on. He became too ambitious and tried to light three bombs at once. He managed to throw one. Either the second or the third exploded as it left his hand. Both his hands were blown to pulp; he appears to have lost his right hand entirely. His left eye was blown out, his cheek gashed and his chest and one leg burnt. He talked cheerfully and drank tea after they carted him off and announced that he would soon recover. He died, aged 33, a few days later on a hospital ship and was buried at sea. Afterwards there was another of those clerical mix-ups. His wife, Rose, was at first told that he had been wounded and was returning to Australia.

Who receives the VC? Who qualifies for mythology? There is not always a lot of sense to it, particularly in actions as frantic and fast-moving as Lone Pine or the British landing at W Beach. One bomber who had been with Private Hamilton had both his hands blown off. The doctor who treated him was reported as saying: 'After I had fixed him up for the beach he said: "Goodbye, Doc, old sport. Sorry I can't shake hands." '

The action for which Tubb, Dunstan and Burton received their VCs involved much bomb-catching by Corporal F. Wright, a labourer from Melbourne, and Corporal H. Webb, an orphan from the Melbourne suburb of Essendon. Wright eventually clutched at a bomb that burst in his face and killed him. Webb shortly after had both hands blown off as he tried to catch a bomb. He walked as far as Brown's Dip, the valley behind the old Australian trenches, and died. Webb received the Distinguished Conduct Medal, Wright nothing.

With its thick limestone pylon and its sweep of lawn, Lone Pine is one of the most arresting cemeteries on the peninsula. When there is a sprinkle of late-winter snow it can even look beautiful. Yet it is not an evocative place like Gully Ravine or Baby 700. These two have changed so little from 1915; if you stand around long enough and alone, the ghosts come out. Lone Pine has changed too much for this to happen. It was a rabbit warren and a mass grave. Photographs taken at the time show that the Australians who fought here and lived afterwards stood around in shock. The whites of their eyes are huge and their cheekbones are taut against skin that seems like marble. Now, in this same place, there are rows of pine trees and gravelled paths and white walls and flowers that give off sweet scents. Lone Pine has become wholesome.

It is asking too much to imagine this place as it was, even though you can still make out Turkish trench lines in what is left of the Cup. And it all seems so small – too small. Thousands of men, Turks and Australians, died here in a space not much bigger than a few suburban building blocks. Once this place was about anarchy and maggots; now it has an air of triumph and formality. And yellow daisies sway in the wind near Oliver Cumberland's grave.

Lone Pine is mostly for the 3700 Australians and New Zealanders who, like Burton, have no known grave and the 1200 who, like Shout, were buried at sea. Their names are on stone panels at the foot of the pylon. Private James Martin is listed here. He was a farmhand from Victoria who left for Gallipoli on June 28. He spent some hours in the water after the *Southland* was torpedoed near Lemnos and reached Anzac on September 8. A month later he picked up a pencil and wrote in a boyish scrawl to his parents in the Melbourne suburb of Hawthorn.

Just a line hoping all is well as it leaves me at present. Things are just the same here the only difference we are expecting a bit of rain which will not be welcomed by us. This place will be a mud hole when the rain does come. We had a bit of a shower last night but it was nothing to speak of. Occording [sic] to an account of a Turkish

Officer who gave himself up the other night says that the Turks are getting very badly treated by the German Officers and are only getting one meal a day and that was in the evening. There was one Turk who tried to give himself up the other night and got shot by the sentry. We dragged him into our Trenches to bury him in the morning and you ought to have seen the state he was in. He had no boots on an old pair of trousers all patched and an old coat. The pioneers took him down the gully to bury him and one got shot in the thigh by a sniper in the Turks Trenches. We are not doing bad for food we got that little present from Lady Ferguson [wife of the Australian Governor-General] that was 2 fancy biscuits, half stick Chocolate and 2 sardines each. I think I have told you all the news so I must draw to a close with Fondest love to all.

Private Martin craved a letter. Across the top of his letter he scrawled: 'Write soon. I have received no letters since I left Victoria and I have been writing often.' A little over a fortnight later he died from heart failure, probably caused by enteric fever, and was buried at sea.

His enlistment papers gave his age as 18. At the time of his death he was 14 years and 9 months. Among his effects was a scrap of red and white streamer that he had picked up as his troopship left Melbourne.

21

The breakout

The success in the stinking holes of Lone Pine produced a sequel that Birdwood could not have foreseen. Essad sent his local reserves, such as Zeki Bey's battalion and 5th Division troops from the village of Kojadere, to Lone Pine. That could have been foreseen. Essad was so worried he also summoned two regiments of Colonel Hans Kannengiesser's 9th Division, which was guarding the coast at Kum Tepe south of Anzac. This also could have been foreseen. And it wouldn't have mattered too much, so long as Kannengiesser's men stayed at Lone Pine.

But Kannengiesser, who arrived ahead of his troops, was told about midnight on August 6 that his men would not be needed at Lone Pine. Bigger things were happening. The British were landing at Suvla. And something was going on out on the northern flank, out in the foothills where the Turks had only two battalions and a few scattered trenches. The Anzacs appeared to be trying for the heights. Since he was now at Anzac, Kannengiesser should go on to Chunuk Bair. The summit was virtually undefended. Kannengiesser headed off ahead of his regiments, just as the New Zealanders of the right assaulting column were heading for the same place.

Kannengiesser must have been an exceptional soldier. Kemal was a cruel judge of men and no admirer of Germans. Yet he said of Kannengiesser: 'He was one of the most valuable German officers in our army.'

Birdwood soon had a second success. The two covering forces went out to clear the foothills and did the job with verve. The only trouble was that they took longer than they were supposed to.

The right assaulting column, all New Zealanders, was to creep up on Chunuk Bair from Rhododendron Ridge. Sazli Dere, which had a fork in it, ran up the southern side of Rhododendron. Chailak Dere, narrower and shorter but without a fork, ran up the northern side and around a little hill called Table Top, which was an offshoot of Rhododendron. The Turks had outposts on Table Top and further down the line of Rhododendron at Old Number Three Outpost and Destroyer Hill. On the northern side of Chailak Dere they had trenches on Bauchop's Hill. If these positions were overrun, and as quietly as possible, the way was clear to Chunuk Bair.

They were overrun by Brigadier-General Andrew Russell's covering force, 2000-strong and made up of his New Zealand Mounted Rifles Brigade (the Wellington, Auckland and Canterbury regiments), plus the Otago Mounted Rifles and the Maori Contingent. The force left the northern end of Anzac at 8.30 pm. The Auckland and Wellington regiments headed up Sazli Dere and took Old Number Three, Destroyer Hill and Table Top. The Otagos and Canterburys and the Maoris went up Chailak Dere, turned left, and took Bauchop's.

Old Number Three fell first. The trenches here were roofed, as at Lone Pine. For three weeks before the offensive a destroyer would shine her searchlight on the post at 9 pm and shell it for precisely 30 minutes, sending the Turks deep into their shelters. Then the searchlight would be switched off. There was a routine to it; there was meant to be. On the night of August 6 the routine was repeated, except that the moment the search-light was switched off the Auckland regiment stormed the trenches with bayonets before the Turks could emerge from underground. More than 100 Turks were killed and the others taken prisoner. The New Zealanders lost six killed.

A squadron of the Wellington regiment took Destroyer Hill and the rest of the regiment climbed the cliff-like slopes of Table Top in single file, cutting steps with entrenching tools. This hill fell too, but the climb took so long that the larger plan was now behind schedule. It was after midnight. The right assaulting column, which was to follow the covering force, was supposed to leave Anzac at 10.45 to be on Chunuk Bair by dawn. At this time of the year the first streaks of light came at 4 am.

The Otagos and Canterburys met rougher opposition at Bauchop's; there were more Turkish posts than expected. Just before 1 am the summit was taken with a bayonet charge, but at heavy cost. The New Zealanders lost around 100, including Lieutenant-Colonel Arthur Bauchop, the sawmiller who commanded the Otagos.

The right covering force had taken two-and-a-half hours longer than expected to complete its work. Even so, during the whole of the Gallipoli campaign few troops showed a flair to match that of the New Zealand Mounteds on the night of August 6.

The left covering force, two battalions of the New Army from the 13th Division, also did well. Their task was to go past Sazli and Chailak Deres, turn right up Aghyl Dere, and take the heights of Damakjelik Bair, the spur that tumbled down from near Hill Q and pointed towards Suvla. Damakjelik formed the left hand rampart of Aghyl Dere, the valley along which the left assaulting force would move. By 12.30 am the Turks on Damakjelik had surrendered.

The Turks in the foothills had been routed. There were hardly any Turks further up the range. Three hours of darkness remained. The way was open for both the right and left assaulting columns. Birdwood's plan, though running behind time, was very much alive.

The right assaulting column, under Brigadier-General Francis Johnston, moved out at 11.30 pm, even though the sounds of fighting, including Maori *hakas*, could still be heard in the foothills. Johnston had his New Zealand Infantry Brigade (the Canterbury, Otago, Wellington and Auckland battalions), a mountain battery and a company of engineers. The Canterburys advanced up Sazli Dere; the other three battalions, the mountain battery and the engineers went up Chailak. The idea was that after passing Table Top, both would climb the range and join up in a saddle between Table Top and the western shoulder of Rhododendron Ridge. From there they had to climb only 1000 yards along the crest of Rhododendron to see the Narrows from the summit of Chunuk Bair.

Command of the New Zealand force was riven by factions and feuds. It didn't help that Godley commanded the New Zealand and Australia Division. Unlike Birdwood and Walker, he was loathed by the rank and file. He also favoured regular officers, such as Johnston and his brigade-major, Arthur Temperley, and Lieutenant-Colonel Athelston Moore, commander of the Otagos, over citizen-soldiers like Malone. Godley, Johnston and Moore had bungled the attack on Baby 700 early in May.

Johnston appears to have been unwell and was said to drink heavily. There is a suggestion that he had been drinking on the morning of August 7. In his *Gallipoli*, Robert Rhodes James quotes Aspinall writing of Johnston in a private letter: 'I did, of course, know the truth, though, as official historian, I could not blurt it out . . . it was nothing but a national calamity that he was allowed to continue in command.' What was 'the truth'? The private correspondence of John North, author of *Gallipoli: The Fading Vision*, also contains a claim that Johnston was 'fighting drunk' when his brigade arrived below Chunuk Bair.

Temperley later described Johnston as a 'capable tactician' – whatever that means – but 'no genius'. He 'erred on the side of recklessness and inability to weigh the situation calmly'. Temperley said Johnston was 'always rather inarticulate'. His loyalty to the views of his superiors was 'complete and unswerving whatever his own personal opinions might be', an approach that would have endeared him to Godley.

Johnston and Temperley didn't get along with Malone. 'He was not a man of many ideas,' Temperley said. He was 'a picturesque rugged figure, a typical old New Zealand pioneer with a powerful jaw and an appearance of great strength and determination'. Malone didn't think the preparations for the attack on Chunuk Bair were thorough enough.

The Brigadier [Johnston] will not get down to bedrock. He seems to think that night attack and the taking of entrenched positions without artillery preparation is like 'Kissing one's hand'. Yesterday he burst forth. 'If there's any hitch I shall go right up and take the place myself.' All as it were in a minute and on his own! . . . He is an extraordinary man. If it were not so serious, it would be laughable. So far as I am concerned, the men, my brave gallant men, shall have the best fighting chance I can give them or that can be got. No airy plunging and disregard of the rules and chances.

Hughes and Young, the commanders of the Canterbury and Auckland battalions respectively, were out of favour because they were seen as 'Malone men'. Moore was all right; he was a regular.

The brigade, with a theoretical strength of 4000 men, was down to about 2800. The troops had been in the May struggle for Baby 700 and the Second Battle of Krithia; they had garrisoned Quinn's and other haunted houses at the head of Monash Gully. They had great spirit but they were worn out before they marched off to take the heights. Many – maybe 75 per cent, Temperley thought – had dysentery.

As the Otagos moved up Chailak Dere, leading the Wellingtons and the Aucklanders, they heard Turks on Table Top. These Turks had apparently been missed when the covering force cleared the hill. As two companies of Otagos climbed the hill to investigate, they heard hand clapping and cheering. The Turks wanted to surrender. More time was lost in this comic interlude, but now the moon was up and the column moved faster. A Turk ran out of the darkness. Temperley shot him dead with a revolver. He was the only Turk they saw after Table Top. The column climbed towards Rhododendron Ridge, where they would meet the Canterburys.

The Canterburys had become lost in Sazli Dere, which is harder to navigate than Chailak. An order was misinterpreted and most of the battalion ended up back at its starting point. In daylight around 4.30 am

Johnston was still waiting for the Canterburys.

Malone's Wellingtons had reached a position that came to be known as the Apex, where Chailak Dere ended and Cheshire Ridge ran into Rhododendron Ridge. Malone was just 500 yards from the summit of Chunuk Bair. There were only about 20 Turkish infantrymen there protecting an artillery battery. The battery commander was asleep.

At 4.30 am Australian light horsemen were supposed to charge the Nek. The idea – and here we use a noun rather loosely – was that the Australians would be attacking up the range as the New Zealanders, having captured Chunuk Bair, were coming back down. The attack on the Nek was a lunatic idea, close to wicked: even if the New Zealanders were coming down the hill, the Australians still had to charge at line after line of trenches bristling with machine guns. When Johnston paused to wait for the Canterburys, the attack on the Nek became entirely pointless.

The New Zealand line was strung out and the Canterburys were still missing when, around 5.30 am, Johnston and Temperley joined Malone at the Apex. Temperley appears to have wanted the Wellingtons and Aucklanders to attack Chunuk Bair. Malone was said to be against this. Temperley appeared to be doing the thinking and talking for Johnston. As Temperley wrote of a later interlude in the battle: 'As his staff officer I had learnt to know the working of his mind and to interpret him. This had become much accentuated since the battle started; he sat for hours in absolute silence; he was frequently barely coherent and his judgment and mind were obviously clouded.'

We don't really know what happened here. Temperley was one of the few senior officers present to survive the war. He tries to be fair but cannot disguise his bias towards 'regular officers'. There should have been no discussion and Johnston should not have waited for the Canterburys. Birdwood had said all commanders were to push on to the heights regardless of what was happening around them. If Malone did object, it may have had nothing to do with flouting the spirit of Birdwood's order. Malone may have simply lacked confidence in Johnston. And what *was* wrong with Johnston? Was he affected by alcohol? Or physically exhausted? Or having some form of breakdown? Or simply not up to commanding this sort of operation?

Temperley wrote in his personal narrative of the battle of Chunuk Bair that he advised Johnston to delay the assault. He didn't know what was happening on the right or left and a pause seemed sensible. He couldn't see the Indian Brigade coming up to attack Hill Q or Monash heading for Hill 971. Nothing seemed to be happening at Suvla. And the Turks were now firing from the crest of Chunuk Bair. Temperley sent a message to divisional headquarters saying that he was waiting. Johnston approved the message.

Meanwhile the New Zealanders were lying down eating a breakfast of bully beef and biscuits and trying to forget their thirst, which is hard when you are eating beef in a swill of brine. It was around 8 am.

Fire was coming from the crest of Chunuk Bair because Kannengiesser had arrived there around 7 am. He had ridden ahead of his two regiments and climbed Chunuk Bair on foot. The sun was already hot. Kannengiesser looked over to his right to Suvla and saw an armada of British ships. He could see British troops on the hillock called Lala Baba and out on the salt lake, which was dried hard. There was no sound of firing from Suvla. Chunuk Bair was quiet too; the only gunfire was coming from the old Anzac position. He found the main ridge unoccupied. He eventually came upon the Turkish battery and its 20-strong escort. Kannengiesser woke up the commander and told him to fire on Suvla.

Soon afterwards he spotted Johnston's troops advancing from near the Apex, about 500 yards away.

> The English approached slowly, in single file, splendidly equipped and with white arm bands on their left arms, apparently very tired, and were crossing a hillside on our flank, emerging in continually increasing numbers from the valley below. I immediately sent an order to my infantry – this was the 20-man strong artillery-covering platoon – instantly to open fire. I received this answer: 'We can only commence to fire when we receive an order from our battalion commander.'
>
> This was too much for me altogether. I ran to the spot and threw myself among the troops, who were lying in a small trench. What I said I cannot recollect, but they began to open fire and almost immediately the English laid down without answering our fire or apparently moving in any other way. They gave me the impression that they were glad to be spared further climbing.

The Gallipoli story is full of 'if onlys'. If only the navy had returned to the attack on March 19 when the Turks were short of ammunition. If only the Allies had landed in March rather than April. If only Hamilton had insisted that more troops be landed at Y Beach. The Kannengiesser incident is said to be another of these. 'Thus,' Bean wrote in *Gallipoli Mission*, 'passed by far the best chance of winning a great campaign.' Had they pushed on before Kannengiesser arrived, the New Zealanders could certainly have taken Chunuk Bair. Whether this would have won the war is another matter.

Kannengiesser saw two companies from Kemal's 19th Division on Battleship Hill and appropriated them for Chunuk Bair. The first of his own troops were starting to arrive when, around 9 am, Kannengiesser was wounded in the chest by fire from the Apex.

Meanwhile, Godley had received Johnston's signal. 'Attack at once,' he replied.

As the left assaulting column pulled out of Anzac, Bean was shot.

He had wanted to see the column leave and walked along the beach to Godley's headquarters at Number Two Outpost. Here he witnessed an exchange that tells much. Monash's troops were trudging by. The attack was behind schedule.

'Can I tell army corps that both the brigades have cleared this place?' Godley asked his staff officer, Lieutenant-Colonel Pinwell. Pinwell said he would find out. He reported that Monash's stretcher-bearers were just passing.

'Then I can say both brigades are past here?' Godley said, ever testy with underlings.

'No, no, sir, the Indian Brigade is only arriving.'

'What, are they behind Monash? Good God!'

'But that was the order they were told to go in, sir.'

As Bean noted in his diary, it seemed elementary for a general to know the order in which his attacking troops were supposed to leave. It may have been a lapse. If not, it explains much of what happened over the next few days.

Bean drank Godley's whisky then said he would walk

with the Indian column in the hope of picking up news of Monash's progress. 'Tell him to hurry up,' Godley said.

Bean headed out along the beach. Stray bullets plopped into the ground. He thought he could hear the British landing at Suvla.

> I was moving on again when something gave me a whack (like a stone thrown hard) in the upper part of the right leg. I could feel it whack the right side of the leg and bruise the inner part of the left side. I was pretty sure I had been hit by a stray which had gone in on the right and not come out, but I couldn't feel any blood, and so thought it might not have penetrated at all. Some of the stones from shell bursts had hit me quite as hard earlier this day – but presently I felt my hand greasy in my pants . . .

Bean went back. Godley gave him another whisky and sent him to the dressing station, after which Bean hobbled to Anzac, reaching the Sphinx as a barrage fell on the Nek, sending tails of earth high in the morning sky. This was the prelude to the light horsemen's charge there. Bean slumped into bed without waking Arthur Bazley, his batman. Bazley woke Bean later in the morning. 'I've been hit, Baz,' Bean said.

A doctor told Bean he should leave because of the risk of tetanus. Bean refused and mostly lay in his dugout for three days. Phillip Schuler, the young *Age* correspondent, brought him news. Bean behaved exactly as one would expect him to. He was a man of integrity and understated courage, and stubborn too. He got all his material first hand. That was what made him different from the other journalists. He counted the bullets. Why would he leave just because he had been shot? The bullet was still in Bean when he died in 1968. Long before that he had refused a knighthood. He told a friend that he could not imagine his wife (he married at 41) going to the butcher and asking for the meat for Sir Charles Bean.

The left assaulting column, 5000 strong, left 30 minutes late and infected with a mixture of nerves and crabbiness that is hard to describe but shows up in most accounts of the departure. Major Cecil Allanson, commander of the 6th Gurkhas, wrote: 'There was a feeling of panic and doubt in the air as to where we were and where we were going.' Lone Pine, an old-fashioned frontal assault, had been planned so well that it worked. From the moment the troops started trudging along the beach, this big loop to the left, this flanking attack aimed at nothing less than winning the war, carried the germ of shambles.

Maybe it was the darkness and the strange country. Certainly Monash's Australians were in no condition to undertake this rush at the heights. Monash had asked his medical officers late in July if the brigade was fit for such an operation. Three of the four said it was not; the men were suffering from dysentery, bronchial infections, rapid pulses, heart dilation and loss of weight. Monash chose to go with the minority opinion. He thought the excitement of an offensive might improve the men's condition.

Then there was the planning. Theorists had given this attack the precision of a railway timetable. Trains didn't run out in the bandit country. No-one at Anzac had been down the Aghyl Dere or along Abdel Rahman Spur. No-one knew how confusing this country was, particularly the five forks of the Aghyl Dere. No-one knew that the Aghyl Dere sometimes looked like the Kaiajik Dere and that Kaiajik Dere sometimes looked like Asma Dere. As Cox told the Dardanelles Royal Commission: 'There does not seem to be any reason why the hills should go where

The face of innocence: Private James Martin from Hawthorn, Victoria, lied about his age, joined up and arrived at Anzac in September. Six weeks later he died of enteric fever. He was 14 years and nine months old. *[AWM 00069.001]*

Face of a hero: the ever-cheerful Captain Alfred Shout, VC, MC, Australia's most decorated soldier at Gallipoli. A carpenter who emigrated to Sydney from New Zealand, he had both hands and an eye blown away in the battle for Lone Pine in August. He died, aged 33, a few days later.
[AWM G01028]

Face of a martyr: Lieutenant-Colonel William George Malone, killed on Chunuk Bair. By the standards that applied at Lone Pine, he should have received the Victoria Cross. He was bossy and quick to judge but he had a sense of humour. He took a reporter to the frontline at Quinn's. 'Now we have given them a sporting chance to snipe us, let us retire,' he said. 'I always give a visitor that thrill.' *[Courtesy of Judy Malone]*

The terraces Malone built behind Quinn's Post, the most important – and absurd – position on the Allied line at Anzac. Behind the Allied trenches, the cliff was almost sheer. Russell's Top is on the horizon. *[AWM G01026]*

Private Oliver Cumberland.

Private Joe Cumberland

[Both photos courtesy of Mrs Joan Crommelin]

Lieutenant-General Sir Frederick Stopford: his generalship at Suvla was disastrous and he became the scapegoat for the failure of the August offensive. He was elderly beyond his years and had never commanded men in battle before. His speciality was ceremonial duties. His *Who's Who* entry for 1920 did not mention his time as a corps commander at Gallipoli. In his mind it never happened.

After the Turks, the big enemy at Anzac was the terrain. Charles Bean's shot of troops dragging a water tank up a hill in July shows what the men had to deal with. *[AWM G01117]*

John Monash: after his time as a brigade commander at Gallipoli, he went on to become Australia's most famous general. The mad terrain and sloppy planning at Gallipoli gave him few chances to use his best gifts. The higher he rose in rank, the better he became. *[AWM A01241]*

Anzac officers waiting for Lord Kitchener to arrive in November. Brigadier-General Andrew Russell, commander of the New Zealand Mounted Rifles Brigade, is second from the left. Monash is third from the left. Next along is Brigadier-General Francis Johnston, commander of the New Zealand Infantry Brigade. *[AWM G01325]*

Australian dead at Lone Pine in August. 'Of all the bastards of places...' [AWM A04013]

Lieutenant-Colonel John 'Bull' Antill in a typically aggressive pose. He ordered the third charge by light horsemen at the Nek in August to go ahead even though the men in the first two lines had been shot to pieces. [AWM G01330]

W Beach at Helles, where the Lancashire Fusiliers won six Victoria Crosses on the morning of the landing. Now, a few months into the campaign, W Beach looks like a mining camp. W Beach has today reverted to the way it was before the war, a rising plain of tussocks and scrub. *[AWM 00313]*

A horse boat being unloaded at V Beach ten days into the campaign. This shot was taken from the *River Clyde*. *[AWM H10284]*

Looking towards Suvla from Anzac. The white area is the salt lake.
[AWM H03167]

Gallipoli was always about improvisation. Chaplain Ernest Merrington conducts communion at the Apex late in the campaign. He uses two biscuit boxes and a scrap of cloth for an altar. *[AWM P01875.004]*

Thousands of Australians crowd into Lone Pine cemetery for the memorial service in 2000. Once this place was about bomb-throwing and anarchy; now it has an air of triumph and formality. *[Patrick Carlyon]*

British-issue rifle clips found by the author's party near shallow scrapes around Hill 90. The clips and the scrapes almost certainly belonged to men of Monash's 4th Brigade who died here in August in their failed attempt to reach Hill 971. *[Denise Carlyon]*

The wild country to the north of Anzac, one tawny ridge after another, the battleground for the August offensive. *[AWM G01137]*

Wounded from the 1st Australian Light Horse Brigade and the Welch Fusiliers battalion at the dressing station below Pope's Hill after the failed attacks along the escarpment on August 7. *[AWM C02707]*

Keith Murdoch outside Charles Bean's dugout at Anzac Cove in September. Murdoch is credited in Australian mythology with single-handedly exposing the scandals of the Gallipoli campaign. The truth is rather more complicated. *[AWM A05396]*

Ellis Ashmead-Bartlett, the journalist–adventurer from Fleet Street who had more to do with exposing scandals at the Dardanelles than Murdoch. He was always broke, lived above his means and sometimes forgot that he was supposed to be an observer rather than a participant. Most of his gloomy predictions about the campaign came true. Unlike Murdoch, he put his name to a newspaper article that said the Gallipoli campaign was failing.

Phillip 'Peter' Schuler, the *Age* correspondent at Gallipoli. He took the photograph at Lone Pine that appears on the front jacket of this book. He joined the army in 1916 and was killed on the western front the following year, aged 28.
[AWM G01560]

The path to Pope's Hill on the Anzac escarpment was so steep that steps had to be cut into the hill and strengthened with packing cases. A yellow erosion scar is all that remains of Pope's today. *[AWM H15375]*

A self-firing rifle used during the evacuation. The water dripped from the top tin into the bottom one, which, after about 20 minutes, overbalanced and caused the rifle to fire. [AWM G01291]

Australians playing two-up at Brown's Dip, behind Lone Pine, as a Turkish shell bursts nearby. Four minutes after this photograph was taken, four of the men were killed by another Turkish shell. [AWM H03557]

Part of the final accounting: bones of Turkish soldiers collected at Gallipoli in 1919. The Turks put their casualties at 251,309, including 86,692 dead. Allied casualties were more than 140,000. Britain lost 21,255 dead, France 10,000, Australia 8,709 and New Zealand 2,701. *[AWM H11907]*

they do . . . It is mad-looking country . . .' The route chosen amounted to 5 miles; it was the equivalent of 25 miles of flat country. Many officers had been shown the north flank from the decks of destroyers. This was a waste of coal: one can only begin to understand this wilderness by walking the ridges.

And Cox's column itself was unwieldy: so many different units, commanders who hardly knew each other and wore their jealousies like badges. Cox was 55 and recovering from some form of 'breakdown' caused by his long stint in Hunter-Weston's butcher's shop. Monash described Cox as 'one of those crotchety, peppery, livery old Indian officers, whom the climate has dried and shrivelled up into a bag of nerves'. Monash misread the nature of what he was being asked to do so badly that he drew up a timetable that had his first troops arriving on Abdel Rahman Spur at 1.40 am, just three hours after striking off. And the culmination of the attack was a mystery. Cox had decided that orders for the final assault on 971 were to be issued, in the dark and with the men inevitably scattered, when the 4th Brigade reached Abdel Rahman.

Cox's column consisted of his 29th Indian Brigade, Monash's brigade, a mountain battery and a company of New Zealand engineers. The column would march along the coast, past Walden Point, then turn right into Aghyl Dere. It would head down this valley for three-quarters of a mile, its left flank protected by the New Army battalions of the covering force on Damakjelik Spur. Then the two leading Australian battalions would head out to the left to form a line of posts to Abdel Rahman. The main column would head up the last main tributary of Aghyl Dere. At the head of this, two battalions of Gurkhas would veer off to the right to attack Hill Q. The two remaining

Australian battalions, along with Allanson's Gurkhas and a battalion of Sikhs, would cross Asma Dere and climb Abdel Rahman. Anyway, that was what was supposed to happen.

The first serious check came when the column approached Walden Point. Major Percy Overton, the New Zealand scout at the head of the column, was using a Greek miller as a guide and talking to him through an interpreter. Instead of going around Walden Point, the Greek wanted to take a shortcut through Taylor's Gap, a narrow pass between Walden's and Bauchop's Hill. The Greek said this would save half an hour. Overton argued with him, then agreed to the 'shortcut'. The gorge turned out so narrow that the column had to move in single file. Turks began sniping from the hills. Engineers were sent ahead to hack a path through the dwarf oak. Taylor's Gap is only 600 yards long but the head of the column took three hours to pass through it and reach Aghyl Dere. It was now 2 am. By Monash's timetable the Australians should have been on Abdel Rahman. Nerves were fraying along the column that stretched all the way back to Anzac. Rumours buzzed up and down the line.

Monash became frustrated. Cox had told him to march in the centre of the brigade, which meant he had no notion of what was happening up front. He sent staff officers forward. One impaled himself on a bayonet. None returned. Monash obtained Cox's permission to go to the front of his column, which had inexplicably stopped at the mouth of the Aghyl Dere. He found Lieutenant-Colonel Tilney, commander of the 13th Battalion, 'conferring and arguing' with Overton and a staff officer, 'apparently unable to decide what to do'. Monash remembered saying: 'What damned nonsense! Get a move on, quick.'

Monash led the two leading platoons across Aghyl Dere into a field of stubble that became known as Australia Valley. As the moon came up the Turks opened fire. It was now 2.30, and this is where the big mistake of navigation seems to have occurred. The Australians didn't know where they were. As has been mentioned, the two leading battalions, the 13th and 14th, were supposed to break off to the left. Monash now sent these battalions out into Australia Valley. Peter Pedersen in *Monash as Military Commander* suggests these battalions were detached 700 yards too early, and the evidence, untidy as it is, supports his conclusion. Overton was no help; he didn't know where he was either. Trying to follow the plan, Monash then sent his other two battalions, the 15th and 16th, along Aghyl Dere.

Around 3 am Lieutenant-Colonel James Cannan, commanding the 15th, thought he was near the point where the 15th and 16th were supposed to strike off towards Abdel Rahman while the Gurkhas swerved to the right for Hill Q. Overton and his Greek guides told Cannan that Abdel Rahman was about 15 minutes away. Overton then left with the Gurkhas for Hill Q. The 15th, blundering around in broken country, now came under Turkish fire. The Turks, quite likely, were part of the force the New Zealanders had driven off Bauchop's. The 16th, under Lieutenant-Colonel Pope, came up on Cannan's right. Around dawn Cannan and Pope, feeling their battalions could go no further, dug in, even though the Turkish opposition was light.

The Australians could see spurs rising ahead across a valley; the valley had to be Asma Dere, the spurs the start of Abdel Rahman. Pope actually thought he was on Abdel Rahman. In truth the valley was Kaiajik and the spurs were part of the northern arm of the Damakjelik outcrops that marched towards Hill 60. The men were exhausted. All they wanted to do was sleep. Cox told Monash to attack 971 at 11 am.

Allanson arrived at Monash's headquarters around 7 am. He had been ordered to support Monash with his Gurkhas. Monash, Allanson said, had lost his head. He was running about saying: 'I thought I could command men, I thought I could command men.' He told Allanson the operation was a 'hopeless mess' and 'you are no use to me at all'. Allanson said he was anxious to get away quickly, 'as I felt thoroughly upset by what I had seen'.

Cox arrived around dawn, having lost his headquarters staff. He was bleeding from a slight wound and had one Gurkha as an escort. He and Monash argued about whether the attack on 971 should go ahead. He eventually allowed Monash to go on with his entrenching. But what do we make of Allanson's portrait of Monash? Allanson's letters show him to be a man of robust opinions. He appears to have written his account of Monash's outburst in the 1930s and only after he felt Monash had slighted the Indian Brigade in a book. Allanson didn't mention the outburst in his published diary. He made no criticism of Monash when Bean interviewed him a few weeks after the August offensive. Allanson disliked Australians and thought New Zealanders 'charming'. In one of his letters he says the Australians lack discipline and 'their habits are just too disgusting and filthy for words'. In another he says the Australians are 'immeasurably superior' to the New Army, which is full of 'rotters'. Field Marshal Lord Slim, who served alongside Allanson that August as a subaltern in the Warwickshire Regiment, later described him as an unreliable witness and inclined to 'embroider'. No-one else, it seems, heard Monash say: 'I thought I could command men.' Monash may indeed have said it;

but context is everything. Monash was entitled to be disillusioned and ill-tempered that morning.

Bean in his official history also damned Monash's leadership on that morning. Monash owned a fine mind and was a good organiser. 'But he was not a fighting commander of the type of Walker, M'Cay or Chauvel, and the enterprise in which he was now engaged was one calling for still more – the touch of a Stonewall Jackson, and the recklessness of a J. E. B. Stuart.' This misses the point. Monash, as he would later prove in France, was the opposite of Hamilton: better at planning battles than carrying them out in the field. But this had little to do with why his column was stalled. His men couldn't lift their legs; it is not usual for soldiers to want to fall asleep in strange country with bullets kicking up dust around them. And this first leg to Aghyl Dere was the easier part. These men could not have climbed Abdel Rahman, where the slopes were much steeper than Chunuk Bair, even if Stonewall Jackson was leading them and 'Jeb' Stuart had galloped up with a wagonload of scaling ladders.

Bean didn't like Monash; he certainly didn't understand him and this was partly Monash's fault. Monash was what these days would be called a self-promoter; he saw little virtue in modesty. He gave Bean 'a good talking to' in June for failing to give the 4th Brigade enough publicity. There are few surer ways of getting a journalist offside. Bean, however, carried his own prejudices. He had a romantic notion of how senior officers should be. Country lads with modest ways who came from good English-Australian families with clergymen or schoolteachers close up in the pedigree – these were fine. This Monash, the son of a Polish merchant, a city man, middle-aged and portly, an engineer who knew how to play political games – he didn't fit the Bean template.

In 1918 Bean lobbied against Monash being made commander-in-chief of the Australian Corps. 'He is not the man,' Bean wrote in his diary. 'Besides, we do not want Australia represented by men mainly because of their ability, natural and inborn in Jews, to push themselves.'

By mid-morning on August 7 both flanking attacks out of Anzac had failed to reach their objectives. They might yet succeed, but surprise had been lost.

Meanwhile four British battalions had landed at Suvla. The only casualty was a naval rating killed by a stray bullet from the shore.

22

The voyage of the *Jonquil*

It is doubtful if any corps commander, before or since, has gone to war with the languor of Frederick Stopford. It was no small thing, this first battle of his, this Suvla business, whatever it was about. Hard to know what it was about, really. Depended on who you talked to. It involved 20,000 troops and an amphibious landing at night and they said he was in charge of it and it was all so hard to understand. All these ships. Destroyers, these new things they called beetles, trawlers, paddle steamers, horse-boats, luxury liners turned into transports, tugs from the Thames. Had to land heavy guns and mules and water. Yes, water. It was so hot out here. Left a fellow with no energy at all. Hamilton says this Suvla thing will be fine, but Johnny was always an optimist. Seems to flit from here to there, from this to that, without ever lingering long enough to tell you much. Watching him dart about makes a fellow tired. Hard to get near him too. That Braithwaite fellow seems to protect him. Reed says we don't have enough artillery. Fellow should know. Been on the western front. Knows about new things like telephones. Mahon says the plans are too complicated and probably won't work. Mahon should know. He's a lieutenant-general, though not as senior as some of us. And now there is this damned knee. Dashed rotten luck. All a chap wants to do is lie down.

Stopford had sprained his knee on the morning of August 6. The duck was lame. One of Hamilton's staff officers – almost certainly Aspinall – visited Stopford that evening. He found the corps commander lying on his valise, spread out on the floor of his tent.

'I want you to tell Sir Ian Hamilton that I am going to do my best, and that I hope to be successful,' Stopford said. 'But he must realise that if the enemy proves to be holding a strong line of continuous entrenchments I shall be unable to dislodge him till more guns are landed.' Then he added a piece of wisdom: 'All the teaching of the campaign in France proves that continuous trenches cannot be attacked without the assistance of large numbers of howitzers.' Reed, Stopford's chief-of-staff, had used almost those same words 11 days earlier.

The staff officer said that GHQ was sure there were no continuous trenches at Suvla. All the 11th Division, which would land first, had to do was grab the high ground around the bay before the Turks brought up reinforcements. From his bed of pain the general wasn't so sure.

Hamilton had wanted Stopford to stay on Imbros during the Suvla landings and go ashore on the morning of August 7. Stopford wanted to be close to his men. He would arrive off Suvla around midnight on the sloop *Jonquil*, flying the flag of Rear-Admiral Christian. There was room for Stopford's general staff on the *Jonquil* but not his administrative staff, which would be on the liner *Minneapolis*. The mistakes of Anzac were being repeated. The *Jonquil* could talk to Imbros by radio, although it wasn't set up to handle heavy traffic. A ship would lay a cable from Imbros. The Suvla end of it would go ashore with the first troops; the Imbros end would be connected to a clock-faced dial at GHQ. When the needle on the dial trembled, Hamilton would know the troops were ashore.

The first two brigades of Hammersley's 11th Division started to land at B Beach, south of Nibrunesi Point, shortly before 10 pm while Russell's New Zealanders were still clearing the Anzac foothills. The beach was undefended, which was just as well because, as usual, orders had been issued late. Most of the men didn't find out what they were supposed to do until they were on the lighters headed for Suvla. When they landed, the men had been on their feet for 17 hours. Some were sore from a cholera inoculation they had been given the day before. The night was incredibly dark and no-one much knew where anything was. It was just as well the Turks had no machine guns and were merely firing the odd rifle. The hillocks called Lala Baba and Hill 10 were to be seized first. The 34th Brigade of the 11th would land within Suvla Bay at A Beach around 10 pm. Then the troops from all three brigades would climb Kiretch Tepe to the north and attack Chocolate Hill to the east.

Two companies from the 6th Yorkshire Battalion of the 32nd Brigade cleared the Turks from Lala Baba, although the defenders were only fighting a delaying action. Outnumbered worse than ten-to-one, Willmer wasn't going to waste men in suicidal stands. The attack of the Yorkshires was the first by New Army troops in the Great War. The casualties were heavy: all the officers bar two juniors and one-third of the men. No-one knew it then, but this was a foretaste: the New Army men would be slaughtered in similar fashion all over France. The two Yorkshire companies were supposed to move on to Hill 10. With their senior officers dead or wounded, and not knowing what they were supposed to do, the men lay down.

At GHQ on Imbros, Aspinall, Dawnay, Orlo Williams and Mackenzie sat waiting for news. Three hours after the landing at B Beach they were still waiting. A telegram arrived from Bulgaria. The British Military Attaché in Sofia wanted to know what was happening at Gallipoli. Mackenzie remembers Aspinall laughing and saying he would like to tell him. A telegram came in about stores, then one from Anzac: 'When does the next hospital ship come? This one is full.' The wounded were being shuffled around again. Mackenzie decided to take the telegram to Surgeon-General W. E. Birrell, the Director of Medical Services.

Mackenzie had met Birrell in May. The Surgeon-General, thin and elderly with a grey moustache, had approached him in a mood of incredulity. Someone had told Birrell that Mackenzie made a living writing novels. Was this true? Yes, said Mackenzie. 'Well, it's the most extraordinary thing I ever heard,' said the general. 'Why, I never bought a book in my life!' How did one think of a book? 'Do you just sit down and think?' The general explained he didn't want to seem inquisitive 'but I've never come into contact with this kind of thing before'.

Now Mackenzie headed for the Philistine surgeon's tent. He read out the telegram. Birrell's breath came in puffs of indignation from the bedclothes. 'Tell them General Birrell does not know.'

Mackenzie said the general would have to send such a telegram himself.

'What time is it?' the general asked.

'Close on two o'clock.'

'And do you mean to tell me I've been woken up at such an hour to answer a question like that? I never heard of anything so completely ridiculous in my life.'

They continued to argue. 'I feel most strongly that I have been woken up in a totally unnecessary way,' the general said.

'I expect they are feeling rather strongly about things on the beach at Anzac just now,' Mackenzie told him.

The general eventually shuffled off, grumbling to himself, to send a reply.

The wounded suffered outrageously throughout the campaign and this was partly Birrell's fault. He had helped reinvent the medical nightmare of the Crimea. This conversation, trivial though it may seem, probably tells us more than columns of statistics about the hell of the hospital ships.

Mackenzie returned to GHQ. Still no word from Suvla. Aspinall had drawn beards and moustaches on all the women in the London illustrated weeklies. Dawnay was making cocoa. Mackenzie read the *Tatler*. Someone produced a bottle of Horlick's Malted Milk Lozenges and, according to Mackenzie, 'we all sat sucking them in a melancholy'. Aspinall was now drawing women on sheets of foolscap. 'Good God!' Aspinall said suddenly. 'They must be ashore by now.'

Grey streaks of dawn appeared. Mackenzie ran down to the signals tents and asked if there was any news from Suvla. 'Only this, sir,' said the sergeant. He had a message from the Suvla signaller saying he could hear rifle and shell fire. This is how GHQ found out that the Suvla force was landing: a signaller at the front talking to his mate on Imbros.

Mackenzie tried to sleep but couldn't. He now believed that the Suvla landing would fail.

I felt as if I had watched a system crash to pieces before my eyes, as if I had stood by the deathbed of an old order . . . The war would last now until we had all turned ourselves into Germans to win it. An absurd phrase went singing through my head. *We have lost our amateur status tonight.* It was foolish for me who had been old enough to appreciate the muddle of the South African War to go on believing in the practical value of the public-school system. I had really for long mistrusted it, but since coming out here I had fallen once more under its spell as I might have fallen under the spell of a story by Rudyard Kipling. Yes, the war would go on now. I must remember to write home tomorrow for more woollen underclothes.

The landing of Brigadier-General William Sitwell's 34th Brigade at A Beach, inside Suvla Bay, went badly. In something close to a re-run of the Anzac landing, the destroyers anchored nearly 1000 yards south of where they should have been. This meant the lighters were headed for a spot where shoal water had been suspected. Two lighters struck a reef about 50 yards from the coast and the troops had to wade ashore in water up to their necks and holding their rifles above their heads. There was sporadic rifle fire from the coast. Battalions became badly mixed up once ashore. A battalion of Manchesters rushed two small posts on the northern horn of Suvla Bay, climbed Kiretch Tepe ridge, battled with Turks who were falling back in front of it, and by 3 am held a position two miles east of Suvla Point. This was easily the best work done in the whole of the Suvla landing.

At 3 am Sitwell and the second half of his force had not landed. The moon was up and the New Army lads with their white armlets were easy to hit. Sitwell's lighter struck a reef 100 yards offshore. Small boats were needed to land the troops. Sitwell landed at about 3.30 am and found that the redoubt on Hill 10, one of his brigade's first objectives, had not been captured. Worse, no-one knew where it was. A party of Lancashire Fusiliers rushed back to the beach pursued by Turks.

Sitwell sent troops out to take Hill 10 as dawn broke. A sand dune could be seen: that must be it. The troops charged the hillock, and came under fire from the real Hill 10, 400 yards to the north. In the words of Aspinall: 'It was now broad daylight and the situation in Suvla Bay was verging on chaos.' The beach was still under rifle fire and two or three Turkish guns were peppering the beach and the ships.

Apart from the capture of Lala Baba and the advance of the Manchesters on Kiretch Tepe, Stopford's force had not reached its objectives. It was lost and disorganised. No-one was truly in charge of the landing. No-one seemed to *want* to be in charge, least of all Stopford. Groups of men wandered around trying to find out where they were and what they should be doing. Hammersley and his 11th Division staff had reached B Beach about 12.45 am. Aspinall, the master of politesse, said in his official history that the general was 'feeling the climate severely' and 'rather exhausted'.

Runners were sent out to discover where the forward troops were. The first news came in a message received well after daybreak. It read: 'The Ridge. 7th. 32nd Brigade holds Lala Baba. W Yorks on right. Yorks and West Ridings on ridge. York and Lancs. in hollow behind ridge in reserve.'

The note had not been signed. There was no mention of the time at which it had been written. It was not addressed to anyone.

*　　*　　*

The *Jonquil* anchored in Suvla Bay soon after midnight. Stopford and Admiral Christian heard rifle fire from the shore. In an official report a week later the admiral wrote: 'Very little firing having been heard on shore, it was assumed that the force had landed unopposed.' It was a hot night. Mattresses were brought on deck.

Here our narrative lurches into the bizarre. No-one would think to write it as fiction because it goes against the way people are expected to behave. This interlude says that curiosity is not part of the human condition, that Darwin and Freud and Shakespeare got the big things wrong. Languor is the most powerful of human emotions. Stopford lay down on the deck to sleep. It was only 14,000 men and a night landing. No officer was sent ashore to find out what was happening. No message was sent to GHQ. Stopford had said he wanted to be close to his men. Why, then, didn't he talk to them?

Commander Edward Unwin was in charge of the landing craft. He brought the first news of the landing to the *Jonquil* about 4 am. He didn't know much about what was happening onshore. He did know about grounded lighters and chaos in Suvla Bay. The 10th Division was now arriving. It could not be landed within Suvla Bay; the reefs had caused too much trouble.

Again we lurch into the paranormal. Back on Imbros, Hamilton paced back and forth, hoping for news. No official report came from Suvla all night. All Hamilton had was a few words from a telegraphist talking to his mate. The telegraphists on Imbros asked the Suvla operator for more news. He could say only that things seemed quiet, that he knew nothing, that he had been given no official messages to send. Hamilton took this to mean that the landing was going well. He was the commander-in-chief. If this expedition failed, he would take the blame. But he was also a gentleman. He was not going to pick up paper and scribble out a demand that a subordinate tell him what was happening at a landing. Stopford was in a trance and his knee hurt; he didn't know real from unreal. Hamilton did. He must have known, before dawn on August 7, that Stopford was a dud. But, as was his way, he saw what he wanted to see.

Von Sanders knew exactly what was happening. Major Willmer had sent him a succinct message at 6 am. The enemy was still landing but the Turkish positions in the hills were safe. Reinforcements were urgently needed. If these English continued to muddle, von Sanders might get the reinforcements there in time.

23

Goodbye, cobber. God bless you

On June 27, 40 days before Birdwood began his August offensive, the Turks began shelling the trenches at Walker's Ridge held by the 8th Light Horse Regiment from Victoria. The 8th was part of the 3rd Light Horse Brigade that arrived in late May. There were two other regiments in the brigade: the 9th from South Australia and the 10th from Western Australia. In the light horse a regiment was the equivalent of a battalion, except that its full strength was nearer 500 men than 1000. The 3rd Brigade was holding Walker's and Russell's Top. Those Turkish shells on June 27 killed 7 and wounded another 15, including Lieutenant-Colonel Alexander White, a 33-year-old maltster, who grew up at Ballarat before moving to the Melbourne suburb of Elsternwick. A shell fragment hit White in the head. It was removed on a hospital ship where, as compensation for his agonies, White received a hot bath, pyjamas and a sleep.

White loved soldiering, or what he understood of it as a citizen-soldier. He had joined the Mounted Rifles at Ballarat after leaving school and had been steadily promoted. He was full of quiet idealism and the men liked him. The rankers called him 'decent' and 'a good man'. He wore a locket containing a photograph of his wife and infant son, 'Young Bill'. He went off to war with a poem he had cut from a newspaper and placed in his Bible.

> Let me be a little braver
> When temptation bids me waver,
> Let me strive a little harder
> To be all that I should be.
> Let me be a little meeker
> With the brother that is weaker
> Let me think more of my neighbour
> And a little less of me.

White, like so many others, soon discovered at Anzac that war wasn't the way they said it was in Fitchett's *Deeds That Won the Empire* and Shakespeare's *Henry V*. Rotting hands and booted feet poked through the earthworks at Russell's Top and the hill smelt like a flyblown sheep. As a teenager White had been smitten by light cavalry. There were no horses here, no arched neck bobbing with ears pricked, no tang of sweat on leather, no pomp and lousy circumstances. Just a rabbit warren that stank of rot and dysentery. It lay opposite another rabbit warren, owned by the Turks, that looked and smelt the same. That was the prize here. Not Jerusalem or El Dorado, just a dog-legged trench 50 yards up the hill that smelt as ripe as the one you were in. White had a sense of duty; he kept his disappointments for his diary.

> Dear little wife and kiddie I seem so far away from you all; I do not want to speak about the war; it's horrible. If I let myself think too much about it my nerves would go. Have seen things and done things I want to forget.

The Turkish barrage that wounded White was part of a softening up of the Australian line for a frontal attack. Three days later, shortly after midnight, the Turks came howling down the hill from the Nek. Packed shoulder-to-shoulder in the front trench, the Australians fired as fast as they could work their bolts. Troops who couldn't find room in the front trench knelt in the open. A few Turks briefly got into the saps thrown forward of the Australian line and the so-called 'secret sap' that ran out to the left. A few made the parapet of the main trench only to die there.

By 2 am the charge had failed. A second attack around dawn also failed. The Turks spoke of the 'black night'. Enver Pasha, the Minister of War, was visiting Essad's headquarters on Scrubby Knoll. Enver didn't know much about war but he knew the rhetoric. He told the survivors that their charge had been 'most useful in engaging the attention of the English at a critical moment'.

We should not be too hard on him; shortly we will hear an English general dressing up an Australian attack, just as futile, in similar terms. This is the way of politicians and generals, and still is. Of course there was no 'critical moment', and of course Enver didn't believe what he was saying. He told Kemal privately that the attack was wasteful. Kemal briefly resigned. Turkish dead lay everywhere in front of the Australian trenches; the casualties probably ran to 800. The Australians had lost 7 dead and 19 wounded. A sergeant in the Light Horse wrote:

> I went around the trenches in the morning and the sight that met one's gaze was horrible. Dead Turks and some not quite dead were lying about just like rabbits after a night's poison being laid.

There was much to be learned from this attack of Kemal's. The idea was good. If the Turks took Russell's Top, they split the Anzac line and could fire into the back of Pope's and Quinn's. The execution of the attack, the way it was thought out – or not thought out – was a throwback to the Turkish siege of Vienna in 1683. In the new warfare of the 20th century the advantages were with the defenders in the trenches with their machine guns. Assaults against positions like these could only work if the attackers first put down such a barrage that most of the defenders were either killed, wounded or out of their minds. The Turks had not done this. To make things worse, they were attacking on a narrow front. The Nek is about 30 yards wide at the Baby 700 end, with cliffs on both sides.

After the Turkish offensive of May 19, Godley had ordered the New Zealand Mounted Rifles to counter-attack towards the Nek, over the very ground where the Turks had been slaughtered. The commanders of both the Wellington and the Auckland regiments 'objected', thereby undoubtedly saving the lives of hundreds of their countrymen. Russell, the brigade commander, agreed with them and apparently talked Godley out of the attack.

Godley didn't like being stood up. He was a robotic soldier. If he thought at all, it was only about important things, such as how to cadge a smart horse for a day's fox-hunting. Godley was made for drill and good order and the rituals of the officers' mess, for training grounds and peacetime. He was not made for this war where part of the trick was to know which of the old ways to discard. Grit and dash and discipline – they were fine things – and when Godley began his military career they might have been enough to take an objective, particularly if it was held by Sudanese with spears. Machine guns and quick-firing artillery now chewed up men with bayonets; it didn't matter that these men were brave, good at drill and always did as they were told. The world had changed and Godley had not. He was not alone.

Godley took orders from his superiors without question. That, he apparently thought, was the way to get on. He expected the same dumb obedience from those beneath him. After the New Zealanders had stood him up in May, Lieutenant-Colonel Charles Mackesy, commander of the Auckland Mounted Rifles, was sent back to Egypt to advise on an outbreak of disease among the horses there. This was assumed to be a reprisal for Mackesy's refusal to sacrifice his men.

As part of the August offensive Alexander White's 8th Regiment and Lieutenant-Colonel Noel Brazier's 10th were to charge at the Nek at dawn on August 7. Godley had learnt nothing from the Turkish failures of May 19 and June 30, and he clearly didn't understand what the New Zealanders had objected to in May. Brigadier-General Frederic Hughes, commander of the 3rd Light Horse Brigade, and Lieutenant-Colonel John Antill, his brigade-major, discussed the plan with Godley and Andrew Skeen of Birdwood's staff. The two Australians didn't think much of it and said so.

Hughes, a company manager and sharebroker, was 57; he should not have been commanding a brigade in wartime, and this had nothing to do with his age. His rise through the ranks as a citizen-soldier owed much to nepotism. The army had seduced him with its ceremonies and uniforms and the social standing it gave him. As one of his officers later told Bean: 'In time of war, as in peace, our brigadier's idea of soldiering was to salute smartly, roll a greatcoat correctly, and note the march discipline.' Hughes soon became ill at Anzac. He was evacuated with pneumonia in June and with a second illness in July. Bean wrote in the official history that Birdwood had 'little confidence' in Hughes. But Birdwood wasn't going to remove him. Such things weren't done. That was part of the old ways too.

Jack Antill was a professional who had served prominently in the Boer War. In the Transvaal he had carried the whiff of Custer: he liked to gallop at enemy guns. 'Banjo' Paterson mentioned him frequently in his reports for the *Sydney Morning Herald* and the *Argus*. 'In the taking of Pretoria,' Paterson wrote in 1900, 'the New South Wales Mounted Infantry under Captain Antill achieved a performance which General Ian Hamilton – a cool-headed man, and not one prone to overpraise things – described to me as "one of the most brilliant things of the war".' Antill hit his peak in South Africa. When he returned to the army in 1911 he was more famous as a martinet and a bully. 'Bull' Antill they called him, and he was a fearsome sight. In a photograph taken at Anzac he seems to be dressing down the camera, arms akimbo, mouth set, a toreador taunting a shy bull. He may have been sour because his career had stalled; if so, it was his own fault. Chauvel and Brudenell White had been to South Africa and their minds had continued to grow. Antill had become like Godley, stiff and mechanical. In the 3rd Light Horse Antill was more powerful than he should have been. This was because Hughes was less powerful than he should have been. Both men bickered with Brazier, the commander of the 10th, who was contrary and quick to take offence.

Hughes and Antill were not the men to tell Godley his proposed attack on the Nek was folly. Godley apparently reassured them, and this would have been easy enough. Hughes and Antill had been on the peninsula 11 weeks without being in a major attack. Neither thought much about tactics or strategy. Godley and Skeen explained that there would be other attacks at the same time. The 1st Light Horse Brigade would jump out of Pope's and rush the Chessboard opposite. Others from the 1st Brigade would break out of Quinn's in 4 waves of 50 men. Australians at Steele's Post would attack German Officers' Trench and try to knock out machine guns that enfiladed the ground in front of the Nek. Besides, the New Zealanders would be streaming down Battleship Hill from Chunuk Bair, firing into the back of Baby 700.

Revisionism doesn't need to come into judgements about the attack on the Nek. If the assault seems futile now, it was just as futile in 1915. Birdwood told Walker to attack Lone Pine and Walker, after objecting fiercely, found ways to make the thing work. Birdwood told Godley to attack the Nek and Godley went ahead blindly, just as he was told, handing the task to two reactionaries in Hughes and Antill and ignoring all Gallipoli's lessons.

There was the simple matter of the Turkish attack of June 30. Did Godley think Australians were different from Turks? The Turks had charged down the hill in darkness to be slaughtered. Why would Australians charging up the hill in daylight, and into the rising sun at that, do any better? The Turkish trenches on the Nek and Baby 700, eight deep and covered by machine guns on both flanks, were much stronger than the Australian works opposite.

And this business of the New Zealanders attacking the Turks from behind? We know now that this couldn't happen because Johnston was still 500 yards from Chunuk Bair at 4.30 am on August 7, the time set for the Australian rush at the Nek. Let's assume, however, that the New Zealanders *had* been coming back down

Battleship Hill. They would have been skirmishing all the way. At 4.30 am they would still have been a long way from the eight lines of Turkish trenches in front of the Australians. The Turks, even if they had been a little panicked by the news that New Zealanders were behind them, could still have brought hundreds of rifles and five machine guns to fire on Australians running uphill with long bayonets and sawn-off hopes.

We should also now mention that the attack on German Officers' Trench failed. On the morning of August 7 the pre-conditions for the charge at the Nek no longer existed. Birdwood and Godley knew this before 4.30 am. They knew the New Zealanders were short of Chunuk Bair, yet they let the attack go ahead. In his autobiography, a book of surpassing shallowness, Godley wrote that the attack at the Nek fulfilled its object of drawing the enemy's reserves away from the main attack. Godley didn't know much but, like Enver, he knew the rhetoric one falls back on to dress up defeat as victory, the words that make murder sound like an act of statecraft.

The written orders for the charge made it seem easy, one logical step after another. Because of the narrowness of the Nek, only 150 men could go forward in one rush. The first line would take the trenches at the Nek with bayonets and bombs. The second line would 'sweep on', past the first, and take the lower trenches on Baby 700. These two lines would come from White's 8th Regiment. The third and fourth lines, from Brazier's 10th, would drive further into the Turkish lines; the fourth would bring up the picks and shovels. As Peter Burness wrote in *The Nek*, 'Godley was proposing to use the light horsemen in a massed bayonet attack of a kind which had been rendered in-effective by weapon developments back at the time of the

American Civil War.' Rifles were to be unloaded, and one has to wonder why. True, there would be no time to fire during the rush up the hill, but wouldn't there be some advantage in having ten rounds in the magazine on reaching the trench? Why were the planners trying to turn back time? Why didn't someone suggest carrying clubs?

Letters and diaries suggest the light horsemen in the ranks thought they could succeed. Antill sold the idea strongly. His half-literate written orders spoke of the need for 'DASH and DETERMINATION'. 'No time to waste on prisoners – no notice of tricks of the enemy such as "cease fire" . . .' The brigade had never been in a big attack before and innocence begets hope. These men had joined up to fight, not to burrow in the ground and disinter bodies. They were horsemen and here they were, without horses, living like troglodytes. Bean says they saw the attack as the path to 'green and open country'. The clamorous victory at Lone Pine had inspired them. That too was a frontal assault; they did not know it had been planned differently to theirs. And they believed the New Zealanders would be attacking the Turks from the rear.

So keen were the light horsemen that some hid their illnesses to stay in the lines and others returned from hospital. White was still recovering from his head wound. A corporal whose nerves were gone told the doctor he was staying. Captain Vernon Piesse, a West Australian farmer, returned from a hospital ship on the eve of the attack. 'I'd never have been able to stand up again if I hadn't,' he said.

The light horsemen shivered before the attack, too cold to sleep, although their chests were warmed briefly around 3 am when a double issue of rum was poured from stone jars. Through a piece of administrative stupidity their woollen tunics had been taken from them four days earlier. Shirtsleeves, shorts and English-style sun helmets were fine during the hot days; the nights were still chilly. The men were to charge carrying 200 rounds of ammunition, a field dressing pinned inside their shirts, full water bottle, six biscuits and two empty sandbags. Some would also carry wire-cutters, periscopes, planks, scaling ladders and picks and shovels. All wore white patches on their shirts so the Allied artillery could identify them. With each line went four red-and-yellow marker flags. These were to be planted in captured trenches. Personal belongings, letters, books, photographs, keepsakes, the little things that reminded the men they were strangers on this yellow hill and that home was in Kalgoorlie or Hamilton – these were left behind in the men's packs.

As the men shivered they heard firing from Lone Pine, out to the right, and on the foothills to the left. Just before dawn they heard rifle-fire at Suvla. This was the big one. Today they were going to break out of the Anzac jail. They didn't know that the attack on German Officers' Trench had failed, that Monash was lost in the countryside and Johnston in the muddle of his own mind.

The bombardment of the Turkish trenches at the Nek and beyond sounded ferocious to all who heard it. Bean said it was the heaviest since the prelude to the attack on Baby 700 on May 2. The barrage sounded better than it was. There were no battleships firing as there had been on May 2 and, because the opposing frontlines were so close, many of the shells had to be lobbed deep into the Turkish position. Major Carew Reynell of the 9th Regiment (the reserve) wrote in his diary that the bombardment was 'desultory' and a 'joke'.

The Australian line below the Nek ran for more than 100 yards. On the right there was a conventional trench, directly facing the Turks across relatively flat ground; pegs had been driven into the wall so that the men could get out quickly. The left-hand end of the line was in dead ground. This was the so-called 'secret sap', a ditch without a parapet or parados and hidden by scrub and a slight mound.

At 4.23, seven minutes ahead of schedule, the artillery barrage stopped. Watches had apparently not been synchronised. Any hope of surprise was now lost. The Turks in the front trench were packed two-deep and ready, bayonets bobbing. The Turkish machine gunners further up the hill and off to the flanks fired off a few test bursts. One light horseman later wrote to his mother that at that moment 'we knew we were doomed'.

Alexander White had decided to lead the first wave over. He didn't have to. It would have been good sense for a commanding officer to wait behind. White had a quixotic sense of duty and unusual courage. He knew exactly what he was doing. He offered his hand to Antill. 'Goodbye,' he said.

White stood in the trench, every now and then dropping his eyes to his watch. Finally he shouted: 'Go!'

In the half-light the Turkish rifles and machine guns belched flames. Bean heard it and called it 'one continuous roaring tempest'. Sergeant Lawrence heard the same roar, so loud that, even out near Lone Pine, one could not shout over it. White ran ten paces and was killed. He got further than most. Most died within three paces of the parapet; some were hit before they cleared it. An Australian watching from Pope's Hill told Bean the line fell 'as though the men's limbs had become string'. The killing was worse on the unprotected right.

Three men actually reached the Turkish parapet on the right. One of them crawled back two nights later with an ankle wound. On the other side Lieutenant E. G. Wilson, a grazier from Warrnambool, also reached the parapet. Then a bomb killed him. It was his 23rd birthday.

Sergeant Cliff Pinnock went down in the first line and admitted that afterwards, when the regiment's roll was called, he 'cried like a child'.

> I was in the first line to advance and we did not get ten yards. Everyone fell like lumps of meat . . . All your pals that had been with you for months and months blown and shot out of all recognition . . . I got mine shortly after I got over the bank, and it felt like a million ton hammer falling on my shoulder. However I managed to crawl back and got it temporarily fixed up till they carried me to the Base hospital. I was really awfully lucky as the bullet went in just below the shoulder blade round by my throat and came out just a tiny way from my spine very low down on the back . . . It was simply murder.

Pinnock arrived in an Egyptian hospital and suddenly realised he had come from an unearthly place. He was overjoyed to see a woman's face and hear a piano.

Major Thomas Redford, a Warrnambool merchant, was shot in the brain. 'He died with a soft sigh,' a sergeant wrote, 'and laid his head gently on his hands as if tired.' Trooper Lionel Simpson was running holding on to one end of a plank. He felt the trooper on the other end holding back; the man had been hit in the leg. 'I could see the knee coming out and machine-gun bullets going into it,' Simpson recalled when he was in his nineties. Simpson was hit in the head and shoulder. Thought to be the last survivor of the charge, he died in 1991 at the age of 100.

Reynell watched. Machine guns did most of the damage, he wrote. 'Some men's legs were completely severed by this fire.' Thirty seconds, no more, and the first line had been wiped out. But a red-and-yellow marker flag had been seen in the right-hand corner of the Turkish frontline. It fluttered for a few minutes then disappeared. The flag's appearance said much about the human spirit; otherwise it was meaningless. All it signified was that someone, ever briefly, had beaten the odds. It was evidence of grit and luck, not occupation.

The second line at the Nek should never have gone. At Quinn's, also around 4.30 am that morning, the Queenslanders of the 2nd Regiment of Chauvel's 1st Light Horse were to charge in 4 lines of 50 men. The first line at Quinn's ran into a firestorm. Forty-nine of the 50 men were either killed or wounded. Major G. H. Bourne told the second line to stand fast, talked to his immediate superior and stopped the attack. Chauvel confirmed Bourne's action.

At the Nek the second line went without hesitation two minutes after the first. It went even though Turkish fire was still thudding into the bodies of the first line, causing them to convulse in front of the parapet.

The second line was cut down like the first. Maybe if White had not gone with the first line he would have chosen as Bourne had. Maybe. Didn't matter now. White, good man that he was, was dead.

Captain George Hore, a barrister, got further than most in the second line. He said he bent low and ran as hard as he could. He could see the trench ahead aflame with rifle fire. Bullets kicked up dust around him. Hore felt a 'sting' in his shoulder. He flung himself down, alone. He would have been picked off easily had he not fallen near a fold in the ground and the swollen body of a Turk killed in the attack of June 30. He crept close to the corpse as though it were a perfumed angel. What should he do? Rush the Turkish trench alone? A bullet struck him in the foot and removed that option. He edged his way back to the Australian line and lived.

Trooper Walter McConnan wrote home that he had a graze on the back from a piece of red-hot shrapnel or bomb. 'While waiting about the dressing station . . . I came over young Sanderson of Benalla with a shattered leg. He was patient and brave. Australians can die I can tell you.'

Two-and-a-half minutes and a whole regiment had been destroyed for no gain and not a single Turkish casualty that we know of. The wounded cried out from no-man's land. A fierce sun was climbing behind the Turkish trenches.

Two Turkish field guns were starting to burst shrapnel over no-man's land as the West Australians of the 10th filed into the trench that was thick with dead, dying and wounded Victorians. Its floor and walls were spattered with gore and the place reeked of cordite, the incense of war. Flies swarmed; it was going to be a good day for flies. Unlike the first line of Victorians, many of whom ten minutes earlier went forth in a surge of hope, these West Australians knew they were going to die. Mates shook hands.

Major Tom Todd, in charge of the third line, told Brazier, the regimental commander, that his men had no hope of making the Turkish trenches. Brazier knew this well enough; he had watched the carnage through a periscope. To him it all now seemed senseless. At 4.40 he went to brigade headquarters. Hughes wasn't there – he had gone to an observation post at about the time the second line ran to its death – but Antill was. Antill was a literalist most of the time and didn't like Brazier any of the time. Now Brazier was telling him that the attack was pointless. Antill's written account of the day is confused.

He does, however, appear to have been furious that an underling, and particularly this prickly West Australian, could actually query an order. Antill told Brazier the marker flag had been seen in the Turkish trench. Brazier afterwards told Bean that Antill then shouted at him: 'Push on!' Antill acted alone. He did not refer the decision to Hughes or Godley's headquarters.

Brazier said he returned to the frontline and said: 'I am sorry, lads, but the order is to go.' Trooper Harold Rush turned to his mate. 'Goodbye, cobber,' he said. 'God bless you.' These words are on Rush's headstone in Walker's Ridge Cemetery, and 85 years on visitors to the peninsula stare at the words and wonder why, when they open their mouths, no words come out.

Around 4.45, in Bean's words, 'the 10th went forward to meet death instantly'. Piesse, who had returned from the hospital ship, died in this wave. So did Sergeant J. A. Gollan, the farmer who talked the doctor into letting him stay, although he lingered until August 30. So did two brothers, Gresley Harper, a barrister, and Wilfred, a farmer. Wilfred was either 25 or 26. He was last seen 'running forward like a schoolboy in a foot race'. He was the inspiration for the Archie Hamilton character in Peter Weir's film *Gallipoli*. Killed too was Lieutenant A. P. Turnbull, a Rhodes scholar from Perth.

Major Todd survived the third rush. He was lying out there somewhere. He sent back a message scribbled on pink paper. He was pinned down. What should he do?

Brazier took the pink paper to Antill. Brazier said that Antill refused to listen to him. 'Push on!' he repeated. Brazier now went looking for Hughes and says he told him the attacks were 'murder'. Hughes said: 'Try Bully Beef Sap.' This seemed to indicate Hughes was thinking of an attack from a new direction. Bully Beef Sap ran off the right hand side of the Russell's Top trenches towards the plunging wall that led down to Monash Valley.

The fourth line under Major Joe Scott was lined up ready to go to its death. Without orders the troops on the right rose and rushed over the parapet. 'By God, I believe the right has gone!' Scott said. Many of the officers knew Brazier was trying to have the fourth charge called off; the men did not. No-one seemed to know quite what happened, except that the men on the right thought they had been ordered to go. Major Scott managed to stop some men leaving the trench, but the fourth slaughter had begun.

Sergeant W. L. Sanderson rose in this rush. He saw a captain wave and assumed this was the signal to go. The captain fell dead a second or so later. Sanderson told Bean that as he ran forward he could see the Turks standing two deep in the front trench. Machine-gun fire was coming in from both flanks. The bullets had chewed up the bushes and left them spiky. Sanderson tripped over a bush near the Turkish parapet and fell on a dead Turk. Two dead Australians lay on the parapet. They looked like the Harper brothers. After about 30 minutes Sanderson, slightly wounded from a Turkish bomb, began to edge back towards the secret sap. He came on a Victorian from the 8th, lying on his back smoking. 'Have a cigarette,' the Victorian said, 'it's too ---- hot.'

Sanderson then came on a Victorian lieutenant. A bullet had hit the bombs he had been carrying and his hip had been blown away. Sanderson and the Victorian with the cigarette tried to drag him back. The lieutenant begged them to leave him. 'I can't bloody well stand it,' he said. They got him into the secret sap, where he promptly died. The lieutenant may have been Ted Henty, from the family that provided Victoria's first white settlers. Sanderson made his way along to the main trench to see Lieutenant Turnbull, the Rhodes scholar, dying. 'About 50 yards of the line had not a man in it except the dead and wounded – no-one was manning it.'

So it was over, this piece of madness. Dead and wounded were still lying out there. Bean wrote:

> At first here and there a man raised his arm to the sky, or tried to drink from his waterbottle. But as the sun of that burning day climbed higher, such movement ceased. Over the whole summit the figures lay still in the quivering heat.

Bean returned to the Nek in 1919 and found bones bleached by the sun lying on a piece of ground the size of three tennis courts. The 8th had virtually been wiped out: 234 casualties, including 154 dead, out of 300. The 10th had 138 casualties, including 80 dead. No ground had been gained, no strategic purpose served. We don't know what the Turkish casualties were, but they would have been negligible.

The marker flag that flew briefly in a Turkish trench also caused losses among two companies of Royal Welch Fusiliers from the British 13th Division. They were to climb along the steep wall of Monash Valley, between Russell's Top and Pope's, and attack the Chessboard. The British assault was conditional on the Australians taking the Nek, because the Turks there could shoot into the backs of the Fusiliers from close range. Antill allowed the Fusiliers to go forward on hearing about the red and yellow flag. The Turks rolled bombs down the valley wall. The Fusiliers' commander eventually called the assault off after losing 65 men.

As already mentioned, the attack by the 1st Light Horse at Quinn's was called off after the first wave had been wiped out. The 1st also attacked from Pope's and got into a bomb-fight with the Turks. The light horsemen had to retreat after three hours, mainly because there weren't many of them left. One hundred and fifty-four of the 200 who went out became casualties. Every officer except one was hit.

The three assaults by the two light horse brigades had failed, even though the men had shown unreasonable courage and, in the case of the last three lines at the Nek, an acceptance of death that almost defies understanding. But courage was not enough; it was never going to be enough. The assaults failed mainly because Birdwood, Godley and Skeen had not thought them through carefully. Skeen showed that he understood nothing of the terrain and very little about real life by announcing, when the killing at the Nek was at its worst: 'It is not the light horse I am anxious about. I think they will be all right. What I hope is that they will help the New Zealanders.'

What happened at the Nek, however, went beyond failure. The attack there could have been called off, as occurred at Quinn's, after the first line had been shot down. Yet it went on mindlessly, so that it truly became what Brazier and others called it: murder.

Peter Weir's 1981 film *Gallipoli* is elegiac, well written and beautifully scored; it captures an Australia that no longer exists and a brief age of innocence. The film is so well done that for many Australians it is the reference point on the Gallipoli campaign. Yet its final scenes, built around the fourth charge at the Nek, are inaccurate and unfair to the British. The film suggests the Australians at the Nek were being sacrificed to help the landing at Suvla. It also suggests that a British officer was ordering successive waves of Australians to run out and commit suicide.

The scale of the tragedy of the Nek was mostly the work of two Australian incompetents, Hughes and Antill. Hughes was the brigade commander and he didn't command; Antill wasn't the brigade commander and he did. Responsibility rattled Hughes and, either consciously or unconsciously, he walked away from it. Antill behaved as he always did, like a bull strung up in barbed wire. Antill gave orders without finding out what was happening. He could easily have justified calling the attack off: the failure of the first line proved the objective was unattainable. Antill could also have argued successfully that the scale of casualties bore no relationship to anything that might be gained. One also has to wonder whether Antill's judgements were influenced by his dislike of Brazier.

Hughes came down with enteric fever, left the peninsula forever in October, returned to Australia and retired as a major-general. Antill was promoted to brigadier-general and served with the Light Horse in Sinai. Here, according to Burness in *The Nek*, he again showed that he lacked the ability to think quickly, which is even more important when directing horsemen in open country. He was sent to France to command infantry. His health broke and he returned to Australia. He was made a Companion of the Order of St Michael and St George for his war service and left the army in 1924 as an honorary major-general.

The incident at the Nek was like incest: no-one in the family much wanted to talk about it. Everyone in authority felt guilt that such a thing could happen. They became a mutual protection society and offered the occasional alibi.

Hamilton doesn't mention the charges at the Nek in his *Gallipoli Diary*, which runs to 2 volumes and 700 pages.

Godley gives it one sentence in his autobiography, although he devotes 11 pages to the August offensive. Godley gives the Nek two sentences in his official summary of operations at Anzac from August 6 to August 10. He mentions the 8th Light Horse but not the 10th, as though the last two charges never happened. In his official report of January, 1916, Hamilton also fails to mention the 10th. He says some of the Turkish positions were carried but that it was impossible to hold them. Hamilton was always an optimist.

Birdwood said in his autobiography that the position was too strongly held to be taken, but the attack 'had been of value in pinning the Turks to the spot and preventing them from sending reinforcements to their right'. The Turks could, of course, have been 'pinned to the spot' by a long artillery barrage and the *threat* of a charge.

Hughes complained he did not receive 'proper support'. Antill said the attack might have been worthwhile 'had the people at Suvla done their job'. Bean's account of the charge in the *Argus* in September was inconclusive. It did not say the attack was a failure and suggested that the Turks had lost heavily too. The report was subject to censorship. Bean told the truth in his official history, to the annoyance of Hughes and Antill. In the British official history Aspinall reports Brazier's attempts to have the later charges called off but not the parts played by Hughes and Antill.

After a few days the corpses of the Australians lying at the Nek began to stink. Swarms of flies crawled over them. Three months later, only skeletons remained. Skeletons with packs on their backs and rifles nearby. Men from Victoria's Western District and the wheat lands of Western Australia. Carrion on some foreign field.

* * *

It is March, 1998, and you stand on this same carrion-field and look out on a scene of silent beauty. Snowflakes are dancing and whirling out of a pale grey sky that glowers just above your head. The breeze smells of salt. Snow festoons the old Australian trenches, which dogleg through the holly. They have been shored up with pine logs and the iced-over uprights rise like stalagmites. Over to your left the Aegean shows its surly face, inky blue and flecked with whitecaps. Straggles of snow lie on the flutes and runnels of Malone's Gully. Even erosion looks dainty today.

Up ahead is the Turkish memorial. This is roughly where the Turkish trenches were when the light horsemen charged on August 7. This is also where Captain Joseph Lalor and others of the 12th Battalion dug in on the day of the landing.

It is like going back to the family farm: everything seems smaller than it should be. Bean was right: this place isn't much bigger than a couple of tennis courts. Other fabled places are so close, over to the right, and they are tiny too: The Bloody Angle, Dead Man's Ridge, Pope's with its 'waterfall' of erosion, Quinn's, the Chessboard. Walk carelessly and you will pass some hellhole where for eight months men lived like moles and died in their thousands. So much killing, so little ground.

The secret sap would have been over there, in the holly towards the Aegean. Bully Beef Sap would have been on the other side and further back, pointing towards Monash Valley. It is difficult to work things out now. The monuments, the paths, the sad little Australian cemetery, the pine trees – all make for confusion. When you walk up Baby 700, the snow crunching underfoot and turning to yellow slush, you begin to see the battlefield more clearly. The Nek is exactly that: a neck of land, about 30 yards wide at its narrowest point and with cliffs on both sides, joining Russell's Top to Baby 700. What you also see from here is that the Turkish machine gunners had a perfect field of fire. Because of those cliffs, the Australians could spread neither left nor right. They were jammed in a funnel.

Beneath your feet in the Nek cemetery lie 300 Australian dead, most of them killed on August 7. Here life ended for several accountants, two former Duntroon cadets, a Perth architect, a bunch of farm kids from Victoria's Western District, a schoolmaster from Geelong, a vigneron from Rutherglen, a string of barristers, an ironmonger, a grocer, a Rhodes scholar, old boys from Scotch and Melbourne Grammar – and four sets of brothers. A lost generation.

Two years later you return to the Nek. No snow today. It is the day after the Anzac Day service of 2000. The ground is greasy from the overnight rain. Three plastic roses, protected by cellophane and carrying tags that announce they were made in China, lie among the headstones. No-one else is here. Yesterday thousands swarmed over the beach and Lone Pine. Those two places are seen to be rich in symbolism. The Nek is something else, too hard to explain.

24

Loitering without intent

Ashmead-Bartlett was off Suvla on the *Minneapolis* at dawn on August 7. As he headed for the saloon and breakfast – iced melons, fish, eggs and bacon – he passed an old steward cleaning the carpet with a vacuum cleaner. Ashmead-Bartlett was struck by this. Constantinople was hanging in the balance and all this old bloke could think to do was to fuss over the carpet. The force of habit and discipline on the humble mind. 'It is this same spirit amongst the rank and file which alone enables modern warfare to be carried on,' Ashmead-Bartlett decided.

He gazed on Suvla Bay as the sun began to melt the haze. The bay was packed with warships, transports, landing craft, hospital ships, trawlers and other small craft, and the *Jonquil*, which carried Frederick Stopford, who was in charge of this enterprise, although it helped if every now and then people reminded him this was so. The warships were thundering away at the Anafarta hills, not really knowing what they were aiming at. All they knew was that there were guns up there somewhere. There had to be: clouds of Turkish shrapnel kept bursting over the beach. Ashmead-Bartlett could see dark objects on the salt lake. Dead Turks. He could not see any live Turks or gun emplacements.

He was troubled that the New Army troops ashore seemed half-hearted, as though they were loath to go for their objectives. From Anzac came an incessant rumbling, like distant thunder on a summer's day, and white clouds of smoke hung over the hills. Here at Suvla the war seemed too quiet. 'No firm hand appeared to control this mass of men suddenly dumped on an unknown shore.' And when one looked at the great sweep of country these men were supposed to occupy in the first day, there didn't look to be too many men. What Ashmead-Bartlett didn't know then was that units were intermixed, as they had been at Anzac on the first day, and that there *was* no firm hand in charge of the landing. The men ashore were tired, hot and thirsty. Their offensive was already paralysed, not by the Turks but by mismanagement and confusion within the British command.

Von Sanders was seeing the same panorama as Ashmead-Bartlett through the eyes of Major Willmer, his local commander. Willmer told von Sanders the British soldiers moved 'bolt upright, as if on parade', tended to bunch up and made little use of cover. Von Sanders was in the same position he had been in on April 25. Before moving his troops he had to be sure where the main threat lay. Was it the breakout into the foothills north of Anzac? Or maybe this landing at Suvla? Or were these feints too, like Lone Pine? Was the main landing going to come at Bulair?

When the first streaks of dawn lit up an armada off Suvla, von Sanders knew the answer. The heights of Sari Bair: that's what this offensive was about. He moved decisively.

He told Feizi Bey, the commander at Bulair, to hurry south with most of his 7th and 12th divisions. He ordered every soldier on the Asian side of the Dardanelles to march to Çanakkale, whence they would be shipped across the Narrows to Anzac. He told Wehib Pasha at Helles to send a second division to Anzac. Von Sanders' moves, as they had been after the April 25 landings, were just about impeccable, but he could not get around one problem. The reinforcements would take time to arrive. The first division he had taken from Wehib would arrive in a few hours. The two divisions from Bulair and the second division he had taken from Wehib would not arrive until tomorrow morning, August 8. The troops from the Asian side would not cross the Narrows until tomorrow night. Throughout today he had only Kemal's division to throw against the two columns marching on Sari Bair. He had only Willmer's 3 battalions, maybe 1500 men now, to hold up the 20,000 British troops who had come ashore at Suvla. Von Sanders headed for Suvla to see for himself.

Today, August 7, had become the crucial day for the Allies. Things had gone wrong. The attacks at the Nek, Pope's and Quinn's had failed. The New Zealanders had done well to get within reach of Chunuk Bair, but Johnston had dithered and the advance was held up. Cox's assaulting column was hours behind schedule, tired, lost and scattered. The Suvla landing had succeeded only in the sense that the men were ashore; as Ashmead-Bartlett could see from the *Minneapolis*, they weren't doing much. The Allied offensive was a tangle of problems, caused mainly, it should be noted, by the terrain and failures of command rather than Turkish opposition. And yet, even though surprise had been lost, there was still a chance it could succeed – so long as the assaulting columns and the Suvla troops raced for their objectives before von Sanders' reinforcements arrived. Today was the crucial day.

*   *   *

We left Johnston and the other New Zealander commanders on the early morning of August 7 debating whether to attack Chunuk Bair, deciding they wouldn't, telling Godley so, only to be told by the general that they wanted to attack the hill at 10.30 am after an artillery barrage. Johnston had bungled, but it would be unjust to blame him for the slaughter of the Light Horse at the Nek. Johnston must, however, take much of the blame for what now happened to the New Zealanders.

When Godley's order to attack arrived, Temperley urged Johnston to disobey it. Johnston said, no, he would carry it out. Around this time two companies of Gurkhas arrived. They had lost contact with their own column and offered to help the New Zealanders.

Johnston's column was at the Apex, a small rocky lump about 500 yards from the summit. Beyond the Apex, Rhododendron Ridge falls down a narrow saddle before rising to another rocky lump known as the Pinnacle. From here to the crest of Chunuk Bair the approach dips again then widens out into a steep climb of perhaps less than 300 yards. The narrow ridge joining the Apex to the Pinnacle falls away to the head of Sazli Dere on the right. On the left it falls to the end of Aghyl Dere. About halfway down the left-hand slope is a little tableland with mysterious gullies on either side. There was a sheepfold here in 1915 and this ledge rejoiced in the name of the Farm.

Lieutenant-Colonel Young, commander of the Auckland Battalion, had gone forward to reconnoitre before Godley's order to attack arrived. Bullets zipped past him as soon as he passed the Apex. And the ground worried him. It was so narrow that only 100 or so men could go forward at any time. He told Johnston the attack should be at night. Young was told he would be leading the attack in daylight with three companies of his Auckland Battalion; the Gurkhas would be on his left.

More than six hours behind schedule, the New Zealanders went for Chunuk Bair. Rhododendron Ridge was only a useful way to Chunuk Bair if the attackers had surprise on their side. It was too narrow, as the Nek was, for an assault against an enemy that had had time to prepare. The Aucklanders began to fall ten yards past the Apex. Temperley said the leading Auckland platoons were 'simply devastated'; the sight was 'sickening'. About 100 Aucklanders reached the unoccupied Turkish trench at the Pinnacle and hastily began to deepen it. Every time a shovelful of earth rose in the air the Turks let fly with a mountain gun. Behind the Pinnacle the dead and the wounded lay in the sun, perhaps 300 of them, nearly as many as at the Nek. Wounded were still crying out when darkness came. The Gurkhas on the left ended up down in Aghyl Dere.

Johnston had undergone a character change. Around dawn he was silent and morose. Now he was out on the ridge behind the Apex cheering his men on like a barracker at a football match. And now he wanted the Wellington Battalion to follow the Aucklanders.

Malone refused. The men crowded around the Apex heard him do so. Corporal Charlie Clark was nearby. There was a 'big row', he recalled in 1982. Malone was 'stern and strong-faced'. He shouted to his men: 'Stop where you are.' Clark recalled that Malone said: 'No. We are not taking orders from you people. Wellington is not going up there. My men are not going to commit suicide.' Malone said he would take responsibility for his action. 'I will take all risk and any punishment.' The Wellingtons would take Chunuk Bair at night, not in daylight, he said.

The Canterbury Battalion had suffered heavy casualties from artillery and machine-gun fire as it moved up towards the Apex. According to Temperley, Hughes, the Canterbury commander, had formed up his battalion in close order in full view of the Turks. Hughes arrived at the Apex with tears pouring down his cheeks. The Otago Battalion also suffered. A private told how he was looking at the face of a comrade when suddenly a mark the size of a sixpence appeared between the man's eyes, and he fell spurting blood. Only the Wellington Battalion was relatively untouched. Malone looked after his men. (It is an irresistible speculation: what would he have done if he had been at the Nek a few hours earlier?)

Johnston told Godley the attack had failed. Godley agreed to delay a fresh attempt until nightfall. He would reinforce Johnston with two New Army battalions from Shaw's 13th Division, the 7th Gloucesters and the 8th Welch Pioneers. Russell was told to send up the Auckland Mounted Rifles and the Maori Contingent as a reserve. Johnston decided to attack again at 4.15 am after a 45-minute barrage. Malone's Wellingtons and the Gloucesters would lead the attack.

For the New Zealanders the seventh had been a wasted day.

Far out on the left General Cox's battalions were so scattered he didn't know where they all were, let alone what they were doing. It wasn't Cox's fault. For most of the campaign the British planners had under-estimated the fighting spirit of the Turks; in the case of this left assaulting column they had underestimated the roughness of the terrain.

Monash's Australians were too tired to go anywhere much; they certainly weren't going to take Hill 971 today.

They were going to lie down and scrape holes as protection against snipers and think about how thirsty they were. If Monash was frustrated, as Allanson's account suggests, he was in an even bigger muddle than he realised. Monash, the engineer who knew how to figure angles and estimate distances, was not where he and his battalion commanders thought they were. He was one valley, or dere, further back than he thought he was. He was about 700 yards nearer the sea than he thought he was. He was also further north than he thought he was. Monash was looking at Kaiajik Dere and thinking it was Asma Dere. He was looking at the northern arm of Damakjelik Spur and thinking it was Abdel Rahman Spur.

The error was serious. Seven hundred yards is an eternity in this country. And if Monash didn't know where he was, that meant Cox and Godley didn't know where he was either.

The right-hand side of Monash's line was bothered by fire from snipers and artillery throughout August 7. Things were quieter on the left. A group of men loaded themselves up with water bottles, crossed Hill 60, and walked about a mile-and-a-half towards Suvla. They found a farm hut, filled the water bottles, picked blackberries and raided beehives, then headed back, bothered only by the odd sniper. If the Australians were tired, the scrounging instinct was alive.

Cox briefly thought his Gurkhas might make Hill Q on the seventh. Then he realised they were also too widely scattered, although, unlike Monash's troops, they had managed to keep moving. Cox obtained permission to take the 39th Brigade of the 13th Division – Warwickshires, Gloucesters, Cheshires, Wiltshires and others – from Godley's reserve to help capture Hill Q and Chunuk Bair. The Gloucesters, as already mentioned, headed off to join up with Johnston's New Zealanders. The rest of the 39th Brigade became lost. The Indian Brigade had become so scattered that it was not a fighting force but a series of raiding parties heading towards Q. The sun was fierce and the water scarce. Cox's army was wearing itself out slogging over country it couldn't begin to understand.

Three battalions from Monash's brigade were to assault what they thought was Abdel Rahman at 3 am on August 8. Monash told Cox he didn't have enough men. Cox gave him a battalion from Baldwin's 38th Brigade. This battalion and Monash's 13th would hold the present line. That would leave Monash's 14th, 15th and 16th battalions free to attack Abdel Rahman.

Godley sent Monash two messages. One was a polite reprimand.

> I feel confident that after today's rest and starting comparatively fresh, your brigade will make a determined effort to capture the key of the position tomorrow morning. In selecting it for this task I had the original brigade in mind and I hope you will ask your excellent COs to let the men know from me that we all expect the reconstituted brigade to live up to the traditions of the original.

Godley, as he would be throughout this offensive, was out of touch. True, the brigade had not moved during the day, but the men had been dodging bullets, digging scrapes, looking after their wounded and thinking about their thirst; they were looking at four hours' sleep at best. Why would they start 'comparatively fresh' on the eighth?

Godley's other message said Monash's troops should be well up the slopes before dawn so that they could take the crest as soon as the artillery barrage lifted at 4.15 am. 'The assault should be carried out with loud cheering,' Godley explained.

The flaw in the plan was that Monash was 700 yards farther away from Abdel Rahman than he thought he was. Even if the opposition was light, he could not reach and climb Abdel Rahman by 4.15. There was another matter that no-one could know, because this country had not been scouted. Abdel Rahman was a fearsome climb, one of the toughest on the peninsula.

Monash now introduced other flaws into the plan. Pope, commander of the 16th, was to command the attack. Pope also had to command his own battalion. He was given no extra staff to help him lead three battalions and keep in touch with Monash, who would stay back above the Aghyl Dere.

Monash's decision was curious. No, he should not have been up with the leading troops in the fashion of Alexander White, who was so brave at the Nek and perhaps not very wise; it is hard to look after your men if you have already become the martyred dead. But Monash had to be at least in the centre of those three attacking battalions. The nature of the country dictated this. If he stayed behind, he would have little idea of what was happening. If the telephone line from Pope was cut, he would have no idea.

The medical arrangements were not thought through properly. The brigade's own field ambulance had become lost in Taylor's Gap. The 3rd Light Horse Field Ambulance had been clearing the brigade's wounded from a station in Aghyl Dere. The light horsemen were not told an attack was about to be made.

Cox had had two bad days in a row. He had men – New Army, Indians, Australians – wandering over the

valleys and ridges north of Anzac like lost tribes. He had
not reached any of the objectives he should have reached
on the morning of the seventh. Godley, who may as well
have been in Athens for all he knew about what was going
on, was becoming impatient. Maybe tomorrow would be
better. For Cox, as for Johnston, the seventh had been a
wasted day.

Stopford finally sent his first message to GHQ from the
Jonquil on the morning of the seventh. He had landed
20,000 men on an enemy coast – well, in a manner of
speaking. He hadn't actually stood around supervising the
landing, getting his boots wet and cracking out orders.
Other chaps had done that. He'd been sleeping and
dashed hard it was too with those rifles going off all the
time. But chaps had dropped by the *Jonquil* and told
him things. He had told Hamilton he wanted to be with
his men at the landing and he had been – well, in a
manner of speaking. Apparently his men had taken this
hill with a funny name. Lala something. Might have taken
another hill as well. Hard to tell. Navy fellows got into a
bit of trouble with their new landing barges. Never had
that trouble in the Sudan. Lot to be said for paddle
steamers.

Stopford's cable arrived at Imbros about noon. He
should have sounded relieved, even a touch confident, but
he wasn't. The cable ended: 'As you see, we have been
able to advance little beyond the edge of the beach.' He
should have sounded relieved because the demons that
had been troubling him on Imbros had not appeared.
There weren't many Turks ashore; those who were around
tended to fight delaying actions and melt away. And there
were no continuous trenches, so he didn't need all those
howitzers. Yet Stopford's message was glum. To say he

was going through the motions is to attribute to him an energy he didn't own.

If Hamilton had failed to see Stopford's character flaws before, why couldn't he see them now? Why didn't he reprimand Stopford for taking so long to send his first message? Why didn't he go to Suvla himself and order Stopford to take the encircling hills? Had Hamilton done so, Aspinall wrote in the official history, the duration of the Great War might have been shortened. This is an exaggeration: the August offensive was going to be won or lost from high in the Sari Bair range, not Suvla. Yet it is astonishing that Hamilton did nothing to shake Stopford out of his trance. By 4.20 pm on the seventh, Hamilton had apparently become a little fretful. He had Braithwaite send a message: 'Have only received one telegram from you. Chief glad to hear enemy opposition weakening, and knows you will take advantage of this to push on rapidly.'

Push on rapidly . . . What happened at Suvla on the seventh can be told briefly. Stopford did not go ashore. He thus had no first-hand knowledge and was separated from his administrative staff. On shore, orders were issued and cancelled, troops marched this way then the other. Hammersley kept changing his mind and was shaken when a Turkish shell burst nearby. The 10th and 11th divisions were badly mixed up. General Mahon found himself commanding only three battalions of his 10th. The troops mostly huddled around the beach. Every now and then, Turkish snipers picked one off. The temperature was around 90 degrees Fahrenheit. A few troops became crazy with thirst. They used bayonets to cut into the hoses from the ships to get a drink of water. Admiral Christian seems to have been infected with Stopford's languor. No guns were landed on the seventh, which gave Stopford another reason to delay, and only 50 mules instead of 564. As darkness came Stopford's force finally captured Chocolate Hill and Green Hill.

The profit-and-loss account for the day went something like this. Stopford's men had taken Hill 10, Chocolate Hill and Green Hill, and the Turkish outposts on the two horns of the bay. The hills that commanded Suvla – Kiretch Tepe ridge to the north, Tekke Tepe ridge in the centre and the Anafarta Spur to the south – were still with the Turks. Stopford's casualties for the first 24 hours stood at around 1700, or more than the whole of the Turkish garrison opposing them. This figure is all the more astonishing when one remembers there had been no pitched battle, that Willmer's force didn't own one machine gun and that most of his artillery had not been firing.

The biggest casualty, however, was leadership. Hamilton was on Imbros, out of touch. Guy Dawnay had been sent to Suvla and returned to GHQ full of pessimism; he was regarded as being 'unduly impatient'. Stopford was on the *Jonquil*, out of touch. Hammersley was just above the beach, out of touch and decidedly jumpy; he didn't know his men had captured Chocolate Hill until midnight; next morning he discovered they had also taken Green Hill. The brigadiers in charge of the capture of these two hills were two miles behind the fighting, out of touch. So instead of chasing the Turks and perhaps obtaining a foothold on the Anafarta Spur, the successful troops waited on the hills they had taken. As Major-General J. F. C. Fuller wrote in *The Decisive Battles of the Western World*, Hamilton and Stopford waited for victory or defeat as if the whole operation were a horse race. Such generalship, he continued, defied definition.

One had to feel sorry for the New Army troops. All of them were new; most were very young. They were confused by their baptism to war, tired from their long sea trip, hot and thirsty and not particularly robust. Yet they might still have fought well. They couldn't fight well because they were badly led.

One could say Willmer had bought 24 hours with his delaying actions and sniping; another 18 hours, give or take, and he would receive massive reinforcements. But to say this is to give Willmer too much credit, even though he had deployed his tiny force intelligently and kept his head throughout. Willmer had not bought 24 hours; the English generals had handed him 24 hours.

At 7 pm Willmer sent von Sanders a message that summed up the day splendidly: 'No energetic attacks on the enemy's part have taken place. On the contrary, the enemy is advancing timidly.'

At Suvla the seventh had been a wasted day.

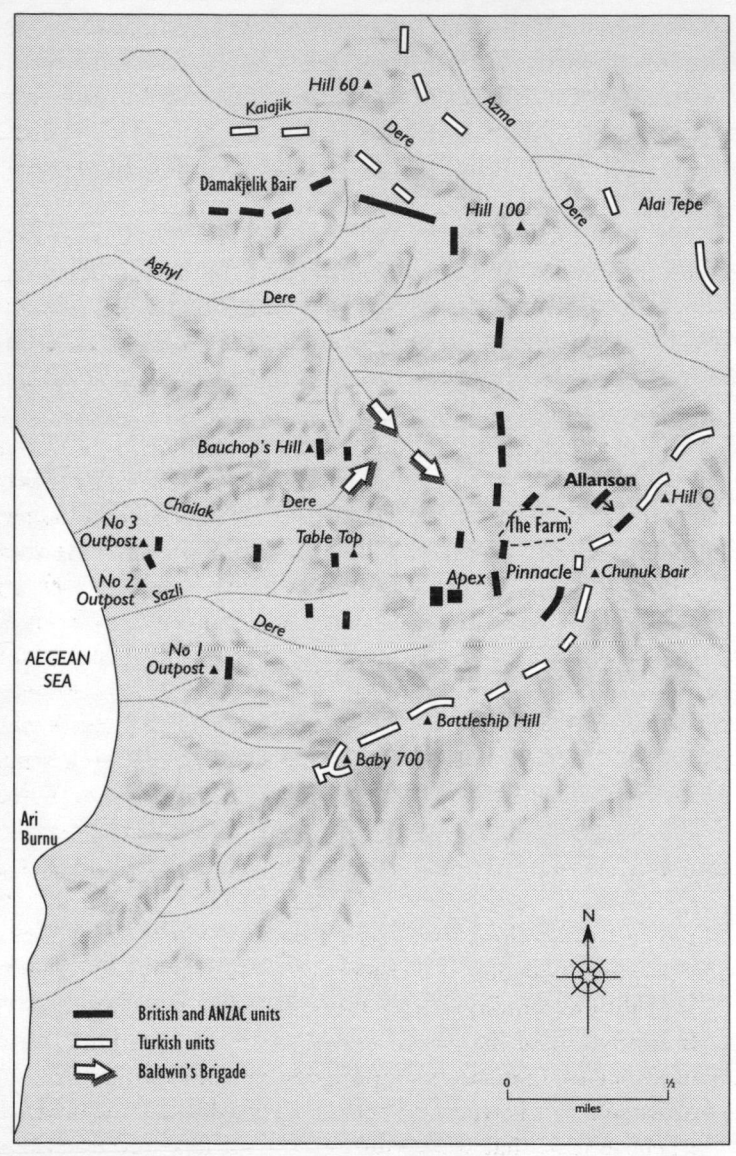

Positions before the Turkish counter-attack

25

The martyr of Chunuk Bair

The day before he tramped out of old Anzac for the assault on the heights, the tough and tender New Zealander who was William George Malone wrote to his wife. Her name was Ida but he called her 'Mater'. She was his second wife. His first, Elinor, died in childbirth in 1904. Two of Malone's sons from that first marriage, Edmond and Terry, were fighting at Gallipoli. Malone had found time to write to his two sons, aged nine and seven, by Mater. 'I see lots of strange things here,' he told them, 'big ships and little ones, aeroplanes and all sorts of guns and things. Soldiers and sailors. The other day a tortoise called on me.' That was in May. Now, on August 5, he wrote to Mater. 'My sweetheart,' he began.

> I expect to go through all right but dear wife if anything untowards happens to me there are our dear children to be brought up. You know how I love and have loved you . . . If at anytime in the past I seemed absorbed in 'affairs', it was that I might make proper provision for you and the children . . . It is true that perhaps I overdid it somewhat. I believe now that I did, but did not see it at the time. I regret very much now that it was so and that I lost more

happiness than I need have done. You must forgive me; forgive also anything unkindly or hard that I may have said or done in the past . . . I have made a will and it is in the office in Stratford . . . I am prepared for death and hope that God will have forgiven me all my sins . . .

Now, three days later, on the last morning of his life, in the dark below the surly lump of Chunuk Bair, Malone prepared to rush the summit with his Wellingtons. As well as being a land agent and a solicitor with five offices, Malone was a farmer. He owned about 2000 acres around Stratford on the North Island. New Zealand has some of the kindest dirt in the world. One would have liked to know what Malone thought of this run of country he was on now, rock-strewn and rain-scored, the soil a hungry yellow, as though the goodness had been sucked out, the few trees bent and mean, as though they had arthritis. He must have thought it strange that every day they asked him to offer up his life not for the hedged fields of home, not for the hearth and the roses and the willows, but for a wilderness that would cripple a goat.

Malone, tall and straight-backed, didn't fit any of the stereotypes. He was born near London but saw himself as a New Zealander. He was of Irish descent and the temper of his adopted land was Scottish. He was a Catholic in a predominantly Protestant society. He spoke French and loved classical music. He liked soldiering but he was never going to make general: he was ambitious but not in the sense that he was prepared to win promotions over the bodies of his men; he was always going to be more popular with his men than with his superiors. He was bossy and petty, a man of tidy habits that bordered on fetishes, yet his men loved him. Sixty years after Chunuk Bair old men who had served with 'Molly Malone' spoke of him with reverence. He was their father; he had looked after them.

Malone awakened his batman, Private Benjamin Smart, at 3 am on August 8 and gave him the address of his wife in case he should be hit or killed. Then he shook hands with Smart and said goodbye.

Malone knew exactly where the summit was. The navy and the Anzac batteries were lighting it up with red and orange flames. Malone and his men advanced 16 abreast along the ridge linking the Apex to the Pinnacle, past the dead and wounded from the previous day's battle, past the shallow trench at the Pinnacle, down the dip, then up towards the summit itself, spreading out as the hill opened out in front of them. Behind the Wellingtons came the Gloucesters and Welch Pioneer battalions Johnston had picked up the previous day. Not a shot was fired as the Wellingtons climbed. When the barrage ended they charged the summit.

It was the sweetest of anti-climaxes. There was only a Turkish machine-gun crew below the summit. Most of the defenders higher up had fled the artillery barrage because their trenches were too shallow to protect them. Kannengiesser, their commander, had been carted off wounded the previous day; his replacement had been wounded shortly after. A bearded Turk, who looked to be about 70, went for his rifle. 'We had to shoot him, poor old joker,' Corporal Clark said. Two sentries who threw bombs were killed. Twenty Turks, and a German petty officer from the *Goeben*, were taken prisoner. It was that easy.

And when dawn came, Malone and his men saw, beyond Bigali and Mal Tepe, what Tulloch had seen on the first day, the silvery waters of the Narrows. From Chunuk Bair one can see two stretches of water, both close to Çanakkale. As with Tulloch, thoughts of victory teased. As with Tulloch, they teased briefly.

What the New Zealanders also saw was that this summit was going to be hard to defend. It wasn't a sharp peak so much as two humps with a saddle between them. The ground was rocky and hard; that's why the Turkish trenches were so shallow. Worst of all, the summit was open to fire from north and south. The Turks on Battleship Hill to the south could fire across Sazli Dere into the back of the Wellingtons. The Turks on Hill Q to the north were slightly above Chunuk Bair. The Wellingtons and the New Army troops following them suddenly came under heavy fire.

In theory there should have been no fire from Hill Q; General Cox's columns should have captured it at dawn, and Hill 971 too. Or so the plan said.

Cox had a few little problems on the early morning of the eighth. He had a wound to the ankle. He was running 13 battalions, more than a conventional division, but with virtually no staff. He did have his brigade signals section but this wasn't much help: it was made up of Gurkhas who didn't speak English. Godley wanted him to capture Hill Q and Hill 971 today and preferably early. It didn't look much of a distance to travel, not on a map anyway. Godley was running the operation from his headquarters at Number Two Outpost and didn't know what was happening; in one sense, he was more remote than Stopford, who from the deck of the *Jonquil* could at least watch ant-like figures running hither and thither above the beaches. Anyway, Cox was out there, and *he* didn't know what was happening.

He did know that his force – Sikhs, Australians, Gurkhas and New Army boys – was intermingled and scattered over 1000 acres or so. Some were simply lost. It was hard to get the wounded out and nearly as hard to get ammunition and water in. The sun was cruel. Cox thought he at least knew where Monash's brigade was, just one valley away from Abdel Rahman Spur. It would be 11 days before Monash discovered he had been *two* valleys away from Abdel Rahman.

For the purpose of writing orders for the assault of August 8, Cox decided to regard his 13 battalions as 4 separate columns. We will not linger on these because as the day unfolded, three of them didn't – couldn't – operate as discrete forces; but their composition gives an idea of the tangle of Cox's command.

Column One included South Lancashires from the 38th Brigade, Warwicks from the 39th, and the Gurkhas who had joined up with Johnston at the Apex before falling back to the Aghyl Dere. This column was going to take the northern slopes of Chunuk Bair.

Column Two included two battalions from the 39th Brigade and Cecil Allanson's battalion of Gurkhas. Allanson knew how to get across bad country; he was way out in front of the other two battalions. This column was going to take the southern peak of Hill Q.

Column Three comprised the 14th Sikhs and another Gurkha battalion. It was going to take the northern peak of Hill Q.

Column Four comprised Monash's brigade and the battalion of New Army reinforcements Cox had given him. This force was going to take Abdel Rahman Spur, then Hill 971.

We needn't worry about columns One and Three. They were pretty much lost and scattered when the day began. Aspinall doubts whether they moved at all. They were 'columns' on paper only. So was Column Two. It doesn't matter much either. But one of its component parts – Allanson's Gurkha battalion – does.

Major Allanson, a 38-year-old regular from Wales, was at the foot of Hill Q. He waited for the other two battalions of Column Two to catch up, but the Staffords and Worcesters were lost somewhere on the upper reaches of the Aghyl Dere. Allanson decided to attack Q with his own battalion and started to climb. About 300 feet below the crest he and his Gurkhas came under fierce fire.

A lieutenant in the Warwicks watched Allanson's climb. Lieutenant William Joseph Slim, in his early twenties, had found himself commanding a company because he was the only surviving officer. The future Lord Slim also had some Gurkhas with him. Slim led his men across to Allanson. The two shared a dirty envelope of raisins and decided to merge their forces. Allanson also picked up men from the North Staffordshire and South Lancashire battalions. He took his force another 100 feet higher. The Turkish fire became intense. Allanson wrote:

> I lay without moving till 6 pm, with every conceivable shot flying in the air about me, shrapnel, our own maxims, rifles, and our own high-explosives bursting extremely close, which told me how near we were to the top. I lay between two British soldiers; the man on my left had a Bible, and read it the whole day; the man on my right I found was a corpse. I wondered if I ought to make good resolutions for the future, and did not.

Allanson was Cox's one success; but throughout the day, Cox didn't know where Allanson was.

If you walk the track that nowadays runs along the crest of Abdel Rahman Spur you come upon a promontory that pokes off the main ridge like a lumpy pier. This is Alai Tepe, its sides streaked a washy yellow by the winter waterfalls. It commands just about all the country Cox's men were moving through. Far away to the right is Suvla Bay, where, in the words of Ashmead-Bartlett, General Stopford sat with orders all over his breast and disorders all over his command. To the left lies the saddle of Hill Q, beneath which Allanson crouched, and beyond that Chunuk Bair, where Malone lay under a tempest of bullets.

Most of all, Alai Tepe commands the Asma Dere and the line of flat-topped knolls that run away towards Suvla. These knolls were probably once part of a continuous spur, like Rhododendron, that ran off the main range near Hill Q towards the sea at Suvla. Erosion has turned the spur into a series of islands. They are, for want of a better title, the northern arm of the Damakjelik Spur and they peter out before Hill 60. The two sizeable knolls at the top end of this island chain are Hill 100 and Hill 90. Alai Tepe sits about 100 feet above them. It commands their flat tops and eastern flanks and the Asma Dere that winds around them. The Turks had four machine guns here on August 8. As Zeki Bey told Bean in 1919, the machine gunners had 'great effect because they were not themselves under fire, and could therefore shoot very calmly'.

The Turks here did shoot very calmly. In just an hour or so they wrecked Monash's brigade, shot it up and broke its heart. And, as Bean wrote, they produced 'one of those "black days" which most deeply affect the spirits of soldiers'.

The story of Monash's three attacking battalions that morning is like that of the air traveller who lands in Los Angeles and thinks he is in St Louis, then goes on to St Louis and swears he is in New York. The 15th Battalion led off in the dark, followed by the 14th and the 16th, led by Pope, who was also commanding the column. The column crossed the Kaiajik Dere and thought it was crossing Asma Dere. It began to climb the northern arm of Damakjelik, those 'islands' mentioned above, and thought it was climbing Abdel Rahman. It turned sharply right, heading east, towards Hill 100 and thought it was heading for Hill 971. The column entered a field of oaten stubble around 4.15 am and the dawn threw a soft golden light on the stalks. According to the orders, the men should have been on 971 by now.

While the 15th was still crossing the stubble the machine guns opened up on the men caught in the golden light. The guns were on Alai Tepe. Colonel Cannan, leading the 15th, thought *he* was on Alai Tepe. Turkish infantry now appeared. The 14th got through the oat field and reached Hill 100. The 16th avoided the oat field. Soon these two battalions were ahead of the 15th, which was being shot up badly. The left-hand side of the 15th, that nearest to Alai Tepe, broke.

The column had been pulled up around Hill 90 and Hill 100. This is where Monash and most of his senior officers believed they were *starting* from. Shrapnel was now bursting over the Australian positions. Close to 400 men had been hit in the 15th and about 250 in the 14th. Pope had to decide whether to dig in or withdraw. He was out of touch with Monash at the old frontline: the telephone wire had been cut. It was repaired around 7 am and Monash told Cox what was happening. Cox ordered a withdrawal.

The brigade's machine-gun section came up to cover the retreat, which was a shambles. Wounded were lying everywhere. Some had to be left. John Brotchie of the 14th was 44 and the father of nine children. His mates called him 'Dad'. He wrote home:

The coming back was awful, wounded men being carried in various ways, all stretchers employed now and gone ahead. On comrades' backs with foot wounds, others on improvised stretchers formed of rifles, of wood, of coats, of bagging, of anything that could possibly help. Poor helpless, heart rending sights these, desperate remedies, desperate straights. As we got round, the shells got us once more, hard and often, the men with the wounded struggling up the hills and through the narrow gullies, gullies where a lean man could hardly squeeze through, and many a wounded man on a man's back got a nasty jar through these narrow sections. I tried to help in places, but was not up to carrying a wounded man.

Isolated troops were unaware of the retreat. Corporal George Kerr, shot through the left thigh and right arm, was part of a group of 13 Victorians who ended up fighting from behind a barricade of ammunition boxes before surrendering. Only 2 of the 13 were unwounded. Kerr wrote that his Turkish captors wore tattered uniforms and some were barefoot. A wounded Australian was bayoneted and another bashed unconscious with a rock. The Turks prepared to roll several wounded men over a cliff.

Two officers – one German, one Turkish – appear to have saved the Australians. An old Turk, grey-haired and wearing a uniform that was too small for him, walked to Kerr and inspected his wounds. The Turk pulled out a large dagger. He walked over to a pine tree, tore off a branch, whittled it into a rough crutch, and threw it to Kerr.

'If you do not use this, I'm going to have to shoot you,' the old Turk said in crude French. Kerr hobbled off, bleeding and light-headed. He spent three years as a prisoner, most of the time working on the Berlin–Baghdad railway in the Taurus Mountains.

Before noon all three of the Australian battalions, what was left of them, were back in their old lines. There had been 765 casualties. The 15th had left old Anzac 850-strong; it was down to 280. The brigade was a shambles; it could never take Hill 971 now.

So ended a battle that, even today, has a surreal quality. There are missing pieces and questions for which there are no answers. Many of the 4th Brigade thought they had been on Hill 971. One wrote to his mother: 'I caught a bullet in the left knee about ten minutes after the big charge of Hill 971.' In his summary of the August offensive Godley wrote that the 4th Brigade had advanced *from* the Asma Dere against the lower slopes of Abdel Rahman. The Australians had never been on Abdel Rahman. Godley said the Australians withdrew to their previous line on the Asma Dere. They withdrew to above the *Aghyl Dere*. Monash said on August 9 that his troops had been on the promontory the Turks called Alai Tepe. On August 19, after 'numerous reconnaissances', he decided he had all along been about half a mile west of where he thought he had been. 'Much worried about previous error,' Monash wrote in his diary, 'for which Eastwood and Locke [two of his staff officers] are to blame.'

This left the mystery of where his men *had* got to. Bean solved this in 1919 by riding along the Asma Dere. He climbed the knolls of the northern arm of the Damakjelik Spur. On Hill 90, under Alai Tepe, he came on huddles of Australian dead, some with the colours of the 14th Battalion on their sleeves. He found Australians and Turks lying together on Hill 100. One Australian had a small Bible with the name 'H. Wellington' on the fly leaf.

Few went there after Bean. For the Australians, this was a good battle to forget. For the Turkish farmers, the land, apart from an acre here and there, is so useless it wouldn't feed an anorexic goat. Unlike old Anzac, it remains today much as it was in 1915.

And those questions for which there are no answers? Why did Monash hand the attack to Pope? Why didn't Monash at least go forward when the telephone line was cut? Why did he neglect the medical arrangements, so that some wounded had to be abandoned and others carried to the beach on the backs of their comrades? Why did he let things happen that destroy the morale of troops and their trust in their leaders? Was he tired? (He slept for nine hours after the attack.) Was he simply too old to be slogging through this country? Had he realised by the night of the seventh that this assault on Hill 971 had been so carelessly conceived that nothing, including his leadership from the front, could have saved it?

These questions wouldn't matter too much if Monash had been a lesser soldier. The tease is that everything Monash did, or didn't do, on August 8 was out of character. All his life Monash was a busy diarist; one suspects he was often writing for posterity and his biographers. He never explained what happened on the eighth. After the Great War was done, he didn't have to. He was properly famous for triumphs elsewhere.

Monash's troops – or those of anyone else, for that matter – could not have succeeded under the machine guns of Alai Tepe. You know that when you walk the country, although 'walk' is too dainty a verb. By the time you reach the flat-topped knolls beneath Abdel Rahman, you lurch on legs of jelly, your ribcage rising and falling like a bellows.

Four of us – two Australians and two Turks, Kenan Çelik and his son Ahmet – started off from Bauchop's Hill. We would descend into Taylor's Gap, the 'shortcut' to Aghyl Dere, then try to find where Monash's battalions ended up on August 8.

Bauchop's gives a fine panorama; on a spring day in 2000 it all makes sense from here. There's the Anzac ridge, coming off Hill 971 like a spoke and tumbling down to the sea at Ari Burnu. There's another spoke, coming off Chunuk Bair this time, and petering out short of the sea: Rhododendron Ridge. There are the two valleys along which the New Zealanders advanced: Sazli and Chailak, each side of Rhododendron. And there, on the other side of Bauchop's, are the valleys where the Australians became lost: Aghyl, Kaiajik and Asma.

You lose your sense of direction as soon as you start to descend. The scrub is much thicker than at old Anzac. In the washaways, with their bulrushes and baritone frogs and mud holes, you lose sight of the ridge line and know what it is for a blind man to be robbed of his cane. Near the olive groves of Australia Valley we are suddenly in a little amphitheatre. The rearing walls block out the Sari Bair ridges. We have gone only a little way and already the Australian element of this party doesn't know where it is. And you recall that Cox's column was in here in the dark.

The heavy clay here preserves animals' footprints like fossils. That was a rabbit and those belong to a dog, probably wild. These? They have to be a pig's. A few days later we come on a party of Turks, all bearing shotguns, near Big Anafarta village. They have just shot a wild boar. What hasn't been shredded by pellets, which isn't much, will be fed to the dogs.

This country is nothing like Anzac: no monuments, no roads, no people, just wild dogs that are too clever to be seen and lots of snakes that aren't. Apart from odd pieces of shrapnel, we have seen no clues that for a few days in 1915 this was a battlefield. It is as though we are lost in antiquity, which is pretty much the truth of it. Anyway, the trip had been worthwhile, if only to understand how rough the country is. Then, suddenly, there are clues everywhere.

Kenan and Ahmet, who actually know where they are, have brought us up on the southern shoulder of Hill 90. We have come on a warren of shallow scrapes, just big enough for a hip and a shoulder and washed smooth by the rains. They were dug 85 years ago and, preposterous as it sounds, you can sense the urgency of the morning they were dug. The ground here says panic and fear. The holes are scattered about willy-nilly. There is no line. It is as though those who scraped them were so frantic that they burrowed like rabbits trying to escape a terrier. The Australians were here all right. Ammunition clips are strewn about, dozens of them, British issue, four vents down the back, three down each side, packed with earth and rusty. Sometimes they disintegrate softly in your hand and the metal drifts off in the breeze, seeds from the plant of war. Here is a Turkish bullet with a batter of rust. There's another one in the clay over there. It has hit something hard, most likely a rock; its nose is splayed like a tiny cauliflower. There's a buckle with the tongue eaten away, possibly off a watchband. And there, that round thing, slightly concave on the underside – it is too rusted for one to read the insignia but it has to be a button. There are slivers of bone everywhere, grey-white, smoothed by wind and rain and showing scorch marks from a scrub fire a few years back.

We go on to the flat-topped Hill 100, our thirst and tiredness forgotten. From the top you see Little Anafarta village on one side and Hill 971 on the other. Hill 971 is close and far, far away. And the climb to it, up Abdel Rahman, is so steep. You now know one thing: the books on the campaign, the maps, the written orders – all are meaningless. It would have been impossible for the 4th Brigade to make the top of Abdel Rahman by the early morning of August 7 (the first day of the offensive) even if there had been no Turks here. There didn't need to be Turks; the terrain is enemy enough.

We come on deep trenches on Hill 100. Turkish. The ammunition clips here have no vent down the back; the shells carry a circle of Ottoman script around the firing cap. We come upon a thigh bone and lots of smaller bones in a pathetic huddle under a bush. Ahmet squats and stares at them. 'Martyr,' he says softly. 'Poor man.'

Next day we take the fire track along the top of Abdel Rahman to a point opposite Alai Tepe, so as to come at Hill 100 from the other side. Kenan goes down to Alai Tepe alone; the rest of us are too sore. He finds the deep trenches where the four Turkish machine guns commanded about 400 acres of country that, in normal circumstances, no-one would want to own.

Nothing has been done with this land. Apart from the odd olive grove and pine trees that have been planted to hold the soil together, this country is just about as it was in 1915. If you were standing here in August, 1915, you would have seen Allanson's Gurkhas huddled under Hill Q, the New Army divisions stalled at Suvla, groups of British troops beneath Chunuk Bair near the Farm, Malone's New Zealanders on Chunuk Bair itself, Australians who survived the battle that had taken place in front of you stumbling back towards the Aghyl Dere, Turkish reinforcements trudging down from Bulair. You would have heard the rumble of ships' guns and the tap-tap of rifles.

The silence is almost spooky. Kenan, on Alai Tepe, bends down to pick up a stick with which to poke the earth. He is 400 yards away and you hear the crack as he snaps the branch. From near the crest of Chunuk Bair a huge statue of Mustafa Kemal looks out over these mean valleys. There is something proprietorial about it.

Some New Zealanders who fought on Chunuk Bair never saw the Narrows. Malone didn't stare at them for long. He was a practical man; he knew that looking at the Narrows was not the same as owning them. He had to hold this awkwardly shaped summit: that was the first thing. And after 5 am, when the haze lifted and the Turkish riflemen could see their targets, clinging to that summit became one of the epics of the Gallipoli campaign.

Malone had to decide where to site his trenches. There is still argument about where they were. Temperley afterwards damned Malone for wasting two hours digging in on the reverse side of the crest. Hamilton's brief diary entry for August 10 talked about the trenches being 'badly sited', although he is not to be taken seriously. He was remote from this battle and obsessed with Stopford. A British pamphlet, written for the war on the western front, had recently arrived at Anzac. It recommended that in the age of quick-firing artillery, trenches were better sited on the reverse rather than the forward sides of crests. Malone and Temperley had discussed this idea at old Anzac. Malone saw sense in it; Temperley said it didn't apply to Gallipoli.

The best evidence of where Malone's trenches were comes from Malone's adjutant, Captain Ernest Harston. He says Malone decided to put two of his four companies forward of the crest in the existing Turkish trench; the other two would dig a new trench behind the crest and then drive saps forward to join the two lines.

Temperley visited the frontline in the evening of August 8 and called it a 'hopeless position'. No observation was possible. Malone had followed the ideas set out in the pamphlet. 'The convictions previously formed in Malone's stubborn rather narrow mind overrode and obliterated the memory of all orders, discussion, argument or reasoning.' We should remember, however, that when Temperley arrived the lines of the morning had changed. We should also note that while Temperley damns Malone for narrow-mindedness, Temperley admits that later in the battle Johnston was 'no longer in a condition to exercise command efficiently'. But Temperley wasn't going to tell Godley this. It would have been a 'terribly disloyal' thing for a regular officer to do and 'I am certain I could not have done it.' Who had the narrower mind? Malone or Temperley? How many mistakes did Johnston have to make before Temperley realised there were larger things at issue here than the loyalty of one clubman to another?

By 5 am the Turks were starting to pick off the Wellingtons. The Gloucesters and Welch Pioneers were shot down as they came up to reinforce Malone. The Gloucesters on Malone's left broke as they tried to dig in. The Turks could creep to within 20 yards of the Wellingtons before being seen. The front trench, which was too shallow anyway, became clogged with dead and wounded. By 6.30 am Malone was running a tremendous battle. At this stage he had no contact with Johnston at the Apex.

Private Reginald Davis was in the front trench. In 1919 he told how he became a prisoner of the Turks.

A Taranaki man named Surgenor was the only man left firing besides myself . . . Private Surgenor was hit in the head somewhere, but kept on firing with his face streaming with blood, until he got another hit in the head, which dazed him for a time, and knocked him back in the trench. This time I thought he was killed, but he partly came to soon after, and loaded rifles for me to fire. At that time I was using three rifles and each was burning hot.

Davis was shot in the elbow. Surgenor bound the wound. The Turks arrived. One lunged at Davis five times with a bayonet. Davis deflected four of the thrusts but the fifth went through his arm. The Turk prepared to shoot Davis but was distracted. Davis and William Surgenor spent three years in Turkish prisons.

These two may have been on the left of the front trench. The Wellingtons on the right hung on to their forward trench. Harston went back looking for reinforcements. He found a signaller with a telephone in front of the Pinnacle. He said afterwards that he had 'the greatest difficulty' convincing Johnston's headquarters that the casualties were heavy. It shouldn't have been that hard. Wounded were everywhere behind the Wellington line, hundreds of them, Wellingtons, Gloucesters, Welch Pioneers. Many crawled into Sazli Dere. They called out for water and died in the blazing sun. Many were never seen again.

Private Nicholson remembered taking the Turkish trench on the downhill side. 'But it was not very long, probably two or three hours, before that was too full of dead or wounded bodies to use, and so we finished up really standing on them.' Nicholson never saw the Narrows: he didn't have time to look. 'Our field of fire was between us and Turk heads coming over the hill. The first thing we saw of them was heads. Heads were our targets.'

The New Zealanders' rifles became too hot to hold. Some of the Wellingtons used three or four rifles.

Wounded men reloaded them. Nicholson said the bayonet fighting seemed to last weeks, although 'I suppose it was only minutes'.

I don't remember any charges. It was all stand and defend with the bayonet, just a mad whirl. In the back of my head I could hear the words: 'Get the bastard before he gets you. Get him or he'll get you!' ... I don't remember bayonets going in. Perhaps I shut my eyes. I don't know who I killed and who I didn't ... The Turks were heaving bombs at us too ... And it was hot, hard and thirsty. It's only when your tongue actually rattles round in your mouth that you can say you are thirsty. That's no fable. Actually rattling round in your mouth. We stripped off our tunics and we were fighting in singlets and in the buff ... The Turks were the same. Soon it was so you could only identify a Turk by his hat, his whiskers and swarthy complexion.

Nicholson lost his dearest friend. Teddy Charles ran forward and Nicholson never saw him again. 'Later, in the dark, I thought I heard Teddy's voice calling for his mother, then for me.' Nicholson couldn't get to him. 'He's still on Chunuk Bair, a pile of bones.'

Nicholson said that if he had been asked to describe the colour of the earth on Chunuk Bair, he would have said it was a dull or browny red. 'And that was blood. Just blood.'

He saw Malone through the day. 'He was moving about a fair amount. He kept boosting our morale, and he always had a kind word, an encouraging word. "It'll ease off shortly," he promised. "They'll get tired of this." Little nothings.'

Charlie Clark was playing poker over the crest in a

Turkish gunpit when the Turks first attacked. He took off towards the crest.

> I heard thump, thump, thump and it was fellows falling around me. Nine or ten of them, suddenly wounded or dead, all the jokers I'd been playing poker with just a minute or two before. I couldn't see where the bullets was coming from. Then I sighted a Turk, just standing up, shooting among us . . . I pushed my rifle over a sandbag, got a sight on this Turk, and shot him in the face.

Clark was moments later hit in the leg. 'When I looked at it, the wound was so big I couldn't cover it with my hand.' He crawled away to a ravine where 200 other wounded lay under shell fire.

The Wellingtons made short bayonet charges at the advancing Turks. Those who made it back to the trench found themselves walking on dead and wounded, so that if they stood upright the trench only protected them to their knees. Johnston sent the Auckland Mounted Rifles and the Maori Contingent forward as reinforcements. The Maoris, like the Gurkhas the day before, were pushed down the hill to the Farm. The Auckland Mounted could only send forward a dozen or so men at one time.

Malone had resorted to using a bayonet himself. A bullet buckled his bayonet. Malone said this proved that it was lucky and kept it with him. An officer told him he should not be leading bayonet charges. Malone replied: 'You're only a kid – I'm an old man – get out yourself!'

About 5 pm Malone was hit by a misdirected shrapnel burst fired either from an Anzac battery or a warship. According to an officer present, the shrapnel made a swishing noise. 'Col. M was killed the other side of me . . . he collapsed into the adjutant's [Harston] or

Cunningham's arms.' Harston thought the shell came from a destroyer. He had seen the puffs from her guns just before Malone was hit.

So died one of the grand and original figures of the Gallipoli campaign, a free spirit who could stretch his mind beyond the clubby world of the Godleys and Johnstons and would stretch his integrity for no man. It seems unconscionable that he received no posthumous decoration for his day on Chunuk Bair. By the standards set at Lone Pine, he should have received the Victoria Cross. In death, as in life, Malone was not much loved by those in authority. He was always going to be an outsider. Mater took her three children to England during the war and never returned to New Zealand. Malone's farms were sold and his large family home 'The Farlands' burned down. His son Edmond died of wounds in France in 1918.

The Turks had been bringing up reinforcements all day, including the 8th Division, taken from Helles. Turkish numbers between Battleship Hill and Big Anafarta village more than doubled in the 24 hours to the afternoon of August 8, and that was before the 8th arrived. There was panic among the Turks even though they had managed to win back most of their side of the Chunuk Bair crest. Kemal was certainly receiving panicky messages, as he tells in his memoir of the battle. One read:

An attack has been ordered on Conkbayiri [Chunuk Bair]. To whom should I give this order? I am looking for the battalion commanders but I cannot find them. Everything is in a muddle. The situation is serious. At any rate someone who knows the ground must be appointed. There are no reports and no information. I am confused as to what I should do.

Another said:

All the officers are killed or wounded. I do not even know the name of the place where I am. I cannot see anything by observation. I request in the name of the safety of the nation that an officer be appointed who knows the area well.

An old friend of Kemal's telephoned to say he had been ordered to take his regiment to Chunuk Bair. He was worried that no-one seemed to be in command there. 'Advance at once to Conkbayiri,' Kemal told him. 'Events will appoint a commander.'

Kemal knew that Chunuk Bair was a 'dangerous situation' that needed a strong leader. Von Sanders' chief-of-staff telephoned him. The commander-in-chief wanted to know what Kemal thought about Chunuk Bair. 'There is one moment left,' Kemal told him. 'If we lose that moment, we are faced with a general catastrophe.'

'What should be done?' the chief-of-staff asked.

'The only remedy is to put all the available troops under my command.'

'Won't that be too many?'

'It will be too few,' Kemal told him.

That evening (as a result of another incident that had nothing to do with the conversation above) von Sanders gave Kemal command of all troops at Suvla and on Sari Bair.

Kemal was made for crises. In his diary that night he wrote a Tolstoyan homily: 'The actions and conduct of the participants in great historical events reveal their true moral characters.' One senses that Kemal couldn't wait to get to Suvla. When he had dealt with the English there, he would come back and deal with Sari Bair. He had not slept for three nights and he had malaria; he was thin and his face looked haunted. Yet his spirit was soaring. It was *his* battle now.

At Chunuk Bair the Turkish fire eased off as darkness came. The Otago Battalion and the Wellington Mounteds moved up without a casualty to take over the trench line.

Of the 760 Wellingtons who had arrived on the crest that morning, only 2 officers and 47 men remained unwounded. They looked like the nightshift leaving a clandestine abattoir. Their uniforms were torn and spattered with blood. They had drunk no water since dawn and hardly slept for two days. According to Bean, they talked in whispers, trembled and cried. The Welch had lost 417 men, the Gloucesters 350. Every officer and sergeant among the Gloucesters had been either killed or wounded.

Wounded lay on the crest itself, in Sazli Dere, on the saddle back towards the Pinnacle, and between the Pinnacle and the Apex. Hundreds of them. Some bled to death and others went mad with thirst. Some asked when the stretcher-bearers were coming and were told they weren't. Others prayed or hallucinated or passed out. The problem wasn't merely that there were so many wounded and so few stretcher-bearers; it was also how to carry so many men to the beach. This was true everywhere on the left. Like the military commanders, the medical authorities had not thought enough about the terrain. Some of the wounded from August 8 took three days to travel down Chailak Dere, attacked by flies the whole way, thirsty the whole way, covered in dust and with bloodied clothes stuck to their bodies. Six men were sometimes needed to carry one stretcher over the rougher parts, often under shrapnel fire. When, finally, these broken men, some now showing the first black blotches of gangrene, were lifted on to a lighter, they sometimes had to be shopped around overcrowded ships where surgeons hacked off arms and legs in a few minutes because that was all the time they had. The limbs were tossed into baskets and burnt.

Aspinall, always careful with his words, calls the sufferings of the wounded at Anzac in August 'indescribable'. A medical officer told of scenes worse than those that followed the April 25 landings.

> . . . it was a shock to me when four lighters pulled up alongside and we saw the poor shattered figures, with bloody bandages, grimy faces and dirty clothes . . . men were dying every minute . . . lighters kept coming alongside with their burden of suffering humanity and the man in charge would shout – 'For God's sake take this lot, we've been going about from ship to ship and no-one will have us, and more men are dying.' We worked, one and all, until we could no longer tell what we were seeing or doing, all day and all night, picking out the cases where the dreaded gangrene had set in . . . Even the clean open decks stank with the horrid smell of gangrenous flesh . . . The operating room . . . was a stinking, bloody shambles . . .

When the stretcher-bearers reached the beaches they dipped their stretchers in the sea to wash off the blood, then headed back into the hills. Aubrey Herbert was buzzing about the beaches, interviewing Turkish prisoners and passing clearing station after clearing station. He met a man with ten bayonet wounds. 'He was extremely cheerful,' Herbert wrote in *Mons, Anzac and Kut*.

> I stumbled on poor A. C. (a schoolfellow), who had been wounded about 3 am the day before, and had lain in the sun on the sand all the previous day. He recognised me, and asked me to help him, but was light-headed. There were 56 others with him . . . It was awful having to pass them. A lot of the men called out: 'We are being murdered.'

They were. And it wasn't over yet.

General Godley nearly took himself to the Apex on August 8. This would have been useful. Orders tend to be written more sensibly when the general has actually seen the ground. Godley *meant* to go to the Apex. There was to be a divisional conference there with Johnston and Brigadier-General Anthony Baldwin to discuss tactics for the next day. Godley even started walking up the dere from his headquarters at Number Two Outpost. Then the phone rang. Urgent message from General Cox. By the time Godley had dealt with Cox's problem it was too late to go. Or at least this is the way Godley tells it in his autobiography. Nor was there time, it seems, to send a staff officer in his place. Staff officers were apparently very busy shuffling paper and answering phones. Kemal, one imagines, would have thought these people quaint, just as he might have been puzzled by a blacksmith who found ways to avoid going near a forge.

Godley must have known by noon on the eighth that Chunuk Bair was his best and only hope. Far out on the left Monash's attack had failed so quickly and completely that the capture of Hill 971 now seemed improbable.

Those two columns in the centre, the two that were supposed to be attacking the southern and northern peaks of Q? They weren't attacking anything. There was a good chance they were lost. Suvla? Nothing happening there. Chunuk Bair was the only foothold on the main range. By default, Chunuk Bair *was* the August offensive.

Godley had decided to renew the attack there on August 9 with four of five battalions from the corps reserve under Brigadier-General Baldwin. They would attack up the range towards Hill Q. Cox's Indian and New Army troops would attack Q from below. The New Zealanders, meanwhile, would turn back down the range towards Battleship Hill. How should Baldwin get his battalions to Chunuk Bair so that they could attack at 5.15 am tomorrow? Godley told Baldwin he thought they should follow the path of the New Zealanders, the high road along Rhododendron Ridge. But he thought he and Baldwin should see the ground and hear Johnston's thoughts. The three would meet at the Apex on the afternoon of the eighth. Johnston, Godley felt sure, would agree with him.

Johnston didn't agree when he met Baldwin at the Apex, although he probably would have had Godley been present. Johnston advised Baldwin to take the low road: along Chailak Dere, across Cheshire Ridge and into Aghyl Dere, then climb to the Farm and from there to Hill Q. The advice, as we will see, was lethal. One can't blame Baldwin for accepting it: he didn't know the ground; he was entitled to think Johnston did.

Historians and others usually portray the Suvla landing and what followed as black comedy. Stopford plays the buffoon and he's a natural. W. S. Gilbert could have worked three or four operas around him. But why, you wonder, isn't this episode at Anzac seen the same way?

Here's Godley playing at de facto corps commander. Apart from a certain lack of ability, he doesn't have the staff for the job. Each night he produces a new sheaf of orders; each day he tries a new way to make the August offensive work, except that it doesn't. Now, thanks to Malone and the Wellingtons, there's a chance, something better than a tease, that it could work. But only at this one place. Only at Chunuk Bair. If Godley is ever going to be famous as a general, it is here, on this hill. This is his place and his moment. It is only a mile from his headquarters. Does Godley realise this is his moment? Probably not. Does he go to Chunuk Bair? No, he takes a phone call about a lesser thing. Does he send a staff officer who can tell him about the ground and appraise what the New Zealanders are up against? No. Does it occur to him that those are his troops up there and that it might do them good if he were briefly seen with them? He doesn't have to stick his head up or show off, just turn up. If this thought does occur to him, it's not as important as taking a phone call from Cox.

So he lets Johnston run the conference. Johnston who was barely coherent the day before, who has made a mess of everything he has done at Anzac. Godley lets Johnston act as a de facto divisional commander. He lets him write a script for a disaster.

Godley admits to few regrets in his autobiography, but he knows he got this one wrong.

I have never ceased to regret that I did not stick to my original intention of going to see the ground for myself. I feel sure I should have insisted on the advance being made by the high ground, and it is possible that it might then have succeeded.

He goes on to say, as if this explains all, that Mustafa Kemal was in command of the Turks and 'he was to dash our hopes of victory'. Kemal didn't have to think about going to the firing line; an instinct told him that was where he should be.

While Godley was fussing over his typing pool on the eighth, von Sanders was at Suvla, riding over the ground from which he would launch his counter-attack. Von Sanders didn't know Stopford, so he assumed, quite reasonably, that the general's force would try to join up with the Anzac force beneath the Sari Bair heights. Von Sanders would attack Stopford with Feizi Bey's two divisions, which were arriving from Bulair. The German wanted to throw them in that evening. Feizi Bey said that his divisional commanders thought their men were too tired and hungry. They didn't know the ground and the artillery support was inadequate. Better to wait until tomorrow.

'You are the group commander,' von Sanders said. 'What do *you* say?'

'I am of the same opinion,' Feizi replied.

Whereupon von Sanders sacked him. Which is how Mustafa Kemal came to be in command at both Suvla and on the northern flank of Anzac.

Kemal began riding north around midnight. It would be unthinkable to try to run the Suvla operation from Anzac. Kemal was happy. 'For the first time in four months,' he wrote in his diary, 'I was breathing air which was more or less pure and clear.' Anzac, he wrote, was polluted 'by the corruption of human corpses'.

Hamilton also went to Suvla on the eighth, which meant, though neither knew it, he and von Sanders were within four miles of each other. Hamilton didn't go to look at the ground; he went to look at Stopford. Six hours earlier, Aspinall and Maurice Hankey had gone to Suvla. Aspinall wanted to have a look at Stopford too. He didn't like what he saw.

By the time Aspinall arrived Stopford had more or less decided to do nothing with his 22 battalions for the day. He had not yet been ashore and one had to marvel at his lack of curiosity. He had been told before the landing that Turkish reinforcements from Bulair would probably reach Suvla today. This did not seem to be bothering him, even though he had not taken any of the heights. At 9.30 am he sent a message to both divisions ashore congratulating them on their achievements. Then he cabled Imbros. His troops, he told Hamilton, deserved 'great credit for the results obtained against strenuous opposition'. Achievements? Results? Strenuous opposition? If he lacked curiosity, Stopford had imagination. He also told Hamilton: 'I must now consolidate the position held.' This panicked Hamilton. He decided to go to Suvla himself.

Aspinall came ashore around noon and his spirits rose. The bay was at peace and its shores fringed with bathers. He and Hankey assumed that the heights had been taken. There was nothing to worry about; the place was secure. The pair walked inland looking for corps headquarters. They were told the frontline troops were not on the ridges but several hundred yards ahead. No, there weren't any orders to push forward. No, they would not find corps headquarters here; headquarters was on the *Jonquil*. Aspinall began to panic. Meeting Hammersley didn't help. The commander of the 11th Division said his troops were tired out and had suffered heavy casualties. He hoped to do something tomorrow.

Aspinall hurried to the *Jonquil*, where he found Stopford in 'excellent spirits'.

'Well, Aspinall, the men have done splendidly, and have been magnificent.'

'But they haven't reached the hills, sir.'

'No, but they are ashore.'

Aspinall said GHQ would be disappointed the heights had not been taken. The general should advance before the Turkish reinforcements arrived from Bulair.

Of course he realised the importance of time, Stopford said. But he couldn't move until the men were rested and more guns were ashore. He would order an advance tomorrow.

Aspinall hurried to de Robeck's flagship and cabled Hamilton.

Just been ashore, where I found all quiet. No rifle fire, no artillery fire, and apparently no Turks. IX Corps resting. Feel confident that golden opportunities are being lost and look upon the situation as serious.

Hamilton did not receive the cable, but he was on his way to Suvla anyway. Hankey was forming pictures in his mind for the letter he would write to the Prime Minister. Four days later, he sent it.

A peaceful scene greeted us. Hardly any shells. No Turks. Very occasional musketry. Bathing parties round the shore. An entire absence of the expected bustle of a great disembarkation. There seemed to be no realisation of the overwhelming necessity for a rapid offensive, or the tremendous issues depending on the next few hours . . . As an irresponsible critic I don't want to be hard, but I must confess I was filled with dismay, as was the G. S. man whom I accompanied.

Aspinall's manner had worried Stopford. The general went ashore at 4 pm intending to order a general advance. He couldn't find Hammersley. Told that Hammersley was intending to attack the W Hills the next morning, Stopford decided to leave things as they were. He returned to the *Jonquil* to find another telegram from Hamilton saying the Turks were not entrenched on the high ground, 'but hardly likely this state of affairs will continue'. Whereupon Stopford changed his mind again and ordered a general advance on Tekke Tepe Ridge and the Anafarta Spur and W Hills. Hammersley was to decide when this would happen.

When Hamilton arrived, de Robeck, Keyes and Aspinall at once told him how badly things were going. Hamilton, Keyes and Aspinall headed for the *Jonquil*.

Stopford, Hamilton wrote, seemed happy. He said everything was going well, although the men were thirsty and tired.

'And where are they now?' Hamilton asked.

'There,' said Stopford, pointing to a line running north to south on a map. 'Along the foot of the hills.'

'But they held that line, more or less, yesterday.'

'Yes,' said Stopford. The men were tired, so he had decided to postpone the occupation of the main ridge, which might lead to a regular battle, until tomorrow.

Hamilton wrote that he was inclined to say: 'A regular battle is just what we are here for.' Here we touch on one of Hamilton's failures as a commander-in-chief: he seldom says what he is inclined to say. The conversation was nevertheless becoming strained.

Hamilton said: 'We must occupy the heights at once. It is imperative we get Ismail Oglu Tepe [the W Hills] and Tekke Tepe *now*.'

Stopford objected. Orders would have to be re-written.

A night advance was not feasible. The generals ashore had told him their men were too tired. They may not have got their water yet. More guns needed to be landed.

Hamilton said he must see Hammersley himself. Stopford agreed. According to Hamilton, Stopford asked to be excused from coming ashore because his knee was hurting. According to Stopford, he was not invited along and felt slighted.

Hamilton had watched Stopford turn into a defeatist before the landing, and done nothing. He – and Aspinall, for that matter – had allowed Stopford to water down the orders for the landing. Now Hamilton seemed hurt that Stopford was letting him down. Now, too late, Hamilton had decided he needed to provoke and push. He was also in a tizz. He says he 'nipped' down the *Jonquil*'s ladder, 'tumbled' into Keyes' boat and 'shot' across the water to Hammersley. Aspinall says Hamilton 'bounded' into the general's headquarters.

Hamilton and Hammersley bickered politely. Hammersley said much the same as Stopford. He couldn't get orders out in time; he would prefer to wait for daylight; his battalions were scattered. Hamilton overruled him. There had never been a greater crisis in any battle than this one, he said. The heights must be occupied before the Turks got there. And they were coming all right: British aircraft had spotted their columns. Hamilton couldn't believe what he was hearing. He had seen attack orders dictated to a division from the saddle in less than five minutes. Here was a division unable to stir itself without 12 hours' notice. Hamilton admits to thinking this but, as was his way, didn't say it. Kitchener would have fixed Stopford and Hammersley with his icy stare and told them they were nincompoops. Hamilton was trying but he was not made for thuggery.

He eventually persuaded Hammersley to send the 32nd Brigade to Tekke Tepe Ridge during the night. Hamilton was so worried he decided to spend the night offshore on de Robeck's yacht *Triad*.

What Hamilton and Hammersley didn't know was that the 32nd Brigade was not in one place. It had been pushing forward on its own initiative. One battalion was on Scimitar Hill, just north of the W Hills. Orders were now sent out for the brigade to concentrate. Scimitar Hill, an important position, was abandoned. The brigade was missing one battalion half an hour before dawn, but the commander still gave the order to advance on Tekke Tepe.

Too late. Kemal had ridden in from Anzac after 1 am. Turkish troops headed for Tekke Tepe shortly afterwards. They got there before the British. The Suvla commanders had wasted 48 hours in which they could have taken this ridge; now they had lost it by 30 minutes.

And now, on the morning of August 9, the battle for Suvla took on a different face. All the advantages of a surprise landing had been squandered. Stopford had lost his numerical superiority. It was now two divisions versus two divisions, except that the Turks were on the high ground. Suvla too was headed for a siege, and it should never have gone like this.

26

A man alone

It was obvious why Suvla was going wrong. Stopford should not have been in charge of fighting troops anywhere. Like the eunuch ordered to arouse the harem, he was beaten in mind and body before he started. He was such an affront to soldierly ideas that he often becomes the scapegoat for all that went wrong at the Dardanelles in August. We need to remember that the offensive was always going to be won or lost on the ridges above Anzac by Birdwood and Godley. These two were not like Stopford, yet they were failing as surely as he was. Their failure is not so easy to explain.

There are a few clues but they don't explain enough. Neither Birdwood nor Godley had the staff to control so many fronts. They were both men of courage yet, unlike von Sanders and Kemal, they ran their battles from too far back. Rhododendron Ridge, the Apex, Chunuk Bair, the Aghyl Dere, the spurs of Damakjelik – these were new places. Birdwood and Godley had to see them before they could begin to understand them. Instead they stayed at their headquarters and each day reacted to a dozen crises. The plan would fail by lunchtime and they would start on a modified version for the next day. When that failed they scratched up a third version for the following day. They often didn't know where their troops were or what condition they were in. Their response to a crisis was (as Allanson put it years later) to throw reinforcements at the commander concerned. All through they were too confident.

They couldn't seem to understand the importance of Chunuk Bair; they certainly didn't understand what was happening there. Temperley received 'from the coast' a funeral oration to be read over Malone's body. Temperley was also asked what he proposed to do with the body. He sent back a message saying that Chunuk Bair was littered with bodies, mainly because a terrible battle was still going on. He should not have had to tell headquarters such things.

On the morning of August 9, as Stopford began to fight his first serious battle, Birdwood and Godley began their third version of the August offensive. This time they were going for Hill Q.

We left Major Allanson huddled just under the saddle that joins Chunuk Bair to Hill Q. He had his 6th Gurkhas, and a few South Lancashires and Warwicks, including the future Lord Slim. Allanson had tried to obtain more men from the battalions near him.

The whole of the South Lancs. and Warwicks could have joined me in the attack on the morning of the 9th, but the result of my pleadings with their C.Os. was only to get a company of each; it was courageous of them even to give me that, as I neither belonged to their brigade or even their division, they had never seen or heard of me before, and I must have appeared like a demented man demanding from them their units.

Alone among General Cox's commanders, Allanson had got close to his objective, except Cox didn't seem to know where Allanson was. During the night of August 8 brigade headquarters ordered Allanson to move his men within assaulting distance of Q. He was already there, 70 feet below the saddle. He was short of food, water and ammunition. He had been told he could have these things if he sent men down for them.

The Turks knew he was there; their bullets threw up dust around his dugout all night. 'The roar was incessant,' he wrote. 'I was rather weak from want of food, and I trembled most of the night.' Allanson's orders said he was to join in the general assault at 5.15 am when the bombardment lifted.

The shells thudded into Q and the hill seemed to leap underneath him. 'The trenches were being torn to pieces; the accuracy was marvellous, as we were only just below.' Allanson looked about for the troops who were supposed to be helping him. Not a sign. The barrage stopped at 5.20.

Allanson waited three minutes before deciding his men would attack alone. 'Then off we dashed all hand in hand, a most perfect advance, and a wonderful sight . . .'

Allanson was alone because Baldwin's four battalions had become lost in the dark. Baldwin's first battalion didn't reach the Farm until 6 am. This caused a chain reaction. Apart from Allanson's party, Cox was supposed to be attacking Q with another battalion of Gurkhas, the Warwicks and two battalions from Shaw's 13th Division. This was the left arm of the attack. It had been ordered not to advance until Baldwin's battalions came into line. Baldwin was the centre of the general assault. The right was the New Zealand force just behind the crest of

Chunuk Bair. The New Zealanders had been told to go forward when Baldwin began his attack. Baldwin's troops were still spread out over Aghyl Dere when dawn broke.

The New Zealanders at Chunuk Bair couldn't go forward anyway. After dawn the Turks attacked them with bombs and rifles. The Turks knew that Chunuk Bair was everything in this battle. When Baldwin's troops eventually reached the Farm they immediately came under fire. Baldwin decided to dig in on the edge of the plateau.

This meant that shortly after 6 am, and despite all those elaborate plans drawn up at headquarters, the August offensive on the third day amounted to Allanson, his Gurkhas and the few New Army men he had picked up. One battalion and two or three companies – that was the 'general assault'.

Allanson's wrote his account of the attack on Hill Q two days after the event.

> At the top we met the Turks: [Lieutenant] Le Marchand was down, a bayonet through the heart. I got one through the leg, and then, for about ten minutes, we fought hand to hand, we bit and fisted, and used rifles and pistols as clubs; blood was flying about like spray from a hair-wash bottle. And then the Turks turned and fled, and I felt a very proud man: the key of the whole peninsula was ours, and our losses had not been so very great for such a result. Below I saw the straits, motors and wheeled transport, on the roads leading to Achi Baba.
>
> As I looked round I saw we were not being supported, and thought I could help best by going after those [Turks] who had retreated in front of us. We dashed down towards Maidos, but had only got about 300 feet down when I saw a flash in the bay and suddenly our own navy

put six 12" [inch] monitor shells into us, and all was terrible confusion; it was a deplorable disaster; we were obviously mistaken for Turks, and we had to get back. It was an appalling sight; the first hit a Gurkha in the face; the place was a mass of blood and limbs and screams, and we all flew back to the summit and our old position just below. I remained on the crest with about 15 men; it was a wonderful view; below were the straits, reinforcements coming over the Asia Minor side, motor cars flying. We commanded Kilid Bahr, and the rear of Achi Baba and the communications to all their army there . . .

I was now left alone much crippled by the pain of my wound, which was now stiffening, and loss of blood. I saw the advance at Suvla Bay had failed . . . I now dropped into the trenches of the night before, and after getting my wound bound up, proceeded to try and find where my regiment was; I got them all back in due course, and awaited support before moving up the hill again. Alas; it was never to come, and we were told to hold our position throughout the night of the 9th-10th.

Again, one of the Gallipoli 'what ifs'. What if Baldwin's force had been able to join Allanson? That would have put five battalions on the saddle of Q. If they had been able to join up with the New Zealanders behind Chunuk Bair, this would have been some foothold on the main ridge. Allanson's attack was in the Gallipoli tradition. His little party, so resolute when others were irresolute, was alone; Allanson didn't have enough men to make a difference. One cannot argue, as some have, that a mistake by the navy changed the course of the war. (It is more likely, incidentally, that the shells came from Anzac gunners who could see the inland slopes of Q and assumed the specks on the hill were Turks.)

Allanson knew he couldn't do too much. He said in a private letter in 1934 that it occurred to him that the attack was 'fatuous' because it did not appear to 'offer any hope of permanent success'. But one had to do something. 'Certainly those around me did all they could to discourage me . . . but it appeared to me then, as it does today, that it was my bounden duty to attempt it, and indefensible for me to do nothing.'

Allanson's force suffered about 200 casualties on the hill. Those hit by the salvo were stained yellow from the lyddite in the shells. Slim had been wounded and lost a lot of blood. The future Governor-General of Australia was carted off to an Australian field ambulance. There, as he put it, he lay in the sun and got shelled. Allanson, also carted off, said he told 'the general' (presumably Cox) that if his Gurkhas were forced to retreat, 'we gave up the key of the Gallipoli Peninsula'. The general told him the Gurkhas would be withdrawn next morning. The attack had failed nearly everywhere else, he explained.

Allanson's papers in the Imperial War Museum and the Liddell Hart Centre reveal a man of strong opinions: idealistic, erratic, bitter, proud of his Gurkhas and disenchanted with the general staff and the way they ran the August battle. In September he wrote home:

Sir Ian Hamilton came over our line the other day: you know Lord Pentland wrote to him. He never said one word about that: nor did he say one word about ours being the only regiment in the force to reach the Chunuk Bair, nor that we had done well or anything. It was a little discouraging and nearly made one feel what a cipher one is . . . I do not think one can say too much to regiments & the officers. It is all you can do & they deserve it & appreciate it & after all the staff are safe. We have to carry out their plans, good or bad, & every advance is at great cost & those whose lives are always in jeopardy & stick it out deserve the kind word.

Allanson had seen the letter recommending him for the Victoria Cross.

I do not think for a moment I shall get my VC: the operation was not a successful one as a whole, & it should have been had there been proper co-ordination: hence very little will be said of it & not much will be given.

Allanson received the Distinguished Service Order.

The general assault of August 9 had failed by early morning. To the north, however, a curious thing happened. The Turks attacked Monash's 4th Brigade, and New Army battalions reinforcing it, on Damakjelik Spur. Why do this? The Turks had a crisis at Chunuk Bair and they knew it. Monash's brigade wasn't threatening anything.

Von Sanders, at Suvla, thought Monash's troops were part of Stopford's corps. He also thought Stopford's objective was Hill 971. He had decided to use one of Feizi Bey's divisions to attack towards Suvla Bay; the other division would attack south, towards 'Stopford's' forward positions on Damakjelik. The two New Army battalions and Monash's troops fought well and held off the Turkish division. The other Turkish division, fighting the real Stopford, did better.

The casualties from the August offensive among the Anzac troops were now probably more than 10,000. Those unwounded were worn out, hungry and thirsty. The offensive was failing, but Hamilton, Birdwood and Godley didn't seem to know this. General Shaw took charge of the front at Rhododendron Ridge, Chunuk Bair and the Farm after the general assault petered out on August 9. That night the New Zealanders – what was left of them – were pulled out of the line and replaced with New Army battalions, the Loyal North Lancashires and the Wiltshires, both from Shaw's division. Meanwhile Turkish reinforcements were massing behind Chunuk Bair. The Turks were moving from the defensive to the offensive.

War, as distinct from skirmishing, came to Suvla at dawn on August 9. Ashmead-Bartlett was at Lala Baba and sensed something was different. The Turkish fire was much heavier and their artillery better directed. Reinforcements had obviously arrived. Stopford had received reinforcements too. The 53rd Division had begun landing the previous night. One brigade arrived on the morning of the ninth. None of its officers had seen a map of Suvla. On the beach, according to Aspinall, the new-comers found 'a general air of depression, confusion and indifference' that turned out to be infectious. There were no orders waiting for them. The brigade staff climbed Lala Baba to see if they could work out what was happening. They looked out on the dry salt lake and saw crowds of British soldiers hurrying back to the beach. One of them wrote in his diary that the scene reminded him of 'a crowd streaming away from a football match'.

This crowd turned out to be men driven back from Scimitar Hill. Below Tekke Tepe ridge, the troops ordered up as a result of Hamilton's intervention the previous night had been routed. Around noon fires started in the scrub on Scimitar Hill. British wounded tried to crawl ahead of them. Ashmead-Bartlett watched.

I watched the flames approaching and the crawling figures disappear amidst dense clouds of black smoke. When the fire passed on little mounds of scorched khaki alone marked the spot where another mismanaged soldier of the King had returned to mother earth.

Ashmead-Bartlett later came on hundreds of stragglers who had left the front because of thirst.

They were completely done, burnt black, begrimed with dirt, with their tongues blackened, shrivelled, and lolling out of their mouths, their clothes in shreds, and many only in their shirt sleeves. Some, when they reached the sea, rushed into it, even swallowing the salt water ... Confusion reigned supreme. No-one seemed to know where the headquarters of the different brigades and divisions were to be found. The troops were hunting for water, the staffs were hunting for their troops, and the Turkish snipers were hunting for their prey. Late in the evening I ran across Sir Ian Hamilton standing all by himself somewhere near Ghazi Baba. His face was pale and worried, his gaze was directed on the columns of smoke rising leisurely from the smouldering fires along the front of Anafarta. To the Commander-in-Chief it must have been obvious at this hour that his final effort to reach the Narrows had failed.

The Turks under von Sanders and Kemal had done what they set out to do. On the morning of the ninth they confined Stopford's force to a semi-circle in front of Suvla Bay and the salt lake; they denied him the heights. They turned Suvla into a siege, much like Helles and old Anzac, except that to say this is misleading. It is more accurate to say Hamilton and Stopford allowed Suvla to become a siege. The Turkish official account virtually says this. Suvla failed, it says, because the force that landed there 'did not attack vigorously and swiftly the weak force opposed to it'.

Hamilton went looking for Stopford in the morning and found him supervising the building of 'splinter-proof' huts for himself and his staff. He was absorbed like a weekend handyman. He told Hamilton it was important to do things right as he expected to be here for a long time. Had the Turks discovered where Stopford's head-quarters lay, they would surely have issued an order that on no account was it to be shelled.

Hamilton went to Anzac to see Birdwood, Godley and Shaw. His account of their luncheon has an air of un-reality that matches anything at Suvla. The Suvla generals were pessimists: they saw lines of Turkish trenches that had never existed. The Anzac generals were optimists: they had just failed for the third day in a row, but this was nothing much. Stopford was part of the problem, they said. If he had got moving, the Turks could not have spared the men to reinforce the ridge above Chunuk Bair. The generals felt Chunuk Bair was safe. Birdwood refused Hamilton's offer of his last reserve, the 54th Division; Birdwood said he couldn't water and feed them. The Anzac generals were 'in tip-top spirits and immensely pleased with the freedom and largeness of their newly conquered kingdom', Hamilton wrote. 'They are sure they will have the whip hand of the Narrows by tomorrow.'

The upbeat mood of the lunch made Hamilton feel better. He briefly forgot about Suvla, then remembered. You can almost hear him thinking: 'Why can't Stopford be a good fellow like Birdie or Godley? Why can't he make me feel good?' The lunch emboldened Hamilton. That night he wrote Stopford a note that was uncharacteristically direct. The commander-in-chief was concerned by the want of energy and push in the 11th Division. What was wrong? Was it the general [Hammersley], or the brigadiers, or both? Hamilton told Stopford to get a move on or the whole plan would fail. He had to take Teke Teppe ridge; he had to accept the inevitability of casualties.

Stopford sent back a note the next day. He wanted to push on, he said. And he would get those hills, but to do so he needed more water and artillery.

27

Death by avalanche

On August 10, the day after Birdwood, Godley and Shaw reminded Hamilton that soldiering could still be fun if you picked the right luncheon companions and that Chunuk Bair was safe, Chunuk Bair fell. The Turks came howling over the crest, swept away the New Army battalions that had replaced the New Zealanders, then rolled on down the hill and massacred Baldwin's force at the Farm. Death by avalanche.

Kemal returned from Suvla to lead the attack. It would be wrong to say he 'masterminded' it. It wasn't that crafty. It was the sort of thing that had failed all over the peninsula: a frontal attack with bayonets against a position protected by machine guns and artillery. It was the sort of thing Kemal had failed at before, notably on the 'black night' of June 30 when he tried to overrun Russell's Top. There was an even bigger gamble this time. Kemal didn't know much about the ground on the other side of the Chunuk Bair crest; he didn't know how steeply it fell to the Farm or how many machine guns the New Zealanders had at the Apex. Some of his officers tried to talk him out of it. Too heavy-handed, too risky, they said. Better to try a flanking attack. Kemal conceded afterwards that the officers were right – in theory. He listened to them and waved away their qualms with the serenity of a man who knows exactly what he is doing, why he is doing it, and what will happen to him if he fails.

He had worked out most of the detail before he left Suvla. Not that there was much; blood sacrifices aren't sophisticated. Kemal had a conviction rather than a plan. He wrote in his diary that he couldn't reconcile the idea with logic and reason. It sprung 'from what we feel in the blood and the fiery moments of battle'. Kemal invested his hope in surprise. The British behind Chunuk Bair wouldn't expect the Turks to come surging over the top without an artillery barrage or anything in the way of a softening up. Terror – that would be part of it, thousands of men boiling over the skyline like a storm, wild and fanatical. And surprise – that would be the bigger part. 'To achieve this,' Kemal wrote, 'we needed more than numbers, we needed a cool and courageous command.' Kemal wasn't that cool: he still had malaria. His face was pinched and he hadn't slept for four nights.

He considered surprise had worked for him at Suvla the morning before. The British had gone out expecting skirmishes and Kemal had given them a battle. Not a big one but enough to break their nerve. The Turks rushing down Tekke Tepe provided the terror and the burning scrub helped too. Kemal noticed the indecision of the British commanders, 'that fear of responsibility that leads to defeat'. He knew he had contained Stopford by noon. Chunuk Bair concerned him more. Stopford was a nuisance; Chunuk Bair was the biggest threat since the landings of April 25.

Kemal went to see von Sanders. The German favoured a flanking attack against the Anzac columns, maybe along the Aghyl Dere. Kemal wanted a frontal assault on

Chunuk Bair. Take back Chunuk Bair and the Aghyl Dere didn't matter, he said. Von Sanders didn't want to argue.

Kemal rode to Chunuk Bair. He put one regiment in the front trench, which in places came within 20 or 30 yards of the British line. He put another about 30 yards behind the first. All this was done as quietly as possible. This was the risky part. If the British thought the Turks were massing and opened up with artillery, Kemal's tightly packed force would be wiped out and Godley's troops would stroll up to Hill Q. Bayonets only would be used in the first stage of the attack.

Kemal looked at his watch. Nearly 4.30. Dawn was minutes away. Kemal moved towards the front of the line. He spoke softly. 'Soldiers,' he said with a nod towards Napoleon, 'there is no doubt at all we are going to defeat the enemy in front of you. But do not hurry. Let me go ahead first. As soon as you see me raise my whip then you will all leap forward.'

On the other side of that crest the 6th Loyal North Lancashires had taken over the New Zealanders' trenches after dark. New Zealand dead and wounded lay all about and the trench smelt of blood and cordite, burnt earth and maggots. The Loyals, New Army volunteers, had only been in action a few days and already they knew the truth: war wasn't the way the recruiting people had sold it back home.

The New Zealanders had pulled back beyond the Apex. The casualties in the infantry brigade were worse than 40 per cent. With 700 casualties, Malone's Wellington Battalion, the surrogate child he had loved so well, had been almost wiped out. Casualties among the mounted brigade were worse than 25 per cent. The New Zealanders had fought with rare heart. It seems a denial of what they did that only one Victoria Cross was awarded for their time on the summit. This went to Corporal Cyril Bassett, a signaller. Bassett, a humble man, knew the truth about Chunuk Bair. 'All my mates ever got were wooden crosses,' he said long afterwards.

Two-and-a-half companies from the 5th Wiltshires, the other relieving battalion, arrived from the Farm after 2 am, panting from their climb. There was no room for them in the trenches, so they trudged to the cliff-like slopes of Sazli Dere, just behind, peeled off their webbing, stacked their rifles and tried for their first sleep in four days. A company of the Loyals took over the Pinnacle and New Zealand machine gunners stayed on at the Apex. Like all the columns out to the left of Anzac, this one was now intermixed and difficult to command, about 2000 men from 4 different brigades. Johnston was still in charge but he was now receiving his orders from Shaw, who, like Godley, had not seen the ground.

Baldwin's force at the Farm, more than 3000 strong, was similarly intermixed: Hampshires, Wiltshires, Royal Irish Rifles, Warwicks, East Lancashires, men from four brigades of the New Army. At dawn they huddled around the terrace, bare except for its sheepfold, and stared up at the gullies, dark and sinuous, plunging down from Chunuk Bair.

Then they heard it. The sounds of skirmishing had been drifting down for 30 minutes. This was something else. Shouts at first. Then rifle shots. Then the tap-tap-tap of machine guns. And this rumble, as though an avalanche was coming down the hill.

Kemal carried his riding whip with its looped-over flap. Another officer, knowing what Kemal was about to do, picked up a shovel. Kemal raised his whip, the officer raised his shovel, and other officers lifted their swords. The line surged forward. 'Allah! Allah!' the Turks shouted. The men leapt into the darkness like lions, Kemal said.

We don't know for sure what happened to the Loyals because so few survived. The lie of the land suggests they would have been lucky to get off one shot each before the Turks reached them. It wouldn't have mattered if they had got off several. This was a wave rolling over the hill, unstoppable, thousands of men in cloth helmets and rag-tag uniforms, calling on their god, bayoneting everything that moved in front of them and heading for the Pinnacle.

The Wiltshires behind the Loyals tumbled down Sazli Dere without grabbing their rifles from the stack. It is a steep descent. The Wilts probably didn't think about it. The fear of heights tends to evaporate when a mob with bayonets and lots of bad intent is chasing you. Besides, in the dawn gloom they probably didn't have any idea the valley floor was 200 feet below.

For a fortnight a group of them lay down there, including a major shot in the spine, taking water from a spring and food from the dead. Turks came on them but refused to take them prisoner; once they gave them some water. The major died. After a fortnight the survivors were starving. All bar seven tried to make a rush down the valley. Light horsemen on August 27 fired on a disorderly body of 'Turks' coming down the valley. Bean says there is little doubt the 'Turks' were the Wilts. They ran away and died, probably shot by real Turks. Of the seven who stayed behind, two climbed to a New Zealand position on Rhododendron Ridge. The New Zealanders climbed down and rescued the last five Wilts.

The Turks overran the Pinnacle about five minutes after they ripped through the Loyals' trenches. Now the New

Zealand machine guns at the Apex were knocking the Turks over by the hundred. Temperley admits, 'with deep regret', that he ordered the machine gunners to fire on 300 or 400 New Army troops who ran towards the Turks with their hands up.

The right wing of Kemal's line swung down towards the Farm. The navy was now dropping shells into the Turks, but they kept going, crashing through the thick bush, slipping and sliding down the slopes, their blood up. They had taken back Chunuk Bair; they would count their casualties afterwards.

Kemal was hit by shrapnel at the old Turkish frontline. 'The heavy naval shells sank into the ground, then burst, opening huge cavities all about us,' he wrote. 'The whole of Chunuk Bair was enveloped in thick smoke and fire.' Dead Turks lay all around him. Kemal asked a commander where his troops were. 'Here are my troops,' the officer said. 'Those who lie dead.'

The way the story goes, the shrapnel hit Kemal on his breast pocket. It smashed a watch inside and left Kemal with a minor wound. He later presented the broken watch to von Sanders; in return, the German gave Kemal a chronometer that worked.

We don't know too much about what happened at the Farm. Again there were few survivors. High-ranking officers fought shoulder-to-shoulder with their men. Baldwin was killed early on. The brigadier-general who succeeded him was immediately shot through the lungs. His successor, in turn, was wounded. Nearly all the Warwicks were killed and maybe half the Irish Rifles. By 10 am more than 1000 New Army men were lying dead and wounded on this little terrace where sheep once camped.

Some of Baldwin's men headed for Cheshire Ridge.

Others fled into the gullies alongside the plateau, became lost and died there. Having wiped out the threat, the Turks climbed back to the main ridge; the Farm didn't matter any more.

Hamilton used to say he had been born several hundred years too late and maybe he had. He believed in the magnificent intangibles: courage, will, character, sacrifice. Nothing wrong with this. Except that Hamilton seemed to think that in 1915 these things *alone* could win battles, as they once did in the Highlands. He didn't realise war was now about the triumph of technology and organisation as well as the triumph of the spirit. More likely, he did realise this but refused to accept it. It made war seem like commerce.

Analytical exercises seemed to bore him. He couldn't quite think a problem through to a conclusion, particularly if it was a conclusion he didn't want to reach. So often in *Gallipoli Diary* he starts to review a situation and before he has completed four or five sentences, he is offering classical allusions, homilies, half-truths and slogans. The exercise peters out in a welter of sentimentality.

After the loss of Chunuk Bair the August offensive had failed. Hamilton had run up 25,000 casualties on 3 fronts in 4 days. Tragic as this was in human terms, it might not have been so bad if the original objectives had been reached. But Hamilton did not have the heights at Anzac or Suvla. His Anzac troops were spent; so were the Helles divisions. The Suvla troops were unlikely to succeed anywhere until Stopford and others were sacked. Yet here is Hamilton writing of the events of August 10:

Well, we had Chunuk Bair in our hands the best part of two days and two nights. So far the Turks have never retaken trenches once we had fairly taken hold. Have they done so now? I hope not. Birdie and Godley are at work on a scheme for its recapture. The Turks are well commanded: that I admit. Their generals knew they were done unless they could quickly knock us off our Chunuk Bair. So they have done it. Never mind: never say die. Meanwhile we have the East Anglian Division [the 54th] available tomorrow, and I have been over in the G.S. marquee working out ways and means of taking Kavak Tepe [a hill north of Tekke Tepe] which may also give us an outlook, more distant, but yet an outlook, on to the Dardanelles.

This is Hamilton at his most foolish and most admirable. How are Birdie and Godley going to take back Chunuk Bair? What troops are they going to use? The Turks are well commanded. Why is this? What are they doing differently? How is he going to take Kavak Tepe, or anything else at Suvla, so long as Stopford is in charge?

Hamilton had underestimated the extent of his failure. But it was worse than that. He didn't understand what had happened. As someone once said, an optimist sees an opportunity in every calamity.

If you stayed at one of the waterfront hotels in Çanakkale and never stepped outside, you would still know why Chunuk Bair mattered. Once the haze lifts, you see it from the hotel window, over the water and far away, high above the white houses and minarets of Eceabat, hulking and black-green. It dominates this part of the peninsula. You look at it every day and realise why Hamilton had to hold it and why von Sanders had to take it back.

On the ground at Chunuk Bair it is hard to visualise what once was. This was a bald hill in 1915; now it is a muddle of pine trees, memorials, plaques, statues, cemeteries, stone walls, souvenir stalls and tourist buses. For obvious reasons this is the most popular spot on the battlefield for Turkish visitors. The New Zealand monument, a pylon of white stone, stands on the crest, a little ahead of the line held by the New Zealanders. Down the crest towards Hill Q stands a statue, massive and intimidating, of Kemal clasping his riding whip. This is roughly where he stood to order the attack. The spot where he spent the night of August 9 is marked, about 200 yards back from the New Zealand trenches, which wind drunkenly through the pines. Because of those trees, and the tourist buses, this no longer looks like the place where Malone died.

Malone's remains probably lie in the New Zealand cemetery. It is the same here as at the Australian cemetery at the Nek. Many of the New Zealanders, Gloucesters and Loyals who occupied these trenches are undoubtedly in the ground here, but no-one knows where. Only ten graves are known; 620 bodies are unidentified. When Bean arrived in 1919 he found that the Turks had buried the dead from the August battles in rows. The graves on the first three rows had been ransacked and the bones were lying on the surface. He found the bones and kit of the Wiltshires in Sazli Dere. He found bones between the Apex and the Pinnacle, probably those of the Aucklanders killed on August 7.

The Apex looks just the way it appears in photographs taken in 1915. The New Zealand trenches are still there. Sazli Dere is particularly steep here. A few years back an Australian visitor lost his footing near this spot and toppled into the gorge. As he tumbled down the slope, he thought he spotted something interesting in the scrub. He climbed back and picked up a periscope.

The Farm was a sheepfold that became an abattoir; now it smells of lavender. The wind rustles in the pine trees and the Aegean glistens and merges into the sky so well that you cannot tell where one ends and the other begins. There are 645 buried here but no-one knows who they are, except that most were undoubtedly from Baldwin's force. Bean found no dead on the terrace itself but on the slope below bodies lay thickly: Royal Irish Rifles, Hampshires, Wiltshires. Except at the Nek, Bean had nowhere seen the dead lying so close together and, because of the altitude, the bodies had not decomposed as completely as those at old Anzac. For the first time on his return to Gallipoli, the scenes 'got us down'.

Where Allanson and his Gurkhas reached the saddle below Hill Q is several hundred yards from the Farm. If Allanson was where we think he was, and dashing *down* towards Maidos, as he put it, it is difficult to see how he could see 'a flash in the bay'. Heavy lumps of shrapnel litter the ground and lizards scurry in the Turkish trenches. From here you can see a large stretch of the Dardanelles. You understand why, briefly, Allanson felt elation.

Back in Australia, the war produced flashes of humour in the press. In the *Age*, a New Zealand officer told how the Maori Contingent danced a *haka* for Godley. The Turks watched perplexed. Shortly after a Turkish newspaper reported: 'For the first time in the history of the straits, they have had to endure an attack by cannibals!'

Mostly, though, the war continued to be misreported. On August 12, two days after the story above appeared, the *Argus* gave the first hint of the August offensive. Hamilton, who seemed to get more words published than Bean or Ashmead-Bartlett, reported that a fresh landing had taken place 'and considerable progress made'. On August 24, this heading appeared in the *Argus*:

ON GALLIPOLI
SUVLA BAY LANDING
'MOST BRILLIANT FEAT'
GREAT FORCE DISEMBARKED

The text beneath described the Suvla landing as 'the most brilliant work yet carried out in this war'. General Stopford would have been pleased.

28

One fine class

The August offensive at Anzac wobbled to a stop like a crippled horse. It had produced sublime moments that still challenge the imagination: the light horsemen at the Nek, Allanson and his Gurkhas, Malone and his Wellingtons, Walker and his Australians at Lone Pine. But it had still failed.

The New Army troops had struggled as best they could. Bean wrote in his diary that the Anzac officers had no confidence in them and neither did he. These Englishmen were too short and delicate. 'The truth,' Bean pronounced, 'is that after 100 years of breeding in slums, the British race is not the same . . . It is breeding one fine class at the expense of all the rest.' This is an interesting theory – a touch of Darwin, a whiff of Marx – and it may even have been true. As an explanation of why the offensive failed it is too glib. The New Army men had been asked to do too much too soon. They were often badly led. They took their orders and were lying dead and wounded up and down the gullies north of Anzac and on the Suvla plain. Bean might have been looking at the wrong end of the English social order. What about that 'one fine class'?

The offensive had failed but the rank and file, and even

a few colonels, had had their moments; the generals, with the exception of Walker at Lone Pine, had not. A curious thing had happened which Pugsley alludes to in his account of the New Zealanders' war. The men had started to outgrow their generals. The citizen-soldiers had moved on; they now knew the difference between drill and war. Most of the generals had not learnt much since the landing. They were still part of a club with arcane rules. With the exception of Walker, they had for five days played at war from a distance and on sheets of paper because they thought this is what generals did. Unhappily for them, their opponents worked to different rules.

Temperley returned to the coast after nearly a week at Chunuk Bair and ran into Braithwaite. 'You'd better come along and see Godley,' Braithwaite said.

'Where shall we find him?' said Temperley.

'Oh, we always know where to find Godley. Ever since this show started he's made a point of being at Number Two [Outpost] round about certain times of the day, war or no war.'

Braithwaite explained that despatch riders were now galloping along the coast between Suvla and Anzac. The Turks in the hills took pot shots at them. Temperley and Braithwaite found Godley and Shaw at No. 2 Outpost. A galloper was approaching from Suvla. In a confidential letter to Bean in 1936, John North, author of *Gallipoli: The Fading Vision*, said Temperley had told him the conversation went like this:

Braithwaite: Here's Temperley.

Godley: Hello, Temperley. Been fighting a battle, haven't you? By God, Shaw, that was a close shave! They'll get the blighter before he gets much farther!

Temperley (a little icily): Yes, we *have* been fighting a battle. The brigade has lost nearly two-thirds of its men.

Godley: Don't talk like a bloody fool. By God, Shaw, I believe this fellow *will* get away with it, after all! [To Temperley] A man who's been in action always comes out with some cock-and-bull story about thousands of casualties. [To Shaw] Christ, did you see him duck that time! [To Temperley] You'd better go and get yourself a drink. [To Shaw] By God, Shaw, look – look! – they've got him at last, by God, they have! That *was* a bloody fine shot! When's the next one due to come along? And where's that fool . . .

Thus did the commander of the Sari Bair operation conduct himself. A New Zealand private who had served in the infantry brigade's headquarters reflected on Godley in 1982.

Would I say we disliked our General Godley more than the Turks? I don't know but he wasn't very popular. I certainly didn't like him. He was too hidebound, a parade-ground soldier. He was nicely dressed and very good on the parade ground, and no good off it.

And then there was Stopford. What to do about him? Once the offensive failed at Anzac, Hamilton and Stopford began to grate against each other even more. It was as though Hamilton was compensating for his slowness in realising that Stopford was a dud. He had let him get away with too much; now he was going to niggle him, shame him into doing something. Stopford's corps was all Hamilton had left if he wanted to keep the offensive going. In any case, IX Corps couldn't sit on the plain while the Turks dug trenches in the hills.

But Hamilton didn't understand that everything had changed at Suvla. Stopford had no reason to be gun-shy on the first two days; now that the Turks had brought up reinforcements, however, he really did have to move carefully. He couldn't expect to take hills with perhaps a few hundred casualties, as he might have on the first two days. It didn't matter that he lacked artillery on the first two days; now it did.

Hamilton poked and prodded and Stopford was as stubborn, as unearthly, as ever. He was up and down, despairing and hopeful on the same day. He could still find reasons for not doing things. And he could still deliver lines that belonged to comic opera.

Hamilton had given Stopford two fresh divisions, the 53rd, which had begun to land on August 8, and the 54th, which landed on the tenth. Hamilton wanted them to attack the Tekke Tepe Ridge. Stopford said the two divisions were 'sucked oranges'; they were unreliable. There was, he explained, a 'want of leadership by the officers'. The argument went back and forth for days. Then Stopford raised another objection. The Turks, he said, were 'inclined to be aggressive'. This observation ranks with that of the nurse on the hospital ship *Gascon* who, after watching hundreds of wounded being lifted aboard, wrote in her diary on August 10 that this was 'a dreadful war . . . more like wholesale murder'. Sister Kitchen, overworked and despondent, had merely come up with an awkward form of words; Stopford actually meant what he was saying.

On August 11 Hamilton told Stopford the 54th Division was to take Tekke Tepe Ridge at dawn the next day. Back came a long letter from Stopford. No mention of the next day's attack. The new divisions, Stopford said, were no good. They couldn't take anything. 'This letter,' Hamilton wrote, 'has driven me very nearly to my wits' end.' He rushed off to Suvla to 'wrestle' with Stopford. Stopford won a delay: the attack was postponed until the

13th. Stopford pointed out that the foothills were now teeming with Turkish snipers. Even if the 54th made the summit of Tekke Tepe, it could be cut off. The point was good, but Hamilton didn't want to know about it. He wanted a win somewhere. He wanted to be able to tell Kitchener he had taken a hill – or anything.

Stopford sent word next day that he didn't want to attack. He wanted to clear the ground in front of the foothills first with a brigade of the 54th; then maybe the whole division could go on and take the hill. Hamilton had just received a cable that 'makes me feel *sick*' from Kitchener. Could not Hamilton 'ginger up' the Suvla troops? 'The utmost energy and dash are required for these operations or they will again revert to trench warfare,' the great man said. Hamilton had promised him an attack for the next day. Now Stopford wasn't sure if he wanted to attack. Hamilton sent Braithwaite to Suvla. If Stopford wasn't going to try for Tekke Tepe, Braithwaite was to tell him to attack the W Hills instead. Stopford told Braithwaite that the probing action by the 163rd Brigade towards Tekke Tepe was going ahead, but that he could attack neither Tekke Tepe nor W Hills tomorrow. Hamilton cabled Kitchener that the general advance had been postponed but that a brigade was out there making a 'small attack'. He left the good news for the last sentence: 'This morning the 10th Division captured a trench.'

The 163rd Brigade – Suffolks, Hampshires, Norfolks, including a company recruited from King George's estate at Sandringham – went out on the plain, bayonets glittering in the sun and carrying maps that depicted another part of the peninsula, to be shot down from the scrub. The Norfolk company disappeared in the smoke, never to be seen again. The soldiers' bodies were found years later well inside the old Turkish lines. Conspiracies attend this incident, including the suggestion, aired a few years back in a British television programme, that the Turks executed the Sandringham company. There is nothing to support this. It merely sounds more attractive than the probability that the King's farm hands, like so many others at Gallipoli, died as a result of incompetence. The survivors of the 163rd Brigade fell back to the start line.

Next day Stopford told GHQ the 53rd Division was looking shaky after being shelled. The division might 'bolt at any minute', he said. He also made his famous pronouncement about the Turks being inclined to aggression. Hamilton went to Suvla again. A few days earlier Hamilton had felt that Stopford's spirits were picking up; he was in 'better form'. Now he found him without hope. The 53rd Division, Stopford said, was finished; the 54th was incapable of attack; the rest of IX Corps was immovable. He needed more time before he could think about a general attack.

Hamilton left reproaching himself for not having stood up to Kitchener when the leadership of IX Corps was being discussed. 'Ought I to have resigned sooner than allow generals old and yet inexperienced to be foisted on me?' A more relevant question might have gone something like this: 'Why didn't I realise that Stopford was the wrong man when, before the landing, he moped around Imbros talking about defeat and difficulty?'

Hamilton cabled Kitchener that the Suvla generals were 'unfit for it', which was unfair to Mahon, who was up on Kiretch Tepe with his 10th Division and who had, to this point, done nothing wrong. Hamilton said that he would have to give IX Corps time to rest and reorganise.

Hamilton thought Stopford was going to do no more than that. But on August 14, Stopford, without talking to

GHQ, told Mahon to push forward along the Kiretch Tepe ridge. Mahon did so next day, only to find that the three Turkish companies in front of him had been re-inforced. The British made ground but the fighting became desperate. Next day the Turks counter-attacked. The Irish troops had no bombs to throw back, so they threw rocks. The Irish fought well, as did a brigade from the 54th. The British eventually retreated to the old front-line with 2000 casualties.

Von Sanders took this attack seriously. In his memoirs, he talks about August 15 as a day of crisis. If the British took the ridge, they might be able to push right across the peninsula and outflank his army.

Stopford's headquarters didn't take the battle nearly so seriously. A brigade commander on Kiretch Tepe asked urgently for reinforcements on August 16. Corps head-quarters at first told him no help could be sent. Headquarters didn't seem to know what was going on. There was a reason for this. It was no longer Stopford's headquarters. The general had been sacked. And Mahon had walked off in a huff while his men were battling for their lives on Kiretch Tepe.

Hamilton's cable to Kitchener about the Suvla generals had brought a fast response.

> If you should deem it necessary to replace Stopford, Mahon and Hammersley, have you any competent generals to take their place? From your report I think Stopford should come home. This is a young man's war, and we must have commanding officers that will take full advantage of opportunities which occur but seldom. If, therefore, any generals fail, do not hesitate to act promptly. Any generals I have available I will send you.

Kitchener promptly followed this with another cable. He had plucked three generals from the western front, including Byng, for Hamilton. 'I hope,' Kitchener said, 'Stopford has been relieved by you already.'

Kitchener had two months earlier told Hamilton he could not have Byng. Kitchener had so much believed this was a young man's war that he had sent Stopford, who was elderly beyond his years. But Kitchener could do this; he had been doing it for years. He did not behave like a military commander or a cabinet minister so much as a king. His highness has had a whim – two actually. Not only are young generals desirable; they are also plentiful.

One wonders whether Hamilton would have sacked Stopford if Kitchener had not made it so easy for him. He might have; but how long would he have waited? Hamilton decided that Major-General Beauvoir de Lisle, commander of the 29th Division at Helles, should relieve Stopford until Byng arrived to take over IX Corps. Stopford left Suvla on August 16.

Hamilton asked Mahon to waive his seniority and serve, temporarily, under de Lisle. Mahon hated de Lisle and apparently had trouble even writing his name. Mahon told Hamilton: 'I respectfully decline to waive my seniority and to serve under the officer you name. Please let me know to whom I am to hand over the command of the division.' Mahon packed up and headed for Mudros. His division was fighting on Kiretch Tepe and needed help. Mahon didn't 'desert' – Hamilton gave him permission – but it was moral desertion and it showed all the humbug of the old British army and its rules for different classes. Three British soldiers were executed for offences during the Gallipoli campaign; the French executed many more there. A private could not leave his post or fall asleep on guard duty, but a general could sulk off in the middle of a battle. Hamilton conceded that a general 'chucking up' his command while his division was under fire was a 'very unhappy affair'. He wasn't going to sack him for it, though. Mahon was a good chap; he would cool down. He did, and eventually returned to command what was left of his division. If Mahon's tantrum was disgraceful by the standards of any era, he didn't suffer for it. He was in the club.

Major-General John Lindley voluntarily resigned command of the 53rd; he had the grace to tell Hamilton his division had gone to pieces and he didn't think he could pull it together again. Sitwell, a brigade commander in Hammersley's 11th Division, was sacked. As someone said, Sitwell had been well-named. Hammersley, who had been as useless as Stopford, was recalled.

All this came too late. De Lisle was a fighting general – a brute, Birdwood called him – and he had been promised an extra division, the 2nd Mounted, which would come from Egypt without its horses. It took de Lisle only a day, however, to realise Hamilton had underestimated the difficulties at Suvla. The force was more confused and exhausted than anyone had realised. De Lisle told Hamilton he needed time to reorganise; Hamilton didn't have time to give him.

One can only live with delusions so long. An air of crisis was enveloping the expedition. There were too many disasters and they could not be hidden.

De Robeck had sensed the mood and thought that perhaps he should be seen to be doing something. The submariners had been intrepid, forcing their way into the Marmara and even torpedoing a collier at Constantinople, but the rest of the navy had been passive. De Robeck now seemed to be saying to Hamilton that it was time for the fleet to try something. He appeared to be fishing, hoping Hamilton would say, yes, we can't do this job without you. Braithwaite put aside the rulebooks on protocol and told Hamilton to encourage de Robeck to try to force the straits again. Commodore Keyes and Rear-Admiral Wemyss were for the scheme; de Robeck wasn't, but he wanted to hear what Hamilton had to say. Hamilton wouldn't help him. He wouldn't presume to tell the navy what to do. He still believed that, with reinforcements, the army could open up the straits.

He had already asked for those reinforcements – and a lot more. Hamilton also sensed that a crisis was developing. De Lisle's glum report appears to have convinced him it was time to tell Kitchener what was really happening. He sent Kitchener a long report on the August offensive. About 1000 words into the document, he ran up to the truth: 'The result is that my coup has so far failed.' Hamilton estimated that the Turks had 110,000 troops to his 95,000. He admitted that the Turks had the 'moral ascendancy' over some of his new troops. He asked for 45,000 reinforcements to bring his existing force up to strength, and for another 50,000 as fresh divisions. The demand was direct and uncompromising, not at all like Ian Hamilton.

In London, people in power began to wonder afresh about this Hamilton and his Dardanelles expedition. If there is one thing worse than a man who deals in half-truths, it is a man who decides things are so bad he needs to tell you the truth.

29

All for nothing

All battles are sad: people who don't deserve to die always do. There is something beyond sadness in the battles for Scimitar Hill and Hill 60 on August 21. They killed so many for so little. They were not going to change any of the big things. On that hot and misty afternoon when these two battles were going on less than two miles apart, Hamilton could no longer take the heights. He didn't have enough men left. And if he couldn't take the heights, he couldn't get across the peninsula. But by now perspectives had become skewed. Capturing a vineyard at Helles, bundling Turks off a foothill north of Anzac, an advance of a few yards at Suvla: these had come to be seen as evidence of progress, what Hamilton would call a 'big tactical scoop'. The Gallipoli campaign was conceived as a strike across the peninsula; now it was about a yard here and a trench there.

These two battles of August 21 were about tidying up, about securing the Suvla beachhead by taking the country around the W Hills and joining Suvla to Anzac by clearing the Turks off the mound known, rather extravagantly, as Hill 60. De Lisle had grown confident again. Hamilton had promised him the 29th Division from Helles and the

2nd Mounted Division, a yeomanry formation, had arrived from Egypt. The yeomanry was a throwback to the days of Crécy and Agincourt; its heartland was in the fox-hunting shires and many of the officers came from the rural aristocracy. This was the Mounteds' introduction to war. The Turks, unhappily, were not sporting chaps.

De Lisle had become so upbeat that he wanted to make the general advance that had so terrified Stopford. Hamilton had become less confident. He knew he was running out of chances. He must also have been wondering whether he was running out of friends in Whitehall. There had been no reply to his cable asking for more men. He couldn't afford heavy casualties. He told de Lisle to limit his attack to the W Hills and the nearby Scimitar Hill, so named because the plateau on its summit curled like a crescent. De Lisle decided that the 29th would take Scimitar while the 11th Division took the W Hills. The Mounteds were in reserve.

The artillery barrage before the attack looked terrific but didn't hit much, mainly because the gunners didn't know where to aim. Ashmead-Bartlett, watching from Chocolate Hill, said the Turks' positions seemed to go up in one vast cloud of smoke and flame. Trees, scrub and great chunks of earth flew in the air. As nearly always happened, the Turks survived well; it is not too hard to sit these things out when the shells are landing nowhere near you. The infantry attack was timed for 3 pm. The idea was that the sun would be behind the British as they charged and in the eyes of the Turks. This advantage was lost when the sky clouded over and an Arthurian mist rose from the Suvla plain. The Turkish gunners opened up and knew exactly what they were aiming at. Suvla is an amphitheatre designed by an artilleryman: the British were on the stage and the Turks in the balcony.

Ashmead-Bartlett decided to shoot some movie film. He saw a flash and found himself in darkness. He had been buried. A spot of light appeared. A kindly soldier was digging him out. Ashmead-Bartlett's still-camera, walking stick, binoculars and water-bottle had been blown up. He was tired of lugging the movie camera about, yet it was untouched. Ashmead-Bartlett felt the Turks had no sense of what to hit.

The 11th Division's attack on the W Hills had failed by 5 pm. To the left Irish troops from the 29th briefly took the summit of Scimitar Hill, which the British had abandoned on August 8, but it was no good having Scimitar if you did not also control the higher hills to the south-east. Shrapnel and machine-gun fire ripped into the Irish troops and they broke and ran back down the hill. Dead and wounded lay all over the western slopes. Bushfires broke out. Hamilton, watching from Kiretch Tepe, thought the ancient gods were against him. 'Mist and fire still hold their own against the inventions of man,' he decided.

The Mounteds were ordered forward. They marched across the dry salt lake as if on parade as white puffs of shrapnel burst over them and arrived at Chocolate Hill about 5 pm. Smoke from the scrub fires stung their nostrils as wounded men staggered towards them out of the false twilight. The yeomen didn't know where the front was, what they were supposed to do or what had happened to the 29th Division. The haze was so thick they could barely see Scimitar Hill. Some of them nevertheless got to the top, only to be driven off by Turkish fire. Further south, Sir John Milbanke, VC, a colonel in the 2nd Mounted, was told to attack a redoubt. 'I don't know where it is,' he told his officers, 'and don't think anyone else knows either, but in any case we are to go ahead and attack any Turks we meet.' Milbanke did what he was told and died.

When darkness came de Lisle's troops briefly owned a small plot on the western side of Scimitar Hill and, further south, part of a Turkish trench. Now the wounded had to be dragged out of the smoke and the flames.

Trooper Frederick Potts of the Mounteds was wounded in the thigh as he charged up Scimitar Hill. Trooper Arthur Andrews crawled up to him. Andrews was shot in the groin. The two lay there that night and the next day, mad with thirst. They tried to move on the second night and Potts was shot in the ear. They found water in the bottles of dead men and Potts said the water was like wine, even though it was nearly boiling. Potts and Andrews heard 'terrible screams and groans'; they presumed the Turks were finishing off the wounded. Andrews couldn't crawl and urged Potts to leave him. Potts put him on a shovel and used it as a sledge to drag him down the hill to the British lines. Potts received the Victoria Cross. He died in 1943; Andrews outlived him by 37 years.

The casualties had been terrible: 5300 out of the 14,300 troops who took part. The 29th Division had been ruined – again. The casualties from the August offensive and its aftermath, including those evacuated because of illness, were now running at around 40,000. Churchill wrote of the battle for Scimitar Hill: 'On this dark battlefield of fog and flame Brigadier-General Lord Longford, Brigadier-General Kenna, VC, Colonel Sir John Milbanke, VC, and other paladins fell. This was the largest action fought upon the peninsula, and it was destined to be the last.'

Not quite. The battle for Hill 60, which began on the same afternoon, went on for more than a week. It was as heroic and as pathetic as any battle at Gallipoli.

* * *

The force Birdwood cobbled together to attack Hill 60 tells how badly his corps had been cut up in the August offensive. He had lost 12,500 men, one-third of his force, in four days. For the assault on Hill 60, Birdwood used Monash's brigade (down to 1400 men from a nominal strength of 4000), 2 regiments of the New Zealand Mounted Rifles (down to 200 men each), Cox's Indian Brigade (now only 1300 strong) and 3 New Army battalions (one of which, the 10th Hampshire, could muster only 330 men).

Hill 60 is a long rise 200 feet high and so insignificant that it barely qualifies as a hump. Birdwood wanted to take it to make safe the link between Anzac and Suvla and to obtain a view north towards the two Anafarta villages. His troops had to attack across the Kaiajik Dere, which was exposed to the Turks on Hill 100. Of the 150 Australians from the 13th Battalion in the first wave, 110 were killed or wounded at once and others were hit shortly afterwards. The 14th Battalion, which supplied the second wave, suffered similarly. As at Suvla, the artillery barrage was next to useless; its main effect was to warn the Turks an attack was coming. As at Suvla, the scrub caught fire. Wounded men were roasted; others died when their ammunition pouches exploded. At nightfall Cox's force had a small foothold on the lower slopes of the hill. Cox needed reinforcements. Godley reluctantly sent him the 18th Battalion from the 2nd Australian Division, which had just begun to arrive at Anzac.

The 18th had been ashore three days. The survivors of the 1st Australian Division were gaunt and haunted. These new men were big and rosy-cheeked; they had never been under fire and were full of hope. They arrived a few hundred yards west of Hill 60 at dawn on August 22.

Their officers were called to a conference and told they were to attack with bombs and bayonets only. But they had no bombs, an officer interjected. Well, they'd just have to do their best without them. They charged the Turkish trenches 750-strong and came out with 383 casualties, half of them dead. Hill 60 was still unconquered and a new battalion had been ruined. Troops were short and compromises inevitable; there was still something contemptible about the way the 18th had been sent out to die.

Birdwood tried for the hill again on August 27. This time the attacking force had to be scratched up from nine battalions. The Australians, New Zealanders and New Army troops took a strong position on the lower slopes but the summit defied them. The 9th Light Horse Regiment was sent up as reinforcements. Next day the 10th Light Horse Regiment was brought in and the men who had survived the charges at the Nek fought magnificently. This time the Turkish trenches were taken, but it turned out that they did not encircle the hill. The Turks still had more than half of the summit; there would be no view to the north.

Private James Grieve from Kellyville, New South Wales, had arrived with the 18th. He wrote to his parents that he would have enjoyed the voyage from Alexandria to Lemnos 'only that I had a bad attack of toothache and I had to have it pulled out and the Dr. nearly pulled my head off'. He was in the first attack on Hill 60.

It was awful to hear the moans & groans of the wounded and dying. One poor chap lying a few feet away from me was wounded in the knee. I bandaged it up for him as well as possible and he started to crawl back but I heard after that he was shot dead while crawling back 'poor fellow'. There were bullets and machine guns whizzing all around, also shrapnel which is worst of all. It fell all around me and several chaps fell around me and yet I escaped. It was marvellous how I came out without a scratch, but I expect it was my luck.

After the charge, I got into a trench which about 60 of our Batt. were in and there we had to stop for about 35 hours & keep the Turks at bay. In that trench things were awful. Our own dead, and also dead Turks lying all around & the smell was awful but that was not the worst. We were in such a cramped position & it was almost impossible to get water & I never felt the want of water so much in my life before. I would have given all I possessed in this world to have had a real good drink of water.

James Grieve's letter ended with a row of 15 kisses. It was found in a dugout near Hill 60. Grieve was killed in the attack of August 27, the date of the letter.

He was one of 2500 casualties at Hill 60. Monash's brigade had been reduced to 968 men, the size of a battalion. The four regiments of the New Zealand Mounted Rifles were down to a total of 365 men. The 18th Battalion had been reduced from 1004 to 386 men in 11 days. Monash wrote in his diary: 'The whole was a rotten, badly organised show . . .'

It was not without humour, however. Monash wrote to Godley after the first attack asking that some of his 'survivors' be taken out of the line. Godley was angered by the word 'survivors'. The use of words like that, he said, could cause morale to slip. In his *Gallipoli*, Robert Rhodes James tells of his uncle, a lieutenant attached to a Gurkha battalion, who lay for hours in the scrub seriously wounded in the throat. Two Australians found him after dusk. One kicked him. 'Aw, leave the dead 'uns till later,' said the other. Lieutenant Lemon lived.

* * *

Lieutenant Hugo Throssell of the 10th Light Horse had been in the charge at the Nek on August 7. Throssell knew the charge was hopeless. He called out to his men to lie down on dead ground. 'A bob in and the winner shouts,' he yelled as his men huddled around him in a hollow. 'Jim' Throssell liked to joke. And he was lucky. He managed to crawl back unharmed. His brother, Ric, was wounded.

Now, on August 29, Throssell was in a trench at Hill 60 in a bomb-fight with the Turks that was as desperate as anything that happened at Lone Pine. Throssell and his men were on one side of a barricade, the Turks on the other. Ten yards separated them at times. Both sides pelted each other with bombs. The Australians fired until their rifles became so hot they had to throw them down and grab replacements from the dead and wounded. Throssell was shot in the shoulder and the neck. Corporal Syd Ferrier had an arm blown off by a Turkish bomb. He kept throwing bombs with his other arm until he collapsed. He died on a hospital ship.

Throssell held the trench, came out of the line and tried to smoke a cigarette. His wounds had stiffened and he could not raise his hand to his mouth. His shirt was shredded by bomb fragments and one of his 'Australia' badges had been driven into his shoulder. Throssell returned after having his wounds dressed. Captain (later Lieutenant-General) Horace Robertson ordered him to leave and not come back.

Throssell, a 31-year-old farmer, won the Victoria Cross. He rejoined the Light Horse in Palestine in 1917 and was wounded in the thigh and foot during the Battle of Gaza. His brother was killed in the same action. Throssell spent the night searching unsuccessfully for his brother's body. After that he seemed to change. The joy of life was gone.

Throssell married the writer Katharine Susannah Prichard and they settled on a farm near Perth. Throssell started to go broke as the Great Depression took hold. He thought a war-service pension would bring financial security to his family. In November, 1933, aged 49, the man who went off to war with a mischievous smile sat down on the verandah and shot himself in the head.

Suvla is the kindest country on the peninsula. No erosion gutters as at Helles, no razorbacks as at Anzac. Here are beaches of white sand, green fields of wheat, plots of tomatoes and peppers criss-crossed with black irrigation pipes, red poppies along the roadsides, hedges and copses and little white farmhouses. Once there was a Greek city here, probably on Nibrunesi Point. Black goats graze the hills and their bells tinkle across the plain. A fisherman sets his nets in the pastel blue waters of Suvla Bay then settles in the stern and rubs his stubble. Men sip coffee in the village cafes and talk about the important things: tractors and tomatoes.

Suvla is also the saddest battlefield on the peninsula. Anzac and Helles have their pilgrims and their soaring monuments. Suvla carries a taint. 'Suvla generals' has become a collective noun for timidity. Suvla is the relation we don't talk about.

Yet the men in the ground here, and there are about 5000 of them, had no say in who led them. They had honour, as they proved in the battles of Scimitar Hill and Kiretch Tepe; they are just as dead as the men at Anzac and Helles but hardly anyone comes to their graves. You know this because the cemeteries have no tracks worn by footfalls. You stand here and listen to the creaks and sighs of the cypresses and read the names of boys from Manchester and Yorkshire and Wales who responded to

Kitchener's accusing finger and ended up in the ground here – for nothing, really. The lawn at Lala Baba cemetery is hungry and thick with daisies. Here is the grave of Private T. Downing of the South Wales Borderers, aged 17; he died the day before Suvla was evacuated. Here is Private W. Ringrose of the Welch Regiment; he was 46. Over there is the grave of a 16-year-old. Here lies Brigadier-General Paul Kenna of the 2nd Mounted. He was 53 and won the Victoria Cross at Omdurman in 1898. Beside him lies a lance-corporal from the South Notts Hussars.

Scimitar Hill is hardly a commanding position, just another scrubby hill with nothing to tell you that hundreds of men were burnt alive here. You look out over wheat fields and hedges, a patchwork quilt as pretty as Norfolk. Somewhere out there the Sandringham Company disappeared. A Turkish guide a few years ago picked up a Norfolk button near that hedge there.

A farmer has recently ploughed a field of deep brown earth on Chocolate Hill and the neck of an English rum jar sits up like an unearthed fossil. An artillery shell complete with its warhead lies next to a farmer's woodheap. Roosters crow and goat bells jangle and clunk.

You approach Hill 60 through fields of wheat, as the soldiers did in 1915. The pine trees planted on the summit now make the hump seem bigger than it is but it still doesn't seem tall enough to qualify as a hill. The old trenches are either side of the cemetery. There are 712 unmarked graves here. Lieutenant-Colonel Carew Reynell is definitely here; Private James Grieve from Kellyville is probably here. New Zealanders have been to the cemetery today. They have left cards with plastic poppies attached. 'We will remember them,' the cards say.

No-one leaves cards at Suvla.

30

The pen *is* mightier

Hamilton slept badly at Imbros on the night of September 1. He thought he was being drowned in the Hellespont. A hand gripped his throat, water closed over his head. He woke up trembling. Now he felt that some visitor had entered his tent. He could see the form but a shadow hid the face. 'Never had I suffered from so fearful a dream,' Hamilton wrote.

Was it a dream or a premonition?

The following day Hamilton did have a visitor, an Australian journalist on a short visit to Gallipoli. Hamilton said he seemed a sensible man, well spoken and with dark eyes. He briefly made Hamilton uncomfortable by offering an 'elaborate explanation of why his duty to Australia could be better done with a pen than with a rifle'. The journalist was Keith Murdoch. He is credited in Australian mythology with single-handedly exposing the scandal of the Dardanelles campaign.

To fall for this is to step around the truth about Murdoch, but was he the spectre Hamilton saw in the dark? Hamilton never saw a face. The man didn't have to be a stranger. On the day Murdoch arrived Guy Dawnay, one of Hamilton's staff officers, left for a brief visit to

London. Dawnay, an old Etonian, knew the right people; he was friendly with the royal family and the Asquiths. Hamilton thought Dawnay could put the case for reinforcements, tell the King and the politicians what was happening, kill the rumours and have a rest.

In truth Dawnay had become a double-agent. He didn't want to be, and his conscience was uneasy. Like Brutus, he had finally bought the for-the-good-of-the-nation argument. There didn't seem any other way. On behalf of several staff officers, he was going to London to tell the truth. He would not make a fuss nor be disloyal to Hamilton and when asked questions he would merely answer honestly. That would be enough. He and the staff officers in the plot still liked Hamilton; he was easy to like. They simply no longer believed in him as a commander. Not after Suvla and Stopford. And they knew the truth could never reach London so long as Hamilton was sending the cables. As Dawnay put it, Hamilton was Mr Micawber.

Before Dawnay left the Dardanelles and Murdoch arrived, those in power in London had begun to wonder about Hamilton. Ashmead-Bartlett had given his version of the Dardanelles campaign to just about everyone who mattered in London in June. The failure of the August offensive made him look a good prophet. George V had lost faith in Hamilton. Stopford had returned home and filed charges with the War Office against Hamilton and his staff. Kitchener ordered four generals to investigate the charges. Hamilton was not even given the chance to read them. Hankey had written an account of his visit. His views were moderate but he was not Mr Micawber. Asquith read Hankey's report and told Kitchener that the generals and staff involved in the Suvla operation should be court-martialled and dismissed from the army.

Bulgaria, having watched the Dardanelles conflict carefully, decided the Turks were going to win and finally came into the war on Germany's side. Serbia now had to be protected from the Greek port of Salonika. With Bulgaria as an ally, Germany would soon have an unimpeded route to Constantinople. If the Germans brought siege guns, the Allies would be blown off the peninsula. Some in Cabinet, notably Lloyd George, saw the new front at Salonika as more important than Gallipoli. Meanwhile, at Imbros and on the peninsula, senior officers whispered to journalists that Hamilton and Braithwaite were bunglers.

It wasn't over when Hamilton stopped trembling in the gloom of his tent that September morning. It was just starting. They were going to drown him. They would do it slowly.

When Keith Murdoch was trying to break into Fleet Street in 1908 he wrote home to Melbourne: 'I'll be able to learn ever so much here. That's very evident and with health I should become a power in Australia.' It was an odd thing for a young journalist to say. He might have said he expected to become a better reporter. What was this about being a power? In describing the 30-year-old Murdoch of 1915, Bean wrote: 'He was a man of forceful personality, combining keen love of power with an intense devotion to his country . . .'

Murdoch couldn't get the job he wanted in Fleet Street, not because he lacked ability but because he had a stammer that sometimes rendered him inarticulate. He was lonely and homesick and rejection made everything seem blacker. He shared a small room with fleas and held bread on his penknife over a gas ring to make toast. He hated the fogs and the squalor. And there was something else. 'A shocking feature of London,' he wrote home, 'is the immorality stalking the streets.' Keith Murdoch was a high-minded young man.

He was tall and heavily built with dark-brown eyes that twinkled. His parents had migrated from Scotland to Melbourne in 1884. His father was a Presbyterian minister. Young Keith worked for the *Age* as a stringer before heading off to London and failure. On his return he covered Federal Parliament, then sitting in Melbourne, and cultivated Andrew Fisher, the Prime Minister, and Billy Hughes, who would become Prime Minister in 1915. Murdoch tried to become the official Australian war correspondent but lost to Bean, who had better credentials. Murdoch was appointed editor of a cable service supplying the Sydney *Sun* and the Melbourne *Herald* from *The Times* building in London. On his way to London to take the job he would do a little work for the government. Fisher and George Pearce, the Defence Minister, asked him to stop in Egypt and investigate complaints about delays in soldiers' mail. For this, he would be paid £25.

He wrote to Hamilton from Cairo asking to be allowed to visit 'the sacred shores of Gallipoli'. Hamilton later described the letter as 'wheedling', although on the Murdoch-scale it wasn't particularly so. Murdoch arrived at Imbros and signed the same form Bean and the other correspondents had signed. He agreed not to correspond by any route other than through the chief censor. How long Murdoch spent on the battlefields is unclear. Bean's diary has him at Anzac on four days. Murdoch wrote a windy article about men charging 'with the light of battle in their eyes'; the Australians, he said, were 'stoical, but not contemptuous'. It was a typical Murdoch piece: lots of generalisations, not many facts, more a sermon than a news story. Murdoch certainly spent much time in the press camp on Imbros. There he met the man who was going to change his life.

Ellis Ashmead-Bartlett captivated the Australian. Murdoch was a journeyman; Ashmead-Bartlett was the master craftsman, a natural writer now covering his seventh war, sipping champagne and giving instructions to the cook he had imported from Paris as he explained important matters of strategy. He was such a good talker – Bean described him as 'the cleverest conversationalist I have ever known' – and he didn't hold back. He explained how the campaign was being mismanaged, how Hamilton and his staff were out of touch, how it was all doomed. Murdoch rightly concluded that there was a story here that no-one was writing. Australians were being misused and Murdoch was an Australian nationalist.

There are two versions of what happened next. Desmond Zwar, one of Murdoch's biographers, says Ashmead-Bartlett came to Murdoch and asked him to carry a letter to Asquith. Zwar says Murdoch did not ask what was in the letter. In his *The Uncensored Dardanelles*, Ashmead-Bartlett says Murdoch was alarmed by what he had seen but did not feel that his word would carry weight with the authorities. 'He, therefore, begs me to write a letter which he will carry through uncensored, telling the plain truth, which he can hand over to the government.' Ashmead-Bartlett said he had 'coached' Murdoch, 'but he says he wants something definite under my own signature'.

Ashmead-Bartlett's letter was cool and forensic, although he allowed himself a few flourishes. The August offensive 'was the most ghastly and costly fiasco in our history since the battle of Bannockburn . . . the muddles and mismanagement beat anything that has ever occurred in our military history . . . my views are shared by the large majority of the army'. The power of the document, however, lay in the way Ashmead-Bartlett stitched one argument to another, building a case like a barrister. He predicted another disaster if the army stayed in its present positions during the winter. The 'supreme command' needed to be changed to restore the confidence of the troops. He told Asquith he knew he was breaking the censorship rules by sending the letter. He asked that the liberty be forgiven.

When Murdoch landed in Marseilles an army officer with an escort of British troops and French gendarmes met him and forced him to hand over the letter. Asquith never received it. The plotters had been betrayed. Hamilton said he had been tipped off by a journalist (others have identified him as Henry Nevinson, the representative of the English provincial press) who was worried about 'the honour of his profession'. Hamilton thought the letter was addressed to Harry Lawson, the proprietor of the *Daily Telegraph*. On September 28 Braithwaite called in Ashmead-Bartlett, told him that the letter had been seized, and that he, Ashmead-Bartlett, must return home.

'May I leave at once?' said Ashmead-Bartlett.

Braithwaite had not thought this out carefully. While he was on Imbros, Ashmead-Bartlett was a nuisance; from London, he could drown Hamilton and Braithwaite.

Murdoch, meanwhile, had arrived in London determined to write his own letter, which he would send to *his* Prime Minister. It was much longer than Ashmead-Bartlett's and utterly different in style. While he was completing it in *The Times* building, Murdoch lunched with Geoffrey Dawson, *The Times* editor, and told him how bad things were at Gallipoli. Dawson led a double life: he didn't know whether he was an editor or an arm of government, as he later proved during Edward VIII's abdication saga. This Australian might fit into some of the games he and others were playing. Lord Northcliffe, the proprietor of *The Times*, for instance, was against the Dardanelles campaign.

Dawson led Murdoch to Sir Edward Carson and Carson led him to Lloyd George. Murdoch might just as well have been walking around with the sign 'Pawn' on his back. Powerful men who wanted Britain out of the Dardanelles would push him all around the board. Lloyd George wrote to Carson.

> I saw Murdoch the Australian yesterday. He struck me as being exceptionally intelligent and sane. That made the account he gave me of his visit to the Dardanelles much more disquieting . . . I agree that Murdoch's report does not differ in essentials from that furnished to us by Colonel Hankey . . . As you know, I always opposed this Gallipoli enterprise, and so have you . . .

Lloyd George suggested that Murdoch send a copy of his letter to Asquith, who did a curious thing. Without checking the accuracy of it or giving Hamilton a chance to answer it, he had the letter printed as a state paper. Perhaps Asquith was trying to appease Lloyd George; perhaps he was just tired of the Dardanelles and Ian Hamilton.

Murdoch's letter is a farrago of fact and gossip, sense and nonsense, sometimes fluttery and sometimes tough, pro-Australian and anti-British, hysterical rather than cool, sentimental rather than analytical. It is adolescent and middle-aged, over-cooked and puffed up with the author's sense of his own importance.

'From what I saw of the Turk . . .' Murdoch writes. He

didn't see any Turks. His is mostly second-hand knowledge masquerading as first-hand. Nowhere is
Ashmead-Bartlett mentioned even though the document
bubbles with his ideas. Murdoch gives the impression that
he picked all this up by walking around for a few days.
The letter bristles with factual errors, particularly about
troop numbers (Murdoch has 90,000 landing at Suvla
instead of 30,000), casualties (he overstates them by
about 40 per cent) and the terrain (he has Gurkhas on Hill
971). It is inconsistent: Murdoch writes that Hamilton has
failed as a strategist (one can hear Ashmead-Bartlett talking here) and must go; a few sentences later, he writes: 'It
is not for me to judge Hamilton.' And there is this
muddle: 'Sedition is talked round every tin of bully beef
on the peninsula, and it is only loyalty that holds the
forces together.'

Perhaps the worst factual error was this: 'I do not like
to dictate this sentence, even for your eyes, but the fact is
that after the first day at Suvla an order had to be issued
to officers to shoot without mercy any soldiers who
lagged behind or loitered in an advance.' It was true that
troops occasionally had to be stood over: Bean once saw
M'Cay threaten to shoot an Australian NCO and
Temperley ordered English troops shot at Chunuk Bair.
Murdoch had turned prattle around an Imbros campfire
into a field order at Suvla. No such order existed.

There was a 'grandeur' about the Australians, Murdoch
wrote. 'It is stirring to see them, magnificent manhood,
swinging their fine limbs as they walk about Anzac.' The
British at Suvla were 'toy soldiers'.

The physique of those at Suvla is not to be compared with
that of the Australians. Nor is their intelligence. I fear
also that the British physique is very much below that of

the Turks . . . They [the Suvla troops] are merely a lot of childlike youths, without strength to endure or brains to improve their conditions.

Of the generals, Maxwell in Egypt had 'a poor brain for his big position'. The men had faith in Birdwood and Walker but not much in Godley. 'Birdwood struck me as a good army corps commander, but nothing more. He has not the fighting quality nor the big brain of a great general.' Braithwaite was 'more cordially detested in our forces than Enver Pasha'.

It was a diatribe, full of errors and a quality that might be described as well-meaning arrogance. All these things tend to divert us from a larger matter. *So much of what Murdoch wrote was true.* He had caught the mood of dissent in the Gallipoli command. For all its errors and pomposities, this was a more accurate portrayal of what was happening there than any of Hamilton's reports to London.

Some of Murdoch's points were good. Too much reliance had been placed on 'floating artillery'. Naval guns with flat trajectories weren't much use against narrow trenches. How was this army going to hang on when the winter rains began to flood its summer trenches? The treatment of the wounded had been disgraceful. Sir James Porter, the Principal Hospital Transport Officer, should be recalled. 'Oh! no Australian has the heart to tell of the fearful wreckage of lives due to this man's incompetency.'

Murdoch saved his best abuse for the general and administrative staffs.

The conceit and self-complacency of the red feather men are equalled only by their incapacity. Along the line of communications, and especially at Mudros, are countless high officers and conceited young cubs who are plainly only playing at war. What can you expect of men who have never worked seriously, who have lived for their appearance and for social distinction and self-satisfaction, and who are now called on to conduct a gigantic war? Kitchener has a terrible task in getting pure work out of these men, whose motives can never be pure, for they are unchangeably selfish . . . appointments to the general staff are made from motives of friendship and social influence. Australians now loathe and detest any Englishmen wearing red.

Of this, Hamilton later said, 'No gentleman would have said it, and no gentleman will believe it.'

Murdoch's journalistic career was made, and in such an unusual way. On a piece larded with factual errors; on a piece based on the thoughts of another who was not acknowledged; and, strangest of all, not on a published story but on a private note to a politician. Murdoch was soon hosting dinner parties in London for Billy Hughes, the new Australian Prime Minister. He became, as Zwar wrote in his biography, Hughes' fixer, speech editor and errand boy. He finally had what he wanted: power. Like Dawson at *The Times*, Murdoch had become an arm of government. What copy he did produce from the war in France was mostly flat and lazy; he got around the work he hadn't done with generalisations, homilies and the liberal use of the perpendicular pronoun.

But it didn't matter. Murdoch was a man to know. The most useful friend he had made in London was Northcliffe, the operatic figure who, before he went completely mad, was a true genius at popular journalism. Murdoch later used Northcliffe's ideas to transform the Melbourne *Herald*. There, Murdoch was much better as an editor than he had ever been as a reporter. Before he left London he wrote Northcliffe a letter (and this one did qualify as wheedling): 'My dear Chief, I address you as such as the Chief of All Journalists (of all ages) and on returning to my desk today wished again (as I often have) that I could call you such in another way . . .'

Asked about the Gallipoli letter in 1989, Murdoch's son, Rupert, said: 'Oh sure, it may not have been fair, but it changed history, that letter.'

Two other men arguably changed history more. Ashmead-Bartlett arrived in London on October 10. Dawnay had begun talking to everyone from King George to Churchill ten days before Murdoch arrived in London.

Ashmead-Bartlett found the Cabinet and the military in confusion. Some wanted to evacuate the Dardanelles at once; others wanted to stay, not because they thought the Allies could win but because they were worried about a loss of British prestige in the East; others thought that now that Bulgaria had joined Germany and Turkey, Salonika was the important front. No-one much believed in Hamilton. It wasn't personal: he was simply seen as a loser.

Looking back, it all seems so amateurish. The politicians were muddling and improvising, hoping that the next soldier or journalist who walked through their door would lay out some magic solution, or at least make up their minds for them. One must be fair, however. There had never been a world war before; the politicians were still learning how to run one. They were just realising that men like Kitchener and, to a lesser extent Hamilton, belonged to a way of doing things that was as quaint as powdered wigs. They sensed there was a new way of doing things but they didn't know what it was. They sensed a few other things. The Germans were not like the hill tribes. The military club was got up for Omdurman rather than the Somme. Muddling through wouldn't get you through any more. This war was too big, too complex, to be run like a feudal estate by a cross-eyed man with a scowl.

There was another problem with Gallipoli, so simple that in the era of the jumbo jet it seems absurd. The people making the decisions had not been there. And one had to see those battlefields to understand them. Once you saw the land you understood why the fleet's guns were no substitute for artillery. Hill 971 didn't look far from Anzac on a map; if you were standing on Rhododendron Ridge looking out over those yellow hills and black gullies, you knew, at once and instinctively, that 971 might as well have been in Bulgaria. This was why Ashmead-Bartlett was worried about the winter: he knew the country. He knew the winter rains would flood the trenches, that thousands of bodies would be washed out of their shallow graves and into the Allied lines.

Ashmead-Bartlett was not like Murdoch, who was content to write a private note that made him lots of useful friends. Ashmead-Bartlett wanted to see his byline on a story; in the best tradition of his craft, he wanted to lay something on the line. He also knew that the way to put pressure on the government was through public opinion. And you couldn't have public opinion if the public didn't know what was going on. He had to find a newspaper that would defy the censors and print his copy. The Berry brothers, who ran the *Sunday Times*, were game. To get around the censorship rules, they decided to publish Ashmead-Bartlett's story as an interview. This appeared on October 17 and caused what Ashmead-Bartlett called a 'sensation'. Northcliffe telephoned him and asked for permission to reproduce the piece in *The Times* and the *Daily Mail*. Most of Monday's Fleet Street papers carried extracts, as did the Australian papers. The *Argus* paraphrased Ashmead-Bartlett as saying: 'The results attained at Gallipoli were highly unfavourable to ourselves.'

Australia's leaders didn't want to know what had gone wrong at Gallipoli. Ashmead-Bartlett was bad for recruiting. The journalist, who was broke, was planning a lecture tour of Australia. Munro-Ferguson, the Governor-General, privately referred to him as an 'undesirable'. Ashmead-Bartlett gave a lecture on Gallipoli to 2500 people at Queen's House, London, late in October. He praised the Anzac troops but said the initial attacking force was too small and called Gallipoli a failure. The day that this was reported in the *Argus*, Billy Hughes, who had just become Prime Minister, was asked in Parliament about Ashmead-Bartlett's views.

> I am sorry you have put that question. (Hear, hear) We have no responsibility of directing the campaign. Our business is only to carry out the instructions of the Imperial Government . . . and to give it what assistance we can. At all events, we owe the Imperial authorities this duty to refrain from criticising their actions (Cheers) . . . I do not pretend to understand the situation but I do know what the duty of this government is, and it is to mind its own business (Hear, hear), to provide our quota of men for the Imperial Government, and to see that they are efficiently led, fed, and equipped. (Loud cheers).

The *Argus* editorial of the same day said Hughes was right. Federation might have come in 1901 but, for the moment, Australia was still a self-governing colony.

* * *

Dawnay saw Kitchener on September 13, Churchill the next day, Bonar Law and George V two days later. The King told him that he had feared Stopford was too old. Dawnay saw Churchill several more times and Lloyd George and Sir Edward Carson. Then he talked with the Prime Minister. Asquith's questions suggested he no longer believed in Hamilton and seemed bewildered by the war in general. Dawnay answered several questions about the Murdoch letter. The Prime Minister nodded and seemed satisfied. Then he returned to the letter. He said parts of it were doubtless false or exaggerated but other parts were certain to be true. He told Dawnay that Stopford's version of events at Suvla differed from Hamilton's. He asked Dawnay why Hamilton did not go ashore at Suvla at the start of the offensive.

Two days later Dawnay again saw Kitchener. The War Minister had been close to charming at their first meeting; now he was gruff and restive. He said the Dardanelles campaign had not been well managed. He referred to Murdoch's letter and, according to Dawnay's papers, 'said that the fact that such complaints were made proved that things were not well. His view was that the *morale* of the troops was not good.'

Hands were reaching down into the water and pushing Hamilton under.

Kitchener tossed Hamilton a rope. Hamilton might save himself if he was willing to drown Braithwaite. There had been a 'flow of unofficial reports from Gallipoli', the War Minister cabled. 'They adversely criticise the work of the headquarters staff and complaints are made that its members are much out of touch with the troops. The War Office also doubt whether their present methods are quite satisfactory.' Kitchener suggested sending Braithwaite home. 'Should you, however, decline and desire to remain as at present, may we assume that we are quite safe in regarding these unofficial reports as not representing the true feelings of the troops?'

This was unfair. How could Hamilton rebut 'unofficial reports' when he hadn't seen them and didn't even know who was making them. Hamilton knew Kitchener was playing at Pontius Pilate. 'He is trying to save me,' he wrote. Braithwaite didn't deserve to be saved. Hamilton, decent man that he was, saved him. 'My confidence in that officer is complete,' he cabled back. 'I did not select him; you gave him to me . . .'

Kitchener asked Hamilton on October 11 for an estimate of casualties if the battlefields were evacuated. Hamilton was upset: evacuation was unthinkable. Before Hamilton answered the cable Dawnay returned from London and, it seems, tried to warn his commander. 'Dawnay thinks some queer things are happening,' Hamilton wrote. 'He could – or would – say nothing more.' Dawnay *knew* some queer things were happening. Hamilton cabled Kitchener next day saying that half the force could be lost in an evacuation. What Hamilton was really saying was that he didn't want to know about an evacuation.

The Dardanelles Committee met on October 14 and the mood was tense. German airships had bombed London the night before. Forty-seven people had been killed; there was much panic and the symbolism was worse than the casualty list. Bonar Law and Lloyd George had circulated notes before the meeting saying they wanted to abandon Gallipoli. Carson had resigned because, as he was to say a few days later, his colleagues could never make up their minds about anything. And now this wretched Hamilton fellow was saying he would lose half his force in an evacuation. The committee decided Hamilton had to go. Kitchener was asked to do the drowning.

Meanwhile Hamilton had finally received the Murdoch letter. He thought it 'an irresponsible statement by an ignorant man', so he didn't attempt to demolish it point by point. His cable in reply was dignified but lame. In his diary, he wondered how the letter had become a state paper. What was Asquith doing? 'Is K still the demi-God, that is the question?'

Kitchener answered that question on the night of October 15. Hamilton was 'ferreted out of bed' by a messenger. Kitchener had cabled to say that Hamilton was to decipher the next message himself. Did the general want to be woken up when the second message arrived? Hamilton guessed what the message would say. He behaved in character. No, he didn't want to be woken. He would decipher the message in the morning. But he had time for a few metaphorical flights about cups of hemlock and the bowstrings that were once used to strangle Ottoman generals who failed.

In the morning Hamilton picked up the cipher book and decoded this:

> The War Council held last night decided that though the Government fully appreciate your work and the gallant manner in which you personally have struggled to make the enterprise a success in face of the terrible difficulties you have had to contend against, they, all the same, wish to make a change in the command which will give them an opportunity of seeing you.

Kitchener had taken 64 words and arranged them in a back-to-front sentence to say one word. Sacked.

It meant more than that, of course. Hamilton was a

62-year-old general. All his life, all his reputation – and it had been a very fine one before Gallipoli – was wrapped up in the army. From this moment his past would count for nothing. He was the most debased currency that war throws up, a failed general. In a sense he had always been an outsider, too kindly, too bookish. Now he was officially an outsider. When he returned to London people would 'cut' him and his wife in the street.

Hamilton had moral as well as physical courage. 'He is, I must say, most wonderfully good about it,' Birdwood wrote to his wife. 'No ranting and raving that it is someone else's fault, etc . . .'

Hamilton left the day after he decoded the cable. He rode over to the journalists' camp to say goodbye. Bean felt sad.

The poor chap looked to me very haggard – almost broken up; so were some of the staff . . . I am honestly very sorry to see Hamilton go. He is a gentleman and has always been courteous and considerate to us. The British Army has never believed in him, but he is a good friend to civilians, and has breadth of mind which the army does not in general possess.

It is rather fault of character than of intellect that has caused him to fail. He has not strength to command his staff – they command him; especially Braithwaite . . . Braithwaite is a snob . . . If Hamilton had had a loyal, agreeable, capable Chief of Staff his success might have been very different . . . Hamilton has not the strength to give those with whom he is surrounded a straight out blow from the shoulder . . . To mix the metaphor – he has an unlucky ability for gilding the pill. He can't administer a pill unless it is golden . . .

It is a most fatal aptitude this gilding the pill, and

Hamilton, with his beautiful style in literature and kind gentlemanly manners, is hopelessly weakened by it – poor old chap.

Hamilton boarded the cruiser *Chatham* and went to his cabin. He wondered whether he could stand going on deck and watching Imbros and the camp 'fade into the region of dreams'. A message arrived. Could he come on deck? The *Chatham* was steering a corkscrew course among the anchored ships. As Hamilton passed each ship the sailors stood and cheered him.

A few weeks later, Dawnay wrote to his wife.

Last night your letter came – so I have your dear hand-writing before me, beloved. It is interesting to hear that Sir Ian is thought to be badly used. He probably was, in the sense that the authorities' reasons for recalling him may have been all wrong. But the salient fact is that he was *no use*.

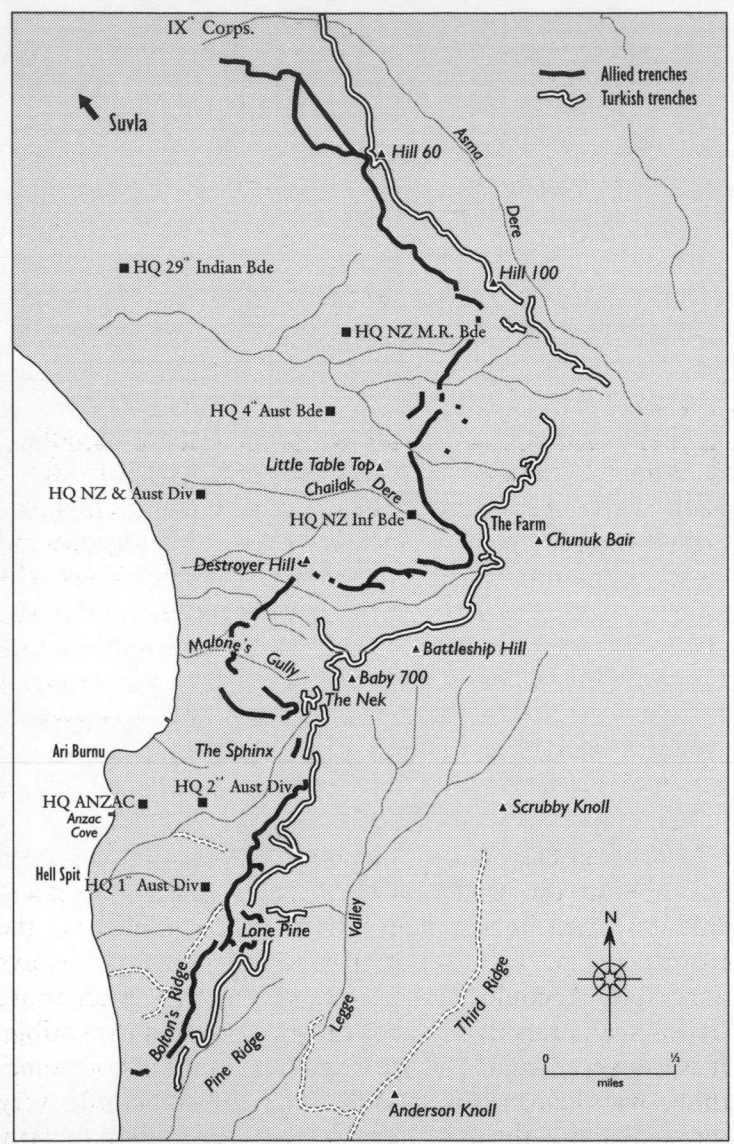

The opposing trenches at Anzac prior to the evacuation

31

We go, we stay, we freeze

Hamilton had been a soldier, big-hearted and willing, for 42 years; it took Gallipoli to prove that he didn't have the temperament to be a commander-in-chief. He lacked the certitude of generals of lesser intelligence and rougher manners. Asked to play Henry V at the Dardanelles, he turned in a memorable Hamlet. He probably would have got away with commanding an army in France. He needed a father figure close by, a Kitchener or Roberts just across the Channel. In his tent on Imbros in 1915 Hamilton was more desolate than an astronaut on the moon in 1969: Neil Armstrong could at least talk to Houston whenever he wished.

There had been a case for replacing Hamilton a month or so before the August offensive. In military terms there was less point in removing him now. He didn't have the troops to go on the offensive and he was always amenable: he could have been talked into an evacuation. In political terms the case for sacking him was irresistible. It was a spectacular gesture. It gave the impression something was being done about Gallipoli, something very serious. It hid the fact that Cabinet really didn't know whether to stay or leave and that Kitchener had finally been exposed as an improviser, and not a very good one.

One of the myths that has travelled down the ages has Kitchener as the master of organisation. As Hamilton wrote – with affection, it should be said – Kitchener 'hated organisation with all his primitive heart and soul, because it cramped his style'. Kitchener, Hamilton explained, was an individualist, 'a master of expedients'. Expediency had brought him this mess at the Dardanelles. Ever since he had bustled Hamilton out there in March, Kitchener had been redefining objectives as the whim struck him. Hamilton was to garrison Constantinople; Hamilton was to occupy the Gallipoli Peninsula. He could have more men; he could not have more men. He had to take Achi Baba and any other Turkish hills he ran into, but he couldn't have proper artillery; artillery was for France. Kitchener had a war in France, another at Gallipoli, another in Egypt and now a Balkans front was opening at Salonika. He juggled men and *matériel* between them as one emergency arose and another subsided. No-one knew how he did this: the process was as mysterious as the man himself. Now, in the month after Hamilton's sacking, as the Gallipoli adventure began to frighten just about everyone in the Cabinet, Kitchener's behaviour became erratic.

He appointed Sir Charles Monro to replace Hamilton. Nothing erratic here. Monro had commanded the Third Army in France. He was shrewd and pragmatic and difficult to rattle once he had made up his mind. As Hamilton said: 'He was born with another sort of mind from me.' Monro was a 'Westerner': the war, he believed, would be won or lost in France; Gallipoli was a sideshow. He thought the peninsula probably should be evacuated; he would decide when he arrived there. Unlike Hamilton, Monro wasn't going to be hustled away. He spent several days at the War Office looking at reports and figures; he talked with Kitchener four times. And he obtained clear instructions. He had to decide whether to leave or fight. If he wanted to leave, he had to estimate the likely losses. If he wanted to stay, he had to say how many extra troops he needed. Sensible instructions, but there was still a problem: Kitchener didn't want to leave Gallipoli. Roger Keyes had arrived in London. He had a new plan to force the straits. De Robeck didn't believe in it. If the Admiralty said yes to Keyes, de Robeck would ask that another admiral be put in charge.

The war at Gallipoli had gone back to stalemate. Lines were straightened out, tunnels dug, bombs thrown. Allied guns were rationed to two shells a day; one in three Turkish shells failed to burst. Both armies were tired; the Turks could afford to be: they were on the high ground. Sickness among the Allied troops became worse. Evacuations for sickness during October from the three battlegrounds ran at better than 600 a day. The arrival of all of the 2nd Australian Division helped at Anzac, but the Mediterranean Expeditionary Force was fading away. On October 10 there were 114,000 men at or near the battlefields; had all formations been up to strength, there would have been 200,000.

And now winter was coming; the first gale had already arrived. The glassy Aegean of the spring was turning dark and boisterous. The men couldn't live in the open trenches in winter. Orders went out for 5000 tons of galvanised iron, for all the timber that could be got in Egypt and England as well as trench pumps and horse rugs.

Monro arrived at Imbros on October 28 and the general staff at once presented him with a paper to help him make up his mind. An attack on the Narrows, the paper said, could not start until spring; it would require

400,000 men. An evacuation could result in a loss of half the fighting troops. Monro wanted to see the terrain. Before he could do so, Kitchener sent him a cable that stopped just short of bullying: 'Please send me as soon as possible your report on the main issue at the Dardanelles, namely, leaving or staying.' Next day, October 30, Monro made a quick tour of the battlefields. Aspinall went with him.

> The local conditions to which the Gallipoli army had long since grown accustomed – the open beach, the crazy piers, the landing of stores by hand from bumping lighters, the strings of kicking mules, the heavy dust, the cramped spaces, the jostling crowds on the narrow beach within range of the enemy's guns – filled him with blank amazement. Arriving later at Anzac Cove, where conditions were still more difficult, his wonder only grew. To the staff officer beside him he remarked with a whimsical smile: 'It's just like *Alice in Wonderland*, curiouser and curiouser.'

At each battlefield he stayed just long enough to visit the headquarters offices close to the beaches and to glance at the country beyond. He posed identical questions to the corps commanders. Were their troops fit for an offensive? Assuming that no new troops could be sent to them and that the Turks would be reinforced and supplied with heavy guns from Germany, could they hang on through the winter?

To the first question, the generals said their troops could only sustain an offensive for 24 hours. To the second, they shrugged their shoulders; they would do their best.

Monro had made up his mind. He recommended

evacuation to Kitchener next day. The general staff agreed with him. They had known Monro only a few days but they liked him. As Dawnay put it, he saw down to the *root* of things. Monro's cable was a masterpiece of economy and good sense. 'We merely hold the fringe of the shore,' he said. The Turks had 'all the advantages of position and power of observation of our movements'. Monro said he was leaving to see Maxwell in Egypt. Then he would look at Salonika.

Monro has been criticised for deciding too quickly and for not going beyond the beaches. Churchill wrote: 'He came, he saw, he capitulated.' It is a cracking line – and unjust. Kitchener was pushing Monro to decide. An experienced general didn't need to go much beyond the beaches to understand what would happen when the winter rains and the German guns came. All one had to do was stand on the beach, close one's eyes, and see the Allies, bedraggled and water-logged, being blown off the peninsula.

Monro must have known his advice would upset Kitchener, and it did. Kitchener was clutching at Keyes' half-baked scheme to force the straits again. Kitchener asked whether Monro's corps commanders were also for evacuation. Davies at Helles and Byng at Suvla said they were for leaving; Birdwood was against. He agreed it was just about impossible to break out of the present positions. He was worried about the likely loss of British prestige in the Islamic world and the risks of taking men off in bad weather. Monro cabled these views to Kitchener, plus his own estimate of losses in an evacuation. Monro thought 40 per cent of the men might be lost.

Kitchener didn't like this either. Keyes' scheme teased him, but there was now a rider that rendered it absurd.

Balfour, the First Lord of the Admiralty, said the Admiralty probably would support the scheme 'if the army meant business'. How could the army mean business? Monro had just reported it incapable of an offensive beyond 24 hours. Keyes felt the navy had let the army down since the sea battle of March 18. He was right, but it was too late to make amends now.

The strategic conduct of the war had now been put in the hands of a War Committee made up of three to five members of Cabinet. Churchill was excluded. This new body met on November 3 and decided it could not yet accept Monro's advice. Kitchener should go to the Dardanelles to see for himself. In truth the Prime Minister and others wanted to get Kitchener away.

Kitchener was rattled, so badly that he showed Birdwood a small corner of his soul. He sent him a cable that began: 'Most secret. Decipher yourself. Tell no-one . . .' He told Birdwood, who was acting as commander-in-chief while Monro was away, that he was leaving for the Dardanelles. The Admiralty, Kitchener said, would probably agree to a fresh attempt to force the straits. The army had to help. Birdwood was to examine the best place for a new landing near Bulair. To find the troops for this landing, Birdwood was to run down the garrisons at Anzac and Helles and, if necessary, evacuate Suvla. Birdwood would be in command.

We must do it right this time. I absolutely refuse to sign order for evacuation, which I think would be greatest disaster and would condemn a large percentage of our men to death or imprisonment. Monro will be appointed to command the Salonika force.

A War Office cable followed saying that Birdwood was

now the commander of the Mediterranean Expeditionary Force.

Here was Kitchener, master of expedients. Monro had given the wrong advice, so he was being sent away. Kitchener had a new scheme to take the peninsula. He had just thought it up himself. Birdwood, like Hamilton before him, could work out the details and carry it out. Kitchener had also put Birdwood in an awkward position: Monro, his commander-in-chief, was away. None of this mattered. He was Kitchener of Khartoum; he could do these things.

Birdwood was appalled. He told Kitchener an attempt to land at Bulair would be disastrous. He said Monro should remain in command. 'He has already established confidence in those who have seen him, and his experience in France, which I lack, will be absolutely invaluable. He will, I know, carry out any orders of the Government better than I can.' Birdwood suppressed the order that promoted him to commander-in-chief.

On the same day Kitchener sent Birdwood a fresh cable. 'I fear the navy may not play up,' he said. 'The more I look at the problem the less I see my way through, so you had better very quietly and very secretly work out any scheme for getting the troops off.'

On the morning of November 4, Birdwood was to attack Bulair; in the evening, he was to work out a plan to evacuate. To make everything worse for him, two peers had stood up in the House of Lords and asked whether the Government was considering abandoning the peninsula. The Germans and Turks thought the incident so bizarre that they assumed it had to be a trick. Monro learnt of his 'punishment' from Maxwell in Cairo. Before going to Salonika, Monro would see Kitchener at the Dardanelles.

*　*　*

Kitchener arrived, set himself up on the battleship *Lord Nelson*, went ashore and discovered what everyone does when they walk around the Allied beachheads. They aren't the way they seem on the maps. 'The country,' Kitchener cabled to Asquith on November 15, 'is much more difficult than I imagined, and the Turkish positions . . . are natural fortresses which, if not taken by surprise at first, could be held against very serious attack by larger forces than have been engaged.' Or, to put it another way, while sitting in London for the previous six months and dashing off instructions as the whim struck, the Minister of War hadn't known what he was talking about. 'To gain what we hold,' he told Asquith, 'has been a most remarkable feat of arms . . . Everyone has done wonders . . .' On his return from Anzac, Kitchener noticed Guy Dawnay, whom he had last seen in London. 'Young man, you were right,' he said.

Kitchener came ashore at Anzac on the afternoon of November 13, hulking and red-checked, carrying a walking stick and wearing a brilliant red band on his cap. The senior officers knew he was coming and had tidied up their uniforms and put on Sam Browne belts; the troops didn't know Kitchener was coming and as usual were wearing torn shorts and dirty singlets. When they saw him on the end of the pier, just about the best-known face in the British empire after King George, they left their dugouts and ran to the beach and cheered him. No officer led them; it just happened. Kitchener told them: 'The King asked me to tell you how splendidly he thinks you have done – you have done splendidly, better even than I thought you would.' Bean was there.

The men would not have cheered many men – they would never have cheered Ian Hamilton like it, for all his kindness and gentle manners. K. is the sort of man every Australian admires – not a polished man but a determined one, an uncompromising worker. These men honestly admire him far more than the British do; the British really admire a man who has more display about him, but these men honestly and quite sincerely like the absence of display . . . K. received a welcome which I doubt whether he knows the value. There are not many men that Australians would honour in that way.

Bean wrote that in his diary, probably the same night. The incident seems strange, child-like even, to us now: these men with big hearts, haggard and wasted by dysentery, coming to cheer the man whose block-headedness had led them to this dusty shore, this dead-end, these holes in the ground. But neither they nor Bean knew of Kitchener's part in their downfall. It would be decades before Kitchener's public reputation began to crumble.

Kitchener climbed Walker's Ridge on a long stride, winding the portly Maxwell, and walked along trenches 30 yards from the Turks, his red cap bobbing just below the parapet. The men at the firing line cheered him, which must have made the Turks ask themselves what was going on and whether they should throw a couple of bombs, just in case. According to Bean, Birdwood and White were so worried about Kitchener's safety that they could barely speak.

Kitchener didn't recommend evacuation in his cable to Asquith on November 15. He didn't recommend staying either. He had embraced a half-thought-out scheme for a new landing in southern Turkey near Alexandretta. This was meant to save face: the British would leave Gallipoli only to land at Ayas Bay. Monro's staff, particularly

Dawnay, promoted the Ayas Bay plan on the basis that it would never happen but that the prospect might make Kitchener, Birdwood and Maxwell feel easier about leaving Gallipoli. The ruse worked. Monro, though suffering from a broken ankle from a boating accident, was making the running. Kitchener had now decided Monro was a bright chap. He intended to place him in command of all the Mediterranean forces outside Egypt. Birdwood would command at Gallipoli.

These were crazy times. Kitchener bent this way and that and became 'fidgety' as he awaited Asquith's reply to his telegram of November 15. Monro didn't bend at all; he, not Kitchener, was the strong man out here. Birdwood still wanted to stay. Davies now thought he could hold on at Helles. Keyes still wanted to force the straits, Wemyss wanted to stay and de Robeck still didn't want to risk a single ship. It was much the same in London. Asquith, Lloyd George and Bonar Law wanted to go; others, notably Lord Curzon, the former viceroy of India, wanted to stay, and others didn't know what they wanted. Hankey argued to stay; he wanted the four divisions at Salonika sent to Gallipoli. Others thought Salonika more important than Gallipoli. Churchill said he 'knew too much and felt too keenly to be able to accept Cabinet responsibility for what I believed to be a wholly erroneous conception of war'. He left the Government to serve with the Grenadier Guards in France.

Cabinet eventually told Kitchener that the Ayas Bay scheme was out and that he had to say whether he was for or against an evacuation without face-saving schemes. Kitchener was on the slide: he used to tell Cabinet what to do.

Kitchener on November 22 recommended the evacuation of Anzac and Suvla and the retention of Helles 'at all events for the present'. Asquith cabled back that the War Committee wanted a complete evacuation, Helles too. Cabinet had to confirm this.

The big storm came to Gallipoli on November 27 and lasted three days. The seas were so wild no vessel could approach the battlefields. Forked lightning blazed and the sky rumbled and roared. First came the hail, followed by 24 hours of pelting rain. Then a hurricane began to blow from the north. Heavy snow began to fall. It was the worst blizzard on the peninsula for 40 years. Any blizzard on the peninsula is fearsome because there is nowhere to hide. Suddenly you understand why the scrub never grows much higher than eight feet, why the pine trees are so small and twisted.

Only one man died from exposure at Anzac, although there were hundreds of cases of frostbite. It was the first snow many Australians had seen. They threw snowballs to keep warm and enjoyed an extra ration of rum. A lieutenant, newly arrived, wrote in his diary: 'It is actually snowing this morning. The first I have ever seen – it looks beautiful and covers over so many things which are not.'

The water poured out of the hills at Suvla and turned the trenches into surging creeks. Dead Turks and pack horses came bobbing into the British trenches. Turks and Englishmen forgot about the war and climbed out of their trenches in full view of each other. Nature was more terrifying than bullets; the rifles probably wouldn't have fired anyway. When the snow came, both sides lit fires in the open and huddled around them until their faces became black from smoke. Men were found frozen to death on the firesteps. More than 200 died at Suvla, drowned or frozen; another 5000 came down with frostbite. If there was going to be an evacuation, it had to be done quickly.

Cabinet was wavering. Wemyss and Keyes were still urging the Admiralty to rush the straits. Curzon had written a strong memorandum against leaving. He made the nice point that, apart from Monro, the other army commanders changed their minds so often there was really no consensus. He envisioned the leaving as a Biblical calamity.

> . . . a disorganised crowd will press in despairing tumult on to the shore and into the boats. Shells will be falling and bullets ploughing their way into this mass of retreating humanity . . . Conceive the crowding into the boats of thousands of half-crazy men, the swamping of craft, the nocturnal panic, the agony of the wounded, the hecatombs of slain.

Salonika was going badly; Kitchener thought the four divisions there could go to Gallipoli. Kitchener was for staying again; he wanted to attack at Suvla. Monro held firm for going. Kitchener asked for the views of Birdwood and Byng. Neither could recommend Kitchener's new plan.

How different it was to March. Back then Kitchener issued a fiat and Hamilton and an army rushed to the Aegean to do whatever Kitchener decided they would do. There was hardly any planning and other Cabinet ministers were not consulted. They didn't want to be: Kitchener knew about these things. Now, seven months later, everyone demanded to be consulted, everyone had a view. Kitchener wasn't the final answer. He might not even last too long as War Minister.

But a decision had to be made quickly because of the weather. On December 7 Cabinet decided to evacuate Anzac and Suvla. Helles was to be held for now. Helles was the face-saver. All Monro had to do was get two corps off two beachheads while the Turks watched.

32

Goodbye to all that

The Turks threw a note into the Australian lines at Lone Pine one day in November. The note read: 'We can't advance; you can't advance. What are you going to do?' It was a loaded question: the Turks had received new howitzers. They had also received fresh ammunition: now all their shells were going off. The road to Berlin through Bulgaria was opening up. In mid-November the Turks set up a battery of four Austrian howitzers above Suvla. Late in the month howitzer shells screamed into the Australian frontline, mostly around Lone Pine. This was a new side to the war, as Bean said, a 'modern' bombardment. The Australian trenches, narrow and shallow, had stood up to Turkish field guns well enough, particularly when the Turks were only firing shrapnel. The howitzers, with their lobbing angle of fire and explosive warheads, wrecked trenches, smothered men and blocked communications saps.

Sergeant Pinnock, of the 8th Light Horse, wrote home: 'My God, I cannot imagine how those poor unfortunates in France ever stuck it. Where they dropped and exploded a hole was left as big as your drawing room, the explosion was simply fearful.'

It was time to go. As the Turkish note had said, the Australians couldn't advance. Migrating birds were flying over the peninsula every day now. When the true winter came the Allied troops at Anzac and Suvla would start to die from cold and exposure, if they didn't drown first. Now there were these howitzers and this new German ammunition that went off every time.

It was time to go because the Turks were making it easier to do so. Their frontline troops seemed half-hearted. They too were worn out and cold; they too had watched thousands of the their comrades run to their death in frontal assaults. As their note said, they knew it was a stalemate. Kemal was ill with malaria and exhaustion. Just as he was convinced in June that the Allies would go for the Sari Bair heights, he now believed they were preparing to leave. Time to attack, he told his superiors. Time to destroy the invaders before they got away. 'We have no forces, not even a single soldier, to waste,' he was told. Kemal felt there was nothing more for him to do. He left for Constantinople in early December to get well again and spend his arrears of back pay. Kemal liked to drink and talk; he had no interest in money except for the things it could buy, particularly *raki* and books.

Von Sanders said he thought the conflict was in stalemate too. It was an agreeable stalemate because he owned all the good ground. Now that the road was open to Berlin he didn't believe the Allies could advance even if they were reinforced. 'We of course knew nothing of the intended withdrawal and did not learn of it up until the last minute,' he wrote. One finds the first part of this hard to believe. Von Sanders' frontline troops certainly suspected a withdrawal. Lieutenant Mehmed Fasih, near Lone Pine, wrote in his diary on November 27 that he had just received a 15-day-old Turkish newspaper. 'It contains very good news. The English are definitely withdrawing from the Dardanelles . . . It is in fact confirmed by the results of our probes.' On the same day he records that Turkish troops are reluctant to attack. The lieutenant's diary, written in Ottoman script, has only recently been published in English. Two days before the entries above, Fasih wrote that Turkish officers were 'amazed' at how passive the enemy had become. It seems probable that the Turkish frontline troops believed the Allies were, at the least, winding down their offensive as well as doing some curious things. Maybe the Turks felt there was no point playing at heroics with an enemy who was on his way home.

Other things were working for the Allies. God smiled on the expedition now that it was packing up. The weather settled down. The sea was like glass again. The nights lasted 12 hours and mists and fog rolled in before dawn and this mattered because all the men had to come off in the dark. Now that Birdwood had taken over Hamilton's command, the cold-eyed Godley had been confirmed as commander of the Anzac Corps, despite having demonstrated over the previous seven months that he was spectacularly unfit for such a post. This was as good a reason to go as any.

Birdwood had to get 80,000 troops off two battlefields. He had to do it at night. He had to do it so well that each day when the sun came up everything looked the same as it had the day before. He had to get off 200 guns, 2000 vehicles, more than 5000 horses and mules and great piles of stores. He had to keep the evacuation a secret among his rank-and-file until as late as possible. At the very end he had to get men away from positions that were 20 yards from the Turkish lines. If the seas turned rough and the ships could not get in, there was nothing he could do. He now knew how Moses felt as he approached the Red Sea. All through there was the fear that if the scheme was discovered, it could end up the way Lord Curzon had predicted, with thousands of men slaughtered on the beaches. In one respect Anzac was riskier than Suvla. If the Turks suspected something and broke through strongly at Russell's Top, they could shoot down into the beach north of Anzac Cove.

Monro, however, had done things that made planning easier. He had asked for schemes for the evacuation long before Cabinet sanctioned it. He had brought his general staff and administrative staff together, as Hamilton should have done. He had put Aspinall and Brudenell White in charge of planning. Both were good at this sort of thing and there was no Braithwaite to fuss around them. Birdwood visited Anzac most days and suggested modifications to the plans. This distinguished him from Hamilton. Hamilton had left detail for others.

The plan was for withdrawal by stages. Half the men would be off by December 18, leaving a garrison of about 20,000 at each beachhead. These garrisons would come off on the nights of December 18 and 19. The Turks had to be convinced that things were normal, even though they weren't. They had to be made used to silence. White devised the 'silent stunt' carried out at Anzac over three days from November 24. The Anzacs stopped shooting and stayed quiet for three days. Private Donald Lechte of the 2nd Australian Division in 1973 told his daughters what happened:

> . . . every man was to stay as much as possible in his dugout . . . no rifles were to be fired nor any noise made day or night; no tins or dixies were to be thrown about to

make the least noise. On the third day an aeroplane from the Turks flew over on our side & flew up & down low down trying to observe why the sudden quietness; everybody was ordered to stay in their dugouts & not look up so that they wouldn't see a sea of white faces looking at them . . . that night we were all called out to maintain the front trenches & be prepared for the Turks to come over & see if we were gone or still there; sure enough about 4 am we saw a few men in no-man's land & we waited until quite a number showed up; we had been instructed not to fire any shots till told to, so we waited for a while & somebody got excited or nervous & opened fire; then, of course, everybody opened fire, and that was that. The Turks, of course, realised they had been tricked.

Lechte said the troops were not told the reason for the stunt. They were told they were leaving two weeks later. Monash was told on December 12.

It is of course an absolutely critical scheme, which may come off quite successfully, or may end in a frightful disaster . . . I need not say I feel very unhappy . . . I am almost frightened to contemplate the howl of rage and disappointment there will be when the men find out what is afoot, and how they have been fooled. And I am wondering what Australia will think at the desertion of her 6000 dead, and her 20,000 other casualties.

It was important to keep the fact of the evacuation from the men as long as possible. Stories were put about that the garrisons were being thinned out for winter, but rumours flew along the trenches. As early as November 30 a staff officer from GHQ, who himself knew nothing officially, stopped to talk to an Irish soldier at Suvla.

'You fellows had a bad time in the blizzard,' the officer said.

'We had indeed, sir,' the soldier replied, 'but this grand news about evacuation is putting new life into us!'

The weather held and the Turks stayed quiescent. Each night the ships came in and the men and stores went off. Each morning the beaches looked normal as the mists blew away. By the morning of December 18 half the men had been taken off at the two fronts. Now the last 40,000 had to be got off over the next two nights. Trench floors were broken up with picks so that footfalls would not be heard. Self-firing rifles were set up at Anzac. A kerosene oil tin was filled with water. Underneath it was an empty tin with a string attached to the rifle trigger. On the night of December 19–20 holes would be punched in the bottom of the upper tin. After about 20 minutes the lower tin would fill with water, over-balance and fire the rifle. Men were told to stand about smoking and yarning within sight of the Turkish observers on Gaba Tepe.

Bean left on the night of December 17 after smashing his home-made furniture and ripping his waterproof sheets with a knife. 'Somehow I don't like to think of that furniture as a curiosity in some Turkish officer's home,' he scribbled in his diary. That day he had watched the light horsemen play cricket on Shell Green in another display of 'normalcy'. A photograph shows a batsman driving hard off the front foot, the spirit if not quite the elegance of Victor Trumper – while three puffy clouds of shrapnel burst overhead. Bean found himself on the *Grafton*, which would stay until the evacuation was complete. The captain turned out to be a son of W. G. Grace, England's fabled cricketer. Next day Bean wrote in his diary: 'So I have left old Anzac. In a way I was really fond of the place.'

On the night of the 18th another 20,000 men left Suvla and Anzac on a sea 'as smooth as unruffled silk'. Those remaining became tense. The Turks could now break through the lines. Anzac seemed so deserted. Some visited the graves of their mates and tidied up around the crooked crosses they would never see again. Birdwood came ashore on the last morning and his thoughts must have been confused. He knew he had to go; he knew this had been a military failure. But he also knew something that those who had not been here could never understand. There *had* been a triumph here. It was simply that the Australians and New Zealanders he liked so well had held on to this forlorn bit of dirt for so long and with such good humour. That was why the place, this beach just about deserted, wriggled into your heart and wouldn't go away. The hanging on: *that was the thing*. Birdwood met a soldier who pointed to a cemetery. 'I hope *they* won't hear us marching back to the beach,' the soldier said.

After 11 pm less than 2000 men were holding the entire Anzac line. Sergeant Pinnock was still there, freezing and cursing the moonlight because it allowed him to imagine too much.

> . . . you imagined wherever you fixed your eyes for a minute you saw a Turk. Unfortunately I was in an exposed position, pretty close up, and had instructions not to fire unless I was certain a Turk was there. My God, I would have given anything in the world to have been able to open up and let go a hundred or so rounds just to ease my nerves . . . I never in all my life thought that imagination could carry one so far.

At 2.15 am Pinnock received the order to move out. Trails of salt and flour had been laid to mark the way to the beach and shaded candles spluttered in biscuit boxes. Blankets and bags had been laid to deaden the noise. The troops pulled barbed wire across the paths behind them. They lit fuses that an hour later would set off a charge to wreck a sap or a tunnel. The leaving had precision the way the landing had panic.

Pinnock said not a word was spoken in the 20 minutes it took the men to reach the beach. One boat was waiting for them. They waited in it for three minutes while staff officers tossed to decide who would be the last to leave. Once on the ship, Pinnock bribed a steward to get a bath. He got rid of his lice and clothes by throwing them through the porthole.

The 24th Battalion of the 2nd Australian Division was at Lone Pine. The evacuation was going so well the men were ordered out 20 minutes early at 2.40 am. According to the battalion's official history, the officers took a last look along the line. A lieutenant saw a figure crouching over the parapet. He pointed his revolver at him and challenged him quietly. It was one of his own men 'having just one more pot at them'. Then the officer heard the sound of bombs exploding. He found a lone Australian trying out the new Mills bomb grenades, which had only just arrived and were rationed because they cost the fabulous sum of 17 shillings and sixpence each. 'It's a pity not to use them,' the lone bomber explained, 'they're great.'

Another officer saw two Turkish scouts emerging from a tunnel. With a sergeant he prepared to ambush them. 'A bonzer night,' said one of the 'Turks'. 'It'll be a pity to leave the old joint.' The two Australians had lost their way in the trenches and were sauntering towards the beach, unaware they had 20 minutes to catch the last boat. Some of the men were so tired from two nights without sleep that they fell down exhausted. There was nothing to do but to kick and prod them to keep them moving. The men passed a cemetery and the crosses stood out in the bright moonlight. As the men reached the beach engineers fired a huge pile of explosives planted in tunnels under the Turkish frontline at the Nek.

The explosion was so tremendous a tremor ran through the sand on the beach. Bean, on the *Grafton*, saw a brilliant red glare reflected on the under-surface of two clouds of dust and smoke. The Turks opened fire with rifles and machine guns. They thought this was the start of an attack. The mines at the Nek killed 70 Turks, probably wounded hundreds more, left two great craters and rattled the bones of the light horsemen lying in the open after the four charges of August 7. The Turks felt wronged when they later discovered that these mines had been fired when the evacuation was almost over. They thought this ungracious. Many present-day Turkish historians take the same view.

Monash watched the Nek go up from a transport ship.

. . . a couple of hundred Turks must have gone up in the air, but nothing could be seen except a volcano of dust. Instantly a most terrific tornado of rifle and machine gun fire burst forth along the whole length of Sari Bair . . . Thus, dramatically, with the bullets . . . whistling harmlessly overhead, we drew off in the light of the full moon, mercifully screened by a thin mist – and so ended the story of the Anzacs on Gallipoli . . . It [the evacuation] was a most brilliant conception, brilliantly organised, and brilliantly executed – and will, I am sure, rank as the greatest joke in the whole range of military history.

Joke? It was certainly a masterpiece. At 4.10 am it was

complete. An hour later the Turks were still shooting at ghosts. There had been two casualties: one man wounded early in the evening, another hit in the arm by a spent bullet as he left the beach.

Godley left a letter for the Turkish commander asking him to preserve the Anzac graves. He said he felt sure the Turks would do this; they had behaved 'most honourably' during the fighting. Australian soldiers left their own notes. One said: 'You didn't push us off, Jacko, we just left.' A light horseman set up a table for four. There was jam, bully beef, biscuits and cheese. And a note: 'There are no booby traps in this dug-out.' It was almost true. He had added black powder from cartridges to the packet of tobacco he left behind. Many left meals for the Turks. Von Sanders misunderstood this. He thought it was evidence of how abruptly the Anzacs had been ordered away.

The evacuation had gone just as well at Suvla. It was a good place to leave. It was a byword for ineptitude; it had no folklore, except as a killing ground for generals. Stopford, Hammersley, Braithwaite and Hamilton all metaphorically died here, caught loitering without intent.

The last troops left at 5 am. The supply depot was soaked with petrol and fired on the beach. Commander Edward Unwin, the hero of *River Clyde*, was the Naval Transport Officer for the withdrawal. He was the last to leave as the blazing stores sent sparks high above the beach. A soldier fell overboard and began to flounder as one of the lighters approached a transport. Unwin dived in and saved him. This meant there had not been a single casualty at Suvla.

The war went on at Helles. The day after the northern battlefields were abandoned, Joseph Murray of the RND was sapping near Gully Ravine. When he emerged from the tunnel, the troops on the frontline told him the Turks were crawling forward to attack. Suddenly hundreds of Turks ran forward. The Dubliners went over the parapet to meet them with bayonets. The Turks and the Irishmen fought in no-man's land for an hour. Then Murray realised it was over except for a personal bayonet fight between a Dublin and a Turk.

First the Dublin had a slight advantage, then clever foot-work gave the advantage to the Turk. Both bayonets were pointing to the sky, then pointing to the ground. Advantage to the Irishman; the Turk pushed him away; both thrust, both parried – and so it continued until both men sank to their knees, absolutely exhausted. They faced each other, gasping for breath, with determination on their faces but no sign of anger. After a few moments we moved forward to collect our man and the Turks did likewise. We were within arm's length of each other but no-one spoke . . . Both parties turned and walked slowly away to their respective trenches. Not a shot was fired from either line . . . As we assisted our lad over the parapet, the boys gave a resounding cheer for the safe return of their conquering hero. I am certain I heard a similar cheer from the Turkish line.

The 29th Division, one would have thought, had done enough in the Gallipoli campaign. It had been mauled in the landings at V and W beaches, then patched up and hurled time and again at Krithia. Its soldiers had died copiously in the greatest hellhole of all Gallipoli: Gully Ravine. The division had been taken to Suvla and thrown at Scimitar Hill, then left out in the blizzard. It had been evacuated from Suvla, leaving behind another 2500 of its dead. When the 29th left Egypt for the Helles landings, it had been 17,000 strong. Now, after Suvla, it had taken 34,000 casualties, including more than 9000 killed or missing. In arithmetic terms the division had been wiped out twice. Its 86th Brigade reached Mudros from Suvla less than 1400 strong – the size of one-and-a-half battalions – and with only four regular officers who had lost everything in the Suvla flood except the clothes they wore. But the division was bigger than mere arithmetic; it was cobbled together again and again, and its spirit soldiered on. Now, in mid-December, it was being sent back to Helles to plug another hole and suffer again. The 29th had to go because the French were leaving Helles, regardless of what the British did. Monro wanted to take the British off too, but he didn't yet have Cabinet approval. Then, on December 28, it came.

Curious things were happening at Helles. The four British divisions there should have been under fierce pressure from the Turks, who could now throw all their artillery, all their troops, at one place. It was said that the British had finally established a 'moral ascendancy' over the Turks. This may have been so: the Turks had always been better defending than attacking. It may also have been that the Turks in the frontline thought that the urgency had gone out of their war. Even if these Englishmen stayed, they were not going to capture the Narrows, let alone Constantinople.

Until December 13 Wemyss and Keyes still thought the Narrows could be forced and a great victory won. As usual there was a catch: the Helles troops had to take Achi Baba first. Once the hill was taken the navy could attack the Narrows with 'every hope of success'. Fortunately the scheme was turned down. Monro knew Achi Baba couldn't be taken, not before and not now. And there was another flaw that would only be discovered when the

Great War ended. Achi Baba didn't command the Kilitbahir forts; it was not the 'key' to the peninsula. Which leads to another retrospective judgement. Helles had perhaps never been a good place to land. It was too far from the forts, not in miles but in terms of the hills and gorges and plateaus that had to be taken first.

Von Sanders wanted to throw the British off. He was bringing up another eight divisions to do so. Yet he admits seeing a clue that the British were leaving. Turkish troops on the Asian side of the straits had observed British guns being taken off.

The ruses of Anzac and Suvla were now employed at Helles. The artillery kept firing, no tents were struck, self-firing rifles were set up, troops were paraded at places where Turkish observers could see them, horses plodded up and down the bog that was Gully Ravine. And each night the boats took men off. By the morning of January 7 the garrison had been reduced from 35,000 to 19,000.

That day von Sanders attacked. It was a preliminary to the big assault he was planning; he wanted first to straighten out the Turkish line on Gully Spur. The Turkish artillery barrage was perhaps the heaviest ever seen at Helles. British warships returned the fire. Saving ammunition didn't matter now. The cruiser *Edgar* let fly with 1000 six-inch shells and the destroyer *Wolverine* fired every round she carried. Hundreds of bayonets wavered above the Turkish trenches, but in most places the infantry attack never came. Turkish officers could be seen trying to urge men forward. The men refused to move everywhere except near Fusilier Bluff. The attack petered out after 5 pm. That night another 2300 British troops left. The garrison was below 17,000. They all had to come off on the next night.

Five hundred mules that could not be embarked were

shot, to the distress of the troops. Bad weather looked to be on the way but the navy decided to go ahead. Battleships, a cruiser, six destroyers, cross-Channel steamboats, a cargo boat, two hospital ships, a dozen or so lighters and strings of cutters approached the beaches for the last time. By 9 pm the wind was gusting at 35 miles an hour and waves thumped into the trembling piers. There was the prospect of disaster and yet the storm was also working for the British. The Turks wouldn't expect them to leave on a night like this.

As the last men embarked and the seas continued to rise, dashing the last boats against the piers, fuses were lit to blow the main magazine and piles of stores were set alight on the beach. General Maude, commander of the 13th Division, was missing. He had gone back to Gully Beach to pick up his valise. The general turned up after 3.30 am, his valise and bedding role bumping along on a wheeled stretcher. The last boat left at 3.45. When it was 100 yards offshore the main magazine blew, as someone said, 'like St Paul's Cathedral being fired out of a howitzer'. The Turks now realised what had happened. It was too late. The adventure was over.

Joe Murray left on the last night. He had three miles to walk to the beach, his boots wrapped in sandbags. He couldn't believe he was leaving. He expected any moment to be told to about-turn. When the column halted at control posts, he fell asleep. The whole column was walking in a stupor. Murray approached V Beach. No-one spoke.

> We were all living in the past. The future did not exist any more – it was so very far away and the past so near, so fresh in our minds. I imagined all my pals were with me as

they had been on the day we landed. We had been a motley crowd, full of hope then and anxious to do our best for Britain. Our colonel had told us the eyes of the world would be upon us. The eyes of the Turks certainly were but the rest of the world forgot us.

At midnight Murray made for the pier near the *River Clyde* and boarded an iron lighter. It was so crowded that some men fainted but could not fall. Others threw up and some fell asleep.

Perhaps as the years roll by we will be remembered as the expedition that was betrayed by jealousy, spite, indecision and treachery. The Turks did not beat us – we were beaten by our own High Command!

Soldiers always say that. This time it was probably true.

33

A terrible beauty

Gallipoli, the war that got away from its handlers, is a tale of all that is fine and all that is foolish in the human condition. If it made more sense, it would be a lesser story. The tale is mostly about frailty. This, along with the beauty of its setting, helps explain why it lingers in the imagination after larger and more important wars are forgotten. Tragedies have more layers than epics and Gallipoli has somehow become bigger than the sum of its facts.

We should not try to bring too much order to it, beyond noting three obvious things about the British strategy, if indeed that is the right noun. Churchill, Kitchener and Hamilton never had the means to reach their end: they were always about five divisions and a couple of hundred heavy guns short. Second, the political resolve in London was never strong enough. And, third, Gallipoli was always an adventure and never a scheme. John Lee, Hamilton's biographer, probably got it right when he wrote that 'we do not need to hunt out individuals to blame, but rather see a failure of the British political and military system to cope with the demands of a mass, industrialised warfare with which it was wholly unfamiliar'.

Kitchener would nevertheless have been hunted out had he lived. Gallipoli exposed him as something short of the genius for war that he was supposed to be. He had failed to live up to the promise he had never shown. Cabinet was tired of him. He didn't pass on information; he made up policy as he went along like a man delivering an endless off-the-cuff speech; he wanted to be commander-in-chief and a Cabinet minister at the same time. He could not last as War Minister, but there was a problem: how did one get rid of a public idol?

The problem solved itself in June, 1916. Kitchener sailed for Russia on an official visit. The cruiser *Hampshire* struck a mine off the Orkneys. Kitchener drowned and a pall fell over the nation. To the people of the empire he had been the rallying point: he *knew* about war; he was going to get us through. Alistair Cooke, the celebrated journalist and broadcaster who grew up in Manchester, recalled hearing as a child the news from his mother that Kitchener was dead. 'It was one of those typical days when the sun slants through the coal dust after heavy rain. We walked home hand in hand, and I thought the bottom had dropped out of our world.' Now there was a new problem. The Dardanelles campaign had left Kitchener with a case to answer, but his name could not be sullied now that he had found martyrdom in the North Sea.

There had to be inquests, however. The press was querulous and the public sniffed scandal. The British surrender to the Turks at Kut-al-Amara in Iraq in 1916 made everything worse. Some of the Gallipoli players, notably Churchill, wanted state papers published in the belief that these would repair their reputations. Others wanted to undermine Asquith; the Gallipoli campaign had damaged him as much as it had Kitchener. And there was the matter of casualties. Casualties always look worse when they belong to a defeat.

We cannot be sure of all the figures even today. About one million men from both sides served at Gallipoli and between one-third and one-half of them became casualties. The Turks put their losses at 251,309, including 86,692 dead. This suggests a degree of precision; everything else suggests the Turks were not counting that carefully. The French weren't counting carefully either and admitted it with round figures: 27,000 casualties, 10,000 of them dead. British losses came out at 73,485, including 21,255 dead. The Australians lost 8709 dead and 19,441 wounded. The New Zealand figures were frightful: of the 8556 who served at Gallipoli, 2701 died and 4752 were wounded (the latter figure includes those wounded more than once). In all, the Allied casualties were worse than 140,000. This was a modest figure by the standards of the stalemate in France; it was a very bad figure for a defeat.

The Asquith Government in 1916 ordered commissions of inquiry into the defeats at Gallipoli and Kut, mainly to give the impression that it was responding to public disquiet and also to avoid publishing state papers. Australia, even though it now sensed Gallipoli had been mismanaged, didn't want an inquiry; the *Age* and the *Argus* condemned it before it began. There was concern that the empire might be harmed if Kitchener and Churchill were seen to have blundered. Australia seemed to be saying that she didn't mind making sacrifices for the empire, even if those directing the war in London weren't too bright. Besides, the Anzac legend had taken hold. Australia didn't want officialdom spoiling the poetry. New Zealand was more inclined to criticise the imperial authorities.

Godley sent Hamilton a copy of his written statement to the inquiry. 'I have tried to say as little as possible,' he explained, ever the good clubman. A lawyer told Hamilton that his best defence was to attack Kitchener. Ever chivalrous, Hamilton refused to do so. The interim report of the inquiry came out in March, 1917. It covered events up until five days after the failed naval attack. Its criticisms were muted and smudged by the passive voice. Kitchener did not use the Imperial General Staff as he might have, 'with the result that more work was undertaken by him than was possible for one man to do, and confusion and want of efficiency resulted'. Asquith, Churchill and the War Council should have sought more advice from naval experts. Asquith (he had now been replaced by Lloyd George as Prime Minister) should have called a meeting of the War Council between March 19 and May 14, when the nature of the Dardanelles commitment changed utterly. The commissioners concluded with an each-way bet. The expedition had not succeeded but 'certain important political advantages' had been secured. The Northcliffe press asked when Asquith's 'old gang' would be prosecuted. *The Times* called Churchill a 'dangerous enthusiast'. Australian reaction was softer.

Now the inquiry turned to the land campaign and called 170 witnesses. The final report came out in 1919. The censures were again polite and vague, rather like the final orders for the Suvla landing, and the players could often interpret the words to mean what they wanted them to mean. Hamilton thought he came out well. The commissioners, in effect, said that Hamilton's task was made harder because the authorities in London had not understood the nature of the conflict. Hamilton had regarded Kitchener as a commander-in-chief rather than as a Cabinet minister. Hamilton should have 'examined the situation as disclosed by the first landings in a more critical spirit'; he should have analysed the chances of success more rigorously and told Kitchener what he thought. The commissioners thought the difficulties of the operation had been underestimated, as had the fighting spirit of the Turks. The enterprise could only have worked if the Government had diverted more men and guns from the western front. The plan for the August offensive was impractical (there was no mention of the charges at the Nek). Stopford received a gentle reprimand.

Australia saw the Anzac landing as a piece of nation-building. Here was proof that the 14-year-old Commonwealth was more than an appendage of Britain. Australia had stepped out into the world for the first time in 1915 and afterwards people were inclined to cheer. The Australians and New Zealanders had not won, but they had hung on when they had no right to. They had fought as well as any 'British' troops and in the grottoes of Lone Pine and on Chunuk Bair they had done things that were imperishable. The Anzacs went on to fight on the western front (as did the 29th Division and the RND) and in Palestine, and they were better troops again in those places because of what they had learnt at Gallipoli. Innocence had been among the Anzac casualties at Gallipoli. If one was going to fight the Great War out to its finish, innocence was a good thing to be rid of. Gallipoli certainly gave Australia a sense of the worth of its people; whether it was the nation-building experience it could have been is less certain.

Gallipoli should have been a revelation. It should have told Australians that the British empire wasn't quite the flawless instrument they thought it was, that it was possible for Australia to build a civilisation of its own that borrowed heavily from Britain but also cherished values that, like those of the Americans, were homespun. But in the nineteen-twenties Australia (and New Zealand, for that matter) lapsed back into her old ways as a self-governing colony. Australia looked back to Gallipoli, which was proper, but didn't much look forward to what she might do as an independent nation. The fall of Singapore in 1942 proved that the imperial planners still knew how to make a big mistake and that, as in 1915, Churchill didn't care too much about Australia and New Zealand. Singapore was a bigger turning point for Australia than Gallipoli, but it is not so well remembered. Only when the Second World War ended and the Cold War began, when the British empire was seen to be breaking apart and European migrants began pouring into Australia – only then did Australia start to take on an identity of its own. The British society in the south seas finally became the Australian society. There was still an imperial city across the seas but now it was called Hollywood.

The war was hard on the next generation of Australians. Men came home morose and bitter and sometimes violent, everything made worse because they couldn't explain what made them that way; they had demons but the demons didn't have names. The historian Bill Gammage in 1994 spoke of 'dreams abandoned, lives without purpose, women without husbands, families without family life, one long national funeral for a generation and more after 1918'. The great-grandchildren of the men of Gallipoli didn't have to endure all that; they can see the campaign with a gentler eye.

Gallipoli has become Australia's Homeric tale. There is now more interest in the campaign than there was half a century ago. Alan Moorehead wrote in 1956 that hardly anyone visited the Gallipoli cemeteries. Even as late as 1984 the dawn service at Ari Burnu attracted only 300 people. In 2000 the crowd topped 15,000 and a new site for the service had to be built at North Beach. The end of the Cold War has brought a change in perceptions. Gallipoli is no longer linked, as it was for decades, to the military causes of the day. Finally it stands alone.

There is such a thing as the Anzac spirit or tradition, although no-one can define it neatly. It is compounded of many ideas: refusing to give up no matter how hopeless the cause, dry humour and irreverence, mateship, fatalism, stoicism and more again. Sometimes the spirit is misappropriated. The Australian yacht was trailing by three races to one in the America's Cup of 1983. Alan Bond, leader of the Australian syndicate, still thought victory possible. He made reference to Gallipoli, then said: 'We had our back to the wall there, and we won that one.'

For Turkey, Gallipoli truly was about nation-building. The Gallipoli campaign helped restore Turkish pride. The Ottoman empire was old and rotten and spent; the Gallipoli battles rather proved that the Turkish people were not. More important, those battles brought Mustafa Kemal to prominence. The British and the Anzacs knew about Enver and von Sanders and often mentioned them in their letters and diaries; they didn't know they had also been fighting Kemal until after the war. Enver didn't like to see Kemal's name mentioned in the Turkish press and Kemal's reputation mostly spread by word of mouth. He was perhaps not the military genius he is sometimes made out to be (a military genius is hard to define, as Napoleon proved in 1812), but he was that rarest of things, a natural leader. He always knew what he had to do; there was a certitude about him that was at once unnerving and inspiring.

Kemal was promoted to general after Gallipoli and

served on the Russian front; in 1918 he was commanding the 7th Army near Aleppo when General Allenby's forces, including the Australian Light Horse, advanced into Syria. Kemal was by then getting ready for another war. With the armistice, the vultures were finally trotting towards that great piece of carrion. The Ottoman empire was no more and Turkey itself was going to be carved up. The peace deal was punitive and cynical. France wanted southern Anatolia, Italy wanted the east. The Greeks, who had come into the war in 1917, moved on Smyrna (now Izmir) and its hinterland, but they wanted a lot more, as much as they could get, and Lloyd George encouraged them to take it; Lloyd George didn't like Turks. Thanks to the arrival of Lenin, the Russians missed out on Constantinople (the British occupied it in 1920), but the Dardanelles came under international control. The Greeks spread inland towards Ankara.

Kemal led the revolt that became the War of Independence. He was running what was left of the country from Ankara where he had set up a parliament. He began to roll the Greeks back towards Smyrna. The Greeks scorched the earth behind them, torching village after village. Kemal arrived in Smyrna behind his cavalry-men in September, 1922, a hero wearing no badges of rank. The people of Smyrna presented him with a car and sacrificed an ox in his honour. Later, when Kemal strolled into a hotel, the waiter didn't recognise him and told the saviour of Turkey that there were no tables free.

Kemal now turned towards the place that had made him, the Dardanelles. He was taking the Turks back into Europe. Lloyd George decided to resist Kemal with force at Çanakkale; Churchill, in Cabinet again, backed him. London called on the empire for support and 14,000 New Zealanders volunteered. Britain and Churchill were on the edge of another war over the Dardanelles, only this time the *Turks* were threatening Constantinople. At a peace conference the Turks won the right to occupy eastern Thrace and reclaim Constantinople. A week or so later, in October, 1922, Lloyd George resigned and Churchill went down with him, later losing his seat in the Commons. Patrick Kinross, Kemal's biographer, wrote:

> After three years of fighting, the despised Turkish rebel had helped to bring down a British Government and a renowned Prime Minister. The romantic had fallen to the realist. The Macedonian had defeated the Celt.

In short, it had been a rerun of Kemal versus Hamilton at Suvla and Chunuk Bair. Kemal, president of the new Turkey, began a series of tremendous reforms. Turkey became a republic, the Islamic form of government ended, secular schools sprang up, women were emancipated, hats replaced the fez, the Ottoman script was scrapped for Roman characters, and family names were introduced (Kemal became Atatürk, meaning father of the Turks). Kemal even bullied bewildered Muslims into getting up and doing the foxtrot. His rule was often severe, more Oriental than Western in style, but he kept a sense of humour. Alcohol had always calmed him. A French journalist wrote that Turkey was governed by a drunkard, a deaf man (Ismet, who would become president on Atatürk's death) and 300 deaf-mutes (the deputies). 'This man is mistaken,' Kemal announced. 'Turkey is governed by one drunkard.'

Kemal became difficult and moody in his mid-fifties. Adoration followed him, but he was lonely – his marriage had failed long ago – and his body seemed to be rebelling. He became seriously ill in 1937; his abdomen blew up and his face turned pale. He had cirrhosis of the liver and eventually fell into a coma. On November 10, 1938, he opened his eyes, those blue eyes that had stared down the world so uncompromisingly, then closed them and died.

Before Turkey signed an armistice in October, 1918, Enver, Talat and Djemal fled to Berlin. Talat stayed there and lived modestly under another name. More than anyone, he had been blamed for the Armenian massacres of 1915, in which perhaps 600,000 people died, cast out into the countryside, robbed, raped, beaten and stripped of their clothes. One day in Berlin Talat felt a hand on his shoulder and turned to stare into the eyes of an Armenian student who had lost his parents and sisters in the massacres. The youth had been bothered by a dream in which his mother said: 'You know Talat is here. But you seem quite heartless and are not my son.' The boy looked into Talat's eyes, then took out a revolver and killed him with a bullet to the brain. Blood cascaded down Talat's white shirt, which, with its rusty stains, is now in a military museum in Istanbul.

Enver left Berlin for Russia. He may not have been a Bolshevik but he was always an adventurer and the intrigues of Russia's Asian lands were his natural game. He turned against the Russians, took part in a revolt in Turkestan in 1922, and was killed by Red Army machine-gun fire at the age of 40. Djemal also went to Russia and was assassinated in Georgia. Von Wangenheim, the German ambassador who had courted Enver so well, died of a stroke in Constantinople. Von Sanders, whom some regard as the best general of the Gallipoli campaign, was held at Malta by the British until August, 1919. Nine years later he published *Five Years in Turkey*, a cold and matter-of-fact book that leaves the reader certain the general is holding a lot back. He died, aged 74, in Munich four years before Hitler came to power.

Hunter-Weston, Godley and Braithwaite all commanded corps in France. Hunter-Weston might have 'broken down' at Gallipoli but his vanity was intact; after the war he composed a *Who's Who* entry for himself that took almost a column and included the important news that he was the honorary colonel of the 1/1st Hunts Cyclist Battalion. Godley became Governor of Gibraltar and died in 1957. One cannot condemn Hunter-Weston and Godley for failing to understand the new warfare of the 20th century; few generals did in 1915. One can, however, condemn them for faults that are timeless. They were careless and arrogant and not very good.

Sir John Maxwell, the commander in Egypt, was sent to Ireland early in 1916 to deal with the Easter Rising. The rebels didn't have much popular support until Maxwell executed 14 of them. Maxwell thus played a big part in starting Ireland's war of independence and also ensured that Billy Hughes' attempts to introduce conscription in Australia would fail.

Allanson became the British consul in Monte Carlo and Dawnay, having reached the rank of major-general, left the army to become a merchant banker when that calling was respectable. Stopford was, as they say, not asked to serve again. Keyes directed the raid on the German base at Zeebrugge, Belgium, in 1918, became an admiral of the fleet, a member of parliament and a baronet. As commander of the Mediterranean Fleet in 1925 he finally sailed through the Dardanelles. Aspinall, who was with him, said Keyes became emotional. 'My God,' he said, 'it would have been even easier than I thought; we simply *couldn't* have failed.' Keyes was always a believer.

The *River Clyde*, despite being hit by countless shells,

was refloated in 1919, renamed the *Angela* and then the *Maruja y Aurora*, and sailed back and forth across the Mediterranean for 40 years as a Spanish tramp. In 1936, near Gibraltar, she passed a liner on which Gallipoli veterans, including Birdwood and Keyes, were returning home from a pilgrimage. The *Maruja y Aurora* dipped her ensign and the liner dipped hers. Thirty years later the ship that had been the *River Clyde* was broken up for scrap.

Monash went on to become the greatest military commander Australia has produced. If he has never quite received the recognition he deserves, it is perhaps because (as Geoffrey Serle, Monash's biographer, suggests) Australians prefer to celebrate sportsmen and bush-rangers. The mad terrain and sloppy planning of Gallipoli gave Monash few chances to use his gifts; battle orders tended to be better when he wrote them himself. The higher he rose in rank, the better he became. In France he led an Australian corps of 150,000 men to a series of victories in 1918. The United States decorated him after he had commanded two American divisions during the capture of the Hindenburg Line. He finished the war heavy with honours and exhausted. He died in Melbourne in 1931, aged 66. More than 250,000 people turned out for his funeral.

Sinclair-MacLagan, so bewildered, as anyone would have been, on the morning of the Gallipoli landing, also did his best work in France, particularly at Hamel in 1918, when his 4th Division led a counter-attack that overran the German positions in 93 minutes. Harry Chauvel, the light horseman, liked the desert better than the claustrophobia of Pope's Hill. He rose to command of the Desert Mounted Corps in Palestine, the first Australian to command a corps, ordered the famous attack at Beersheba in 1917 and the following year took Damascus and Aleppo.

Birdwood stayed with his Anzacs until 1918, when he took over the 5th Army. He made a long tour of Australia in 1919–20 and his affection for the men he had led was obvious. He badly wanted to become Governor-General in the early nineteen-thirties and had George V's blessing, but the moment was wrong. James Scullin, the Australian Prime Minister, persuaded the King that Sir Isaac Isaacs should become the first Australian-born Governor-General. Birdwood was one of four future field marshals to serve at Gallipoli (the others were Slim, Blamey and John Harding, who had been a lieutenant in the 54th Division). Birdwood survived all the Gallipoli commanders bar Godley and died in 1951, aged 85.

Harold Walker, arguably the finest of the Allied generals at Gallipoli, was wounded there in September and October, the second time seriously. He commanded the 1st Australian Division until July, 1918. For some reason – perhaps because he was modest, or because he didn't write much – he figures little in the Australian folklore of Gallipoli. He deserves to be better remembered; Australia owes him more than it has acknowledged. Francis Johnston, commander of the New Zealand Infantry Brigade, was killed in France in 1917. Bernard Freyberg of the RND, present at the burial of Rupert Brooke and famous as the one-man diversion at Bulair, ended up with a VC and three bars to his DSO after being wounded nine times. He commanded the New Zealand forces in World War II and later became Governor-General of New Zealand.

Ashmead-Bartlett was so broke during his Australian lecture tour of 1916 that he sold the diary he had kept at Gallipoli to the Mitchell Library, Sydney, for several hundred pounds. He later covered the war in France, which must have made a great many generals nervous, but he still needed money. For a large fee, he left journalism to help the Hungarians fight the Bolsheviks. He married in 1919 and fathered two sons, but the marriage soon foundered. He spent two years as a Conservative MP, then had to resign because he was broke again. He died in Lisbon in 1931 while covering the turmoil in Spain for the *Daily Telegraph*.

Bean produced volume after volume of war history, remarkable for its accuracy, detail and democratic temper; his narratives often rambled about like the Darling in flood but that was thought to be part of their charm. Forty-four years to the day after he had risked death to help the wounded of Krithia, Bean received an honorary doctorate from the Australian National University. Bean, much-loved by all who knew him, died in 1968. The Australian War Memorial in Canberra is his memorial too.

The Melbourne *Herald* prospered under Keith Murdoch, who became the kingmaker he always wanted to be. Opinions about him were polarised: some said he was a fine newspaperman and a high-minded citizen; others said he was a calculating seeker of power and wealth. In 1940 the author of the 'Gallipoli letter' became the chief censor for Robert Menzies' wartime government. Murdoch wanted the power to compel newspapers to publish statements he put out. The newspapers protested and Murdoch shortly afterwards resigned as Director-General for Information. He died in 1952. The text of his Gallipoli letter was not published until 15 years later, which may have been just as well. As William Shawcross wrote, neither its tone nor its accuracy reflected well on him.

The *Age*'s Phillip Schuler was the first Australian to write about the scandal of the wounded. He wrote a book about Gallipoli in 1916, then joined the army. He died on the western front in 1917, 27 years old, hit in the face, throat, left arm and right leg. His father, who was editor of the *Age*, eventually received his son's effects, which included a typewriter, a pair of spurs, a pipe, two erasers, a dictionary and a riding crop.

The Dardanelles had twice wrecked Churchill's career. It was fashionable in the nineteen-twenties to blame him for the defeat of 1915. Bean reflected a considerable body of opinion when he wrote in the first volume of his war history: 'So, through a Churchill's excess of imagination, a layman's ignorance of artillery, and the fatal power of a young enthusiasm to convince older and more cautious brains, the tragedy of Gallipoli was born.' Later, when it became known that the Turks were almost out of ammunition after the naval battle of March 18, some decided that the Dardanelles adventure had been a good idea that – if only the Allies had been luckier – could have shortened the war. Then they would trot out the 'what ifs', the way gamblers tell of horses that were certainties beaten. In recent times the mood has perhaps swung back the other way. The one thing that is clear is that, whether it was a good idea or not, Churchill imposed the Dardanelles adventure on a government that had no notion of how to carry the idea through. And the one thing that has never been explained is this: how, precisely, was the appearance of British battleships off Constantinople going to shorten the war in France and Belgium?

World War II was made for Churchill and he for it. He was not only rehabilitated but seen as one of the political giants of the century; his part in the Dardanelles campaign became a footnote to a fabulous life. As a politician, Churchill was mostly a liability in peacetime: he got too many things wrong and perhaps cared more for posterity than for people. But he was always right about Hitler.

There had never been any question about Ian Hamilton's physical bravery; after his sacking he showed a higher form of courage. He had reason to be bitter – whatever his failings as a commander, he had been let down by Kitchener and Cabinet – but he refused to play the victim. On his return to London he discovered that Kitchener had never told Cabinet that he, Hamilton, had requested younger generals in preference to Stopford. Moreover, Kitchener had never shown Cabinet Hamilton's requests for reinforcements and artillery. By late 1916 most accepted that the case against Kitchener was stronger than the case against Hamilton – except the case against Kitchener could not be put because the nation was in mourning for him.

Hamilton stumped back and forth across the country opening war memorials. He wrote books of charming prose, railed against capitalists, lamented that so many men who had fought in the trenches now couldn't find jobs and argued for the Allies to be generous in their treatment of Germany. The harsh terms imposed on Germany at Versailles in 1919 upset him. Opening a war memorial a few years later, he said: 'Don't be too hard on your enemies. Don't grind them down now that they're beaten.' In another speech around the same time, he said: 'These boys of yours did not die for reparations; nor for Mesopotamia; nor even for Jerusalem. They had hoped, God bless them, to kill war.' Hamilton was a complex man: he was beguiled by the beauty of war and repelled by its cruelties.

The Hamiltons had no children. In 1919 Jean fostered

two babies, Harry and Rosalind. Harry was killed in action in North Africa in 1941. Hamilton bought a farm in Sussex from Churchill and bred Belted Galloway cattle, although he and Jean continued to live at 1 Hyde Park Gardens. In 1924 he was sounded out as a possible candidate for Secretary of State for War in a Labour government. He declined. He admitted he had made mistakes at Gallipoli, though not in his battle tactics. He had 'culpably neglected the ceaseless internecine war raging on the home front of Whitehall and Fleet Street'. He went to Germany in 1938 to lay wreaths at German war memorials and a few days later met Hitler at Berchtesgaden. They talked for 90 minutes. Hamilton knew the Führer was trying to charm him, but he still came away believing Hitler meant well. Hamilton was now so in thrall to pacifism that he failed to see that Hitler was a bigger threat than Kaiser Bill or Enver Pasha had ever been.

Hamilton was 86 when World War II broke out, still lively and curious, still the charming companion, witty and courtly and a touch unworldly, the same man who had made that fateful walk from Horse Guards in 1915, merely older and frailer. Gallipoli had hurt him but he wouldn't let it crush him. Some still thought him to blame and some didn't. It didn't matter too much now. He was old and he was easy to like and even to admire.

In temperament, he had been the wrong commander for the Gallipoli campaign, but one has to wonder who could have succeeded there under the conditions Kitchener imposed. Hamilton's bad luck was that he was sent forth when Britain hadn't learnt how to fight a world war. His big mistake was in not telling Kitchener in the fortnight after the landings that he had nothing like the numbers of men and guns needed to win. But that was not his way. He could always see hope somewhere. His strength of character as a man, that blithe spirit, was his weakness as a commander.

Hamilton stayed in London throughout the war – he wasn't going to run away from a few bombs – and wrote another book. He died at Hyde Park Gardens in 1947, aged 94. Years later a memorial to him was opened in St Paul's Cathedral. Churchill spoke of a brilliant and chivalrous man. He was not wrong.

The Gallipoli Peninsula went back to how it always was when there wasn't a war going on. There were more ghosts now and the new ones whispered in the voices of Manchester and Ballarat. That was the only difference, that and the debris that had been left. Oxen were hitched to ploughs and the mouldboards scuffed the bones of someone's lost love and brought up clunking pieces of shrapnel and badges with weird scrawl on them, and wheat and olives grew again in the blood and the bone. The winter gales came and after them the rude scents of spring, and the land came alive again and tortoises, shy and careful, grazed near what had been the Anzac telephone exchange, and at Quinn's Post the rain washed Malone's pretty terraces into the Aegean. An Australian sergeant carried home a cone from the lone pine that had once stood on 400 Plateau and four trees sprouted from the seeds and they, in turn, produced hundreds more that now rustle and whisper in parks and school grounds across Australia.

In the early nineteen-twenties an official of the Imperial War Graves Commission noted that at the end of Brighton Beach lay a valley filled with rhododendrons in their season and hollyhocks in theirs. Shrapnel Gully was quiet now. Near where it met the sea there was a great cemetery.

A Turkish shepherd boy, bored and lonely, stood by the stone wall carelessly pronouncing the names of those who lay on the other side. One generation passeth away and another generation cometh: but the earth abideth forever.

Endnotes

The final stanzas of Patrick Shaw-Stewart's poem, which appear at the start of the book, were written when he was on three-days' leave from Gallipoli, presumably at Imbros. The poem was untitled.

Part One Of mice and men

Chapter 1
Page
15.   'Waste landscape': Liman von Sanders, *Five Years in Turkey*, p. 59.
15.   'Wouldn't feed a bandicoot': Captain W. H. Sheppard, letter to his parents dated 28 August, 1915, Australian War Memorial.

Chapter 2
Page
30.   'Fascinated and repelled by the modern': John Lee, *A Soldier's Life: General Sir Ian Hamilton 1853–1947*, p. 269.
31.   'Too much feather in his brain': Lee, p. 143.

31. 'A breadth of mind . . .': Kevin Fewster (ed.), *Gallipoli Correspondent: The Frontline Diary of C. E. W. Bean,* p. 169.

32. 'One of those revolving lighthouses . . .': quoted in Robert Rhodes James, *Gallipoli,* p. 21.

33. 'Apart from one romantic attachment': Philip Magnus, *Kitchener: Portrait of an Imperialist,* p. 10.

33. 'Calvary beckoned and beguiled': for a fascinating assessment of Gordon's mindset at Khartoum, see Lytton Strachey's *Eminent Victorians.*

34. 'It was not like the Great War': Winston Churchill, *My Early Life,* p. 120.

36. 'It is the suicide of nations': quoted in Paul Fussell, *The Great War and Modern Memory,* p. 72.

38. 'The one-man show': Ian Hamilton, *Gallipoli Diary,* vol I, p. 13.

38. 'We are sending a military force . . .': Hamilton, p. 2.

39. 'But my knowledge of the Dardanelles': Hamilton, p. 2.

39. 'We have done this sort of thing before': Hamilton, p. 3.

40. 'But half that number of men . . .': Hamilton, p. 6.

41. 'K. turned on him': Hamilton, p. 8.

42. Kitchener's written instructions for the Mediterranean Expeditionary Force: *see* Appendix 1 in Cecil Aspinall-Oglander's official history, *Military Operations: Gallipoli* (two volumes, plus maps and appendices).

43. 'Actually my heart went out to my old chief': Hamilton, p. 15.

43. 'If the fleet gets through . . .': Hamilton, p. 16.

43. 'I haven't a notion of who they are': Hamilton, p. 16.

43. 'This is going to be an unlucky show': quoted in Alan Moorehead, *Gallipoli,* p. 84.

44. 'What pluck': Hamilton, p. 19.

45. 'There is a man . . .': quoted in Patrick Kinross, *Atatürk: The Rebirth of a Nation,* p. 58.

45. The quality he most admired in a woman: Kinross, p. 260.

45. Kemal as an amalgam of East and West: Kinross, p. 292.

Chapter 3
Page

52. The empire's early genius for lightness: Jason Goodwin, *Lords of the Horizons,* p. 209.

53. 'Today arbitrary government has disappeared': quoted in Henry Morgenthau, *Secrets of the Bosphorus,* p. 7.

55. 'There was Enver . . .': quoted in Alan Moorehead, *Gallipoli,* p. 14.

55. 'Whenever I think of Talat . . .': Morgenthau, p. 13.

55. 'I do not expect to die in bed': Morgenthau, p. 14.

56. 'A light in his eyes . . .': quoted in Moorehead, p. 15.

56. 'Man of destiny' and 'the little Napoleon': Morgenthau, p. 19.

58. 'Fundamentally ruthless, shameless and cruel': Morgenthau, p. 5.

58. 'The jovial enthusiasm of a college student': Morgenthau, p. 4.

60. Churchill's version of the seizure of Turkish ships: Winston Churchill, *The World Crisis,* vol II, pp 436–37.

60. 'The greatest opportunity of his life': Morgenthau, p. 49.

61. 'Something is distracting you': Morgenthau, pp 45–46.

62. 'We heard the clanking of the portcullis': quoted in Robert Rhodes James, *Gallipoli,* p. 9.

62. 'Then, momentarily checking his enthusiasm': Morgenthau, p. 46.

64. The decision to close the straits: Aspinall-Oglander, *Military Operations: Gallipoli,* vol I, p. 16, and Morgenthau, p. 69.

64. 'He presented a pitiable sight': Morgenthau, p. 68.

65. 'I know nothing about it': Morgenthau, p. 81.

65. 'Enver and I prefer that the war shall come now': Morgenthau, p. 82.

66. 'The bombardment of November 3 warned me': quoted in Aspinall, p. 35.

67. 'At the conclusion of our conversation . . .': Liman von Sanders, *Five Years in Turkey*, p. 39.

69. Callwell's plan 'intended to be dissuasive': quoted in Robert Rhodes James, p. 10.

Chapter 4
Page

71. 'I was up till 2 am with Winston': quoted in Trumbull Higgins, *Winston Churchill and the Dardanelles*, p. 19.

72. 'Old and worn-out and nervous': quoted in Higgins, p. 90.

73. 'But only if it's immediate': quoted in Winston Churchill, *The World Crisis 1911–1918*, vol II, p. 530.

73. 'Do you consider the forcing of the Dardanelles . . . ?': Churchill, p. 532.

73. 'I do not consider Dardanelles can be rushed': quoted in Churchill, p. 533.

74. 'Churchill suddenly revealed his well-kept secret': quoted in Robert Rhodes James, *Gallipoli*, p. 32.

75. 'There is only one way out': quoted in Higgins, p. 91.

75. 'I just abominate the Dardanelles operation': quoted in Rhodes James, *Gallipoli*, p. 34.

75. Dardanelles scheme is 'unjustifiable': quoted in Higgins, p. 93.

77. 'A good army of 50,000 men . . .': quoted in Rhodes James, p. 11.

77. 'Unless a strong military force is ready': quoted in Higgins, p. 105.

78. 'We blew No 1 fort to a perfect inferno': Lieutenant Harry Minchin RN in a letter to his grandfather, Imperial War Museum.

79. 'There are not six men . . .': Henry Morgenthau, *Secrets of the Bosphorous*, p. 130.

80. 'Who is co-ordinating and directing this great combine?': quoted in A. J. P. Taylor (ed.), *History of World War I*, p. 71.

81. 'I have already informed you ...': quoted in Cecil Aspinall-Oglander, *Military Operations: Gallipoli*, vol I, p. 85.

82–3. 'The position is' and 'To put it briefly': Commodore Roger Keyes in a letter to his wife, quoted in Tom Frame, *The Shores of Gallipoli: Naval Aspects of the Anzac Campaign*, p. 84.

84. 'Everyone ... knew really that it would be madness': Diary entry of Commander Worsley Gibson, Imperial War Museum.

84. 'A most delightful man ...': Ellis Ashmead-Bartlett, *The Uncensored Dardanelles*, p. 29.

85. 'One could not feel that his training ...': Churchill, p. 636.

85. 'Gallipoli looks a much tougher nut': Ian Hamilton, *Gallipoli Diary*, vol I, p. 27.

Chapter 5
Page

87. 'The Turks and the Germans care nothing for each other': Henry Morgenthau, *Secrets of the Bosphorous*, p. 136.

88. 'After the war ...': Morgenthau, p. 140.

91. 'The situation had become very critical': this account from the Turkish official accounts appears in Aspinall-Oglander, *Military Operations: Gallipoli*, vol I, p. 97. (The Turkish official history of the Gallipoli campaign, which contains some splendid maps, has not yet been published in English.)

91. *Bouvet* 'was seen to be in distress': quoted in Winston Churchill, *The World Crisis 1911–1918*, vol II, p. 644.

93. 'Except for the searchlights ...': Commodore Keyes quoted in Robert Rhodes James, *Gallipoli*, p. 63.

94. Operation was a 'complete failure': Cecil Aspinall-Oglander, *Military Operations: Gallipoli*, vol I, p. 98.

95. De Robeck's cable to Churchill: quoted in Churchill, p. 645.

95. 'Constantinople expected another 'go': Morgenthau, p. 147.

95. Talat readies for a 'protracted journey': Morgenthau, p. 150.

96. 'After losing so many ships': quoted in Tom Frame, *The Shores of Gallipoli*, p. 87.

Chapter 6
Page

103–6. Hamilton's diary entries in *Gallipoli Diary* for the four days run to 12 pages.

107. 'What has happened since the 21st?': Winston Churchill, *The World Crisis 1911–1918*, vol II, p. 652.

108. 'I had something better to do . . .': Liman von Sanders, *Five Years in Turkey*, p. 58.

109. 'The place of greatest danger': von Sanders, p. 59.

111–12. Hamilton's two diary entries: Ian Hamilton, *Gallipoli Diary*, vol I, pp 79–80.

113. 'Have just dictated a long letter to Lord K.': Hamilton, p. 62.

114. 'You should supply any troops': Cecil Aspinall-Oglander, *Military Operations: Gallipoli*, vol I, p. 124.

115. 'The comedy was ended by a party of Turkish cavalry': quoted in Aspinall, p. 53.

116. 'It will be grim work to begin with': quoted in Robert Rhodes James, *Gallipoli*, p. 86.

117. 'News of the arrival and departure of transports': Aspinall, p. 110.

117. 'The Germans have tabulated the experiences . . .': Hamilton, p. 65.

118. 'Have you any good and recent information': Aspinall, p. 121.

118. Hankey's memorandum to Asquith: quoted in Aspinall, pp 101–102.

119. 'All goes well . . .': quoted in Rhodes James, p. 82.

120. Compton Mackenzie's encounter with Hunter-Weston:

Compton Mackenzie, *Gallipoli Memories*, pp 150–52.

122. 'The enemy is of a strength unknown': Hamilton, p. 93.

122. 'The truth is . . .': Hamilton, p. 94.

122. 'Gallipoli gives us no liberty of manoeuvre': quoted in Rhodes James, p. 82.

122. 'When Nelson saw a fort': Hamilton Papers, Liddell Hart Centre.

123. 'The more, I said, I had pondered over the map': Hamilton, p. 95.

124. 'There will be and can be no reconnaissance': Hamilton, p. 96.

124. The 'Unspeakable Turk': Hamilton, p. 101.

125. 'With luck, then, within the space of an hour . . .': Hamilton, pp 97–98.

126. 'Once ashore . . .': Hamilton writing in 1924, quoted in Rhodes James, p. 89.

130. 'It's too wonderful for belief': quoted in Alan Moorehead, *Gallipoli*, p. 109.

130. 'If I should die, think only this of me': opening lines of Rupert Brooke's sonnet *The Soldier*.

131. 'Rupert Brooke is dead': Hamilton, pp 124–25.

'Joyous, fearless, versatile . . .': quoted in Michael Hickey, *Gallipoli*, p. 94.

Chapter 7

Page

133. The story of the two New Zealand prisoners has appeared in Turkish publications and is part of the Turkish oral tradition.

134. An 'independent Australian Briton': quoted in Gavin Souter, *Lion and Kangaroo*, p. 13.

135. 'There was not one of those glorious young men . . .': Compton Mackenzie, *Gallipoli Memories*, p. 81.

135–6. Bean's Lone Pine anecdote: Charles Bean, *Official History of Australia in the War of 1914–18*, vol I, p. 6.

137. 'This bill marks . . . the beginning of a new phase of

civilisation': quoted in Paul Kelly, *The End of Certainty*, p. 7.

137. 'The crimson thread of kinship': quoted by Malcolm Turnbull, *Age*, January 4, 2001.

138. 'Australians did not need to pause': Geoffrey Blainey, *A Shorter History of Australia*, p. 153.

138. 'Whatever happens, Australia is a part of the empire . . .': quoted in Souter, pp 262–63.

139. 'We are strongly opposed to the present government . . .': quoted in Ernest Scott, *Official History of Australia During the War of 1914–18*, vol XI, p. 22.

140. 'Upon that sense of right . . .': Bean, p. xivi.

141. 'Once in a generation . . .': Hamilton, p. 34.

141. 'The representative of the King and of the race': quoted in Souter, p. 256.

142. 'Would it not be well . . .?': quoted in Ernest Scott, p. 8.

144. Figures on wages and religion: from the *Official Year Book of the Commonwealth of Australia, No. 8, 1915*.

144. Story concerning Henry Montgomery, Bishop of Tasmania: quoted in Blainey, p. 151.

145. 'The bush still sets the standard': Bean, pp 46–47.

146. Population figures: from the *Official Year Book*, 1915.

146. Figures on enlistments: from Scott, Appendix 5, p. 874.

146. Random sample of the 11th Battalion: Suzanne Welborn, *Lords of Death*, pp 188–190.

147. 'The force to be at the complete disposal of the Home Government': quoted in Bean, p. 29.

147. 'There is indescribable enthusiasm . . .': quoted in Souter, p. 264.

148. Alan Moorehead and Uncle Harry: Alan Moorehead, *New Yorker*, April 2, 1955.

149. 'We are expecting to leave at any moment': letter of John Simpson Kirkpatrick, dated October 14, 1914, Australian War Memorial.

149. Accounts of 'Snowy' Howe's enlistment appear in Souter, p. 269, and Charles Bean, *Gallipoli Mission*, p. 15.

150. 'I was dead scared when I went to join up': quoted in Patsy Adam-Smith, *The Anzacs*, p. 19.

150. 'I got in by the skin of my teeth': letter of Oliver Cumberland, dated October 17, 1914, Australian War Memorial.

150. 'If the boys are prepared to die . . .': letter of Joe Cumberland, dated January 13, 1915, Australian War Memorial.

151. 'A class of men not quite the same . . .': Bean, p. 43.

152. Composition of the 1st Division: Bean, pp 54, 60.

153. 'Am briskly engaging enemy': quoted in Bean, pp 105–106.

154. 'A small, thin man, nothing striking or soldierly about him': quoted in Geoffrey Serle, *John Monash: A Biography*, p. 209.

155. There are several versions of the 'sentry joke'. It appears in a letter a New Zealand gunner wrote to his mother, and in Lady Godley's correspondence with her husband.

155. 'An exceptionally able man on paper': quoted in Serle, p. 209.

157. 'A competent Jew': quoted in John Robertson, *Anzac and Empire*, p. 35.

157. 'The typical Hebrew mouth and the typical Hebrew eye': quoted in Serle, p. 181.

157. 'Lord Kitchener recently sent me a certain amount of nasty correspondence': quoted in Serle, p. 209.

157. Bridges' fall from his horse: Bean, pp 66–67.

157–8. Character of Bridges: Bean, pp 66–67.

159. 'Oh, go along with you': Bean, p. 244.

159. Godley as bad tempered, pernickety and selfish: quoted in Serle, p. 258.

160. 'Out of sight and out of mind': Alexander Godley, *Life of an Irish Soldier*, p.137.

160. 'He was too clever . . .': Godley, p. 9.

160. 'Our honeymoon objective . . .': Godley, p. 63.

161. Composition of the New Zealand contingent:

Christopher Pugsley, *Gallipoli: The New Zealand Story*, pp 360–61.

162. 'They are of all classes': quoted in Pugsley, pp 55–56.

PART TWO Attrition

Chapter 8

Page

166. 'Just like little birds, ain't they, Snow?': Charles Bean, *Official History of Australia in the War of 1914–18*, vol I, p. 254.

169. 'Look at that!': Bean, p. 252.

170. Clarke's conversation with Laing: paraphrased in Bean, p. 272.

170. 'Landed 0420 . . .': Ivor Margetts, diary, Australian War Memorial.

170. 'It was a wonderful sight': Margetts letter, dated May 23, 1915, Australian War Memorial.

172. 'Soon I came upon Col. Clarke . . .': Margetts letter.

172. 'Steady you fellows!': Bean, p. 273.

173. 'Col. Clarke, who was about 20 yards to my right . . .': Margetts letter.

173. 'Don't come here!': Bean, p. 274.

175–6. For an analysis of navigational problems with the landing, *see* Tom Frame, *The Shores of Gallipoli: Naval Aspects of the Anzac Campaign*, pp 198–210.

176. 'Tell the colonel . . .': Bean, p. 252.

177. Braithwaite's instruction on the Anzac landing: Cecil Aspinall-Oglander, *Military Operations: Gallipoli*, Appendix 5.

177. Birdwood's order for the Anzac landing: Aspinall, Appendix 14.

177. General Bridges' order for the Anzac landing: Aspinall, Appendix 16.

177. 'I had originally intended landing . . .': Birdwood's report

on Anzac landing to Braithwaite, dated May 8, 1915, Birdwood Papers, Imperial War Musuem, London.

179. 'The beach was very rocky': letter of Arthur Blackburn VC, dated June 3, 1915, Australian War Memorial.

180. 'However we pushed on . . .': Blackburn letter.

180. 'Up till now I had seen no one . . .': Blackburn letter.

181. Bean's conclusions about the advance of Blackburn and Robin: Bean, p. xii.

183. 'As the Australians got in among them': Bean, p. 338.

Chapter 9
Page

187. 'The day was just breaking over the jagged hills': Ian Hamilton, *Gallipoli Diary*, vol I, p. 128.

188. Von Sanders' reactions to the landings: Liman von Sanders, *Five Years in Turkey*, p. 63.

189. The 'unforgettable picture' at Bulair: von Sanders, p. 64.

191. 'I do not order you to attack; I order you to die': Kemal Atatürk, 'Memoirs of the Anafartalar Battles', p. 9, Imperial War Museum, London.

192. Adil Şahin's account of the Anzac landing: told to the author by Kenan Çelik, Gallipoli, March 1998.

193. 'Both from this report . . .': Atatürk 'Memoirs', p. 5.

193. 'On the little maps . . .': quoted in Charles Bean, *Gallipoli Mission*, p. 135.

194. 'Let me tell you the conversation as it took place: Atatürk 'Memoirs', pp 6–7.

195. 'May well have decided the fate of the peninsula': Patrick Kinross, *Atatürk*, p. 76.

195. 'The force which the enemy had landed': Atatürk 'Memoirs', p. 8.

196. 'Every soldier who fights here with me': quoted in Kinross, p. 78.

199. 'I want you to take your whole brigade: Bean, pp 364–65.

200. 'Then began the strain of waiting': quoted in Ronald McNicoll, *Walter Ramsay McNicoll 1877–1947*, a

private biography kindly loaned to the author by D. D. McNicoll.

201. 'It was galling . . .': McNicoll biography.

203. 'One met small parties . . .': McNicoll biography.

203. 'They needed no epitaph': Bean, p. 421.

204. 'The beach was crowded with all sorts of beings': Jock Phillips, Nicholas Boyack, E. P. Malone, *The Great Adventure*, p. 33.

206–7. Margetts' trips to Baby 700: Ivor Margetts letter, dated May 23, Australian War Memorial.

207. Lalor's conversation with Margetts: quoted in Bean, p. 308.

207. 'Now then, 12th Battalion . . .': Bean, p. 309.

209. Braund's message: Bean, p. 318.

209. 'Reinforcements are on their way': Bean, p. 319.

210. 'I rolled down into the gully': Margetts letter.

211–12. The principal source for the dispute about straggling is Alistair Thomson's article ' "The Vilest Libel of the War": Imperial Politics and the Official Histories of Gallipoli' in *Australian Historical Studies*, October, 1993.

Chapter 10
Page

216. 'Wars are only carried on . . .': Ellis Ashmead-Bartlett, *The Uncensored Dardanelles*, p. 41.

216. 'In conversation with me that evening . . .': Charles Dix, 'Efficient Navy: How Troops Were Landed', in *Reveille*, March, 1932.

217. 'I climbed ashore over some barges . . .': Ashmead-Bartlett, pp 48–49.

218. Text of Birdwood's message to Hamilton: Ian Hamilton, *Gallipoli Diary*, vol I, p. 143.

219. 'In terms which could have jeopardised his career': appears as a footnote in Robert Rhodes James, *Gallipoli*, p. 129. Charles Bean says in *Official History of Australia*

in the War of 1914–18, vol I, that Walker 'fought like a tiger against evacuation', p. 455.

220. Account of Hamilton's reaction to Birdwood's message, including dialogue: Hamilton, pp 142–44.

221. Hamilton's 'gallant reply': Alexander Godley, *Life of an Irish Soldier,* p. 172.

221. Godley's 'wonderfully good innings': Godley, p. 344.

223. 'When he was nearly 50 he took us on a 23-mile march': told to the author by a member of Blackburn's World War II battalion.

227. 'The Australians who were about to go into action . . .': This account of Ashmead-Bartlett's report of the landing is taken from the *Age*; versions in other newspapers vary slightly from this.

228. Figures on enlistments: Ernest Scott, *Official History of Australia in the War of 1914–18,* vol XI, p. 871.

228. For an account of Bryce's report and its aftermath see Phillip Knightley, *The First Casualty*, pp 83–84.

229. 'Lady doctors' not wanted: *Age*, May 8, 1915.

Chapter 11
Page

235. The 'utterly indescribable' condition of the wounded: Aubrey Herbert diary, entry for May 10, 1915.

236. 'We are holding the ridge . . .': Ian Hamilton, *Gallipoli Diary*, vol I, pp 146–47.

236. Content of Matthews' frantic messages: Cecil Aspinall-Oglander, *Military Operations: Gallipoli*, vol I, p. 212.

237. 'We looked for a long time . . .': Hamilton, p. 168.

238. 'Would you like to get some more men ashore?': Hamilton, p. 133.

239. 'Had the suggestion been acted upon . . .': Aspinall, p. 205.

239. Sami Bey's order: quoted in Aspinall, p. 255.

240. 'Will you please send help': Aspinall, p. 209.

241. 'Situation critical': Aspinall, p. 212.

241. Hunter-Weston was 'cheery, stout-hearted': Hamilton, p. 137.

242. Hunter-Weston's message and the dead tortoise: Aspinall, p. 254.

243. 'I never knew blood smelt so strong before': George Drewry, VC, letter, Imperial War Museum.

243. Corpses 'like a shoal of fish': Turkish commander at V Beach, quoted in Robert Rhodes James, *Gallipoli*, p. 122.

243. The sea 'absolutely red with blood': Commander Charles Samson, who flew over V Beach, quoted in Alan Moorehead, *Gallipoli*, p. 143. Hamilton also reports the sea red with blood, p. 135.

244. 'Wasteful rascals!': Compton Mackenzie, *Gallipoli Memories*, p. 150.

245. Result of trials at the Musketry School in Kent: quoted in Michael Evans, *From Legend to Learning: Gallipoli and the Military Revolution of World War I*, p. 21.

246. Lieutenant-Colonel Weir de Lancy Williams' diary notes: quoted in Aspinall, p. 232.

249–50. Career and character of Unwin: Stephen Snelling, *VCs of the First World War: Gallipoli*, pp 46–49.

250. 'I told him I was full up': quoted in C. V. Usborne, *Smoke on the Horizon*.

251. The hand of a dying man: quoted in Michael Hickey, *Gallipoli*, p. 129.

251. 'But he was again shot in our arms': George Drewry, VC, letter, Imperial War Museum.

251. 'The wounded cried out all day': quoted in Rhodes James, p. 122.

252. 'I stayed on the lighters': Drewry letter.

252. 'Through our glasses . . .': Hamilton, p. 131.

254. 'You can't possibly land!': quoted in Aspinall, p. 240.

254. Hamilton's signal to Hunter-Weston: Aspinall, p. 240.

254. 'I can't stand it': quoted in Snelling, p. 40.

255. 'I 'listed to get killed': R. R. Willis, VC, *Gallipoli Gazette*, 1934.

256. 'It might have been a deserted land': quoted in Geoffrey Moorhouse, *Hell's Foundations: A Town, Its Myths and Gallipoli*, p. 63.

256. 'There was one soldier between me and the wire': quoted in Moorhouse, p. 64.

256. 'The front of the wire was now a thick mass of men': quoted in Moorhouse, p. 64.

258. Hunter-Weston's message to S Beach: Aspinall, p. 237.

260. Issuing 'many orders in great anxiety': quoted in Rhodes James, p. 126, and confirmed for the author by Turkish sources.

261. 'The whole thing was a misunderstanding': Aspinall, p. 262.

Chapter 12
Page

263. 'The beautiful battalions of the 25th': Ian Hamilton, *Gallipoli Diary*, vol I, p. 209.

265. Birdwood's view of the landing: Kevin Fewster (ed.), *Gallipoli Correspondent: The Frontline Diary of C. E. W. Bean*, p. 75.

265. 'I don't know how Joe is at present': Oliver Cumberland letter, dated May 8, 1915, Australian War Memorial.

267. 'What trenches are these?': Charles Bean, *Official History of Australia in the War of 1914–18*, vol I, p. 485.

268. 'For goodness sake come down here, sir': Bean, p. 486.

269. 'Seemed to think so much': Ellis Ashmead-Bartlett, *The Uncensored Dardanelles*, p. 29.

269–70. Doughty-Wylie's career: Stephen Snelling, *VCs of the First World War: Gallipoli*, pp 75–77.

270. Doughty-Wylie's letters to his wife and to Gertrude Bell: the L. O. Doughty-Wylie Collection, Imperial War Museum, and Gertrude Bell letters, Newcastle University.

271. 'I happened to be quite close': *Regimental Records of the Royal Welch Fusiliers*.

272. 'The men round about were full of admiration': quoted in

Snelling, pp 72–73.

272. 'Alas, for that faithful disciple of Charles Gordon': Hamilton, p. 156.

273. 'The shock was terrible': L. O. Doughty-Wylie Collection.

274. 'The Turks are coming': Bean, p. 511.

274. 'Will hold it until otherwise ordered': Bean, p. 514.

275. 'It's my business to be sniped at': Bean, p. 521.

275. Turks 'did everything imaginable to raise their courage': Ivor Margetts letter, dated May 23, 1915, Australian War Memorial.

278. Malone's account of his relief of Braund: Jock Phillips, Nicholas Boyack and E. P. Malone, *The Great Adventure*, pp 36–37.

279. 'It was practically impossible for everyone to understand . . .': Cecil Aspinall-Oglander, *Military Operations: Gallipoli*, vol I, p. 287.

279. 'Alarmist messages have been sent to me': Aspinall, p. 294.

279. Hamilton's thoughts after the First Battle of Krithia: Hamilton, pp 174, 176.

280. Aspinall on the door being bolted and barred: Aspinall, p. 295.

280. 'Least said, soonest mended' and 'all goes well': Hamilton, p. 181.

281. Hamilton's force 'insufficient': Aspinall, p. 304.

281. 'If you want more troops . . .': Hamilton, p. 164.

281. 'Thanks to the weather . . .': quoted in Aspinall, p. 304.

282. 'No message was more gratifying': Ivor Margetts letter, dated May 23, 1915, Australian War Memorial.

282. 'Such *boys* they look': Malone's diary in *The Great Adventure*, p. 42.

283. McNicoll 'captured' by British marines: Ronald McNicoll, *Walter Ramsay McNicoll*.

284. 'Bearded, ragged at knees and elbows . . .': Bean, p. 535.

284. 'We were all surprised to see each other . . .': Margetts letter.

285. 'I am quite well now . . .': Oliver Cumberland letter, dated May 31, 1915, Australian War Memorial.

287. 'I spoke to as many of them as I could . . .': Hamilton, p. 184.

287. Hamilton's description of Anzac: Hamilton, pp 178–79.

288. 'Imbros and Samothrace begin to show up grey . . .': *Gallipoli Correspondent*, p. 82.

289. 'Five hundred of our fighting men . . .': Hamilton, p. 177.

290. 'Soldiers! You must drive into the sea the enemy . . .': quoted in Robert Rhodes James, *Gallipoli*, p. 144, and Aspinall, p. 317.

293. Godley belonged to the 'Army Clique': quoted in Geoffrey Serle, *John Monash*, p. 258.

294. Monash 'seemed a little shaken': *Gallipoli Correspondent*, p. 85.

294. 'The net result as regards gain of ground was nil': quoted in Christopher Pugsley, *Gallipoli: The New Zealand Story*, p. 183.

Chapter 13
Page

297. 'In France these reports would have been impersonal messages': Ian Hamilton, *Gallipoli Diary*, vol I, p. 207.

298. 'Trust to our bayonets when we get in': Hamilton, p. 201.

300. 'It is important to push on': quoted in Cecil Aspinall-Oglander, *Military Operations, Gallipoli*, vol I, p. 335.

300. 'Unaware of the enemy's positions . . .': Aspinall, p. 339.

301. 'Four weak battalions of New Zealanders . . .': Aspinall, p. 343.

301. 'The grassy slopes that crown the cliffs . . .': Aspinall, p. 343.

302. Ashmead-Bartlett on Achi Baba: Ellis Ashmead-Bartlett, *The Uncensored Dardanelles*, p. 85.

303. 'It is a relief to get in where war is being waged scientifically': Malone's diary in *The Great Adventure*, p. 44.

304. 'I was starting with the last platoon . . .': quoted in Christopher Pugsley, *Gallipoli: The New Zealand Story*, p. 195.

304. 'A sledgehammer blow on the foot . . .': quoted in Pugsley, p. 195.

305. 'At 4 pm I issued orders . . .': Hamilton, p. 211.

305. 'I am quite satisfied that the New Zealand officer . . .': quoted in Pugsley, p. 198.

305. 'I was never in the midst of such an uproar . . .': Kevin Fewster (ed.), *Gallipoli Correspondent*, p. 91.

306. McNicoll wounded, and the charge of the Australians at Krithia: *Gallipoli Correspondent*, pp 92–93.

307. 'The manner in which these Dominion troops went forward . . .': Ashmead-Bartlett, p. 91.

308. Death of Sergeant Greig: diary and letters of George Fergus Greig, Australian War Memorial.

309. Malone and Johnston bicker at Krithia: Malone's diary in *The Great Adventure*, p. 45.

310. 'Well that was too much for me': quoted in Pugsley, p. 197.

310. 'Bayonets sparkled all over the wide plain': Hamilton, p. 211.

311. 'The puppet figures we watched began to waver': Hamilton, p. 212.

312. 'I thought I had a charmed life': quoted in Ron Austin, *As Rough as Bags*, p. 88.

313. Bean rescues McNicoll: *Gallipoli Correspondent*, pp 94–95.

313. McNicoll's operation in London: Ronald McNicoll, *Walter Ramsay McNicoll*.

314. Bean rescues the wounded at Krithia: *Gallipoli Correspondent*, pp 95–99.

315. 'They had been sent off from the beach': Hamilton, pp 216–17.

316. 'One feels fearfully lonely . . .': quoted in Pugsley, p. 199.

317. 'And they were blubbering . . .': quoted in Maurice

Shadbolt, *Voices of Gallipoli*, p. 38.

318. Hamilton's summary of the Second Battle of Krithia: quoted in John Lee, *A Soldier's Life*, p. 175.

Chapter 14
Page

324. The worry that Bridges would get White killed: Charles Bean, *Two Men I Knew*, p. 72.

324. 'General, you'll be caught . . .': quoted in *Two Men I Knew*, p. 72.

325. 'I don't quite know how it happened': quoted in *Two Men I Knew*, pp 73–74.

325. 'Were he a young man . . .': Ian Hamilton, *Gallipoli Diary*, vol I, p. 229.

326. 'There is a general impression . . .': *Argus*, September 3, 1915.

326. 'A brigade is really the last command . . .': quoted in *Two Men I Knew*, p. 75.

327. 'Now, if I was a mucking canary . . .': Compton Mackenzie, *Gallipoli Memories*, pp 80–81.

328. 'Get me a good dinner when I come back': Charles Bean, *Official History of Australia in the War of 1914–18*, p. 554.

329. Letters of John Simpson Kirkpatrick, his mother and sister: Australian War Memorial.

335. 'Sulphurous' mood at War Council: Winston Churchill, *The World Crisis 1911–18*, vol II, p. 754.

335. 'The War Council would like to know . . .': quoted in John Lee, p. 177.

336. Hamilton's 'soliloquies' and misinterpretation of Kitchener's cable: Hamilton, pp 230–31, 235–36 and 238.

338. Fisher's note of resignation: quoted in Churchill, p. 762.

338. 'The temper of the Turkish army . . .': quoted in Churchill, p. 743.

339. Fisher's 'nervous exhaustion': Churchill, p. 745.

339. Kitchener in a 'queerer mood': Churchill, p. 757.

339. 'You are bent on forcing the Dardanelles': quoted in Churchill, pp 764–65.

Chapter 15
Page

342. 'I wonder what it means': Kevin Fewster (ed.), *Gallipoli Correspondent*, p. 105.

342. 'Play ya again next Saturday': Charles Bean, *Official History of Australia in the War of 1914–18*, vol II, p. 143.

343. 'Better than a wallaby drive': letter of Jack Merivale, dated May 31, 1915, Australian War Memorial.

343. 'Our men were sitting on top of the parapets': diary of J. H. L. Turnbull, Australian War Memorial.

343. 'One out – got him': Bean, vol II, p. 148.

343. 'I want two or three' and 'I managed to get the beggars, sir': Bean, vol II, pp 149–50.

344. 'Lieut Crabbe informed me . . .': quoted in I. Grant, *Jacka VC*.

344. 'I saw one head wound like a star': *Gallipoli Correspondent*, p. 106.

345. 'On both sides the losses were so great': Liman von Sanders, *Five Years in Turkey*, p. 76.

346. 'We may not find it advisable to press on further from the south': Cecil Aspinall-Oglander, *Military Operations: Gallipoli*, vol II, p. 24.

346. 'The smell of the dead Turks outside our trenches . . .': diary of Reg Garnock, Australian War Memorial.

Chapter 16
Page

347. Von Sanders' version of the truce: Liman von Sanders, *Five Years in Turkey*, p. 76.

347. Hamilton's version of the truce: Ian Hamilton, *Gallipoli Diary*, vol I, p. 239.

347. Sergeant Lawrence's description of General Walker:

Ronald East (ed.), *The Gallipoli Diary of Sergeant Lawrence*, p. 66.

348. 'It is extraordinary how the men have changed . . .': Kevin Fewster (ed.), *Gallipoli Correspondent*, p. 110.

349. Mackenzie's account of the Anzac truce: Compton Mackenzie, *Gallipoli Memories*, pp 79–83.

350. Herbert's account of the truce: Aubrey Herbert, *Mons, Anzac and Kut*, pp 138–42.

351. Ranford on the truce: diary of J. M. Ranford, Australian War Memorial.

351. Nicholson on the truce: quoted in Nicholas Boyack, and Jane Tolerton, *In the Shadow of War*, p. 82.

351. Fenwick on the truce: quoted in Christopher Pugsley, *Gallipoli: The New Zealand Story*, pp 230–32.

352. Turnbull on the truce: diary of J. H. L. Turnbull, Australian War Memorial.

352. Malone on the truce: Malone diary in *The Great Adventure*, p. 54.

353. Bean on the truce: *Gallipoli Correspondent*, p. 119.

353. 'In one trench there is an archway . . .': *Gallipoli Correspondent*, p. 117.

354. 'We could notice the Turks . . .': Cuthbert Finlay letter, Australian War Memorial.

354. Turkish prisoners encouraged to escape: diary entry of Cecil McAnulty for June 20, 1915, Australian War Memorial.

355. 'Such a dirty, dilapidated, unorganised post . . .': Malone's diary in *The Great Adventure*, p. 58.

355. 'The art of warfare . . .': *Gallipoli Correspondent*, p. 139.

355. Charlie Clark on Quinn's Post: quoted in Maurice Shadbolt, *Voices of Gallipoli*, p. 61.

356. Dan Curham on Quinn's: quoted in Shadbolt, p. 45.

356. 'I didn't cry . . .': quoted in Shadbolt, p. 90.

356. 'Wouldn't carry a bandicoot to the square mile': letter of Will Sheppard , dated August 28, 1915, Australian War Memorial.

357. 'Before us passed the unique panorama of Anzac . . .':
diary of Chaplain E. N. Merrington, Australian War
Memorial.
358. 'He was a little infantry lad . . .': Ion Idriess, *The Desert
Column*, pp 376, 378, 389.
359. 'I went swimming with two men . . .': diary of J. K.
Gammage, Australian War Memorial.
359. Sergeant Lawrence on life at Anzac: Lawrence, pp 28, 33.
360. Hamilton on life at Anzac: Hamilton, pp 256–58.

Chapter 17
Page

364. Ashmead-Bartlett's adventures before during and after the
sinking of the *Majestic*: Ellis Ashmead-Bartlett, *The
Uncensored Dardanelles*, pp 105–18.
364. Content of Ashmead-Bartlett's letter to the press:
Ashmead-Bartlett, Appendix I, pp 269–77.
367. 'There's the *Triumph* sinking': Aubrey Herbert, *Mons,
Anzac and Kut*, p. 142.
367. 'Gentlemen, the *Triumph* has gone': Ashmead-Bartlett,
pp 110–11.
368. 'What a change since the War Office sent us packing . . .':
Ian Hamilton, *Gallipoli Diary*, vol I, p. 263.
369. 'He was in a terrible mess': Joseph Murray, *Gallipoli As I
Saw It*, p. 73.
370. 'His fresh troops won't have to be very fresh . . .': Murray,
p. 75.
370. 'Once a day, if you are lucky . . .': Murray, p. 76.
370. Compton Mackenzie's visit to Helles: Compton
Mackenzie, *Gallipoli Memories*, p. 125.
371. 'We have got used to this now . . .': quoted in Pugsley,
Gallipoli: The New Zealand Story, p. 200.
372. 'Dead Englishmen, lines and lines of them . . .': John
Carey (ed.), *The Faber Book of Reportage*, pp 451–52.
372. 'I caught hold of him with much difficulty . . .': Murray,
p. 91.

373. Hunter-Weston is 'more hated than most of the generals': Aubrey Herbert's diary entry for July 25, 1915.

375. 'Dead leaves in autumn': quoted in Robert Rhodes James, *Gallipoli*, p. 213.

377. Circumstances of Moor's VC: Stephen Snelling, *VCs of the First World War: Gallipoli*, p. 122, and C. T. Atkinson, *History of the Royal Hampshire Regt.*

377. 'Sir Ian Hamilton has been sneered at . . .': Mackenzie, p. 121.

378. Ashmead-Bartlett's parody of Hamilton's battle reports: Ashmead-Bartlett, p. 158.

378. 'A look in his eyes not of pain exactly . . .': Mackenzie, pp 96–97.

379. 'Are you convinced that with immediate reinforcements . . .': Hamilton, p. 266.

380. 'The 'only prize that lies within reach this year': Winston Churchill, *The World Crisis 1911–1918*, vol II, p. 808.

382. 'By the way all the bunkum about Turkish atrocities is wrong': letter of H. R. McLarty, dated May 22, 1915, Australian War Memorial.

382. 'The flies are simply unbearable': diary of Cecil McAnulty, Australian War Memorial.

382. 'We literally fought them for a quarter of an hour . . .': Kevin Fewster (ed.), *Gallipoli Correspondent*, p. 129.

383. 'Two men had just passed pulling a Turk by a leg . . .': *Gallipoli Correspondent*, p. 121.

383. 'It's absolutely piteous to see great sturdy bushmen . . .': Ronald East (ed.), *The Gallipoli Diary of Sergeant Lawrence*, pp 46, 48.

384. 'That smell!': Adil Şahin, interviewed for the Australian Broadcasting Commission television documentary *Gallipoli: The Fatal Shore*.

385. Turkish letters: in papers of H. R. McLarty, Australian War Memorial.

386. 'The Turks are also busily engaged sapping or trenching': Cecil McAnulty diary, Australian War Memorial.

386. 'Come on, you bastards': Lawrence, p. 50.

386. Schuler's account of an Anzac funeral: Phillip Schuler, *Australia in Arms*, p. 171.

386. Schuler on Birdwood: Schuler, p. 7.

386. Dentistry at Anzac: Lawrence, p. 51.

387. Lawrence on tunnelling; Lawrence, pp 37, 41.

388. 'On Gallipoli, from first to last, I lived with fear . . .': quoted in Maurice Shadbolt, *Voices of Gallipoli*, p. 37.

388. Nicholson on fear: quoted in Shadbolt, p. 95.

388. Lawrence on the New Army troops; Lawrence, pp 55, 58.

389. Bean on Ashmead-Bartlett: *Gallipoli Correspondent*, p. 138.

Chapter 18
Page

391. Churchill's thoughts on the naval battle: Ellis Ashmead-Bartlett, *The Uncensored Dardanelles*, pp 122–25

392. Ashmead-Bartlett's conversation with Balfour: Ashmead-Bartlett, p. 126.

393. Ashmead-Bartlett's conversation with Kitchener: Ashmead-Bartlett, pp 130–31.

394. Ashmead-Bartlett returns to Imbros, talks to Hamilton: Ashmead-Bartlett, pp 135–36, 138; also see Ian Hamilton, *Gallipoli Diary*, vol I, p. 334.

396. 'The cliff line and half a mile inland . . .': Hamilton, p. 343.

398. 'The place was in a fearful mess . . .': Memoirs of Captain L. R. Grant, Imperial War Museum, pp 57–58.

399. Egerton's comment on Mackenzie's propaganda: quoted in Michael Hickey, *Gallipoli*, p. 222.

399. Hunter-Weston talks of 'blooding the pups': quoted in Robert Rhodes James, *Gallipoli*, p. 231.

399. Hamilton on Gurkhas cutting off Turkish heads: Hamilton, p. 359.

400. 'The trenches are packed with debris': Ashmead-Bartlett, pp 143–44.

400. Hamilton refuses truce: Hamilton, p. 387.
403. Von Sanders on British attacks: Liman von Sanders, *Five Years in Turkey*, p. 79.
404. Hamilton on Hunter-Weston's illness: Hamilton, vol II, pp 22, 26, 32.
404. 'It is pitiful to see men . . .': Joseph Murray, *Gallipoli As I Saw It*, pp 103–104.

PART THREE The last throw

Chapter 19
Page

407. Kitchener's warning about Hammersley: Ian Hamilton, *Gallipoli Diary*, vol I, p. 328.
408. Hamilton rules out Mahon as a corps commander: Hamilton, p. 285.
408. Hamilton rules out Ewart: Hamilton, pp 306–307.
409. A 'placid, prudent, elderly, English gentleman': Winston Churchill, *The World Crisis 1911–1918*, p. 839.
409. Compton Mackenzie meets Stopford: Compton Mackenzie, *Gallipoli Memories*, pp 352–53.
410. Kemal's note to Essad: Atatürk Memoir, Imperial War Museum.
411. Kemal's conversation with Essad: Atatürk Memoir, and Patrick Kinross, *Atatürk*, p. 81.
413. Stopford 'keen' on good plan: Hamilton, vol II, p. 26, and Cecil Aspinall-Oglander, *Military Operations: Gallipoli*, vol II, p. 149.
414. Von Sanders and the shop window in Constantinople: Liman von Sanders, *Five Years in Turkey*, p. 82.
418. Australians 'uncivilised': Aubrey Herbert's diary entry for May 1, 1915.
418. Birdwood flees Australian dugout: Phillip Schuler, *Australia in Arms*, p. 176.
422. Hamilton's passion for secrecy: Charles Bean, *Official*

History of Australia in the War of 1914–18, vol II, p. 469.

423. Details of original scheme for Suvla landing: Aspinall, vol II, p. 148.

425. Details of revised plan for Suvla landing: Aspinall, Appendix 3.

427. Hammersley's 'imprecise' order: Aspinall, vol II, p. 154.

428. An incompetent with 'no conception of what generalship meant': J. F. C. Fuller, *The Decisive Battles of the Western World*, pp 245, 248.

430. Mackenzie's talk with Hankey: Mackenzie, pp 361–62.

431. 'The same intoxicating mixture of danger and desire': Hamilton, vol II, p. 53.

Chapter 20
Page

433. A capable officer with 'one blind spot': Cecil Aspinall-Oglander, *Military Operations: Gallipoli*, vol II, p. 169.

434. Davies 'horrified': Aspinall, p. 171.

435. Von Sanders urged to abandon Helles: Aspinall, p. 177.

437–8. Zeki Bey at Lone Pine: Charles Bean, quoted in *Gallipoli Mission*, pp 185, 190.

439. Gammage on Lone Pine: John Gammage diary, Australian War Memorial.

441. McAnulty on Lone Pine: Cecil McAnulty diary, Australian War Memorial.

441. Lawrence on Lone Pine: Ronald East (ed.), *The Gallipoli Diary of Sergeant Lawrence*, pp 68–69, 75.

443. Margetts at Lone Pine: Ivor Margetts letter of August 20, 1915, Australian War Memorial.

444. The loss of 'all those talented people': Geoffrey Blainey, *A Shorter History of Australia*, p. 159.

444. An unknown officer's account of Lone Pine: Jack Merivale papers, Australian War Memorial.

445. Oliver Cumberland dies at Lone Pine: Cumberland brothers papers, Australian War Memorial. (The letters of the Cumberland brothers have been collected in an

excellent booklet published by the Scone and Upper Hunter Historical Society Museum.)

446. Oliver Cumberland's body re-interred: Patrick Carlyon, 'Blood Brothers', *Bulletin*, May 2, 2000.

446. Idriess on Lone Pine: Ion Idriess, *The Desert Column*, pp 392, 396.

447. Tubb on the death of Burton: quoted in Stephen Snelling, *VCs of the First World War: Gallipoli*, p. 168.

447. 'It was always presumed the events were so terrible . . .': Keith Dunstan, 'Unsung Hero's Number Comes Up', *Bulletin*, April 30, 1996.

448. Shout at Lone Pine: Charles Bean, *The Official History of Australia in the War of 1914–18*, vol II, p. 565, and Snelling, p. 163.

449. 'Goodbye, Doc, old sport . . .': quoted in E. Wren, *Randwick to Hargicourt*.

450. Private Martin's letter: James Martin, letter of October 9, Australian War Memorial.

Chapter 21

Page

457. 'I did, of course, know the truth . . .': quoted in Robert Rhodes James, *Gallipoli*, p. 269.

457. Temperley on Johnston and Malone: A. C. Temperley, 'A Personal Narrative of the Battle of Chunuk Bair', Kippenberger Military Archive and Research Library, Army Museum, Waiouru, New Zealand.

457. 'The Brigadier will not get down to bedrock': Malone's diary in *The Great Adventure*, p. 65.

459. Johnston, Temperley and Malone at the Apex: Charles Bean, *Official History of Australia in the War of 1914–18*, vol II, p. 637.

459. Johnston's behaviour: Temperley narrative.

460. Temperley advises Johnston to delay: Temperley narrative.

461. 'The English approached slowly . . .': quoted in Charles

Bean, *Gallipoli Mission*, p. 220.

461. 'Thus passed by far the best chance of winning . . .': *Gallipoli Mission*, p. 220.

462. Godley–Pinwell dialogue: Kevin Fewster (ed.), *Gallipoli Correspondent*, p. 146

463. Bean shot: *Gallipoli Correspondent*, pp 146–47.

465. 'It is mad-looking country': quoted in Peter Pedersen, *Monash as Military Commander*, p. 94.

465. 'One of those crotchety, peppery, livery old Indian officers . . .': quoted in Pedersen, p. 96.

466. 'What damned nonsense!': quoted in Geoffrey Serle, *John Monash*, p. 234.

467. Battalions detached 700 yards too early: Pedersen, pp 101, 108.

468. 'I thought I could command men': John North Papers, Liddell Hart Centre for Military Archives, London; also mentioned in Robert Rhodes James, *Gallipoli*, p. 272.

468. Allanson's dislike of Australians: North Papers.

468. Allanson's views of Australians: Harry Davies, *Allanson of the 6th*, pp 82, 88.

468. No-one else heard Monash say: 'I thought I could command men': North Papers.

469. 'But he was not a fighting commander . . .' Bean, *Official History*, vol II, p. 589.

469. Monash gives Bean a 'good talking to': quoted in Pedersen, p. 106.

470. 'He is not the man': quoted in Pedersen, p. 216.

Chapter 22

Page

472. 'I want you to tell Sir Ian . . .': Cecil Aspinall-Oglander, *Military Operations: Gallipoli*, vol II, p. 234.

474. Mackenzie and Surgeon-General Birrell: Compton Mackenzie, *Gallipoli Memories*, pp 66–67 and 369–70.

476. 'I felt as if I had watched a system crash . . .': Mackenzie, p. 373.

477. 'Chaos' at Suvla: Aspinall, p. 245.

478. 'Very little firing having been heard . . .': quoted in Aspinall, p. 246.

Chapter 23

Page

482. White's poem: quoted in Peter Burness, *The Nek*, p. 44.

482. 'Dear little wife and kiddie . . .': quoted in Burness, p. 75.

483. Enver's rhetoric about the Turkish charge: Charles Bean, *Official History of Australia in the War of 1914–18*, vol II, p. 316.

483. 'I went around the trenches in the morning . . .': Sergeant William Cameron, quoted in Burness, p. 82.

485. 'Our brigadier's idea of soldiering . . .': quoted in Burness, p. 30.

486. Birdwood had 'little confidence' in Hughes: Bean, vol II, p. 617.

488. Godley's claim that the attack at the Nek fulfilled its objective: Alexander Godley, *Life of an Irish Soldier*, p. 180.

488. 'Godley was proposing to use the light horsemen . . .': Burness, p. 94.

489. Antill's written orders: quoted in Burness, p. 95.

489. The path to 'green and open country': Bean, vol II, p. 610.

489. 'I'd never have been able to stand up again . . .': Bean, vol II, p. 610.

490. Bombardment was 'desultory' and a 'joke': diary of Carew Reynell, Australian War Memorial.

491. 'We knew we were doomed': quoted in Burness, p. 101.

491. White offers his hand and says 'Goodbye': Bean, vol II, p. 612.

491. The line fell 'as though the men's limbs had become string': Bean, vol II, p. 614.

492. 'I was in the first line to advance . . .': letter of C. C. D. Pinnock, dated August 15, 1915, Australian War Memorial.

492. 'He died with a soft sigh . . .': quoted in Burness, p. 102.

492. 'I could see the knee coming out and the machine gun bullets going into it': interview with Lionel Simpson for the ABC television documentary: *Gallipoli: The Fatal Shore.*

492. 'Some men's legs were completely severed . . .': Reynell diary.

493. Captain George Hore's story: Burness, p. 105, and Bean, vol II, p. 618.

494. Trooper McConnan's letter: quoted in Burness, p. 108.

495. Death of the Harper brothers: Bean, vol II, p. 618.

495. Brazier's conversations with Antill and Hughes: quoted in Burness, p. 115.

496. The fourth line charges without orders: Bean, vol II, p. 619.

496. Sergeant Sanderson's story: Bean, vol II, p. 620.

497. 'At first here and there a man raised his arm to the sky . . .': Bean, vol II, p. 633.

498. Skeen's view of the charges: Bean, vol II, p. 606.

499. Antill's later career: Burness, pp 146–47.

500. Birdwood's view of the charges: quoted in John Robertson, *Anzac and Empire*, p. 128.

500. Hughes complains he did not receive 'proper support': quoted in Burness, p. 142.

500. Antill says attack may have been worthwhile: quoted in Robertson, p. 129.

Chapter 24
Page

503. 'It is this same spirit . . .': Ellis Ashmead-Bartlett, *The Uncensored Dardanelles*, p. 181.

504. 'No firm hand appeared to control this mass': Ashmead-Bartlett, p. 183.

504. The British soldiers moved 'bolt upright': quoted in Cecil Aspinall-Oglander, *Military Operations: Gallipoli*, vol II, p. 266.

507. Aucklanders 'simply devastated': A. C. Temperley, 'A Personal Narrative of the Battle of Chunuk Bair'.

507. Clark on Malone's refusal to attack: quoted in Shadbolt, *Voices of Gallipoli*, p. 62.

508. Canterburys' heavy losses: Templerley narrative.

508. 'A mark the size of a sixpence . . .': quoted in Christopher Pugsley, *Gallipoli: The New Zealand Story*, p. 287.

510. Godley's two messages to Monash: quoted in Peter Pedersen, *Monash as Military Commander*, p. 108, and Charles Bean, *Official History of Australia in the War of 1914–18*, vol II, p. 654.

512. Stopford's cable: Cecil Aspinall-Oglander, *Military Operations: Gallipoli*, vol II, p. 264.

513. Duration of the Great War might have been shortened: Aspinall, p. 264.

514. Dawnay regarded as being 'unduly impatient': quoted in Robert Rhodes James, *Gallipoli*, p. 283.

514. Waiting as if the whole operation were a horse race: J. F. C. Fuller, *The Decisive Battles of the Western World*, p. 255.

515. 'The enemy is advancing timidly': quoted in Aspinall, p. 266.

Chapter 25
Page

517. Malone's letter to his two young sons: quoted in the foreword to Malone's diary in *The Great Adventure*, p. 18.

517. 'I expect to go through all right . . .': Malone's diary, *The Great Adventure*, p. 66.

519. Malone says goodbye to his batman: quoted in Christopher Pugsley, *Gallipoli: The New Zealand Story*, p. 288.

519. 'We had to shoot him . . .': quoted in Maurice Shadbolt, *Voices of Gallipoli*, p. 63.

522. 'I lay without moving . . .': Harry Davies, *Allanson of the 6th*, pp 45–46.

523. 'One of those "black days" which most deeply affect the spirits of soldiers': Charles Bean, *Official History of Australia in the War of 1914–18*, vol II, p. 663.

525. 'The coming back was awful . . .': published in *The Genealogist*, September, 1996.

525. Corporal Kerr taken prisoner: Greg Kerr, *Lost Anzacs*, pp 97–99.

526. 'I caught a bullet in the left knee . . .': letter of Gunner F. Garth, dated August 11, 1915, Australian War Memorial.

526. 'For which Eastwood and Locke are to blame': quoted in Geoffrey Serle, *John Monash*, p. 238.

531. Siting of Malone's trenches: A. C. Temperley, 'A Personal Narrative of the Battle of Chunuk Bair', and Ian Hamilton, *Gallipoli Diary*, vol II, p. 86.

531. Harston on where Malone's trenches were: quoted in Pugsley, p. 291.

532. Malone's 'narrow-mindedness': Temperley narrative.

532. 'A Taranaki man named Surgenor . . .': quoted in Pugsley, pp 296–97.

533. Harston's difficulty in convincing HQ that casualties were heavy: quoted in Pugsley, p. 298.

533. 'But it was not very long . . .': Nicolson interviewed in Boyack and Tolerton, *In the Shadow of War*, p. 82, and Shadbolt, p. 92.

534. 'I don't remember any charges . . .': quoted in Shadbolt, p. 93.

534. 'And that was blood. Just blood': quoted in Shadbolt, p. 94.

535. 'I heard thump, thump, thump . . .': quoted in Shadbolt, pp 64–65.

535. 'You're only a kid . . .': Bean, vol II, p. 677.

535. 'Colonel M. was killed . . .': quoted in Pugsley, p. 304.

536. Panicky messages to Kemal: Atatürk's 'Memoirs of the Anafartalar Battles, Imperial War Museum'.

537. Kemal asked about Chunuk Bair: Atatürk 'Memoirs', and Patrick Kinross, *Atatürk*, p. 86.

537. 'The actions and conduct of the participants . . .': Atatürk 'Memoirs', and Kinross, p. 86.

538. Casualties among the Wellingtons, Gloucesters and Welch: Cecil Aspinall-Oglander, *Military Operations: Gallipoli*, vol II, p. 214, and Bean, vol II, p. 679.

539. Suffering of the wounded 'indescribable': Aspinall, p. 309.

539. 'It was a shock to me . . .': Lieutenant N. King Wilson, Bush Papers, Imperial War Museum.

540. 'I stumbled on poor A. C. . . .': Aubrey Herbert, *Mons, Anzac and Kut*, p. 179.

540. Why Godley didn't go to the Apex: Alexander Godley, *Life of an Irish Soldier*, p. 185.

542. 'I have never ceased to regret . . .': Godley, pp 185–86.

543. The sacking of Feizi Bey: Atatürk 'Memoirs', and Kinross, p. 87.

544. Stopford's cable to Hamilton: *Gallipoli Diary*, vol II, p. 59.

544. Aspinall goes to Suvla: Aspinall, vol II, pp 276–78.

545. Hamilton goes to Suvla: *Gallipoli Diary*, vol II, pp 63–67.

Chapter 26
Page

550. Funeral oration to be read over Malone: John North Papers, Liddell Hart Centre for Military Archives, London.

550. 'The whole of the South Lancs . . .': North Papers.

552. Allanson's account of the attack on Hill Q: Harry Davies, *Allanson of the 6th*, pp 51–52. Note: Allanson gave several versions of the attack and the details vary considerably.

554. Attack was 'fatuous': North Papers.

554. 'Sir Ian Hamilton came over to our line . . .': Davies, pp 73, 83.

556. 'A general air of depression . . .': Cecil Aspinall-Oglander, *Military Operations: Gallipoli*, vol II, p. 289.

557. 'I watched the flames approaching . . .': Ellis Ashmead-Bartlett, *The Uncensored Dardanelles*, pp 189–90.
558. Turkish official account of Suvla: quoted in Aspinall, vol II, p. 482.
558. Anzac generals in 'tip-top spirits': *Gallipoli Diary*, vol II, pp 81, 83.

Chapter 27
Page
562. 'What we feel in the blood . . .': quoted in Patrick Kinross, *Atatürk*, p. 90.
563. 'There is no doubt at all we are going to defeat the enemy . . .': quoted in Kinross, p. 91.
564. 'All my mates ever got were wooden crosses': quoted in Christopher Pugsley, *Gallipoli: The New Zealand Story*, p. 314.
564. The Wiltshires in Sazli Dere: Charles Bean, *The Official History of Australia in the War of 1914–18*, vol II, p. 714.
566. Temperley orders machine gunners to fire on New Army troops: A. C. Temperley, 'A Personal Narrative of the Battle of Chunuk Bair'.
566. 'The heavy naval shells . . .': quoted in Kinross, p. 92.
567. 'Well, we had Chunuk Bair . . .': Ian Hamilton, *Gallipoli Diary*, vol II, pp 89–90.
570. The scenes 'got us down': Charles Bean, *Gallipoli Mission*, p. 234.

Chapter 28
Page
573. 'One hundred years of breeding in slums . . .': Kevin Fewster (ed.), *Gallipoli Correspondent*, p. 153.
574. The men had started to outgrow their generals: Christopher Pugsley, *Gallipoli: The New Zealand Story*, p. 306.
574. Godley watches the despatch riders: John North Papers, Liddell Hart Centre, London.

575. 'Would I say we disliked our General Godley ...?': quoted in Maurice Shadbolt, *Voices of Gallipoli*, p. 40.

576. Stopford explains why he cannot attack: Ian Hamilton, *Gallipoli Diary*, vol II, pp 91–92, and Cecil Aspinall-Oglander, *Military Operations: Gallipoli*, p. 319.

577. Hamilton asked to 'ginger up' the Suvla troops: Hamilton, vol II, pp 95–97.

578. Stopford says 53rd Division might 'bolt': Aspinall, p. 319.

578. 'Ought I to have resigned ...': Hamilton, vol II, p. 100.

578. Hamilton tells Kitchener the Suvla generals are 'unfit for it': Hamilton, vol II, p. 102.

579. 'If you should deem it necessary to replace Stopford ...': Hamilton, vol II, pp 104–105.

580. 'I respectfully decline to waive my seniority': Hamilton. vol II, pp 107, 109.

582. 'The result is that my coup has so far failed': Hamilton, vol II, p. 114.

582. Hamilton asks for 95,000 additional troops: Hamilton, vol II, p. 117.

Chapter 29
Page

585. 'I don't know where it is ...': Cecil Aspinall-Oglander, *Military Operations: Gallipoli*, vol II, p. 353.

586. How Trooper Potts won the VC: Potts' account published in Reading newspapers.

586. 'On this dark battlefield of fog and flame ...': Winston Churchill, *The World Crisis 1911–18*, vol III, p. 845.

588. 'It was awful to hear the moans & groans of the wounded ...': letter of James Grieve, dated August 27, Australian War Memorial.

589. 'The whole was a rotten, badly organised show ...': quoted in Peter Pedersen, *Monash as Military Commander*, p. 119.

589. 'Aw, leave the dead 'uns ...': Robert Rhodes James, *Gallipoli*, p. 310.

590. 'A bob in and the winner shouts': quoted in Peter Burness, *The Nek*, p. 117.

590. Throssell's wounds: Snelling, p. 225.

Chapter 30
Page

593. Hamilton's nightmare: Ian Hamilton, *Gallipoli Diary*, vol II, p. 163.

593. Murdoch explains that he is better with a pen than rifle: quoted in Desmond Zwar, *In Search of Keith Murdoch*, p. 25.

595. 'I'll be able to learn ever so much here': quoted in Zwar, p. 10.

595. Bean's description of Murdoch: Charles Bean, *Official History of Australia in the War of 1914–18*, vol II, p. 782.

596. 'A shocking feature of London . . .': quoted in Zwar, p. 13.

596. Murdoch's 'wheedling' letter: quoted in Zwar, p. 24.

597. Genesis of the Ashmead-Bartlett letter: Zwar, p. 28, and Ellis Ashmead-Bartlett, *The Uncensored Dardanelles*, p. 239.

597. Full text of Ashmead-Bartlett letter, Ashmead-Bartlett, pp 240–43.

599. 'I saw Murdoch the Australian yesterday': quoted in Robert Rhodes James, *Gallipoli*, p. 314.

600. The Murdoch letter: a copy is held by the National Library of Australia; it was published in full in Margaret Jennings, *Australia and the Great War* in 1969.

602. 'No gentleman would have said it, and no gentleman will believe it': quoted in Zwar, p. 47.

602. Murdoch as Hughes' fixer: Zwar, p. 50.

603. Murdoch's note to Northcliffe: quoted in William Shawcross, *Murdoch*, p. 39.

603. 'Oh sure, it may not have been fair . . .': Rupert Murdoch interview with Gerard Henderson, quoted in Shawcross, p. 36. (For other accounts of the Murdoch affair, *see*

Phillip Knightley, *The First Casualty*; John Avieson, 'The Correspondent Who Stopped a War', *Australian Journalism Review*, January–December, 1986; and Kevin Fewster, 'Ellis Ashmead-Bartlett and the Making of the Anzac Legend', *Journal of Australian Studies*, June, 1982. For an example of Murdoch's wartime reporting, see Harry Gordon, *An Eyewitness History of Australia*, p. 208.)

605. 'I am sorry you have put that question': *Argus*, October 30, 1915.

606. Dawnay's London interviews: Dawnay Papers, Imperial War Museum.

607. Hamilton saves Braithwaite: *Gallipoli Diary*, pp 235, 236, 240.

608. Hamilton's response to the Murdoch letter: *Gallipoli Diary*, p. 259.

608. Kitchener sacks Hamilton: *Gallipoli Diary*, pp 271–72.

609. 'The poor chap looked to me very haggard . . .': Kevin Fewster (ed.), *Gallipoli Correspondent*, pp 169–70.

610. 'Last night your letter came . . .': Dawnay Papers.

Chapter 31
Page

614. 'He was born with another sort of mind from me': Ian Hamilton, *Gallipoli Diary*, p. 273.

616. Monro's tour of the battlefields: Cecil Aspinall-Oglander, *Military Operations: Gallipoli*, vol II, p. 401.

617. 'He came, he saw, he capitulated': Winston Churchill, *The World Crisis 1911–18*, vol III, p. 878.

618. 'If the army meant business': Aspinall, p. 408.

618. 'We must do it right this time': Aspinall, p. 409.

619. 'I fear the navy may not play up': Aspinall, p. 410.

620. Kitchener's cable to Asquith: Aspinall, p. 417.

620. 'Young man you were right': quoted in Robert Rhodes James, *Gallipoli*, p. 331.

620. 'The men would not have cheered many men . . .': Kevin

Fewster (ed.), *Gallipoli Correspondent*, p. 177.

622. Churchill's reasons for leaving the Cabinet: Churchill, vol. III, p. 884.

623. 'It is actually snowing this morning': diary of R. A. McInnis, Australian War Memorial.

624. 'A disorganised crowd will press in despairing tumult . . .': Aspinall, p. 430.

Chapter 32
Page

627. 'We can't advance; you can't advance': quoted in W. J. Harvey, *The Red and White Diamond: The History of the 24th Battalion AIF*, p. 38.

627. 'My God, I cannot imagine how those poor unfortunates in France . . .': letter of C. C. D. Pinnock, Australian War Memorial.

628. Kemal leaves: Patrick Kinross, *Atatürk*, p. 94.

628. Von Sanders claims to know nothing of the intended evacuation: Liman von Sanders, *Five Years in Turkey*, p. 97.

628. 'It contains very good news . . .': Lieutenant Mehmed Fasih, *Lone Pine Diary*, p. 137.

630. 'Every man was to stay as much as possible in his dugout': recollection of Donald Lechte in State Library of Victoria.

631. Monash on the intended evacuation: quoted in Geoffrey Serle, *John Monash*, p. 247.

632. 'You fellows had a bad time . . .': quoted in Cecil Aspinall-Oglander, *Military Operations: Gallipoli*, p. 452.

632. Bean leaves Anzac: Kevin Fewster (ed.), *Gallipoli Correspondent,* pp 195, 197.

633. 'I hope *they* won't hear us . . .': quoted in Aspinall, p. 453.

633. 'You imagined wherever you fixed your eyes . . .': Pinnock letter, Australian War Memorial.

634. Evacuation stories: W. J. Harvey, pp 56–57.

635. Monash on the evacuation: quoted in Serle, p. 250.

637. 'First the Dublin had a slight advantage...': Joseph Murray, *Gallipoli As I Saw It*, p. 178.

640. 'Like St Paul's Cathedral being fired out of a howitzer': quoted in Robert Rhodes James, *Gallipoli*, p. 346.

640. Joe Murray leaves Gallipoli: Murray, pp 191–92.

Chapter 33

Page

643. 'We do not need to hunt out individuals to blame...': John Lee, *A Soldier's Life*, p. 269.

644. 'It was one of those typical days...': *Nick Clarke, Alistair Cooke: The Biography*, p. 7.

645. 'I have tried to say as little as possible': quoted in John Robertson, *Anzac and Empire*, p. 232.

648. 'Dreams abandoned, lives without purpose...': quoted in Craig Wilcox (ed.), *The Great War, Gains and Losses: Anzac and Empire*, p. 6.

651. 'After three years of fighting, the despised Turkish rebel ...': Patrick Kinross, *Atatürk*, p. 339.

651. 'Turkey is governed by one drunkard': quoted in Kinross, p. 261. (For a thoughtful account of the legacy of Gallipoli, *see* Bill Gammage, 'Anzac's Influence on Turkey and Australia', *Journal of the Australian War Memorial*, April, 1991.)

652. Account of Talat's death: Alan Moorehead, *Gallipoli*, p. 358.

653. Keyes in 1925: quoted in Moorehead, p. 363.

657. 'So, through a Churchill's excess of imagination...': Charles Bean, *Official History of Australia in the War of 1914–18*, vol I, p. 201.

658. 'Don't be too hard on your enemies': Hamilton Papers, Liddell Hart Centre.

658. 'These boys of yours did not die for reparations...': Hamilton Papers.

659. Hamilton admits his mistakes: Hamilton Papers.

661. The Turkish shepherd boy carelessly pronouncing names: Roy Elston, *The Traveller's Handbook for Constantinople, Gallipoli and Asia Minor*, p. 101.

Select bibliography

BOOKS

Adam-Smith, Patsy, *The Anzacs,* Thomas Nelson, 1978.
—— *Australian Women at War,* Thomas Nelson, 1984.
—— *Prisoners of War,* Viking, 1992.
Andrews, E. M., *The Anzac Illusion,* Cambridge University Press, 1993.
Ascherson, Neal, *Black Sea: The Birthplace of Civilisation and Barbarism,* Jonathan Cape, 1995.
Ashmead-Bartlett, Ellis, *The Uncensored Dardanelles,* Hutchinson, 1928.
Aspinall-Oglander, Cecil, *Military Operations: Gallipoli,* two volumes plus appendices and maps, Heinemann, 1929, 1932.
Atkinson, C. T., *History of the Royal Hampshire Regt,* Vol II, Gale and Polden, 1950.
Austin, Ron, *As Rough as Bags, History of the 6th Battalion 1914–1919,* R. J. & S. P. Austin, 1992.
—— *Cobbers in Khaki, History of the 8th Battalion 1914–1918,* Slouch Hat Publications, 1997.
Australian Imperial Force: Staff Regimental and Graduation List of Officers, Government Printer, Melbourne, 1914.
Bean, Charles, *On the Wool Track,* Hodder & Stoughton, 1916.
—— *The Anzac Book,* Cassell & Co, 1916.
—— 'The Story of Anzac', volumes I and II of *Official History*

of *Australia in the War of 1914–18,* Angus & Robertson, 1940.

—— *Anzac to Amiens,* Australian War Memorial, 1946.

—— *Gallipoli Mission,* ABC, 1990.

—— *Two Men I Knew,* Angus & Robertson, 1957.

Benson, Irving, *The Man with the Donkey: The Good Samaritan of Gallipoli,* Hodder & Stoughton, 1965.

Blainey, Geoffrey, *A Shorter History of Australia,* Heinemann, 1994.

—— *The Causes of War,* Sun Books, 1998.

—— *A Short History of the World,* Viking, 2000.

Bowers, Peter, *Anzacs,* Australia Post, 1999.

Boyack, Nicholas and Tolerton, Jane, *In the Shadow of War,* Penguin, 1990.

Burness, Peter, *The Nek,* Kangaroo Press, 1996.

Butler, A. G., *Official History of the Australian Army Medical Services 1914–18. Volume I,* Australian War Memorial, 1938.

Carey, John (ed.), *The Faber Book of Reportage,* Faber & Faber, 1987.

Churchill, Winston, *The World Crisis 1911–18,* four volumes, Odhams Press, 1938.

—— *My Early Life,* Odhams Press Ltd, 1960.

Cochrane, Peter, *Simpson and the Donkey,* Melbourne University Press, 1992.

—— *Australians at War,* ABC Books, 2001.

Curran, Tom, *Across the Bar: The Story of 'Simpson',* Ogmios Publications, 1994.

Cutlack, F. M. (ed.) *War Letters of General Monash,* Angus & Robertson, 1935.

Davie, Michael, *Anglo-Australian Attitudes,* Secker & Warburg, 2000.

Davies, Harry, *Allanson of the 6th,* Square One Publications, 1991.

Dennis, Peter, et al, *Oxford Companion to Australian Military History,* Oxford, 1995.

Denton, Kit, *Gallipoli Illustrated*, Rigby, 1981.

Downing, W. H., *To the Last Ridge*, Duffy & Snellgrove, 1998.

Droogleever, Robin, *From the Front: A. B. (Banjo) Paterson's Dispatches from the Boer War*, Macmillan, 2000.

East, Ronald (ed.), *The Gallipoli Diary of Sergeant Lawrence*, Melbourne University Press, 1983.

Elston, Roy, *The Traveller's Handbook for Constantinople, Gallipoli and Asia Minor*, Thos Cook & Son, 1923.

Facey, A. B., *A Fortunate Life*, Fremantle Arts Centre Press, 1981.

Fasih, Mehmed, *Lone Pine (Bloody Ridge) Diary of Lt Mehmed Fasih*, Denizler Kitabevi, 2001.

Fewster, K. (ed.), *Gallipoli Correspondent: The Frontline Diary of C .E. W. Bean*, Allen & Unwin, 1983.

Fewster, K., et al, *A Turkish View of Gallipoli: Canakkale*, Hodja Educational Resources Co-operative.

Frame, Tom, *The Shores of Gallipoli. Naval Aspects of the Anzac Campaign*, Hale & Ironmonger, 2000.

Fuller, J. F. C., *The Decisive Battles of the Western World*, volume III, Eyre & Spottiswoode, 1956.

Fussell, Paul, *The Great War and Modern Memory*, Oxford University Press, 1977.

Gammage, Bill, *The Broken Years*, Penguin, 1975.

Godley, General Sir Alexander, *Life of an Irish Soldier*, E. P. Dutton, 1939.

Goodwin, Jason, *Lords of the Horizons*, Vintage, 1999.

Gordon, Harry, *An Eyewitness History of Australia*, Rigby, 1976.

Grant, I., *Jacka, VC*, Macmillan and AWM, 1989.

Gullett, H. S., 'The Australian Imperial Force in Sinai and Palestine', volume VII of *Official History of Australia in the War of 1914–18*, Angus & Robertson, 1923.

Hamilton, Ian, *Gallipoli Diary*, two volumes, George H. Doran Co, 1920.

—— *Listening For The Drums*, Faber & Faber, 1944.

Handbook of the Turkish Army, 1916, IWM and Battery Press

(reprint of 1916 edition).

Hargrave, John, *The Suvla Bay Landing*, Macdonald, 1964.

Harvey, Sgt W. J., *The Red and White Diamond: Official History of the 24th Battalion AIF*, McCubbin, 1920[?]

Haythornthwaite, Philip, *Gallipoli, 1915*, Osprey Publishing Ltd, 1991.

Herbert, Aubrey, *Mons, Anzac and Kut*, Arnold, 1919.

Hickey, Michael, *Gallipoli*, John Murray, 1995.

Higgins, Trumbull, *Winston Churchill and the Dardanelles*, Heinemann, 1963.

Hill, Anthony, *Soldier Boy: The True Story of Jim Martin the Youngest Anzac*, Penguin, 2001.

Holmes, Richard, *Epic Land Battles*, Octopus Books, 1976.

Horner, D. M. (ed.), *The Commanders*, Allen & Unwin, 1984.

Idriess, Ion, *The Desert Column*, Angus & Robertson, 1932.

Inglis, K. S., *Sacred Places*, Miengunyah Press, 1999.

James, Robert Rhodes, *Gallipoli*, Pimlico, 1999.

Jennings, Margaret, *Australia in the Great War*, two parts, Hill of Content, 1969.

Johnson, Carl and Barnes, Andrew (eds), *Jacka's Mob: A Narrative of the Great War by Edgar John Rule*, Military Melbourne, 1999.

Keegan, John, *Warpaths*, Hodder & Stoughton, 1995.

—— *The Face of Battle*, Pimlico, 1998.

—— *The First World War*, Hutchinson, 1998.

Kelly, Paul, *The End of Certainty*, Allen & Unwin, 1992.

Kerr, Greg, *Lost Anzacs*, Oxford University Press, 1997.

—— *Private Wars*, Oxford University Press, 2000.

Kinross, Patrick, *Atatürk: The Rebirth of a Nation*, Orion, 1995.

Knightley, Phillip, *The First Casualty*, Harcourt Brace Jovanovich, 1975.

Laffin, John, *Damn the Dardanelles*, Sun Books, 1985.

Lapping, Brian, *End of Empire*, Granada, 1985.

Lee, John, *A Soldier's Life: General Sir Ian Hamilton 1853–1947*, Macmillan, 2000.

Liddle, Peter, *Men of Gallipoli,* David & Charles Military Book, 1988.

Macdonald, Lyn, *1915, The Death of Innocence,* Penguin, 1997.

Mackenzie, Compton, *Gallipoli Memories,* Cassell & Co, 1929.

McDonald, Roger, *1915,* Fontana, 1982.

McKernan, Michael, *The Australian People and the Great War,* Collins, 1984.

McNicoll, Ronald, *Walter Ramsay McNicoll 1877–1947* (private biography).

Magnus, Philip, *Kitchener: Portrait of an Imperialist,* John Murray, 1958.

Masefield, John, *Gallipoli,* Heinemann, 1935.

Matthew, Colin (ed.), *Brief Lives,* Oxford University Press, 1999.

Mills, Harry, *The Road to Sarajevo. Origins of the First World War,* Macmillan,1985.

Moorehead, Alan, *Gallipoli,* Hamish Hamilton, 1956.

Moorhouse, Geoffrey, *Hell's Foundations: A Town, Its Myths and Gallipoli,* Hodder & Stoughton, 1992.

Morgenthau, Henry, *Secrets of the Bosphorus,* Hutchinson, 1918.

Murray, Joseph, *Gallipoli as I Saw It,* William Kimber, 1965.

North, John, *Gallipoli: The Fading Vision,* Faber & Faber, 1966.

Observer Appreciation, *Churchill by his Contemporaries,* Hodder & Stoughton, 1965.

Official Year Book of the Commonwealth of Australia, No. 8, 1915.

Pedersen, Peter, *Monash as Military Commander,* Melbourne University Press, 1992.

Phillips, Jock, Boyack, Nicholas and Malone, E. P., *The Great Adventure,* Allen & Unwin, 1988.

Pimlott, John, *The British Army (The Guinness History of),* Guinness World Records Ltd, 1993.

Pocock, Tom, *Alan Moorehead,* The Bodley Head, 1990.

Pugsley, Christopher, *Gallipoli: The New Zealand Story,* Hodder & Stoughton, 1984.

Robson, L. L., *Australia and the Great War,* Macmillan, 1982.

Robertson, John, *Anzac and Empire,* Hamlyn Australia, 1990.

Sanders, Liman von, *Five Years in Turkey,* Battery Press, 2000.

Sandys, Celia, *Churchill Wanted Dead or Alive,* HarperCollins, 1999.

Schuler, Phillip, *Australia in Arms,* T. Fisher Unwin, 1916.

Scott, Ernest, 'Australia During the War', volume XI of *Official History of Australia in the War of 1914–18,* Angus & Robertson, 1936.

Serle, Geoffrey, *John Monash: A Biography,* Melbourne University Press, 1985.

Shadbolt, Maurice, *Voices of Gallipoli,* David Ling Publishing, 2001.

Shawcross, William, *Murdoch,* Random House, 1992.

Snelling, Stephen, *VCs of the First World War: Gallipoli,* Sutton Publishing, 1999.

Souter, Gavin, *Lion and Kangaroo: The Invitation of Australia,* Text Publishing, 2000.

Steel, Nigel, *Battleground Europe: Gallipoli,* Leo Cooper, 1999.

Steel, Nigel and Hart, Peter, *Defeat at Gallipoli,* Macmillan, 1985.

Stephens, Tony, *The Last Anzacs,* Allen and Kemsley, 1996.

Strachey, Lytton, *Five Victorians,* Reprint Society, 1942.

Sulzberger, C. L., *The Fall of Eagles,* Crown Publishers, 1977.

Swifte, Tim, *Gallipoli: The Incredible Campaign,* Magazine Promotions, 1985.

Taylor, A. J. P. (ed.), *History of World War 1,* Macdonald & Co, 1988.

Taylor, Phil and Cupper, Pam, *Gallipoli: A Battlefield Guide,* Kangaroo Press, 1997.

Tuchman, Barbara, *August 1914,* Constable & Co, 1962.

—— *The Proud Tower,* Papermac, 1980.

Usborne, C. V., *Smoke on the Horizon,* Hodder & Stoughton, 1933.

Wanliss, Newton, *The History of the Fourteenth Battalion AIF,* The Arrow Printery, 1929.

Ward, D., *Regimental Records of the Royal Welch Fusiliers,* Vol 4, 1928.

Welborn, Suzanne, *Lords of Death,* Fremantle Arts Centre Press, 1982.

Wilcox, Craig, *The Great War, Gains and Losses: Anzac and Empire,* AWM and ANU, 1995.

Winter, Denis (ed.), *Making the Legend: The War Writings of C. E. W. Bean,* University of Queensland Press, 1992.

Winter, Denis, *25 April 1915,* University of Queensland Press, 1994.

Wren, E., *Randwick to Hargicourt: History of the 3rd Battalion, AIF,* 1935.

Zwar, Desmond, *In Search of Keith Murdoch,* Macmillan, 1980.

ARTICLES

Ashmead-Bartlett, Ellis: Account of the Anzac landing in the *Age* of May 8, 1915.

Age, Melbourne, all issues from August, 1914 to December, 1915.

Argus, Melbourne, all issues from August, 1914 to December, 1915.

Australasian, all issues for 1914 and 1915.

Avieson, John, 'The Correspondent Who Stopped a War', *Australian Journalism Review,* January–December, 1986.

Barrett, John, 'No Straw Man: C. E. W. Bean and Some Critics', *Australian Historical Studies,* April 1988.

Bastiaan, Ross, 'Gallipoli Plaques'.

Bean, Charles, 'The Anzac People: Firmest Comradeship of the War', *Reveille,* March, 1931.

Carlyon, Patrick, 'Blood Brothers', *Bulletin,* May 2, 2000.

Dean, Arthur and Gutteridge, Eric, 'The Seventh Battalion AIF', 1933.

Dix, Charles, 'Efficient Navy: How Troops Were Landed', *Reveille*, March, 1932.

Doyle, Peter and Bennett, Matthew, 'Military Geography: The Influence of Terrain in the Outcome of the Gallipoli Campaign', *The Geographical Journal*, Royal Geographical Society, March 1999.

Dunstan Keith, 'Unsung Hero's Number Comes Up', *Bulletin*, April 30, 1996.

Ekins, Ashley, 'Historical Guide to the Battlefields of the Gallipoli Campaign', Australian War Memorial, 2000.

—— 'A Ridge Too Far: Military Objectives and the Dominance of Terrain in The Gallipoli Campaign', paper delivered at Onsekiz Mart University, Canakkale, Turkey, April 2000.

—— 'The Assault on Lone Pine, 6 August, 1915: Feint or Folly?', paper delivered at Australian War Memorial symposium, 'Gallipoli: The August Offensive', August, 2000.

Evans, Michael,: *From Legend to Learning: Gallipoli and the Military Revolution of World War 1*, Land Warfare Studies Centre, 2000.

Fewster, Kevin, 'Ellis Ashmead-Bartlett and the Making of the Anzac Legend', *Journal of Australian Studies*, June 1982.

Gammage, Bill, 'Anzac's Influence on Turkey and Australia', *Journal of the Australian War Memorial*, April 1991.

Hamilton, Ian, 'Lack of Guns in Gallipoli Campaign', *Reveille*, September, 1932.

Inglis, Ken, 'The Anzac Tradition', in *Meanjin Quarterly*, Autumn, 1965.

—— 'C. E. W Bean: Australian Historian', the 1969 John Murtagh Macrossan Lecture, published by University of Queensland Press, 1970.

—— 'The Australians at Gallipoli' (two parts), *Australian Historical Studies*, April and October, 1970.

—— 'Gallipoli Pilgrimage', in *Journal of the Australian War Memorial*, April, 1991.

James, Robert Rhodes, 'A Visit to Gallipoli', *1962*, *Stand-To*, March–October, 1964.

King, Jonathan, 'Our Last Anzacs', *Weekend Australian*, November 8–9, 1997.

McKernan, Michael, 'The Warriors', *Weekend Australian*, August 7–8, 1999.

McNicoll, Walter, 'Eerie: Armada's Approach', *Reveille*, March, 1931.

Moorehead, Alan, 'Return to a Legend', *New Yorker*, April 2, 1955.

Pedersen, Peter, 'The Ghosts of Anzac', *Journal of the Australian War Memorial*, April, 1983.

Prior, Robin, 'The Suvla Bay Tea-Party: A Reassessment', in *Journal of the Australian War Memorial*, October, 1985.

Prior, Robin and Wilson, Trevor, 'The Warriors', *Australian*, August 28, 1999.

Reid, Richard, et al, 'A "duty clear before us" ', Department of Veterans' Affairs, 2000.

Roberts, Chris, 'The Landing at Anzac: A Reassessment', *Journal of the Australian War Memorial*, April 1993.

Robertson, J. C., 'The Landing: Epic Feat', *Reveille*, March, 1931.

Sydney Morning Herald, selected issues for 1914 and 1915.

Sun, Sydney, selected issues for 1915.

Thomson, Alistair, ' "The Vilest Libel of the War?": Imperial Politics and the Official Histories of Gallipoli', *Australian Historical Studies*, October, 1993.

Thursby, Cecil, 'Power of the Navy: Made Landing Possible', *Reveille*, March, 1932.

Travers, Tim, 'The Other Side of the Hill', a Turkish perspective on the Gallipoli campaign, in *MHQ*, Spring 2000.

Turnbull, Malcolm, 'Where was the Queen?', *Age*, January 4, 2001.

Willis, R. R., 'The Landing in Gallipoli', *Gallipoli Gazette*, July 1934.

PRIVATE PAPERS AND MATERIAL RELATING TO INDIVIDUALS

Australian War Memorial, Canberra
Lieutenant Henry Allen 1DRL0029
Colonel J. M. Antill 3DRL6458
Bean diaries 3DRL606
Private Arthur Blackburn VC 2DRL0650
Field Marshal Sir Thomas Blamey 3DRL/6643
Lieutenant-Colonel Noel Brazier 1DRL0147
Lord Casey 3DRL/3267 and 3DRL2030
Private Mawer Cowtan PR90/051
Private Joe Cumberland PR86/147
Private Oliver Cumberland PR86/147
Captain Cuthbert Finlay 1DRL284
Private A. C. Fricker PR00956
Private J. K. Gammage PR82/003
Lieutenant Reg Garnock PR91/166
Gunner F. Garth 1DRL/0306
Lieutenant Alfred Glasson PR90/085
General Godley correspondence 3DRL/2233
Sergeant George Greig PR00277
Private James Grieve PR91/079
Private P. H. Harrison PR91/005
Private Cecil McAnulty 1DRL042
Lieutenant R. A. McInnis 1DRL/0438
Lieutenant H. R. McLarty 3DRL/3339
Captain Ivor Margetts 1DRL/0478
Private James Martin PR83061
Colonel L. C. Maygar VC 1DRL/0491
Lieutenant J. L. Merivale 3DRL3961
Chaplain E. N. Merrington 1DRL0496
Sergeant Cliff Pinnock 1DRL547
Lieutenant Jack Playne PR83/067
Corporal J. N. Ranford 1DRL/0551
Major Thomas Redford PR85/64

Major Carew Reynell PR86/388
Lieutenant E. J. Richards 2DRL/0301
Corporal W. V. Rusden 3DRL/2287
Private John Simpson [Kirkpatrick] 3DRL/3424
Captain W. H. Sheppard 2DRL/0314
Private Albert Tew PR00576
Private J. H. L. Turnbull PR91/015

LaTrobe Library, State Library of Victoria
Lieutenant-General William Birdwood MS 10930
Private (later Sergeant) John Brotchie MS 11628
Private Donald Lechte MS10701

Imperial War Museum, London
Allanson Papers
'Atatürk's Memoirs of the Anafartalar Battles' (typescript)
Birdwood Papers
Captain E. W. Bush Papers
Dawnay Papers
L. O. Doughty-Wylie Papers
Lieutenant G. L. Drewry, VC, letters
Rear-Admiral I. W. Gibson, diary
Captain L. R. Grant, memoirs
Hunter-Weston Papers
Commander H. F. Minchin, letter
Rayfield Papers
Orlo Williams Diaries

Liddell Hart Centre for Military Archives, London
Ian Hamilton Papers
John North Papers

Kippenberger Military Archive and Research Library, Army Musuem, Waiouru, New Zealand
A Personal Narrative of the Battle of Chunuk Bair by Colonel
    A. C. Temperley

Churchill College, Cambridge
Churchill Papers
Fisher Letters
Hankey Papers

Newcastle University Library, England
Special Collections: Gertrude Bell Papers 35 and 38

Film and video
Australians at War (episode two), Beyond Productions, 2001. Australian Broadcasting Commission documentary series.

Forgotten Men: The Human Experience of World War I, presented by Sir John Hammerton and introduced by Sir Ian Hamilton, Canal+Images International, 1999. (Originally made in 1934 from footage at the Imperial War Museum.)

Gallipoli, feature film directed by Peter Weir, 1981.

Gallipoli: History in the Depths, Turkish documentary. English translation by SBS Australia.

Gallipoli: The Fatal Shore, reported by Chris Masters for the Australian Broadcasting Commission.

Gallipoli: The Last Crusade, Ed Skelding Productions, 1999.

Gallipoli 1915: The Bloody Peninsula, Castle Communications PLC.

Great Military Blunders, Channel Four Television Corporation, UK.

Heroes of Gallipoli, Australian War Memorial. Of 20 minutes duration, this is Ellis Ashmead-Bartlett's surviving movie film from Gallipoli with titles by Charles Bean.

Kitchener: The Empire's Flawed Hero, a Brook Lapping Production for the BBC.

The Anzac Legend, Interface Productions and Direct Video, 1990.

Acknowledgements

Myths are charming; truths are more interesting and harder to find. In Australia, fact and myth about Gallipoli are interwoven so well that sometimes one cannot tell where one ends and the other starts. Gallipoli is part of the folklore, bigger than the facts. In writing this book I have tried to find the truth (although I know I have not always succeeded) and to step around the myths. This is not necessarily evidence of honest intent. Gallipoli is a true tragedy in three acts; it doesn't need the embroidery of myths. And the men who fought there don't need myths to make them look good.

Of the many people who helped me with this book, two should be mentioned before all others. Kenan Çelik of Çanakkale took me all over the battlefields, day after day, week after week, both sides of the Dardanelles, in 1998 and 2000. We ate bread and tomatoes on the beach near Dardanos, sat out a blizzard at Krithia and wheezed through the mad hills north of Anzac. Kenan knows the ground the way a farmer knows his paddocks, but he has a better gift, and that is his wisdom. I thank him, his wife Hamiyet and their son Ahmet for so many kindnesses. Ashley Ekins, a senior historian at the Australian War Memorial, has also been a good friend. So many times he pointed me towards promising material; he gave generously of his time and knowledge, even though he had his own book to write. Like Kenan, he knows the Gallipoli story is full of subtleties. As with Kenan, I owe him much. I should stress, however, that if this book contains any errors of fact or judgement, neither Kenan nor Ashley, nor indeed anyone other than myself, is responsible.

It is impossible to write about Gallipoli without relying on a handful of books: the official histories of Bean and Aspinall; the diaries of Hamilton and Bean; Chris Pugsley's story of the New Zealanders; Peter Burness's account of the tragedy at the Nek; Stephen Snelling on the VC winners; and Patrick Kinross on Atatürk. I acknowledge my debt to all of them and particularly to Hamilton, whose honesty and literary style make him the rarest of military diarists.

I thank the staff at the Australian War Memorial, particularly Ian Kelly and Paul Mansfield, and at the State Library of Victoria. The staff at the Australian Racing Museum were kind enough to allow me to go through their collection of the *Australasian*. Dolores Ho at the Kippenberger Military Archive and Research Library in New Zealand helped with the provision of the Temperley narrative, which tells so much about the battle for Chunuk Bair and the tensions among the New Zealand commanders. The staff at the Liddell Hart Centre for Military Archives in London helped with the John North and Ian Hamilton papers. I am also grateful for the help and guidance I received from the staff at the Churchill Archives, Cambridge, and the Special Collections Library at the University of Newcastle, Newcastle upon Tyne. Nigel Steel of the Imperial War Museum pointed me towards the more interesting collections there and gave me much good advice. I am also indebted to Anthony Richards at the IWM, Helen Arkwright at Newcastle University, Alan Kucia at the Liddell Hart Centre and Allen Packwood at the Churchill Archives.

Patrick Walters helped me time after time, particularly when it came to finding obscure material or tracking down relatives of Gallipoli veterans. His great-uncle, Carew Reynell, watched the charges at the Nek, wrote a fine diary and died at Hill 60. I hope Patrick will some day write his own book about Gallipoli. Judy Malone, widow of E. P. Malone, Colonel Malone's grandson, was wonderfully helpful with sources in New Zealand, as were Nicholas Boyack and Jock Phillips. Christopher Pugsley permitted me to quote material that is available only in his splendid book *Gallipoli: The New Zealand Story*. Kevin Fewster allowed me to quote extensively from his edited version of Bean's diaries, published as *Gallipoli Correspondent*. One, of course, still needs to see Bean's own words, which I did, but Kevin Fewster's book made the navigation so much easier. Peter Burness of the Australian War Memorial allowed me to quote from *The Nek*, which also contains material not available elsewhere.

Dr Margaret Heese of South Africa, daughter of Sergeant Cyril Lawrence, was kind enough to help me with extracts from her father's diary, which ranks as just about the best thing written at Anzac. D. D. McNicoll obtained for me the private biography written on his distinguished grandfather, Walter Ramsay McNicoll. I am grateful to Betty Durre and Colin Bennett, the grandchildren of Sir John Monash, for their help, and to Jessie Serle, widow of Professor Geoffrey Serle, author of *John Monash: A Biography*. Mrs Joan Crommelin allowed me extensive use of the letters of her uncles, Joe and Oliver Cumberland. Jack Harris, nephew of Private James Martin, the youngest Australian to die at Gallipoli, allowed me to quote from his uncle's letter; Anthony Hill, author of *Soldier Boy: The True Story of Jim Martin the Youngest Anzac,* also helped with Private Martin. Bill Gammage allowed me to quote from the diary of his great-uncle 'Jack' Gammage. Ron Austin helped with material on the 6th Battalion at Krithia. Phil Brotchie gave me access to his grandfather's reminiscences; Mrs Ray Gay allowed me to use the recollections of her father, Donald Lechte. Professor Geoffrey Blainey allowed me to quote from his histories and, better still, several times gave me the benefit of his fine mind.

In the United Kingdom, Stephen Snelling, author of *VCs of the First World War: Gallipoli*, not only permitted me to quote from his book but also helped me find original material. In the UK, I am also grateful to Major Harry Davies, nephew of Colonel Allanson; Mrs Bridget Grant, daughter of Aubrey Herbert; Colonel D. Gibson; Brian Minchin; Charles Grant; Una Kroll, joint executor of the estate of the L. O. Doughty-Wylie Papers; and the heirs of George Drewry, VC.

Bruce Ruxton loaded me up with maps and contacts for my two visits to Turkey and, as is his way, always wanted to help. I am grateful to my old friend John Hamilton, a Gallipoli buff, who several times pointed me towards some interesting material that he had come upon, and to another old friend, Keith Dunstan, son of Bill Dunstan, who won the VC at Lone Pine. Rod Cameron found obscure books for me. I also wish to thank Ross Bastiaan, Andrew Clark, Pauline McIntyre, Greg Kerr, Ian Clarke, Professor Ken Inglis, Dr Selwin Crick, Lambis Englezos, Desmond Zwar, Paul Bailey, Barbara Bessant and others who supplied me with material and ideas.

For permission to quote from collections, my thanks to: The Australian War Memorial; The State Library of Victoria; Kippenberger Military Archive and Research Library, Army Museum, Waiouru, NZ; The Imperial War Museum, London; Trustees of the Liddell Hart Centre for Military Archives, King's College, London; Churchill Archives, Churchill College, Cambridge; The Special Collections Librarian, Newcastle University Library, Newcastle upon Tyne.

The following extracts from books are reproduced with permission: extracts from Charles Bean, *Two Men I Knew*, Angus & Robertson, 1957, reproduced with permission of HarperCollins; extracts from Winston Churchill, *The World Crisis 1911–1918*, Odhams, 1938, and *My Early Life*, Odhams, 1960, reproduced with permission of Curtis Brown Ltd, London, on behalf of the Estate of Sir Winston Churchill; extracts from Michael Hickey, *Gallipoli*, 1995, reproduced with permission of John Murray Publishing; extracts from Trumbull Higgins, *Winston Churchill and the Dardanelles*, Heinemann, 1963, and Robert Rhodes James, *Gallipoli*, Pimlico, 1999, used by permission of The Random House Group; extracts from John Lee, *A Soldier's Life: General Sir Ian Hamilton 1853–1947*, 2000, reproduced with permission of Macmillan, London; extracts from Compton Mackenzie, *Gallipoli Memories*, Cassell, 1929, reproduced with permission of the Society of Authors as the Literary representative of the Estate of Compton Mackenzie; extracts from the private biography of Walter Ramsay McNicoll, 1877–1947, reproduced with permission of the trustees of the estate of Ronald Ramsay McNicoll; extracts from Geoffrey Moorhouse, *Hell's Foundations*, 1992, and C. V. Usborne, *Smoke on the Horizon*, 1933, reproduced with permission of Hodder & Stoughton Ltd; extracts from Peter Pedersen, *Monash as Military Commander*, 1992, reproduced with permission of Melbourne University Press; extracts from

ACKNOWLEDGEMENTS

Geoffrey Serle, *John Monash: A Biography,* 1982, reproduced with permission of Melbourne University Press; extracts from Maurice Shadbolt, *Voices of Gallipoli,* 2001, reproduced with permission of David Ling Publishing; extracts from Gavin Souter, *Lion and Kangaroo: The Initiation of Australia,* 2000, reproduced with permission of Text Publishing.

Garry Linnell was always there when I needed a kindred spirit to talk to. Patrick, my son, helped me with the proofs and Belle, my granddaughter, helped me stay more or less sane. Deborah Callaghan, my literary agent, looked after me wonderfully; it is fair to say she believed in the book before I did. The same is true of Tom Gilliatt, the non-fiction publisher at Pan Macmillan. It was a pleasure to work with Tom and Bernadette Foley, who edited this book; both have a true sense of craft.

Denise, my wife, did an outlandish amount of work on this book and put up with a great deal, including an encounter with two snakes below Bauchop's Hill. To thank her for all she has done is somehow inadequate; this is her book too.

Index

THE TRENCH
by Richard Van Emden

A vivid and harrowing recreation of life in the trenches of the Great War.

What did it feel like to be a soldier on the front line in 1916? What was it like to see the trenches for the first time? What did you do to pass the time once you got there? How did you deal with trench routine? And the deaths of your friends? How did you treat injuries? Or trench foot? Or lice? What did you eat? How did you sleep?

How did you stay alive?

The Trench recreates the experience of day-to-day life for soldiers during the First World War. Based on many hours of original research and interviews with veterans, as well as extant records which describe daily events in extraordinary detail, its aim is to present an accurate picture of how it actually felt to be in the Front Line in 1916.

Awe-inspiring and deeply moving first-hand testimony from veterans of the Great War combines with the experiences of the modern day volunteers who occupied a specially reconstructed trench in northern France to bring us face-to-face with the unimaginable daily tragedies of the conflict and offer a profound new insight into the realities of war.

'A serious investigation into what life was really like in this subterranean world . . . a fascinating book that provides new insights into that terrible conflict'
Good Book Guide

0 552 14968 3

1421
The year China discovered the world
by Gavin Menzies

On 8 March 1421, the largest fleet the world had ever seen set sail from China. The ships, some nearly five hundred feet long, were under the command of Emperor Zhu Di's loyal eunuch admirals. Their orders were 'to proceed all the way to the end of the earth'.

The voyage would last for two years and by the time the fleet returned, China was beginning its long, self-imposed isolation from the world it had so recently embraced. And so the great ships were left to rot, and the records of their journey destroyed. And with them, the knowledge that the Chinese had circumnavigated the globe a century before Magellan, reached America seventy years before Columbus, and Australia three hundred and fifty years before Cook. . .

The result of fifteen years research, *1421* is Gavin Menzies' enthralling account of this remarkable journey, of his discoveries and the incontrovertible evidence to support them: ancient maps, precise navigational knowledge, astronomy, surviving accounts of Chinese explorers and later European navigators as well as the evidence the fleet left behind – from sunken remains to votive offerings left by the Chinese sailors wherever they landed, giving thanks to Shao Lin, goddess of the sea.

Revised and updated with new evidence for its paperback edition, *1421* is a brilliant, epoch-making work of historical detection that radically alters our understanding of world exploration and rewrites history itself.

'Exhaustively researched . . . an intriguing and highly persuasive thesis, told with passion and energy'
Evening Standard

'Menzies has come up with something entirely new . . . it is a startling claim'
Guardian

A Bantam Paperback

0 553 81522 9

THE LAST MISSION
The Secret History of World War II's Final Battle
By Jim Smith and Malcolm McConnell

14 August 1945. As Japan's Emperor Hirohito recorded his message of surrender, rebel troops commanded by elite officers from the War Ministry burst into the imperial palace. Their intention was to stage a coup, destroy the recording and issue forged orders for Japan to continue the war. Had they succeeded there would have been massive *kamikaze* attacks on allied forces, possibly provoking America to drop a third atomic bomb. . .

But on that fateful night, in the skies approaching Tokyo, a stream of B-29B 'Superfortress' bombers were heading towards Japan's last functioning oil refinery. Fearing that they could be carrying another atom bomb, Japanese air defences ordered a total blackout of the city and the imperial palace. In the hours of chaos that followed, the rebels were foiled and soldiers loyal to the emperor wrested back control. At midday on 15 August 1945, the imperial message of surrender was broadcast. The war was finally over.

The result of more than twenty years research by Jim Smith, who took part in that final air raid, *The Last Mission* is gripping work of speculative investigation into one or the least known yet profoundly significant episodes of the Second World War.

'Skilfully weaving personal and archival history, *The Last Mission* gives us a haunting glimpse of just how close we came to the brink of waging a final desperate war on Japanese soil'
Hampton Sides, author of *Ghost Soldiers*

'Fascinating . . . a breathtaking blend of memoir, investigative research and imagination'
Iris Change, author of *The Rape of Nanking*

A Bantam Paperback

0 553 81610 1

IN HARM'S WAY
by Doug Stanton

'A thoroughly researched, powerfully written account of a nightmare at sea, one of the most poignant tragedies and injustices of World War II'
Mark Bowden, author of *Black Hawk Down*

On 30 July 1945 the USS *Indianapolis* was steaming through the South Pacific, on her way home having delivered the bomb that was to decimate Hiroshima seven days later, when she was torpedoed by a Japanese submarine. Of a crew of 1196 men an estimated 300 were killed upon impact; the remaining 900 sailors went into the sea. Undetected for five days they struggled to stay alive, fighting off sharks, hypothermia and dementia. By the time rescue arrived, only 317 men were left alive.

Interweaving the stories of some of these survivors, Doug Stanton brings this incredible human drama to life in a narrative that is at once immediate and timeless. The definitive account of a near-forgotten chapter in the history of the last war, *In Harm's Way* is destined to become a classic.

'Superb . . . it's the stuff about the men in the sea that'll make you weep. Four days without water, being picked off one by one by sharks . . . and no-one in the world even realising they are missing. Gripping'
FHM

'The best thing we've read in years . . . their entire ordeal, from the initial fireball to the 1968 suicide of the captain is spelt out here in vivid, horrific detail. Brilliant stuff'
Later

A Bantam Paperback

0 553 81360 9

A SELECTED LIST OF NON-FICTION TITLES AVAILABLE FROM CORGI AND BANTAM BOOKS